Alfresco 3 Enterprise Content Management Implementation

Install, use, customize, and administer this powerful, Open Source Java-based Enterprise CMS

Munwar Shariff

Vinita Choudhary

Amita Bhandari

Pallika Majmudar

[PACKT] PUBLISHING

BIRMINGHAM - MUMBAI

Alfresco 3 Enterprise Content Management Implementation

Copyright © 2009 Packt Publishing

All rights reserved. No part of this book may be reproduced, stored in a retrieval system, or transmitted in any form or by any means, without the prior written permission of the publisher, except in the case of brief quotations embedded in critical articles or reviews.

Every effort has been made in the preparation of this book to ensure the accuracy of the information presented. However, the information contained in this book is sold without warranty, either express or implied. Neither the authors, Packt Publishing, nor its dealers or distributors will be held liable for any damages caused or alleged to be caused directly or indirectly by this book.

Packt Publishing has endeavored to provide trademark information about all the companies and products mentioned in this book by the appropriate use of capitals. However, Packt Publishing cannot guarantee the accuracy of this information.

First published: May 2009

Production Reference: 1020609

Published by Packt Publishing Ltd.
32 Lincoln Road
Olton
Birmingham, B27 6PA, UK.

ISBN 978-1-847197-36-8

www.packtpub.com

Cover Image by Ninoslav Babić (nbabic@net.amis.hr)

Credits

Authors
Munwar Shariff
Vinita Choudhary
Amita Bhandari
Pallika Majmudar

Reviewers
Michael Uzquiano
Vinita Choudhary
Adrián Efrén Jiménez Vega
Peter Monks

Acquisition Editor
David Barnes

Development Editor
Dilip Venkatesh

Technical Editors
Mehul Shetty
Gaurav Datar

Copy Editor
Leonard D' Silva

Production Editorial Manager
Abhijeet Deobhakta

Editorial Team Leader
Akshara Aware

Project Team Leader
Lata Basantani

Project Coordinator
Rajashree Hamine

Indexer
Hemangini Bari

Proofreader
Dirk Manuel

Production Coordinators
Adline Swetha Jesuthas
Aparna Bhagat

Cover Work
Adline Swetha Jesuthas

About the Author

Munwar Shariff is the CTO of CIGNEX. CIGNEX is the leading provider of open source Enterprise Content Management (ECM) solutions for businesses and government agencies.

He has worked as the chief architect and manager of engineering teams for eighteen years in the field of system software, Internet applications, and mobile applications for clients in the United States, Japan, Germany, UK, Hong Kong, Malaysia, and India.

He is an expert in Content Management Systems (CMS). Since co-founding CIGNEX in late 2000, he has successfully delivered more than 80 CMS applications using various open source technologies. He has written a number of articles on open source CMS, is an experienced trainer, and a frequent speaker at conferences related to this topic.

Munwar earned his MS in Digital Electronics and Advanced Communications from REC Surathkal in India. He has authored two technical books on open source CMS—"*Plone Live*" and "*Alfresco Enterprise Content Management Implementation*".

About the Co-Authors

Vinita Choudhary is a senior consultant at CIGNEX. She has extensive experience in working in a variety of environments with cross-functional, multi-cultural teams as a business analyst and has provided feedback on usability and functional gaps in process flows and proposed solutions.

She has re-organized existing repository of documentation, written guidelines for document creation, filing and change control, wrote reference and training material for software developers and published the same. She is involved in providing pre sales support to the sales team and has worked on process streamlining for the company and various documentation aspects. Vinita holds a Masters in Computer Applications degree from Gujarat University, India.

Amita Bhandari is a senior consultant at CIGNEX. As a senior developer, she has rolled out numerous Alfresco deployments world-wide. She has extensive experience in implementing Enterprise Web Applications using J2EE technologies such as JSP, Servlets, Spring, Hibernate, Web Services, Web Scripts and MVC Frameworks.

She has worked with clients in media and gaming, healthcare and e-governance. She trained many students in Java and advanced Java technologies. She holds a Masters in Computer Applications from Rajasthan University, India.

Pallika Majmudar is a consultant at CIGNEX Technologies. She is very experienced in Java/J2EE domain including the frameworks such as Struts, Spring, Hibernate, Web services, and Web scripts.

She has worked on various CMS applications for the customers in United States, Hong Kong and India. She has implemented Alfresco for clients across verticals like Media, Healthcare, Hi-tech and Communications. Pallika has earned her Masters in Computer Application degree from Gujarat University, India.

Acknowledgements

We would like to thank John Powell, CEO of Alfresco for providing support to the CIGNEX team. Thanks to John Newton, Ian Howells, Matt Asay, Phil Robinson, Paul Holmes-Higgin, David Caruana, Janine Eastwood, Martin Musierowicz, Luis Sala, Joe Van De Graaff, Floyd Spencer, and Natasha Woodhouse for all of the support. They are great partners to work with.

We thank Michael G. Uzquiano, Director of Alfresco Web Content Management, for providing critical feedback and suggesting improvements.

Our special thanks to all of our team members at CIGNEX for making this book a reality. We would like to thank Paul Anthony, CEO of CIGNEX for his encouragement. Our sales, presales, and inside sales teams at CIGNEX helped us to understand what customers are looking at. We have learnt a lot through numerous discussions with them. We owe them a party. Our consulting team at CIGNEX presented us with the various flavors of Alfresco implementations that we could not have possibly imagined, with real-life examples as they worked on the production projects. We are thankful to them.

We sincerely thank and appreciate David Barnes, Senior Acquisition Editor at Packt Publishing for giving us this opportunity. A BIG thanks to Dilip Venkatesh, Development Editor, and to the entire team at Packt Publishing. It is a pleasure to work with them.

Our special thanks to our families and friends.

About the Reviewers

Michael G. Uzquiano is the director of Web Content Management at Alfresco Software. He has developed the Alfresco Surf and Alfresco Web Studio presentation tier technologies for Alfresco, and guides the WCM and Network product strategies today.

He has over 12 years of experience in the ECM industry, having pioneered product and services efforts at Trilogy Software, Epicentric, and Vignette. He's worked in the fields of engineering, consulting, sales, and products. He has also founded a gaming company and a small non-profit organization (with a focus on South America).

Michael holds a Master's degree in Management from Northwestern University's Kellogg Graduate School of Management, where he had concentrated on Finance and Strategy. He also holds a Bachelor as well as a Master of Science degree in Electrical Engineering from Cornell University.

Adrián Efrén Jiménez Vega works at the Center of Information Technologies (CTI) of the University of the Balearic Islands, in Mallorca (Spain). For three years, he has built and deployed various applications based on Alfresco.

Since registering on the Alfresco Spanish forum approximately one year ago, he has dedicated time and openly shared his experience by posting more than 600 messages, and has contributed many practical solutions and useful hints to members of the Community. The 'mini-guides' that he developed are now widely used and referenced among developers in Spain and other Spanish speaking countries. He obtained the "Alfresco Chumby Awards for Community Achievement" in November 2008.

Adrián won the "Web Script Developer Challenge" by developing a Web Script solution to limit the space for users, including e-mail notification.

At present, in parallel with these tasks, he is doing a Computer Engineering study project, and is basing his work on document management with the Alfresco platform.

I would like to thank all of the people who made possible my participation in this project. In particular, my parents, my sister, my friends at CTI, and specially Maribel Barceló and Xavier Pons for their help and contributions.

This book is dedicated to Amit Babaria, head of U.S. business, and to Manish Sheladia, General Manager for India operations at CIGNEX, without whom this book would not have existed.

Table of Contents

Preface   1

Chapter 1: Introduction to Alfresco   9
  An overview of Alfresco   10
    Leveraging the benefits of open source   10
    State-of-the-art content repository   11
    Scalable architecture   12
    Open standards-based underlying components   12
    Globalization support   13
    Security and access control   13
    Business process automation   14
    Enterprise integration   14
  Alfresco Enterprise 3.0—An overview   15
    Alfresco Network   16
    Alfresco Web Studio   16
    Alfresco Share   17
    Alfresco Surf   18
    Alfresco Repository Public API   18
    Alfresco Draft CMIS Implementation   19
    Microsoft SharePoint Protocol support   19
  How you can benefit from Alfresco   19
    Using Alfresco for document management   19
    Using Alfresco for records management   21
    Using Alfresco for web content management   22
    Using Alfresco for collaboration management   23
    Using Alfresco for enterprise content search   25
    Applications of Alfresco   25
  How does the future look like with Alfresco?   26
    Enterprise versus Community Labs   26

Better support options	27
Free upgrades	28
Implementing an example solution using Alfresco	**28**
Where do you get more information?	**28**
Summary	**29**
Chapter 2: Installing Alfresco	**31**
Installing Alfresco	**31**
Out of the box installation architecture	32
Client Applications layer	32
Repository Services layer	33
Data Storage layer	33
The components of Alfresco applications	34
Accessing the application	34
Choosing the right installation option	35
Enterprise and community editions	35
Operating systems—Windows, Linux, UNIX, and MacOS	36
Databases—MySQL, Oracle, MS SQL Server, and PostgreSQL	36
Application servers—Tomcat and JBoss	37
Portals (optional)—JBoss Portal and Liferay	38
Choose the appropriate software for your installation	38
Installing on Microsoft Windows	39
Full installation	39
Installation of the Alfresco Tomcat bundle	42
Installation of other Alfresco Components	43
Installation folder structure	51
Starting and stopping Alfresco as a console application	52
Configuring Alfresco as a Windows service	53
Installing on Linux	54
Installing extensions with AMP Install	55
Summary	**56**
Chapter 3: Getting Started with Alfresco	**57**
Introduction to Alfresco Explorer	**57**
Log in to Alfresco as an Administrator	58
Screen layout	58
Tool Bar	59
Navigator	59
Breadcrumbs	61
Header	61
Detail	61
Administration Console	62
User and groups management	62
Category management	63
Data management	63
System information	63
Getting started with content creation	**63**

Create space	63
Create content	64
Create a link to content	65
My Alfresco dashboards	**66**
Choosing the My Alfresco dashboard as the start location	66
Configuring personal dashboard using wizard	67
Step one: Selection of layout	68
Step two: Selecting components	68
Start with basic configuration	**70**
Extend Alfresco configuration	70
Alfresco ConfigRoot folder	71
Alfresco extension folder	71
Configuration approach	71
Packaging and deploying Java extensions	73
Install the enterprise license file	74
Change the default administrator password	74
Configure the content store	74
Configure the relational database	75
Configure the email service and email server	76
Outbound email service	76
Inbound email server	77
Configure the log files	77
Configure the Alfresco virtual file system	78
Configure the file systems	78
Configure the default logos	78
Customize the look and feel using CSS	80
Configure multilanguage support	80
Creating a blue print for your application	**82**
Enterprise intranet as a theme	82
Features you are going to implement	83
Summary	**83**
Chapter 4: Implementing Membership and Security	**85**
The Alfresco membership and security model	**86**
Users and groups	86
Permissions and roles	87
Authentication	88
How is security imposed in Alfresco?	88
Manage system users	**89**
Creating new users	90
Search for existing users in Alfresco Explorer	92
Modify user details	93
Deleting a user	93

Individual user access	**94**
New user log in and my homepage	94
Update personal details and password	95
Search for existing users in Alfresco share	96
Modify user details using share	96
Manage user groups	**97**
Create groups and subgroups	97
Add users to a group	98
Remove users from a group	99
Extend security permissions and roles	**99**
Default permissions	100
Default roles	100
Create a custom role	101
Secure your spaces	**101**
User roles on a space	102
Invite users to your space	103
Define and secure your spaces	105
Secure your content	**106**
User roles for content	106
Invite users to your content	107
Choosing the correct security model for you	**107**
Use Alfresco's out of the box membership system	108
Configuring LDAP for centralized identity management	109
LDAP configuration with active directory	110
LDAP synchronisation	112
Daisy chaining	113
Configuring NTLM for Single sign-on	115
SSO with active directory	116
SSO with CAS	118
Migrate existing users to Alfresco	**119**
Using command-line scripts for the bulk uploading of users	120
Bootstrapping the Alfresco repository with predefined user data	123
Using web services API to create users	124
Summary	**125**
Chapter 5: Implementing Document Management	**127**
Managing spaces	**128**
Space is a smart folder	128
Why space hierarchy is important	129
Editing a space	130
Editing space properties	130
Deleting space and its contents	132

Moving or copying space by using the clipboard	132
Creating a shortcut to a space for quick access	132
Choosing a default view for your space	132
Sample space structure for marketing project	133
Managing content	**134**
Creating content	134
Creating text documents	134
Uploading binary files such as Word, PDF, Flash, Image, Media	136
Editing content	138
Online editing of HTML, text, and XML	138
Offline editing of files	139
Uploading updated content	141
Content actions	141
Deleting content	142
Moving or copying content using the clipboard	142
Creating a shortcut to the content for quick access	142
Managing content properties	142
What is Content Metadata?	142
Metadata extractors	143
Editing metadata	143
Adding additional properties	144
Library services	**144**
Versioning	144
Auto Versioning	145
Check In and Check Out	146
Checking out documents	146
Checking in the working copy	147
Undo Check Out to unlock a document	148
Categorizing content	**149**
Managing categories	149
Adding categories to content	150
Search content by category	151
Managing multilingual content	**152**
Versions of Multilingual Content	153
Deleting Multilingual Content	154
Using network drives to manage content	**154**
CIFS	154
Mapping the drive	155
Drag-and-drop documents in Alfresco through CIFS	157
Check Out and Check In documents in CIFS	157
File Transfer Protocol	158
WebDAV	159
Microsoft Office 2003 add-ins	**160**
Support for Microsoft Office 2007	160
Installation	160

Configuration	161
Features of MS Word add-in	162
Editing a file in Word	163
Recovering deleted content	**163**
The Data Dictionary and space templates	**165**
The Data Dictionary space	165
Space templates for a reusable space structure	167
Creating a new space template for reuse	168
Using an existing space template to create a new space	168
Discussions on spaces and documents	**170**
Discussion forums for collaboration	170
Forum space	170
Creating discussion forums in the forum space	171
Creating topics in the forum	171
Replying to topics	172
Departmental forums and security	172
Defining forums for groups within a department	173
Inter-department collaboration through spaces	174
Managing space users	174
Space collaboration through email	174
Starting a discussion on a specific space	174
Content collaboration	175
Owner invites individuals to collaborate on content	175
RSS syndication	**175**
Using RSS feeds	176
RSS templates	177
Migrating existing content into Alfresco	**177**
Drag-and-drop content to the network drive	177
Using web services to migrate content	177
The ACP Generator's bulk upload utility	178
Summary	**178**
Chapter 6: Implementing Business Rules	**179**
Using business rules on spaces	**179**
Organize documents automatically	180
Run rules in the background	188
Dynamically add properties to a document	188
Automatic versioning of documents	190
Send notifications to specific people	191
Chaining all of the business rules	192
Built-in business rules	**193**
How these business rules work	194
Checking the conditions	194

Table of Contents

What are the actions that are executed?	195
When are these rules triggered?	197
Applying actions to individual content	**198**
Removing an aspect from a content	198
Handling content transformations	**199**
Transforming a Word document to PDF	199
Resizing and transforming images	201
OpenDocument Format	203
Converting Microsoft Office documents to ODF	203
Built-in transformations	206
Executing JavaScript as business rules	**206**
Use built-in JavaScript as actions	206
Extend business rules with custom JavaScript	206
Set up the Corporate Forms space	207
Create custom JavaScript	208
Execute custom JavaScript as an action	209
JavaScript API	210
Scheduled actions	**211**
Example of archiving expired content	211
XML configuration file for scheduled actions	215
The cron expression	216
Summary	**217**
Chapter 7: Extending the Alfresco Content Model	**219**
Custom configuration	**220**
Configuration files for the default content model	220
Configuration files for custom content model	222
Custom model context file	223
Custom model file	224
Custom web client configuration file	224
Hierarchy of configuration files	224
Custom aspect	**225**
The need for a custom aspect	225
Steps for adding a custom aspect	226
Define a custom aspect	226
Extend the content model with the custom aspect	227
Configure the web client for the custom aspect	229
Use custom aspect as a business rule	230
Constraints	**232**
Constraint types	232
REGEX	233
LIST	233
MINMAX	233
LENGTH	234

[vii]

Applying a constraint	234
Advanced property sheet configuration	**237**
Display labels	237
Conditional display of properties	238
Converters	238
Component generators	238
Custom content type	**239**
When do you need a custom content type	239
Steps to add a custom content type	239
Define the custom content type	240
Extend the content model with the custom content type	240
Configure the web client for the custom content type	241
Add custom content type	242
Create a Press Release as HTML content	244
Create business rules targeting the custom content type	245
Custom associations	**246**
When do you need an association?	246
Define a custom association	246
Use a custom association	248
Presentation Template for custom content types	249
Association example	252
Dynamic models	**253**
Dynamic custom model	253
Deploying a custom model	254
Activating and deactivating a custom model	254
Updating a custom model	255
Dynamic web client	255
Deploying web client customizations	256
Reloading web client customizations	256
Dynamic models in a multi-tenancy environment	257
Summary	**257**
Chapter 8: Implementing Workflow	**259**
Introduction to the Alfresco workflow process	**260**
Simple Workflow	**260**
Out of the box features	261
Define and use Simple Workflow	261
Identify spaces and security	262
Defining the workflow process	263
Adding simple workflow to items	263
Sending a notification for approval to the Manager	265
Test your simple workflow	266
Email notification templates	268

Implementing complex workflows	269
The workflow process	270
Advanced workflows	**271**
Workflow user interactions	272
Out of the box features	273
Creating custom advanced workflows	276
Defining the workflow process	277
Step 1: Create and deploy the task model	278
Step 2: Create and deploy the workflow resource bundles	282
Step 3: Create and deploy the process definition	285
Step 4: Display the workflow images	292
Step 5: Create and deploy the Alfresco Explorer task dialogs	293
Step 6: Test the workflow	295
Track the status of this workflow through a customized dashlet	297
Out of the box features of the workflow task list's dashboards	299
List of My Tasks To Do	299
Reassign Adhoc Task	300
Manage Adhoc tasks	301
List of My Completed Tasks	302
View the Status of or Cancel a Workflow	302
Integration with rules	303
Summary	**304**
Chapter 9: Integrating External Applications with Alfresco	**305**
The Alfresco content platform	**305**
Embeddable enterprise content management system	306
Integrated enterprise content management system	306
Various protocols for integration	307
Using web service as an integration solution	308
Using FTP, WebDAV, and CIFS protocols for integration	308
RESTful web services	308
Web Scripts	**309**
What is a Web Script	309
How to implement Web Scripts	310
Hello World example	312
Sample out of the box portlet Web Scripts	313
Myspaces portlet	313
Document list portlet Web Script	313
Web Script to list the latest documents	314
Daily dose integration Web Script in detail	315
Integrating Web Script with an external Java application	317
Web Script to integrate document search	318
Document search Web Script in detail	318
Calling the Web Script from external application	325

Various application integration examples	**326**
Integrating with Liferay	326
Various available options	326
Liferay built-in Portlet for Alfresco	328
Using your own API	328
Integrating with Drupal	329
Integrating with Joomla!	330
Integrating with Adobe Flex	331
Email integration: MS Outlook, Lotus Notes, Novell, and Thunderbird	332
Integrating with iPhone	333
Integrating with iGoogle	335
Steps to integrate iGoogle Gadgets with Alfresco	336
Using iGoogle Gadgets	337
Integrating with FFMPEG video transcoder	339
Various options for video transcoding	339
Various options for audio transcoding	340
Integrating transformation as an action in Alfresco	340
Integrating with ViewOnePro image viewer	343
Integrating with the Facebook social network application	346
Creating a new Facebook application	347
Registering the Facebook application with Alfresco	350
CMIS	**352**
Scope of CMIS	353
Alfresco CMIS implementation	354
Sample Alfresco CMIS dashlet	354
Summary	**357**
Chapter 10: Advanced Collaboration Using Alfresco Share	**359**
Alfresco Share	**360**
My Dashboard	363
Customize your dashboard	363
My Profile	365
Viewing your full profile	365
Editing your profile	366
Changing your password	367
Sites	368
Creating a site	368
Searching for a site	369
Managing your site membership	370
Deleting a site	370
People	370
Searching for a user	370
Using your personal dashboard	371
Entering a site	371
Configure the personal dashboard RSS feed	371

View scheduled events	372
Using the Alfresco Network	373
Using a site	**373**
Getting Started	374
Site Profile	374
Site Colleagues	374
Site Calendar	374
Site Activities	374
Recently Modified Documents	374
Wiki	374
RSS Feed	375
Customize a site	**375**
Customizing a site's dashboard	376
Editing the site details	377
Configuring the site dashboard RSS feed	378
Configuring the Wiki site dashlet	378
Subscribing to an RSS feed	378
Tagging site content	379
Selecting a page	379
The Wiki page	380
The Document Library page	386
Working with multiple library items	400
The Calendar page	401
The Blog page	406
The Discussions page	414
Managing site users	420
Benefits of using Alfresco Share	**426**
SharePoint protocol support with Alfresco Enterprise 3.0	**426**
Handling documents within Microsoft Office	427
Creating a Document Workspace	427
Editing a document	430
Document Versions	431
Adding content to a document library	433
Collaborating on a document	434
Saving a document to the Document Workspace	435
Customize the Document Workspace	436
Manage the Document Workspace membership	437
Working with a Document Workspace document locally	439
Deleting the Document Workspace	442
Document Workspace dashlet in Share	442
Summary	**442**
Chapter 11: Customizing the User Interface	**443**
Configuring Alfresco Explorer	**444**
Configuring views	444
Configuring space views	444
Applying a Custom View to a space	446
Configuring forum topics sort direction	448

Table of Contents

Adding a custom icon to a space	449
Configuring HTML links to appear in Alfresco Explorer	450
User configurable dashboards	450
Writing custom dashlets	450
Using webscripts as dashlets	454
Using a FreeMarker dashlet from the repository	457
Presentation templates	457
The FreeMarker template engine within Alfresco	458
The Alfresco objects available to FreeMarker	458
FreeMarker template node model API	460
FreeMarker directives	460
Custom template to preview web pages	461
Custom template for XML content	463
Custom templates for custom space view	465
Customizing Alfresco Share	466
Presentation templates	466
Custom template	468
Configure custom webscripts	469
Configure custom dashlets	471
Configure custom components in Alfresco Share	474
Rich user interface using Flex	477
Alfresco Share 3.0 Integration support	477
Customizing JSP Client	479
Various user interface options	**483**
Summary	**483**
Chapter 12: Search	**485**
Overview	**485**
Search using Alfresco Explorer	**486**
Simple search	486
Search file names only	487
Advanced search	488
Search by content location	489
Search by content category	489
Search by content properties	490
Extending the search form	490
Configure the web client user interface	491
Search custom content and properties	491
Save a search as a report	492
Define complex search criteria	492
Save search criteria as public or private report	493
Reuse a saved search	494
OpenSearch	**494**
Alfresco's open search engines	495
Keyword search description	495
Sample keyword search in HTML	496

Sample keyword search in RSS	496
Alfresco Explorer as an OpenSearch aggregator	497
Registering new search engines	497
Federated search	499
Configuring the Alfresco search engine	**500**
The theory behind the search engine	500
Limit search results	500
Indexing properties	501
Configuring Lucene in Alfresco	502
Summary	**503**

Chapter 13: Implementing Imaging and Forms Processing — 505

Electronic imaging and the paperless office	**506**
Forms processing	**507**
Alfresco for imaging and forms processing	508
Sample imaging solution with workflow	**509**
Setting up space and security	510
Business rule to extract important metadata	511
Transform documents into the required format	513
Define the workflow process	514
Connecting the scanner to network folder	515
Bulk upload scanned documents into the repository	515
OCR integration	**517**
Intelliant OCR-Alfresco bundle	518
Integration with Kofax Ascent Capture	**519**
Kofax release script configuration	519
Release script functionality	522
Integration with an eCopy-enabled scanner	**522**
Summary	**523**

Chapter 14: Administering and Maintaining the System — 525

Exporting and importing content	**526**
Alfresco Content Package (ACP)	526
Exporting and importing space content	527
Export of a department space using Alfresco Explorer	527
Importing a department space using Alfresco Explorer	528
Using business rules to import data	529
Using command line tools	530
The export tool	530
The import tool	531
Data backup	**531**
List of items to backup	532
The content stored in the filesystem	532
The metadata stored in the relational database	533

Customization files	533
Membership data	534
Log files	534
Backup frequency	**534**
Backing up based on the Alfresco deployment	**535**
Alfresco deployed as a repository application server	535
Alfresco deployed as a Clustered Repository Server	536
Alfresco deployed as hot backup	537
Upgrading to newer versions of Alfresco	**537**
Upgrading to a minor release	538
Upgrading to a major release	539
General maintenance tips	**541**
Regular maintenance of deleted items	541
Examining log files	541
Resetting the administrator password	542
Resetting the complete repository data	542
Migrating servers	543
User quota system	**543**
Multi-Tenancy	**544**
Enabling Multi-Tenancy	544
Creating tenants	544
Tenant use case	545
Managing tenants	547
Exporting and importing tenant data	547
Full auditing	**548**
Controlling audit information	548
Simple audit template for displaying auditing information	549
Summary	**550**
Index	**551**

Preface

For the past ten years, we have been implementing various Content Management Systems. We talk to customers who have made multi-million dollar implementations of proprietary software, and faced all kinds of challenges, including vendor lock-in, a rigid code base, and expensive upgrades. At CIGNEX, our focus has been provide value to our customers by using open source alternatives to commercial CMS products.

Alfresco 3 offers true Enterprise Content Management (ECM) by providing an open source alternative to Microsoft SharePoint, Documentum, and Interwoven. It is the most popular Java-based CMS, with over 1.5 million downloads, 50,000 live sites, 74,000 community members, and more than 150 application extensions in Forge.

Unlike most other open source CMSes, which offered only web content management, Alfresco provided a wide range of solutions to Enterprise customers, with an impressive roadmap. Most importantly, it is created using entirely open standards. This excited us a lot, and we started implementing Alfresco in many enterprises. We became the Platinum System Integration partner of Alfresco. As part of an implementation, we also train our customers so that they are equipped with all of the information required to manage their systems. We have trained many users, administrators, and developers in Alfresco. This book distils the hands-on approach of my training courses into a concise, practical book.

This book focuses on business needs rather than technical syntax. We start by showing the reader how to do something—a step by step example. We explain how that process worked. Then, we explain what other options are available, and how they fit into the overall picture. We hope this helps the reader to 'generalize' from such examples. We hope that you take advantage of this book by setting up a flexible enterprise Content Management System for your company and customers.

Preface

Your feedback is very valuable to us. You can contribute by reporting any errors that you find in this book, making suggestions for new content that you'd like to see in future updates, and commenting and blogging about this book

What this book covers

This book will take you through the complete cycle of implementing, customizing, and administering your ECM installation. The topics that this book covers are as follows:

Chapter 1 includes an overview of the Alfresco architecture and the key features of the software. It explains various use cases for using Alfresco for your document management, records management, web content management, and collaboration requirements, and also provides a future roadmap.

Chapter 2 provides valuable tips on how to to choose the right installation for you, and also describes installation of the software and how to start using it.

Chapter 3 gives the basic information about Alfresco Explorer and also provides you with various ways of configuring Alfresco, according to your business needs.

Chapter 4 describes working with users and setting up security, including LDAP and Active Directory integration. This chapter also introduces concepts such as "Single Sign-on", and the daisy chaining of multiple membership sources.

Chapter 5 describes how to use Alfresco as a smart document repository, providing automatic version tracking and control, and accessing the repository from the Web, shared network folders, or FTP. It also includes a description of searching and editing documents directly from Microsoft Office Tools.

Chapter 6 teaches you how to automate document management tasks by using business rules and various content transformations.

Chapter 7 explains how to design custom content types.

Chapter 8 teaches you how to automate your business process by using the advanced workflow concepts of Alfresco 3.

Chapter 9 integrates Alfresco with external applications. This chapter also includes examples of integrations with Liferay Portal, iPhone, Facebook, iGoogle, Microsoft Outlook, Adobe Flex, and the Ffmpeg video transcoder.

Chapter 10 explains how to build collaborative web sites by using document libraries, wikis, blogs, forums, calendars, discussions, and social tagging.

Chapter 11 explains how to customize the user interface and create your own dashboard layouts, presenting content in custom ways that are relevant to your business.

Chapter 12 explains how to content easy to find by using search, content categorization and metadata. It also includes a description of Alfresco's Open Search features.

Chapter 13 describes how to collect paper documents and forms, transforming them into accurate, retrievable information, and delivering content into an organization's business applications.

Chapter 14 explains effective administration and the maintenance of the system for efficient performance and high availability. It also explains how administrators can set up Alfresco 3 for multiple business units in a single-instance, multi-tenant environment.

What you need for this book

The default installation of Alfresco software requires installing the Windows Enterprise version, `Alfresco-Enterprise-<version>-Full-Setup.exe`, which can be downloaded from the SourceForge project location (`http://sourceforge.net/project/showfiles.php?group_id=143373`). Now, Alfresco is hosting its own community download area, so you can also download it from `http://www.alfresco.com/products/ecm/enttrial/`. Select the download package, and you will be asked for a user name and password for the Alfresco content community.

At the time of writing this book the latest version is Alfresco Enterprise 3.1 and the installer file **Alfresco-Enterprise-3.1-Full-Setup.exe** is approximately 350 MB in size.

This installer will install:

- Java Development Kit (JDK) [If no JDK is currently installed on your machine]
- Apache Tomcat 6.0.18
- Portable Open Office 3
- The Alfresco Explorer web application, packaged as a Web Archive (WAR)
- The Alfresco Share web application, packaged as a Web Archive (WAR)
- SharePoint Protocol support

To install and run Alfresco, you need at least 500 MB of disk space and at least 512 MB RAM on the desktop or server.

Who this book is for

This book is designed for system administrators, and experienced users or developers who want to install and use Alfresco in their teams or businesses. Because Alfresco is free, many teams can install and experiment with its ECM features without any up-front cost, often without management approval. This book assumes a degree of technical confidence, but does not require specialist system administration or developer skills in order to get a basic system up and running.

Alfresco is particularly suitable for IT consultants who want to or need to set up a flexible enterprise Content Management System for their clients, whether this is for demonstration, development, or as a mission-critical platform. This book gets you to that result quickly and effectively.

This book also helps business users to make decisions about migrating from an existing proprietary ECM to Alfresco 3.

This book is not a developer's guide. However, various examples in the book will help developers to extend Alfresco's functionality and to integrate Alfresco with external systems.

Although no knowledge of Alfresco is presumed, exposure to HTML, XML, JavaScript, and related web technologies will help users to get the most from this book.

Conventions

In this book, you will find a number of styles of text that distinguish between different kinds of information. Here are some examples of these styles, and an explanation of their meaning.

There are three styles for code. Code words in text are shown as follows: "Note that the `scheduled-action-services-context.xml` file has two blocks of XML configuration."

A block of code is set as follows:

```
<cm:person view:childName="cm:person">
<cm:userName>fredb</cm:userName>
<cm:firstName>Fred</cm:firstName>
<cm:lastName>Bloggs</cm:lastName>
<cm:email>fredb@alfresco.org</cm:email>
```

When we wish to draw your attention to a particular part of a code block, the relevant lines or items are set in bold:

```
        </property>
        <property name="stores">
            <list>
                <value>workspace://SpacesStore</value>
            </list>
        </property>
        <property name="queryTemplate">
            <value>PATH:"/app:company_home"</value>
        </property>
        <property name="cronExpression">
            <value>0 0/15 * * * ?</value>
        </property>
        <property name="jobName">
            <value>jobD</value>
        </property>
        <property name="jobGroup">
            <value>jobGroup</value>
        </property>
```

Any command-line input or output is written as follows:

```
> chmod a+x ./alfresco-<version>-linux-community.bin
```

New terms and **important words** are introduced in a bold-type font. Words that you see on the screen, in menus or dialog boxes for example, appear in the text like this: "Go to a space and add a file by clicking on the **Add Content** link."

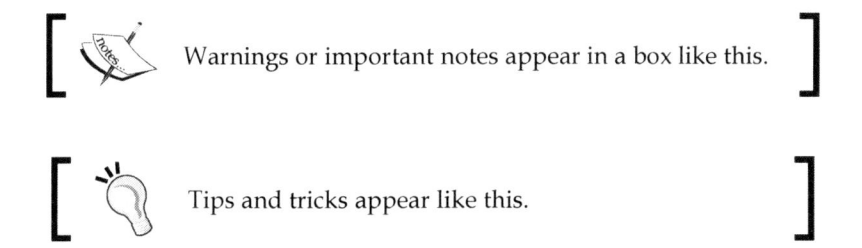

> Warnings or important notes appear in a box like this.

> Tips and tricks appear like this.

[5]

Reader feedback

Feedback from our readers is always welcome. Let us know what you think about this book—what you liked or may have disliked. Reader feedback is important for us to develop titles that you really get the most out of.

To send us general feedback, simply drop an email to feedback@packtpub.com, and mention the book title in the subject of your message.

If there is a book that you need and would like to see us publish, please send us a note via the **SUGGEST A TITLE** form on www.packtpub.com or email suggest@packtpub.com.

If there is a topic that you have expertise in and you are interested in either writing or contributing to a book on, see our author guide on http://authors.packtpub.com/.

Customer support

Now that you are the proud owner of a Packt book, we have a number of things to help you to get the most from your purchase.

Downloading the example code for the book

Visit http://www.packtpub.com/files/code/7368_Code.zip to directly download the example code.

The downloadable files contain instructions on how to use them.

Errata

Although we have taken every care to ensure the accuracy of our content, mistakes do happen. If you find a mistake in one of our books—maybe a mistake in the text or the code—we would be grateful if you would report this to us. By doing so, you can save other readers from frustration, and help us to improve subsequent versions of this book. If you find any errata, please report them by visiting http://www.packtpub.com/support, selecting your book, clicking on the **let us know** link, and entering the details of your errata. Once your errata are verified, your submission will be accepted and the errata added to any list of existing errata. Any existing errata can be viewed by selecting your title from http://www.packtpub.com/support.

Piracy

Piracy of copyright material on the Internet is an ongoing problem across all media. At Packt, we take the protection of our copyright and licenses very seriously. If you come across any illegal copies of our works, in any form, on the Internet, please provide us with the location address or website name immediately so that we can pursue a remedy.

Please contact us at `copyright@packtpub.com` with a link to the suspected pirated material.

We appreciate your help in protecting our authors, and our ability to bring you valuable content.

Questions

You can contact us at `questions@packtpub.com` if you are having a problem with any aspect of the book, and we will do our best to address it.

Introduction to Alfresco

Enterprise Content Management (**ECM**) is the fastest growing category of enterprise software. Customers who are implementing or upgrading ECM systems are facing issues such as vendor lock-in, high maintenance costs, and a lack of standardization. Open source technologies and open standards are becoming powerful alternatives to commercia closed-source ECM software. Alfresco—a relatively new player in this market—has already gained a lot of momentum by providing content management solutions to enterprises, by using open standards and open source based technologies.

The latest release of Alfresco has an Enterprise Edition as well as a Labs Edition. The Alfresco Community Labs product, formerly known as the Community version of Alfresco, is an unsupported product, and is designed for use by developers and technical enthusiasts in noncritical environments. It serves as the research vehicle for new features, and as the platform for the Alfresco Community. Constant innovation of Alfresco Community Labs renders a daily build that offers the latest functionality.

The Alfresco Enterprise Edition is a production-ready, stress-tested certified build that is supported by Alfresco Software Inc. It is a fully-supported Alfresco Product that can be used by corporations and governments that require commercial **Service Level Agreements** (**SLA**s). With the release of Alfresco Enterprise Edition 3.0, Alfresco adds Alfresco Share, which is a new collaborative content solution, a draft implementation of the CMIS specification, and Microsoft Office SharePoint Protocol support to Alfresco's innovative ECM platform.

This chapter provides an introduction to Alfresco and outlines the benefits of using it for your enterprise's content management requirements. It also introduces the features of Alfresco Enterprise 3.0.

In this chapter, you will see:

- The overview and features of Alfresco Enterprise 3.0
- Key features of Alfresco software
- How to use Alfresco for your document management, records management, web content management, and collaboration requirements
- The future roadmap

An overview of Alfresco

Alfresco was founded in 2005 by John Newton, co-founder of Documentum, and John Powell, former COO of Business Objects. Its investors include the leading investment firms Accel Partners and Mayfield Fund. A combination of the proven track record of its leaders, the features of the technology, the open source business model, and good venture capital backing of the team makes Alfresco unique.

Leveraging the benefits of open source

Enterprise customers can reduce costs, minimize business risks, and gain a competitive advantage by adopting the right open source based business software solutions. Based on publicly-available pricing from a range of vendors, a white paper from Alfresco shows how it is possible to save, in the first year of implementation (based on a 1,000 user configuration) up to 89 percent of the cost of SharePoint purchases, and up to 96 percent of the cost of other ECM solutions, by using Alfresco's open source ECM. You can reduce the cost of software solution acquisition, deployment, and maintenance by bringing the community into the development, support, and service process.

Alfresco is the leading open source alternative for Enterprise Content Management. It couples the innovation of open source with the stability of a true enterprise-class platform. The open source model allows Alfresco to use the best-of-breed open source technologies. It also allows contributions from the open source community to get higher-quality software produced more quickly, and at a much lower cost.

State-of-the-art content repository

The following diagram provides an overview of the Alfresco content repository and its integration with external systems such as Virtual File Systems, Web Applications, Knowledge Portals, and Web Services.

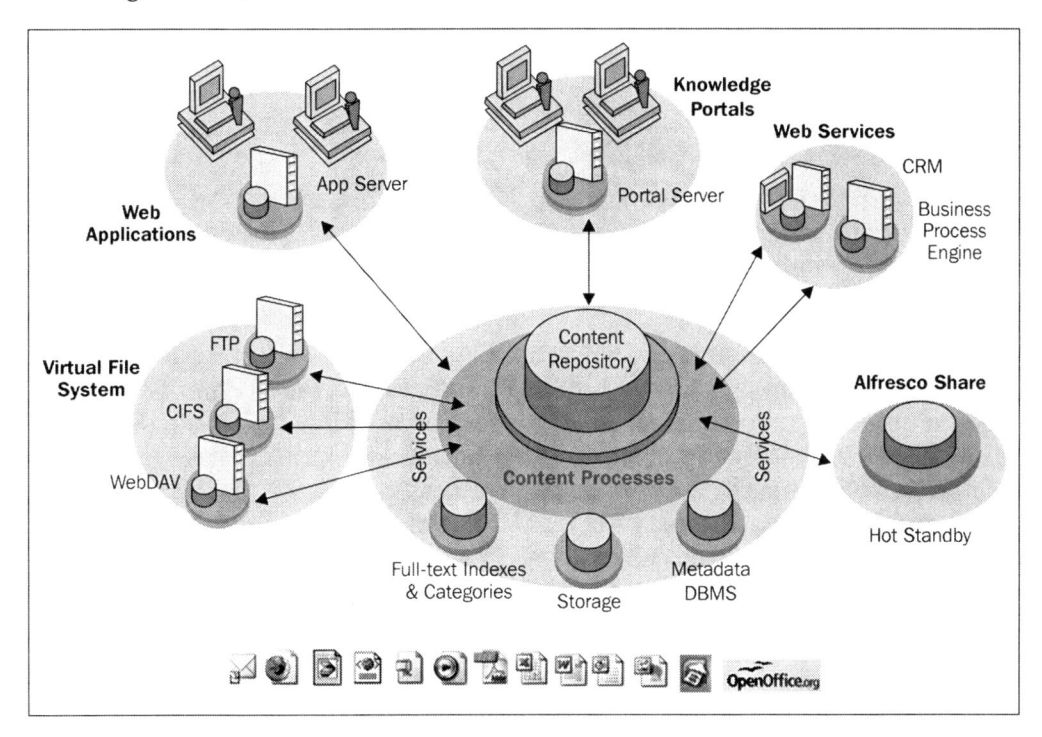

A content repository is a server or a set of services that is used to store, search, access, and control content. The content repository provides these services to specialist content applications such as document management systems, web content management systems, image storage and retrieval systems, records management, and other applications that require the storage and retrieval of large amounts of content. The repositories provide content services such as content storage or import, content classification, security on content objects, control through content check-in and check-out, and content query services to the content applications.

What distinguishes content management from other typical database applications is the level of control exercised over individual content objects, and the ability to search content. Access to these services requires wrapping the calls in security to prevent unauthorized access or changes to content or its metadata. The finer the granularity of this security and the complexity of its relationship with other objects such as people and folders requires a more sophisticated mechanism than that provided by traditional database security.

The complex requirements of these services imply that much of the business logic of the content repository can be as large as, or larger than, the database itself. Almost all of the content repository vendors provide proprietary service interfaces to encapsulate the breadth of functionality required. Despite having tried over the last ten years to standardize these interfaces, it is only over the last two years that any progress has been made. In 2005, the Java community adopted the **JSR-170** standard interface, and Alfresco's content repository is based on this standard.

Scalable architecture

The single most important aspect of any ECM system is the underlying architecture. Alfresco supports pluggable aspect-oriented architecture out of the box by leveraging open source standards and components such as Spring, Hibernate, Lucene, CMIS, JSR 168, JSR 170, and JSE6.

The architecture is based on open standards. Hence the applications built using Alfresco can be deployed on any environment, such as Windows, Linux, Mac, and so on. It can use any relational database, such as MySQL, Oracle, and so on. The scalable architecture can run on various application servers, such as JBoss Application Server, Apache Tomcat, and so on. It can work with any browser, such as, Mozilla Firefox, Microsoft Internet Explorer, and so on. Also, it can integrate with any portal such as JBoss Portal, Liferay Portal, and so on.

In any enterprise, the amount of content that you will manage will keep on increasing. In some organizations such as media, pharmaceutical, healthcare, and so on, the content increases exponentially every year. Hence, scalability is a critical issue when evaluating ECM solutions.

Due to its modular and light-weight architecture, Alfresco is highly scalable. Alfresco provides horizontal scalability by having each tier in the architecture deployed on multiple servers. Similarly, Alfresco can scale up vertically by supporting partitioning and load-balancing in multi-server environments.

Alfresco server can scale up information by using complex search, structure, and classification of information. Alfresco server can scale up activities by using complex information per activity with dynamic views and full object-level security.

Open standards-based underlying components

Open standards protect enterprise investment, promote innovation, and make it easier for IT departments to support the software. By adopting open standards for their ECM requirements, enterprises can lower the risk of incompatibilities with existing technologies. Enterprise application integration becomes easier with open standards.

Alfresco is completely built on the following open standards:

- Java 1.6
- Java Content Repository API
- Java Portlet Integration
- Spring 2.0 Aspect-Oriented Framework
- ACEGI Aspect-Oriented Security Framework
- Hibernate 3.2 ORM Persistence
- Lucene 2.1 Text Search Engine
- AIFS (Alfresco Intelligent File System) supporting Windows Files sharing (SMB/CIFS), NFS, FTP
- WebDAV
- Jakarta POI – Java API for accessing Microsoft file formats
- PDFBox iText – Open source Java PDF libraries
- Open Office 2.x
- JSR-223 Java Language Integration – Scripting for Java platform
- JBPM 3.2

Globalization support

If your enterprise has a global business model, it is very important for you to provide content in multiple languages. Most enterprises look beyond their geographic borders for new markets. The majority of web users speak little or no English. Hence, ECM systems should be designed with globalization in mind.

Alfresco out of the box supports several major languages, including Chinese, Dutch, English, French, German, Italian, Russian, and Spanish.

Security and access control

Protecting unauthorized access to content is a key requirement for enterprises. This is true for corporate web sites, intranets, extranets, front office, and back office applications.

A nice thing about Alfresco is that permissions can be applied at a space (folder) level, or can be set for each individual content item. Out of the box, Alfresco supports a relational database-based membership system, and also supports external identity management systems such as LDAP, NTLM, Kerberos, and Active Directory.

Essential library services

Library services are required if you want to manage, leverage, modify, and control the content in an ECM system. Alfresco provides library services such as Check-in and Check-out, version control, auditing information, and content streaming.

Using Alfresco, you can define the library services to be executed automatically, based on business rules. For example, every edit to the content can version the content automatically. Or every Check-out can move the content to a specific location, again based on business rules.

Alfresco provides additional intelligence on the content by adding metadata (data about data), business rules, security rules, and collaboration rules dynamically, by using aspect-oriented programming. Alfresco also provides features such as content metadata extractors, content transformers, translations, and auto categorization, to make the content intelligent.

Business process automation

Business process automation increases productivity, reduces costs, streamlines processes, and shortens operation cycles. Alfresco includes **JBoss Business Process Manager (JBPM)** as a business process management and automation solution. This helps to manage the document life cycle by providing security and audit trails capabilities.

Enterprise integration

Alfresco provides open standards based protocols for integrating with external applications. Some of the application integration examples are mentioned in this book in Chapter 9. Alfresco can be used either as an embedded repository, or as an external content repository. Because it is open source, you can re-use the integration components for your business applications, thereby saving time and money.

Alfresco, now integrates with applications such as Facebook, ViewOne Pro, and iGoogle, and gadgets such as iPhone.

Quark Publishing System 8 and Alfresco are working together towards bringing web-based storage and collaboration for Quark assets. Alfresco integration with Joomla! is a perfect example of how cooperation between open source projects can yield innovative solutions more rapidly than a proprietary model.

Alfresco integrates with Kofax Ascent Capture and offers customers access to a comprehensive production capture solution, including automatic document classification, data extraction, and validation for both Internet-based distributed capture or centralized environments.

Alfresco integrates with an open source J2EE-based leading portal framework called Liferay. The Alfresco-Liferay bundle is an out of the box solution that provides an excellent portal-based ECM solution.

Drupal, a free and open source modular framework and **Content Management System** (**CMS**) written in the PHP programming language, can also be integrated with Alfresco to yield effective solutions.

Alfresco integrates with external identity management systems such as LDAP and Active Directory, and supports centralized security and single sign-on.

Alfresco Enterprise 3.0—An overview

Alfresco Enterprise 3.0 is built on the Alfresco Surf platform. This platform enables you to build dynamic, REST-oriented web applications and collaborative web sites. . The Surf platform is designed to work in a number of different web environments. It includes content-oriented components designed around the **Yahoo! User Interface** (**YUI**) Library and Adobe Flash for dynamic uploads and the preview of content and other information. These new user interface components make it much simpler for users to develop new collaborative web applications. It is also designed so that it can work as a Web Part in Microsoft SharePoint Portal.

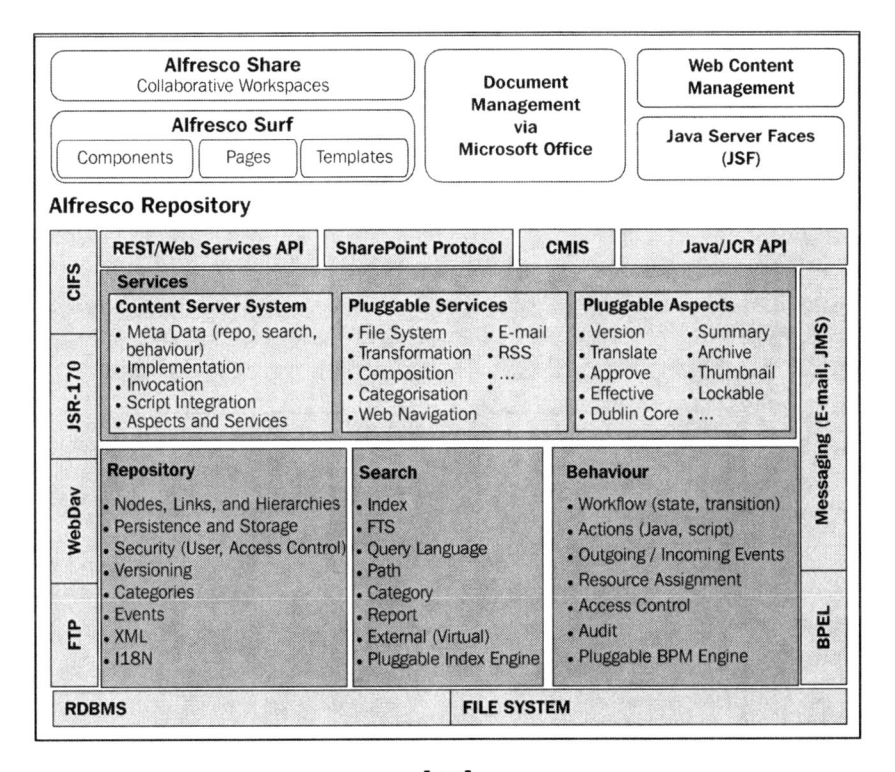

Alfresco Network

Alfresco Enterprise subscription customers are provided with access to Alfresco Network. Alfresco Network provides an easy-to-navigate portal frontend through which customers can access enhanced Enterprise features, including the following:

- Alfresco Knowledge Base: This is a repository of certified solutions, recommendations, and best practices for building with and configuring Alfresco's Enterprise product.
- Alfresco Call Tracking: This supports the creation and tracking of support tickets through to resolution.
- Documents and Downloads: This provides full access to Enterprise-certified product releases and their associated documentation.
- Extensions / Add-on Library: This provides access to officially certified and supported extensions and add-ons that can be plugged into your existing Alfresco Repository or Alfresco Surf presentation layer.
- Enhanced Support Experience: This provides live interaction with support engineers, document lockers, and also provides integrated call tracking history.
- Heartbeat and Monitoring: These provide remote support for the Alfresco Repository in order to monitor the heartbeat and health of the system, collect log files, and provide a quicker resolution turnaround.
- Enterprise News Feeds: These provide access to all of the latest updates, consolidated into feeds around product, support, and community news.

Alfresco Web Studio

Alfresco Web Studio is a visual, drag-and-drop, designer for building web sites using the **Alfresco Surf** platform. It features graphical overlays that facilitate the building of your web site's pages, navigation structure, templates, and presentation layout. Web components snap into your site's pages through simple drag-and-drop interactions. Using **Alfresco Web Studio**, you can quickly create custom web sites while leveraging the strengths of the Alfresco Web Content Management runtime and repository.

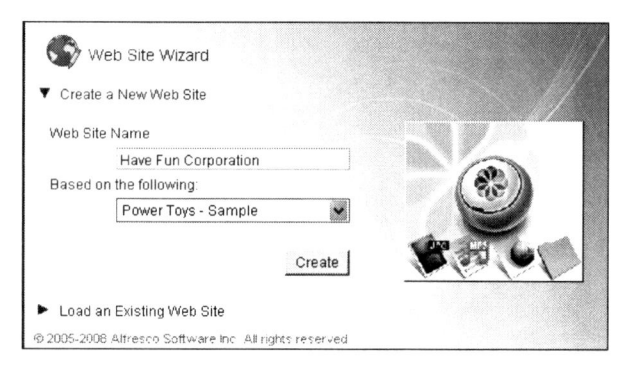

Alfresco Web Studio is available for Surf designers who want to build Surf applications by using a visual, drag-and-drop designer. By using Alfresco Web Studio, application designers are able to browse a library of Alfresco Web Components and visually assemble their web experience.

This puts the full-breadth of Alfresco Collaboration, Document Management, and Web Content Management functionality at their fingertips. It also opens the doors for Web Component provisioning from other open source and open standards vendors (that is, Google Gadgets and so on).

Alfresco Share

Alfresco Share delivers out of the box, collaborative content management. Alfresco Share simplifies the capturing, sharing, and retrieval of information across virtual teams, boosts productivity, and reduces network bandwidth requirements and email volumes between project team members.

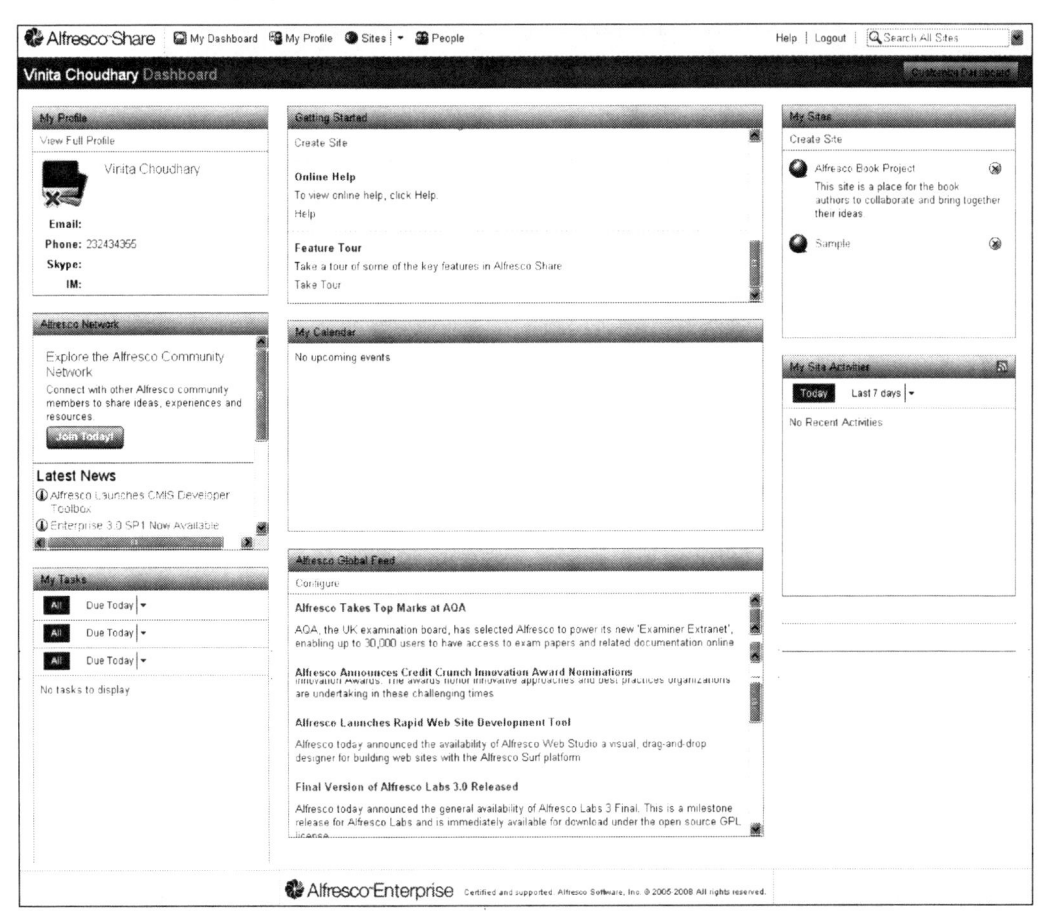

Introduction to Alfresco

Alfresco Share is built on Alfresco's innovative ECM repository. Additionally, Alfresco Share introduces a new, simplified, easy-to-use and easy-to-adopt knowledge worker UI. The current JSF client will still be available and unchanged, but, the migration to the new UI will be paced by the community and by the community's self-migration to the new UI infrastructure and user experience.

Now, you can share content in a document library and also have access to that content via thumbnails. You can upload project content in bulk and let others choose content via thumbnails and view content in a Flash viewer—allowing users to view content regardless of the originating application or product version (for example, Microsoft Office 2007). It is also possible to search rich metadata for document properties and tags. The content can be tagged, and access to the tags can be shared. Social tags can also be shared and filtered. Discussions can be created on sites, documents or even topics, and the content can also be provided via an RSS feed.

Alfresco Surf

Alfresco Surf is the presentation tier technology utilized by Alfresco for its entire 3.x product suite.

Alfresco Surf works hand-in-hand with Alfresco Web Content Management, and provides virtualized content retrieval, preview, and test support for user sandboxes and web projects. Applications built with Alfresco Surf can be deployed from Alfresco Web Project spaces to production servers while taking full advantage of Alfresco WCM's Enterprise class features.

Alfresco Repository Public API

The Repository Public API provides content and collaboration services for customizing and developing Alfresco applications. It was introduced with Labs 3b, and offers services such as site management, site activities, tagging, commenting, thumbnails, blogs, wikis, and forums for supporting social collaboration. These new REST APIs are based on ATOM Publishing. The Repository Public API has two forms:

- A RESTful API for remotely connecting to the Repository (as used by Alfresco Share.)
- A Javascript API for developing extensions to the Repository (as used in Web Scripts, Actions etc.)

Alfresco Draft CMIS Implementation

The Alfresco Enterprise 3.0 release includes a Draft CMIS Implementation. The **Content Management Interoperability Services (CMIS)** specification defines a domain model and a set of API bindings that can be used by applications to work with one or more Enterprise Content Management repositories or systems. The Alfresco Draft CMIS Implementation includes: CMIS REST API binding, CMIS Web Services API binding, CMIS query language, Apache Abdera CMIS Extension, and CMIS REST API Binding Test Harness. The CMIS implementation will provide the following benefits:.

- Being a write once, run-anywhere application
- Integrating multiple repositories
- Supporting business processes across repositories
- Requiring users to learn only one UI for all repositories

The CMIS technical draft specification (v0.5), announced on September 10th 2008, has been developed jointly by EMC, IBM, Microsoft, Alfresco, Open Text, Oracle, and SAP.

Microsoft SharePoint Protocol support

Alfresco was the first ECM to offer Microsoft Office SharePoint Protocol support. vailable at a lower cost and with no additional client installation, this is remarkable. It also allows a choice for hardware, database, operating system, application server, and portal products.

How you can benefit from Alfresco

Alfresco offers Enterprise Content Management (ECM), such as document management, collaboration, records management, knowledge management, web content management, and imaging. You can configure and customize Alfresco to address your specific business requirements. Some of these are listed below for your reference.

Using Alfresco for document management

Using Alfresco, you can implement document management solutions such as Enterprise Document Management, Digital Asset Management, and Contracts Management.

Alfresco document management features provide organizations with all of the services necessary for creating, converting, managing, and sharing electronic documents. Built on industry-standard open source platforms, Alfresco provides version management and search capabilities.

The document management administrator interface allows you to import and export workspaces and documents, define security, and provide user management through the definition of users, groups, and roles. Cost effective upgrades and data migration administration are some of the key benefits.

A built-in data management and transformation engine provides you with the ability to transform the data into required formats, based on business rules. Integrated workflow provides you with full control over the document life cycle, management, and process flow.

Presentation templates and dashboard views provide you with a personalized and real-time reporting of your content. The preview feature is useful for viewing the content in combination with other content elements. Similarly, the composite document feature helps you to logically group documents and digital assets for your marketing projects.

Digital Asset Management provides a single access point for all of your rich digital media and their underlying metadata information throughout the extended enterprise. Alfresco centralizes storage and provides easy, efficient, enterprise access to digital assets, and allows them to be quickly repurposed, which streamlines processes and saves money.

Whether it's an employment contract, a purchase agreement, a maintenance contract, or a collaboration agreement with a business partner, in order to protect a company's commercial interests, one should guarantee completeness, validity, traceability, and inalterability. Alfresco's document lifecycle management features ensure that people in various departments, divisions, or regions of a company can work together to support all of the processes relating to a contract throughout its lifecycle—from creation, through fulfillment and modification, to termination.

Key features include:

- Flexible metadata management
- Full audit control
- Transformation of data
- Security and version control
- Indexing and full text search
- Locking, Check-in and Check-out
- Offline briefcase synchronization to allow offline access content

- Taxonomy and categorization of content
- Advanced search with combined metadata, location, and multi-category search
- Soft deletes and deleted documents recovery support
- Scheduled jobs and actions
- Management of web assets

Using Alfresco for records management

Using Alfresco, you can implement records management solutions, such as enterprise records management, compliance, imaging, forms management, and business process management.

Alfresco's record management features provide a secure, auditable environment for creating, declaring, classifying, retaining, and destroying records. Organizations can ensure compliance by defining and enforcing policies for records use, storage, and disposition, with a legally-defensible audit trail.

Records management capabilities are modeled to support the US Department of Defense 5015.2 Records Management standards. Alfresco provides file plan templates for numbering, classification, disposition, and other metadata-driven population of records. Disposition includes the transfer of records and/or the ultimate destruction of the records.

Predefined reports will provide you with information about recent records, records due for cut-off, records due for expiry, records due for transfer, and records due for destruction.

The lifecycle determines the disposition of the record, including when the records will be cut off or grouped together, how long the records will be held, and what happens to the record after the holding period expires—whether they are transferred to a records holding area, or whether they should be destroyed.

By integrating with scanning and OCR technologies, Alfresco provides an end-to-end solution for collecting paper documents and forms, transforming them into accurate, retrievable information, and delivering the content into an organization's business applications. The information then becomes full-text searchable, and goes through various lifecycles based on the organization's defined business process

Emails are considered as records in some organizations. Alfresco enables you to drag-and-drop emails from Microsoft Outlook into the file plan space. The system will extract the metadata from email files and populate information such as who the e-mail is from, who the recipients are, and the subject of the email. Email content is stored in a secure and scalable repository, and is also full-text searchable.

Introduction to Alfresco

Key features include:

- Record plans
- Automatic conversion from proprietary office formats to long-term vendor neutral formats such as **Open Document Format (ODF)** and **Portable Document Format (PDF)**
- Vital records information management
- Record cut-off information management
- Record holding and retention management
- Record transfer process
- Record destruction management
- Record lifecycle management
- Archival policies
- Disposition schedules
- Restriction of user functions
- Audit trails

Using Alfresco for web content management

Using Alfresco, you can implement web content management solutions with a scalable content repository, a web 2.0 AJAX-based user interface, flexible workflow, multi-language support, and a robust search engine.

Alfresco web content management features provide a rich environment for creating, managing, and publishing web content, along with an infrastructure for supporting multiple sites. This managed content can include text, HTML, XML files, graphics and photos, video or audio, and specialized programming required for user interaction. Through this solution, organizations can integrate multiple disparate sites and data formats, and give users (often sales people, partners and customers) rapid access to information, and in a timely manner. Because, Alfresco web content management is built on open source platforms, supporting, managing, and expanding these systems can be straightforward and cost-effective.

Alfresco supports a wide range of protocols, such as HTTP, HTTPS, WebDAV, web services, XML-RPC, FTP, and RMI for the exchange of content with external systems. With the help of technologies such as RSS and web services, the content is delivered to various channels such as public internet sites, internal marketing sites, and portals.

Alfresco leverages the existing infrastructure for membership such as LDAP, Active Directory, and Relational databases. A granular level of security enables content authors to secure a single web page and also the files, embedded images, and videos within a web page.

Users of the Alfresco web content management system are typically nontechnical business users, or subject matter experts who do not understand HTML syntax. Alfresco includes inline editors to edit text, HTML and XML content, and connectors to edit the office documents using desktop tools of your choice. The transformation engine is used to transform content from one form to another. For example, all of the incoming images of various types and sizes can be transformed to a standard format and size.

Drag-and-drop layout development lets users customize the look and feel of web sites without waiting for assistance from developers. Alfresco speaks your language and supports multilingual content management.

A robust, full-text search engine lets you search your web content (HTML, PDF, MS-Word, PowerPoint slides, and so on) based on your security access permissions. Advanced search features enable you to search web content based on its metadata and keyword values.

Key features include:

- Standards-based forms for creating content
- An e-mail based workflow and approval process
- An in-context review or view of changes in the context of a live site
- Managing branches and support for parallel branching
- Pre-built templates for both web sites and web site components
- The integration of enterprise systems
- The re-use of existing sites–easily re-use an existing look and feel
- High-availability, fault tolerance, and scalability support for any number of sites, auto failover, and clustering of the delivery tier
- Multi-site change set management–support for projects, sandboxes, change sets, layers, and snapshots
- A preview feature with presentation templates
- The management of web assets
- Brand management
- A Digital Image Library

Using Alfresco for collaboration management

Using Alfresco, you can implement collaboration solutions, such as corporate and departmental intranets, knowledge management, and client and project extranets.

Introduction to Alfresco

Alfresco collaboration features provide the infrastructure, integration points, and tools required for accessing, sharing, and distributing content among users or systems. Built upon industry standards, open source platforms, Alfresco helps you to quickly define and develop environments for teams (project teams, associations, research, and so on) that will streamline processes, reduce costs, and improve time to market. Users can manage and collaborate on documents, web information, and forms within a single system through a consistent user interface.

A comprehensive security model that is based on individuals, groups, projects, and team spaces provides you with the highest level of control. The solution leverages the existing infrastructure, such as LDAP or Active Directory, for authentication and authorization.

A web-based rules engine enables business users to define the business and content rules appropriately, without the help of programmers and IT. Alfresco supports a graphical tool for defining the workflow and business process management for content flow in collaborative environments.

Users can discuss content by using the discussion forums and discussion threads tied to the content. Users can subscribe to content and receive email notifications when content is added or updated. The solution supports both inbound and outbound RSS syndication for sharing content beyond the corporate firewalls.

Interfaces such as **Common Internet File System (CIFS)** and WebDAV allow each team member or department to map the folder on the server as a local network drive. This enables the bulk transfer of files between your local system and the central server repository. Users can use their favorite editors to edit the content that is mapped in the local network drive.

Knowledge Management (KM) refers to a range of practices used by organizations to identify, create, represent, and distribute knowledge for re-use, awareness, and learning across the organization.

Key features include:

- Team spaces
- Full audit control
- Discussion forums
- Message boards
- RSS syndication
- Ad-hoc security
- A version controlled content repository

- Full-text search of various content items
- User-controlled routing
- Integration of enterprise systems
- High availability, fault tolerance, and scalability
- Business process-driven content management

Using Alfresco for enterprise content search

Most ECM systems do not consider search to be an important part of Enterprise Content Management. Search functionality helps us to locate information quickly, to generate business reports, and to make business decisions. The following features of Alfresco will provide you with an enterprise search solution:

- Single-point access to an enterprise content repository
- Full-text search of documents
- The ability to index documents and provide metadata search capabilities
- The ability to build and share reports by using saved searches
- The ability to search for users and collaborative groups
- The ability to search archived content

Applications of Alfresco

Because the architecture is flexible and extensible, you can build various applications using Alfresco, such as:

- Enterprise document repositories
- Intranets
- Enterprise knowledge management portals
- Scalable content repositories
- Corporate web sites
- Marketing communications
- On demand publishing
- Compliance and records management
- Financial applications that involve security, forms handling, and an approval process
- Research portals for collaboration and the sharing of information

Alfresco's web site (http://www.alfresco.com) has a list of customer case studies. Going through these case studies will help you understand the type of applications that you could develop using Alfresco.

How does the future look like with Alfresco?

This book is based on Alfresco Enterprise 3.0. This book is an update to a previous book, which was on the Alfresco 1.4 release. The Alfresco system has evolved towards a state-of-the-art, one-point solution to the ECM needs.

In 2009, Alfresco aimed to focus on five key areas:

- New and enhanced team and enterprise collaboration services
- Publishing and management services for dynamic, Web 2.0-enabled web sites
- Web client usability
- Scalability, performance, and enterprise-readiness
- Standards

There has been so much interest from international organizations, governments, and multinational corporations that translation seems a natural extension of the Alfresco model.

Alfresco has weaved itself into a number of other products. Products such as Quark, Acrobat.com, CAStor and Adobe LiveCycle are just a few to mention who have incorporated the Alfresco ECM into their products in some way.

Enterprise versus Community Labs

Alfresco spent the summer of 2008 releasing Alfresco Labs 3, which includes a version of their new collaboration solution, Alfresco Share, and Surf which is a new development platform. From there, they spent time performing extensive testing to prepare for the release of their latest enterprise version.

The enterprise version is the certified build of Alfresco—the one that is sold to production environments for companies and government organizations that want a stable, supported solution. Alfresco currently has over 700 organizations using the enterprise version.

Enterprise releases are available to customers with an enterprise subscription. Enterprise releases are tested and certified for customer deployment. The releases include a maintenance release train of engineering-led and customer-driven bug fixes to ensure successful operation in an enterprise environment. These bug fixes will periodically be made available in the community code-line, where they are mixed in with upcoming features and other product enhancements. Maintenance release schedules are driven by Alfresco Support.

Enterprise Edition	Community Labs
100% Open Source with Commercial Support	100% Open Source. No Alfresco or Certified Partner Support
High-Availability Cluster Certified	No High-Availability Cluster Testing
Scalability Certified	No Scalability Testing
Stress Tested, Certified and Supported Build	Daily Build with SVN Access
Certified across Combinations of both Open Source and Commercial Stacks	Quality Assurance on Periodic Build on a Basic Open Source Stack

Better support options

Alfresco comes with multiple support options. Firstly, it is supported by the company Alfresco, which gives users direct access to Alfresco's engineering team and the most recent bug fixes. This is currently the best way to receive high-quality support for the Alfresco software. However, as more and more people adopt the software, the options for quality support beyond Alfresco–the company–will improve.

At any given point in time, the following three support alternatives exist for Alfresco open source software:

- In-house development support: Because the source code is open source, you can train your developers in-house to support your application that has been built using Alfresco.

- Community support: Alfresco already has a big community world wide. With a growing community, you can always get help through the Alfresco community forums, although the quality of support can vary.

- Alfresco enterprise network support: As mentioned, Alfresco Inc. currently provides the highest quality option for production and development support. This support is provided to the company's customers who are using the Enterprise product. It includes direct access to the engineers who write the Alfresco code, up-to-date bug fixes, configuration assistance, and a range of other services.

Free upgrades

For every new release, you will receive free, upgraded software. You might have to take care of your specific customization to upgrade to the latest version of the software. It is important to follow best practices while implementing Alfresco, so that upgrades are easier and less expensive to handle.

Implementing an example solution using Alfresco

Subsequent chapters of this book contain examples to help you implement your requirements, such as collaboration, customization, document management and so, on using Alfresco. These examples are an attempt to solve similar content management problems, that are encountered in a typical enterprise.

The idea of providing examples in this book is to:

- Engage the reader, and keep the material feeling realistic.
- Help you apply the features of Alfresco to your business decisions. You will see in the fictional example that decisions are made for particular reasons, and you can compare and contrast these reasons (and thus the decisions) with your own situation.
- Give the book an overall theme, through a narrative engine, to keep things moving and not make this book feel like technical documentation.

Where do you get more information?

The best place to start looking for more information is Alfresco's own corporate web site (`http://www.alfresco.com`). You can find the latest news and events, various training programs that offered worldwide, presentations, demonstrations, and hosted trails on this web site.

Alfresco is 100 percent open source, and all of the downloads are available from the SourceForge.net web site at `http://sourceforge.net/project/showfiles.php?group_id=143373`.

The Alfresco Wiki (`http://wiki.alfresco.com`) contains documentation including a tutorial, user guide, developer guide, administrator guide, roadmap, and so on.

The Alfresco discussion forums (http://forums.alfresco.com) are the best place to share your thoughts, and to get tips and tricks about Alfresco implementation. The discussion forums are available in multiple languages which can be selected on the home page of the Alfresco web site (www.alfresco.com).

If you would like to file a bug or learn more about the fixes in a specific release, then you must visit the bug tracking system at http://issues.alfresco.org/

Summary

Alfresco is the leading open source alternative for Enterprise Content Management. It couples the innovation of open source with the stability of a true enterprise-class platform. The open source model allows Alfresco to use the best-of-breed open source technologies and contributions from the open source community in order to get higher-quality software produced more quickly, and at a much lower cost.

Alfresco provides the key features of a scalable, robust, and secure Content Management System, in order to deliver trusted and relevant content to your customers, suppliers, and employees.

2
Installing Alfresco

One of the remarkable features of Alfresco is the ease with which it can be installed and deployed. The simple out of the box installation is quite straight forward, with preconfigured options that are aimed at having a complete, working content management system in no time. This chapter provides you with a basic understanding of Alfresco architecture, various installation options, and the key terminologies used. By the end of this chapter, you will be well equipped with the information necessary to make a choice of a suitable operating system, database, application server, and other software required for your installation. This chapter is essential reading matter for anyone not already familiar with Alfresco.

By the end of this chapter, you will have learned about:

- The overall architecture of Alfresco
- Determining what is the correct installation option for you
- Out of the box full installation of Alfresco
- Installing Alfresco and all of the required software
- Installing Alfresco Components
- Installing modules with AMP Install

Installing Alfresco

Before delving directly into installation, it is important for you to understand the architecture behind Alfresco and the various installation options available to you. This will help you to make good decisions in selecting the appropriate software for your business application.

Installing Alfresco

Out of the box installation architecture

The Out of the box deployment of Alfresco is a typical web application architecture, consisting of different layers, as shown in the next figure. This new architecture is basically N-tier and delivers scalability without the need for massive hardware and software investment. It can also accommodate more users with the existing hardware resources. The layered architecture of Alfresco provides the benefits of easily manageable, flexible, and highly scalable content management solution.

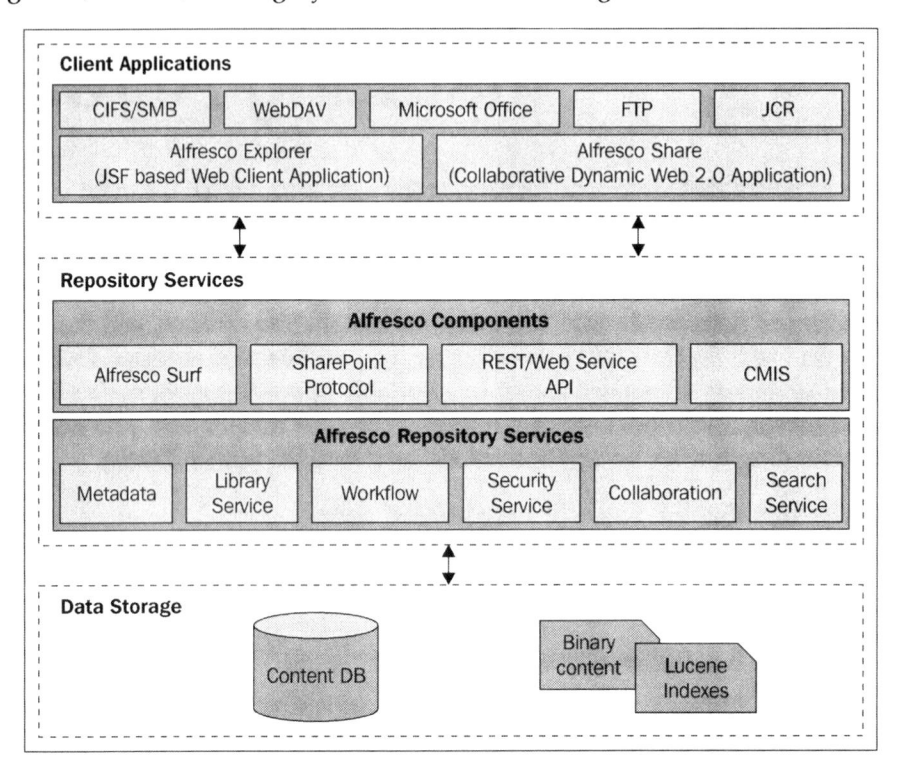

Client Applications layer

The Client Applications layer contains the actual application, as the web browser, on the user's machine, that is, basically the presentation layer. Out of the box, Alfresco provides two client applications: Alfresco Explorer and Alfresco Share. Alfresco Explorer is a pure document management web application, and Alfresco Share is a web 2.0 application, that provides dynamic, collaborative support. In the next couple of chapters, we will talk about these two applications in detail. Along with these two applications, Alfresco provides support for CIFS, FTP, WebDAV, Microsoft office, and so on. Refer to the topic in Chapter 9, named *Integrations*, for more information on the different client applications that are integrated into Alfresco in order to leverage the services provided by Alfresco.

Repository Services layer

The Repository Services layer consists of Alfresco components and services. This new architecture provides a clear separation between the presentation tier and the repository tier. The Alfresco RESTful API provides access to its services via HTTP, which makes it accessible to other tools and applications. The Alfresco Surf platform enables you to build dynamic, REST-oriented web applications and collaborative web sites. More detailed information about Surf platforms are provided in Chapter 11. The SharePoint protocol offers greater choice for Microsoft users, by providing them with the first open source, fully-compatible SharePoint repository. Companies can leverage existing investments in Linux and Java, as well as Microsoft .NET connection software, to significantly reduce their SharePoint total cost of ownership and maximize their hardware and software investments. Chapter 11 describes SharePoint protocol in detail. The **Content Management Interoperability Services (CMIS)** specification defines a domain model and a set of API bindings that can be used by applications, to work with one or more Enterprise Content Management repositories or systems.

Data Storage layer

The Data Storage layer stores the data in a relational database and a file system.

The content in Alfresco is stored in persistent back-end systems such as a database and file system. There is a reason for using both database and a file system as content storage. Any content within Alfresco consists of two elements—the content itself and information about the content (metadata).

The actual content can be anything from simple documents (HTML, XML) to images, audio, and video. The actual content and its related versions are stored as binary files in the file system. Storing content in a file system has its own advantages. It allows a very large amount of content, random-access streaming, and options for different storage devices. It is important to note that Alfresco is agnostic with respect to the file system it utilizes. It is possible to configure Alfresco to use a vast diversity of file systems.

Alfresco uses Lucene—a popular open source search engine, to provide metadata searching, and full text search capabilities of the content. Apart from the actual binary content, Lucene's index files are also stored in the file system.

The content metadata consists of information that includes elements like:

- The format of the content
- The date the content was created
- The language the content is in

The security settings are stored in the relational database.

The components of Alfresco applications

The application server hosts the user interface and domain logic. It provides an abstraction and enables communication between the client and storage layers. In the case of Alfresco, the application server houses Alfresco applications (such as the Alfresco Explorer and Alfresco Share) and the Alfresco repository.

The Alfresco repository provides a set of reusable cross-cutting content management services such as content storage, query, versioning, and transformation, which may be utilized by one or more applications.

An Alfresco application provides a complete solution tailored for a specific area of content management such as document management and records management. The user interfaces for all of these applications are referred to as Alfresco Explorer and Alfresco Share. Alfresco Explorer is the JSF based client, which is highly customizable and configurable according to specific user requirements. The out of the box web client gives you lot of packaged functionality. With the web client management console, you can manage users, security, content, business rules, and so on. Additionally, Alfresco Share introduces a new, simplified, easy-to-use, and adopt knowledge worker UI. The current JSF client is still available and is unchanged.

Accessing the application

There is no installation or configuration required for the Alfresco user interface. Any number of web browsers can connect to the application without prior client installation activities.

The out of box installation comes with Alfresco Share and the Alfresco Share web client, which you can use to connect to the Alfresco repository through web-based applications.

Apart from these applications, Alfresco's out of the box installation supports various client applications for accessing Alfresco content via Web Services or protocols such as FTP, WebDAV, and CIFS:

- **File Transfer Protocol (FTP)**: This is useful for transferring files from your local file system to the remote server.
- **WWW Distributed Authoring and Versioning (WebDAV)**: This is primarily designed for editing and managing files on remote web servers in a structured way. For example, an application like Adobe Photoshop can directly open and edit a file in the Alfresco content repository. This gives you the flexibility of using your own favorite editor to edit the content on the Alfresco server.
- **Common Internet File System (CIFS)**: This maps Alfresco's content as your local file system folder.

Web Services: Most of the ECM products, on the market store content, are in a proprietary format, which is like a **black box**. Alfresco's content is stored as per the **JCR (Java Content Repository-JSR 170)** open standards. Any JCR-compliant client application can read content that is stored in the Alfresco repository. This is one of the key selling points of Alfresco. An API is provided out of the box so that you can connect to the Alfresco repository from your applications, through web services or JCR integration.

Choosing the right installation option

Alfresco is a completely open source application, which is developed using open standards. Hence, it runs on various operating systems, relational databases, application servers, web browsers, and portals, and supports various languages. Let us examine all of the choices, and determine which option is right for you.

Enterprise and community editions

Alfresco currently provides two types of product download options:

- Alfresco Community Lab Network
- Alfresco Enterprise Network

Both of these options have the same code base and features, and are completely open source. For both the options, you can use the Alfresco documentation (Wiki), community support (forums), and community-contributed add-on products. Alfresco Community Lab Network is free. Alfresco Enterprise Network requires a per-CPU license fee.

The Alfresco Community Labs Network is an unsupported product and is mainly designed for developers and technical enthusiasts in non-critical environments. Alfresco Community Lab is released early and often, and renders a daily build, while offering the latest functionality. It doesn't provide scalability or high availability certifications. I would recommend this for use as the research vehicle for new features, and as the platform for the Alfresco Community, and consider it as a test drive before you install the Enterprise edition.

If you are implementing Alfresco for a major corporation or a financial, insurance, government or healthcare organization, I would recommend that you go for Alfresco Enterprise Network support. The primary benefit is that with the support of Alfresco and its certified partners you will get a stable, reliable, certified, and supported application with warranty and indemnity. Your Alfresco version will be certified on all available stacks, such as Linux, Windows, MySQL, Oracle, and so on. You will also benefit from Alfresco support, which includes problem resolution, compatibility advice, migration advice, and upgrade support. For mission-critical applications, you will get 24 x 7 support from Alfresco experts.

Operating systems—Windows, Linux, UNIX, and MacOS

Choosing an operating system to run Alfresco on will be based on various factors. For some companies it depends on in-house expertise. For example, if you have administrators and I.T staff who can easily manage business applications running on a Microsoft windows platform, then your choice could be to go with the Windows operating system. For some companies it is based on the integration requirements with existing systems.

If you do not have any preferences, I would recommend that you go with Linux operating system for production use. Linux source code is freely distributed. Tens of thousands of programmers have reviewed the source code to improve performance, eliminate bugs, and strengthen security. No other operating system has ever undergone this level of review. The key advantages of Linux are listed below:

- It has the best technical support available
- It has no vendor lock-in
- It runs on a wide range of hardware
- It is exceptionally stable
- It supports many tools and applications that you may need
- It interoperates with many other types of computer systems
- It has a low total cost of ownership

Databases—MySQL, Oracle, MS SQL Server, and PostgreSQL

The data access layer of Alfresco is implemented using an open source software component and ORM (Object Relational Mapping) tool called **Hibernate.** Hibernate abstracts the database layer and provides seamless integration between the Alfresco repository and any relational database.

If you have already chosen the Microsoft Windows operating system, then the natural choice for you would be MS SQL Server. If you already have a license for Oracle, then an Oracle database is the best choice for you. Alfresco also supports the PostgreSQL database.

If you do not have any preference, I recommend that you go with the MySQL database, which costs nothing if you go with the open source version. The MySQL database has become the world's most popular open source database because of its consistent, fast performance, high reliability, and easy usability. It's used in more than 10 million installations, ranging from large corporations to specialized embedded applications. MySQL runs on more than 20 platforms, including Linux, Windows, OS/X, HP-UX, AIX, and Netware, giving you the kind of flexibility that puts you in control.

Application servers—Tomcat and JBoss

Alfresco runs on any J2SE 5.0 complaint application server. Hence, there are no application server specific dependencies. However, it is important to make a choice of application server before moving into production.

Alfresco uses the **Spring** framework and not the **Enterprise Java Beans** (**EJB**) framework. This means that there is no dependency on JBoss or any other application server that provides EJB containers. **Spring** is an open source application framework for Java/JEE. The Alfresco repository uses the Spring Framework as the core foundation of its architecture. If you are developing a standalone application, then Apache Tomcat might be a good option. Tomcat powers numerous large-scale and mission-critical web applications across a diverse range of industries and organizations. It is the most widely-accepted web application server on the market.

On the other hand, you should consider using the JBoss application server, which has the highest market capture (> 35%) of J2EE-based application servers in the world. JBoss internally uses Tomcat, and hence you get the benefits of the Tomcat servlet engine as well.

Alfresco utilizes JBoss caching ability to distribute and maintain data caches, making it possible to build large-scale systems that outperform traditional Enterprise Content Management systems. Alfresco also utilizes the clustering, failover and load balancing facilities of the JBoss application server, in order to increase scalability. Alfresco's business process management features are powered by JBoss jBPM tool.

If you have already invested in JBoss, then Alfresco provides complementary industry-leading Enterprise Content Management technology to the JBoss enterprise middleware system suite.

Portals (optional)—JBoss Portal and Liferay

You can go with a portal of your choice; if you already have an enterprise portal then you can integrate Alfresco with it. If you do not have a portal in place and you would like to leverage the portal framework, then you can consider using either the JBoss portal or the Liferay portal. Both of these are based on J2EE technology; both of them are open source and open standards based, and both of them have Alfresco's built-in support.

JBoss Portal provides an open source platform for hosting and serving a portal's web interface, publishing and managing its content, and customizing its experience. Whereas most packaged portal frameworks help enterprises to launch portals more quickly, only JBoss Portal delivers the benefits of a zero-cost, open source license combined with a flexible and scalable underlying platform.

Liferay is the most downloaded and popular open source portal with 40,000 downloads per month. It runs on top of any J2EE servlet, such as Tomcat, so a full installation of JBoss is not required. However, it can be run against most full application-servers out of the box including JBoss, JRun, BEA, WebLogic and Orion. It has full set of web service interfaces to the portal. Liferay supports 800+ portlets (products) and has wider adoption in the market.

Choose the appropriate software for your installation

You need to make the best choice of software to install Alfresco. If you do not have any specific requirements, you might consider a complete open source stack for production usage, and go with Alfresco **Enterprise** Edition on the **Linux** operating system with the **MySQL** database running on the **JBoss** application server with a **Liferay** Portal.

The examples in this book were created and tested with the following choice of Alfresco installation:

- Alfresco Enterprise 3
- Operating System: Windows XP
- Database: MySQL 5
- Application server: Tomcat 6
- JDK 5
- Portal: None

Installing on Microsoft Windows

In our earlier section, you may have noticed that the repository application server is the default deployment option chosen. This means that the out of the box Alfresco installation is a typical web application, where the web application server becomes the host for an embedded repository and is accessible through the HTTP protocol. In this section, we will discuss the requirements and procedures for the two flavors of installation of Alfresco, *Full Installation* and *Installation of Alfresco Tomcat Bundle*.

Full installation

The default installation of Alfresco software requires installing the Windows enterprise version, `Alfresco-Enterprise-<version>-Full-Setup.exe`, downloaded from the SourceForge project location (`http://sourceforge.net/project/showfiles.php?group_id=143373`). Alfresco is hosting its own community download area, so you can also download this from `http://www.Alfresco.com/products/ecm/enttrial/`. Select the download package, and you will be asked for the user name and password of the Alfresco content community.

At the time of writing this book, the latest version was Alfresco Enterprise 3.0.1 and installer file *Alfresco-Enterprise-3.0.1-Full-Setup.exe* is approximately 350 MB in size.

This installer will install:

- Java Development Kit (JDK) — If JDK is not already installed on your machine
- Apache Tomcat 6.0.18
- Portable Open Office 3
- Alfresco Explorer web application, packaged as a Web Archive (WAR)
- Alfresco Share web application, packaged as a Web Archive (WAR)
- Share point Protocol support

To install and run Alfresco, you need at least 500 MB disk space and at least 512 MB RAM on the desktop or server.

The following steps are a simple way of installing all of the software and components required to run Alfresco, through the installation wizard:

1. Start the installation of Alfresco by double-clicking on the Alfresco installer. Select the language `English` from Language Selection dialog.
2. Click **yes** when prompted for installation confirmation, and the installation wizard is launched.

Installing Alfresco

You will see this welcome screen:

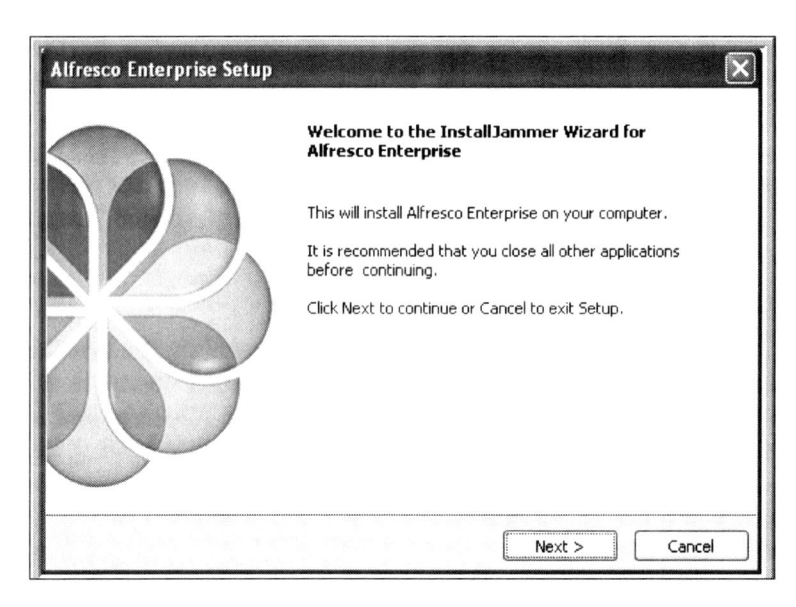

3. After you click **Next**, you will be asked for the type of setup. You will have two options: **Typical** and **Custom**. Typical will install everything, including Default Component, Samples, WCM, Java, OpenOffice. With the Custom option you can select the custom components for installation. For full installation, choose **Typical** and click on **Next**.

4. You will see the option to choose the installation folder. Let us install Alfresco in the default folder proposed by the installer, which is C:\Alfresco. Please note that you have the option to browse and select another folder by clicking on the **Browse** button. Once you are done with the folder selection, click on **Next**.

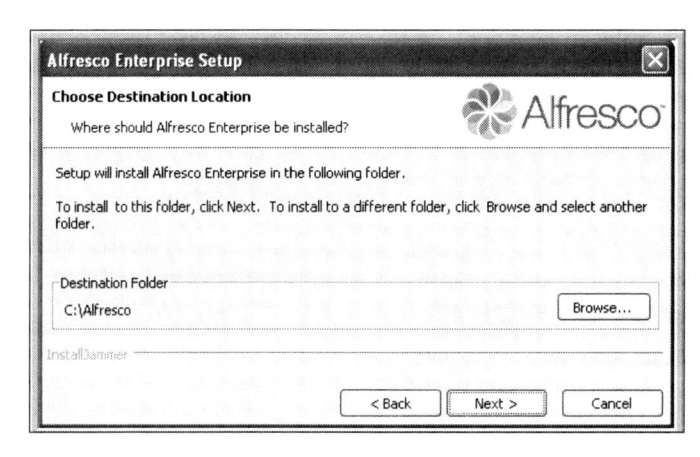

5. In the next window, review the settings and click on **Next** to start installation.
6. On the next screen, select the database `MySQL`. This should be installed and running already on your machine. Click on **Next**.

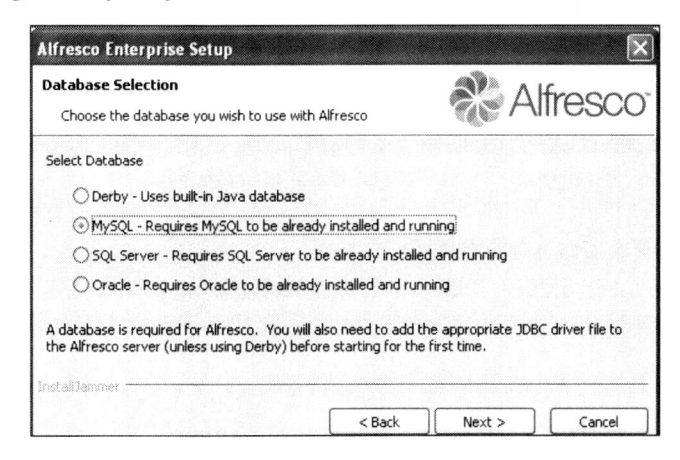

7. On the next screen, provide the password for MySQL installed on your machine, and click on **Next**.
8. The installer will try to establish the connection to MySQL and creates a new database named `Alfresco`. Click on **Next**.
9. You will be notified upon successful creation of the database. On the next screen, you will be asked to put the database JDBC driver file (.jar) in the Tomcat `C:\Alfresco\tomcat\lib` folder.
10. Once you have completed the installation, the final installation screen will be as shown , as in the screenshot below. Do not forget to read the contents of the `Readme` file, as it contains information about using CIFS , along with some troubleshooting tips.

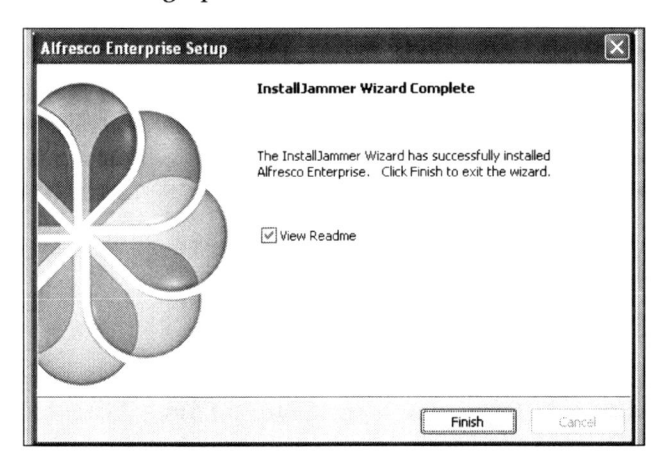

11. Run the `alf_start.bat` file, which is available at `C:\Alfresco`. Wait a few seconds to allow Tomcat to start, and then fire up your web browser and browse to `http://localhost:8080/Alfresco`. Since this is the first time that you are using Alfresco, use **admin** as your username and password.

Installation of the Alfresco Tomcat bundle

This section provides the installation pre-configured Tomcat bundle for Alfresco, which requires JDK to already be installed on your machine.

Installing Java SE Developer Kit

The very first step for installing Alfresco is to install the Java SE Developer kit. Alfresco requires Java 1.5 or higher. If you already have JDK then you can skip this section.

To Install Java SDK, carry out the following steps:

1. Download JDK 5.0 update or JDK 6.0 update from `http://java.sun.com/javase/downloads`.
2. After downloading, double-click the installation file to automatically proceed with the installation.
3. Accept the license agreement. Click on **Next**.
4. In the next window, for a custom set-up, choose **Default**. Click on **Next**.
5. In the next window, choose the desired browsers to install Java for [optional]. Click on **Finish**.
6. Test your installation by issuing the command `C:\> java` –version from the command prompt.
7. Create a `JAVA_HOME` environment variable to set the path of Java SE Developer Kit.

Installing Alfresco bundled with Tomcat

For convenience, Alfresco provides the bundle of Alfresco with Tomcat. This bundle includes a pre configured Tomcat server, together with the Alfresco web application archive (`Alfresco.war`) file, the Alfresco Share web application archive (`share.war`), batch files, database setup scripts, a sample extension folder, and so on.

To download the Apache Tomcat bundled with Alfresco application, carry out the steps shown below:

1. Browse to the customer or partner's portal.
2. Log in to the Alfresco web client and Browse to **Company Home > Downloads > 3.0 Releases > 3.x Enterprise > Installation Files > Alfresco DM**.
3. Download `Alfresco-enterprise-tomcat-<version>.zip`.

To install the Apache Tomcat bundled with Alfresco application, use the following steps:

1. Unzip the downloaded bundle to `C:\`
2. Confirm the creation of the folder `c:\Alfresco`, with unzipped files.
3. The Alfresco application is packaged in a web application archive (WAR file) and is found under the `webapps` folder (`C:\Alfresco\tomcat\webapps`).
4. When installed, the WAR file automatically unpacks itself into a folder named `Alfresco`.

Installation of other Alfresco Components

This section describes the installation of the Alfresco components.

Installing SharePoint Protocol Support

If you have installed Alfresco by using the full setup, then this support will already be there. Otherwise, follow the steps below to add SharePoint protocol support.

To download `Apache vti-module.amp` and `ROOT.war`, use the following steps:

1. Download `vti-module.amp`, Connector functionality for Microsoft SharePoint Protocol support, from `http://process.Alfresco.com/ccdl/?file=build-1342/vti-module.amp&a=y&s=n&t=y`.
2. Download `ROOT.war`, the Microsoft SharePoint Protocol support servlet that forwards Office requests to the main web application, from `http://process.Alfresco.com/ccdl/?file=build-1342/ROOT.war&a=y&s=n&t=y`

To install SharePoint support, carry out the following steps:

1. To install this module, copy `vti-module.amp` to the `<Alfresco_installation_folder>\amps` folder
2. Run the `apply_amps.bat` file, which is available at `<Alfresco_installation_folder>`
3. Copy `ROOT.war` in `<Alfresco_installation_folder>\tomcat\webapps` folder
4. Delete the `Alfresco` and `ROOT` folders in `webapps`, if they exist.

Installing the Alfresco license file

If you want to use Alfresco Enterprise edition, you require a license file. Alfresco Enterprise edition comes up with a 30 day evaluation license. If you don't provide a license file then you can evaluate Alfresco for 30 days. After that it, will be expired and you will only have 'read only' access to the repository.

Installing Alfresco

To download the Alfresco license file, proceed with the following steps:

1. Browse to the customer or partner's portal.
2. Login to Alfresco web client and browse to **Company Home > Downloads > 3 Releases > 3.x Enterprise > Licence Files**
3. Download the customer license, `Alfresco-enterprise-<version>-customer-unlimited.lic`, or partner license, `Alfresco-enterprise-<version>-partner-unlimited.lic`.

To install the license file, use the following steps:

1. Shut down Alfresco, if it's already running
2. Browse to the folder:
   `<Alfresco_installation_folder>\tomcat\shared\Alfresco\extension\license`
3. Place the downloaded license file into this folder.
4. Restart the Alfresco server.

After the successful installation of this license, the suffix '.installed' will be appended to the file name and you can begin to utilize the terms of your license immediately.

Installing and configuring the MySQL database

As mentioned earlier in this chapter, the content in Alfresco is stored in persistent back-end systems, such as a database and a file system. So for the persistence of metadata, we need a database. Alfresco, by default, uses MySQL to persist the metadata.

If you have already installed MySQL on your machine, you can skip this section.

To install MySQL, use the following steps:

1. Download the MySQL package from `http://dev.mysql.com/downloads/` Alfresco requires MySQL 4.1 or higher.
2. After downloading the package navigate to your download location and unzip.
3. Double-click on the `setup.exe` file to automatically start the installation.
4. You will see the welcome message screen, as shown below. Click on **Next**.

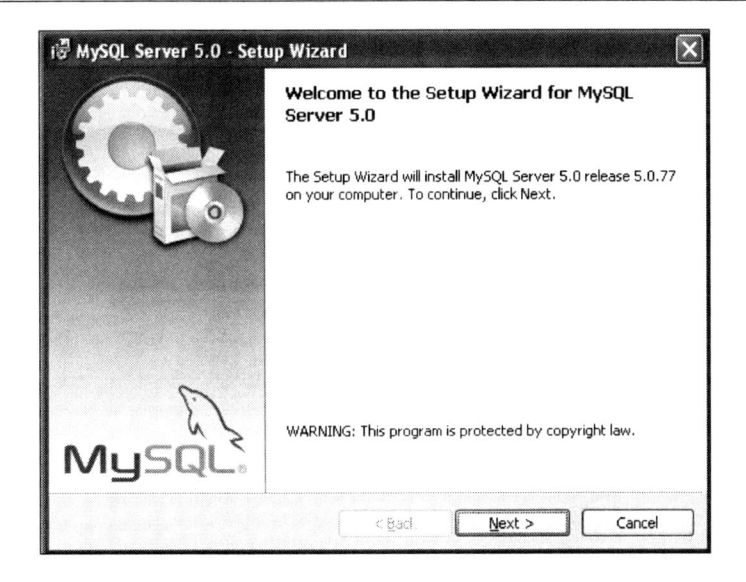

5. Select the **Typical** setup on the next screen.
6. Choose the default options for the remaining screens.
7. Once that wizard completes, you will have the option to configure the MySQL server instance, as shown in the screenshot below. Select **Configure the MySQL Server now** and then click on **Finish**.

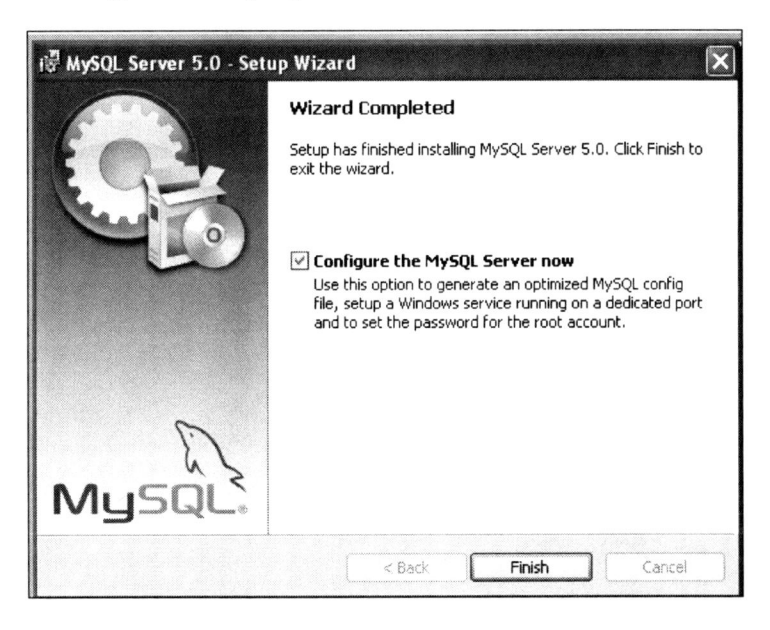

Installing Alfresco

8. You will then see the welcome screen for **the MySQL Server Instance configuration wizard**, as shown below. Click on **Next**.

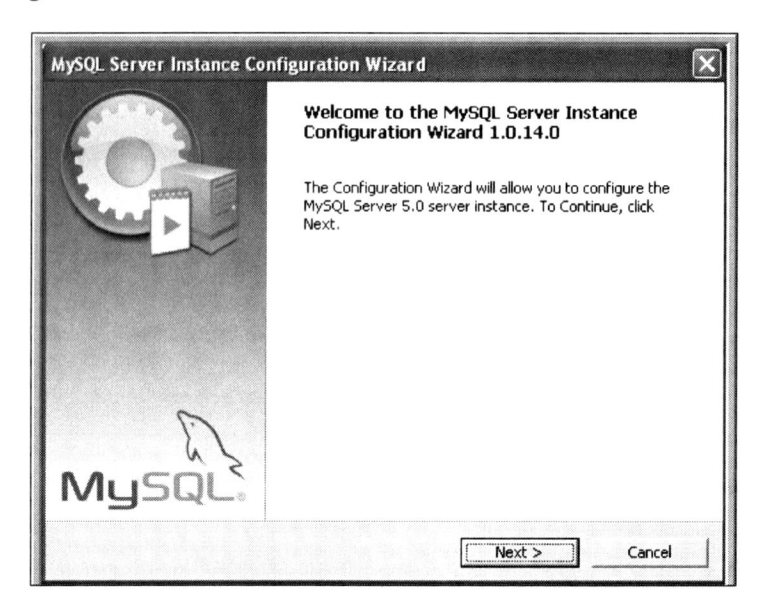

9. Choose the default selected options on the next screens.
10. Select **UTF8 Character** set, when asked.
11. Accept the option: **Install As Windows Service** option, as shown in the screen below. Click on **Next**.

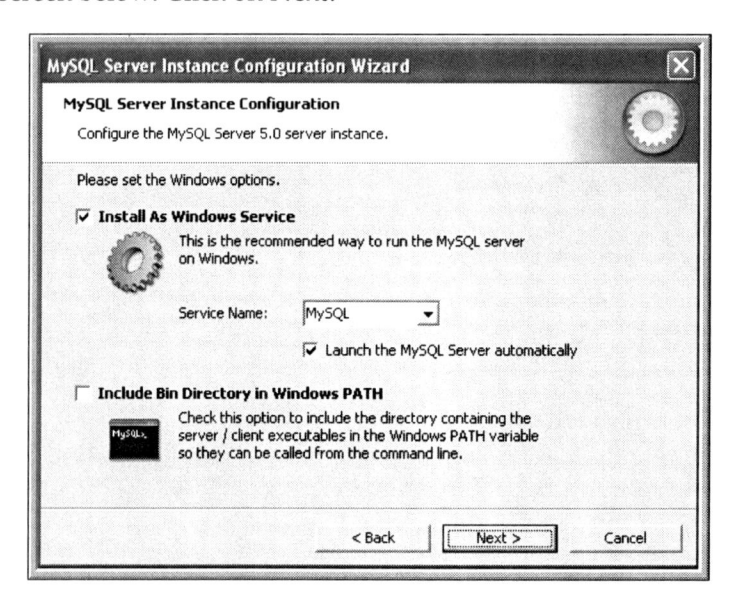

[46]

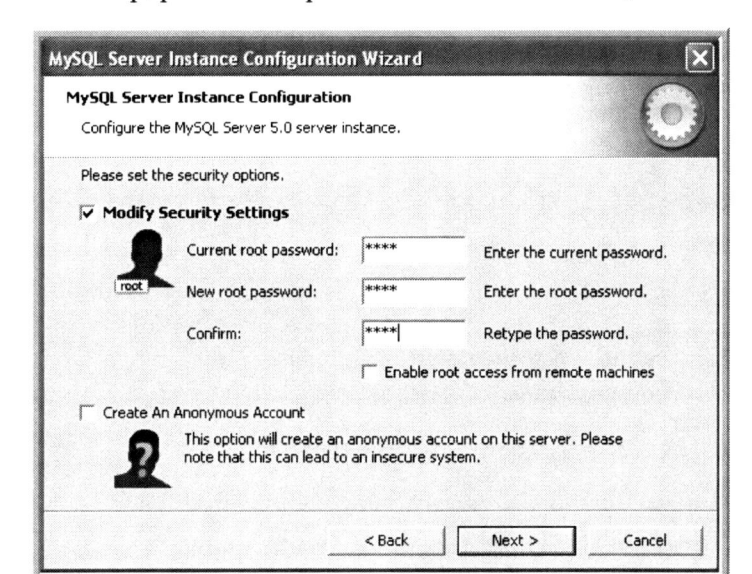

12. In the next step, provide the password for the root user, and then click **Next**.

13. On the next screen, click on **Execute,** to start the configuration
14. Open the MySQL command line client from **All Programs| MySQL| MySQL Server 5.0| MySQL Command Line Client**, and provide the root password.
15. To test your installation, type the following command: `mysql -u root -p`

To set up the MySQL Database for Alfresco, carry out the following steps:

1. At the command prompt, browse to `<Alfresco_installation_folder>\extras\databases\mysql`.
2. Run the `db_setup.bat` file.
3. When asked for a password, enter the root password of MySQL, and then press *Enter*.
4. If `db_setup` fails, this may either be because the MySQL service is not running, or because the MySQL command cannot be found. Either correct this or set up the Alfresco database and user manually, by loading the `db_setup.sql` file into MySQL, for example, `mysql -u root -p <db_setup.sql>`.
5. If the set-up is successful, a MySQL database will be created with the following details
    - Database name: Alfresco
    - Database User Name: Alfresco
    - Database Password: Alfresco

6. To confirm that the database has been created, log in to MySQL by using the following command:

   `mysql -u root -p` command.

7. At the MySQL prompt, execute the command `show databases`. You will find the database created as Alfresco.

To configure the MySQL Database for Alfresco, you need to make the following outlined changes:

To convert the default installation to MySQL, we simple need to modify two files in the `<Alfresco_installation_folder>\tomcat\shared\classes\Alfresco\extension` folder that are set to use default database. The files are `custom-repository.properties` and `custom-hibernate-dialect.properties`.

In the `custom-repository.properties` file, make the following changes:

- Comment out the Derby connection lines by using #
- Uncomment the MySQL connection lines and adjust them as appropriate
- Provide the proper value for database settings connection properties, such as db.name, db.username, and db.password.

In the `custom-hibernate-dialect.properties` file, make the following changes:

- Comment out the Derby line using #
- Uncomment the MySQL line

Copy the Database Connector lib has following 2 steps involved:

- Download the MySQL database connector JAR file
- Copy that JAR file to `<Alfresco-root>\tomcat\lib`.

Installing OpenOffice

For transforming documents such as office to PDF, OpenOffice is used. This is basically a cross-platform office application suite. OpenOffice is an optional installation that provides access to a range of document transformations in Alfresco.

To Install OpenOffice, follow the steps shown below:

1. Download the latest stable version of OpenOffice from

   `http://download.openoffice.org`

2. Run the downloaded installation file, and the installation wizard will start.
3. Accept the license agreement, and then click on **Next**.

4. Provide the required customer information, and then click on **Next**.
5. Select the setup type as **Custom**, and then click on **Next**.
6. Choose the `OpenOffice.org.writer` module, which is the only module used by Alfresco; all others are not required for Alfresco. Change the installation folder to `<Alfresco_installation_folder>\OpenOffice` by clicking on **Change** button, and then click on **Next**.
7. Optionally, select the files for which you want OpenOffice to be the default application, and then click on **Next**.
8. To configure OpenOffice as a headless service, perform the following configuration
    - If this is a fresh Alfresco installation, browse to `<Alfresco_installation_folder>\tomcat\shared\classes\Alfresco\extension\bootstrap`
    - Rename the `openoffice-startup-context.xml.sample` file to `openoffice-startup-context.xml`, or:
    - From the command prompt (or via a .bat file), start OpenOffice by issuing the following command:
    - `soffice "-accept=socket,host=localhost,port=8100;urp;StarOffice.ServiceManager" -nologo -headless`

Installing Image Magick and CIFS

Installing Image Magick

Image Magick is a software suite that can read, convert, and write images in a variety of formats. Alfresco leverages the power of Image Magick for image transformations. Alfresco already has an executable for this, which is, `imconvert.exe`, which available in the `<Alfresco_installation_folder>\bin` folder. To implement Image Magick on the Windows operating system, you are required to add the `imconvert.exe` file to the system path, or you can copy this file to the `C:\Windows\System32` folder.

Installing CIFS

Alfresco supports the virtual file system via CIFS Interface. It already has `win32netbios.dll` available in the `<Alfresco_installation_folder>\bin` folder. To implement CIFS it on Windows operating system, you need to add the file `win32netbios.dll` to the system path, or you can copy this file to the `C:\Windows\System32` folder.

Installing WCM

To download Alfresco WCM, carry out the following steps:

1. Browse to the customer or partner's portal.
2. Log in to the Alfresco web client and browse to **Company Home > Downloads > 3.0 Releases > 3.x Enterprise > Installation Files > Alfresco WCM**.
3. Download the file **Alfresco-enterprise-wcm-<version>.zip**.

To install the Alfresco application on a bundled Apache Tomcat use the following steps:

1. Extract the `Alfresco-enterprise-wcm-<version>.zip` file into the `C:\Alfresco` folder.
2. Copy the `wcm-bootstrap-context.xml` file from the `C:\Alfresco` folder to the `C:\Alfresco\tomcat\ shared\classes\Alfresco\extension` folder.

Installing Microsoft Office Add-ins

To download the Microsoft Office Add-ins, carry out the following steps:

1. Browse to the customer or partner's portal.
2. Log in to the Alfresco web client and browse to **Company Home > Downloads > 3.0 Releases >3.x Enterprise > Installation Files > Office Plugins**.
3. Download the installer file `Alfresco-enterprise-office2003-addins-<version>.zip`. This contains the office installer for all three Add-ins: Microsoft Word, Excel, and Power Point.
4. If you want to install any individual add-in then you can choose the specific installer from `Alfresco-enterprise-word2003-addin-<version>.zip`, `Alfresco-enterprise-excel2003-addin-<version>.zip`, or `Alfresco-enterprise-powerpoint2003-addin-<version>.zip`.

To install the Microsoft Office Add-ins, carry out the following steps:

1. Run the `setup.exe` file.
2. The setup up program will download the required components from the Microsoft web site, if required.
3. Run any of the Office applications.
4. A Welcome window with configuration options will be displayed.
5. Provide the Alfresco WebClient URL, i.e. `http://localhost:8080/Alfresco/` in the Web Client URL area.
6. Specify the WebDev URL by appending `webdev/` to the web client URL in the area for the WebDev URL.

7. Verify the CIFS mapping address in the CIFS server area.
8. If you are using CIFS, authentication is automatic; otherwise, you need to enter your user name and password for Alfresco in the Authentication area.
9. After performing all of the steps mentioned above, click on **Save Settings**.

Installing Flash player

Installing the Flash player is optional, but if you are using Alfresco Share, then it is advisable to install this, as Alfresco Share uses the Flash player for viewing Flash previews. It is also used when you want to make use of its Multi File upload facility.

To install Flash player, carry out the following steps:

1. Download the latest version of the Flash player from Adobe's Flash Player Download site, at http://www.adobe.com/products/flashplayer.
2. Follow the Wizard steps to install the Flash player.

Installing SWFTools

For previewing PDF files, Alfresco Share uses the pdf2swf utility of the SWFTools. This generates one frame per page of fully formatted text inside a Flash movie. Installing SWFTools is optional.

To install SWFTools, carry out the following steps:

1. To install SWFTools, download the latest version from the SWFTools web site at, http://www.swftools.org.
2. Follow the installation Wizard steps to install SWFTools.

Installation folder structure

Let's take a peek into the installation folder <Alfresco_installation_folder>, to look at the folders:

- Alfresco: All of the shortcuts for installing, uninstalling, starting, and stopping Alfresco, are present in this folder as Windows services. In addition, restarting, stopping, and starting of Alfresco, are present as a normal console application. We can access this folder from the **Start** menu of Windows.
- alf_data: All of the Alfresco content and Lucene indexes are stored in this folder.
- Amps: All of the **AMP** extensions files that are required are in here, and then they use the **apply_amps** script to perform the updates.

- `bin`: This folder contains the sub-installations of Alfresco. The main installation scripts in the `Alfresco` folder calls the sub-scripts in this folder in order to start the sub Alfresco `Tomcat` component of the installation, creating and setting up the permissions for the Alfresco MySQL database. This folder is very useful for people opting for the manual installation, rather than using an installer.
- `extras`: This folder contains additional files, such as the space template for record management file plans, which can be imported into the Alfresco repository.
- `java`: As is evident by the name, this folder contains the Java Development Kit. All of the Alfresco development is done by using Java as the core programming language.
- `licenses`: This folder contains the licenses for Alfresco, MySQL, and Apache along with licenses for the other third party applications used inside Alfresco.
- `tomcat`: Once again, as evident from the name, this folder holds the Tomcat installation, where the Alfresco application is deployed as a WAR file. You can see the `Alfresco.war and share.war` files in the `webapps` sub-folder of this folder.
- `Openoffice`: This folder contains the entire portable office suite installation that is used for word processing, spread sheet processing, and so on.
- `virtual-tomcat`: This folder contains the customized Tomcat, which is used for previewing files in WCM.
- `README`: `README` files provide information about using CIFS, and some troubleshooting tips.

You can uninstall any program by double-clicking on the `uninstall.exe` file.

Starting and stopping Alfresco as a console application

The options for starting and stopping Alfresco as a console application can be viewed by selecting **Start | All Programs | Alfresco Enterprise**. The options are as shown in the following screenshot:

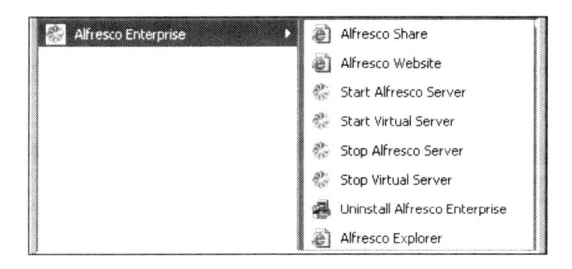

The options there are discussed below:

- **Stop Alfresco Server**: This option is used to stop Alfresco. It stops the MySQL server and the Tomcat application server.
- **Start Alfresco Server**: Use this option to start the Alfresco as a console application. This will start the MySQL server and the Tomcat server.
- **Stop Virtual Server**: This option is used to stop the Alfresco Virtual server. It stops the Virtual Tomcat application server.
- **Start Virtual Server**: Use this option to start the Alfresco Virtual server, mainly used for Alfresco WCM. This will start the Virtual Tomcat Server.
- **Alfresco Explorer**: This option is used to open the Alfresco Web Client in the browser.
- **Alfresco Share**: This option is used to open Alfresco Share in the web browser.
- **Alfresco Web site**: This option is used to open Alfresco's web site in the web browser.

Alternatively, you can always start, stop, and restart the Tomcat application server, and the MySQL database server, manually, by going to their respective folders. This gives more control to the user. However, the console option provides batch files to perform the start and stop procedures in a consolidated way, relieving the user of any unwanted errors.

Configuring Alfresco as a Windows service

You can also configure Alfresco as a Windows service in a standard Alfresco/Tomcat Installation. With the default installation, Alfresco is bundled as a web application that launches within Tomcat. To configure Alfresco to run as a Windows service, you need to set up Tomcat to run as a Windows service.

To configure Alfresco as a Windows service, carry out the following steps:

1. Open a command prompt.
2. Go to the `<Alfresco_installation_folder>`/tomcat/bin folder.
3. Use the following commands:
    - `service.bat install Alfresco`
    - `tomcat5.exe //US//Alfresco` -DisplayName "Alfresco Server"
    - `tomcat5.exe //US//Alfresco` -JvmMs=256 --JvmMx=512 --JvmSs=64

- `tomcat5.exe //US//`Alfresco:-JavaHome`<Alfresco_installation_folder>/java`
- `tomcat5.exe //US//`Alfresco:-Environment ALF_HOME=`<Alfresco_installation_folder>/`
- `tomcat5.exe //US//`Alfresco:-Environment PATH=`<Alfresco_installation_folder>/`bin;%PATH%
- `tomcat5.exe //US//`Alfresco:-StartPath `<Alfresco_installation_folder>`--Startup auto

To uninstall the service, go to the `<Alfresco_installation_folder>/tomcat/bin` and enter the following command: service.bat uninstall Alfresco.

To edit your service settings, go to the `<Alfresco_installation_folder>/tomcat/bin` and enter the following command: `tomcat5w.exe //ES//Alfresco`

To start the service, locate the service named **Alfresco Server** in your Windows Service control panel, and start Alfresco from this control panel.

Installing on Linux

Alfresco provides a nice package that includes all of the programs you need for using Alfresco on your Linux machine. Download this package from the customer or partner's portal by selecting the latest version of the `Alfresco-<version>-linux-community.bin` file.

This installer file contains Tomcat, Open Office and Alfresco. Make sure that you have permissions to execute the installer. Make sure that you have JDK 5 or higher installed on your machine before installing Alfresco.

Use the following command to change the permissions on the installer so that it can be executed:

`> chmod a+x ./Alfresco-<version>-linux-community.bin`

Become the root (super) user, in order to install, by executing the following command (for some platforms that have the super user account disabled by default, you might require "su –s").

`> su`

Next, execute the installer directly on the command prompt as follows.

`./Alfresco-<version>-linux-community.bin`

Follow the instructions presented by the installer:

1. You will be asked for the **language** in the **Language Selection** prompt; select **English,** and then click **OK.**
2. On the next screen you will be prompted off confirmation off the installation. Click on **Yes**. The installation wizard is launched.
3. Click on **Next** in the **Welcome** window.
4. In the next window, provide the JDK installation location via the **Browse** button, and then click on **Next**.
5. In the next screen, of Setup Type, select **Typical,** and then click on **Next**.
6. You will be asked for a location into which you want to install the software, in the next window. If you choose to skip the 'Become root' step above, your home folder is selected by default. If you intend that Alfresco should be run by other users, or start on startup, you should change this to a different location. Exit the installer and become the root user. If you are the root user, the default of /opt/Alfresco-<version> will be selected. If you want to change it, /usr/local/Alfresco-<version> will often be another good choice.
7. Review the settings in the **Start Copying Files** window, and then click on **Next**. The installation starts.
8. In the **OpenOffice Location** window, select the OpenOffice location by clicking on the **Browse** button, selecting the location, and then clicking **OK**. If you do not want to use OpenOffice for your document conversions, then select the Alfresco installation folder as the location.
9. In the **Install Jammer Wizard Complete** window, click **Finish**.
10. In the next window, **Readme**, click **Close**.
11. Run the alf_start.sh file, which is available in the Alfresco root folder. Wait a few seconds to allow Tomcat to start, and then fire up your web browser and browse to http://localhost:8080/Alfresco. Because this is the first time that you are using Alfresco, use the username and password **admin**.

Installing extensions with AMP Install

Alfresco provides extensions as AMP files, which we can install with the help of the Module Management Tool in Alfresco. The Module Management Tool supports the installation of AMP modules, including upgrades to later versions, enabling and disabling of installed modules, uninstallation of installed modules, and listing of currently installed modules.

Installing Alfresco

To install any AMP module in Alfresco, please refer to the following steps:

1. Download the particular AMP file, with the `.amp` extension.
2. Copy the `<extension-module>.amp` file to `<Alfresco_installation_folder>\amps`
3. Run the `apply_amps.bat` file, which is available at `<Alfresco_installation_folder>`. This will install the particular module.
4. Delete the **Alfresco** folder in **webapps**, if it exists, and restart the server.

Some of the extension modules available within Alfresco are `Alfresco-blog-integration.amp` for Blog Publishing, `Alfresco-fb-doclib.amp` for FaceBook integration and `Alfresco-recordsmanagement.amp` for Records Management sample functionality.

Summary

You have many options to choose from when installing Alfresco. Alfresco installers for the Windows and Linux operating systems make the installation process so simple that you could install all of the installation software such as JDK, MySQL, Alfresco, SharePoint protocol, OpenOffice, Microsoft Office Addins and so on, within minutes. On the Windows platform you can run Alfresco as a service or as console application.

3
Getting Started with Alfresco

Now that you have installed Alfresco successfully, it is important to understand the terminology of Alfresco, and configure the Alfresco repository, before we can start using it. This chapter provides you with the basic information about Alfresco Explorer, a web-based client application used to access the repository. The chapter also provides you with various ways of configuring the repository as per your business needs. By the end of this chapter, you will have learned how to:

- Log in to the Alfresco Explorer application
- Use the Administration console to perform system administration tasks
- Use Alfresco for basic document management
- Configure the personal dashboard wizard
- Configure a relational database of your choice
- Configure email and log files
- Configure the file system interface in order to drag-and-drop content into the repository
- Define multi-language support
- Create a blue-print for your application

Introduction to Alfresco Explorer

The Alfresco Enterprise Content Management product is bundled and shipped along with two web-based applications. One is called the **Alfresco Explorer**, which was formerly known as the "Web Client". In this chapter, we will go through a high-level overview of Alfresco Explorer. The other web-based application is called **Alfresco Share**, which enables collaboration. Chapter 10 of this book has a detailed description of Alfresco Share.

By using any web browser, you can connect to the Alfresco Explorer application. Using Alfresco Explorer, you will be able to manage users, security, content, business rules, and everything related to your enterprise content stored in Alfresco.

> In rest of this book, wherever the web-client configuration files are referred to, consider them as Alfresco Explorer related configuration files.

Log in to Alfresco as an Administrator

To begin, if Alfresco is installed by using the Tomcat bundle, then we can access the Alfresco Explorer from `http://localhost:8080/alfresco`. If Alfresco is installed from the JBoss bundle, you may use the same URL as for Tomcat. You can also access the Alfresco Explorer in the portal from `http://localhost:8080/portal`, navigate to the Alfresco Explorer from the page menu, and then maximize the portlet.

When you start Alfresco for the first time, Alfresco creates the initial database content that is required for managing the data. The first time you use Alfresco, your username and password will both be "admin". You can change the password once you log in. Depending on your installation, you may have a choice of languages in the language drop-down menu. This book assumes that your selected language is English.

Screen layout

Once you log in, you will see the **My Alfresco** dashboard. You can browse through the Alfresco Explorer by clicking on the **Company Home** link that is provided on the upper-left of the screen. A typical Alfresco Explorer page is shown in the next screenshot. Let us examine various sections of the Alfresco Explorer layout.

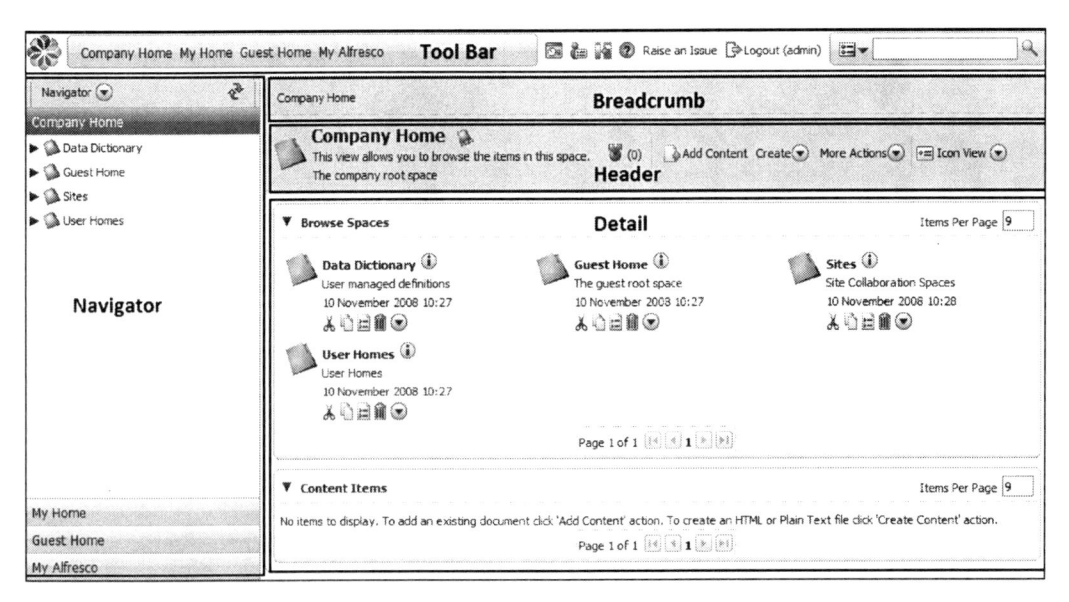

Chapter 3

Tool Bar

The **Tool Bar** at the top provides us with the following information:

- Logo
- Links to home spaces, and the **My Alfresco** dashboard
- Administration Console icon to perform system administration functions
- User Options icon to change your options and settings
- icon to hide or show the shelf
- Help button to launch online help
- **Raise an Issue** link to submit bug reports to Alfresco
- **Login** and **Logout** options
- Search box with basic and advanced search options

Navigator

The **Navigator** window is used to display the Navigator tree view. It consists of **Shelf**, **OpenSearch**, and **Categories** options, as shown in the following figure:

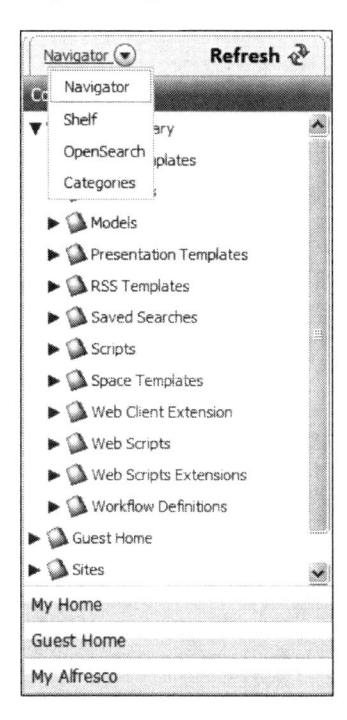

Navigator Tree View

The **Navigator** provides a tree view of the entire repository hierarchy, including folders and sub-folders. There is also a **Refresh** button, as shown in the previous figure, to refresh the navigator tree view with the latest files.

Shelf

The **Shelf** includes Clipboard, Recent Spaces, and Shortcuts.

- **Clipboard** is used to cut or copy content and to paste in multiple spaces. Clipboard also facilitates the creation of links to actual content items or spaces.
- **Recent Spaces** provides a list of recently visited spaces. Therefore, it is useful if you want to go back to a specific space with one click. The information in the Recent Spaces is refreshed every time you log in to the Alfresco Explorer.
- **Shortcuts** are similar to favorites. You can create shortcuts to your frequently visited spaces.

OpenSearch

The **OpenSearch** is Alfresco's implementation of an open standards based search API for sharing search results, and extending existing schemas such as ATOM and RSS.

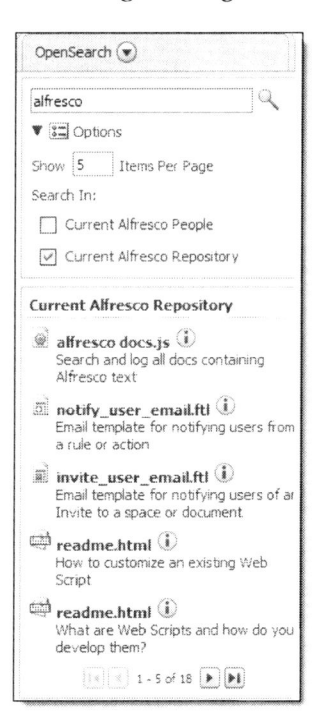

The execution of searches is supported using HTTP requests and responses. For example, the keyword search shown above can also be executed using an HTTP request as given below.

```
http://localhost:8080/alfresco/service/api/search/keyword?q=alfresco
```

More details about **OpenSearch** are provided in Chapter 12 of this book.

Categories logical view

Alfresco content can be categorized to be part of one or more categories. The **Categories** window provides a logical navigation of content according to the category hierarchy.

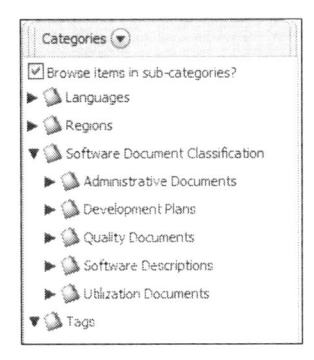

Breadcrumbs

Breadcrumbs help you navigate through various spaces. Typically, breadcrumbs provide paths to parent spaces.

Header

The **Header** screen provides us with information about the current space, number of business rules applied to the current space, options for creating content, menu actions to manage content, and options to use various views to display information about the current space.

Detail

The **Detail** screen provides us with information about the subspaces and content, which are a part of the current space.

You can click on the icon or the title of a space or the content item in the **Detail** screen to access this information.

Actions are listed as icons for each space or content. Additional action items will be listed if you click on the double arrow icon.

Administration Console

The **Administration Console** in the Alfresco Explorer is useful to perform all of the system administration tasks. You can access the **Administration Console** by clicking on the administration console icon on the **Tool Bar**, as shown in the following screenshot. This icon is visible and accessible only to the users with admin privileges. Refer to the following screenshot to view the list of administration functions that can be performed by the system administrator:

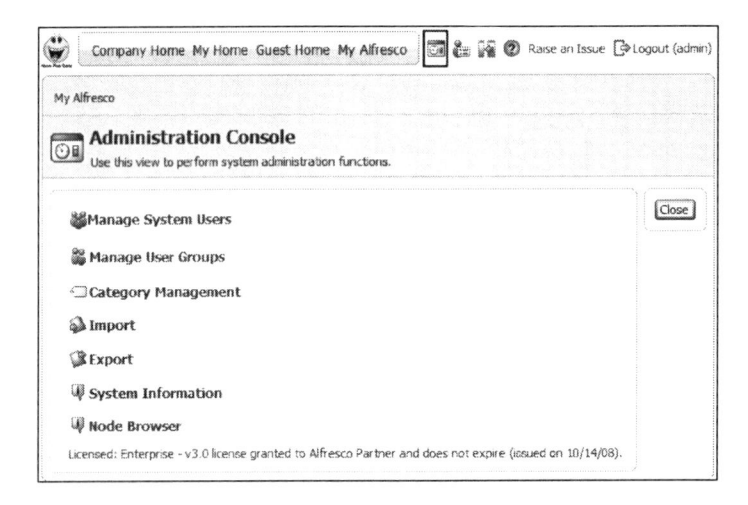

User and groups management

You can add and delete users, and update user information, by using the **Manage System Users** functionality. When you first install Alfresco, there will be two users, namely **admin** and **guest**, created by the installer. You can create new users by using the Manage System Users functionality.

The **Manage User Groups** functionality is useful for creating groups of users and sub groups within the groups. Groups are useful for providing authorization to access the content.

Category management

Categorization allows content information to be classified in a number of ways. This aids searching for content. Categories are editable only by the administrator. Categories can have sub-categories and content can be linked to one or more categories.

Data management

The **Export** and **Import** functionalities are used to extract and load in large amounts, personal or department information and team information, from one location to another within the same repository or to another repository. **Import** and **Export** functionality is covered in detail in Chapter 14.

System information

The **System Information** functionality is used to view session information and the HTTP header information. The content in Alfresco is stored in an industry standard **Java Content Repository (JCR)**, where every folder and file is represented as a **Node**. The subfolders are represented as branches of a node, and are nodes themselves. **Node Browser** functionality is useful to navigate through the entire repository through nodes and subnodes.

Getting started with content creation

The remaining chapters of the book cover the content creation, management, and delivery aspects of Alfresco in detail. In this section, you will be introduced to the key terminology, and you will get a basic understanding of content creation in Alfresco.

Create space

Alfresco space is a folder with additional properties such as business rules and security. Similar to a folder, a space can hold subspaces and any type of content. To create a space within a space, click on the **Create** icon in the header, and then click on the **Create Space** link as shown in the following screenshot:

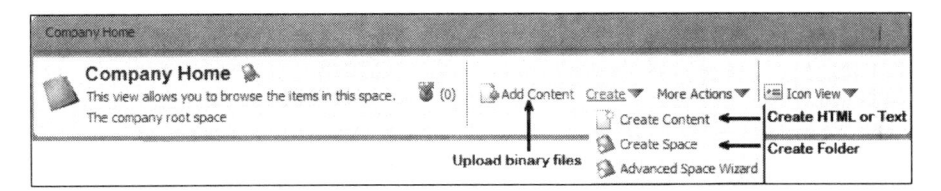

The **Create Space** wizard will be displayed as shown in the following screenshot. **Name** is a mandatory property (as you can notice a small star next to the label), whereas **Title** and **Description** are the optional properties. You can also associate an icon with this space. Fill up the information and click on the **Create Space** button to create the space.

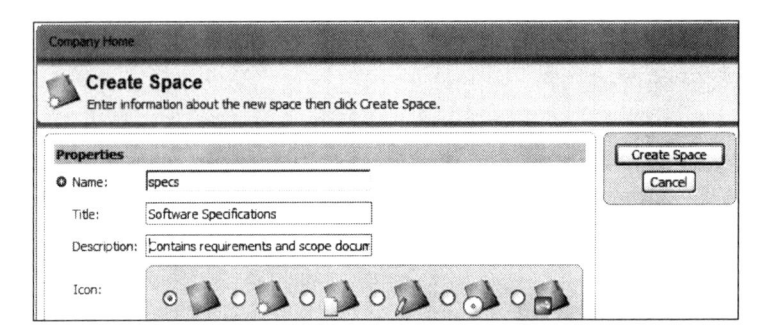

Each space supports various actions such as **Delete**, **Copy** and **Paste All**, as shown in the following screenshot. For each user who is logged-in, the actions for a specific space can be different, as it is based on the user's security permissions. For example, if you do not have permission to delete a space, you will not see the **Delete** link or icon in the **Actions** menu.

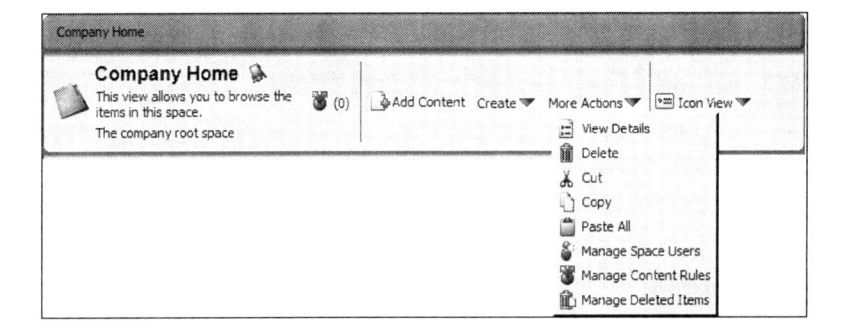

Create content

In Alfresco, content is any kind of document such as a Microsoft Office file, Open Office file, PDF, HTML, XML, text, image, audio, or video file.

Each content item is made of two main elements—the content itself and the information about the content, which is known as metadata or properties. By default, each content item will have properties such as title, description, and author, along with the audit trail information such as creator, creation date, modifier, and modification date. Additional properties can be added as required.

To add a document to a space, click on the **Add Content** link in the header, as shown in the first screenshot under the previous section. To create HTML or text content in a space, click on the **Create** icon and click on the **Create Content** menu link, as shown in the first screenshot under the previous section.

Every content item supports various actions such as **Delete**, **Update**, **Cut**, and **Copy**, as shown in the following screenshot. For each user who is logged-in, the actions for a specific content can be different, based on the security permissions.

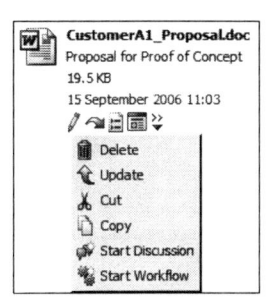

Create a link to content

A link (or shortcut) to content, is a special type of file that serves as a reference to another file. This is similar to the symbolic links commonly used in Unix-like operating systems. A link only contains a symbolic path to the content, which is stored elsewhere in the Alfresco repository. Thus, if a user removes a link, the file to which it points, remains unaffected.

There might be situations where you need to have the same file in two spaces. For example, you might want to have a product data sheet in the engineering department space as well as in the marketing department space. Instead of creating two copies of the same file, you can keep one copy in one space and create links to the target file in other spaces.

Users should pay careful attention to the maintenance of links. If the target of a link is removed, then the document vanishes and all links to it become orphans. Conversely, removing a symbolic link has no effect on its target.

Follow the process mentioned next to create a link to content:

1. Identify the target document and click on the **Copy** action (as shown in the previous screenshot).
2. The document will be placed on the clipboard, as shown in the next screenshot.
3. Go to the space where you would like to create the link to the content.

4. Click on the **Paste as Link** icon in the clipboard to create the link, as shown in the next screenshot.

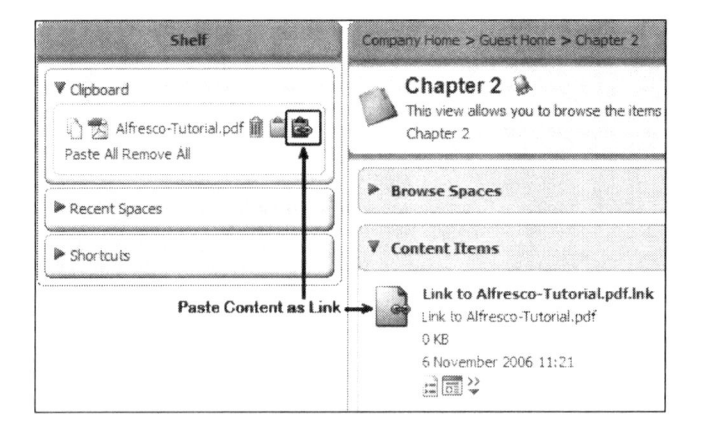

My Alfresco dashboards

In the Alfresco Explorer user interface, the **My Alfresco** area is known as the **Dashboard**. You can construct your own Dashboard page from a list of pre-configured components that are available out of the box.

Choosing the My Alfresco dashboard as the start location

The **Start Location** is the first page that is displayed immediately after you log in to the Alfresco Explorer. You can choose your start location using the user profile icon as shown in the next screenshot. Once you log in to the Alfresco Explorer, the first page you will see is the page that you have chosen as the **Start Location.**

To select the My Alfresco dashboard as your starting page, click on the user options icon in the top menu and select **My Alfresco** as your start location. The next time when you log in, the My Alfresco dashboard will be displayed as your personal homepage. You can also view this dashboard page by clicking on the **My Alfresco** menu item at the top of the screen.

Configuring personal dashboard using wizard

If you click on the **My Alfresco** link provided in the **Tool Bar**, you will see a default dashboard, which contains useful information for beginners. Through the Dashboard wizard, you can configure the dashboard layout and dashboard components (also known as dashlets). The dashboard configuration is very specific to your personal requirements. The dashboard configuration settings you choose will be stored in the database. Every time you log in to the Alfresco Explorer, you will see your personal dashboard as the homepage.

To start configuring your dashboard, click on the **Configure** icon, given in the **My Alfresco Dashboard**, as shown in the next screenshot. The **Configure Dashboard Wizard** will open up (as shown in the first screenshot under the next section), allowing you to select the dashboard layout and dashlets.

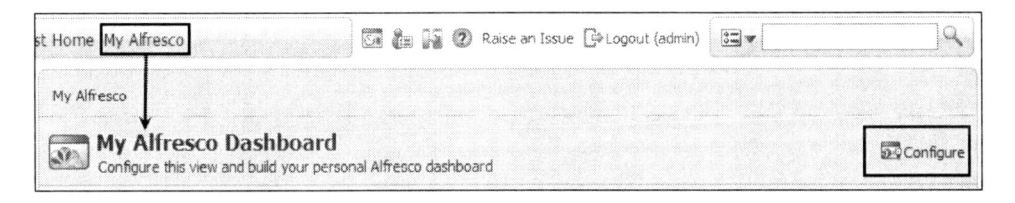

Getting Started with Alfresco

Step one: Selection of layout

The first step is to choose the layout and the number of columns for your dashboard view. There are four styles available for displaying your dashlets. The options are pictorially represented in the following screenshot:

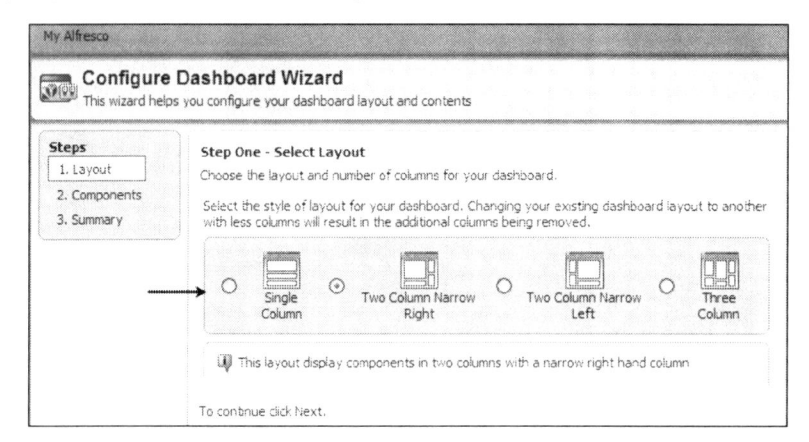

Select the style of layout you wish to have for your dashboard. By changing your existing dashboard layout to another with a lesser number of columns will result in the additional columns being removed.

As an example, select the **Two Column Narrow Right** option, to display your dashboard components in two columns with a narrow right-hand column. Click on the **Next** button to move to the next step, selecting the dashboard components.

Step two: Selecting components

Based on the number of columns that you selected in the previous step, you need to add components to each column, as shown in the following screenshot. Notice the list of available dashboard components. These dashboard components are also called dashlets, as they display certain information in small windows, similar to a portal's portlets. You can also sequence the dashlets by using the **+** and **-** buttons.

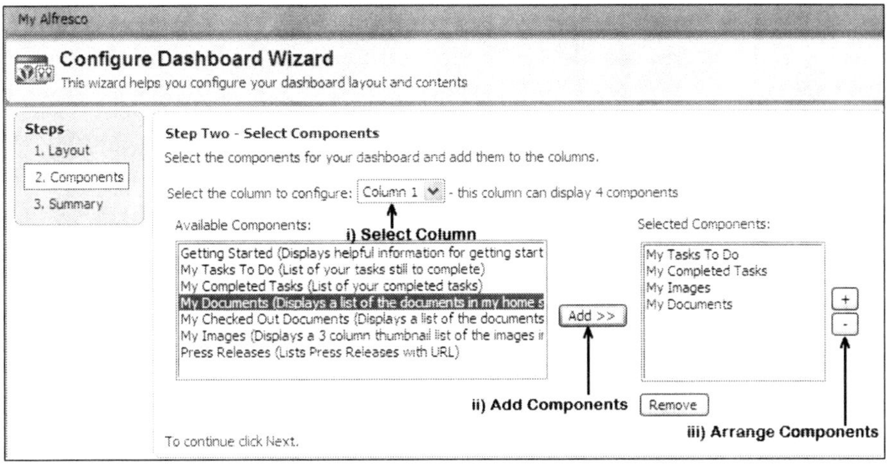
My Alfresco
Configure Dashboard Wizard
This wizard helps you configure your dashboard layout and contents
Steps
1. Layout
2. Components
3. Summary
Step Two - Select Components
Select the components for your dashboard and add them to the columns.
Select the column to configure: Column 1 - this column can display 4 components
Available Components:
i) Select Column
Getting Started (Displays helpful information for getting start
My Tasks To Do (List of your tasks still to complete)
My Completed Tasks (List of your completed tasks)
My Checked Out Documents (Displays a list of the documents
My Images (Displays a 3 column thumbnail list of the images i
Press Releases (Lists Press Releases with URL)
Add >>
Selected Components:
My Tasks To Do
My Completed Tasks
My Images
My Documents
ii) Add Components
Remove
iii) Arrange Components
To continue click Next.

Select the following components for **Column1**:

- **My Tasks To Do**: Lists all the tasks assigned to you that are pending
- **My Completed Tasks**: Lists all the tasks completed by you
- **My Images**: Lists the images in your home space
- **My Documents**: Lists the documents in your home space

Select the following component for **Column2**:

- **My Checked Out Documents**: Lists all the documents that are checked out and locked by you

Getting Started with Alfresco

Click on the **Next** or **Finish** button to save your selection. The selection is effective immediately, and you can see the dashboard with your selections, as shown in the next screenshot:

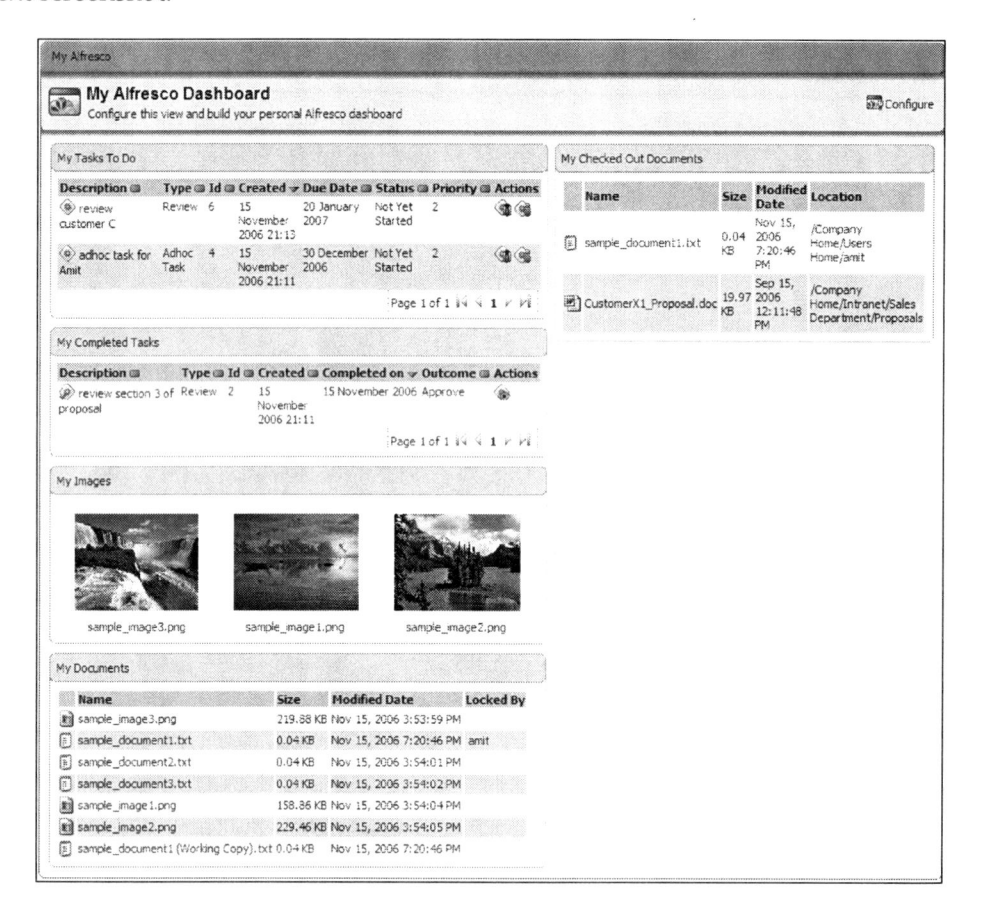

Start with basic configuration

Now that you have planned your implementation, you can start configuring Alfresco according to your business needs. This section covers basic configuration settings that need to be defined before using the system such as relational database, email server, look and feel, and multi-lingual support.

Extend Alfresco configuration

Alfresco configuration items are completely exposed as XML files, so that you can override the default out-of-the-box Alfresco items by customizing individual configuration items.

Alfresco ConfigRoot folder

The default configuration files for Alfresco are in the WAR file format. When the server starts, the files are expanded to `<configRoot>`, which is either:

JBoss: `<JBOSS_HOME>/server/default/tmp/deploy/`

`tmp*alfresco-exp.war/WEBINF/classes`

or

Tomcat: `<TOMCAT_HOME>/webapps/alfresco/WEB-INF/classes`

The default configuration files, maintained by Alfresco, are contained in `tomcat/webapps/alfresco/WEB-INF/classes/alfresco` folder. The repository properties file (`repository.properties`) in this folder defines some of the core system properties, including the following:

- `dir.root`: This is the folder (`alf_data`), where the binary content and Lucene indexes are stored. It is relative by default, but should point to a permanent, backed-up location for data to be stored permanently.
- `db.*`: These are the default database connection properties.

The web-client configuration files are located in the web-client `*.xml` files. You can examine the other configuration files in the `tomcat/webapps/alfresco/WEB-INF/classes/alfresco` folder.

Alfresco extension folder

You can override or extend the Alfresco configuration by placing the custom configuration files in the `<extension>` folder. If you have downloaded one of the bundles (JBoss or Tomcat), you will find the sample files in the corresponding location:

- `<alfresco>/jboss/server/default/conf/alfresco/extension`
- `<alfresco>/tomcat/shared/classes/alfresco/extension`

Configuration approach

When Alfresco starts, it first reads all the default configuration files, and then reads the customized configuration items (in the `extension` folder). So, depending upon the type of item, the customization either extends or overrides the default configuration items.

The example given below extends the advanced search form. The first file contains the default configuration. This file can be found in the folder: `tomcat/webapps/alfresco/WEB-INF/classes/alfresco/web-client-config.xml`:

```xml
<alfresco-config>
...
...
...
  <config evaluator="string-compare" condition="Advanced Search">
    <advanced-search>
      <custom-properties>
        <meta-data aspect="rma:filePlan"
                           property="rma:recordCategoryName" />
        <meta-data aspect="rma:filePlan"
                       property="rma:recordCategoryIdentifier" />
        <meta-data aspect="rma:record"
                              property="rma:recordIdentifier" />
        <meta-data aspect="rma:record"
                                    property="rma:orginator" />
        <meta-data aspect="rma:record"
                         property="rma:orginatingOrganization" />
        <meta-data aspect="rma:record"
                                 property="rma:dateReceived" />
        <meta-data aspect="rma:record"
                         property="rma:supplementalMarkingList" />
      </custom-properties>
    </advanced-search>
  </config>
...
...
...
</alfresco-config>
```

The web-client configuration file in the `extension` folder adds an additional property called `cm:effectivity` to the advanced search form. The `extension` folder could be located at: `tomcat/common/classes/alfresco/extension/web-client-config-custom.xml`.

```xml
<alfresco-config>
  <config evaluator="string-compare"
                                    condition="Advanced Search">
    <advanced-search>
      <custom-properties>
        <meta-data aspect= "cm:effectivity" property="cm:to" />
      </custom-properties>
    </advanced-search>
  </config>
</alfresco-config>
```

Web-client configuration files can contain configuration that either augments the standard configuration or replaces it.

Replacement is performed at the `config` level by adding a `replace= true` attribute to the configuration element, as shown here:

```
<config evaluator="xx" condition="yy" replace="true">
```

Any configuration found within a section marked this way, will replace any configuration found in the Alfresco maintained files. For example, if you wanted to replace the list of languages shown on the login page, you could add the following:

```
<config evaluator="string-compare" condition="Languages"
                                              replace="true">
   <languages>
      <language locale="fr_FR">French</language>
      <language locale="de_DE">German</language>
   </languages>
</config>
```

On the other hand, if you just wanted to add French to the list of languages, you would add the following:

```
<config evaluator="string-compare" condition="Languages">
   <languages>
      <language locale="fr_FR">French</language>
   </languages>
</config>
```

Whenever you make changes to these configuration files, you need to restart Alfresco to see the effect of the changes.

Packaging and deploying Java extensions

If your customization consists only of Alfresco configuration files or properties files, that is, `web-client-config-custom.xml` or `webclient.properties`, then you can place the customization files in the `extension` folder.

However, if you are changing the Java source code, the process is a little different. Java classes are typically packaged within a `.jar` file, which then has to go in the web application's `WEB-INF/lib` directory. If you have Java code, you are more than likely to have at least one other file as part of your extension, that is, configuration files. These too can be contained within the `.jar` file, by simply packaging them within the `.jar` file in the `alfresco/extension` folder.

Another alternative is to add your `.jar` file to the `alfresco.war` file. In JBoss, if you deploy a web application as a WAR file, the application gets exploded to a temporary directory each time the application server starts. Therefore, there is no place to copy the `.jar` file to. One solution is to use an exploded deployment. Create a directory called `alfresco.war` under the `deploy` directory and extract the contents of `alfresco.war` (the file) into it. Then copy your `.jar` file to `deploy/alfresco.war/WEB-INF/lib` and restart JBoss.

Install the enterprise license file

If you have installed the enterprise version of Alfresco, you have to install the enterprise license file. Otherwise, by default, the Alfresco enterprise software expires in thirty days after installation.

Get the `.lic` file from Alfresco. Copy the `.lic` file to the `tomcat/shared/classes/alfresco/extension/license` folder (for example, it is the `tomcat/shared/classes/extension/license` for Tomcat). Once in place, restart the Alfresco server. The information about the license being set will be visible in the logs. The license file is also renamed as `.installed`. The Administration Console within Alfresco also gives details of the license status.

Change the default administrator password

The Administrator is the super user of the system. The administrator user ID, as well as the password, is initially set to `admin`. You can change the password by logging into Alfresco Explorer as the `admin` and change the password.

Another way of overriding this password (during startup) is to update the web-client configuration file in `extensions` folder with the following code:

```
<admin>
    <initial-password>admin</initial-password>
</admin>
```

Configure the content store

Alfresco stores the content (binary files) and search indexes in the file system. By default, on the Windows platform, this location is the `<tomcat_install>/alf_data` folder.

You can manage the file system storage locations by editing the `custom-repository.properties` file in the `tomcat/shared/classes/alfresco/extension` folder. The main property to edit is `dir.root`, which points to the file repository location.

If these properties are not listed in your `custom-repository.properties` file, then copy those properties from the `tomcat/webapps/alfresco/WEB-INF/classes/repository.properties` file into the `tomcat/shared/classes/alfresco/extension/custom-repository.properties` file and edit accordingly, as shown here:

```
dir.root=C:/Alfresco/alf_data
```

> You must use forward slashes for all operating systems

The best practice is to use an absolute path such as `./alf_data`, to avoid confusion.

Configure the relational database

Installation is covered in detail in Chapter 2. During installation, if you use either the Windows installer or the Linux binary, the installer automatically installs a local MySQL database and configures it for you.

If you are installing the database and configuring it manually, you need to follow the steps mentioned next:

To configure the MySQL database:

1. Create a new `alfresco` user and an `alfresco` database.
2. Grant all permissions to the user `alfresco` on the `alfresco` database.
3. Override the database properties in the `tomcat/shared/classes/alfresco/extension/custom-repository.properties` file as follows:
   db.driver=org.gjt.mm.mysql.Driver
   db.url=jdbc:mysql://localhost/alfresco
   db.username=alfresco
   db.password=alfresco
4. In the `tomcat/shared/classes/alfresco/extension/custom-hibernate-dialect.properties` file, unmask the MySQL dialect and mask all of the other dialects.
5. The MySQL database connector is not bundled in Alfresco 3.0. You need to manually install it. Download the database connector file (`mysql-connector-java-5.0.3-bin.jar`) from http://dev.mysql.com and copy it to the `<alf_install>\tomcat\lib folder`.
6. Restart Alfresco.

Alfresco supports MySQL, Oracle, and MS SQL Server databases. The steps to configure a database remain the same for any of these databases.

Configure the email service and email server

Alfresco provides various notifications to the users during the content management process. You need to configure Alfresco to use an existing email server to send outbound emails. You can also use Alfresco as an email server itself for all the inbound emails.

Outbound email service

Follow the steps given below to configure the Alfresco repository to send emails from an SMTP server. Currently, the repository does not support secure SMTP servers.

1. Edit the file `tomcat/shared/classes/alfresco/extension/custom-repository.properties`.
2. Copy the following block of email properties:

   ```
   # Email configuration
   mail.host=
   mail.port=25
   mail.username=anonymous
   mail.password=
   mail.from.default=alfresco@alfresco.org
   ```

3. Modify any property to your required value as follows (you can delete any unmodified property, as it will retain the default value from `tomcat/webapps/alfresco/WEB-INF/classes/repository.properties`):

   ```
   mail.host=<the name of your SMTP host>
   mail.port=<the port that your SMTP service runs on
                              (the default is 25)>
   mail.username=<the username of the account you want e-mail
                              to be sent from >
   mail.password=<the password>
   mail.from.default=<the default FROM email address>
   ```

4. Restart Alfresco.

> **Note**: Throughout this book, whenever you encounter a case where no value is assigned to a parameter under email configuration, this means that the user will need to give details of the SMTP server that is configured on the production server. It will be as specified by the user.

Inbound email server

In order to configure Alfresco as an inbound email server, we must carry out the following steps:

1. Browse the `tomcat/shared/classes/alfresco/extension` folder and unzip the `custom-email-server.sample.zip` file.
2. Extract the two files, the `custom-email-server-context.xml` file and the `custom-email-server.properties` file, into the `tomcat/shared/classes/alfresco/extension` folder.
3. Edit the `custom-email-server.properties` file as follows:

   ```
   email.inbound.enabled=true
   # Email Server properties
   email.server.enabled=true
   email.server.port=25
   email.server.domain=provide domain address of your email server
   ```

Also, there are other settings in the file such as a blocked list and an allowed list, which can be configured according to your needs.

Configure the log files

Log files hold very important runtime system information. In order to install Tomcat, the log files are located in the `<install_folder>` itself. The Tomcat application server creates a log file every day. The current log file is named `alfresco.log`, and at the end of the day it will be backed up as `alfresco.log.YYYY-MM-DD` (for example, `alfresco.log.2008-12-22`).

You can configure the log file by updating the `tomcat/webapps/alfresco/WEB-INF/classes/log4j.properties` file. You can set the level of logging as `info`, `debug`, or `error` according to the amount of information you want to see (for example, `log4j.logger.org.alfresco.web=info`). For example, the option 'debug' will provide you with very detailed information. However, it creates performance issues in high-traffic installations.

Configure the Alfresco virtual file system

One of the unique strengths of Alfresco is the ability to access the repository through a variety of interfaces such as FTP, WebDav, and CIFS. These interfaces are referred to as the **virtual file system**.

To customize the default FTP, WebDav and CIFS file server configuration values, you must extend the `tomcat/webapps/alfresco/WEB-INF/classes/file-servers.xml` file. This is done by modifying values in the `tomcat/shared/classes/alfresco/extension/file-servers-custom.xml` file.

Configure the file systems

In addition to file servers, within the `file-servers-custom.xml` file, you can configure file systems. The default file system is named "Alfresco". However, it is easy to change this, as well as add new file systems. Additionally, you can configure a file system, so that it can be accessed by using only a particular set of protocols such as FTP or CIFS. You can also configure a file system, so that it has only read and write options for a particular user. Carry out the following steps to configure the file system:

1. Within the `file-servers-custom.xml file`, locate the `<config evaluator="string-compare" condition="Filesystems">` element.
2. Add `replace="true"`
3. Within the `<filesystems>` element, copy the existing file system definition (for example, `<filesystem name="Alfresco">` ... `</filesystem>`).
4. Paste at the same element level within the `file-servers-custom.xml` file.
5. Change the file system name from `<filesystem name="Alfresco">` to `<filesystem name="Marketing">`.
6. In the Alfresco Explorer, create a new space called `Intranet` under the **Company Home** space.
7. Configure a new relative path, `<relativePath>/Intranet</relativePath>`, to point to `Intranet` space. Save the file.
8. Restart Alfresco.
9. Test your work by navigating to `\\<your server name>\A` from any window. You will see two file systems—`Alfresco` and `Intranet`.

Configure the default logos

When using the Alfresco Explorer, you would have noticed Alfresco logos appear in the login page, in the web-client tool bar, as shown in the following figure. You can configure the custom logos according to your branding requirements.

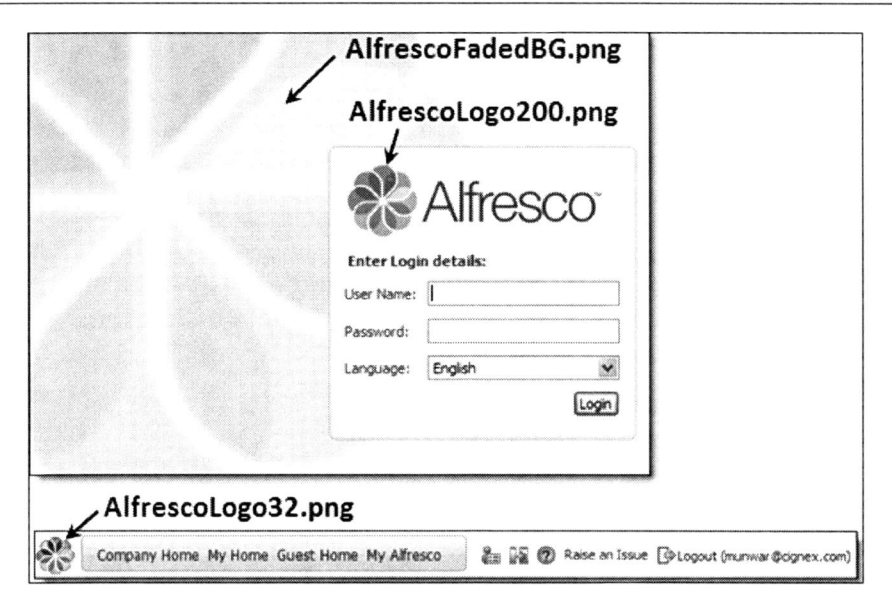

All the logos that appear in the web-client application are kept in a separate folder for logos. In the Tomcat installation, the logo's folder is `<install_folder>\tomcat\webapps\alfresco\images\logo`.

Let's examine some of the logos in this folder:

- `AlfrescoLogo32.png` file is the site logo. This logo is displayed always in the upper-left corner of the Alfresco Explorer. This logo is 32 pixels wide and 30 pixels high.
- `AlfrescoLogo200.png` file is the login page logo. This logo is displayed on the login page, in the login window, along with user name and password. This logo is 200 pixels wide and 60 pixels high.
- `AlfrescoFadedBG.png` file is the login page background logo. This is the blurred logo displayed as a background image on the login page. This logo is 428 pixels wide and 422 pixels high.

To customize these logos, first rename the existing logos to `AlfrescoLogo32_OLD.png`, `AlfrescoLogo200_OLD.png`, and `AlfrescoFadedBG_OLD.png` respectively, for backup purposes. Create three new logos with the original file names and with the same sizes. For example create a custom site logo with the file name as `AlfrescoLogo32.png` (32 x 30 pixels in size).

Now your Alfresco application will display new custom logos, instead of the default old ones. In some browsers you might not immediately see the new logos due to the fact that the old logos are cached in the browser. Refresh the browser cache to view the new logos in the Alfresco Explorer.

Customize the look and feel using CSS

Cascading Style Sheets (**CSS**) files define how to display HTML elements, in other words, the look and feel of the Alfresco Explorer. The font size, font color, background color, font style, text alignment, and table structure—everything is controlled by the CSS files.

The CSS files are located in the `<install_folder>\tomcat\webapps\alfresco\css` folder. You can customize the look and feel by changing the values in the `main.css` file. For example, you can customize the title look and feel by editing the following block in the `main.css` file:

```
headbarTitle
{
  color: #003366;
  font-size: 11px;
  font-weight: bold;
  margin-bottom: 5px;
}
```

> It is a good practice to back up the `main.css` file before making any changes to it.

Configure multilanguage support

You can configure Alfresco to support various languages such as:

- Chinese
- Dutch
- English
- French
- German
- Italian
- Japanese
- Russian
- Spanish

The support for other languages is being developed. The beauty of true open-source development is that most of these language packs are developed and donated by community users.

The following are the steps to configure a specific language support for your Alfresco application:

1. Download the Alfresco language packs from the SourceForge web site: `http://sourceforge.net/project/showfiles.php?group_id=143373`
2. Copy the required language packs to the `tomcat/webapps/alfresco/WEB-INF/classes/alfresco/messages` folder in the file system.
3. Edit the `web-client-config-custom.xml` file in extension folder and include the following XML code to configure the specific languages:

   ```
   <!-- English is the default language.  Add additional languages to
                                       the list in the login page -->
     <config evaluator="string-compare" condition="Languages">
       <languages>
         <language locale="de_DE">German</language>
         <language locale=»es_ES»>Spanish</language>
         <language locale=»fr_FR»>French</language>
         <language locale=»it_IT»>Italian</language>
         <language locale="ja_JP">Japanese</language>
       </languages>
     </config>
   ```

4. Restart Alfresco.

The Alfresco web-client login screen displays all the configured languages in the drop-down list. These languages appear in the login option and will be in the same order as they are defined in the configuration file. Select the language of your choice, as shown in the following screenshot:

Creating a blue print for your application

Now that the configuration is done, the next step is to create a blue print for your application. The blue-print is nothing but a skeleton application in Alfresco, without actual content. This includes the security framework, the folder structure within the Alfresco repository, the categories for taxonomy, the workflow and the business rules, and so on.

Enterprise intranet as a theme

Throughout this book, we will build an intranet for your enterprise, where each department has its own space, document management and security, and business rules. All departments will be able to collaborate on creating an effective enterprise knowledge management portal.

This example-solution is extended in all the chapters. Therefore, reading the chapters in the correct sequence would help you to understand the features of Alfresco in a systematic manner. While reading each chapter, you will understand the concepts of Alfresco, and at the same time you will be developing the solution. Although the extended sample is related to an enterprise intranet, it is introduced in such a way that you would learn all the features of Alfresco.

Let us name our enterprise as **Have Fun Corporation**, which has the following groups of people:

- Administrator: Manages membership, groups, categories, security, business rules, workflow, and templates
- Executive: Has the highest authority over the content and manages approvals
- HR: Manages corporate policy documents
- Corporate Communications: Manages external PR, internal news releases, and syndication
- Marketing: Manages the web site, company brochures, marketing campaign projects, and digital assets
- Sales: Manages presentations, contracts, documents, and reports
- Finance: Manages account documents, scanned invoices and checks, and notifications
- Engineering: Collaborates on engineering projects, workflow, XML documents, and presentation templates

Features you are going to implement

Following are the high level features you are going to implement as a part of solution:

- Security and Access Control: Give de-centralized control to each department to manage their own content and yet share it with others.
- Document Management including version control, Check-in and Check-out, Categorization, notifications, bulk upload, Advanced Search, and so on. Every group will use these features.
- Space templates for engineering projects and marketing projects: Each engineering project will follow a standard structure, workflow, and security rules. Similarly, each marketing project will follow specific workflow, transformation, and publishing rules.
- Content transformations: For marketing and sales material.
- Imaging Solution: The Finance group will use this feature to handle scanned invoices and checks.
- Presentation templates including dashboard views: The corporate communication groups will use this to display news and the latest PR files, finance groups will use these to have thumbnail views of scanned checks, and engineering groups will use these templates to display XML documents.
- Automated Business Rules: Each group uses these in a specific manner. For example: The HR group might send an email notification to a specific group when a document is updated, the sales group will automatically convert a PPT to Flash, the finance group will trigger an approval process whenever a scanned check gets into the system, and so on.

Summary

Alfresco Explorer, one of Alfresco's built-in web application, provides an intuitive user interface, so that even beginners can start using it without any specialized user training.

This chapter introduced you to the key terminology in Alfresco such as the Alfresco Explorer, the administrator console, space, content, category, aspects, actions, and rules.

When Alfresco starts, it reads all of the default configuration files, and then reads the customized configuration items in the extensions folder. So, depending on the type of item, the customization either extends or overrides the default configuration item. You have the flexibility to choose the database and the membership framework of your choice. You can configure email, multi-language support, the look and the feel of the application. The applications that are built on top of Alfresco are highly configurable, customizable, and extendible.

4
Implementing Membership and Security

In this chapter, you will understand the concepts and the underlying framework behind the Alfresco security model and membership system. The Alfresco security model is flexible and allows you to choose either its built-in security or an external security model defined by your organization, using systems such as LDAP and Active Directory. You will understand various security models and learn to choose the one that is most suited to your enterprise's requirements. The Alfresco membership system is highly scalable and can cater to a number of users and content managers.

By the end of this chapter, you will have learned how to:

- Create, update, and delete users
- Group users, based on the activities they perform
- Search for and locate users and groups
- Extend the security policy
- Secure spaces and individual content according to your organization's security requirements
- Choose a suitable security model
- Migrate existing users and groups to Alfresco

The Alfresco membership and security model

A content management system requires a membership system that allows its users to access content, set their preferences, and receive notifications and alerts. Members of the system can collaborate with other members by selectively sharing documents and sharing ideas by using discussion forums. Through workflow, members can control and follow the business process.

Traditional membership models address basic authentication (who can access) and authorization (what they can do). Alfresco extends this model by providing capabilities to manage groups and subgroups of members, member attributes, and member workspaces. It also provides a set of administrative tools to configure and control the membership.

Users and groups

Users are individual members, whereas **groups** are logical categorizations of users.

In Alfresco, a user is identified by a unique user ID, which is also known as the login ID. The administrator is like a superuser of the system. Alfresco identifies the registered users (users not logged in as a guest). The names of such logged-in users are shown on the top righthand corner of the **Alfresco Explorer** screen and the lefthand corner of the **Alfresco Share**.

Alfresco groups logically group a set of users in the system for the purpose of security and collaboration. A group can have any number of subgroups. There is a default group called **EVERYONE**, which represents all of the users of the system.

A user can belong to more than one group and subgroup, as shown in the following diagram. For example, the user **Mike ExecEngg** belongs to two groups—**Executive** and **Engineering**.

A group can have more than one user. For example, the **Sales** group in the following diagram contains two users—**Amit Sales** and **Candace Sales**.

A user belonging to a subgroup will automatically belong to the parent group. For example, **Chi EnggDoc** belongs to the **Engineering Documentation** subgroup, and thus automatically belongs to the **Engineering** group.

This is how a typical organization's hierarchy works. An employee belongs to a particular department, or sometimes, to more than one department.

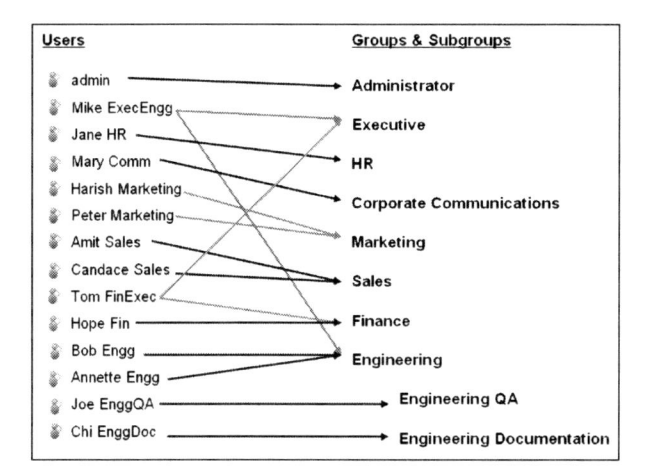

Users	Groups & Subgroups
admin	Administrator
Mike ExecEngg	Executive
Jane HR	HR
Mary Comm	Corporate Communications
Harish Marketing	Marketing
Peter Marketing	
Amit Sales	Sales
Candace Sales	
Tom FinExec	Finance
Hope Fin	
Bob Engg	Engineering
Annette Engg	
Joe EnggQA	Engineering QA
Chi EnggDoc	Engineering Documentation

Permissions and roles

Permissions define access rights on spaces and content. Out of the box, Alfresco supports extensive permission settings on spaces and content. A more detailed description is provided in later sections of this chapter.

Permissions are identified by a string. For example, a particular permission such as `ReadChildren`, may be granted or denied to an authority—a user, a group, an administrator, an owner, and so on. The children of a node—subfolders or files in a folder—will inherit permissions from their parents. So, by default, the files in a folder will inherit their permissions from the folder. Permissions set on a node take precedence over permissions set on the parent nodes. Permission inheritance may be turned off for any node.

A **permission group** is a convenient grouping of permissions such as `Read`, made up of `ReadProperties` and `ReadChildren`. Each one of these permissions is applicable to nodes, spaces, space properties, subspaces, content, content properties, and business rules. The following are typical permission groups:

- Read
- Edit
- Add
- Delete

Roles are collections of permissions assigned to a user. Each role comprises of a set of permissions. Alfresco provides out of the box support for the following roles:

- **Consumer** can read content
- **Editor** can read and edit content
- **Contributor** can read and add content
- **Collaborator** can read, edit, and add content
- **Coordinator** can read, edit, add, and delete content (full access)

The roles and permissions of Alfresco may be extended to support your requirements.

Authentication

Alfresco imposes authentication by using a user name and password pair. Authentication is performed at the following entry points to the Alfresco repository:

- Web client
- CIFS
- FTP
- WebDAV
- Web services
- Spring beans exposed as public services in Java

When a call is made to the repository through the public service API, the caller must first be authenticated. This can be done by logging in using a username and password. Some applications and authentication mechanisms may support single sign-on. For example, a user can access the Alfresco repository through the Explorer program, or another application can access the Alfresco repository through the web services protocol. No matter how a user or an external system connects to Alfresco, they all should go through the same authentication process to access data in the Alfresco repository.

How is security imposed in Alfresco?

Alfresco imposes authorization by assigning a role to a specific user or group for a specific space or content object.

Spaces and content in Alfresco can be secured in a number of ways. By default, a space or content object in Alfresco can be managed only by the owner who created it. For each space, you need to give specific roles (a group of permissions) to specific users (or a group of users) to set the permissions on that space. Subspaces may inherit parent space permissions. Security rules may be specified at the individual content object level, and they may be different from security rules for its parent folder or space.

Let us refer to the previous figure where users **Tom FinExec** and **Hope Fin** both belong to the **Finance** group. Let us say that you have a space called *Finance Department*. You would like to give *full access control* to only those people who belong to the **Finance** group, and give *Read* access to those who belong to the **Sales** and **Executive** groups.

As an administrator for the *Finance Department* space, you can invite the **Finance** group as a *Coordinator* (full access), and **Sales** and **Executive** groups as *Consumers* (read access). Let us refer to the table given below, which shows examples of space structures and the roles assigned to specific groups and individual users on these spaces:

Space Title	Group	Assigned Role
Finance Department	Finance	Coordinator: Full Access
	Sales	Consumer: Only Read Access
	Executive	Consumer: Only Read Access
Company Policies	HR	Coordinator: Full Access
	EVERYONE	Consumer: Only Read Access

Manage system users

You have to log in to the Alfresco Explorer as an administrator (admin) in order to create accounts for each Alfresco user. Only the admin can manage user accounts.

To add users, you need to know the user ID and password, along with other details as listed under *Create New Users* in the next section.

In Alfresco, each user can have his/her individual space. The location and name for a space can be specified while creating a user account. The user for whom a space is created becomes the owner of that space. As an owner, the user can have full access to his/her space.

Creating new users

It is a good practice to create all users in a single space called **User Homes**.

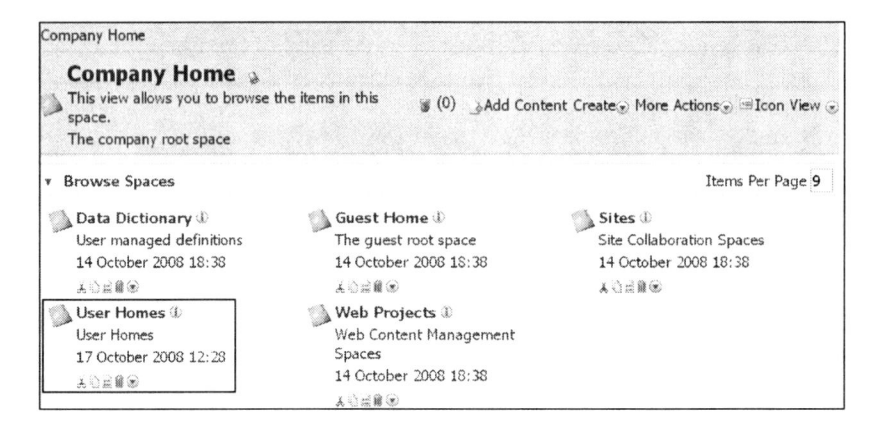

Before adding users, you will need to know the following details about each user:

- First name
- Last name
- Email ID (valid corporate email)
- Company ID (for customer extranet, this could be customer's company name)
- User name (login ID)
- Password
- Home space name (usually the same as the user name)

Refer to the first figure in this chapter for the list of users to be created for your intranet. Follow the following steps to create a user:

1. In any space, click on the **Administration Console** button that is provided at the top of the **Tool Bar**, as shown in the screenshot overleaf:

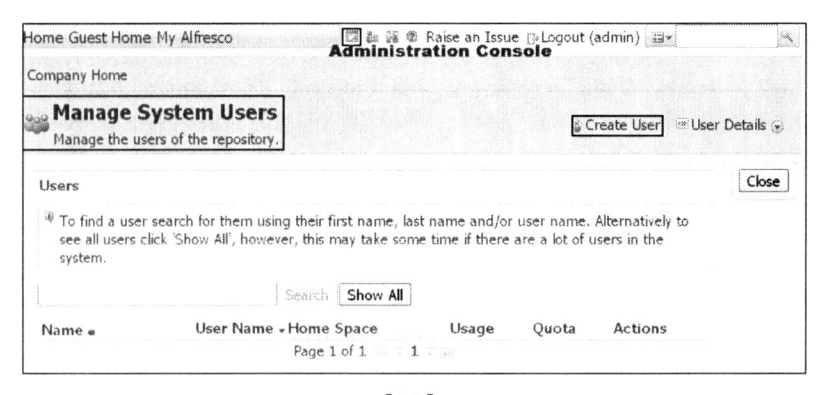

Chapter 4

2. The **Administration Console** pane appears. Click on the **Manage System Users** link. The **Manage System Users** pane appears, as shown in the above screenshot.

3. In the header, click the **Create User** link (highlighted in the screenshot above).

4. The first pane of the **New User Wizard** appears as shown in the next screenshot. This is the **Person Properties** pane, as you can see from the list of steps shown on the leftmost side of the pane.

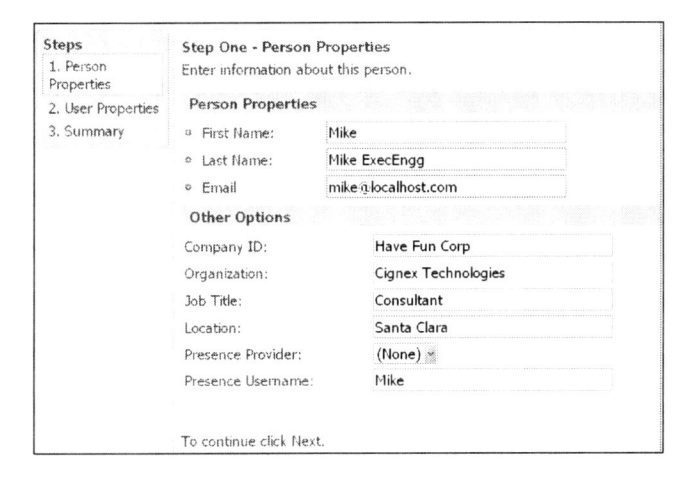

```
Steps                Step One - Person Properties
1. Person            Enter information about this person.
   Properties
2. User Properties   Person Properties
3. Summary             o First Name:       Mike
                       o Last Name:        Mike ExecEngg
                       o Email:            mike@localhost.com
                     Other Options
                       Company ID:         Have Fun Corp
                       Organization:       Cignex Technologies
                       Job Title:          Consultant
                       Location:           Santa Clara
                       Presence Provider:  (None)
                       Presence Username:  Mike

                     To continue click Next.
```

5. For the user **Mike ExecEngg,** specify **Mike** as the **First Name**, **Mike Exec Engg** as the **Last Name**, **mike@localhost.com** as the **Email**, and **Have Fun Corp** as the **Company ID**. In fact, you may also specify the employee ID in the **Company ID** field.

6. Click on the **Next** button appearing at the righthand side of the pane. The second pane of the **New User Wizard** appears as shown in the following screenshot. This is the **User Properties** pane, as you can see from the list of steps on the leftmost side of the pane.

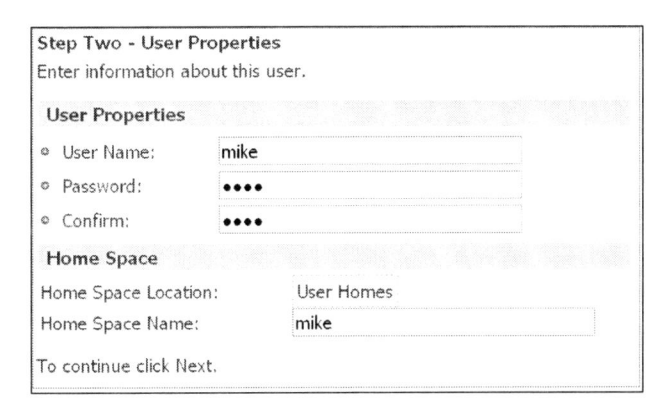

```
Step Two - User Properties
Enter information about this user.

User Properties
  o User Name:         mike
  o Password:          ••••
  o Confirm:           ••••
Home Space
  Home Space Location: User Homes
  Home Space Name:     mike

To continue click Next.
```

7. Specify **mike** (all lower case) as both the **User Name** and **Password**. Choose **User Homes** as the parent space and **mike** as the **Home Space Name**. Note that the username and password must be between 3 and 32 characters in length.
8. Click on the **Next** button appearing on the righthand side of the pane. A third pane will appear. This is the **Summary** pane for the **New User Wizard**.
9. Verify all of the information and click on the **Finish** button to confirm.

> For every wizard in Alfresco, you need to click on the **Finish** button to confirm. Otherwise the information you provided will be lost.

Similarly, create all users (except *admin*, which is already created out of the box) listed in the first figure.

> Do not proceed to the subsequent sections without first creating the users. The remaining sample solution is based on these users and the groups that they belong to.

Search for existing users in Alfresco Explorer

Alfresco provides a "user search" tool to find a user by specifying their first name, last name, and/or user name. Follow the steps below to search for existing users:

1. In any space, click the **Administration Console** icon. The Administration Console pane appears.
2. Click the **Manage System Users** link. The **Manage System Users** pane appears.
3. In the search box, provide the user's first name or last name to search. Alternatively, to see all of the users, click the **Show All** button, without providing any information in the search box.

The search results will be displayed as shown in the next screenshot. If there are many users in the system, the search will return multiple pages with page numbers (as highlighted in the following image).

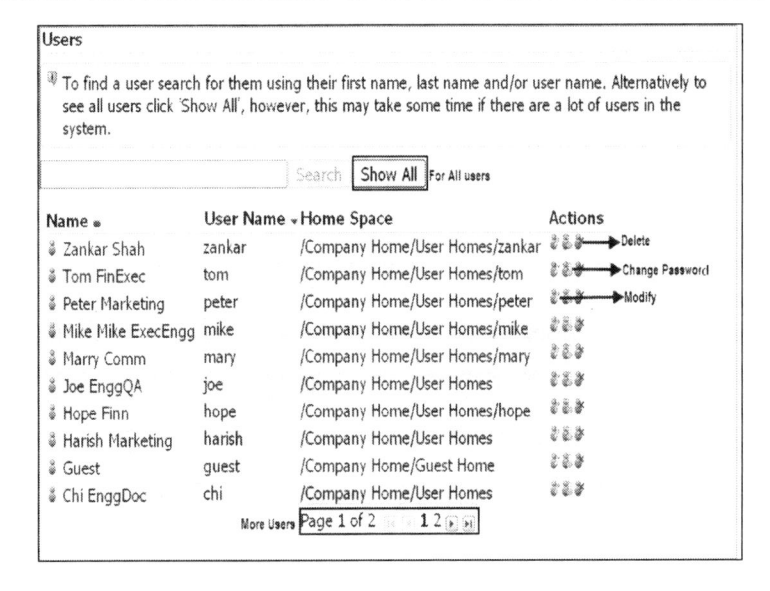

Modify user details

Search for a system user as explained in the previous section. To edit a user's information, click on the **Modify** icon for that user, as shown in the preceding screenshot.

The first pane of the **Edit User Wizard** appears. You can edit and make corrections as required, and then click the **Finish** button to confirm.

Deleting a user

First, search for a system user by following the procedure described under *Search for Existing Users* section. To delete a user's details, click on the **Delete** icon belonging to that user, as shown in the immediately preceding screenshot. You need to be very careful while deleting a user from the system as the user will no longer be able to access the system.

Even if the user is deleted from the system, his/her home space will not be deleted from the system. Therefore, you need to remove the user's space manually if you want to remove the deleted user's content from the system.

Implementing Membership and Security

> Alfresco provides a content recovery tool to recover deleted content. However, there is no way to recover a deleted user. Hence, you need to be careful while deleting a user from the system.

Individual user access

Once a user account is created by the administrator, the user can log in to the system. The administrator can set up an automated script to send an email containing the user ID and password information to the user. You will know more about such email notification template scripts in later chapters.

New user log in and my homepage

Log in to Alfresco, by entering the following URL in your browser:
`http://server_name:8080/alfresco`

If you are already logged in as an administrator, log out by clicking on the **Logout** button in the **Tool Bar**.

The login page appears, as shown in the above screenshot. In the **User Name** text box, enter your user name as **mike**, and enter the same as password in the **Password** text box. Note that the user **Mike ExecEngg** is created as a part of the new user account definition in the previous section.

Depending on your installation, you may have a choice of languages in the **Language** drop-down menu. This example assumes that your selected language is **English**. Click on the **Login** link and enter your credentials. Your home space appears as shown in the following screenshot:

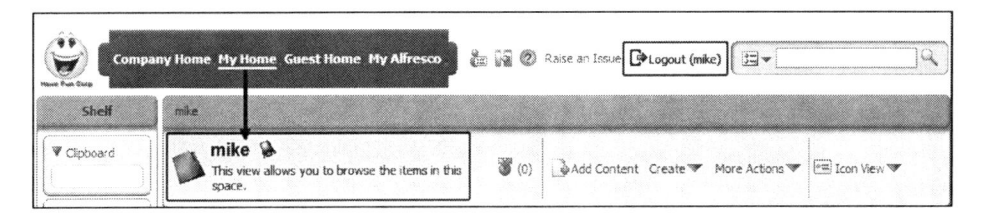

Update personal details and password

You can update your profile information and password by clicking on the user options icon in the **Tool Bar,** as shown in the following screenshot.

Click on the **Edit Personal Profile** icon to update your name and user ID. Click on the **Change Password** link to update your password.

Under the **General Preferences** block, select the **Start Location** as the landing page once you log into the Alfresco Explorer.

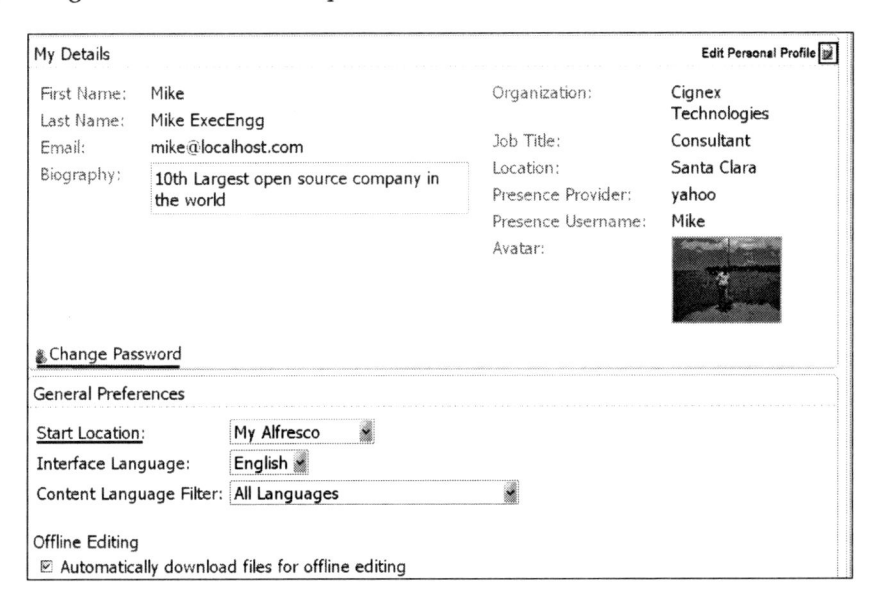

Search for existing users in Alfresco share

You can also search for users in Alfresco share. Click on **People**, and a search pane appears.

In the search box, provide user's first name or last name to search. The search result will be displayed as shown next:

Modify user details using share

Log into Alfresco as mike, by entering the following URL in your browser: `http://server_name:8080/share`

Click on the **My Profile** pane. You can modify the details by clicking on the **Edit Profile** button. You can also change the password by clicking on the **Change Password** link.

The first pane of the **Edit User Wizard** appears. You can edit and make corrections as required, and then click the **Finish** button to confirm.

Manage user groups

Alfresco comes with one default user group called EVERYONE. The EVERYONE group logically includes all of the system users, irrespective of the groups they belong to. This is useful to give *read* access to everyone on certain common spaces—for example, HR Policies. You can create and manage your own groups. In order to create groups, log in to the Alfresco Explorer as an administrator.

Create groups and subgroups

Before adding a group or subgroup (hierarchical groups), you will need to finalize the group names. The group name (identifier) should be unique and cannot be changed once it has been set.

Refer to the first figure in this chapter for the list of groups to be created for your intranet. Follow the steps that are mentioned next in order to create a group:

1. In any space, click on the **Administration Console** icon. The **Administration Console** pane appears.
2. Click the **Manage User Groups** link. The **Groups Management** pane appears.
3. In the header, click **Create | Create Group**. The **Create Group Wizard** appears, as shown in the screenshot below. Specify **Executive** in the **Identifier** field, which is the group used for all company executives. Click on the **Create Group** button to confirm.

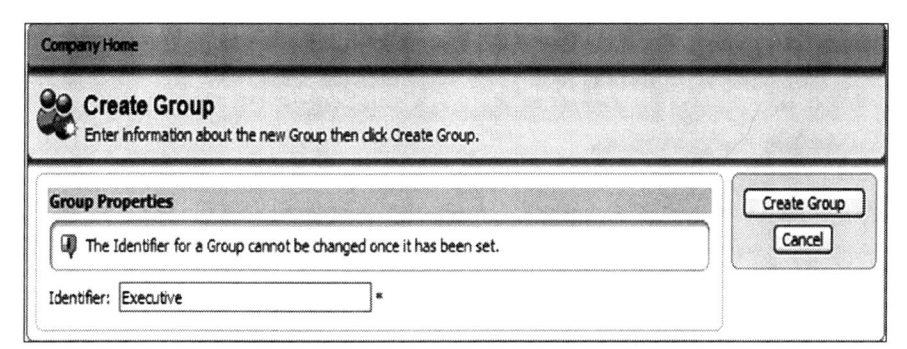

Similarly, create all groups listed in the very first figure (except Administrator, which is already created out of the box).

> Do not proceed to the subsequent sections without creating all of these groups. The remaining sample solution relies on the existence of these groups for security and collaboration.

Implementing Membership and Security

Click on the **Engineering** group, and create two subgroups called **QA** and **Documentation**.

Now you can see the groups at the root level, as shown in the following screenshot. You will notice that **QA** and **Documentation** are not part of the root level groups, as they are subgroups under the **Engineering** group.

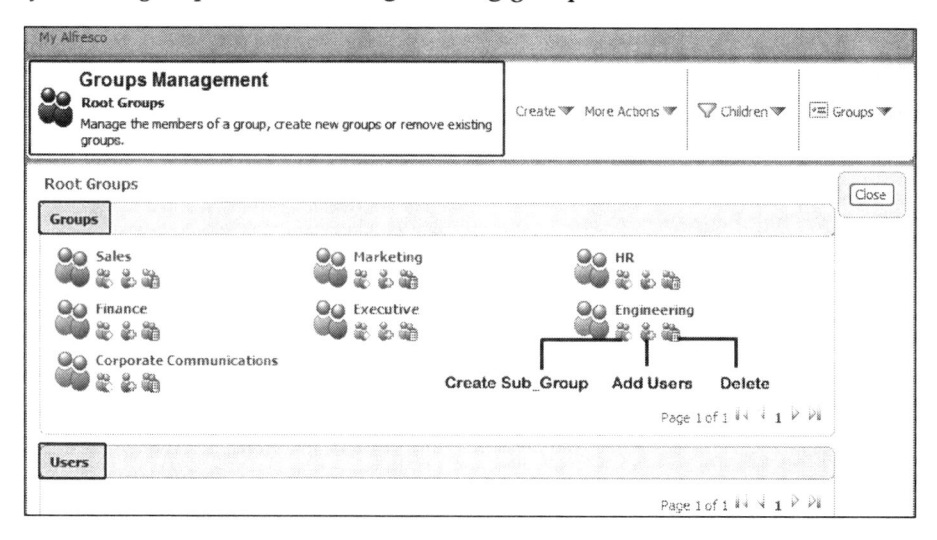

Add users to a group

To add users to a group, click on the **Add Users** icon, as shown in the above screenshot. The **Add User** dialog will pop up. You can search for the system users and add them to a group, as shown in the next screenshot. Click on the **Finish** button to confirm the operation.

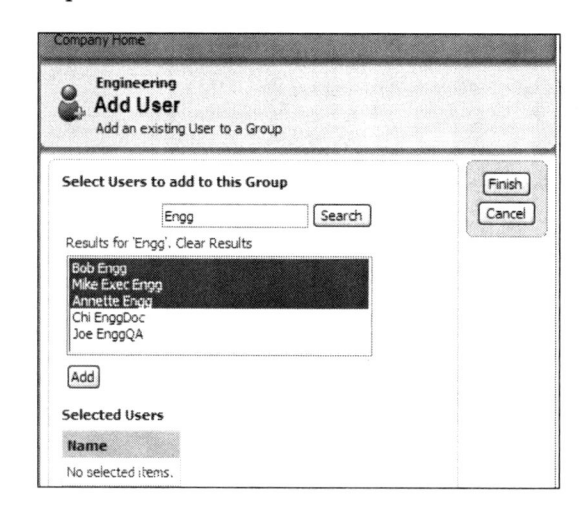

Add users to the newly-created groups as explained in the first figure in this chapter. For example, add user Jane HR to the HR group. Add user Mary Comm to Corporate Communications group. Similarly, add user Joe EnggQA to the QA subgroup of the Engineering group, and so on.

Remove users from a group

Users can be removed from a group by clicking on the **Remove User** icon as shown in the next screenshot.

A user may belong to one or more groups. If the user is deleted from the system users list, he/she will automatically be removed from all of the groups that he or she was a member of.

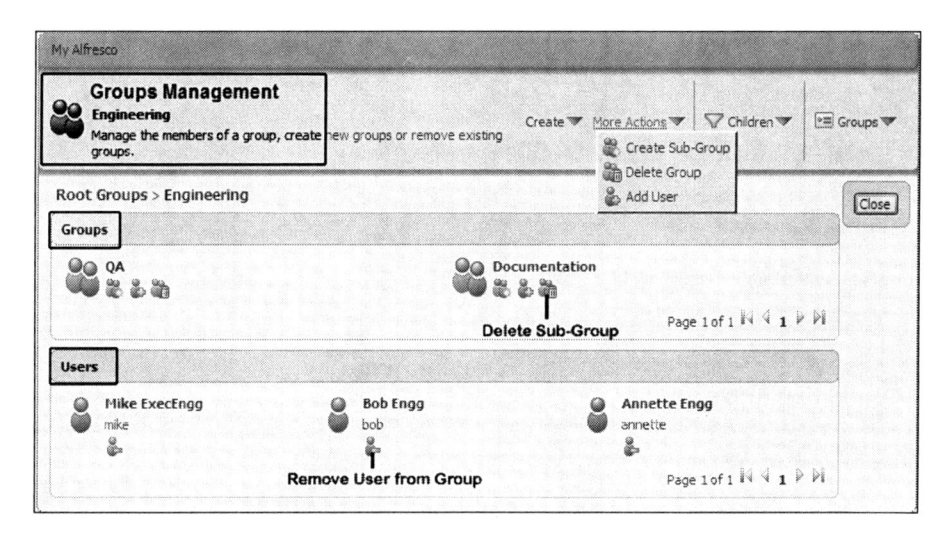

Extend security permissions and roles

Alfresco supports an extensive set of permissions, in order to provide security controls. It also supports a set of roles by grouping these permissions. The security permissions and roles can be extended. However, before extending the permissions and roles, you need to evaluate and understand the existing permissions and roles, and justify the decision for extending them.

Default permissions

Alfresco supports a number of permissions to access the spaces, content, their properties, and so on. The following are some of the permissions for spaces:

- `_ReadProperties`: Reads the space's properties
- `_ReadChildren`: Reads the content within a space
- `_WriteProperties`: Updates properties such as title, description, and so on
- `_DeleteNode`: Deletes the space
- `_DeleteChildren`: Deletes content and subspaces within a space
- `_CreateChildren`: Creates content within a space

The following are some of the permissions for content items:

- `_ReadContent`: Reads the file
- `_WriteContent`: Updates the file
- `_ReadProperties`: Reads the file properties
- `_WriteProperties`: Updates the file properties such as title, description, and so on
- `_DeleteNode`: Deletes the file
- `_ExecuteContent`: Executes the file
- `_SetOwner`: Sets ownership on a content item

A complete list of the default permissions and roles is provided in the Alfresco configuration file—`<config>\model\permissionDefinitions.xml`.

Default roles

Roles are collections of permissions assigned to users in a specific space. Subspaces may inherit permissions from the parent space. Roles may also be applied to individual content items. The following table lists the default roles supported out of the box by Alfresco:

Role	Permission
Consumer	Read spaces and content
Editor	Consumer + edit existing content
Contributor	Consumer + add new content
Collaborator	Editor + Contributor
Coordinator	Full control

Create a custom role

You can add a new custom role according to your security requirements. You will have to include the custom role details in the `permissionDefinitions.xml file`, which is located at `<config>\model\`. For a Tomcat installation, you can find this file at `tomcat\webapps\alfresco\WEB-INF\classes\alfresco\model\permissionDefinitions.xml`.

You need to define your own permissions group (say `TestRole`) and assign permissions as shown below:

```
<permissionGroup name="TestRole" allowFullControl="false"
                                                expose="true" >
  <includePermissionGroup permissionGroup="Read" type="sys:base" />
  <includePermissionGroup permissionGroup="AddChildren"
                                            type="sys:base"/>
  <includePermissionGroup type="cm:lockable"
                                permissionGroup="CheckOut"/>
</permissionGroup>
```

Once you make the changes to the XML file, you need to restart Alfresco to have the new role added to the system.

Secure your spaces

Space can be secured by assigning a role to a specific user (or group) for that space.

A role refers to a set of permissions that can be applied to a folder.

Permissions are identified by a string. For example, a particular permission (say `ReadChildren`) may be granted or denied to an authority, regardless of whether this is a user, a group, an administrator, an owner, and so on. The children of a node will inherit permissions from their parents. So, by default, the files in a folder will inherit their permissions from the folder. Permissions set on a node take precedence over permissions set on the parent nodes. The inheritance of permissions may be turned off for any node. A permission group is a convenient grouping of permissions such as `Read` that is made up of `ReadProperties` and `ReadChildren`.

User roles on a space

Alfresco uses roles to determine what a user can and cannot do in a space. These roles are associated with permissions. The following table lists the allowed permissions for each role on a given space. A user (or group) with the *Consumer* role on a space, can read all of the content within that space. Similarly, a user (or group) with the *Contributor* role on a space can create content within the space.

Permission	Consumer	Contributor	Editor	Collaborator	Coordinator
Read content within space	X	X	X	X	X
Read space Properties	X	X	X	X	X
Read subspaces	X	X	X	X	X
Read forums, topics, posts	X	X	X	X	X
Copy	X	X	X	X	X
Preview in template	X	X	X	X	X
Create content within space	—	X	—	X	X
Create subspaces	—	X	—	X	X
Create forums, topics, posts	—	X	—	X	X
Reply to posts	—	X	—	X	X
Start discussion	—	X	—	X	X
Edit spaces properties	—	—	X	X	X
Add/Edit space users	—	—	X	X	X
Delete space users	—	—	—	—	X
Add/Edit space rules	—	—	X	X	X
Delete space rules	—	—	—	—	X
Cut content/subspaces	—	—	—	—	X
Delete content/subspaces	—	—	—	—	X
Checkout content	—	—	X	X	X
Update content	—	—	X	X	X
Take ownership	—	—	—	—	X

Invite users to your space

You can grant permission to the users (or groups) to do specific tasks in your space. You do this by inviting users to join your space. Each role applies only to the space in which it is assigned. For example, you could invite a user (or group) to one of your spaces as an editor. You could invite the same user (or group) to a different space as a collaborator. That same user (or group) could be invited to someone else's space as a coordinator.

Follow the steps given next to invite a group of users to your space:

1. Click on the **Company Home** menu link in the **Tool Bar** (on the upper-left).
2. In the header, select **Create | Create Space**.
3. Create a new space called **Intranet**.
4. Within the **Intranet** space, create a subspace called **Finance Department**. Ensure that you are in the **Finance Department** space.
5. In the space header, select **More Actions | Manage Space Users**. The **Manage Space Users** pane appears, as shown in following screenshot:

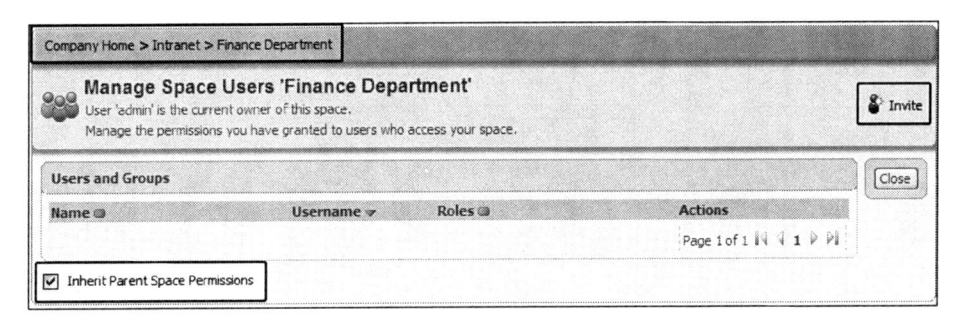

6. Leave the **Inherit Parent Space Permissions** option as checked (selected). If it is not selected, uninvited users cannot see the content item. Only invited users can see the content item, and can access it, according to their assigned role.

Implementing Membership and Security

7. In the header, click the **Invite** link. The **Invite User Wizard** pane appears, as shown in the following screenshot:

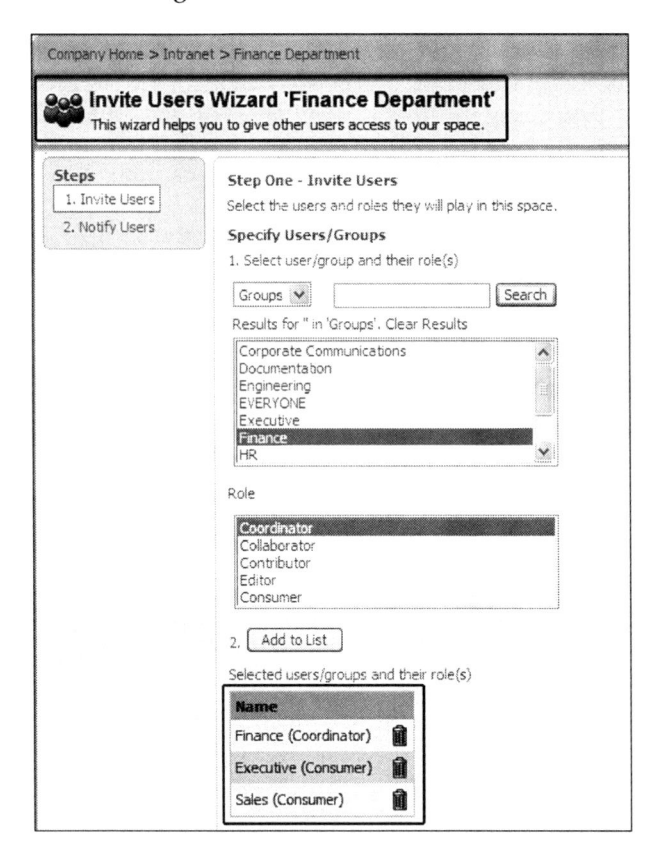

8. Before continuing with your invitation, you can experiment with the **Search** feature. Select the **Groups** option from the drop-down box and click on the **Search** button.

9. From the search results, select the **Finance** group, give it the **Coordinator** role, and click on the **Add to List** button.

10. The finance group is added to the list of invitees.

11. As an administrator of the **Finance Department** space, you can invite the **Finance** group as the **Coordinator** (full access), and the **Sales** and **Executive** groups as **Consumer** (read access).

12. Click on the **Next** button to go to the second pane, where you can notify the selected users.

13. Do not select this option as you do not need to notify these selected users in this sample. Click on the **Finish** button to confirm your selections.

Notice the permissions given to the groups on this space, as shown in the next screenshot:

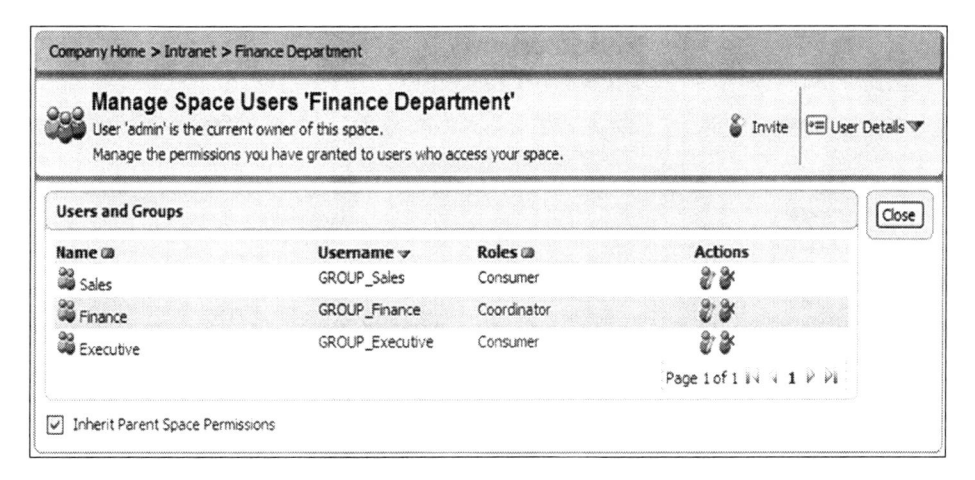

Define and secure your spaces

In the example above, you created a space called **Finance Department**. You assigned the **Coordinator** role (*full control*) to the **Finance** group, and the **Consumer** role (*read access*) to the **Sales** and the **Executive** groups.

Next, go to your **Company Home | Intranet** space and create spaces, as given in the first column of the next table. Invite groups and assign roles as indicated in the second column of the table:

Space name	Group (assigned role)	Individual (assigned role)
Executive and Board	Executive (Coordinator)	—
Company Policies	HR (Coordinator)	—
	EVERYONE (Consumer)	
Press and Media	Corporate Communications (Coordinator)	—
	EVERYONE (Consumer)	
Marketing Communications	Marketing (Coordinator)	—
	EVERYONE (Consumer)	
Sales Department	Sales (Coordinator)	Mr. CEO (Coordinator)
	Executive (Consumer)	

Space name	Group (assigned role)	Individual (assigned role)
Finance Department	Finance (Coordinator)	—
	Sales (Consumer)	
	Executive (Consumer)	
Engineering Department	Engineering (Coordinator)	Mrs. Presales (Coordinator)
	EVERYONE (Consumer)	

Secure your content

Content can be secured by assigning a role to a specific user (or group) on that content.

User roles for content

Alfresco uses roles to determine what a user can and cannot do with the content. These roles are associated with permissions. The table below shows each role and the permissions on the content for that particular role:

Permissions	Consumer	Contributor	Editor	Collaborator	Coordinator
Read Content	X	X	X	X	X
Read Content Properties	X	X	X	X	X
Copy	X	X	X	X	X
Preview in Template	X	X	X	X	X
Start Discussion	—	X	—	X	X
Edit Content	—	—	X	X	X
Edit Properties	—	—	X	X	X
Apply Versioning	—	—	X	X	X
Apply Categorization	—	—	X	X	X
Checkout	—	—	X	X	X
Update	—	—	X	X	X
Take ownership	—	—	—	—	X
Cut	—	—	—	—	X
Delete	—	—	—	—	X

Invite users to your content

Typically, security and access control rules are defined at the space level. It is not advisable to secure individual content items, as this may become unmanageable with a large number of files. It is best to secure the parent space, rather than securing the content itself. However, you can still control the access to a specific content item.

Follow the steps given next to invite users to your content item:

1. Go to a space and add a file by clicking on the **Add Content** link.
2. Click on the **View Details** icon for the file to see the detailed view of the content.
3. From the **Actions** menu on the righthand side, click on the **Manage Content Users** link to assign users to this content item for collaboration.
4. Search and select a user and assign a **Collaborator** role to it.

Now the user can collaborate on the file.

Choosing the correct security model for you

It is very important to choose a suitable security model at the beginning of the implementation of Alfresco. The authentication mechanisms, user profile, data storage, security settings, business rules, and so on, are all based on the security model you choose.

Alfresco imposes authentication through a user's login ID and password. This is where you choose a security model such as Alfresco's built-in membership system, **NTLM (Windows NT LAN Manager)**, or **LDAP (Lightweight Directory Access Protocol)**. These security models are explained in detail in the subsequent sections of this chapter.

Alfresco imposes authorization by assigning a role to a specific user (or group) for a specific space (or content). This will be the same irrespective of which model you choose.

The security model you choose will be based on the requirements of your enterprise. Let us consider the following sample scenarios:

- **Scenario 1**:

    Requirement: I would like to build an extranet as a standalone application to share documents with my customers. I have over 500 customers who will access the site, and I would like to control and manage the security. I need a flexible and highly-scalable membership system.

Probable solution: In this scenario, the out of the box Alfresco membership system would be able to solve the problem.

- **Scenario 2**:

    Requirement: I work in the IT department of a large university. Over the years, the various departments have developed their own sites with local authentication and authorization. Our university has a directory-based central authentication system. How can I consolidate all the sites and provide a central point of authentication and authorization for all our subsites?

    Probable solution: In this scenario, it would make sense configuring Alfresco with LDAP for centralized identity management.

- **Scenario 3**:

    Requirement: In my enterprise we have various systems such as customer support, ERP, proprietary content management systems, and open source ECM Alfresco. Our employees have different accounts for each of these different systems and it is becoming unmanageable for us. We are looking for a single sign-on solution to access all our systems with one log in ID and password.

    Probable solution: In this scenario Alfresco can be configured to use NTML to provide a single sign-on.

Use Alfresco's out of the box membership system

Alfresco's out of the box security system includes the following functionality:

- User management
- Provision of a user's personal information
- User authentication
- Group management
- Ownership of nodes within the repository
- An extendable permission model
- Access control, in order to make sure that calls to public services are restricted to only the authenticated users

Examples in this book are based on the out of the box Alfresco security model.

Configuring LDAP for centralized identity management

LDAP evolved from the X.500 OSI Directory Access Protocol. The LDAP directory is the central authentication engine for the enterprise, and serves as the Yellow Pages for user access and profile information. The biggest advantage of LDAP is that your enterprise can access the LDAP directory on almost any computing platform, using any one of the increasing numbers of readily-available LDAP-aware applications. In fact, LDAP is finding much wider industrial acceptance because of its status as an Internet standard.

You can use LDAP with any directory server such as iPlanet, Novell's eDirectory, Microsoft's Active Directory, or OpenLDAP. If you are planning to implement an LDAP directory in your organization, you may consider OpenLDAP, Active Directory, or eDirectory. OpenLDAP is a stable and widely accepted open-source directory server.

Listed in the following table are the differences between Active Directory and eDirectory:

Sr. no.	Active Directory	eDirectory
1	**Active Directory (AD)** is an implementation of the LDAP directory services by Microsoft.	eDirectory is a Novell product known as **NDS: Novell Directory Service**.
2	It offers a static view of the data.	It supports a logical tree view of data.
3	It supports simple updates without transactions.	It supports hierarchical, object-oriented databases, and referential integrity. However, there is no transactional support.
4	Its main purpose is to provide central authentication and authorization services for Windows-based computers.	Apart from providing central authentication and authorization services, eDirectory can use any other hierarchical data model such as an organizational structure.
5	One can manage AD by using the Active Directory Administrative Tool.	iManager is a supportive Novell product, which is required to manage eDirectory. Using iManager, one can administer Novell eDirectory, along with many Novell and third-party products.

LDAP configuration with active directory

Active Directory supports LDAP-based authentication. It can also support authentication using JAAS+Kerberos and NTLM authentication. Only NTLM will give you a single sign-on solution. We will discuss single sign-on later in this chapter. It is possible to use any authentication methods against an Active Directory server, and extract user and group information using LDAP.

For the LDAP to work with Alfresco, you have to make the some changes in the configuration files.

The custom version of the configurations file given below is available in the following location:

- JBoss: `<alfresco>/jboss/server/default/conf/alfresco/extension`
- Tomcat: `<alfresco>/tomcat/shared/classes/alfresco/extension`

Follow the steps given below to configure LDAP-based authentication with Active Directory.

1. Rename `ldap-authentication-context.xml.sample` to `ldap-authentication-context.xml`.

2. Open the file `ldap-authentication-context.xml` and comment the following block of code:

    ```
    <!-- <bean name="authenticationDao"
      class="org.alfresco.repo.security.authentication.
      DefaultMutableAuthenticationDao" >
        <property name="allowDeleteUser">
          <value>true</value>
        </property>
    </bean> -->
    ```

3. Open the `ldap-authentication.properties` file. Modify the properties to your required values. All other properties can be kept as it is in the file:

    - `ldap.authentication.userNameFormat=CN=%s,DC=company,DC=com`: Map the user ID entered by the user to be passed through LDAP, the %s is replaced with whatever the user types in as their user ID on the login screen.
    - `ldap.authentication.java.naming.provider.url=ldap://openldap.domain.com:389`: The name and port of you LDAP server; the standard port for LDAP is 389.

- `ldap.authentication.java.naming.security.authentication=simple`: The authentication mechanism you want to use.
- `ldap.authentication.java.naming.security.principal=admin`: The user that has read access to the group and people information to be extracted from the Active Directory server.
- `ldap.authentication.java.naming.security.credentials=secret`: The password for the user defined above.

4. Open the `file-server-custom.xml` file. Add the following code:

```xml
<config evaluator="string-compare" condition="CIFS Server"
  replace="true">
     <serverEnable enabled="false"/>
    <host name="${cifs.localname}A" domain="${cifs.domain}"/>
    <comment>Alfresco CIFS Server</comment>

    <!-- Set to the broadcast mask for the subnet -->
    <broadcast>${cifs.broadcast}</broadcast>

    <!-- Use Java socket based NetBIOS over TCP/IP and
         native SMB
    on linux -->
    <tcpipSMB platforms="linux,solaris,macosx"/>
    <netBIOSSMB platforms="linux,solaris,macosx"/>

       <!-- Can be mapped to non-privileged ports,
            then use firewall
     rules to forward requests from the standard ports -->
       <!--
    <tcpipSMB port="1445" platforms="linux,solaris,macosx"/>
    <netBIOSSMB sessionPort="1139" namePort="1137"
    datagramPort="1138" platforms="linux,solaris,macosx"/>
       -->
    <hostAnnounce interval="5"/>

    <!-- Use Win32 NetBIOS interface on Windows -->
    <Win32NetBIOS/>
    <Win32Announce interval="5"/>

    <!-- CIFS authentication -->
    <authenticator type=" passthru ">
     <LocalDomain/>
    </authenticator>

    <!--
    <WINS>
       <primary>1.2.3.4</primary>
```

```
                <secondary>5.6.7.8</secondary>
        </WINS>
            -->
        <sessionDebug flags="Negotiate,Socket"/>
    </config>

    <config evaluator="string-compare" condition="FTP Server"
     replace="true">
            <serverEnable enabled="false"/>
            <!-- Run on a non-privileged port -->
            <!--
            <port>1121</port>
            -->
        <!-- FTP authentication -->
        <authenticator type="alfresco"/>
            <!--       <debug
             flags="File,Search,Error,Directory,Info,DataPort"/> -->
    </config>

    <config evaluator="string-compare" condition="Filesystem Security"
     replace="true">
        <authenticator type=" passthru ">
         <!-- the name of your ldap server   -- >
         <Server> openldap.domain.com</Server>
         </authenticator>
    </config>
```

This authentication mechanism sends user names and passwords in plain text. It is the simplest to set up. This is supported by both Active Directory and OpenLDAP.

LDAP synchronisation

As you have already configured LDAP with Active Directory, the next step would be to extract information from Active Directory. This synchronization of people and groups between the Alfresco repository and LDAP is supported by scheduled jobs. These jobs extract the user or group information from the LDAP repository, and create the appropriate information as an Alfresco import XML file. This file is then imported into the repository.

Follow the steps given below to export users and groups from Active Directory.

1. Rename the `ldap-synchronisation-context.xml.sample` file to `ldap-synchronisation-context.xml`.
2. Open `ldap-synchronisation.properties` file. Modify the properties to the required values, as follows. All other properties can be kept unchanged in the file.
    - `ldap.synchronisation.personQuery=(objectclass=inetOrgPerson)` and `ldap.synchronisation.personSearchBase=dc=company,dc=com`: These two options combine to build the query to find people. In the example above, you will find all objects of type `inetOrgPerson` anywhere in the directory.
    - `ldap.synchronisation.groupQuery=(objectclass=groupOfNames)` and `ldap.synchronisation.groupSearchBase=dc=example,dc=com`: These two options combine to build the query to find groups. In the example above, you will find all objects of type `groupOfNames` anywhere in the directory.
3. Ensure that the changes you made above are saved. Start Alfresco.

On restarting, you will be able to login to the alfresco repository with only LDAP.

Daisy chaining

If you want to login to the Alfresco repository along with Alfresco users too, you have to make some more changes in the configuration files. This concept is known as **Daisy Chaining**.

Alfresco supports a pluggable authentication model. Out of the box, many authenticators are available such as NTLM, LDAP, Kerberos, and Alfresco. Also, you can have your own custom-built authentication system plugged into Alfresco, as shown below:

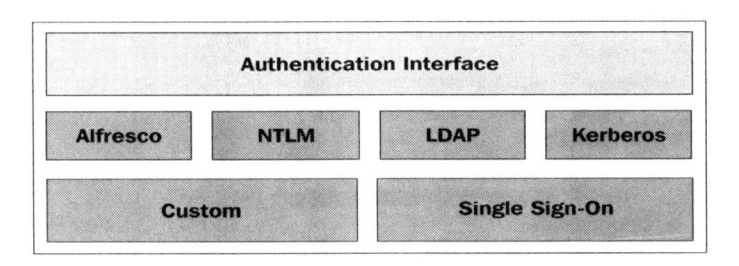

Authentication services may be daisy chained—one instance of Alfresco can have more than one user-source. However, the sequence in which these user data sources are daisy chained is important. When a user logs into the system, Alfresco checks for authentication in a defined sequence, as shown in the next figure:

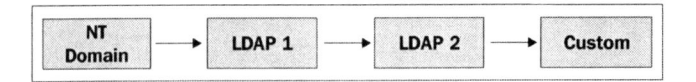

NT Domain → LDAP 1 → LDAP 2 → Custom

Follow the steps given below to implement chaining:

1. Browse the file : `<configRoot>\alfresco\ authentication-services-context.xml`.

2. Copy the following blocks of code :

```xml
    <bean id="authenticationComponentChain"
class="org.alfresco.repo.security.authentication.
ChainingAuthenticationComponentImpl">
        <property name="authenticationComponents">
            <list>
                <ref bean="authenticationComponentAlfresco"/>
                <ref bean="authenticationComponent"/>
            </list>
        </property>
    </bean>
    <bean id="authenticationComponentAlfresco"   class="org.
alfresco.repo.security.authentication.AuthenticationComponentImpl"
parent="authenticationComponentBase">
        <property name="authenticationDao">
            <ref bean="authenticationDao" />
        </property>
        <property name="authenticationManager">
            <ref bean="authenticationManager" />
        </property>
       <property name="allowGuestLogin">
            <value>false</value>
        </property>
        <property name="nodeService">
            <ref bean="nodeService" />
        </property>
        <property name="personService">
            <ref bean="personService" />
        </property>
        <property name="transactionService">
            <ref bean="transactionService" />
        </property>
    </bean>
```

3. Edit the following block, by commenting against an existing property and adding one block of another property.

```
         <bean id="authenticationService" class="org.alfresco.repo.
security.authentication.AuthenticationServiceImpl">
           <property name="authenticationDao">
               <ref bean="authenticationDao" />
           </property>
           <property name="ticketComponent">
               <ref bean="ticketComponent" />
           </property>
           <!--<property name="authenticationComponent">
               <ref bean=" authenticationComponent " />  <This is the
property to be modified to authenticationComponentChain >
           </property> -- >
           <property name="authenticationComponent">
               <ref bean="authenticationComponentChain " />
           </property>
           <property name="sysAdminCache">
               <ref bean="sysAdminCache"/>
           </property>
      </bean>
```

4. Save the changes. You will need to restart Alfresco to see the changes take effect. You can check it by logging in as the Alfresco user as well as the Active Directory user.

Configuring NTLM for Single sign-on

NT LAN Manager (NTLM) is an authentication protocol used in various Microsoft network protocol implementations, and is also used throughout Microsoft's systems as an integrated single sign-on mechanism.

NTLM authentication can be used to provide single sign-on to Alfresco. Using this protocol, the password that is sent over the network is made more secure, than when using basic authentication. NTLM pass-through authentication can also be used to replace the standard Alfresco user database, and instead use a Windows server/domain controller, or a list of servers, to authenticate users accessing Alfresco. This eliminates the task of creating user accounts within Alfresco.

By using NTLM authentication, the web browser can automatically log on when accessing Alfresco and Alfresco WebDAV sites. When NTLM is configured, Internet Explorer will use your Windows log-on credentials when requested by the web server. Firefox and Mozilla also support the use of NTLM. For these, you will be prompted for the username/password details, which can then optionally be stored using the password manager. The Opera web browser does not support NTLM authentication. If an Opera browser is detected, you will be sent to the usual Alfresco login page.

Implementing Membership and Security

Let us consider two scenarios

- SSO with Active Directory: The users who are inside the company network (who are logged into Active Directory) should automatically be logged into Alfresco Repository.
- Two external applications (such as Alfresco and Liferay) achieving SSO through CAS.

SSO with active directory

Follow the steps given below to integrate Single sign-on.

1. Open the `web.xml` file. The location of the file depends on the application server used. For Tomcat this can be found in the `tomcat/webapps/alfresco/web-inf` folder.
2. Modify the existing block of filters, as given below:

```
<filter>
<filter-name>Authentication Filter</filter-name>
<!-- <filter-
class>org.alfresco.web.app.servlet.AuthenticationFilter</
filter-
class> --> <!-- For Novell IChain support use the following
filter -->
<!-- <filter- class>org.alfresco.web.app.servlet.
NovellIChainsHTTPRequestAuthenticationFilter</filter-class>   -->
<!-- For NTLM authentication support use the following
filter -->
    <filter-class>org.alfresco.web.app.servlet.
NTLMAuthenticationFilter</filter-class>
</filter>
<filter>
<filter-name>WebDAV Authentication Filter</filter-name>
<!-- <filter-class>org.alfresco.repo.webdav.auth.
AuthenticationFilter</filter-class> -->
<!-- For NTLM authentication support use the following
filter -->
    <filter-class>org.alfresco.repo.webdav.auth.
NTLMAuthenticationFilter</filter-class>
</filter>
```

Chapter 4

3. Browse the `tomcat\shared\classes\alfresco\extension\ntlm-authentication-context.xml.sample` file. Either rename the file to `ntlm-authentication-context.xml` or create a new file with the name `ntlm-authentication-context.xml` in the same location, and copy the code from sample file.

```xml
<bean id="authenticationDao"
class="org.alfresco.repo.security.authentication.ntlm.
NullMutableAuthenticationDao" />

<bean id="authenticationComponent"
class="org.alfresco.repo.security.authentication.ntlm.
NTLMAuthenticationComponentImpl">
  <property name="personService">
    <ref bean="personService" />
  </property>
  <property name="nodeService">
    <ref bean="nodeService" />
  </property>
  <property name="transactionService">
    <ref bean="transactionComponent" />
  </property>
  <property name="guestAccess">
    <value>false</value>
  </property>
  <property name="servers">
    <value>openldap.domain.com</value>
  </property>
  <property name="useLocalServer">
    <value>true</value>
  </property>
</bean>
```

4. Open the `file-server-custom.xml` file in the same location and add the following code:

```xml
<config evaluator="string-compare"  condition="Filesystem
Security" replace="true">
   <authenticator type="alfresco" />
   </config>

<config evaluator="string-compare" condition="CIFS Server">
  <serverEnable enabled="true" replace="true" />
  <host name="${cifs.localname}A" domain="${cifs.domain}"/>
  <comment>Alfresco CIFS Server</comment>

  <!-- Set to the broadcast mask for the subnet -->
```

[117]

Implementing Membership and Security

```
            <broadcast>${cifs.broadcast}</broadcast>
            <!-- Use Java socket based NetBIOS over TCP/IP and native
            SMB on linux -->
            <tcpipSMB platforms="linux,solaris,macosx"/>
            <netBIOSSMB platforms="linux,solaris,macosx"/>
                <!-- Can be mapped to non-privileged ports, then use
                firewall rules to forward
                        requests from the standard ports -->
                <!--
            <tcpipSMB port="1445" platforms="linux,solaris,macosx"/>
            <netBIOSSMB sessionPort="1139" namePort="1137"
            datagramPort="1138" platforms="linux,solaris,macosx"/>
                -->
            <hostAnnounce interval="5"/>
            <!-- Use Win32 NetBIOS interface on Windows -->
            <Win32NetBIOS/>
            <Win32Announce interval="5"/>
            <!-- CIFS authentication -->
          <authenticator type="alfresco">
          </authenticator>
    <!--
        <WINS>
            <primary>1.2.3.4</primary>
            <secondary>5.6.7.8</secondary>
        </WINS>
    -->
            <sessionDebug flags="Negotiate,Socket"/>
        </config>
```

5. Restart the Alfresco server. If you are logged into Active Directory, you will be automatically logged in to the Alfresco repository.

SSO with CAS

Here is a brief explanation of the integration of Alfresco and Liferay through SSO.

1. Integration of Liferay and LDAP:

    Liferay provides us with facilities to use LDAP for authentication. This can be set up by making changes in the out of the box portlet that is provided by Liferay (the `EnterpriseAdmin` portlet).

2. Integration of Liferay and Alfresco:

    Download the Alfresco WAR file. Refer to the link http://wiki.alfresco.com/wiki/Deploying_2.1WAR_Liferay4 to deploy alfresco WAR.

3. Restart the Liferay server:

   Log into Liferay by entering the following URL in the browser: `http://servername:port/`. Click on the **Auto Deploy** tab of the **EnterpriseAdmin** portlet, locate and browse the `alfresco.war` file. Soon, you will find the alfresco portlet on the Liferay Content Page.

4. Integration of CAS server and Liferay:

   Download the CAS server `liferay-portal-cas-web-4.4.2.war` from `http://sourceforge.net/project/showfiles.php?group_id=49260&package_id=42607`. Download the CAS Client from `http://www.ja sig.org/products/cas/downloads/index.html`. Make changes to the `ssl` section in order to open the port in the `server.xml` file, and provide a location `<liferay>/tomcat/conf`. Finally make the necessary configuration changes to enable filters and authentication.

5. Configure Single sign-on for Liferay:

   Add the entry for the CAS filter in the `web.xml` file that is provided at the location `<liferay>/tomcat/webapps/liferay/web-inf`.

6. Configure Single Sign-on for Alfresco:

   It is already explained in the section *Configuring NTLM for Single sign-on*.

7. Configure the CAS Authentication handler for the CAS server.

8. Log in to Liferay by entering the following URL in the browser: `http://servername :port/`. When you click on **Sign in**, it will redirect you to the CAS server login page. Enter the user ID and password of Active Directory. Once the authentication is done, it will redirect you to the Liferay URL with an already logged in status (with the username that you previously entered).

Migrate existing users to Alfresco

If you are planning to migrate an existing application to Alfresco, you might want to migrate its existing users to Alfresco as well. If you use LDAP or an NTLM-based security model, you don't have to migrate the existing users to Alfresco. Instead, you can directly connect to those user sources from Alfresco. This model is always preferred, as you can manage users and groups at one centralized location, and can access the user information in many applications.

This is applicable if you are using Alfresco's out of the box security model.

Using command-line scripts for the bulk uploading of users

You can bulk upload users to Alfresco using command-line scripts. In order to bulk upload users, follow the steps given below:

1. You have to create home folders for the users that you are importing. Create `fredb` and `sues` folders inside the **User Homes** space.

2. Stop the Alfresco server.

3. You have to create user data XML files in the `/tomcat/webapps/alfresco/WEB-INF` folder. Sample files are shown next, for your reference:

    - `Person.xml`:

        ```
        <view:view xmlns:view="http://www.alfresco.org/view/
        repository/1.0"
                    xmlns:cm="http://www.alfresco.org/model/content/1.0"
                    xmlns:sys="http://www.alfresco.org/model/system/1.0"
                    xmlns:app="http://www.alfresco.org/model/
        application/1.0"
                    xmlns:usr="http://www.alfresco.org/model/user/1.0" >
                    <cm:person view:childName="cm:person">
        <cm:userName>fredb</cm:userName>
        <cm:firstName>Fred</cm:firstName>
                            <cm:lastName>Million</cm:lastName>
                            <cm:email>fredb@alfresco.org</cm:email>
                            <cm:homeFolder>/app:company_home
                                        /app:user_homes/cm:fredb
                            </cm:homeFolder>
                            <sys:node-uuid>4489977c-25b4-4980-ab2e-
        6d6307472bfa
                            </sys:node-uuid>
                    </cm:person>
                    <cm:person view:childName="cm:person">
                            <cm:userName>sues</cm:userName>
                            <cm:firstName>Sue</cm:firstName>
                            <cm:lastName>Sanderson</cm:lastName>
                            <cm:email>sues@alfresco.org</cm:email>
                            <cm:homeFolder>/app:company_home/
                                        app:user_homes/cm:sues
                            </cm:homeFolder>
                            <sys:node-uuid>4489977c-25b4-4980-ab2e-
                            6d6307472bfb
                            </sys:node-uuid>
                    </cm:person>
        </view:view>
        ```

- `UserStore.xml`:

  ```
  <view:view xmlns:view="http://www.alfresco.org/view/
  repository/1.0"
          xmlns:cm="http://www.alfresco.org/model/content/1.0"
          xmlns:sys="http://www.alfresco.org/model/system/1.0"
          xmlns:app="http://www.alfresco.org/model/
  application/1.0"
          xmlns:usr="http://www.alfresco.org/model/user/1.0">
          <usr:user view:childName="usr:user">
              <usr:username>fredb</usr:username>
              <usr:password>fredb</usr:password>
              <usr:enabled>true</usr:enabled>
              <usr:accountExpires>false</usr:accountExpires>
              <usr:credentialsExpire>false</usr:
              credentialsExpire>
              usr:accountLocked>false
              </usr:accountLocked>
          <sys:node-uuid>4489977c-25b4-4980-ab2e-6d6307472bfa
          </sys:node-uuid>
              </usr:user>
              <usr:user view:childName="usr:user">
                  <usr:username>sues</usr:username>
                  <usr:password>sues</usr:password>
                  <usr:enabled>true</usr:enabled>
                  <usr:accountExpires>false</usr:accountExpires>
                  <usr:credentialsExpire>false
                  </usr:credentialsExpire>
                  <usr:accountLocked>false</usr:accountLocked>
              <sys:node-uuid>4489977c-25b4-4980-ab2e-
                  6d6307472bfb
              </sys:node-uuid>
                  </usr:user>
  </view:view>
  ```

4. Open the `repository.properties` file from the path: `tomcat/webapps/alfresco/web-inf/classes/alfresco/`. Modify the properties below to the values that you require:

   ```
   dir.root=C:/Alfresco/alf_data<specify the path of alf data>
   db.schema.update=true
   db.schema.update.lockRetryCount=24
   db.schema.update.lockRetryWaitSeconds=5
   db.driver=org.gjt.mm.mysql.Driver
   ```

```
db.name=alfresco <specify your database name>
db.url=jdbc:mysql:///${db.name}
db.username=alfresco<specify database username>
db.password=alfresco<specify database password>
db.pool.initial=10
db.pool.max=20
```

5. Run a command-line script to upload the users given in the person.xml file and the UserStore.xml file. Change the path to the WEB-INF folder. Run the commands that are given below. The syntax to call the script may change according to the platform of the operating system. Here is a sample script that reads user data from the person.xml file and uploads the data to Alfresco.

```
java -classpath classes;lib\alfresco-repository.
jar;lib\alfresco-linkvalidation.jar;lib\xercesImpl-2.8.0.jar;lib\
alfresco-remote-api.jar;lib\alfresco-vti.jar;lib\alfresco-web-
client.jar;lib\myfaces-api-1.1.5.jar;lib\alfresco-rm.jar;lib\
xmlrpc.jar;lib\jcr-1.0.jar;lib\rhino-js-1.6R7.jar;lib\spring-ws-
1.5.0.jar;lib\subetha-smtp.jar;lib\alfresco-jlan-embed.jar;lib\
JMagick.jar;lib\alfresco-mbeans.jar;lib\hibernate-3.2.6-patched.
jar;lib\jbpm-jpdl-3.2.2.jar;lib\jbpm-identity-3.2.2.jar;lib\
springmodules-jbpm31.jar;lib\spring-2.0.6.jar;lib\alfresco-
core.jar;lib\lucene-analyzers-2.1.0.jar;liblucene-snowball-
2.1.0.jar;lib\alfresco-core.jar;lib\spring-2.0.2.jar;lib\jibx-
run.jar;lib\xpp3-1.1.3_8.jar;lib\commons-logging-1.1.jar;lib\
ehcache-1.4.1-patched.jar;lib\dom4j-1.6.1.jar;lib\acegi-security-
0.8.2_patched.jar;lib\hibernate-3.2.1-patched.jar;lib\quartz-
1.6.0.jar;lib\pdfbox-0.7.3.jar;lib\poi-3.1.jar;lib\jooconverter-
2.1.0.jar;lib\jid3lib-0.5.jar;lib\freemarker-2.3.13.jar;lib\
log4j-1.2.15.jar;lib\cryptix-jce-provider.jar;lib\commons-
codec-1.3.jar;lib\commons-dbcp-1.2.1.jar;lib\commons-pool-
1.4.jar;lib\jta.jar;lib\mail.jar;lib\activation.jar;lib\jug-lgpl-
2.0.0.jar;lib\alfresco-deployment.jar;lib\commons-collections-
3.1.jar;lib\cglib-nodep-2.2_beta1.jar;lib\antlr-2.7.5H3.jar;lib\
tm-extractors-1.0.jar;lib\commons-io-1.1.jar;lib\ridl.jar;lib\juh.
jar;lib\commons-beanutils-1.7.0.jar;lib\jut.jar;lib\sandbox.
jar;lib\jut.jar;lib\lucene-core-2.1.0.jar;..\..\..\lib\mysql-
connector-java-5.1.6-bin.jar;..\..\..\lib\servlet-api.jar;lib\
bsh-1.3.0.jar;lib\saxpath.jar;lib\jaxen-1.1-beta-8.jar;lib\json.
jar;lib\bcprov-jdk15-137.jar;lib\derby.jar;lib\ibatis-2.3.0.677.
jar;lib\truezip.jar;lib\ant.jar;lib\truelicense-1_29.jar;lib\
truexml-1_29.jar;lib\joda-time-1.2.1.jar  org.alfresco.tools.
Import -user admin -pwd admin -uuidBinding UPDATE_EXISTING  -store
workspace://SpacesStore  -path  sys:system/sys:people -verbose
person.xml
```

```
java -classpath classes;lib\alfresco-repository.jar;lib\alfresco-
linkvalidation.jar;lib\xercesImpl-2.8.0.jar;lib\alfresco-remote-
api.jar;lib\alfresco-vti.jar;lib\alfresco-web-client.jar;lib\
myfaces-api-1.1.5.jar;lib\alfresco-rm.jar;lib\xmlrpc.jar;lib\
jcr-1.0.jar;lib\rhino-js-1.6R7.jar;lib\spring-ws-1.5.0.jar;lib\
subetha-smtp.jar;lib\alfresco-jlan-embed.jar;lib\JMagick.jar;lib\
alfresco-mbeans.jar;lib\hibernate-3.2.6-patched.jar;lib\jbpm-
jpdl-3.2.2.jar;lib\jbpm-identity-3.2.2.jar;lib\springmodules-
jbpm31.jar;lib\spring-2.0.6.jar;lib\alfresco-core.jar;lib\
lucene-analyzers-2.1.0.jar;liblucene-snowball-2.1.0.jar;lib\
alfresco-core.jar;lib\spring-2.0.2.jar;lib\jibx-run.jar;lib\
xpp3-1.1.3_8.jar;lib\commons-logging-1.1.jar;lib\ehcache-1.4.1-
patched.jar;lib\dom4j-1.6.1.jar;lib\acegi-security-0.8.2_patched.
jar;lib\hibernate-3.2.1-patched.jar;lib\quartz-1.6.0.jar;lib\
pdfbox-0.7.3.jar;lib\poi-3.1.jar;lib\jooconverter-2.1.0.jar;lib\
jid3lib-0.5.jar;lib\freemarker-2.3.13.jar;lib\log4j-1.2.15.
jar;lib\cryptix-jce-provider.jar;lib\commons-codec-1.3.jar;lib\
commons-dbcp-1.2.1.jar;lib\commons-pool-1.4.jar;lib\jta.jar;lib\
mail.jar;lib\activation.jar;lib\jug-lgpl-2.0.0.jar;lib\alfresco-
deployment.jar;lib\commons-collections-3.1.jar;lib\cglib-nodep-
2.2_beta1.jar;lib\antlr-2.7.5H3.jar;lib\tm-extractors-1.0.jar;lib\
commons-io-1.1.jar;lib\ridl.jar;lib\juh.jar;lib\commons-beanutils-
1.7.0.jar;lib\jut.jar;lib\sandbox.jar;lib\jut.jar;lib\lucene-
core-2.1.0.jar;..\..\..\lib\mysql-connector-java-5.1.6-bin.
jar;..\..\..\lib\servlet-api.jar;lib\bsh-1.3.0.jar;lib\saxpath.
jar;lib\jaxen-1.1-beta-8.jar;lib\json.jar;lib\bcprov-jdk15-137.
jar;lib\derby.jar;lib\ibatis-2.3.0.677.jar;lib\truezip.jar;lib\
ant.jar;lib\truelicense-1_29.jar;lib\truexml-1_29.jar;lib\joda-
time-1.2.1.jar    org.alfresco.tools.Import -user admin -pwd admin
-uuidBinding UPDATE_EXISTING -store user://alfrescoUserStore -path
sys:system/sys:people -verbose UserStore.xml
```

Bootstrapping the Alfresco repository with predefined user data

The Alfresco repository supports a bootstrap process, which is initiated whenever the repository is first started. The process populates the repository with the information that is required upon the first login such as system users, data dictionary definitions, and important root folders.

Detailed information about bootstrapping Alfresco repository is provided in Chapter 14.

Using web services API to create users

You may also use the web services API to programmatically create users in Alfresco. This is useful if you already have another software application to manage users and you would like to create users in Alfresco from that application as and when needed.

The following is sample code provided to create a user `amiranda`, by using the `webservice` API:

```
private void createUsers() throws Exception
    {
        this.userName = "amiranda" ;
        this.password ="amiranda";
        Store store = new Store(Constants.WORKSPACE_
STORE,"SpacesStore");
        String homeFolder = store.getScheme() + "://" + store.
getAddress() + "/app:company_home/app:user_homes"  ;
        NewUserDetails[] newUsers = new NewUserDetails[] {
                new NewUserDetails(
                        this.userName,
                        this.password,
                        createPersonProperties(homeFolder, "Amy",
"Jane", "Miranda", "amiranda@localhost.com", "cignex"))};
// Create the new users
        WebServiceFactory.getAdministrationService().
createUsers(newUsers);
    }
    private NamedValue[] createPersonProperties(
            String homeFolder,
            String firstName,
            String middleName,
            String lastName,
            String email,
            String orgId)
    {
        // Create the new user objects
        return new NamedValue[] {
                new NamedValue(Constants.PROP_USER_HOMEFOLDER, false,
homeFolder, null),
                new NamedValue(Constants.PROP_USER_FIRSTNAME, false,
firstName, null),
                new NamedValue(Constants.PROP_USER_MIDDLENAME, false,
middleName, null),
                new NamedValue(Constants.PROP_USER_LASTNAME, false,
lastName, null),
```

```
                new NamedValue(Constants.PROP_USER_EMAIL, false,
email, null),
                new NamedValue(Constants.PROP_USER_ORGID, false,
orgId, null) };
    }
```

> The complete code can be downloaded from the *Support* section of Packt Publishing's web site.

Summary

The Alfresco membership framework is very secure, flexible, scalable, and customizable. Roles are collections of permissions assigned to users (consumer, contributor, editor, collaborator, and coordinator). You can manage system users and groups through the Administration Console. Security is imposed by assigning a role to a specific user or group for a specific space or content. Authentication is possible using Alfresco's built-in membership system, NTLM, and LDAP. Bulk uploading of users is also possible using command-line utilities and the web services API.

Implementing Document Management

This chapter introduces you to the basic features of creating and managing content in Alfresco by using Alfresco Explorer. With Alfresco, you can manage any type of document, such as HTML, text, XML, Microsoft Office documents, Adobe PDF, Flash, scanned images, multimedia, and video files. You will also understand the concepts of creating and using categories and smart spaces. This chapter also focuses on the most important aspect of adopting a new Enterprise Content Management system, which is migrating the existing data and using it effectively. In this chapter, you will learn various secure ways of sharing your content online, by using syndication features.

By the end of this chapter, you will have learned how to:

- Create spaces and load them with documents
- Automatically control document versioning
- Lock, **Check In**, and **Check Out** documents
- Categorizing content so that you can facilitate searching
- Access documents in the Alfresco repository from your web browser, a network drive, FTP, or WebDAV
- Search and edit Alfresco documents directly from Microsoft Office tools
- Recover deleted content
- Create and use space templates
- Migrate existing documents to Alfresco
- Create and use discussions for spaces and documents
- Enable RSS syndication in order to share content

Managing spaces

A space in Alfresco is nothing but a folder that contains content as well as sub spaces. The space users are the users invited to a space to perform specific actions such as editing content, adding content, discussing a particular document, and so on. The exact capability that a given user has within a space is a function of their role, or rights.

Let's consider the capability of creating a sub-space. By default, in order to create a sub-space, one of the following must apply:

- The user is the administrator of the system
- The user has been granted the Contributor role
- The user has been granted the Coordinator role
- The user has been granted the Collaborator role

Similarly, to edit space properties, a user will need to be the administrator or be granted a role that gives them rights to edit the space. These roles include Editor, Collaborator and Coordinator. For more information about user roles on a space, refer to Chapter 4.

Space is a smart folder

Space is a folder with additional features, such as, security, business rules, workflow, notifications, local search capabilities, and special views. The additional features, which make the space a smart folder, are explained as follows:

- **Space security**: You can define security at the space level. You can designate a user or a group of users who can perform certain actions on the content in a space. For example, on the **Marketing Communications** space in the **Intranet**, you can specify that only users in the marketing group can add content, and other users can only see the content.

- **Space business rules**: Business rules, such as transforming content from Microsoft Word to Adobe PDF and sending notifications when content gets into a space, can be defined at the space level.

- **Space workflow**: You can define and manage the content workflow on a space. Typically, you will create a space for the content that needs to be reviewed, and a space for the content that has been approved. You will create various spaces for dealing with the different stages that the work flows through, and Alfresco will manage the movement of the content between those spaces.

- **Space events**: Alfresco triggers events when content moves into a space, when content moves out of a space, or when content is modified within a space. You can capture such events at the space level, and trigger certain actions, such as sending email notifications to certain users.

- **Space aspects**: Aspects are additional properties and behavior that can be added to the content, based on the space in which it resides. For example, you can define a business rule to add customer details to all of the customer contract documents that are in your intranet's **Sales** space.

- **Space search**: Alfresco search functions can be limited to a space. For example, if you create a space called **Marketing**, then you can limit the search to documents within the **Marketing** space, instead of searching the entire site.

- **Space syndication**: Content in a space can be syndicated by applying RSS feed scripts to a space. You can apply RSS feeds to your **News** space, so that other applications and web sites can subscribe to this feed for news updates.

- **Space content**: Content in a space can be versioned, locked, checked-in and checked-out, and managed. You can specify certain documents in a space to be versioned, and others not.

- **Space network folder**: Space can be mapped to a network drive on your local machine, enabling you to work with the content locally. For example, by using CIFS interface, a space can be mapped to the Windows network folder.

- **Space dashboard view**: Content in a space can be aggregated and presented using special dashboard views. For example, the **Company Policies** space can list all of the latest policy documents, that have been updated in the past one month or so. You can create different views for Sales, Marketing, and Finance departmental spaces.

Why space hierarchy is important

Like regular folders, a space can have child spaces (called sub spaces). These sub spaces can have further sub spaces of their own. There is no limitation on the number of hierarchical levels. However, the space hierarchy is very important for all of the reasons specified above, in the previous section. Any business rules and security defined for a space is applicable to all of the content and sub spaces within that space.

In the previous chapter, you created system users, groups, and spaces for various departments, as per the example. Your space hierarchy should look similar to the following screenshot:

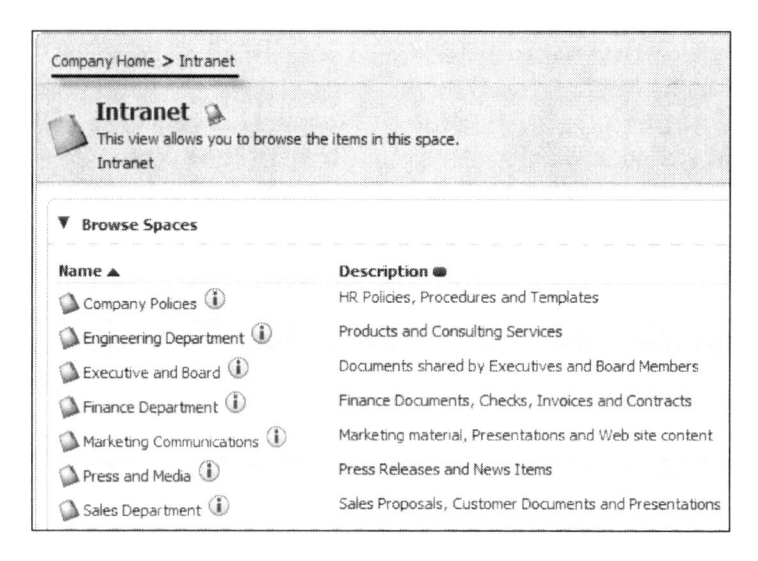

A space in Alfresco enables you to define various business rules, a dashboard view, properties, workflow, and security for the content belonging to each department. You can decentralize the management of your content by providing access to departments at the individual space levels.

The example of the **Intranet** space should contain sub spaces, as shown in the preceding screenshot. If you have not created spaces yet, as per the example given in previous chapter, then you must do it now, by logging in as the administrator. The examples that are used in the remaining chapters of this book refer to these spaces. It is also very important to set the security (by inviting groups of users to these spaces), as explained in the previous chapter.

Editing a space

Using a web client, you can edit the spaces that you have added previously. Note that you need to have edit permissions on the spaces to edit them, as explained in the previous chapter.

Editing space properties

Every space has clickable actions, as identified in the following screenshot:

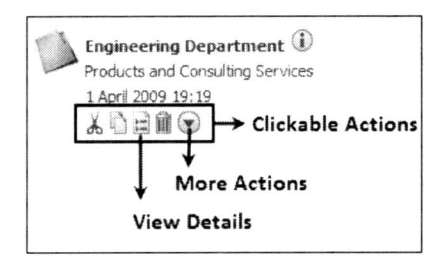

Chapter 5

These clickable actions are dynamically generated for each space—based on the current user's permissions on that space. If you have copy permission on a space, then you will see the copy icon as a clickable action for that space. On clicking the **View Details** action icon, the detailed view of a space will be displayed, as shown in the following screenshot:

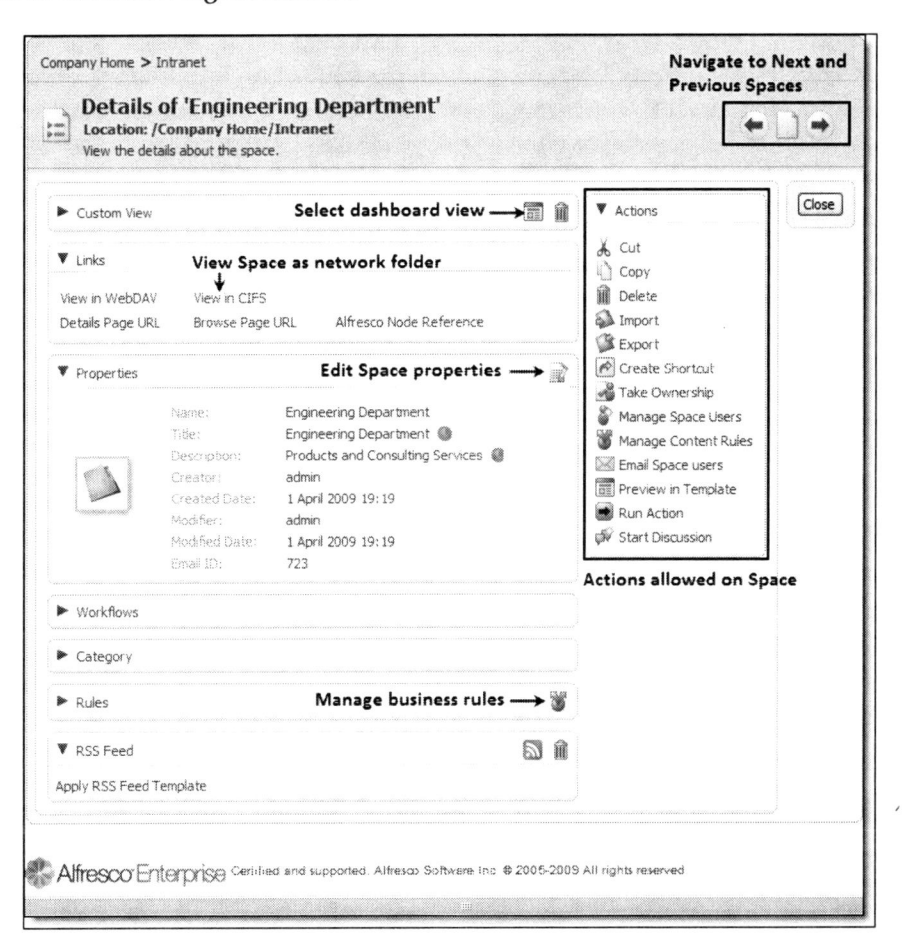

[131]

The detailed view page of a space allows you to select a dashboard view for viewing and for editing existing space properties, to categorize the space, to set business rules, and to run various actions on the space, as shown in the preceding screenshot.

To edit space properties, click on the **Edit Space Properties** icon, as shown in the preceding screenshot. You can change the name of the space and other properties, as needed.

Deleting space and its contents

From the list of space actions, you can click on the **Delete** action to delete the space. You need to be very careful when deleting a space as all of the business rules, sub spaces and the entire content within the space will also be deleted.

Moving or copying space by using the clipboard

From the list of space actions, you can click on the **Cut** action to move a space to the clipboard. Then you can navigate to any space hierarchy, assuming that you have the necessary permissions to do so, and paste this particular space, as required.

Similarly, you can use the **Copy** action to copy the space to some other space hierarchy. This is useful if you have an existing space structure (such as a marketing project or engineering project), and you would like to replicate it, along with the data that it contains.

The copied or moved space will be identical in all respects to the original (source) space. When you copy a space, the space properties, categorization, business rules, space users, all content within the space and, all of the sub spaces, along with their content, will also be copied.

Creating a shortcut to a space for quick access

If you need to frequently access a space, then you can create a shortcut (similar to the **Favorite** option in Internet and Windows browsers) to that space, in order to reach the space in just one click. From the list of space actions, you can click on the **Create Shortcut** action to create a shortcut to the existing space. Shortcuts are listed in the **Shelf** towards the left-hand side.

Choosing a default view for your space

There are four different out of the box **Space View** options (as shown in the following screenshot). These options support the display of the space's information.

- The **Details View** option provides listings of sub spaces and content, in horizontal rows.

- The **Icon View** option provides a title, description, timestamp, and action menus for each sub space and content item present in the current space.
- The **Browse View** option provides a title, description, and a list of sub spaces for each space.
- The **Custom View** is disabled and appears in gray. This is because you have not enabled the dashboard view for this space. In order to enable the dashboard view for a space, you need to select a dashboard view (refer to the icon in the **Custom View** box, shown in the preceding screenshot).

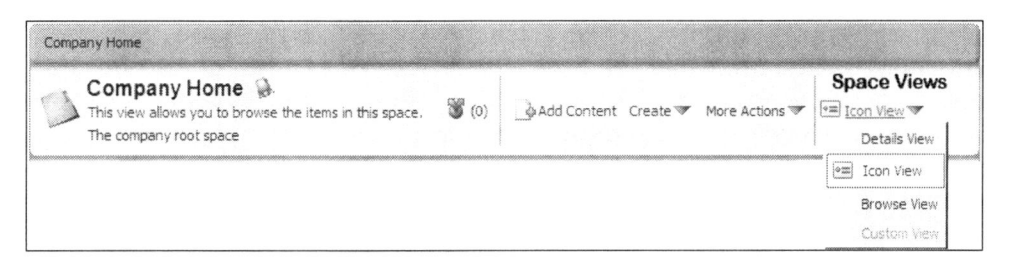

Sample space structure for marketing project

Let us say that you are launching a new marketing project called **Switch to open source ECM**. You can create your own space structure within the **Marketing Project** space to manage content. For example, you can have a space called **Drafts** to house all of the draft marketing documents and so on. Go to the **Company Home > Intranet > Marketing Communications** space, and create a new space called **Switch to open source ECM**, and then create various sub spaces under it, as shown in the following screenshot:

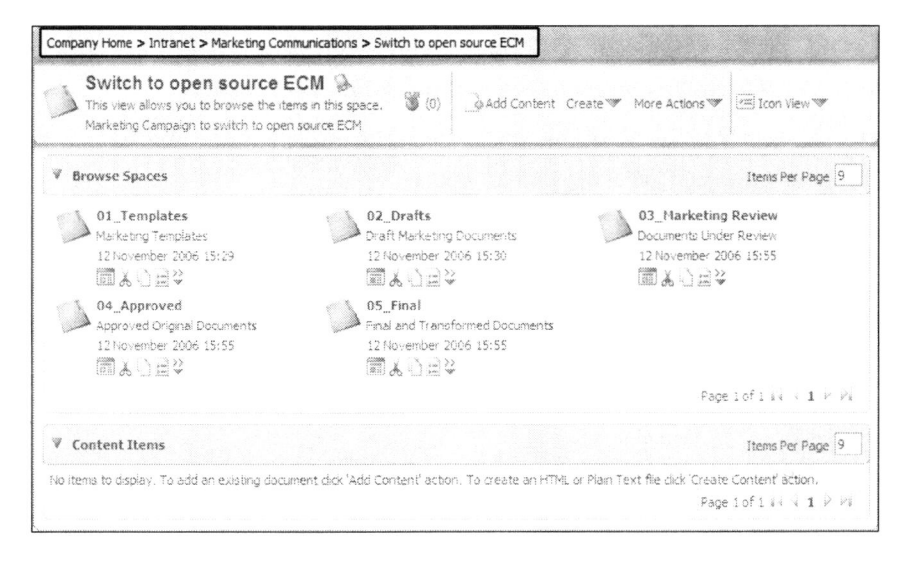

The new marketing project space and the sub spaces created are used in the remaining examples listed in this chapter, in order to manage content.

Managing content

Content can be in any format, as mentioned at the start of this chapter. By using the Alfresco web client application, you can add or modify content and its properties. You can categorize content, lock content for editing, and can maintain several versions of the content. You can delete content, and you can also recover deleted content.

This section uses the space that you have already created as a part of your **Intranet** sample application. As a part of the sample application, you will manage the content in the **Intranet > Marketing Communications** space. Because you have secured this space earlier, only the administrator (**admin**) and the users belonging to the Marketing group (**Peter Marketing** and **Harish Marketing**) can add content to this space. You can log in as **Peter Marketing** to manage the content in this space.

Creating content

A web client provides two different interfaces for adding content. One can be used to create inline editable content, such as HTML, text, XML, and the other can be used to add binary content, such as Microsoft Office files and scanned images.

You need to have one of the the administrator, contributor, collaborator, or coordinator roles on a space to be able to create content within that space. For more information about the user roles on a space, refer to Chapter 4.

Creating text documents

To create an HTML file in a space, carry out the following steps:

1. Ensure that you are in the **Intranet > Marketing Communications > Switch to open source ECM > 02_Drafts** space.

2. In the header, click on **Create > Create Content**. The first pane of the **Create Content** wizard appears, as shown in the following screenshot. In this wizard, and in any Alfresco wizard, you can track your progress through the wizard from the list of steps shown on the leftmost side of the pane.

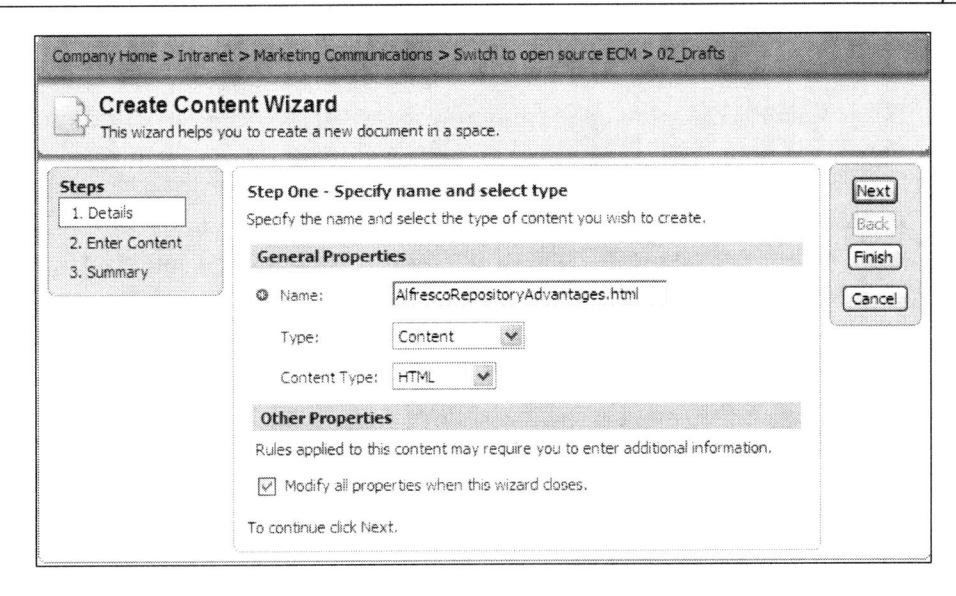

3. Provide the name of the HTML file, select **HTML** as the **Content Type**, and then click on the **Next** button. The **Enter Content** pane of the wizard appears, as shown in the following screenshot. Note that **Enter Content** is now highlighted in the list of steps on the leftmost side of the pane.

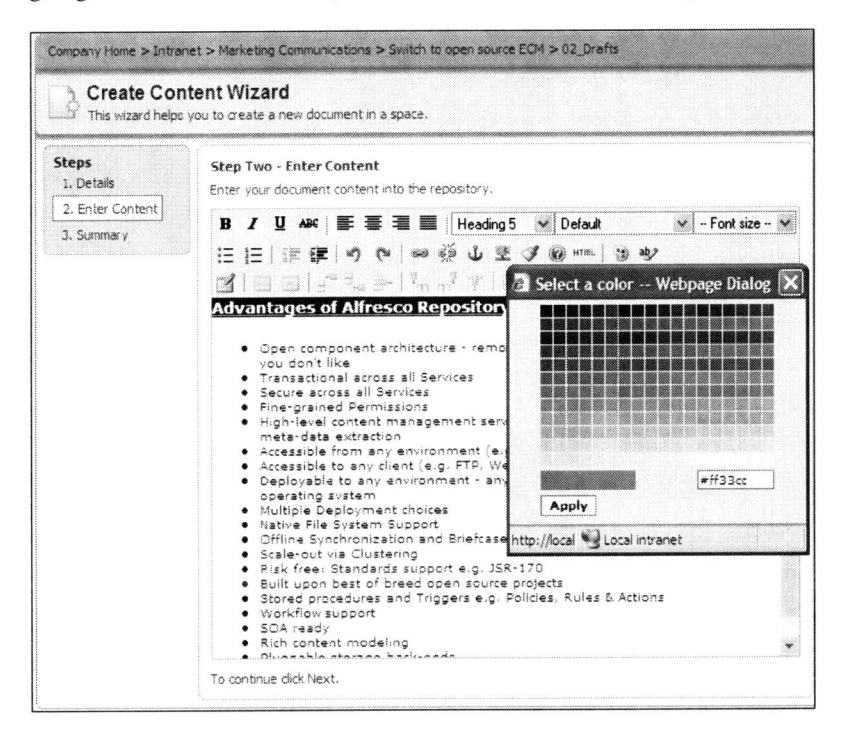

Implementing Document Management

4. You can see that there is a comprehensive set of tools to help you format your HTML document. Enter some text, using some of the formatting features.

5. If you know HTML, then you can also use the HTML editor by clicking on the **HTML** icon. The HTML source editor is displayed. Once you update the HTML content, click on the **Update** button to return to the **Enter Content** pane in the wizard, with the contents updated.

6. After the content has been entered and edited in the **Enter Content** pane, click on **Finish**. You will see the **Modify Content Properties** screen, which can be used to update the metadata that is associated with the content, as shown in the following screenshot:

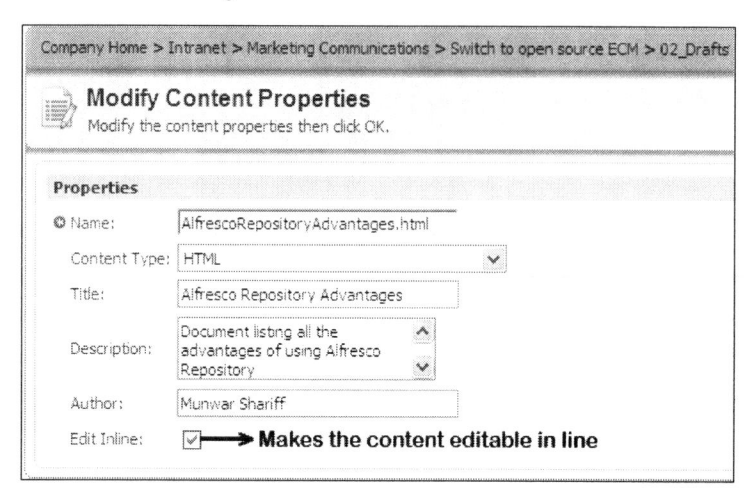

7. If you are satisfied with the properties, then click on the **OK** button to return to the **02_Drafts** space, with your newly-created file inserted in it.

You can launch the newly created HTML file by clicking on it. Your browser will automatically be launched for most of the common file types, which are HTML, text, and PDF. If the browser does not recognize the file, then you will be prompted by a Windows dialog box containing the list of applications, to choose an application. This is the normal behavior if you try to launch a file on any Internet page.

Uploading binary files such as Word, PDF, Flash, Image, Media

Using a web client, you can upload content from your hard drive. Choose a file from your hard disk that is not an HTML or text file. I shall choose the `Alfresco_CIGNEX.doc` file from my hard disk, for the sample application. Ensure that you are in the **Intranet > Marketing Communications > Switch to open source ECM > 02_Drafts** space.

To upload a binary file to a space, carry out the following steps:

1. In the space header, click on the **Add Content** link. The **Add Content Dialog** window is displayed.
2. To select the file that you want to upload, click on the **Browse** button. In the **File Upload** dialog box, browse to the file that you want to upload, select it, and then click on the **Open** button. Alfresco inserts the full path name of the selected file in the **Location** text box.
3. Click on the **Upload** button to upload the file from your hard disk to the Alfresco repository. A message informs you that your upload was successful, as shown in the following screenshot:

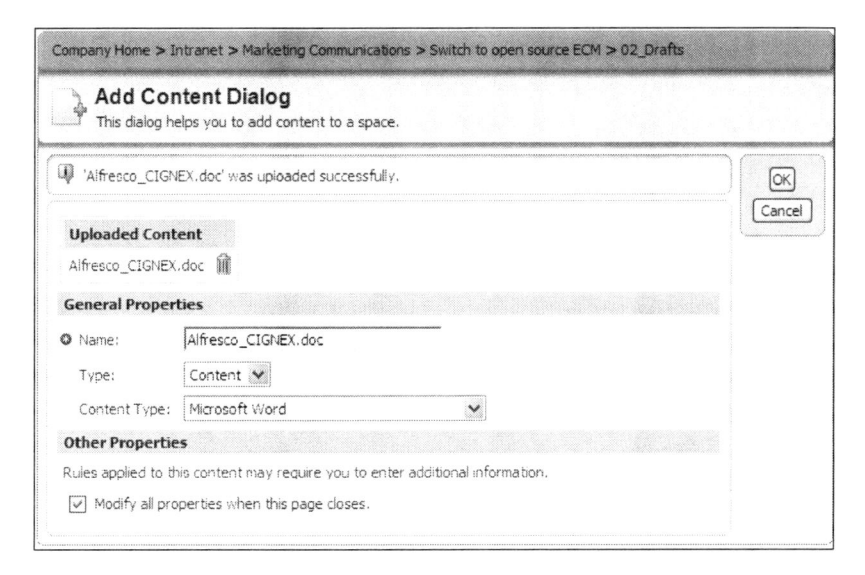

4. Click on the **OK** button to confirm. The **Modify Content Properties Dialog** is displayed
5. Verify the pre-populated properties and enter information in the text boxes as required. Click on the **OK** button to save and return to the **02_Drafts** space.

The file that you have uploaded appears in the **Content Items** pane. Alfresco extracts the file size from the disk properties of the file, and includes the value in the size field. Now that you have two files, you can edit them as you like.

Editing content

You can edit the content in Alfresco in three different ways: by using the **Edit Online**, **Edit Offline,** and **Update** actions. Note that you need to have edit permission on the content to edit them, as explained in the previous chapter.

Online editing of HTML, text, and XML

HTML files and plain text files can be created and edited online. If you have edit access to a file, then you will notice a small pencil (**Edit Online**) icon as shown in the following screenshot:

Clicking on the pencil icon will open the file in the appropriate editor. Each file type is edited in its own WYSIWYG editor. Once you select the option to **Edit Online**, a working copy of the file will be created for editing, and the original file is locked, as shown in the following screenshot:

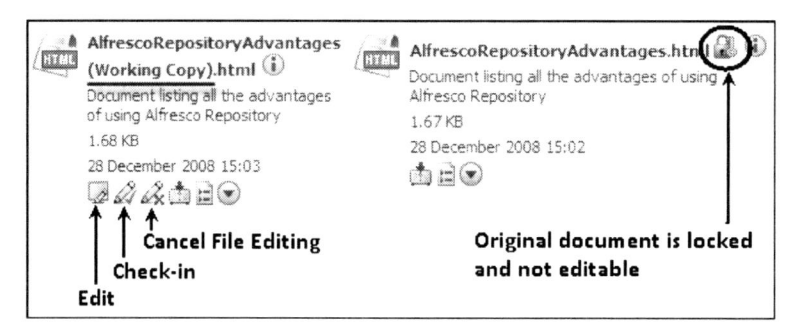

The working copy can be further edited, as needed, by clicking on the **Edit Online** button. Once you are done with editing, you can commit all of the changes to the original document, by clicking on the **Check In** icon.

If, for some reason, you decide to cancel the editing of a document and discard any changes that you have made, then you can do so by clicking on the **Cancel File Editing** button. If you cancel the editing of a document, then the associated working copy is deleted, and all of the changes made to it since it was checked out will be lost.

Offline editing of files

If you want to download a file onto your local machine, edit it locally, and then upload the updated version to Alfresco, then you might consider using the **Edit Offline** option, as shown in the following screenshot:

Once you click on the **Edit Offline** button, the original file is automatically locked. A working copy of the file is created for download. Then a window is displayed, giving you the option to save the working copy of the document locally on your personal computer, as shown in the following screenshot:

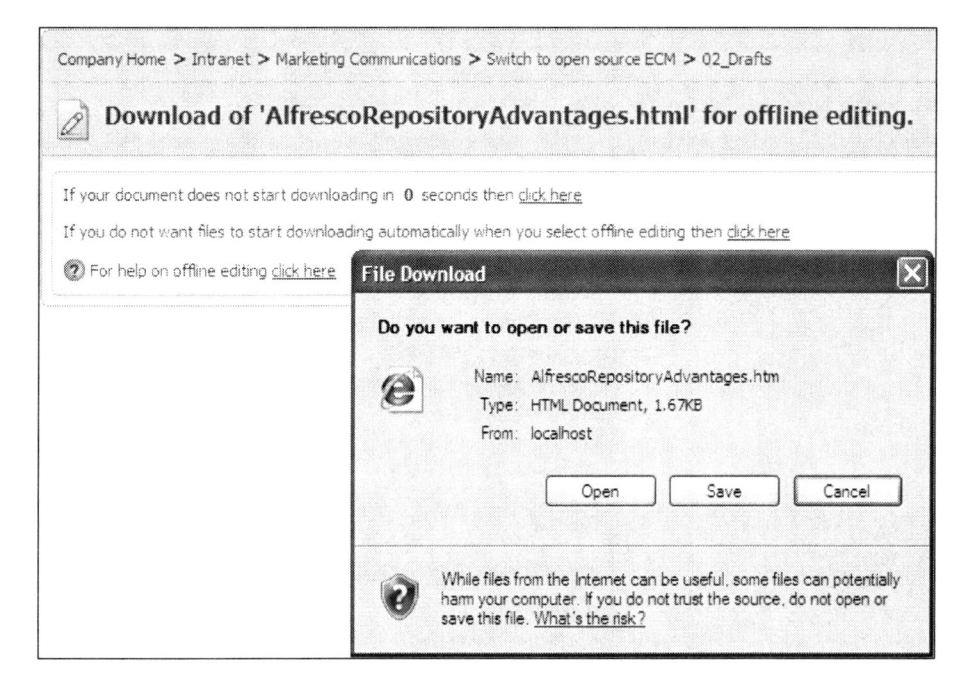

Implementing Document Management

If you don't want to automatically download the file for offline editing, you can turn off this feature. In order to deactivate **Offline Editing**, click on the **User Profile** icon in the top menu, and deselect the option for **Offline Editing**, is shown to be selected in the following screenshot:

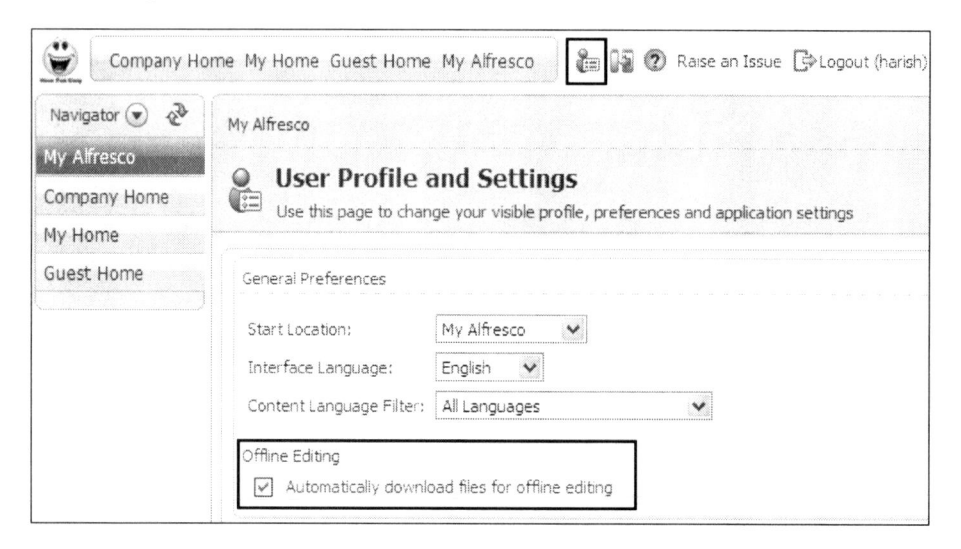

The working copy can be updated by clicking on the **Update New Version** button. Once you have finished editing the file, you can commit all of the changes to the original document, by clicking on the **Check In** icon. Alternatively, you can cancel all of the changes by clicking on the **Cancel File Editing** button, as shown in the following screenshot:

Uploading updated content

If you have edit access to a binary file, then you will see the **Update** action icon in the drop-down list for the **More actions** link, as shown in the upcoming screenshot. If you click the **Update** icon, then the **Update** pane is displayed. Click on the **Browse** button to upload the updated version of the document from your hard disk. It is always a good practice to check out the document and update the working copy, rather than directly updating the document. Checking the file out avoids conflicting updates by locking the document, as explained in the previous section.

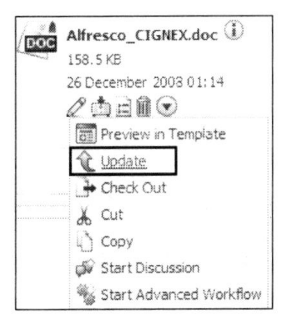

Content actions

Content has clickable actions (icons), as shown in the upcoming screenshot. These clickable actions are dynamically generated for content, based on the current user's permissions for that content. For example, if you have copy permission for the content, then you will see the **Copy** icon as a clickable action for that content.

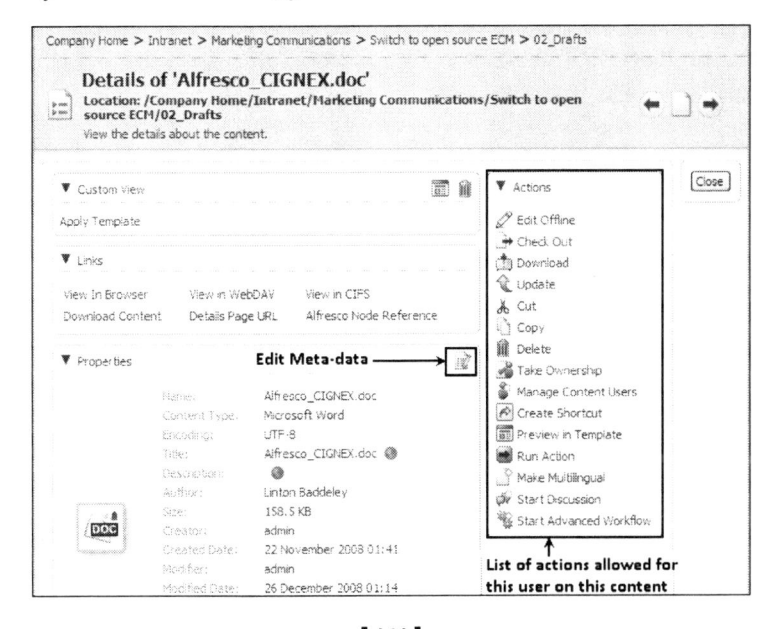

Deleting content

Click on the **Delete** action, from the list of content actions, to delete the content. When the content is deleted, all of the previous versions of that content object will also be deleted.

Moving or copying content using the clipboard

From the list of content actions, as shown in the screenshot above, you can click on the **Cut** action to move content to the clipboard. Then, you can navigate to any space hierarchy and paste the cut content into it, as required.

Similarly, you can use the **Copy** action to copy the content to another space.

Creating a shortcut to the content for quick access

If you need to access a particular content object very frequently, then you can create a shortcut (similar to the way you can with Internet and Windows browser's **Favorite** option) to that content, in order to reach the content in one click. From the list of content actions, as shown in the preceding screenshot, you can click on the **Create Shortcut** action to create a shortcut to the content. Shortcuts are listed in the **Shelf** on the left-hand side.

Managing content properties

Every content item in Alfresco has properties associated with it. Refer to the preceding screenshot to see the list of properties, such as **Title**, **Description**, **Author**, **Size**, and **Creation Date**. These properties are associated with the actual content file, which is named `Alfresco_CIGNEX.doc`.

The content properties are stored in relational database and are searchable using **Advanced Search** options.

What is Content Metadata?

Content properties are also known as **Content Metadata**. Metadata is structured data, that describes the characteristics of the content. It shares many similar characteristics with the cataloguing that takes place in libraries. The term **Meta** derives from the Greek word denoting **a nature of a higher order or more fundamental kind**. A metadata record consists of a number of pre-defined elements that represent specific attributes of the content, and each element can have one or more values.

Metadata is a systematic method for describing resources, and thereby simplifying access to them. If access to the content is required, then it should be described using metadata, so as to maximize the ability to locate it. Metadata provides the essential link between the information creator and the information user.

Although the primary aim of metadata is to improve resource discovery, metadata sets are also being developed for other reasons, including:

- Administrative control
- Security
- Management of information
- Content rating
- Rights management

Metadata extractors

Typically, in most Content Management Systems, once you upload the content file, you need to add the metadata (properties), such as the title, description, and keywords, to the content manually. Most of the content, such as Microsoft Office documents, media files, and PDF documents contain properties within the file itself. Therefore, it is double the effort, having to enter those values again in the Content Management System, as well as in the document.

Alfresco provides built-in metadata extractors for many popular document types, that extract the standard metadata values from a document, and populates the values automatically.

This is very useful if you are uploading the documents through FTP, CIFS, or a WebDAV interface, where you will not have to enter the properties manually, as Alfresco will transfer the document properties automatically.

Editing metadata

To edit metadata, you need to click on the **Edit Metadata** icon in the content details view. Refer to the **Edit Metadata** icon shown in the upcoming screenshot, which shows a detailed view of the file `Alfresco_CIGNEX.doc`. You can update the metadata values, such as **Name** and **Description**, for your content items. However, certain metadata values, such as **Creator**, **Created Date**, **Modifier**, and **Modified Date** are read-only values, and you cannot change them. Certain properties, such as, **Modifier** and **Modified Date** will be updated by Alfresco automatically, whenever the content is updated.

Adding additional properties

Additional properties can be added to the content in two ways. One way is to extend the data model and define more properties for a content type. More information on this is provided in Chapter 7.

The other way is to dynamically attach the properties and behaviour through **Aspects**. By using aspects, you can add additional properties, such as **Effectivity**, **Dublin Core Metadata**, and **Thumbnailable**, to the content. More information on this is provided in Chapter 6.

Library services

Library services are common document management functions for controlling the users through permissions, for creating multiple instances of a document (versioning), and for providing users with access into a document to make the changes (checking-in or checking-out).

Versioning

So far, you have learned about creating spaces, adding files, and editing them. You might have more than one person who can edit a document. What if somebody edits a document and removes a useful piece of information? Well, you can make use of the versioning features of Alfresco to resolve such issues.

Versioning allows the history of previous versions of a content to be kept. The content needs to be **Versionable**, in order for versions to be kept. You can enable versioning in four different ways:

1. **Individually**: To enable versioning for an individual content object item, go to the **View Details** page and click on the **Allow Versioning** link. The screenshot on the next page illustrates how to enable versioning on an individual content item.
2. **Using Smart Spaces**: A business rule can be set for a space to allow versioning of all of the content or selected content within that space. More information about this is provided in Chapter 6.
3. **By Type**: By default, versioning is disabled for all of the content types in the Alfresco content model. Versioning can be enabled for a specific content type, irrespective of the location of the content. More information about this is provided in Chapter 7.
4. **Globally**: Alfresco can be configured globally to enable versioning for all content throughout the site. More information about this is provided in Chapter 7.

Enable versioning for sample file that you have already uploaded to the system. Go to the **Intranet > Marketing Communications > Switch to open source ECM > 02_Drafts** space and view the details of `Alfresco_CIGNEX.doc` file. Click on the **Allow Versioning** link to enable versioning, as shown in the following screenshot. You will immediately notice that a version with a version number of 1.0 is created.

At the time of writing this book (Alfresco version 3.1), reverting back to an older version of the content is not supported. There is a plan to support this feature in future releases of Alfresco. The workaround is to download the older version and upload it again as the current version.

For a checked out content, the version is updated when the content is checked in. The version number is incremented from the version number of the content object that was checked out.

Auto Versioning

Auto versioning can be enabled by editing the content properties and selecting the **Auto Version** checkbox.

If auto versioning is enabled, then each **Save** of the content results in an incremented version number, when the content is edited directly from the repository. Each **Update** (upload) of the content also results in a new version (with an incremented version number) being created.

If auto versioning is not enabled, then the version number is incremented only when the content is checked in.

Check In and Check Out

By using the versioning feature, you can ensure that all of the changes made to a document are saved. You might have more than one person who can edit a document. What if two people edit a document at once, and you get into a mess with two new versions? To resolve this issue, you'll need to use the library services.

Library services provide the ability to check out a document, reserving it for one user to edit, while others can only access the document in read-only mode. Once the necessary changes have been made to the document, the user checks in the document, and can either replace the original, or create a new version of the original.

Check Out locks the item and creates a working copy that can be edited (both the content and the details). **Check In** replaces the original item with the working copy, and releases the lock.

Checking out documents

Ensure that you are in the **Intranet > Marketing Communications > Switch to open source ECM > 02_Drafts** space. Click on the **Check Out** action for the `Alfresco_CIGNEX.doc` file, as shown in the following screenshot:

The **Check Out** pane is displayed, as shown in the following screenshot. You can either check out the file into the current space or to any other pre-defined space. As a best practice, it is recommended that you check out the working copy to your own Home Space.

For the current example, choose to check out the file to the **In the current space** option, and click on the **Check Out** button. You will return to the **02_Drafts** space.

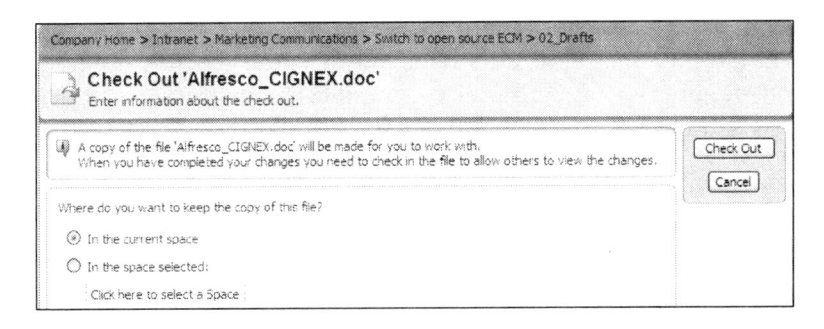

You will see two copies of the same document, as shown in the following screenshot. The original version of the file has a lock. This indicates that no one else can check out this file until you have checked it in again. The original version of the file can't be edited (there is no **Edit** icon) and cannot be checked out (there is no **Check Out** icon). The desired effect of all of these features is that you cannot edit a checked out file, either deliberately or accidentally.

You can only update the working copy. The checked out file has **Working Copy** inserted into the file name. The **Working Copy** can be edited and checked in.

Checking in the working copy

Update the **Working Copy** of the `Alfresco_CIGNEX (Working Copy).doc` file. Updating the document is explained earlier in this chapter in the *Upload updated binary file* section. After you have updated the working copy, you can check in by clicking the **Check In** button, as shown in the screenshot above. Once you click on the **Check In** action, you will see the **Check In** dialog window, as shown in the following screenshot:

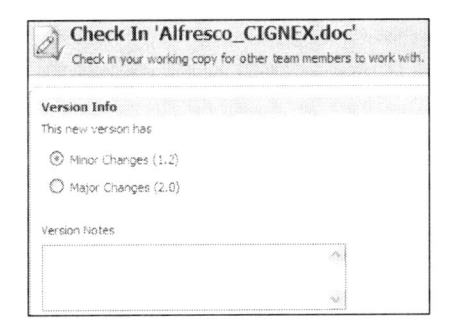

If you have only made a few minor changes to the file, then you should select the **Minor Change** checkbox. By selecting the **Minor Change** checkbox, you will be able to increment only the number after the decimal (for example, from 1.1 to 1.2); otherwise, you will increment the number before the decimal (from 1.0 to 2.0).

For this example, select the **Minor Change** option, and provide some meaningful version notes. Version notes are very important documentation to help understand the differences between various versions of the same document.

There will no longer be a **Working Copy** of the document. Notice the latest modification timestamp of the original document. If you click on the **View Details** action and scroll down to the **Version History**, then you will see that the history has been updated, as shown in the following screenshot:

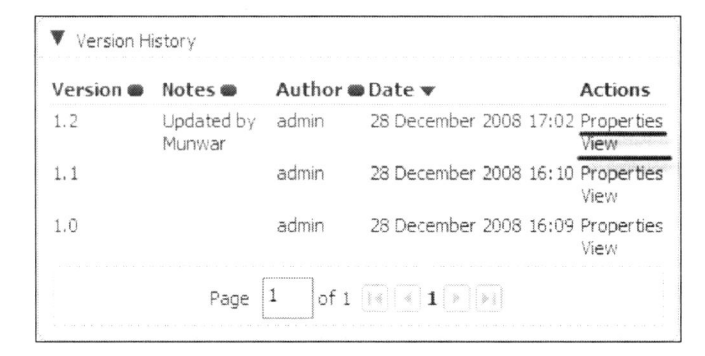

Version	Notes	Author	Date	Actions
1.2	Updated by Munwar	admin	28 December 2008 17:02	Properties View
1.1		admin	28 December 2008 16:10	Properties View
1.0		admin	28 December 2008 16:09	Properties View

Undo Check Out to unlock a document

Now that you are able to use the library services, you might still have questions, such as, how long does a file remain checked-out? Can we see who checked it out and when? And who can cancel the lock?

A document remains in the checked out state (locked), until either the working copy is checked in or somebody cancels the checked out status from the working copy. To cancel a check out, locate the **Working Copy** of the document, and click on the **Cancel File Editing** button, as shown in the following screenshot:

Alfresco_CIGNEX (Working Copy).doc
Information about Alfresco and CIGNEX
158.5 KB
28 December 2008 17:05

This action will delete the working copy and release the lock, as if the **Check Out** had not taken place.

The owner of the document, or a coordinator, or an administrator can unlock the document by executing the **Cancel File Editing** action on the **Working Copy**. Other users, who have read access to the space, can still see the **Working Copy** of the document but they can never edit or check in the document. The possible actions on a **Working Copy** by other users are shown in the following screenshot:

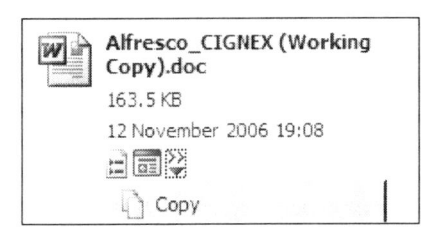

You can enable auditing in the Alfresco repository, and display the audit trail information, such as who locked the content and when. More information about auditing is covered in Chapter 14.

Categorizing content

Categorization allows information to be classified in a number of ways. Various technologies use various terminologies such as hierarchies, taxonomies and ontology for the same concept.

In Alfresco, all of the content can be linked to one or more categories. Categories are defined and managed by administrators only. Categories can have sub-categories, and there is no limitation on the number of categories that can be defined, or depth of the hierarchy. Categorization aids in searching, and the advanced search form in Alfresco allows you to search for content based on categories.

Managing categories

Carry out the following steps to create two new categories called Technology and Products for your sample application:

1. In any space, click on the **Administration Console** icon in the top tool bar. The **Administration Console** pane is displayed.

Implementing Document Management

2. Click on the **Category Management** link. The **Category Management** pane is displayed, as shown in the following screenshot. Notice the existing categories, such as, **Software Document Classification**, **Regions,** and **Languages**.

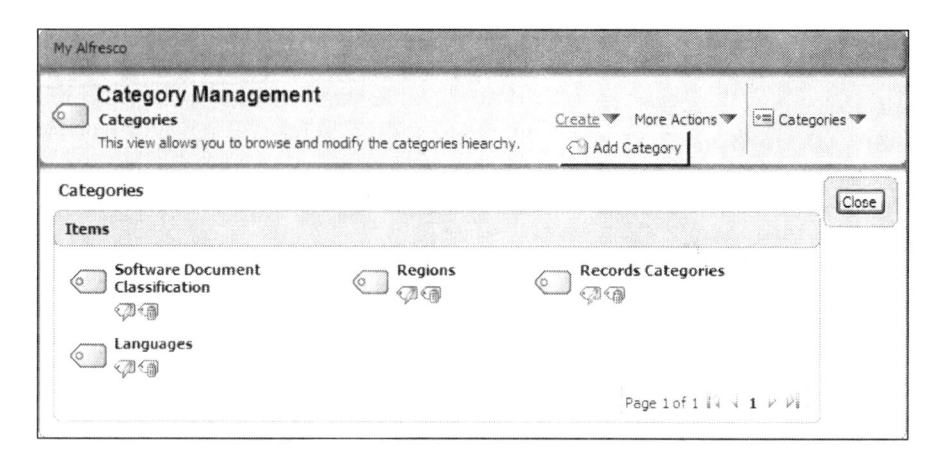

```
My Alfresco
    Category Management
    Categories                                              Create ▼  More Actions ▼   ≡ Categories ▼
    This view allows you to browse and modify the categories hiearchy.   Add Category

Categories                                                                              [Close]
  Items
       Software Document              Regions                Records Categories
       Classification

       Languages

                                                        Page 1 of 1  1
```

3. In the header, click on the **Create | Add Category** link to create a new category.
4. As an example, create a new category called **Open-Source Products**. Under that new category, create a few sub-categories, such as **Alfresco and Plone**.

You can add additional categories and sub-categories, and can edit the existing categories.

Adding categories to content

In order to categorize content, you need to have one of the administrator, editor, collaborator, or coordinator roles, on that content.

To enable categorization for an individual content item (say `Alfresco_CIGNEX.doc`), go to the **View Details** page, and then click on the **Allow Categorization** link. Click on the **Change Category** icon, as shown in the following screenshot, to apply categorization to the content.

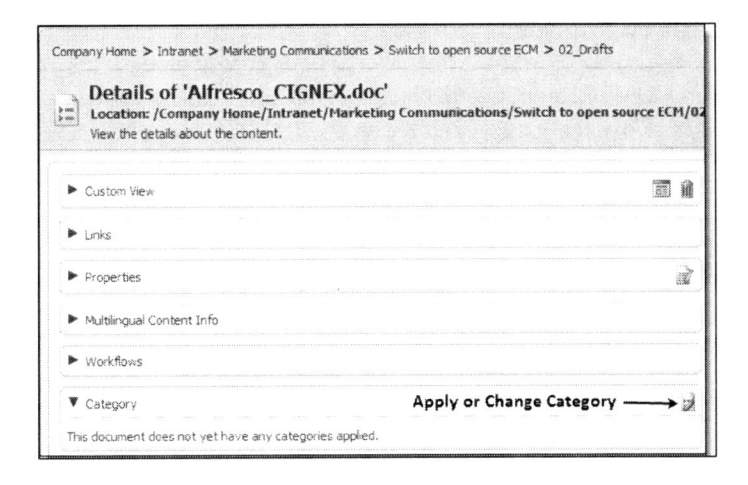

[Screenshot showing Details of 'Alfresco_CIGNEX.doc' with Custom View, Links, Properties, Multilingual Content Info, Workflows, and Category sections. The Category section shows "Apply or Change Category" and notes "This document does not yet have any categories applied."]

You will see the **Modify categories** dialog, as shown in the upcoming screenshot. Apply two different categories to the content. Click on the **OK** button to confirm the assignment. You will see that these two categories are assigned to your document, in the **View Details** page.

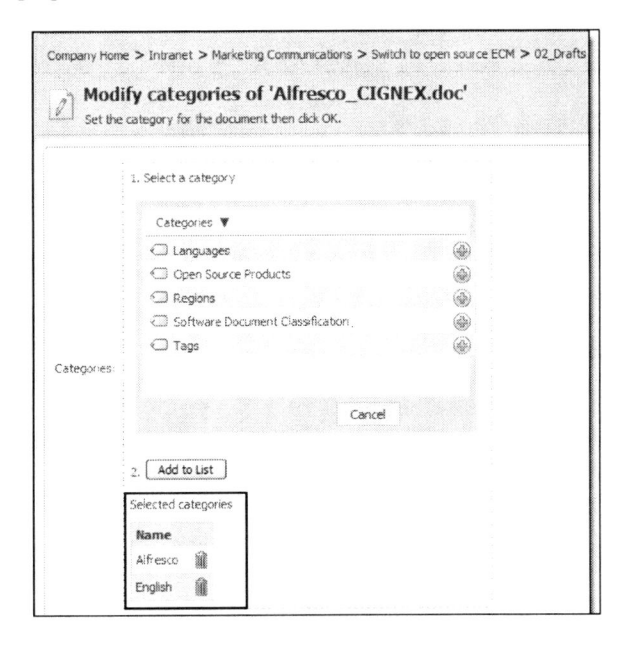

[Screenshot showing Modify categories of 'Alfresco_CIGNEX.doc' with categories: Languages, Open Source Products, Regions, Software Document Classification, Tags. Selected categories shown: Alfresco, English.]

Search content by category

Categorization helps to narrow down a search, or filters the search results. From the earlier example, we will search for marketing documents containing the text **Content**, and categorized under **Open Source Products | Alfresco**.

Implementing Document Management

Click on the **Advanced Search** link from the drop-down list of the search menu. From the form options, click on the **Show me results in the categories** pane. Click on the **Click here to select a category** link. Select the **Open Source Products | Alfresco** category, and provide this text to search for in the **Look For** text box. Then, click on the **Search** button.

Managing multilingual content

You can make content multilingual by selecting the **Make Multilingual** action, as shown in the following screenshot. You need to select the base language (**Pivot Translation**) and, optionally, add other translations.

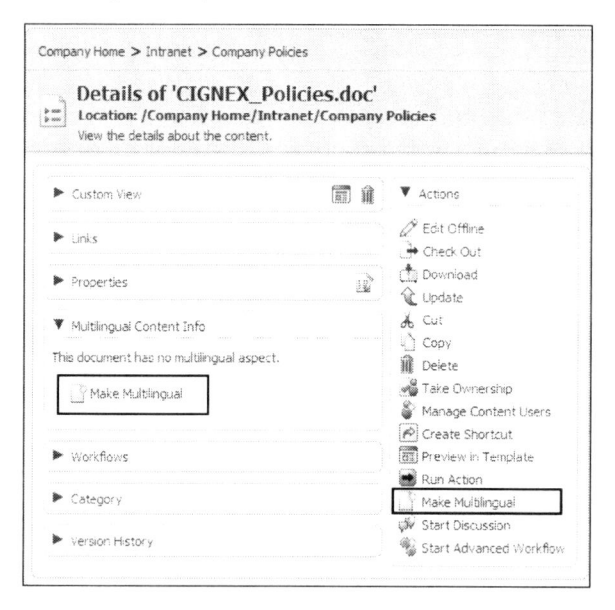

Once multilingual support has been added to a file, you will see the following window in the view details page. You can change the properties, such as **Pivot Translation**, by clicking on the **Edit** button, as shown in the following screenshot:

You can add translations, with or without a file. In either case, a new content object will be created in the selected language. Clicking on the **Add Translation** link will open up a dialog box, enabling you to upload a file with the selected language translation, as shown in the following screenshot:

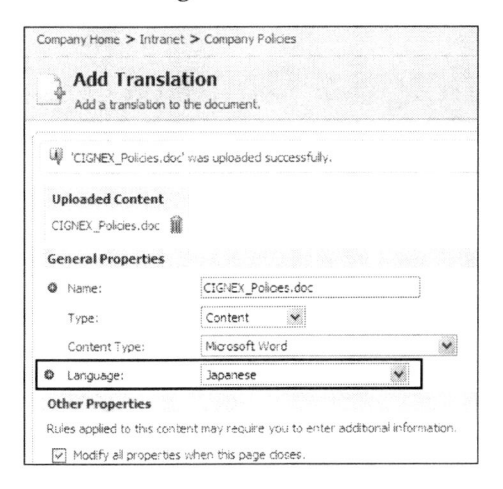

Versions of Multilingual Content

At the time of writing this book, Alfresco's multilingual support is very basic. It is equivalent to associating—and thus, grouping—the documents. All of the latest versions of the documents are associated as one logical document group, as shown in the following screenshot. The latest version of the English document could be 1.0. The German translated version could be 1.1, whereas the Japanese version could be 2.0.

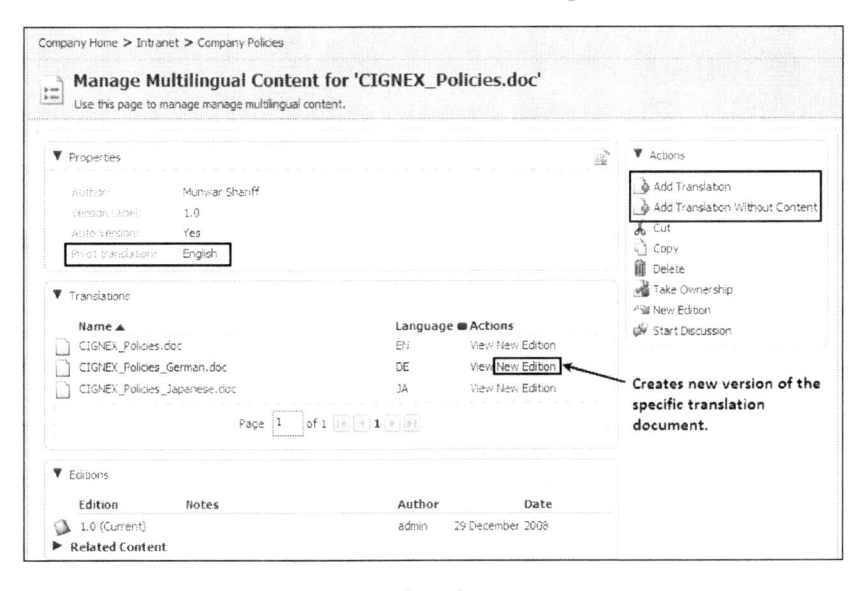

Implementing Document Management

Multilingual files are related to each other, and for all other purposes they are treated as separate files within Alfresco. They can have different versions, different metadata, different categorization, and different workflow processes. All of these translated files will show up in the **Search** result, if they match the search criteria.

Deleting Multilingual Content

You can't delete the base file if it has translated files available for it. In our example (as shown in the following screenshot), the content, with the base language set in English (with the icon **EN**), has two translations available: German (with the icon **DE**) and Japanese (with the icon **JA**). You will see that you cannot delete the base English version. However, you can delete the translated versions. If a particular content does not have translated content, then it can be deleted.

Using network drives to manage content

Out of the box installation includes a web client, that you can use to connect to the Alfresco repository through a web-based application. In addition to a web client, Alfresco supports various client applications for accessing the repository content using protocols such as FTP, WebDAV, and CIFS.

CIFS

CIFS is an enhanced version of Microsoft's **Server Message Block (SMB)**. It is the standard way for computer users to share files across the intranet and Internet. CIFS enables collaboration on the Internet by defining a remote file-access protocol that is compatible with the way that applications already share data on local disks and network file servers.

CIFS supports the usual set of file operations, such as open, close, read, write, and seek. CIFS also supports the locking and unlocking of files and records. CIFS allows multiple clients to access and update the same file, while preventing conflicts by providing file sharing and file locking. CIFS servers support both anonymous transfers and secure, authenticated access to named files.

CIFS helps you to map the Alfresco space to your local file system folder, thus giving you the flexibility of working with files in the repository, as though they are in your local file system. You will be able to bulk upload files to the server and edit them directly by using your desktop applications.

Mapping the drive

As an example, you will now map one of your spaces, say **Intranet | Marketing Communications**, as your local folder.

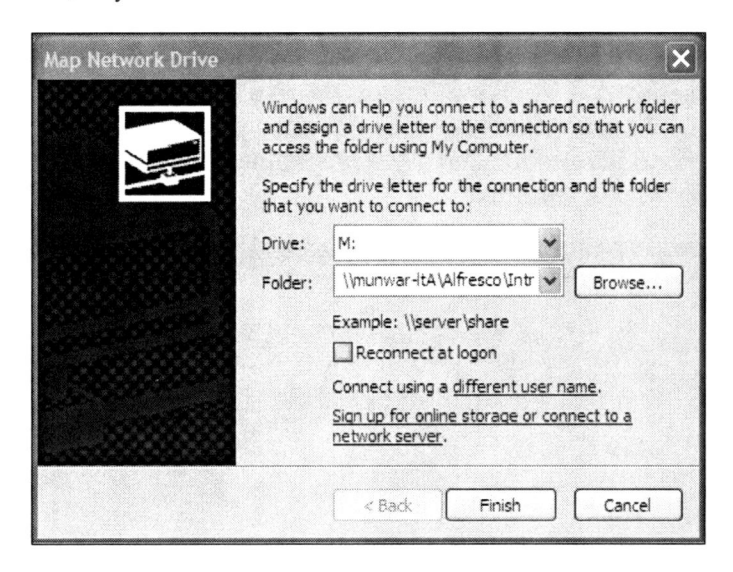

To map a space as a network drive in Windows Explorer, follow the steps given below:

1. In Windows Explorer, click on the **Tools | Map Network Drive** link. The **Map Network Drive** dialog is displayed, as shown in the preceding screenshot.

2. Select an unused drive letter (say, **M** for the **Marketing Communications** space).

3. In the **Folder** text box, type **\\AlfrescoServerNameA\Alfresco\Intranet\Marketing Communications**. Please note that you have to append a capital letter A at the end of your machine name. The syntax is: \\YourMachineNameA\alfresco\YourSpaceName.

4. Click on the **Finish** button. Because the space is secured, the system will prompt you for authentication.

5. Type in your Alfresco username and password when prompted.

Implementing Document Management

Another easy way of mapping your space as a network folder in your local file system is by using a web client. Go to the space and click on the **Open Network Folder** icon, as shown in the following screenshot:

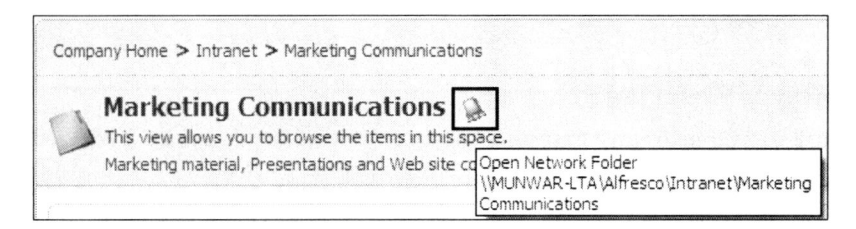

Once a space is mapped as a network folder, you can browse the space as if it is a local folder. The following screenshot illustrates that you could browse your Alfresco content on your local file system, and the server name is `YourMachineNameA`, as shown in the following screenshot:

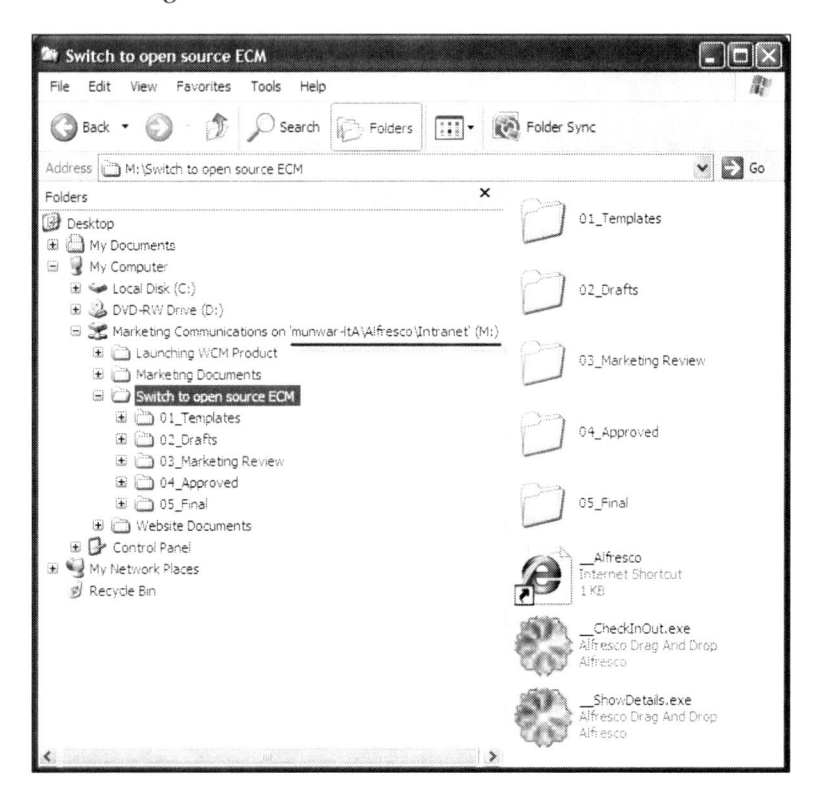

Drag-and-drop documents in Alfresco through CIFS

Once a space has been mapped as a network drive, you can drag-and-drop files from your local hard disk onto the Alfresco server. Similarly, you can copy files from the Alfresco server to your local hard disk.

For example, drag-and-drop an image file from your hard disk into your **Intranet > Marketing Communications > Switch to open source ECM > 02_Drafts** space.

People belonging to a department can map their department-specific space, and can transfer files from their local file system to this space.

As an administrator, you can map the root space (Intranet) to your local drive, and bulk transfer documents between the server and the local machine.

Check Out and Check In documents in CIFS

Carry out the following steps, to try the **Check Out** and **Check In** functions for a document in CIFS:

1. In Windows Explorer, locate the **02_Drafts** folder, and drag-and-drop the **Alfresco_CIGNEX.doc** file (or any other file) onto the **__CheckInOut.exe** file, in order to check out the file.

2. Notice that a working copy of the document is made, and the original document is locked, as shown in the following screenshot.

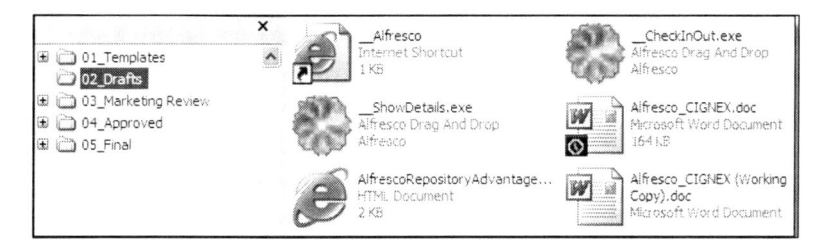

3. Make your changes to the working copy by directly editing it, using your favorite editor.

4. Click on the **__Alfresco** icon (as shown in the preceding screenshot), given in CIFS, in order to open the web client interface directly from your CIFS folder. You can verify that the file has been checked out in the web client interface as well. You will notice that changes made to the Alfresco repository through the CIFS interface are also visible in the web client user interface.

5. Once again, drag-and-drop the working copy onto **__CheckInOut.exe**, in order to check in the file. You will see that the working copy file is checked in and deleted. The original file is updated and unlocked.

If auto versioning is enabled on the document, then you will also notice that the changes made to the document are versioned. This is a great advantage for content authors, as they can edit the documents in their local file system using their choice of editors, as well as maintain various versions in the Alfresco repository automatically.

The sample works fine with Windows Internet Explorer and other web browsers, which already contain the CIFS plugin. If you are using an older version of Firefox or any web browser that does not contain the CIFS plugin, then you need to install the plugin to take advantage of this feature.

For the Firefox (or Mozilla) browser, a plugin is available on the sourceforge.net site. To install the Firefox extension, carry out the following steps:

1. Browse to the URL: http://sourceforge.net/projects/alfresco
2. Click on the green box named **Download**
3. Scroll down to the Firefox extension, and click on the **Download** link
4. Click on the link **alfrescoext-0.9.xpi**
5. In the list of download sites, click on the **Download** link for the site nearest to you
6. Allow permission to install the extension

File Transfer Protocol

FTP is useful for transferring files from your local file system to the remote server. By using any FTP client, you can connect to the Alfresco server, as if it were an FTP site, and you can upload to and retrieve files from it.

If you are connecting to a space, then all of the space's rules are applied and all of the space's permissions are enforced. If versioning is enabled, then content will be versioned, regardless of how it is updated.

Issue the following commands via the DOS command prompt to use FTP, to upload a file from a local hard disk to your **Intranet > Marketing Communications > Switch to open source ECM > 02_Drafts** space.

```
> ftp localhost
Login as: admin/admin
> ls
> cd Alfresco
> ls
> cd Intranet
> ls
> cd Marketing*
```

```
> cd Switch*
> cd 02_Drafts
> put c:\press2A.txt
> ls
```

Verify that the text file is now present in the Alfresco repository. Similarly, you can use any FTP client application to connect to the Alfresco repository and access files.

WebDAV

WebDAV is primarily designed to be used for editing and managing files on remote Web servers in a structured way. For example, an application such as Adobe Photoshop can directly open a file in the Alfresco Content Repository and edit it. This gives you the flexibility of using your own favorite editor to edit content on the Alfresco server.

If you are connecting to a space, then all of the space's rules are applied and all of the space's permissions are enforced. If versioning is enabled, then content will be versioned, regardless of how it is updated.

If you have a WebDAV client, then you can access the Alfresco server by using the URL, `http://localhost:8080/alfresco/webdav/`.

Windows explorer can be used as a WebDAV enabled file mount, by accessing the URL, as shown in the following screenshot:

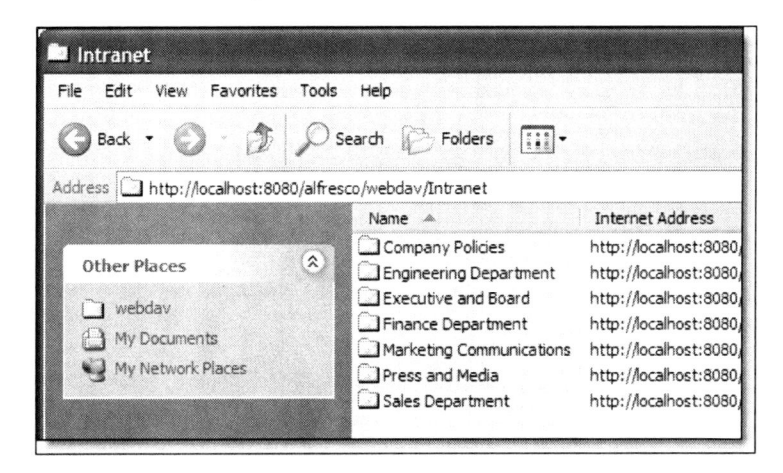

> You can only edit the content and not the metadata of the content by using CIFS, FTP, or WebDAV access.

Microsoft Office 2003 add-ins

For Microsoft Windows users, a natural way of working with the files is by using the Microsoft Office tools. It would be a tedious job for Content Managers to have to search and locate the documents using an Alfresco web client, copy them onto their local desktop, edit them, upload them to Alfresco, and secure them. How about having all of the features mentioned above in your choice of editor itself?

Alfresco provides Office add-ins for MS Word 2003, MS Excel 2003, and MS PowerPoint 2003, to allow them to manage the content directly from those tools. This improves the productivity of Content Managers.

Support for Microsoft Office 2007

Although the Alfresco add-ins were developed for Microsoft Office 2003, they are also compatible with Microsoft Office 2007.

If you are using Microsoft Office 2007 on Windows Vista, then the add-in is not effective, as it provides read-only access to the repository. Unfortunately, this is a known problem with Vista, as Microsoft has rewritten the WebDAV parts of Vista. You may consider the workarounds that are provided at the following URL:

```
http://blogs.msdn.com/sharepoint/archive/2007/10/19/known-issue-
office-2007-on-windows-vista-prompts-for-user-credentials-when-
opening-documents-in-a-sharepoint-2007-site.aspx
```

Installation

Download the Alfresco office add-ins (ZIP file) from the source forge web site, by visiting the following URL:

```
http://sourceforge.net/project/showfiles.php?group_id=143373&package_
id=237030
```

An individual installer (for Microsoft Word, Excel, and Power Point), as well as a combined installer, is available for download. Select an appropriate add-in to download.

Unzip the ZIP file and run the `Setup.exe` file contained within it. The set-up program will download the components that are needed, from the Microsoft web site.

Once the set-up is complete, you can open the Office tool and use the add-in. For example, for MS Word 2003, you will notice a new button named **Alfresco**. For MS Word 2007, you will notice the add-in, as shown in the following screenshot:

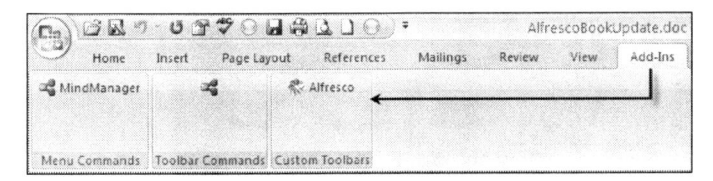

Configuration

Click on the **Alfresco** button to open the add-in window. You need to configure the add-in, by clicking on the link provided at the bottom of the add-in window.

Provide the URL details for the web client, WebDAV, and CIFS, as shown in the upcoming screenshot. No matter how you access the repository, you will still have to go through Alfresco's security rules. Provide the Userid and password for the purpose of authentication. The access to the Alfresco repository will be based on the authorization of the user.

Click on the **Save Settings** button to go the main screen. If you have more than one Alfresco server to connect to, then you might have to manually change the settings as needed. Currently, there is no facility for storing the settings for more than one Alfresco server.

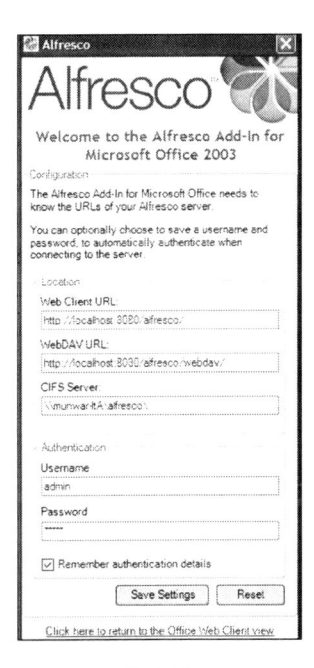

Implementing Document Management

Features of MS Word add-in

The Alfresco add-in allows you to carry out the following activities directly from Microsoft Word. Refer to the following screenshot for more details:

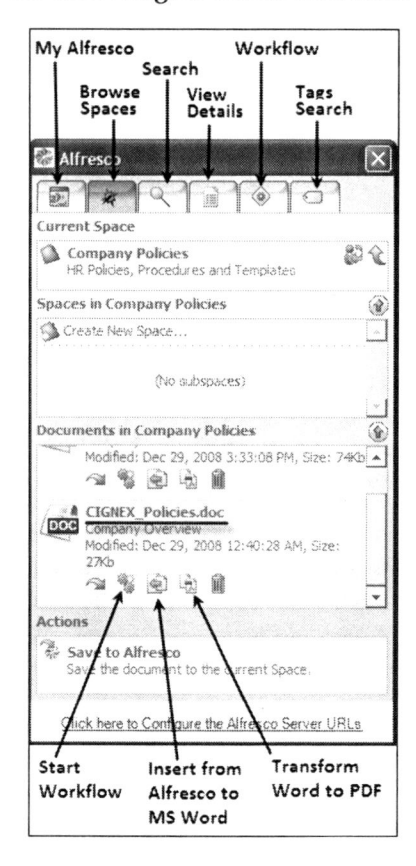

- **My Alfresco**: Displays the **My Alfresco** dashlets.
- **Browse Spaces**: Browses the entire repository for spaces and files.
- **Search**: Searches the repository for keywords.
- **View Details**: Views the details of the selected document.
- **Workflow**: Starts workflow for the active document.
- **Tags**: Allows you to add tags to the document.
- **Transform to PDF**: Transforms the selected MS Word document into PDF.
- **Insert into Word**: Inserts the selected document into Microsoft Word for editing.
- **Save to Alfresco**: Saves the current document to the current space. If the document has not been given a filename yet, then a pop-up panel will prompt you for one.

Editing a file in Word

To edit a file in Microsoft Word, double-click on the file name. The file is opened directly for editing. The MS Word file is locked for others, while it is being edited by you, as shown in the upcoming screenshot. You can perform all of the Alfresco repository activities, such as adding new tags and initiating a workflow approval process. Saving the file in Microsoft Word will directly save it in the Alfresco repository. If auto version is enabled, then it will be versioned automatically.

When you close the file in MS Word, or exit from MS Word, the file will be unlocked in the repository.

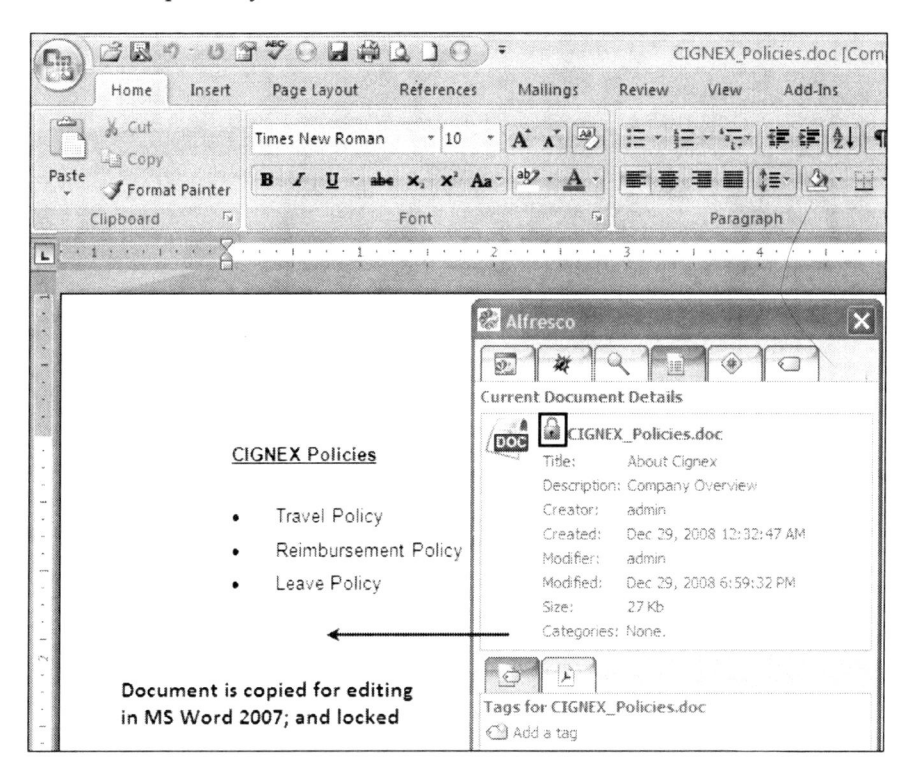

Recovering deleted content

When you delete an item (either content or space) in Alfresco, the item is not deleted from the server, but is moved to a temporary store called **Archive Space Store**. This gives you a chance to recover items that were deleted. Deleted items will be kept in the temporary store forever, until you decide to either recover or purge them. These features are available to administrators through the **Manage Deleted Items** action.

Implementing Document Management

To test these features, log in as an administrator, create a couple of dummy files in any space, and then delete them. Click on the **User Profile Icon** option, located above the menu item, and then click on the **Manage Deleted Items** button. The **Manage Deleted Items** pane appears, as shown in the following screenshot:

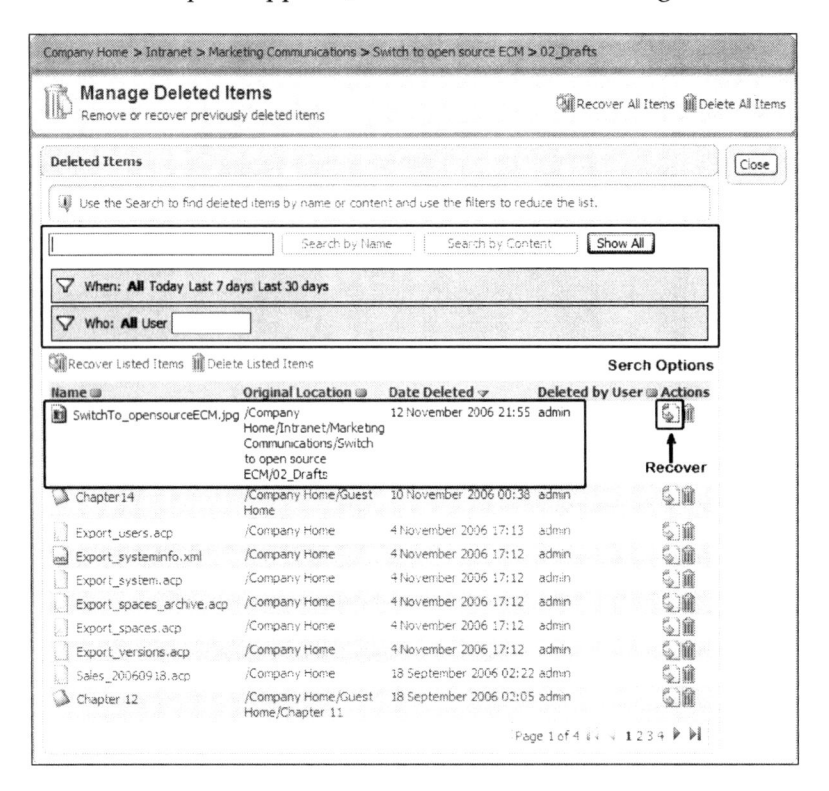

You can list all of the deleted content by clicking on the **Show All** button, as highlighted in the preceding screenshot. You can also search for deleted items by name, by content, by date, or by the person who deleted it, by using the search options provided. Select the item that you previously deleted, and then click on the **Recover Listed Items** icon, as shown in the preceding screenshot. You will notice that the item is recovered to the original space.

When an item is recovered, it is removed from the archive space store and moved to the original space from which it was deleted.

Purged items are deleted forever and cannot be recovered. Because the deleted items will otherwise be in the temporary store forever, it is a good practice to purge them periodically. It is also recommended that you take regular backups of your data. More information about maintenance and backups is provided in Chapter 14.

The Data Dictionary and space templates

The **Company Home** space is the root space. It contains sub-spaces such as **Data Dictionary**, **Guest Home**, and **Users Home Spaces**. Let's learn more about these sub-spaces:

The Data Dictionary space

The **Data Dictionary** space contains all of the user-managed definitions, as shown in the following screenshot:

The scripts and templates contained in these spaces are covered, in detail, in the coming chapters of this book. For the time being, note that the **Data Dictionary** space is a shared resource. All of the scripts and templates provided in the **Data Dictionary** space can be defined by the administrators and can be used by the users. The **Data Dictionary** space contains the following sub spaces:

- **Email Templates**: The **Email Templates** sub space contains email templates for notifying users of an invite to a space or document, and for sending notifications to users based on a rule or an action. Email templates are written in the **FreeMarker** template language, and will have the .ftl file extension.

- **Messages**: The **Messages** sub-space contains message files, which are part of the content model. Message files are nothing but property files that contain multi-lingual messages to be displayed. One of the ways of customizing the messages is to include them in the `<extension>/messages` folder. However, this requires Alfresco to be restarted after they have been included. The message files added to this space do not require Alfresco to be restarted.

- **Models**: The **Models** sub-space contains custom model files. As explained earlier, the model files added to this space do not require Alfresco be restarted. More information about model files is provided in Chapter 7.

- **Presentation Templates**: The **Presentation Templates** sub-space contains presentation templates that are useful for consolidating and viewing content in different ways. Presentation templates are written in the FreeMarker template language and will have the `.ftl` file extension.

- **RSS Templates**: The **RSS Templates** sub-space contains RSS templates, which are useful for providing RSS feeds for spaces. More information about RSS templates is provided in Chapter 10.

- **Saved Searches**: The **Saved Searches** sub-space contains pre-built queries which are saved by the user from the search results page. Each user will have their own private saved searches. This space will also contain all of the saved searches that have been publicly shared by users.

- **Scripts**: The **Scripts** sub-space contains the JavaScript files that are used to perform certain operations on content.

- **Space Templates**: The **Space Templates** sub-space contains space structures that can be used as templates for creating new spaces. Any space can be saved as a space template for future use for a space structure and for data. More about space templates is provided in the upcoming section.

- **Web Client Extension**: The **Web Client Extension** sub-space contains dynamic web client customizations. This newly-added space simply provides an additional source for loading and overriding the web client configuration.

- **Web Forms**: The **Web Forms** sub-space contains Alfresco **Web Content Management (WCM)** web form definition files.

- **Web Scripts**: The **Web Scripts** sub-space contains new custom web scripts. Web Scripts are explained in detail in Chapter 9.

- **Web Scripts Extensions**: The **Web Scripts Extensions** sub-space contains the web script files that are used to override the existing web script files.

- **Workflow Definitions**: The **Workflow Definitions** sub-space contains workflow definition files. The custom workflow files that are added to this space do not require Alfresco to be restarted.

Space templates for a reusable space structure

In the earlier sections of this chapter, you created a marketing project in the **Company Home > Intranet > Marketing Communications > Switch to open source ECM** space. Let us assume that you are going to launch many such marketing campaign projects in your marketing department. Each marketing project space will have a similar structure, used to hold the project information. For example, your marketing project space has marketing templates, draft documentation, and approved marketing collateral. Moreover, each project will have a hierarchy of spaces, security settings, business rules, notifications, and workflows.

Instead of having to repeatedly create the same structure for each project, you can maintain a **Marketing project template**, and simply replicate it for every new project. Therefore, all the work that you do manually can be done in a few seconds, by simply using such a template.

To give you an idea, **Company Home > Data Dictionary > Space Templates** contains a built-in space template called **Software Engineering Project**, as shown in the following screenshot:

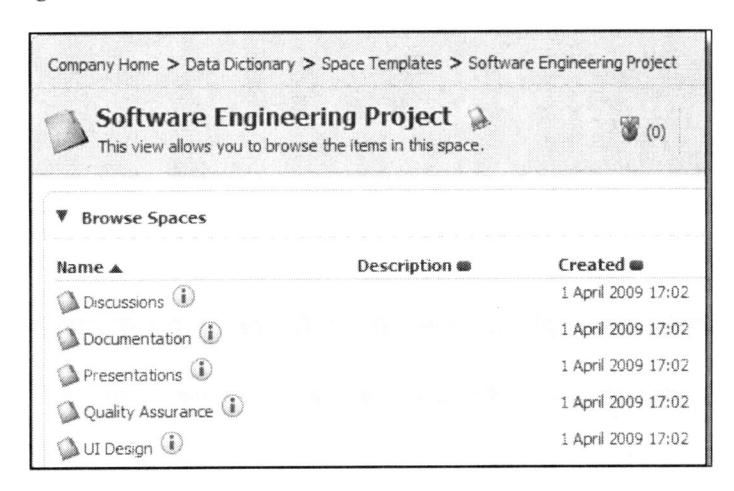

This represents a typical engineering project space structure, with sub-spaces for documentation, discussions, quality assurance, user-interface design, and project presentations. You can use the **Software Engineering project** template and keep on replicating it for every new engineering project. If the template does not exactly match your needs, then you can add or delete some spaces in the template itself.

Note that the **Software Engineering Project** template does not contain rules. This is because the rules will vary from one company to another (for example, because the workflow processes will vary). For your own company projects, adding rules and standard content will increase the value of the space template.

Implementing Document Management

Creating a new space template for reuse

Carry out the following steps to create your own space template for your **Marketing Projects**, using the existing space structure:

1. Log in as an administrator and go to the **Company Home > Data Dictionary > Space Templates** space.

2. Click on the **Create | Advanced Space Wizard** link. The **Create Space Wizard** pane is displayed.

3. Click on the **Based on an existing space** option button, and then click on the **Next** button to go to the second pane, which is titled **Space Options**.

4. Navigate to and select the **Company Home > Intranet > Marketing Communications > Switch to open source ECM** option. Click on the **Next** button to go to the **Space Details** pane.

5. In the **Space Details** pane, enter an appropriate title (such as **Marketing Project**) for your space template, and then click on the **Finish** button to confirm.

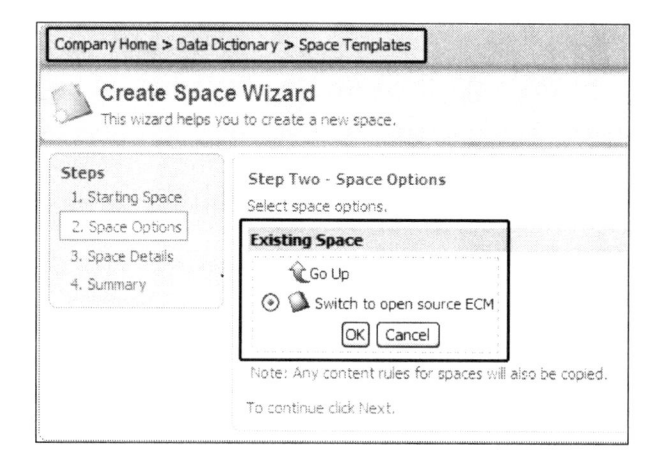

You will notice a new space template called **Marketing Project in Company Home > Data Dictionary > Space Templates**. Examine the space structure.

Using an existing space template to create a new space

You can reuse the **Marketing Project** space template to create new marketing projects. To create a new **Marketing Project**, ensure that you are in the **Company Home > Intranet > Marketing Communications** space, and carry out the following steps:

1. In the space header, click on **Create | Advanced Space Wizard**.

2. The first pane of the **Create Space Wizard** is displayed. Click on the **Using a template** option button, and then click on the **Next** button.
3. The **Space Options** window of the wizard appears, as shown in the following screenshot:

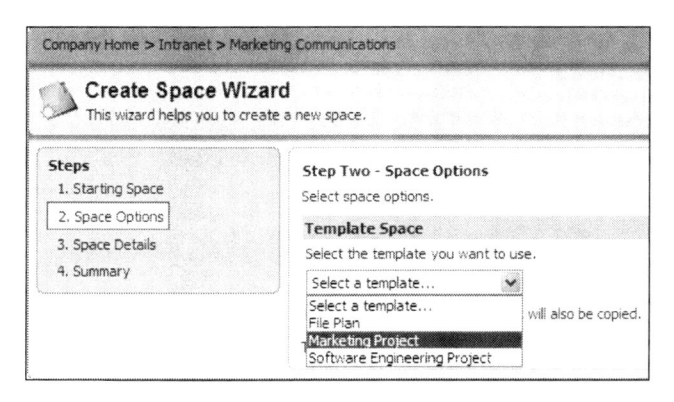

4. Choose the **Marketing Project** template, and then click on the **Next** button.
5. The **Space Details** pane of the wizard appears, as shown in the following screenshot.

6. Specify your new project name, and then click on the **Finish** button to confirm.
7. You can now browse around your new space and compare it with the **Marketing Project** space template. You will notice that the space contents are identical.

Discussions on spaces and documents

Alfresco provides a special type of space called **Discussion forums** for collaboration. You can leverage the extensive security framework to provide access to these spaces in order to promote collaboration. You can also set up inter-departmental collaboration using spaces, allowing multiple people to work on documents within a particular space.

By using the collaborative features, the author of a document can invite others to work on the document and participate in general discussions about the document.

Discussion forums for collaboration

A Discussion forum is a web-based facility for holding discussions, also commonly referred to as Internet forums, web forums, message boards, discussion boards, discussion groups, bulletins, or simply forums.

In Alfresco, a **forum space** is special space that can contain other forum spaces or forums (discussion forums). A forum is essentially a space composed of a number of member-written topics, each comprising a discussion or conversation in the form of a series of member-written replies. These replies can be posted by group members, as defined by the administrator. In some cases, this can be done anonymously or, in the case of a secure forum, only by registered members. These topics remain saved on the web site indefinitely, or until they are deleted by a moderator.

To summarize, you can have one or more forum spaces in Alfresco. Each forum space can have one or more forums. Each forum can have one or more topics. Each topic can have one or more replies. All of the forums, topics, and replies are searchable.

Forum space

A forum space contains a discussion forum. As an example, create a forum space in the **Engineering Department** space by carrying out the following steps:

1. Log in to the Alfresco web client and go to the **Company Home > Intranet > Engineering Department** space.
2. From the **Create** menu drop-down list, choose the **Advanced Space Wizard** option, as shown in the following screenshot:

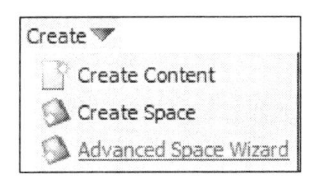

3. The **Create Space Wizard** window is displayed, showing multiple steps. From the options available, select the **From scratch** option, and then click on the **Next** button located on the right-hand side of the screen.
4. You will see a window for step 2, which is to select space options. Choose **Forum Space,** and then click on the **Next** button, to view step 3.
5. In step 3, provide a name for your forum (say **Engineering Discussions**), and then click on the **Finish** button.

Creating discussion forums in the forum space

You can create other forum spaces or discussion forums within a forum space.

Go to the forum space that was created above, which is named **Engineering Discussions**. When you click on the **Create** drop-down menu at the top, you will see options for creating forum spaces, or forums within a forum space, as shown in the following screenshot. Click on the **Create Forum** action, and create a few new forums.

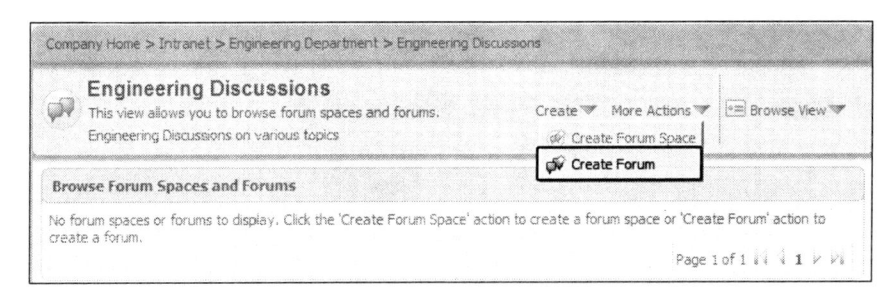

Creating topics in the forum

You can create various topics within a discussion forum. The topics are a type of content item such as a plain-text item.

Click on a forum (say **Alfresco Technology**), and then click on the **Create Topic** button, to create a topic, as shown in the following screenshot:

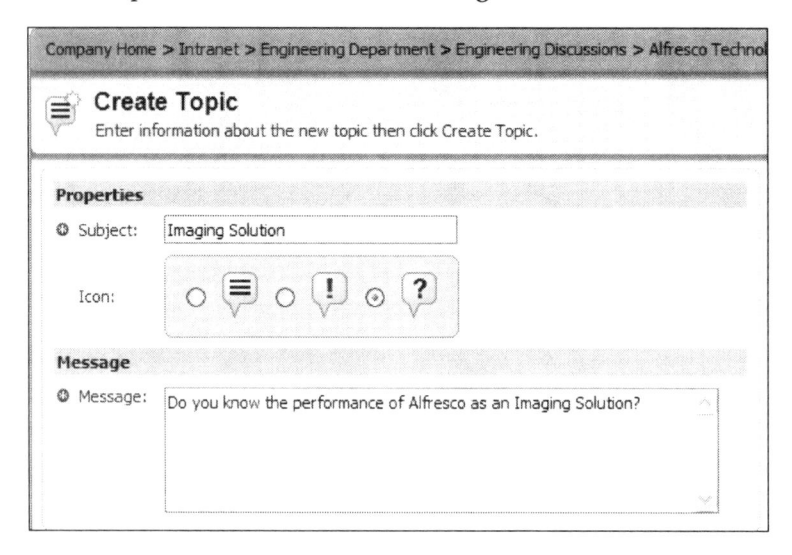

Replying to topics

Users, who have access to this topic can reply with messages. The users can also reply to the replies. There is no limitation on the number of replies. As an administrator, you can edit or delete a particular topic or post (reply).

Departmental forums and security

Forums and topics are types of spaces, and they are governed by the same permissions as other spaces. Users may be invited to the forums and the topics, through the assignment of certain roles.

The following table explains the roles and permissions for forums:

Role	Permission
Consumer	Can copy or view details (of the forum and its topics).
Editor	Consumer permissions, plus can edit posts (within topic). May edit details of forum and topics.
Contributor	Consumer permissions, plus can create a topic in the forum. Can post to a topic or post a reply within a topic.

Role	Permission
Coordinator	Consumer permissions, plus can create a topic.
	Can view or edit details of the forum and topics.
	Can manage the space and the users of the forum and topics.
	Can post to a topic and can cut or delete a topic.
	Can post a reply or edit a post.

The following table explains the roles and permissions for topics:

Role	Permission
Consumer	Can copy or view a topic.
Editor	Consumer permissions, plus can edit a topic.
	Can edit the details of topics.
Contributor	Consumer permissions, plus can post to a topic or post a reply within a topic.
Coordinator	Consumer permissions, plus can post to a topic.
	Can post a reply.
	Can edit a post.
	Can delete a post.

When the option **Inherit parent space permissions** is disabled, no user can view the discussions unless explicitly invited. Even the Coordinators of the forum cannot see the topic. Those users who have been invited, have the access rights (as stated above), corresponding to their role.

Defining forums for groups within a department

By setting the appropriate security, each group within a department can have a discussion forum, and each project can have a separate discussion forum that is specific to that project. As a sample exercise, go to the **Company Home > Intranet > Engineering Department > ProjectA** space, delete the **Discussions** space and create **Discussions** as a forum space. Create a few project-specific discussion forums and topics. Invite various users to participate in the discussions, by giving them the **Contributor** role for the discussion forum. Test this by logging in as various users, and by participating in the discussions.

Inter-department collaboration through spaces

You can use the existing security framework to allow groups and individuals to access certain spaces and collaborate on content.

Managing space users

As an owner of a space, you can invite other users to your space to view, add, or edit content. On any space, the **More Actions | Manage Space Users** link shows a list of users that have permission to work on content in that space. You can click on the **Invite** link to invite individual users or groups, and assign to them the appropriate permissions. More details about securing a space are provided in Chapter 4.

Space collaboration through email

All users who have access to a space, can communicate using email. In order to send an email to the users of a space, click on the **More Actions | View Details** link, and then click on the **Email Space Users** action. As a result, the **Email Space Users** pane appears.

The groups and individual users who have access to this space are listed as email **Message Recipients**. You can choose to email the entire group or only certain users in the group, by expanding the group icon.

Starting a discussion on a specific space

You can start a discussion on a specific space directly, by clicking on the **Start Discussion** action, provided in the actions menu, as shown in the following screenshot:

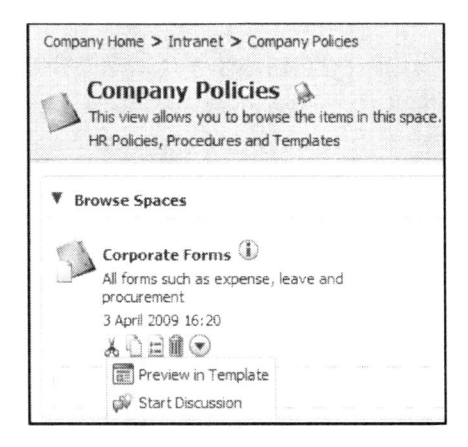

Once the discussion has been started, you will see a discussion forum icon that can be used to view the discussions on the space.

Content collaboration

Similar to collaboration for a specific space, you can collaborate on individual content items as well. You can start a discussion for a specific document directly, by clicking on the **Start Discussion** action, which is provided on the actions menu.

> It is always a good practice to start a discussion for a document in the workflow process. This allows various people to make and review comments, as well as capture all of the review data, as the document goes through various approval steps.

Owner invites individuals to collaborate on content

As an owner of content, you can give the **Editor** role to another individual, to allow them to edit the content. In the content's **View Details** screen, the **Manage content users** action provides a list of users that have permission to work on content.

The process for inviting users to collaborate on content is similar to that for space collaboration. However, the invited users should have the correct roles on the content and the parent space.

RSS syndication

In order to share the information in a space with external systems such as RSS feeds, you need to enable **RSS Feed** for that space.

Go to the details page of the **News** space, and click on the **Enable RSS Syndication** icon, as shown in the following screenshot:

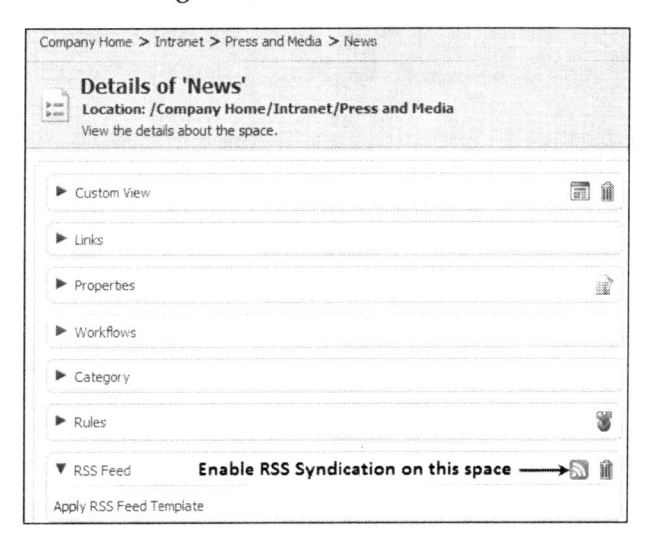

A new window is displayed, enabling you to select the RSS template that is to be applied to the space as an **RSS feed**. The **RSS templates** are custom scripts that determine the content to be shown as feeds. Alfresco comes with a built-in standard RSS template, called `RSS_2.0_recent_docs.ftl`, which renders a valid RSS2.0 XML document, showing the documents in the current space that have been created or modified in the last seven days. Choose the default RSS template from the drop-down menu, and then click on the **OK** button.

In order for anonymous users to be able to view the news feeds, they must have read permission on the **News** space. This means that the **Guest** (anonymous) user must have the **Consumer** role (READ access) for this space, in order for the **RSS feed** to be publicly viewable.

This can be achieved by using the **Manage Space Users** dialog, and inviting the **Guest** user into the **News** space.

> It is very important to ensure that the guest user has the Consumer role on the space to view the RSS feeds of that space.

Using RSS feeds

Let us test the RSS syndication features on the **News** space. Once RSS feeds are enabled on a space, the **RSS Feed Link** icon is visible, as shown in the following screenshot:

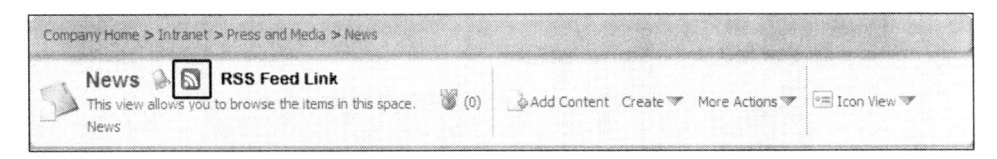

By clicking on the **RSS Feed Link**, you can view the RSS feeds of the **News** space in the web browser. You can view the RSS feeds of the **News** space in any RSS feeds enabled web browser or RSS aggregator.

Version 7.0 of Microsoft Explorer has a built-in RSS feeds viewer. You can receive content automatically by subscribing to a web feed and specifying the interval, at which Internet Explorer should check the web site for updates. To view your feeds, click on the **Favorites Center** button, and then click on the **Feeds** link. This allows you to subscribe to feeds from Internet Explorer, and read them in other programs, such as email clients.

RSS templates

The news information that is displayed as an RSS feed is controlled by the RSS template. **RSS templates** are custom scripts written in the FreeMarker template language. All of the RSS templates in Alfresco are located in the **Company Home > Data Dictionary > RSS Templates** space.

You can either customize an existing template by editing it, or can add a new RSS template by clicking on the **Add Content** link that is provided, as shown in the preceding screenshot.

Migrating existing content into Alfresco

If you want your Enterprise Content Management initiative to be successful, then you need to make sure that you can move your existing content into the new system. Most enterprises will have content in the form of files (on local or shared hard disks), email attachments, faxes (for example, invoices), and scanned images. It is very important to move the content to a centralized and highly scalable content repository such as Alfresco.

Alfresco is a powerful Content Management System for the enterprise, and supports various ways of migrating existing content in the enterprise.

Drag-and-drop content to the network drive

You can drag-and-drop (bulk upload) content from your local hard disks to the Alfresco server by using options such as CIFS, FTP, or WebDAV. Refer to the *Use network drives to manage content* section in this chapter, for details of how to move content from your hard disk to the Alfresco server.

The problem with this approach is that you will have to manually update the metadata (properties) of the content.

Using web services to migrate content

Alfresco provides a very rich web services API. By using this, you can transfer your files, as well as their metadata, to the Alfresco server.

Alfresco also provides RESTful Web Services (known as Web Scripts). By using these, you can easily migrate content to the Alfresco server. RESTful Web Script is a very suitable and flexible solution for integrating Alfresco with any other application, and will most likely be the best solution among all of the available options. More information about Web Scripts is provided in Chapter 9.

The ACP Generator's bulk upload utility

The ACP Generator project provides a tool for bulk uploading content into any Alfresco repository. It reads custom content models, as well as a **comma-separated values** (**CSV**) list of required property and category values for each content item, and then creates an ACP file.

The syntax is as follows:

```
acpGeneratr arg1 arg2 arg3 arg4 arg5
Where:
Arg1: The path and filename of the custom model to be used.
Arg2: The path to the directory where the content to be imported is
      located
Arg3: The destination path
Arg4: The content type we're dealing with
Arg5: The csv file of property values
```

Example:

```
acpGeneratr "D:\PIER\ACPGeneratr\sampleModel.xml"
            \ACPGeneratr\content   ..\ACPGeneratr\testDestDir dm:gqa
                                    "D:\PIER\ACPGeneratr\faqlist.csv"
```

This will create the defined destination folder, and within it, a folder with all of the content and the required `xml` file. All you need to do is zip it into an `ACP` file, and import it to Alfresco. More details about this tool are provided on the Alfresco Forge site, at http://forge.alfresco.com/projects/acpgeneratr/.

Summary

You can customize Alfresco's features, such as smart spaces, library services, and security, in order to implement your enterprise document management requirements. Various interfaces, such as web client, CIFS, FTP, and WebDAV can be used to manage the content in the Alfresco repository. The content can be edited on your local desktop, using your choice of content editors. The Microsoft Office add-in provides a more natural way of managing the content, and thus improves productivity.

You can enable discussions on spaces and individual documents in order to facilitate collaboration. You can enable RSS syndication to share information with external systems or users. Moreover, you can use various ways of merging your existing content into Alfresco, by using free tools and web services.

6
Implementing Business Rules

So far, you have learned how to create system users, create user groups, create spaces, add content, check in and check out documents, use version control with documents, and use network folders to upload content in bulk. In this chapter, you will learn about defining and using business rules according to your business requirements.

By the end of this chapter, you will have learned how to:

- Automatically organize documents into specific spaces when you perform a bulk upload of documents
- Define the sequence of business rules on a space
- Run time-consuming business rules in the background
- Automatically control document versions for specific documents in specific spaces
- Automatically categorize documents based on names
- Send notifications based on a specific event for a document
- Transform documents from one format to another
- Dynamically add custom properties to documents, based on their location
- Configure business rules as scheduled actions to run periodically
- Extend business rules using customized JavaScript files

Using business rules on spaces

You can leverage Alfresco's rules engine to define business rules based on your requirements. You do not need any programming expertise in order to define and deploy a business rule. You can choose to use a business rule from an extensive list of built-in rules, or you can create your own business rules. Business rules can be applied to the entire content or a specific content within a space, based on the conditions that you set. This section will provide you with various real-life examples of business rules, as well as the steps to set and use business rules on spaces.

Implementing Business Rules

Organize documents automatically

In the previous chapter, you learned that you can upload many documents (via a bulk upload) from your local folder to an Alfresco repository. However, each time, you might end up manually moving them to specific spaces in order to organize them inside the repository.

Let us consider a sample scenario. Let us say your finance department receives thousands of documents every day in an electronic format from your customers, vendors, and internal departments. Your finance department receives checks from customers in the form of scanned images, invoices from vendors in the form of PDF documents, and contracts and other documents from various departments in the form of Microsoft Word documents. They would like to upload all of these documents to the Alfresco repository and automatically organize them into various spaces, as shown in the following screenshot:

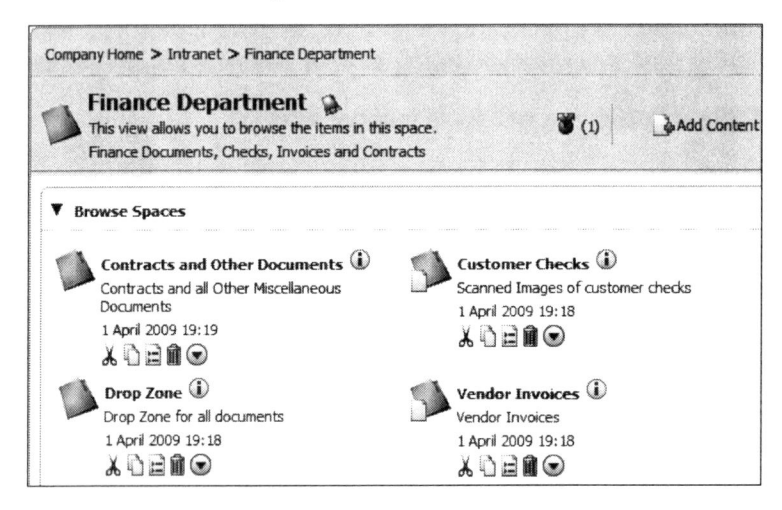

You can consider getting all of these documents as bulk uploads into a **Drop Zone** (a space that is mapped as a network folder). If the document name includes `Check` (say `Client1Check_7003.jpg`), then you would like to move it to the **Customer Checks** space. If the document name includes `Invoice` (say `Vendor2Invoice_20060815.pdf`), then you would like to move it to the **Vendor Invoices** space. You would like to move all other documents (say `Project3Contract.doc`) to the **Contracts and Other Documents** space. You will define a business rule that is triggered as soon as a document gets into the **Drop Zone**; the rule will examine the file name and move it to the appropriate space, automatically.

This example uses the space called **Finance Department**, which you have already created as a part of your Intranet sample application. Because you have secured this space earlier, only administrator (`admin`), and users belonging to the `Finance` group (`Tom FinExec` and `Hope Fin`), can add content to this space. You can log in to the Alfresco Web Client as **Tom FinExec** to manage content in this space. Go to the **Company Home > Intranet > Finance Department** space and create the following four sub-spaces:

- **Drop Zone**
- **Customer Checks**
- **Vendor Invoices**
- **Contracts and Other Documents**

Make sure that you are in the **Company Home > Intranet > Finance Department > Drop Zone** space. Carry the following instructions to define business rules for the **Drop Zone**.

In the **Drop Zone** space, click on the option **More Actions > Manage Content Rules**. You will see the **Content Rules** pane, as shown in following screenshot:

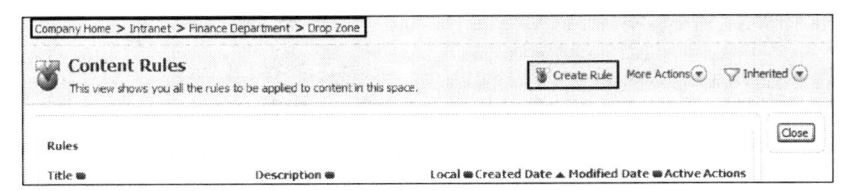

Clicking on the **Create Rule** link (as shown in the screenshot) opens the **Create Rule Wizard** window. As you may notice, the **Create Rule Wizard** window has four steps, as shown in the following screenshot. The first step is to define the condition for selecting the documents, the second step is to define the desired action that will take place, the third step is to define the moment that the rule will run, and the fourth step is to confirm and commit the business rule.

Implementing Business Rules

In the **Step One** window, you will notice that the **Select Condition** drop-down list displays all of the built-in conditions which can be readily-used for your business rules. We will examine all of these conditions in later sections of this chapter. From the **Select Condition** drop-down list, select the **Items which contain a specific value in its name** condition.

Click on the **Set Values and Add** button to set the condition values. You will notice that a new window has popped up, as shown in the following screenshot.

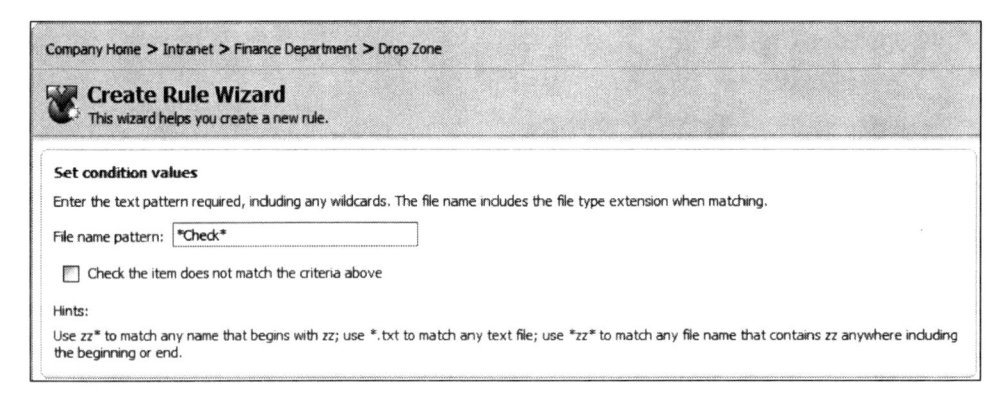

Refer to the figure in order to set the condition values. In **File name pattern**, you can select any of the following options: **Use zz* to match any name that begins with zz; use *.txt to match any text file; use *zz* to match any file name that contains zz anywhere including the beginning or end**.

Select ***Check*** as file name pattern. This means that this rule will be applied to any document that has `Check` anywhere in its file name. For example this rule will be applied to documents which have names such as `Client1Check_7003.jpg` or `Check7003.jpg` and `20060815Client1Check.jpg`. The file name pattern is case insensitive, so the rule will also be applied to documents that have `cHeCk` anywhere in their name.

In the preceding screenshot, you will notice the **Check the item does not match the criteria checkbox**, which changes the criteria so that the rule is applied to files do not match this pattern. This is how you can define the opposite criteria, that is, when `check` is not found within the filename string. For this example, do not select this checkbox. Click on the **OK** button to confirm the condition.

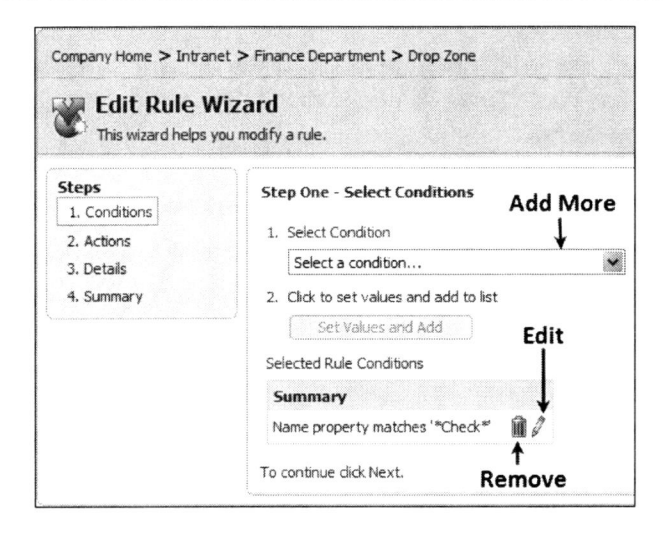

Chapter 6

[Screenshot: Edit Rule Wizard - Step One - Select Conditions, with annotations "Add More", "Edit", and "Remove"]

You may notice the selected rule conditions in the **Summary** section, as shown in the screenshot. You can edit the rule condition by clicking on the **Edit** (pencil) icon, and you can delete the selected rule condition by clicking on the **Remove** icon.

You can define as many conditions as you like by selecting the condition, and then clicking on the **Set Values and Add** button. All of the conditions have to be met in order to apply the actions to the rule. Clicking on the **Next** button will take you to the **Step Two Actions** window, as shown in the following screenshot:

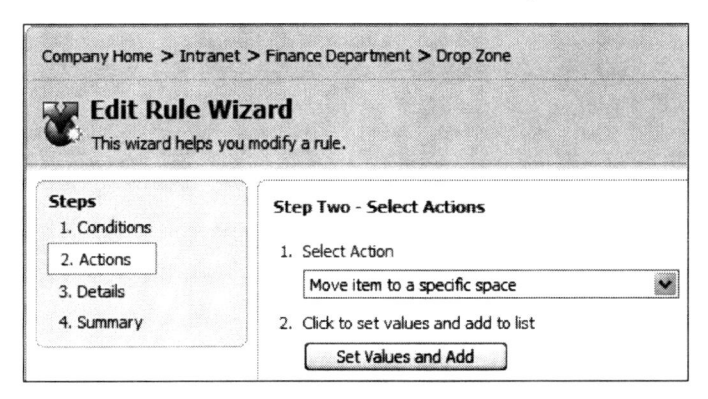

[Screenshot: Edit Rule Wizard - Step Two - Select Actions, with "Move item to a specific space" selected]

In the **Step Two** window, you will notice that the **Select Action** drop-down list displays all of the built-in actions that could readily be used for your business rules. We will examine all of these actions in the later sections of this chapter. From the **Select Action** drop-down list, select the **Move item to a specific space** action.

Implementing Business Rules

Click on the **Set Values and Add** button to set the action values. In the **Set action values** window, click on the **Click here to select the destination** link, in order to select the destination space. You will notice that a new window pops up, as shown in the following screenshot.

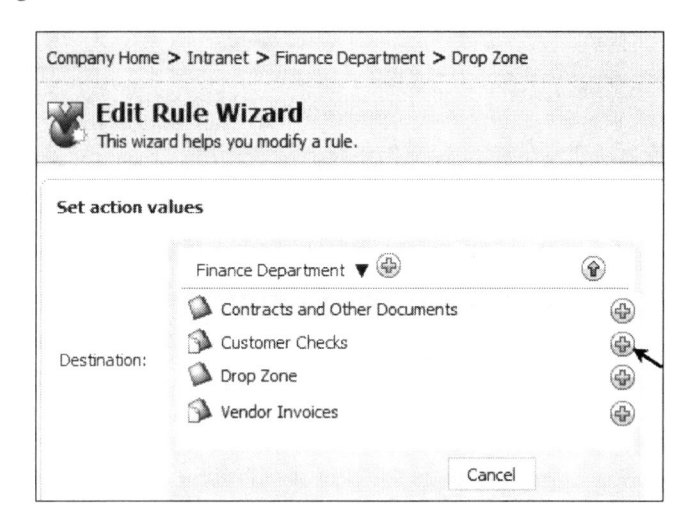

Select **Customer Checks** space as the destination for the selected documents. Click on the **OK** button to confirm the action value.

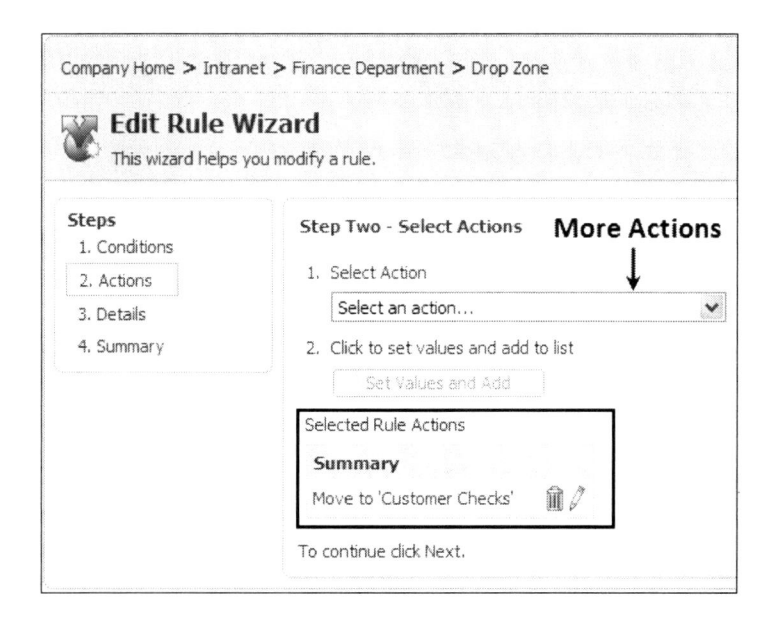

[184]

You will find the **Selected Rule Actions** in the **Summary** section, as shown in the screenshot above. You can define as many actions as you like, by selecting the action and then clicking on the **Set Values and Add** button. All of actions will be run. Clicking on the **Next** button will take you to the **Step Three** window, as shown in the following screenshot.

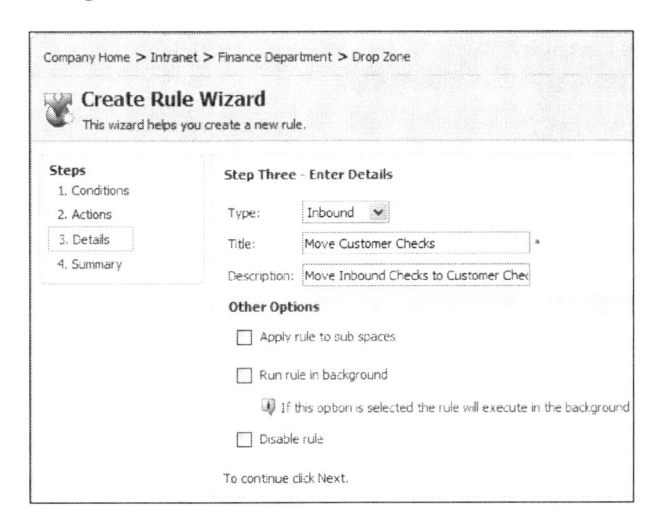

In the **Step Three** window, you will notice the business rule triggering options in the **Type** drop-down list.

- **Inbound** means that this rule is triggered when a document is created (in Web Client), or copied or moved (from some other space), or added (using Web Services API), or dropped (using the drag-and-drop feature of CIFS, WebDAV, FTP) in to the **Drop Zone** space.
- **Outbound** means that this rule is triggered when a document is deleted, or cut (to move to another space) from the **Drop Zone** space.
- **Update** means that this rule is triggered when a document in the **Drop Zone** space is updated. Again, the update can happen by various means, such as manual updating in the Web Client, updating through network drives (CIFS, FTP, WebDAV), and updating through the Web Services API.

Select the **Inbound** type and give a meaningful **Title** and **Description** to your rule. You will notice three checkboxes in the **Other Options** menu. The option **Apply rule to sub spaces** will apply this rule to the **Drop Zone** space as well as all sub-spaces of the **Drop Zone** space. The option **Run rule in background** will execute this rule in the background as a separate process. The option **Disable rule** will allow you to define the rule, but not to activate it yet. You will learn more about **Other options** in the later sections of this chapter.

Implementing Business Rules

Select the **Run rule in background** checkbox, leaving the other checkboxes unselected, as shown in the screenshot above. Clicking on the **Next** button will take you to the **Step Four** window, which displays a summary of the rule.

Click on the **OK** button in the **Summary** window to confirm the rule. You will notice that the rule is now listed for the **Drop Zone** space, as shown in the following screenshot. You can make changes to an existing business rule by clicking on the **Edit Rule** icon, as shown in the screenshot.

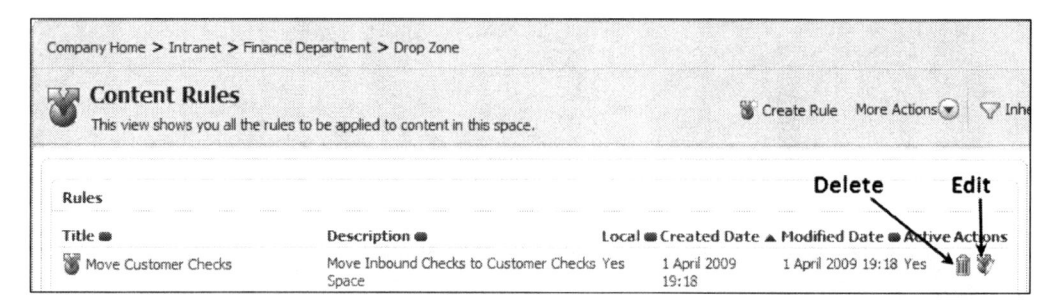

Now, follow the instructions below, and create another new rule in the **Drop Zone** space, to move all of the documents that have 'Invoice' (***Invoice***) in their name, to the **Vendor Invoices** space.

Define a third business rule in the **Drop Zone** space, which moves all of the documents, other than `Checks` and `Invoices`, to the **Contracts and Other Documents** space. When selecting the condition, you have to select two conditions, as indicated in the following screenshot, to eliminate the previous two conditions and select all of the other documents. All of the remaining steps are similar to those for the previous rules.

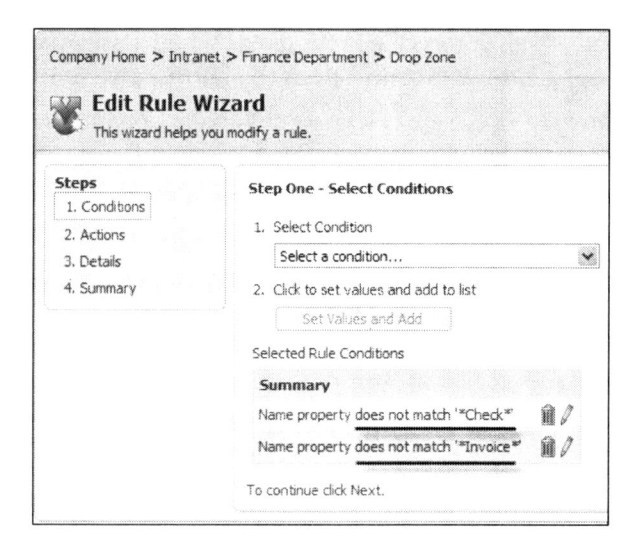

Once you have finished defining the rules, the **Content Rules** window for the **Drop Zone** space should display all of the three rules, as shown in the following screenshot. This is an example of how to set the rules based on the name property of the document. You can think of other useful scenarios that might be applicable to your business.

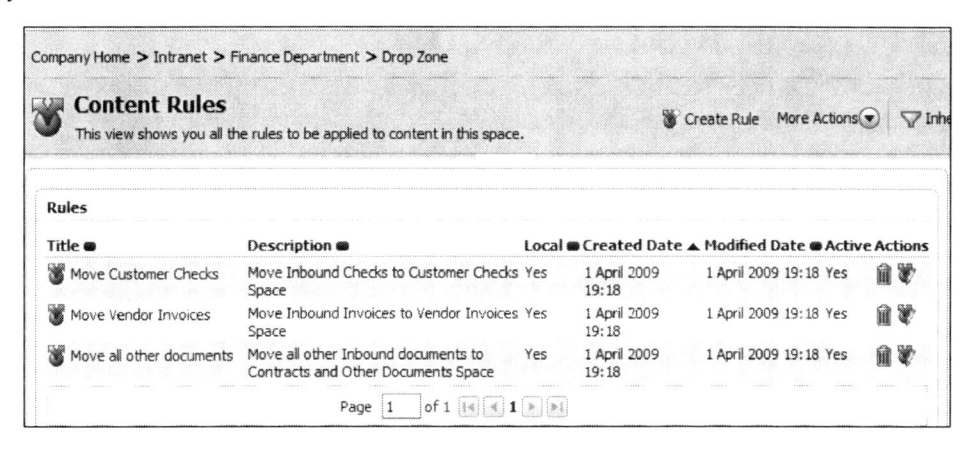

Now, test the business rules that you have defined, by adding documents in the **Intranet > Finance Department > Drop Zone** space. On your personal computer, create files to test your business rules, and choose the file names that match your business rules. For example, create three files named `Client1Check_7003.jpg` (a scanned check), `Vendor2Invoice_20060815.pdf` (a vendor invoice) and `Project3Contract.doc` (a contract document). Drag-and-drop them into the **Drop Zone** space, as shown in the following figure.

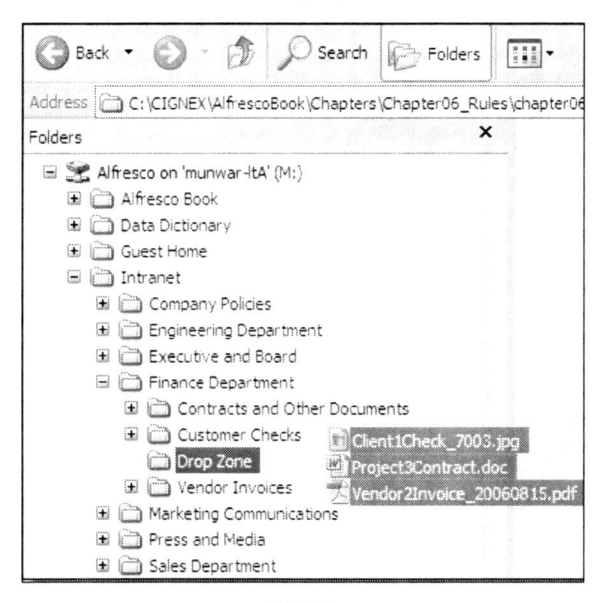

You will notice that the file containing 'Check' has been moved to the **Customer Checks** space, the file containing 'Invoice' has been moved to the **Vendor Invoices** space, and the third file has been moved to the **Contracts and Other Documents** space, automatically.

Run rules in the background

Typically, business rules run in real time. Consider having a business rule that transforms 25 MB (megabytes) of Microsoft Word document to PDF. Consider that rule being applied to hundreds of such files. If you upload a big Microsoft Word document in the Web Client, then you might have to wait for a while before the business rule is completely executed. Similarly, think about having a business rule that sends email notifications to hundreds of people. All of these rules might take a significant amount of time, and the user has to wait for the tasks to complete. Alfresco supports running these rules in the background, so that the user can proceed with other tasks, while the rules are being executed in parallel, in the background.

Refer to the earlier screenshot (under the section describing **Step Three**), where the rule has been selected to run in the background. If this option is selected, then the rule will execute in the background, which means that the results may not appear immediately.

Dynamically add properties to a document

In the previous chapter, you have edited the properties of each document. Those properties are the default properties for every document. There may be situations where you need additional properties for all of the documents in a particular space. You can change the Alfresco content model to assign additional properties to a document. But the issue with this approach is that all of the documents in the repository will inherit these properties, causing unnecessary overhead on the storage.

You can define a business rule on a space to assign additional properties, dynamically, to all or a certain set of documents. Consider the example provided in the previous section, where the **Finance Department** space has various sub-spaces. Let us say that you need to track the effective date and expiration date for all of the documents in these sub-spaces. There is a built-in aspect called **Effectivity**, which adds two properties to a document, namely `effective date` and `expiration date`.

An **Aspect** in Alfresco represents a collection of properties, and also defines the behavior. Out of the box, Alfresco provides a set of Aspects that are ready to be used. Apart from these, you can also define your own aspects as per your business requirements. More details about changing the data model and defining custom aspects are provided in Chapter 7.

Carry the following steps to add the **Effectivity** aspect to all of the documents in the **Finance Department** space.

1. Make sure that you are in the **Company Home > Intranet > Finance Department** space.
2. In the **Finance Department** space, click on **More Actions > Manage Content Rules**.
3. Click on the **Create Rule** link, and you will see the **Create Rules Wizard**.
4. In the **Step One** window, from the **Select Condition** drop-down list, select **All Items**, and then click on the **Add to List** button. Then click on the **Next** button.
5. In the **Step Two** window, from the **Select Actions** drop-down list, select **Add aspect to item**, and click on the **Set Values and Add** button. Select the **Effectivity** aspect, and then click **OK**. Then click on the **Next** button.
6. In the **Step Three** window, select **Inbound Type** and provide an appropriate **Title** and **Description** for this rule. Select the **Apply rule to sub-spaces** checkbox to apply this rule to all of the documents within the sub-spaces as well. Now, this rule will be applicable to all of the sub-spaces, including **Customer Checks**, **Vendor Invoices**, and **Contracts and Other Documents.**
7. **Finish** the Rule.

Test this business rule by adding a document to the **Contracts and Other Documents** sub-space of the **Finance Department** space. You will notice that two additional properties have been dynamically added to the document, as shown in the following screenshot:

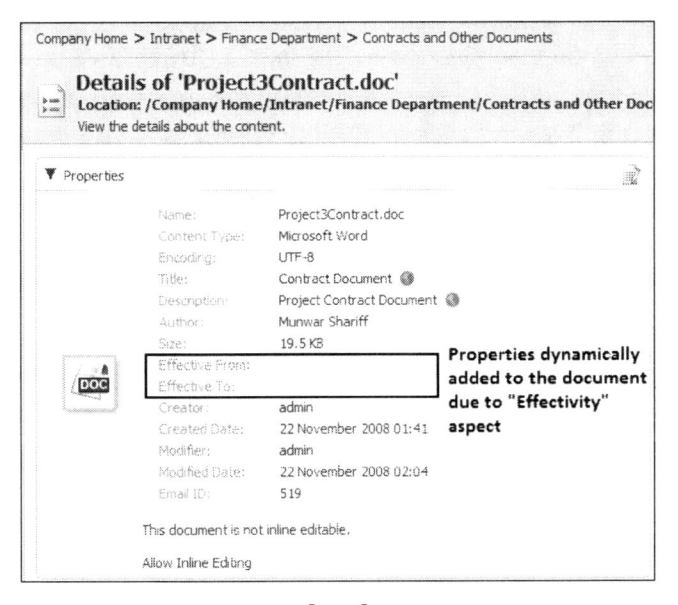

Automatic versioning of documents

In Alfresco, version control is disabled by default. In the previous chapter you enabled versioning for each individual document. It is a tedious job to enable versioning for each document if you have thousands of documents.

You can customize the Alfresco content model to enable versioning for every document. But this approach might be inefficient if you do not want to enable versioning for all of the documents. Consider the example provided in the previous section, where the **Finance Department** space has four spaces, namely **Drop Zone**, **Customer Checks**, **Vendor Invoices** and **Contracts and Other Documents**. **Drop Zone** is a temporary space; hence document versioning is not required. The **Customer Checks** space contains the scanned images of checks and versioning does not make sense, as you need to have only one version of the scanned checks. This is the same with the **Vendor Invoices** space as well. The documents in **Contracts and Other Documents** space do require versioning support. Hence, it makes sense to enable versioning only for the documents in **Contracts and Other Documents** space.

Carry the following steps to enable versioning for all the documents in the **Contracts and Other Documents** space.

1. Make sure that you are in the **Company Home > Intranet > Finance Department > Contracts and Other documents** space.

2. In the **Contracts and Other documents** space, click on **More Actions > Manage Content Rules**.

3. Click on the **Create Rule** link, and you will see the **Create Rules Wizard**.

4. In the **Step One window**, from the **Select Condition** drop-down list, select **All Items** and click on the **Add to List** button. Then, click on the **Next** button.

5. In the **Step Two window**, from the **Select Actions** drop-down list, select **Add aspect to item** and click on the **Set Values and Add** button. Select the **Versionable** aspect and click **OK**. Then, click on the **Next** button.

6. In the **Step Three window**, select **Inbound Type** and provide an appropriate **Title** and **Description** for this rule. Select the **Apply rule to sub-spaces** checkbox to enable versioning for all of the documents within the sub-spaces as well.

7. **Finish** the Rule.

Now, versioning is enabled automatically for all of the documents in this space. Test this business rule by adding a document to this space and then verifying that the document now has a version history.

Send notifications to specific people

Email notification is a powerful feature where specified people can be notified immediately on certain events in the content management system. You can notify people when documents are added to specific spaces or when changes are made to certain documents.

Let us say that in your organization, the Sales Group is responsible for following up on contracts with the customers. Follow the steps below to send email notifications to all of the people in the Sales Group, when a document in the **Contracts and Other Documents** space is updated.

- Make sure that you are in the **Company Home > Intranet > Finance Department > Contracts and Other documents** space.
- In the **Contracts and Other Documents** space, click on **More Actions > Manage Content Rules**.
- Click on the **Create Rule** link and you will see the **Create Rules Wizard**.
- In the **Step One** window, from the **Select Condition** drop-down list, select **All Items,** and then click on the **Add to List** button. Then click on the **Next** button.
- In the **Step Two** window, from the **Select Actions** drop-down list, select **Send an email to specified users,** and then click on the **Set Values and Add** button.

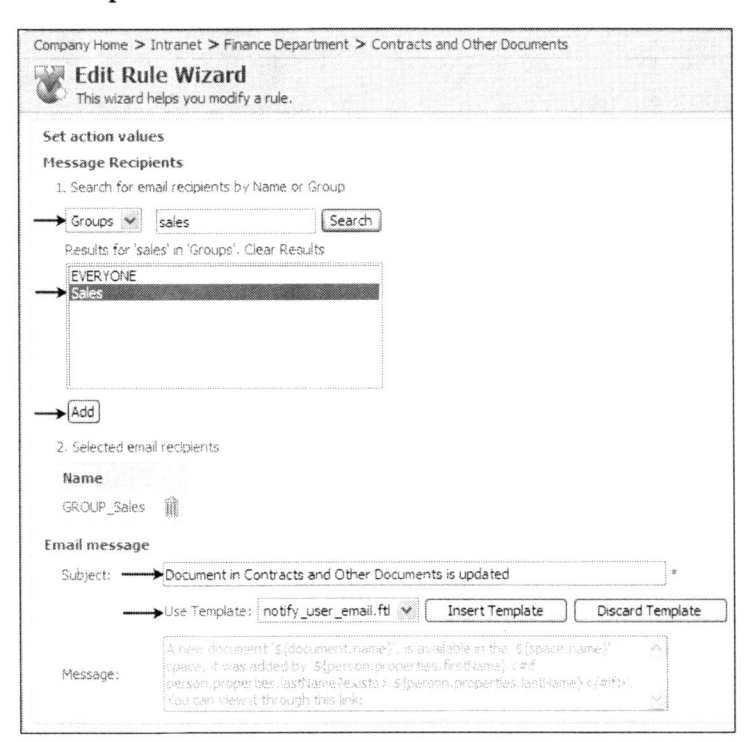

Implementing Business Rules

You will notice a **Set action values** window, as shown in the screenshot. Select the **Sales Group** as the email recipients. Use the built-in template called **notify_user_email.ftl** and click on the **Insert Template** button. Provide an appropriate subject for the email.

- In the **Step Three** window, select the **Update Type**, to send notification upon update of every document.
- **Finish** the Rule.

Test this business rule by updating an existing document in this space. If your email server is configured correctly, then your sales people will receive email notifications, with information about the document that has been updated. Setting up your email server is explained in Chapter 3 of this book.

Chaining all of the business rules

You can have as many business rules as required on a specific space. In a space, all of the rules defined locally in that space, as well as all of the rules inherited from the parent spaces, will be applied. For example, the **Contracts and Other Documents** space contains two local rules and one inherited rule (from its parent **Financial Department** space), as shown in the following screenshot.

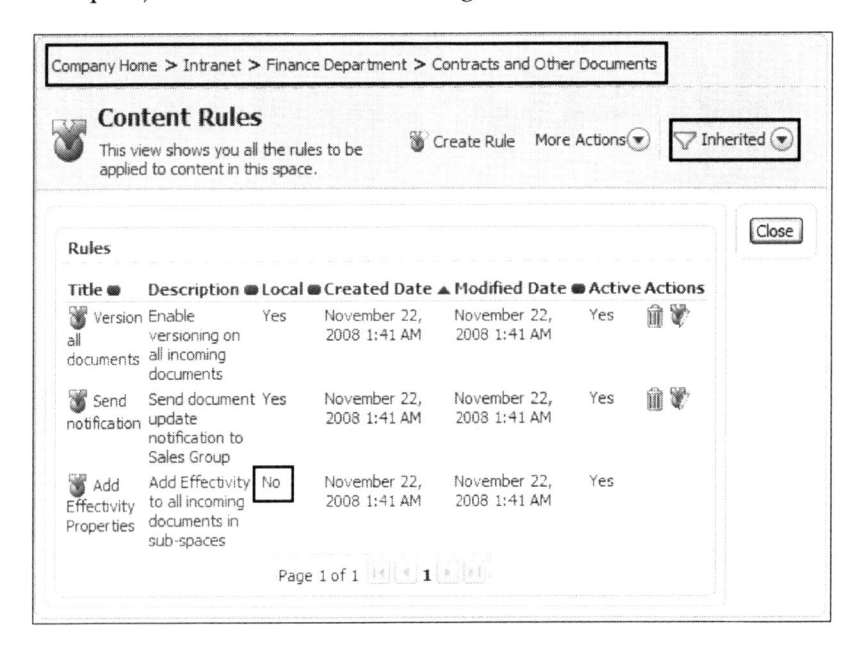

When a document is added to the **Contracts and Other Documents** space, it is automatically versioned due to the **Version all documents** local rule, and two additional properties are added to the document due to the **Effectivity to all documents** inherited (from its parent space) rule. When the document is updated, then the **Send notifications to Sales Group** local rule is executed.

Therefore, you can define business rules on spaces and sub-spaces and chain them together in a sequence to solve your business problem. For example, consider the following sequence of operations, when a document titled `ProjectXYZ_Contract.doc` is dropped in the **Company Home > Intranet > Finance Department > Drop Zone** space.

- Due to the business rules defined in the **Drop Zone** space, the document `ProjectXYZ_Contract.doc` is automatically moved to the **Finance Department > Contracts and Other Documents** space.
- Due to the **Effectivity** rule defined in the parent **Finance Department** space, two properties (Effective From and Effective To) are added to the `ProjectXYZ_Contract.doc` document.
- Due to the **Versioning** aspect rule defined in the space, the document `ProjectXYZ_Contract.doc` is automatically versioned.

However, there are certain things that you need to remember when applying multiple rules on a space.

- The **Inbound** rule will not be applied to documents that are already present in that space, prior to creating the rule. The **Inbound** rule will be applied only to documents that are added after the rule is created.
- If a space has more than one rule, all of the rules will be executed in a sequence.
- The rules defined in the parent spaces (with the **Apply rule to sub-spaces** option selected) will also be executed in the current space.
- A document can be uploaded to a space in different ways, by using Web Client or FTP or WebDAV or CIFS. The **Inbound** rule in a space will be triggered when a document is uploaded to the space, no matter how it is uploaded.

Built-in business rules

You can leverage the built-in business rules by applying them on appropriate spaces. You have already used some of them in the previous sections. This section will provide you with complete information about built-in business rules and the Alfresco rules wizard.

How these business rules work

Alfresco's underlying framework supports the latest technology, which is called **Aspect-Oriented Programming**. This is useful for changing the behavior of the server dynamically, without making changes to the code. Business rules leverage this technology so that you can define them on any space in Alfresco, and change the behavior of the system.

The Alfresco server follows a process to execute business rules.

- Whenever a document is added to the space (Inbound) or removed from a space (Outbound) or updated within a space (Update), the Alfresco server checks whether that space or its parent spaces have any business rules to execute, based on the triggering event type (Inbound, Outbound, or Update). The server checks to see if the business rule condition is satisfied. For example, the business rule can be applied to the documents that have certain patterns in the document names.
- Then the server executes the action defined in the business rule.

The Alfresco Business **Rule Wizard** contains a sequence of screens (as Steps) to capture the following:

- The condition under which to apply the rule
- The action to be performed as a result
- The type of event that triggers the action
- The summary of the business rule to commit

The screens and the built-in features are described in this section.

Checking the conditions

The first step in the Rule Wizard is to select the content items to which the rule should be applied. The following can be checked against the content item:

- Does it have a particular name pattern?
- Is it in a particular category?
- Is it of a specific type or format?
- Does it have a particular aspect?
- Does a property have a specific text or date or integer value?

You can define any number of conditions to select the content items. A content item must meet all the conditions in order to be selected.

You can also select a **Composite Condition,** where you can specify a number of conditions that can be combined by a logical **OR**. This means that a content item must meet at least one of the conditions in order to be selected.

The following screenshot illustrates a **Composite Condition** where a content item will be selected if any of the conditions specified in the summary section are true.

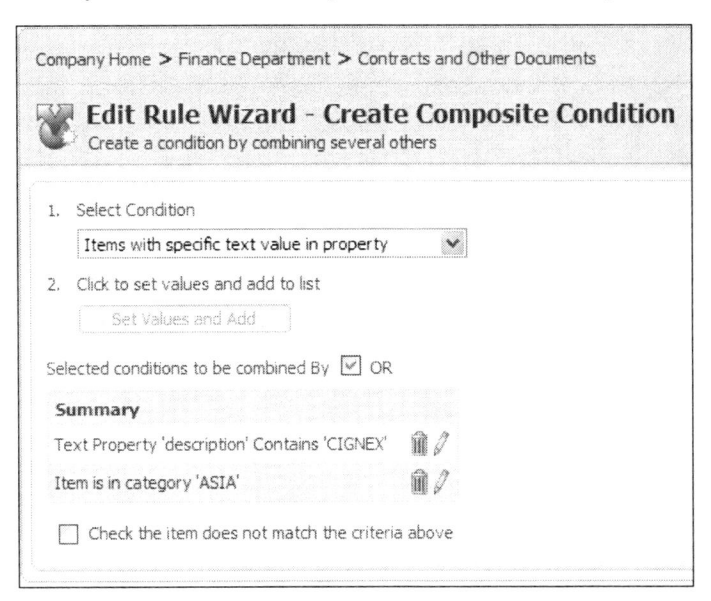

What are the actions that are executed?

The second step in the Rule Wizard is to define the list of actions to be executed as a result. The following is a list of built-in actions that can be selected.

- **Add aspect to item**: Add additional properties and behavior to document
- **Add simple workflow**: Add an approve or reject workflow
- **Check in content**: Check in the document
- **Check out content**: Check out the document to a space
- **Copy item to a specific space**: Copy the document to a space
- **Execute a script**: Execute JavaScript code as an action
- **Extract common metadata fields from content**: Extract document meta data
- **Import Alfresco content package**: Import as a content package
- **Link item to category**: Link the document to a specific existing category
- **Move item to a specific space**: Cut the document from the current space and move it to specified space

Implementing Business Rules

- **Remove an aspect from an item**: Remove a property or set of properties from the document
- **Send an email to specific users**: Send email notifications to specific users or groups of users
- **Specialize the type of an item**: Define the content type for the document
- **Transform and copy content to a specific space**: Transform content, such as DOC to PDF, and move the resultant file to the specified space
- **Transform and copy image to a specific space**: Transform and resize an image, such as from JPG to PNG format, and move the resultant image to the specified space

When you select the **Add aspect to item** action, you will have a list of built-in aspects to choose from, as shown in the following screenshot:

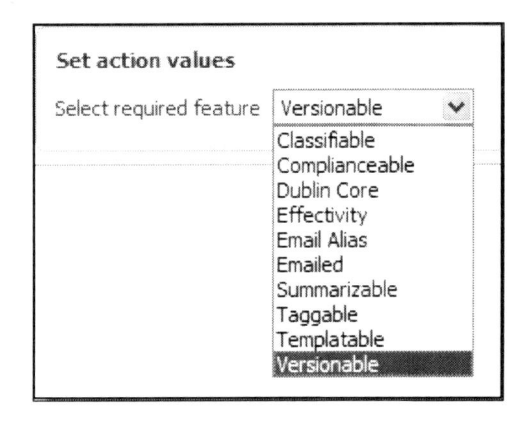

```
Set action values
Select required feature  Versionable
                         Classifiable
                         Complianceable
                         Dublin Core
                         Effectivity
                         Email Alias
                         Emailed
                         Summarizable
                         Taggable
                         Templatable
                         Versionable
```

Each aspect has a different meaning. These are as follows:

- **Classifiable**: Enable Categorization so that categories can be linked to the document.
- **Complianceable**: Add a compliance property called **Remove after** to the document.
- **Dublin Core**: Add Dublin core metadata to the document. Dublin core metadata includes properties such as **Publisher**, **Contributor**, **Subject**, and **Rights**.
- **Effectivity**: Add **Effectivity** properties called **Effective From** and **Effective To** to the document.
- **Email Alias**: Add a property called **Email Alias** to the document or space.
- **Emailed**: Add a set of properties called **Email Data** to the document. This is useful for capturing the email information, if the document is an attachment to an email.

- **Localizable**: Add a property called **Locale** to the document.
- **Summarizable**: Add a property called **Summary** to the document.
- **Taggable**: Add a dynamic, taggable property to the document.
- **Templatable**: Enable the template view.
- **Translatable**: Add a property called **Translations** to the document.
- **Versionable**: Enable versioning.

You can select one or more aspects to be applied as actions on the same document. For example, a document can have an **Effectivity** aspect as well as a **Taggable** aspect, as shown in the following screenshot:

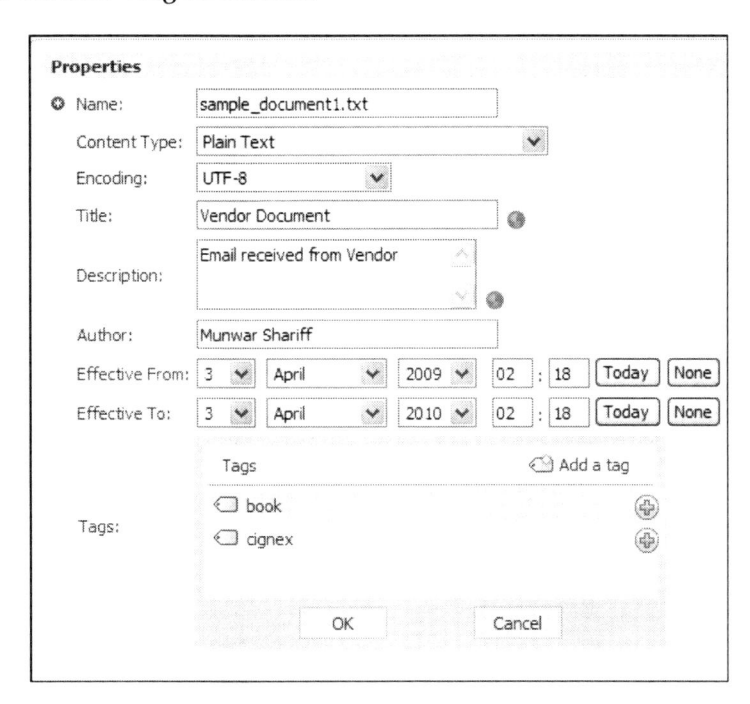

When are these rules triggered?

The third step in the Rule Wizard is to define the triggering event types. The rules are triggered by something happening, as specified by the **Type** field as follows.

- **Inbound**: Content arriving into a space, either new, copied or moved
- **Outbound**: Content leaving a space, either deleted or moved
- **Update**: Content updated, either uploaded or saved

Implementing Business Rules

Applying actions to individual content

In any business, there will always be exceptions, and there will be situations where you need to apply certain business rules to a specific document only. You can execute an action on a specific document directly without defining business rules on the space. This can be useful if you want to execute certain actions on an ad hoc basis for specific documents.

The actions for content are invoked from the **View Details** page of a content item by clicking on the **Run Action** link in the **Actions** box. You are allowed to choose from the range of actions. You can also aggregate actions into a sequence that is applied in one go.

Removing an aspect from a content

You have applied a **Versionable** aspect to all of the incoming documents in the **Finance Department > Contracts and Other Documents** space. Consider a scenario where you would not want a specific document to be versioned, but do want all of the other documents to be versioned. The following are the steps for removing a **Versionable** aspect from a specific document.

Select the document in the **Finance Department > Contracts and Other Documents** space, and then go to the **View Details** page.

1. From the **Actions** box, click on the **Run Action** link, as shown in the following screenshot:

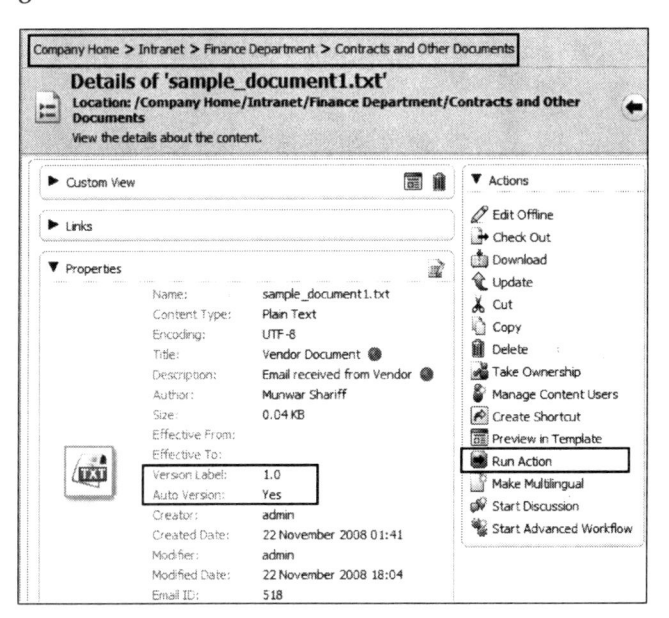

2. The **Run Action Wizard** window is displayed. From the **Select Action** drop-down list, choose the **Remove an aspect from an item** action.
3. Click on the **Set Values and Add** button.
4. From the **Set action values** window, choose the **Versionable** aspect, and then click **OK**.
5. Once you complete executing the action, you will notice that the properties related to versioning have been removed, and the document no longer maintains versions.

Similarly, for a specific document, you can use the **Run Action** option to execute actions such as sending email notifications, adding aspects, and executing scripts.

Handling content transformations

Content transformation simplifies and accelerates the web publishing process by transforming documents into web content. For example, you can leverage the built-in transformations engine to convert Microsoft Word documents into the HTML and PDF formats. Similarly, you can resize and transform images as required. The underlying technology supports a cross-platform environment, including Windows, Linux, and Solaris. You can benefit from the increased consistency across multiple channels including print, Web, wireless, and other content-centric applications.

Transforming a Word document to PDF

Consider the following scenario, as a staff member of the Marketing Department. You want to keep the source document in Microsoft Word format for editing, but you would like to create a PDF version of the document for publishing on the web site. Also, you would like to ensure that whenever you update the source document (in Microsoft Word format), the target document also gets updated (a PDF is generated).

This section uses the space that you have already created as a part of your intranet sample application in Chapter 5. As a part of the sample application, you will manage content in the **Intranet > Marketing Communications** space. Because you secured this space earlier, only the administrator (`admin`), and users belonging to the `Marketing` group (`Peter Marketing` and `Harish Marketing`), can add content to this space. You can log in as `Peter Marketing`, in order to manage content in this space.

Implementing Business Rules

The following are the steps for you to transform and copy a Microsoft Word document from the `Approved` space to a PDF document in the `Final` space.

1. Go to the **Company Home > Intranet > Marketing Communications > Switch to open source ECM > 04_Approved** space.
2. Click on **More Actions > Manage Content Rules**.
3. Click on the **Create Rule** link, and you will see the **Create Rules Wizard**.
4. In the **Step One** window, from the **Select Condition** drop-down list, select **Items with the specified mime type**, and then click on the **Set Values and Add** button.
5. From the **Set condition values** window (shown in the following screenshot), choose **Microsoft Word** as the required source format, and then click on **OK**. Then click on the **Next** button.

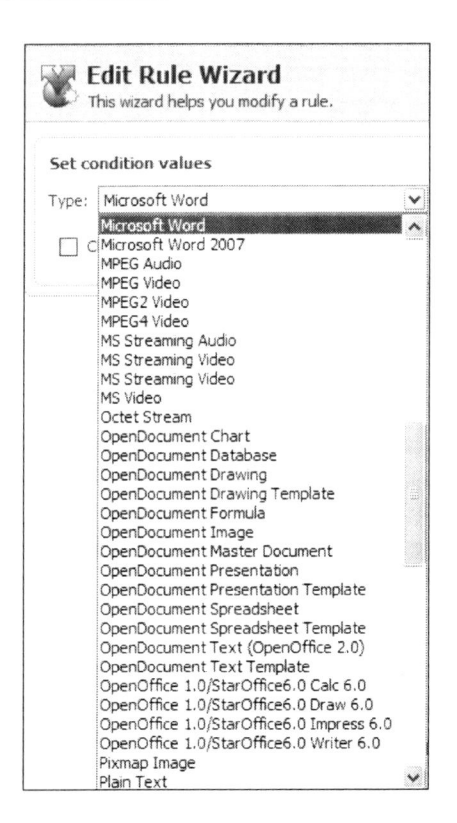

6. In the **Step Two** window, from the **Select Actions** drop-down list, select **Transform and copy content to a specific space**, and click on the **Set Values and Add** button.

7. From the **Set action values** window (shown in the following screenshot), choose **Adobe PDF Document** as the required format, and choose the **05_Final** space as the destination space in which to copy the transformed PDF document.

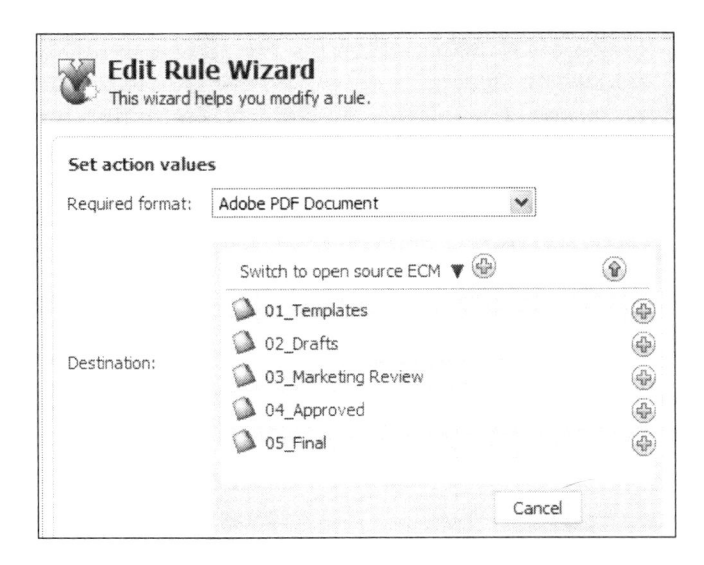

8. In the **Step Three** window, select **Inbound Type,** and provide an appropriate **Title** and **Description** for this rule. You can also select **Update Type**, if you would like to create the destination PDF document whenever you update the source Word document.

9. Select the **Run rule in background** checkbox.

10. **Finish** the Rule.

Now, transformation is enabled automatically for all of the Microsoft Word documents in this space. Whenever a Word document is uploaded or moved to the **04_Approved** space, a PDF version of the document will be created in the **05_Final** space.

Test this business rule by adding a Word document to this space and testing the PDF document in the **05_Final** space.

Resizing and transforming images

Consider a scenario where you would like to keep the source of an image in PNG format and publish a fixed size (say 200 x 200 pixels), JPEG version of the image on the web site.

Implementing Business Rules

PNG is an extensible file format for the lossless, portable, well-compressed storage of raster images. Indexed-color, grayscale, and true color images are all supported, plus an optional alpha channel for transparency.

Joint Photographic Experts Group (JPEG) is a compression method standardized by ISO, and JPEG images are widely used on the Web. The amount of compression can be adjusted to achieve the desired trade-off between file size and visual quality. Progressive JPEG is a means of reordering the information so that, after only a small part has been downloaded, a hazy view of the entire image is presented rather than a crisp view of just a small part. This is a part of the original JPEG specification, but was not implemented in Web browsers until rather later on (around the year 1996). It is now fairly widely supported.

The following are the steps for transforming and resizing an image from PNG format to JPEG format.

1. Go to the **Company Home > Intranet > Marketing Communications > Switch to open source ECM > 04_Approved** space.
2. Click on **More Actions > Manage Content Rules**.
3. Click on the **Create Rule** link, and you will see the **Create Rules Wizard**.
4. In the **Step One** window, from the **Select Condition** drop-down list, select **Items with the specified mime type**, and then click on the **Set Values and Add** button.
5. From the **Set condition values** window, choose **PNG Image** as the required source format, and then click **OK**. Then click on the **Next** button.
6. In the **Step Two** window, from the **Select Actions** drop-down list, select **Transform and copy image to a specific space**, and click on the **Set Values and Add** button.
7. From the **Set action values** window (shown in the following screenshot), choose **JPEG Image** as the required format. In the **Options** box, provide the resize options as **-resize 200x200**. Choose the **05_Final** space as the destination space to which to copy the transformed image.

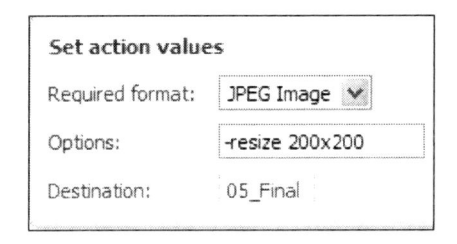

8. In the **Step Three** window, select the **Inbound Type,** and provide an appropriate **Title** and **Description** for this rule.
9. Select the **Run rule in background** checkbox.
10. **Finish** the Rule.

Test this business rule by adding a PNG image to the **04_Approved** space and testing the resized JPEG image in the **05_Final** space.

OpenDocument Format

OpenDocument Format (ODF) is an Open XML-based file format that is suitable for office applications. ODF is an open format for saving and exchanging office documents such as memos, reports, books, spreadsheets, databases, charts, and presentations.

The goal of ODF is to deliver an application-independent format that is vendor-neutral. This helps you to view, use, and update documents in the future when you no longer have software that you bought many years ago when you created the original documents. You will have the advantage of your content being shared across governments, and citizens, or multiple departments and organizations.

Alfresco's Virtual File System offers a simple shared drive interface to any office application. Microsoft Office and Open Office users alike can save or drag content into intelligent **Drop Zones**, where rules and actions transparently convert the incoming content into the ODF vendor-neutral format.

The ability to share documents across organizations without being tied to the technology, strategy, and pricing decisions of a single supplier is critical for businesses and government agencies today. The ability to access content without having a format and technology imposed on all of the users is equally important. Alfresco's ODF Virtual File System addresses these key issues.

Converting Microsoft Office documents to ODF

The example in this section uses the **Intranet > Marketing Communications** space to create and test the ODF Virtual File System. The following are the steps for converting a Microsoft Word document to an ODF office document.

1. Go to the **Company Home > Intranet > Marketing Communications** space.
2. Create a space called **Marketing Documents,** and create two sub-spaces under that space called **Inbox** and **ODF Virtual File System**.
3. Go to the **Company Home > Intranet > Marketing Communications > Marketing Documents > Inbox** space.

Implementing Business Rules

4. Click on **More Actions > Manage Content Rules**.
5. Click on the **Create Rule** link and you will see the **Create Rules Wizard**.
6. In the **Step One** window, from the **Select Condition** drop-down list, select **Items with the specified mime type** and click on the **Set Values and Add** button.
7. From the **Set condition values** window, choose **Microsoft Word** as the required source format and click **OK**. Then, click on the **Next** button.
8. In the **Step Two** window, from the **Select Actions** drop-down list, select **Transform and copy content to a specific space** and click on the **Set Values and Add** button.
9. From the **Set action values** window (shown in the following figure), choose **OpenDocument Text (OpenOffice 2.0)** as the required format and choose the **ODF Virtual File System** space as the destination space to copy the converted document.

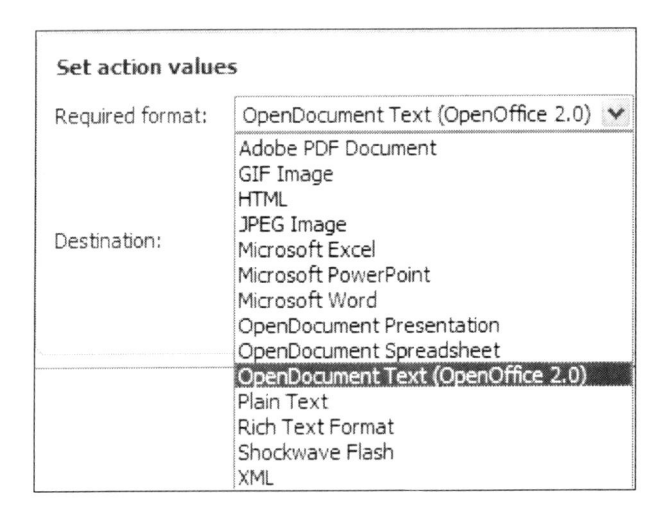

Set action values	
Required format:	OpenDocument Text (OpenOffice 2.0)
Destination:	Adobe PDF Document GIF Image HTML JPEG Image Microsoft Excel Microsoft PowerPoint Microsoft Word OpenDocument Presentation OpenDocument Spreadsheet **OpenDocument Text (OpenOffice 2.0)** Plain Text Rich Text Format Shockwave Flash XML

10. In the **Step Three** window, select **Inbound Type**, and then provide an appropriate **Title** and **Description** for this rule.
11. Select the **Run rule in background** checkbox
12. **Finish** the Rule.

Whenever a Microsoft Word document is uploaded or moved to the **Inbox** space, an ODF version of the document will be created in the **ODF Virtual File System** space.

Add a second business rule to the **Inbox** space that converts incoming Microsoft Excel documents to an **OpenDocument Spreadsheet** format, and copies it to the **ODF Virtual File System** space.

Add a third business rule to the **Inbox** space that converts the incoming Microsoft PowerPoint documents to an **OpenDocument Presentation** format, and copies it to the **ODF Virtual File System** space.

The business rules for the **Inbox** space, should be as shown in the following image.

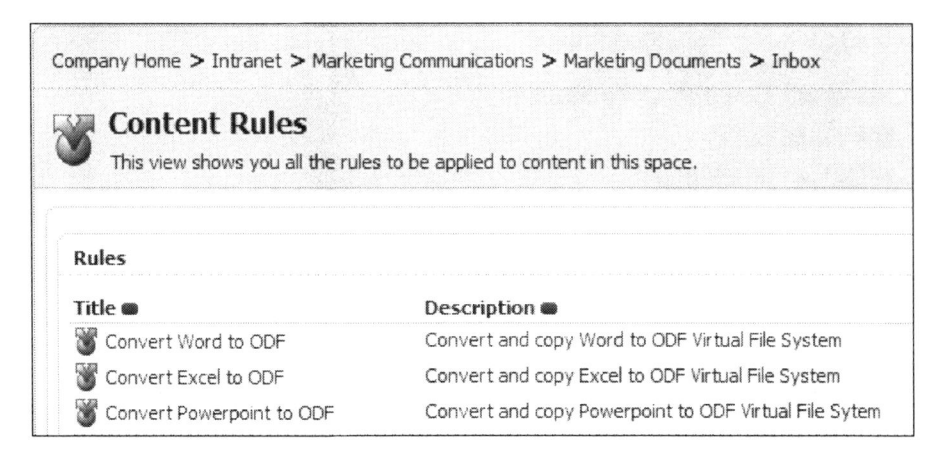

Test the business rules by copying Microsoft Word, Microsoft Excel and Microsoft PowerPoint files into the **Inbox** space. You should see the converted documents in the **ODF Virtual File System** space, as shown in the following screenshot:

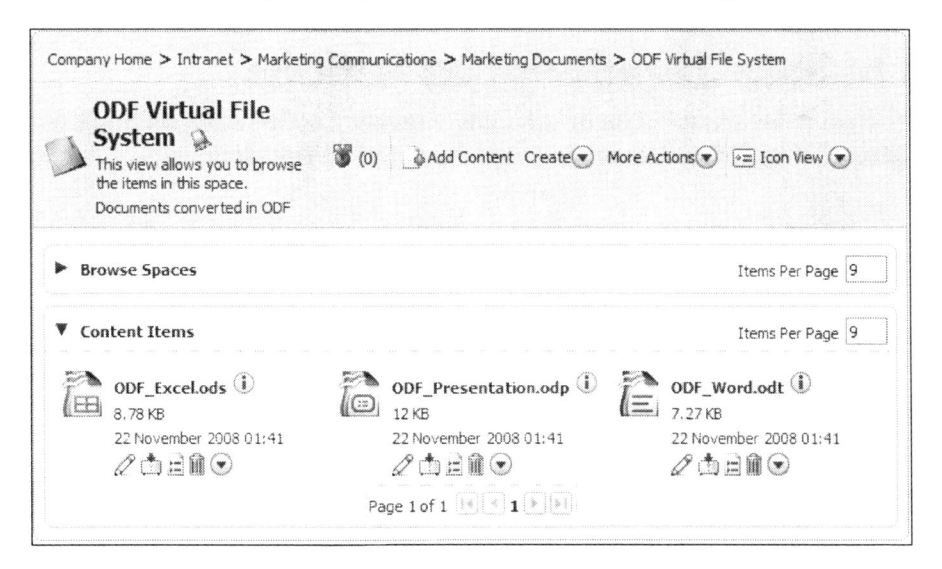

Built-in transformations

You can apply the built-in content transformations in a variety of ways. For example, your marketing department might want to keep source presentations in Microsoft PowerPoint format, and publish a Flash versions of the presentation on the web site.

Try out the following transformations:

- Microsoft PowerPoint to Flash
- HTML to PDF
- HTML to JPEG image
- PDF to Text Document

Try out the various document and image transformations that are available out of the box.

Executing JavaScript as business rules

The built-in rules might not be sufficient to address all of your business requirements. You can execute JavaScript code as an action in your business rule. If you need even more flexibility, you can write business rules in custom JavaScript files and execute them as actions.

Use built-in JavaScript as actions

You can execute JavaScript code by selecting **Execute a script** as an action in the **Rules Wizard**. The **Rules Wizard** displays the list of built-in JavaScript, such as:

- `backup.js`
- `append_copyright.js`
- `backup_and_log.js`

The sample `backup.js` script creates a backup of a file by copying it to a **backup** space. This might be required in some business situations. When using a document in your space, try running `backup.js` as an action and observe the results.

Extend business rules with custom JavaScript

The **Rules Wizard** lists all of the JavaScript files that are available in the **Company Home > Data Dictionary > Scripts** space. You can extend your business rules by writing your own JavaScript files and placing them in this space, so that they are visible to the **Rules Wizard**.

This is a very powerful feature. Consider the following scenario. Let us say your **Finance Department** has received a contract, with a dollar amount as one of the properties. You can trigger JavaScript code, that updates an external financial system with the information extracted from the document.

Consider another example, where your HR group maintains certain corporate forms and policies that are time-bound, that is, which expire after some period or date. The example in this section uses the **Company Policies** space to execute JavaScript code as a business rule. The JavaScript verifies the **Effective To** property of all of the content items in the space and moves the expired content to the **Archived** space.

Set up the Corporate Forms space

To set up a corporate space to implement the example mentioned above, go to the **Company Home > Intranet > Company Policies** space and create a space called **Corporate Forms**. Then create two sub-spaces under this space called **In Use** and **Archived**.

- The **In Use** space will be used to contain forms that are actively in use by the corporation.
- The **Archived** space will be used to contain forms that are no longer used.

Go to the **Company Home > Intranet > Company Policies > Corporate Forms** space, and create a business rule to add the **Effectivity** aspect to all of the incoming documents in the sub-spaces. Refer to the section titled **Dynamically add properties to a document** in this chapter, to set up the business rule for the **Effectivity** aspect.

Now go to the **Company Home > Intranet > Company Policies > Corporate Forms > In Use** space and add a few sample documents. For each document in the **In Use** space, you will notice that two additional properties, namely the **Effective From** and the **Effective To** properties, are present. Update the **Effective From** and the **Effective To** properties of the documents, while making sure that some documents are expired as of today, so that they are ready to be moved to the **Archived** space.

Implementing Business Rules

Refer to the following image for more details:

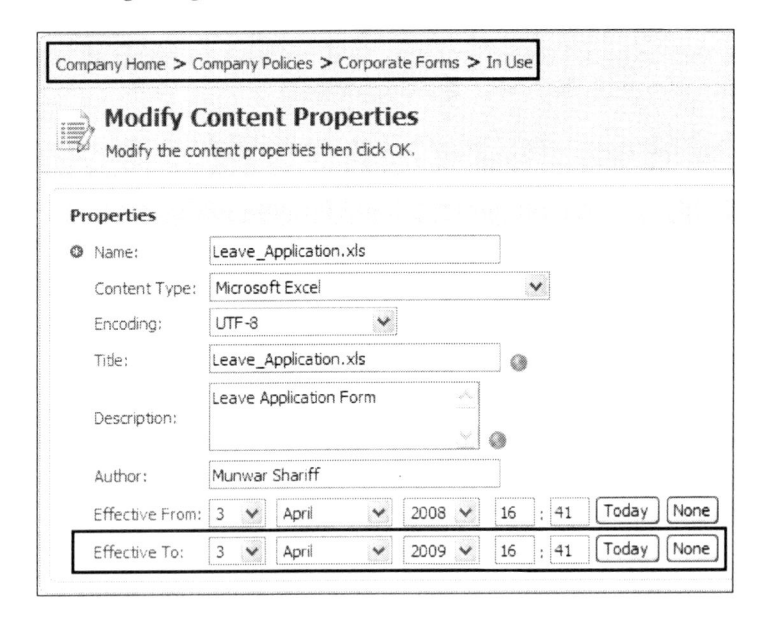

Create custom JavaScript

Create a JavaScript file called `chapter6_archive_expired_content.js`, with the following code. The script verifies the content in the **Intranet > Company Policies > Corporate Forms > In Use** space and moves the expired content—content where the **Effective To** property value is less than or equal to today's date—to the **Archived** space.

```
// -----------------------------------------------------------
// Name: chapter6_archive_expired_content.js
// Description: Moves expired content to Archived space
// -----------------------------------------------------------
var activeFolder   = companyhome.childByNamePath("Intranet/Company
Policies/Corporate Forms/In Use");
var archivedFolder = companyhome.childByNamePath("Intranet/Company
Policies/Corporate Forms/Archived");

if(activeFolder != null)
{
   var i=0;
   var today = new Date();

   activeChildren   = activeFolder.children;
   activeTotal      = activeChildren.length;
```

[208]

```
    for(i=0; i<activeTotal;i++)
    {
       child = activeChildren[i];
       if(child.properties["cm:to"] <= today)
       {
          child.move(archivedFolder);
       }
    }
}
```

Go to the **Company Home > Data Dictionary > Scripts** space, and then click on the **Add Content** link and upload `chapter6_archive_expired_content.js` file that you have created.

Execute custom JavaScript as an action

You can apply a business rule on a space in two different ways. One way is to create a business rule on the space. Another way is to execute the action manually as the **Run Action** command on the space. For this example, let us follow the latter approach.

- Go to the **Company Home > Intranet > Company Policies > Corporate Forms > In Use** space.
- Go to the **View Details** page of the **In Use** space by clicking on the **More Actions > View Details** menu.
- From the **Actions** box, click on the **Run Action** link.
- The **Run Action Wizard** window is displayed. From the **Select Action** drop-down list, choose the **Execute a script** action.
- Click on the **Set Values and Add** button.
- From the **Set action values** window choose the `chapter6_archive_expired_content.js` script and click **OK**.
- Once you have executed the rule, you will notice that all of the expired documents in the **In Use** space have been moved to the **Archived** space.

Note that the script uses the full path of spaces and hence can be executed from any space.

Try creating another custom JavaScript script that moves the effective content (content for which the **Effective To** property value is greater than today's date) from the **Archived** space to the **In Use** space. Test the custom script by applying it on the **Archived** space content. This is useful when you edit the form in the **Archived** space and make it effective again.

JavaScript API

The Alfresco JavaScript API allows script writers to develop JavaScript-compatible files that access, modify, and create the Alfresco repository Node objects. By using the API, script writers can find nodes (via XPath), walk node hierarchies, perform searches (including Lucene full-text searches), examine and modify the value of node properties, and modify the aspects applied to a node. In addition, scripts can create new files and folder objects and copy, move, and delete nodes. All of the usual Alfresco security and ACL permissions apply.

Because JavaScript is a standard language, there are many web resources, online tutorials, and books that can help developers in writing JavaScript files. It is suggested that potential script writers read up on JavaScript before starting to script the Alfresco repository.

The `example test script.js` JavaScript file in the **Company Home > Data Dictionary > Scripts** space lists examples of various Alfresco API Calls.

The following are some of the objects available to scripts in the root scope by default:

Named object	Description
`companyhome`	The Company Home node.
`userhome`	The current user's Home Space node.
`person`	The node representing the current user's Person object.
`space`	The current space node (if any). Note that for a script executing from a rule, the space object will be the space that the rule resides in.
`document`	The current document.
`script`	The node representing the script itself.
`search`	A host object providing access to Lucene and the Saved Search results.
`people`	A host object providing access to people and groups in Alfresco.
`session`	Session related information (session ticket for the authentication ticket).
`classification`	Read access to classifications and root categories.

> A detailed description of the Alfresco 3.0 JavaScript API is available at `http://wiki.alfresco.com/wiki/3.0_JavaScript_API`

Scheduled actions

Now you know how to define and execute actions manually. You can also execute these actions automatically, at a specified time. This will be helpful in use cases such as checking documents' statuses periodically, or for generating reports or executing business rules and notifying certain users.

Alfresco supports **Scheduled actions** so that you can configure certain actions to run at a certain time, automatically. A scheduled action is made up of three parts:

- A cron expression,
- A `query` template, and
- An `action` template.

At the times specified by the cron expression, the query template will generate a query to select a set of nodes (Spaces and Documents). For each of these nodes, the action template applies the action.

The query may be similar to:

- A document has aspect
- It was created in the last month
- It is due in the next month
- It is in a category

Example of archiving expired content

Refer to the sample custom JavaScript (`chapter6_archive_expired_content.js`) you created earlier, which moves the expired content to the **Archived** space.

We have considered a scenario where the HR group maintains certain corporate forms and policies that are time-bound, that is, they will expire after some period or date. In the earlier example, you manually ran the script. In this section, you are going to create a scheduled action that executes the custom JavaScript automatically, every fifteen minutes.

Implementing Business Rules

You need to create a schedule action XML configuration file in your extensions folder, in order to specify the scheduled time, and the custom JavaScript. You will find the scheduled action sample file, `scheduled-action-services-context.xml.sample`, in the location below.

JBoss: `<alfresco>/jboss/server/default/conf/alfresco/extension`

Tomcat: `<alfresco>/tomcat/shared/classes/alfresco/extension`

This file has many good sample scheduled actions for your reference.

Copy the scheduled action sample file as `scheduled-action-services-context.xml` in the same folder, and edit the file as follows:

```
<?xml version='1.0' encoding='UTF-8'?>
<!DOCTYPE beans PUBLIC '-//SPRING//DTD BEAN//EN'
    'http://www.springframework.org/dtd/spring-beans.dtd'>

<beans>

    <!--
    Define the model factory used to generate object models
    suitable for use with freemarker templates.
    -->
    <bean id="templateActionModelFactory" class=
"org.alfresco.repo.action.scheduled.
FreeMarkerWithLuceneExtensionsModelFactory">
        <property name="serviceRegistry">
            <ref bean="ServiceRegistry"/>
        </property>
    </bean>
    <!--
    Example Chapter 6 : Action Definition
    Action is to execute the "Company Home > Data Dictionary >
     Scripts > chapter6_archive_expired_content.js" script
    -->
    <bean id="chapter6_runScriptAction" class=
"org.alfresco.repo.action.scheduled.SimpleTemplateActionDefinition">
        <property name="actionName">
            <value>script</value>
        </property>
        <property name="parameterTemplates">
            <map>
                <entry>
                    <key>
                        <value>script-ref</value>
```

```
                </key>
                <value>${selectSingleNode('workspace://SpacesStore',
'lucene', 'PATH:"/app:company_home/app:dictionary/app:scripts/cm:
chapter6_archive_expired_content.js"' )}</value>
            </entry>
        </map>
    </property>
    <property name="templateActionModelFactory">
        <ref bean="templateActionModelFactory"/>
    </property>
    <property name="dictionaryService">
        <ref bean="DictionaryService"/>
    </property>
    <property name="actionService">
        <ref bean="ActionService"/>
    </property>
    <property name="templateService">
        <ref bean="TemplateService"/>
    </property>
</bean>

<!--
Example Chapter 6 : The query and scheduler definition
Query     - No specific query is used
Scheduler - Run the script for every 15 minutes
Action    - Call chapter6_runScriptAction defined above
-->

<bean id="chapter6_runScript" class=
"org.alfresco.repo.action.scheduled.
CronScheduledQueryBasedTemplateActionDefinition">
    <property name="transactionMode">
        <value>UNTIL_FIRST_FAILURE</value>
    </property>
    <property name="compensatingActionMode">
        <value>IGNORE</value>
    </property>
    <property name="searchService">
        <ref bean="SearchService"/>
    </property>
    <property name="templateService">
        <ref bean="TemplateService"/>
    </property>
    <property name="queryLanguage">
        <value>lucene</value>
    </property>
```

```xml
            <property name="stores">
                <list>
                    <value>workspace://SpacesStore</value>
                </list>
            </property>
            <property name="queryTemplate">
                <value>PATH:"/app:company_home"</value>
            </property>
            <property name="cronExpression">
                <value>0 0/15 * * * ?</value>
            </property>
            <property name="jobName">
                <value>jobD</value>
            </property>
            <property name="jobGroup">
                <value>jobGroup</value>
            </property>
            <property name="triggerName">
                <value>triggerD</value>
            </property>
            <property name="triggerGroup">
                <value>triggerGroup</value>
            </property>
            <property name="scheduler">
                <ref bean="schedulerFactory"/>
            </property>
            <property name="actionService">
                <ref bean="ActionService"/>
            </property>
            <property name="templateActionModelFactory">
                <ref bean="templateActionModelFactory"/>
            </property>
            <property name="templateActionDefinition">
              <ref bean="chapter6_runScriptAction"/>
              <!-- This is name of the action (bean) that gets run -->
            </property>
            <property name="transactionService">
                <ref bean="TransactionService"/>
            </property>
            <property name="runAsUser">
                <value>System</value>
            </property>
    </bean>
</beans>
```

Restart the Alfresco server to ensure that the configuration changes are effective. Now go to the **Company Home > Intranet > Marketing Communications > Website Documents > Staging** space, and add few sample documents. For each document in the **Staging** space, update the **Effective From** date property in such a way that these documents will be moved to the **Production** space at the specified time. Note that the custom JavaScript executes every fifteen minutes to move the effective documents to the **Production** space.

XML configuration file for scheduled actions

The `scheduled-action-services-context.xml` file has two blocks of XML configuration.

The first block, which starts with `<bean id="chapter6_runScriptAction"`, defines the action. This is where you specified the custom JavaScript to be executed. The important things to consider are as follows:

- `actionName`: The name of the action (the bean name for the implementation).
- `parameterTemplates`: A map of names and value templates. These are action specific.

The second block, which starts with `<bean id="chapter6_runScript"`, contains the query and scheduler definitions. This is where you specify the time interval to execute custom JavaScript every 15 minutes. The important things to consider are as follows:

- `transactionMode`: The transaction mode to be used
    - `ISOLATED_TRANSACTIONS`: For each node, the action is run as an isolated transaction. Failures are logged.
    - `UNTIL_FIRST_FAILURE`: For each node, the action is run as an isolated transaction. The first failure stops execution.
    - `ONE_TRANSACTION`: The actions for all of the nodes are run in one transaction. One failure will roll back all executed transactions.
- `queryLanguage`: The query language to be used.
- `stores`: A list of stores to query (currently only one store is supported).
- `queryTemplate`: The template string used to build the query.
- `cronExpression`: The cron expression that defines when the query runs.
- `jobName`: The name of the scheduled job.
- `jobGroup`: The group for the scheduled job.
- `triggerName`: The name of the trigger.

Implementing Business Rules

- `triggerGroup`: The group for the trigger.
- `runAsUser`: The user under whose identity the action will run.
- `templateActionDefinition`: The bean that defines the action.

The cron expression

A cron expression consists of six or seven text fields that are separated by white space.

Field Name	Position	Mandatory	Allowed Values	Special Characters
Seconds	1	Yes	0-59	, - * /
Minutes	2	Yes	0-59	, - * /
Hours	3	Yes	0-23	, - * /
Day of Month	4	Yes	1-31	, - * ? / L W
Month	5	Yes	1-12 or JAN-DEC	, - * /
Day of Week	6	Yes	1-7 or SUN-SAT	, - * ? / L #
Year	7	No	empty, 1970-2099	, - * /

An explanation of the special characters is provided in the following table:

*	All values.
?	No specific value.
-	This is used to specify a range. 1-5 in the day of the week field would mean, "on days 1, 2, 3, 4 and 5". 0-11 in the hour's field would mean, "each hour in the morning".
,	A list of values. In the minutes field, 0,15,30,45 would mean "when the minute is 0, 15, 30 OR 45". In the day field, MON, TUES would mean "on Mondays and Tuesdays".
/	When used after a value, this specifies increments. In the minutes field, 0/15 is equivalent to 0,15,30,45; */15 is equivalent to */15; and 10/15 is equivalent to 10, 25, 40, 55. In the day of the month field 3/7 means "every seven days starting on the third of the month" which is; 3, 10, 17, 24, ...
L	Last.
W	The nearest week day.
LW	The last week day of the month.
#	The nth day of the week.

Here are a few examples for you to your reference:

Daily run at 23:59:00. That is, run the action a minute before midnight each day:

```
0 59 23 * * ?
```

Run every hour from 8 AM to 3 PM on working days:

```
0 0 8-15 ? * MON-FRI
```

Run every 15 minutes for the first 10 days of the month:

```
0 0/15 * 1-10 * ?
```

Summary

Rules make a space smart. Rules are very powerful, and you can use rules very creatively to address your business requirements. You can leverage the **Rules Wizard** to use the built-in rules, as well as define custom rules. Rules can be extended. You can have the rules as scheduled actions, and you can extend them using custom JavaScript files. The best practice is to document the business rules, as they could affect the entire site globally.

Extending the Alfresco Content Model

In the previous chapters, you were able to create content that had standard properties such as name, description, author, creation date, and timestamp. You were able to add aspects such as effectivity and Dublin core metadata to the content by using business rules. What if you need to have custom properties that are very specific to your business? What if you need to have custom content that handles the data and business rules in a way that suits your business needs? The Alfresco content model is highly configurable and easily extendable as per your business requirements. In this chapter, you will understand the process of customizing the content model. You will define your own custom properties and custom content type to extend the capabilities of your business application.

By the end of this chapter, you will have learned how to:

- Configure a custom content model
- Define and add a custom aspect (set of properties)
- Define and use your custom content models
- Define associated documents for your custom content types
- Define constraints for your custom properties
- Preview content using custom presentation templates
- Enable dynamic customization of models without requiring a restart of the Alfresco server

Custom configuration

The Alfresco repository provides support for the storage, management, and retrieval of content. This content may range from coarse-grained documents, to fine-grained snippets of information such as XML elements. The Alfresco repository supports a rich data dictionary, where the properties, associations, and constraints of content are present to describe the structure of such content.

The **Repository Data Dictionary** is, by default, pre-populated with definitions that describe common content constructs such as folders, files, and metadata schemes. However, the data dictionary is extensible—it allows the repository to manage new types of content, as each business application will have its own content requirements. This chapter explains the main concepts behind the data dictionary, and explains how to perform tasks such as defining new types of content and using them in an application.

The following table describes some of the key terms used.

Key Term	Description
Property	A meta-data element that describes the content. For example, **Author** is a property which specifies the person who authored the content.
Content	Binary file (a Microsoft Word or HTML file, or an image) along with a set of properties (meta-data).
Association	Relationship between content items.
Constraint	Constraints control the input property values. For example, you can specify the author's name to be not more than 40 characters.
Aspect	A collection of properties, that and also defines the behavior.
Content Type	Provides a structure for creating content. The structure includes the nature of the content, properties, aspects, constraints and associations

Configuration files for the default content model

The core Alfresco configuration files are present in the application `war` file, and are expanded once the server starts. This location, referred to as `<configRoot>`, varies depending on the environment that Alfresco runs in.

JBoss: `<JBOSS_HOME>/server/default/tmp/deploy/tmp*alfresco-exp.war/WEB-INF/classes`

Tomcat: `<TOMCAT_HOME>/webapps/alfresco/WEB-INF/classes`

A Content Model is a collection of related content types and aspects. The default configuration files for the content model maintained by Alfresco are contained in the `<configRoot>/alfresco/model` folder, as shown in the following screenshot:

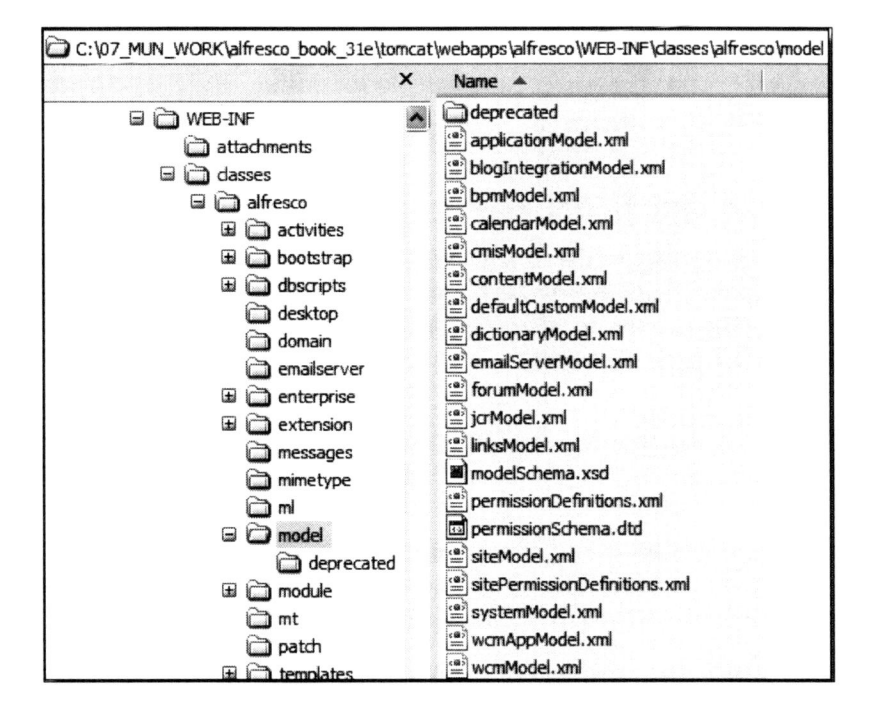

The Alfresco repository is also primed with several domain models, which that are described as follows:

- `contentModel.xml`: This model describes the **Content Domain Model**, such as folder, file, person, category, and dublin core
- `systemModel.xml`: This model describes **system-level Repository** concepts
- `applicationModel.xml`: This model describes the **Alfresco Application Model**
- `dictionaryModel.xml`: This model describes the **Dictionary Meta-model**

Several other models that support the implementation of services are defined by the repository, such as user management, versioning, actions, advanced workflow, collaboration, calendar events, and rules. You can examine the other configuration files in the `<configRoot>/alfresco` folder.

> You should not modify the default content models located in the `<configRoot>/alfresco` folder. This will break the ability of Alfresco to perform automatic upgrades.

The next section explains the correct mechanism for adding custom content models to Alfresco.

Configuration files for custom content model

Alfresco is built on **Spring**, which is a leading platform for building and running enterprise Java applications. A **bean** is simply an object that is instantiated and managed by a Spring container. Alfresco configuration and customization concepts are based on the Spring framework.

> For more information about Spring, refer to the web site http://www.springsource.org/.

You can override or extend the Alfresco content model, by placing the custom configuration files in a folder. This location, referred to as extension, varies depending on the environment that Alfresco runs in.

JBoss: `<JBOSS_HOME>/server/default/conf/alfresco/extension`

Tomcat: `<TOMCAT_HOME>/shared/classes/alfresco/extension`

When you install Alfresco, the sample custom-content files are copied to the extension folder, for your reference. You can also examine the sample custom-configuration files in the extension folder.

The steps to define a custom model in the extension folder are as follows:

1. Create a custom model Spring context file.
2. Create a custom model definition file.
3. Create a custom web client configuration file.

The custom model Spring context file instructs Spring on how to bootstrap or load the custom model definition file. The custom model definition file defines your custom content types, aspects, and associations. The custom web client configuration file contains information on how to to display these custom content types, aspects, and associations. The relationship between these files is shown in the following screenshot::

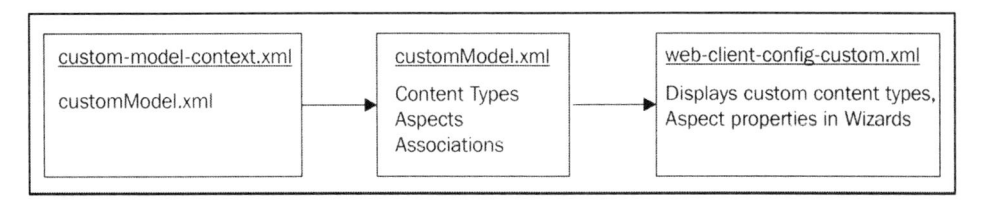

```
┌──────────────────────────┐     ┌──────────────────────────┐     ┌──────────────────────────────────┐
│ custom-model-context.xml │ ──▶ │ customModel.xml          │ ──▶ │ web-client-config-custom.xml     │
│ customModel.xml          │     │ Content Types            │     │ Displays custom content types,   │
│                          │     │ Aspects                  │     │ Aspect properties in Wizards     │
│                          │     │ Associations             │     │                                  │
└──────────────────────────┘     └──────────────────────────┘     └──────────────────────────────────┘
```

Custom model context file

The custom model context file defines the Spring bean that will be used to bootstrap the definition of your custom model. It lists one or more custom model files. When Spring starts up, it will instantiate this bean and will load your model file from disk.

Create a custom model context file and name the file as `<your-custom-model-name>-context.xml`, for example `intranetModel-context.xml`.

> It is very important for you to note that the Alfresco server recognizes context files as being files that end with `-context.xml`.

The following is the content of the `custom-model-context.xml.sample` file in the `extension` folder. Note that the custom model context file defines the `customModel.xml` file as the custom model file.

```xml
<?xml version='1.0' encoding='UTF-8'?>
<!DOCTYPE beans PUBLIC '-//SPRING//DTD BEAN//EN'
   http://www.springframework.org/dtd/spring-beans.dtd'>
<beans>
    <!-- Registration of new models -->
    <bean id="extension.dictionaryBootstrap"
        parent="dictionaryModelBootstrap"
        depends-on="dictionaryBootstrap">
      <property name="models">
          <list>
              <value>alfresco/extension/customModel.xml</value>
          </list>
      </property>
    </bean>
</beans>
```

Custom model file

The custom model file contains the definitions for the custom content types, aspects, and content associations.

A copy of `customModel.xml` file already exists in the `extension` folder. If you examine the `customModel.xml` file, you will notice a custom namespace for all of the variables, called `custom`. XML namespaces provides a method for avoiding element name conflicts. Therefore, every `custom` variable will have the prefix `custom` in this file, as follows:

```
<namespace uri="custom.model" prefix="custom"/>
```

Custom web client configuration file

A copy of the web client configuration file `web-client-config-custom.xml` already exists in the `extension` folder. This web client configuration file ensures that the custom content types and aspects are visible in the Alfresco Web Client application. In this file, you can also override the default web client configuration that is provided out of the box.

Hierarchy of configuration files

The hierarchy of configuration files is shown in the following screenshot::

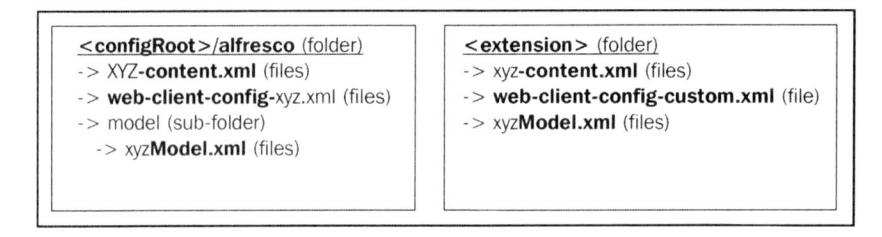

```
<configRoot>/alfresco (folder)        <extension> (folder)
-> XYZ-content.xml (files)            -> xyz-content.xml (files)
-> web-client-config-xyz.xml (files)  -> web-client-config-custom.xml (file)
-> model (sub-folder)                 -> xyzModel.xml (files)
   -> xyzModel.xml (files)
```

During startup, the Alfresco server reads the configuration files in the following order:

- Context files and then the model files in the `<configRoot>/alfresco` folder
- Context files and then the model files in the `<extension>` folder
- Web client configuration files in the `<configRoot>/alfresco` folder
- Web client configuration files in the `<extension>` folder

Custom aspect

Let us assume that your sales people would like to track all of their proposals that are related to a customer. They would like to search the documents and execute business rules, based on the customer details. They would like to capture the following customer details for all of the documents in the sales department space:

- Name of the customer
- Contact's name at the customer's place
- Contact person's phone number
- Project identification number, internally allocated
- Whether this is a new customer

You can extend the Alfresco content model to include the properties listed above as an aspect. You can then apply this aspect to be part of all of your documents in the sales department space.

The need for a custom aspect

The Alfresco content model is designed to be extensible. You can introduce custom properties to your objects in two different ways. The first is to create a custom aspect (in our example, called `Customer Details`) and dynamically attach it to the documents in a specific space. The custom aspect would define the required properties. The other way is to create a custom content type (again, called `Proposal Document`) and define all the required properties on the type itself. The process of creating custom content types is explained in detail in the next section of this chapter.

Choosing a custom aspect over a custom content type is up to you, based on your business requirements.

The following are the advantages of having custom aspect over custom content type:

- **Flexibility**: You will have more flexibility. A custom aspect will give you flexibility to add additional sets of properties to the documents in specific spaces. For example, you can define these additional properties for documents in **Sales Department > Proposals and Finance Department > Customer Checks** spaces.
- **Efficiency**: Because these properties are applied selectively to certain documents in certain spaces only, you will consume limited storage in the relational database for these properties.

- **Behaviors**: A custom aspect can introduce new behaviors for objects. Using Spring's aspect-oriented support, you can define new beans that intercept content-related events and handle them according to your exact needs. This is an advanced capability of aspects. Although this is not covered in this chapter, it is worthwhile to keep in mind when considering the pros and cons of aspects.

The following is the disadvantage of having custom aspect over custom content type:

- **Dependency**: You cannot define a dependency on other aspects. For example, if you want the effectivity aspect to always be associated with the customer details aspect, you need to make sure that you attach both of these aspects to the documents.

Steps for adding a custom aspect

The following process needs to be followed to add a custom aspect to the Alfresco content model:

- Define the custom properties and types of properties.
- Extend the Alfresco Content Model with the custom aspect.
- Configure the Web Client application for the custom aspect.
- Restart Alfresco to make sure that the new changes are effective.

Each one of these steps is explained in detail in the following sections.

Define a custom aspect

You need to define the name of the custom aspect and the properties. For each property, you need to define the type of the property. Some of the property types are listed in the following table. For a complete list of property types, please refer to the <configRoot>/Alfresco/model/dictionaryModel.xml file.

Property Data Type	Description
text	Any string or name
content	Binary document
int	Integer or number
long	Big integer
float	Number with decimal values, such as an nterest rate of 7.5
date	Year, month, and day

Property Data Type	Description
datetime	Timestamp
Boolean	true or false
category	Reference to a category within a classification
path	URL

You may consider calling your custom aspect `Customer Details`, with the following properties:

Property Name	Property Label	Property Type	Mandatory	Default Value
`CustomerName`	Customer Name	text	No	None
`CustomerContactName`	Customer Contact Name	text	No	None
`CustomerContactPhone`	Customer Contact Phone	text	No	None
`CustomerProjectID`	Customer Project ID	int	No	None
`NewCustomer`	New Customer	Boolean	No	True

Extend the content model with the custom aspect

Now that you have identified your custom aspect and the properties, the next step is to extend the Alfresco content model with the XML representation of your custom aspect.

Go to the `extension` folder and rename the `custom-model-context.xml.sample` file to `custom-model-context.xml`. Now examine the contents of the `custom-model-context.xml` file, which includes the name of the custom content model file—`customModel.xml`.

Open the `customModel.xml` file and add your custom aspect, as shown in the following code, before the last line in the file, which is `</model>`.

```
<aspects>
    <!-- Definition of new Content Aspect: Customer Details -->
    <aspect name="custom:CustomerDetails">
        <title>Customer Details</title>
        <properties>
            <property name="custom:CustomerName">
                <title>Customer Name</title>
```

Extending the Alfresco Content Model

```
            <type>d:text</type>
            <protected>false</protected>
            <mandatory>false</mandatory>
            <multiple>false</multiple>
        </property>
        <property name="custom:CustomerContactName">
            <title>Customer Contact Name</title>
            <type>d:text</type>
        </property>
        <property name="custom:CustomerContactPhone">
            <title>Customer Contact Phone</title>
            <type>d:text</type>
        </property>
        <property name="custom:CustomerProjectID">
            <title>Customer Project ID</title>
            <type>d:int</type>
        </property>
        <property name="custom:NewCustomer">
            <title>New Customer</title>
            <type>d:boolean</type>
            <default>true</default>
        </property>
      </properties>
    </aspect>
</aspects>
```

A property can have various elements as shown in the following table.

Property Element	Description
Property name	Unique Id of the property, along with the namespace.
Title	This element will act as a label to display a meaningful name for the property.
Type	Specifies the data type of the property, such as text, int or date
Protected	If this element is set is "true", then it becomes a "read-only" property in the Alfresco web client. The default value is "false", which means that users can edit the property in the web client.
Mandatory	If this element is set to "true", then a value has to be either set or entered by the user before saving the property. The default value is "false", which means the property is optional.
Multiple	If this element is set to "true", then the property can have multiple values set. The default value is "false".
Default	Provides a default value for the property.

Configure the web client for the custom aspect

The content model is extended with a custom aspect called `Customer Details`. You need to make sure that the web client program recognizes this new custom aspect and displays it in the web-based interface. In order to make this happen, you need to configure the web client file `web-client-config-custom.xml` in the `extension` folder.

Open the `web-client-config-custom.xml` file and add the following XML code before the last line, which is `</alfresco-config>`.

```xml
<!-- Lists the custom aspect in business rules Action wizard -->
<config evaluator="string-compare" condition="Action Wizards">
   <aspects>
      <aspect name="custom:CustomerDetails"/>
   </aspects>
</config>
```

This code ensures that the new aspect, called `Customer Details`, is listed in the business rules **Set action values** page, as shown in screenshot under the section Use *Custom Aspect as Business Rule*.

Open the `web-client-config-custom.xml` file and add the following XML code before the last line, which is `</alfresco-config>`.

```xml
<!-- Displays the properties in view details page -->
<config evaluator="aspect-name" condition="custom:CustomerDetails">
   <property-sheet>
      <separator name="sepCust1" display-label="Customer Details" component-generator="HeaderSeparatorGenerator" />
      <show-property name="custom:CustomerName"/>
      <show-property name="custom:CustomerContactName"/>
      <show-property name="custom:CustomerContactPhone"/>
      <show-property name="custom:CustomerProjectID"/>
      <show-property name="custom:NewCustomer"/>
   </property-sheet>
</config>
```

This code ensures that the properties added to the content due to the `CustomerDetails` aspect will be displayed in the content's view details page, as shown in the screenshot in the next section. The `separator` tag that is defined above is useful to group these properties, and to separate them from the other list of properties in the property sheet, by creating a bar with the label **Customer Details**.

Now, restart Alfresco to make sure that the changes are in effect.

Extending the Alfresco Content Model

Use custom aspect as a business rule

Now that the `Customer Details` aspect is available, you can use it to add to your documents as if this aspect was available to you out of the box.

You can define a business rule to dynamically include customer details for all of the documents in a space. Consider the example provided earlier, where the `Sales Department` group needs to maintain the customer details for all of their proposals. Follow the steps provided below to add the `Customer Details` aspect to all of the documents in the **Sales Department > Proposals** space.

- Go to the **Company Home > Intranet >Sales Department** space and create a sub-space for proposals, called **Proposals**.
- Ensure that you are in the **Company Home > Intranet >Sales Department > Proposals** space.
- In the **Proposals** space, click the **More Actions > Manage Content Rules**.
- Click on the **Create Rule** link, and you will see the **Create Rules Wizard**.
- In **Step One**, from the **Select Condition** drop-down list, select **All Items**, and then click on the **Add to List** button. Then click on the **Next** button.
- In **Step Two**, from the **Select Actions** drop-down list, select **Add aspect to item**, and then click on the **Set Values and Add** button.
- In the **Set action values** pane, select the **Customer Details** aspect, as shown in the following image, and then click on OK. Finally, click on the **Next** button.

[230]

- In **Step Three**, select the **Inbound** option from the **Type** drop-down list, and provide an appropriate name and description for this rule.
- Select the **Apply rule to sub spaces** option and then click on **Finish** to apply the rule.

Test this business rule by adding a document in the **Proposals** space. You will notice five additional properties have been dynamically added to the document. Add some meaningful customer data, and then click on the **OK** button.

Navigate to the document and click on the **View Details** icon to view the details page. You will notice that the properties have been added to the document because of the custom aspect are visible in the details page of the document, as shown in the following screenshot:

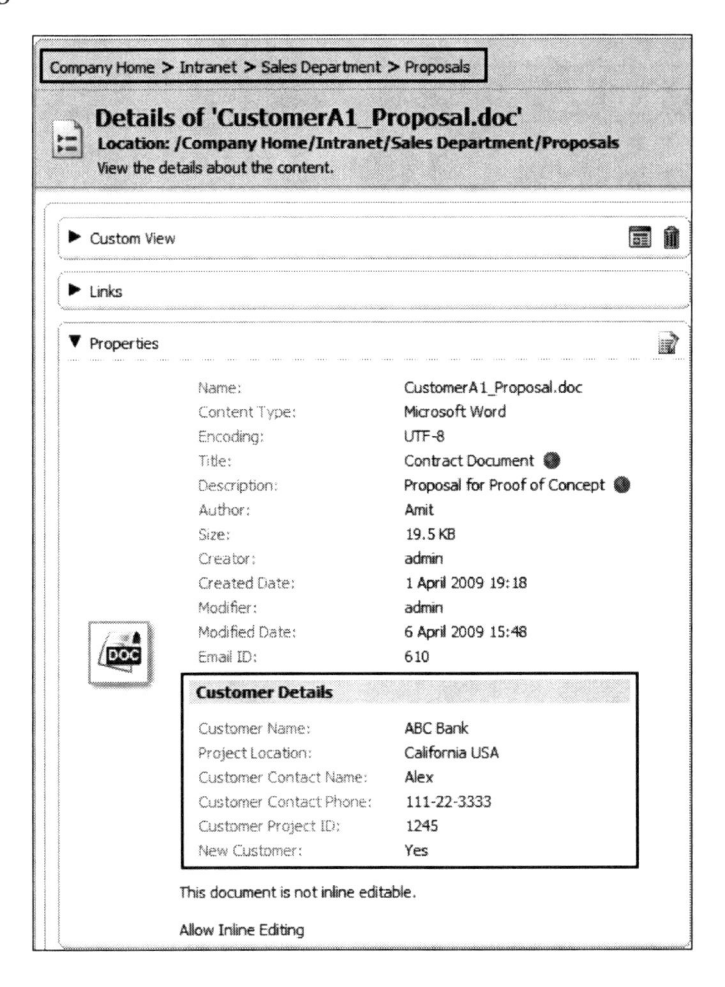

Similarly, create a business rule on the **Company Home > Intranet >Financial Department > Customer Checks** space to add customer details to all of the incoming checks, as shown in the following screenshot. Add an image file (scanned customer check) to this space, and notice that the check has additional properties, as defined by the customer details aspect.

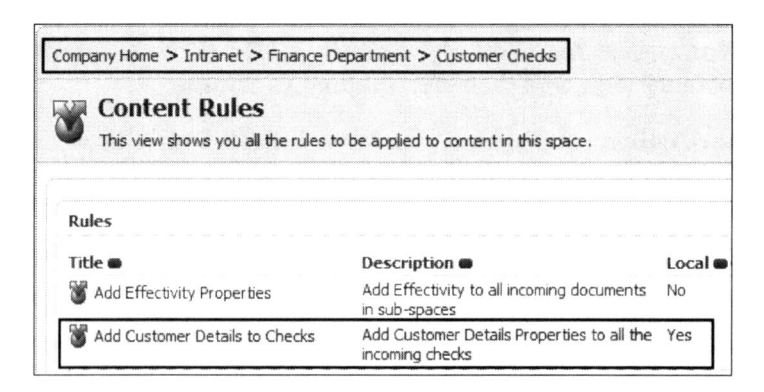

Constraints

A Constraint controls the input value of a property. Constraints can be used to validate input values, and to ensure the use of certain predefined values for the properties. Constraints are defined separately from content types and aspects, and are referenced within a property type definition.

Constraint types

Alfresco provides four types of constraints out of the box, as follows. Apart from these four, the custom constraints can be defined by using Java Programming Language.

- REGEX: ensures that a property value matches a defined regular expression pattern
- LIST: ensures that a property value is picked up from a list of predefined values
- MINMAX: ensures that the given property value falls within a defined numeric range
- LENGTH: ensures that the given property value falls within a defined character length range

REGEX

The following REGEX expression ensures that the property "filename" does not match the defined regular expression pattern. This constraint thus ensures that the file name value entered does not contain the specified special characters:

```
<constraint name="custom:filename" type="REGEX">
      <parameter name="expression">
            <value><![CDATA[[^\"\*\\\>\<\?\/\&\;]+]]></value>
      </parameter>
      <parameter name="requiresMatch">
            <value>false</value>
      </parameter>
</constraint>
```

LIST

The following LIST constraint restricts the property "officelocation" value to one of the predefined values given:

```
<constraint name="custom:officelocation" type="LIST">
      <parameter name="allowedValues">
            <list>
                  <value>California USA</value>
                  <value>New Jersey USA</value>
                  <value>London UK</value>
                  <value>Ahmedabad India</value>
                  <value>Singapore</value>
            </list>
      </parameter>
</constraint>
```

MINMAX

The following MINMAX constraint restricts the property "age" value to a value that is between the minimum and maximum values, as given below:

```
<constraint name="custom:age" type="MINMAX">
      <parameter name="minValue">
            <value>1</value>
      </parameter>
      <parameter name="maxValue">
            <value>100</value>
      </parameter>
</constraint>
```

LENGTH

The following LENGTH constraint restricts the property "password" value to a predefined character length (between 6 characters and 10 characters in length).

```
<constraint name="custom:password" type="LENGTH">
    <parameter name="minLength">
        <value>6</value>
    </parameter>
    <parameter name="maxLength">
        <value>10</value>
    </parameter>
</constraint>
```

Applying a constraint

To apply a constraint, it has to be referred from within a property definition.

Let us add few constraints to the existing Customer Details aspect that we created earlier in this chapter.

Go to the extension folder and open the customModel.xml file and add or change the lines that are highlighted (in the following code). In the following model, we add two constraints named custom:office_list, to provide a predefined list of office locations, and custom:name_length, to restrict the character length of a name. Apply the name_length constraint to the CustomerName property and the office_list constraint to a new property called Project Location.

```
<namespaces>
    <namespace uri="custom.model" prefix="custom"/>
</namespaces>

<constraints>
<constraint name="custom:office_list" type="LIST">
    <parameter name="allowedValues">
        <list>
            <value>California USA</value>
            <value>New Jersey USA</value>
            <value>London UK</value>
            <value>Ahmedabad India</value>
            <value>Singapore</value>
        </list>
    </parameter>
</constraint>

<constraint name="custom:name_length" type="LENGTH">
    <parameter name="minLength">
```

```xml
            <value>3</value>
        </parameter>
        <parameter name="maxLength">
            <value>20</value>
        </parameter>
</constraint>
</constraints>
<types>
   ---------------
</types>
<aspects>
    <!-- Definition of new Content Aspect: Customer Details -->
    <aspect name="custom:CustomerDetails">
        <title>Customer Details</title>
        <properties>
            <property name="custom:CustomerName">
                <title>Customer Name</title>
                <type>d:text</type>
                <protected>false</protected>
                <mandatory>false</mandatory>
                <multiple>false</multiple>
                <constraints>
                   <constraint ref="custom:name_length"/>
                </constraints>
            </property>
            <property name="custom:ProjectLocation">
                <title>Project Location</title>
                <type>d:text</type>
                <constraints>
                   <constraint ref="custom:office_list"/>
                </constraints>
            </property>
            <property name="custom:CustomerContactName">
                <title>Customer Contact Name</title>
                <type>d:text</type>
            </property>
            <property name="custom:CustomerContactPhone">
                <title>Customer Contact Phone</title>
                <type>d:text</type>
            </property>
            <property name="custom:CustomerProjectID">
                <title>Customer Project ID</title>
```

Extending the Alfresco Content Model

```xml
            <type>d:int</type>
        </property>
        <property name="custom:NewCustomer">
            <title>New Customer</title>
            <type>d:boolean</type>
            <default>true</default>
        </property>
    </properties>
  </aspect>
</aspects>
```

In the `<extension>/web-client-config-custom.xml` file, let us include the new property `ProjectLocation`, under the `CustomerDetails` aspect.

Restart Alfresco, to make sure that the changes are in effect. Now log in to the web client application to test the constraints that you added to the `CustomerDetails` properties.

Go to the **Company Home > Intranet >Sales Department > Proposals** space and view the details of one of the existing documents. Edit the properties and enter a value for the **Customer Name** that is more than twenty characters long, and then click the **OK** button. You will see the following message because of the `LENGTH` constraint applied on `CustomerName` property.

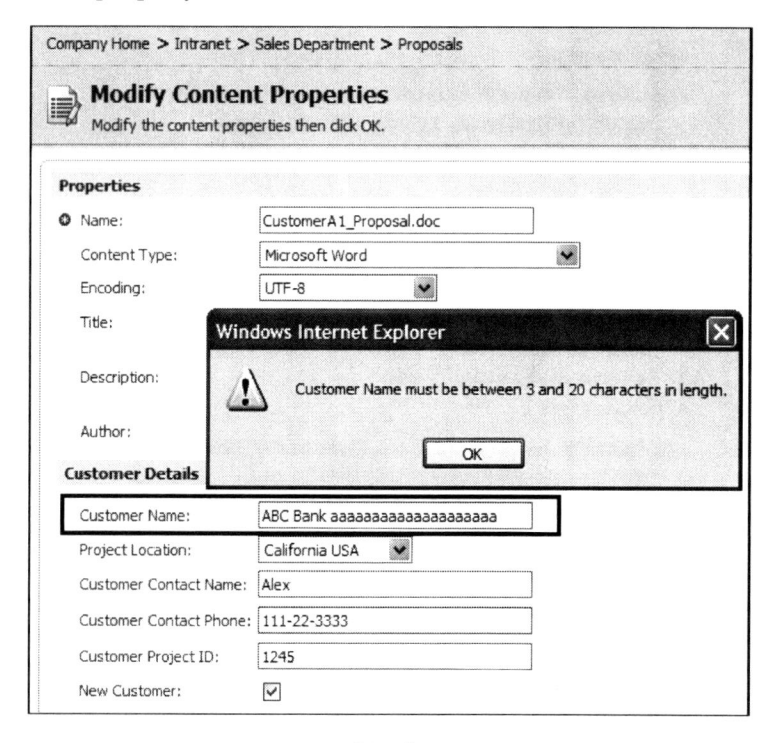

You will see the list of allowed values for the **ProjectLocation** property, due to the `LIST` constraint, as shown in the following screenshot:

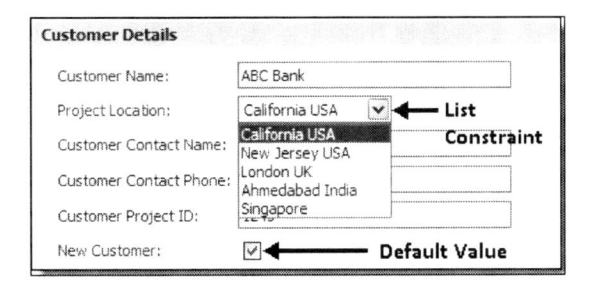

Advanced property sheet configuration

When configuring properties for display in the web client property sheet window, you can control which labels are shown for a specific language, as well as how the properties can be viewed and edited.

Display labels

By default, the property labels are taken from the `<title>` value of the property element, as given in the content model file. Alternatively, it is possible to override this by using the `display-label` attribute in the `web-client-config-custom.xml` file.

However, the property labels displayed are not internationalized (for various languages). In order to achieve internationalized display labels, use the `display-label-id` attribute in the `web-client-config-custom.xml` file, as follows.

```
<property-sheet>
    ------------
    <show-property name="size" display-label-id="size" />
```

The label text will be displayed based on the language selected by the user when they log in to Alfresco Explorer. For example, for English users, the label will be displayed as `"size"`, and for Spanish users the label will be displayed as `"tamaño"`.

All of the label Ids and labels used in Alfresco Explorer are defined in the `<config>/messages/webclient.properties` file. To support a specific language, you need to have a language-specific properties file. For example, the properties file for German language labels is `webclient_de_DE.properties`.

You can add your custom label Ids and label text for specific languages in the `webclient.properties` file, which is in the `<extension>/messages` folder.

Conditional display of properties

By default, all of the properties are displayed when reading and editing the property information. To prevent a property from appearing when editing the property sheet, add the `show-in-edit-mode` attribute, with a value of `false`, as shown below.

```
<property-sheet>
    -----------
    <show-property name="size" display-label-id="size" show-in-edit-mode="false" />
```

Similarly, to prevent a property from appearing when reading the property sheet, add the `show-in-view-mode` attribute, with a value of `false`.

Converters

The property sheet displays the actual values of the properties without manipulating them. For example, if you want to display the property called `size` in a particular format (number of bytes), then you have to use the converters. There are built-in converters, as shown below. For the list of available converters, refer to the `<config>/web-client-config-properties.xml` file. You can also write your own custom converters. However, the converters must be written in the Java language.

```
<property-sheet>
    -----------
    <show-property name="size" display-label-id="size" converter="org.alfresco.faces.ByteSizeConverter" show-in-edit-mode="false" />
```

Component generators

In a web client application, the property sheet will render the appropriate control for the property type. To assign a control other than the default control to a property, you have to use the `component-generator` attribute. For example, the following component generator creates a bar with the tag `Customer Details`, used to separate the properties, and to group them under a specific tag.

```
<config evaluator="aspect-name" condition="custom:CustomerDetails">
    <property-sheet>
        <separator name="sepCust1" display-label="Customer Details" component-generator="HeaderSeparatorGenerator" />
```

The following are some of the built-in generators:

- `MimeTypeSelectorGenerator`: Useful to list select a specific MIME type
- `MultilingualTextAreaGenerator`: Useful for showing a text box
- `SpaceIconPickerGenerator`: Useful for selecting a specific icon for a space

There are built-in generators as shown earlier. You can also write your own custom generators by using the Java language. Refer to the Alfresco wiki page at `http://wiki.alfresco.com/wiki/Component_Generator_Framework` for details of how to implement a custom component generator.

Custom content type

Let us say your Corporate Communications group would like to create press releases and execute certain business rules if the content is of a press release type. They would like to have the additional properties listed as follows:

- PR Person's Name
- PR Person's Email
- PR Person's Phone
- PR Released Date
- Content to be automatically versioned for every update

When do you need a custom content type

Earlier in this chapter, you saw the advantages and disadvantages of having a custom aspect over having a custom content type. You need a custom content type if that type of content has some significance for you, such as in the case of press release. You will be able to add `Press Release` content in any space as you like, without going through the hassles of applying all kinds of business rules on spaces. Similarly, with a custom content type, you will be able to execute business rules based on the content type. For example, you can send notifications to certain people when a `Press Release` is created.

Steps to add a custom content type

The following process needs to be followed in order to add a custom content type to the Alfresco content model:

1. Define the custom content type, the properties, and the mandatory aspects.
2. Extend the content model with the custom content type.
3. Configure the web client for the custom aspect.
4. Restart Alfresco to make sure that the new changes are in effect.

Define the custom content type

You may consider calling your custom content type `Press Release`, with the properties shown in the following table:

Property Type	Property Name	Property Label
text	PRName	PR Person Name
text	PREmail	PR Person Email
text	PRPhone	PR Person Phone
Int	PRDate	PR Released Date

Extend the content model with the custom content type

Now that you have identified your custom content type and the properties, the next step is to extend the Alfresco content model with the XML representation of your custom content type.

Open the `customModel.xml` file and add the following XML code before the `aspects` block:

```
<types>
    <!-- Definition of new Content Type: Press Release -->
    <type name="custom:pressrelease">
       <title>Press Release</title>
       <parent>cm:content</parent>
       <properties>
          <property name=»custom:PRName»>
             <title>PR Person Name</title>
             <type>d:text</type>
          </property>
          <property name=»custom:PREmail»>
             <title>PR Person Email</title>
             <type>d:text</type>
          </property>
          <property name=»custom:PRPhone»>
             <title>PR Person Phone</title>
             <type>d:text</type>
          </property>
          <property name=»custom:PRDate»>
             <title>PR Released Date</title>
             <type>d:date</type>
```

```
            </property>
        </properties>
    </type>
</types>
```

Configure the web client for the custom content type

You need to make sure that the web client program recognizes this new custom content type and displays appropriate dialog screens in the web-based interface. In order to make this happen, you need to configure the web client file `web-client-config-custom.xml`, which is in the extension (`<alfresco_install_folder>\tomcat\shared\classes\alfresco\extension`) folder.

Open the `web-client-config-custom.xml` file and add the highlighted lines of the following code:

```
<!-- Lists the custom aspect and custom content type in business rules Action wizard -->
<config evaluator="string-compare" condition="Action Wizards">
    <aspects>
        <aspect name="custom:CustomerDetails"/>
    </aspects>
    <subtypes>
        <type name="custom:pressrelease"/>
    </subtypes>
</config>
```

This code ensures that the `pressrelease` content is shown in the business rules Action wizard.

Add the following XML code, just before the block shown above. This code ensures that the press release content type is listed when you create new content.

```
<config evaluator="string-compare" condition="Content Wizards">
    <content-types>
        <type name="custom:pressrelease" />
    </content-types>
</config>
```

Extending the Alfresco Content Model

Add the following XML code, just before the block shown above. This code ensures that the properties are available for editing in the **edit properties** window for the `pressrelease` content.

```
<config evaluator="node-type" condition="custom:pressrelease">
   <property-sheet>
      <show-property name="mimetype"
         display-label-id="content_type"
         component-generator="MimeTypeSelectorGenerator" />
      <show-property name="size"
         display-label-id="size"
         converter="org.alfresco.faces.ByteSizeConverter"
         show-in-edit-mode="false" />
      <show-property name="custom:PRName" />
      <show-property name="custom:PREmail" />
      <show-property name="custom:PRPhone" />
      <show-property name="custom:PRDate" />
   </property-sheet>
</config>
```

After making changes to the configuration files, restart Alfresco.

Add custom content type

The new content type, called `pressrelease`, is now available to add anywhere you like. On your personal computer, create a sample press release in HTML format, and save it as `PressRelease1.html`. Follow the steps given below to upload your `pressrelease` content:

1. Go to the **Company Home > Intranet > Press and Media** space, and create a sub-space called **Press Releases**.

2. Ensure that you are in the **Company Home > Intranet > Press and Media > Press Releases** space.

3. In the space header, click on the **Add Content** link. The **Add Content** dialog box appears.

4. To specify the file that you want to upload, click the **Browse** button. In the **File Upload** dialog box, browse to the file that you created earlier, (`PressRelease1.html`) and click the **Upload** button.

5. A message informs you that your upload was successful, as shown in the screenshot on the next page.

6. Select **Press Release** as the **Type**, from the drop-down list.

7. Click the **OK** button to confirm.

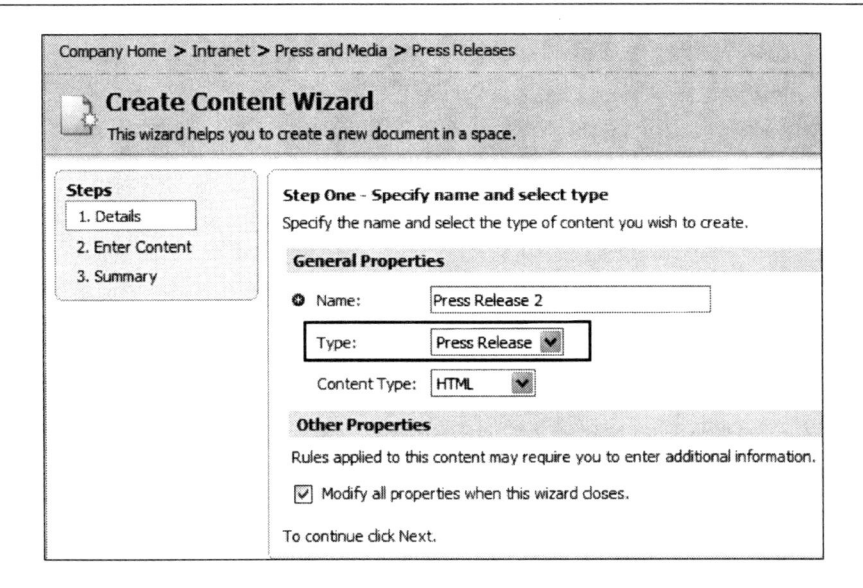

8. The **Modify Content Properties** dialog box appears, as shown in the screenshot below.
9. The **Name**, **Tile**, **Description**, and **Author** properties are basic properties that are populated by default. **Auto Version** is a mandatory aspect that is attached to the `pressrelease` content. The properties **PR Person Name**, **PR Person Email**, **PR Person Phone**, and **PR Released Date** are part of the `pressrelease` content. Also notice that **Edit Inline** is selected for HTML content. Enter the appropriate data for the properties.
10. Click on the **OK** button to save your changes and return to the **Press Releases** space.

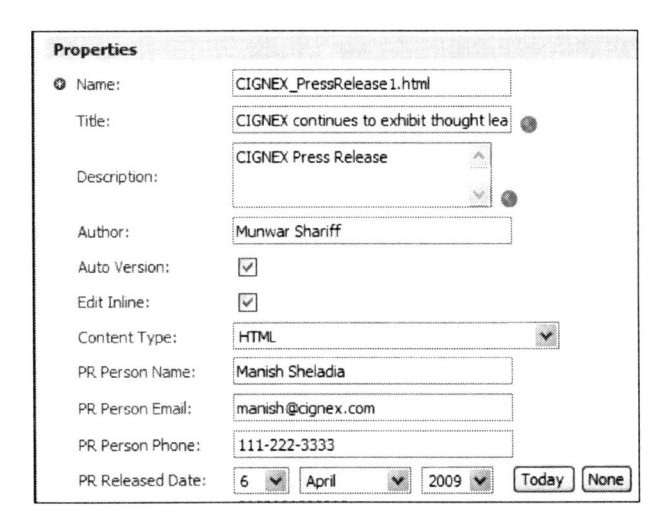

Extending the Alfresco Content Model

Create a Press Release as HTML content

You can also create a `pressrelease` as HTML content, directly in the web client, without uploading the file from your personal computer. To create an HTML file in a space, follow the instructions given below:

Ensure that you are in the **Company Home > Intranet > Press and Media > Press Releases** space. In the header, click on the **Create > Create Content** link. The first pane of the **Create Content Wizard** appears, as shown in the following screenshot:

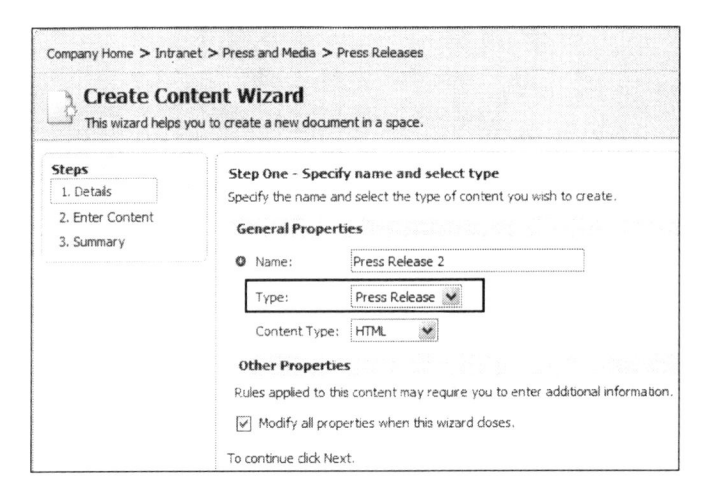

You need to provide the **Name** of the HTML file, select **HTML** as the **Content Type**, and then click on the **Next** button. The **Enter Content** pane of the wizard appears, as shown in the screenshot below.

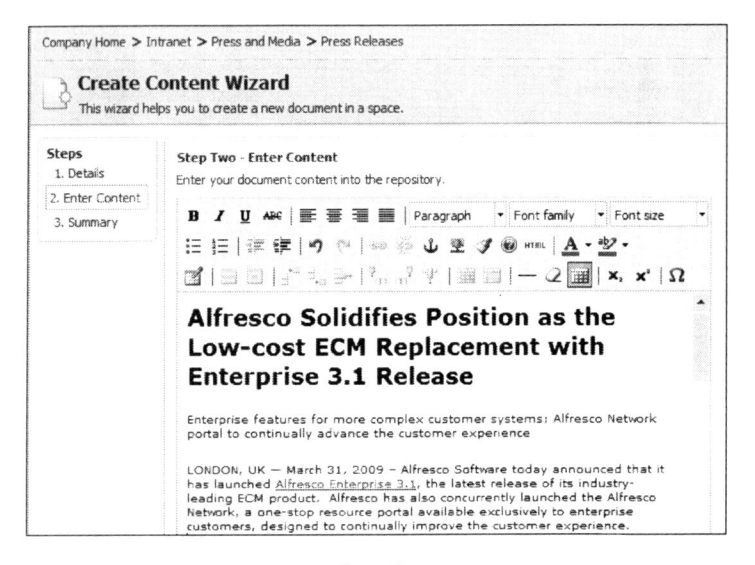

[244]

You can enter some sample press release text by using the text formatting features. After the content has been entered and edited in the **Enter Content** pane, click **Finish**. You will see the **Modify Content Properties** screen used to update metadata that is associated with the content, as shown in the screenshot under the section *Add Custom Content Type*. You can modify the properties as required, and click on the **OK** button. You can preview the newly-created **Press Release** by clicking on it.

Create business rules targeting the custom content type

You can create a business rule targeting a custom content type. For example, you can send notifications to concerned people when a press release is added. When creating the business rule, select the **Items of a specified type or its sub-types** condition, as shown in the following screenshot.

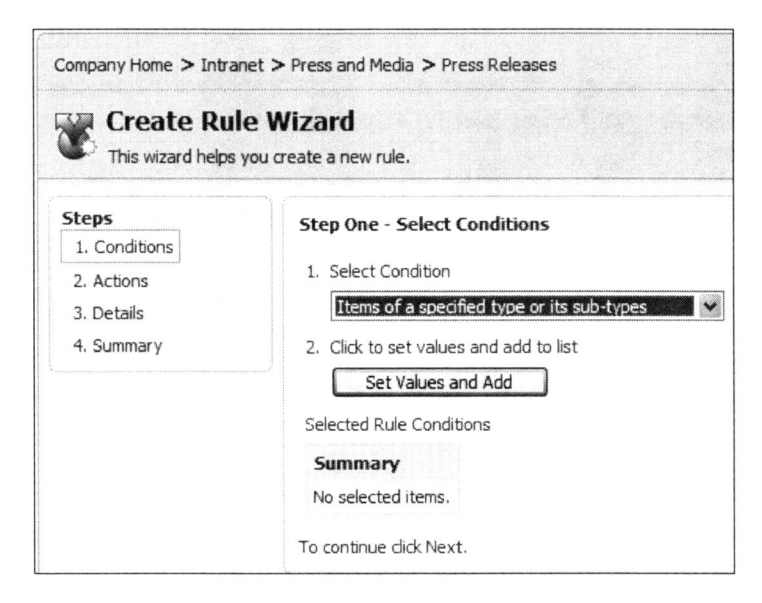

Click the **Set Values and Add** button to set the condition. This will display a dialog box for setting condition values, as shown below. Select the **Press Release** option as **Type**.

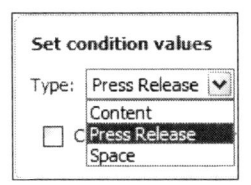

Extending the Alfresco Content Model

Custom associations

You can associate content within the Alfresco repository with one or more content items. An association enables the content to be related to other content.

Alfresco supports two types of associations. The first type is **reference association**, where you refer to other content items within a content item. For example, you can associate a `legal agreement document` with a `master contract` document. Therefore, you can refer to the associated `master contract document` whenever you review the `legal agreement document`. With reference association, if you delete one of the documents, then the other document will not be deleted.

The second type of association is called **child association**, where content (such as space) contains other content items. The child association is employed when we do not want the child source to exist when the source goes away. It is similar to the concept of a cascaded delete in a relational database, or of deleting a folder in Microsoft Windows Explorer. If you delete the parent, then all of their children are deleted too.

You can create your own custom associations according to your business requirements. The process of creating and using custom associations is explained in this section.

When do you need an association?

Reference associations are very useful in various business applications. Let us say that in your engineering department space, if you have a `testing document`, you might want to associate it with an appropriate `requirements document`. Similarly, you might want to refer to some documents in your `Press Release`. Association is required if you want to refer or contain some other content within your content.

Define a custom association

As an example, we will create two associations for the `Press Release` custom content type. The first one uses reference association and is called `Press Release Image`, which refers to an image within the Alfresco repository. The second association is called `Press Release Files`, which refers to one or more files within the Alfresco repository.

In order to define these associations in the content model, open the `customModel.xml` file and insert the highlighted XML code within the `Press Release` content type definition, as follows. For the `Press Release Files` association, the option `<many>` is set to `true`, to indicate more than one reference file.

```xml
<!-- Definition of new Content Type: Press Release -->
<type name="custom:pressrelease">
   <title>Press Release</title>
   <parent>cm:content</parent>
   <properties>
      <property name="custom:PRName">
         <title>PR Person Name</title>
         <type>d:text</type>
      </property>
      <property name="custom:PREmail">
         <title>PR Person Email</title>
         <type>d:text</type>
      </property>
      <property name="custom:PRPhone">
         <title>PR Person Phone</title>
         <type>d:text</type>
      </property>
      <property name="custom:PRDate">
         <title>PR Released Date</title>
         <type>d:date</type>
      </property>
   </properties>
   <associations>
      <association name="custom:PRImage">
         <title>Press Release Image</title>
         <source>
            <mandatory>false</mandatory>
            <many>true</many>
         </source>
         <target>
            <class>cm:content</class>
            <mandatory>false</mandatory>
            <many>false</many>
         </target>
      </association>
      <association name="custom:PRFiles">
         <title>Press Release Files</title>
         <source>
            <mandatory>false</mandatory>
            <many>true</many>
         </source>
         <target>
            <class>cm:content</class>
            <mandatory>false</mandatory>
```

```
            <many>true</many>
        </target>
    </association>
</associations>
<mandatory-aspects>
    <aspect>cm:versionable</aspect>
</mandatory-aspects>
</type>
```

> It is very important to follow a specific sequence when defining the content model, otherwise Alfresco will generate an error during start-up. First define the parent, followed by the properties, associations, and then the mandatory aspects.

You need to make sure that the web client program recognizes these new custom associations in the web based interface. Open the `web-client-config-custom.xml` file and insert the lines of code that are highlighted below:

```
<config evaluator="node-type" condition="custom:pressrelease">
   <property-sheet>
      <show-property name="mimetype"
        display-label-id="content_type"
        component-generator="MimeTypeSelectorGenerator"/>
      <show-property name="size" display-label-id="size"
        converter="org.alfresco.faces.ByteSizeConverter"
        show-in-edit-mode="false" />
      <show-property name="custom:PRName" />
      <show-property name="custom:PREmail" />
      <show-property name="custom:PRPhone" />
      <show-property name="custom:PRDate" />
      <show-association name="custom:PRImage"/>
      <show-association name="custom:PRFiles"/>
   </property-sheet>
</config>
```

Use a custom association

Go to the **Company Home > Intranet > Press and Media > Press Releases** space and upload an image and two text files that you can use to test the custom associations. Click the **view details** icon for one of the press releases (an HTML file) in the space that you created earlier. Click the **edit properties** icon to select the associations, as shown in the following screenshot:

For the `Press Release Image` association, select the image that you uploaded earlier. Similarly, for the `Press Release Files` association, select both of the files that you uploaded earlier. Click on the **OK** button to update the properties. On the **view details** page, you will notice the files associated with the press release.

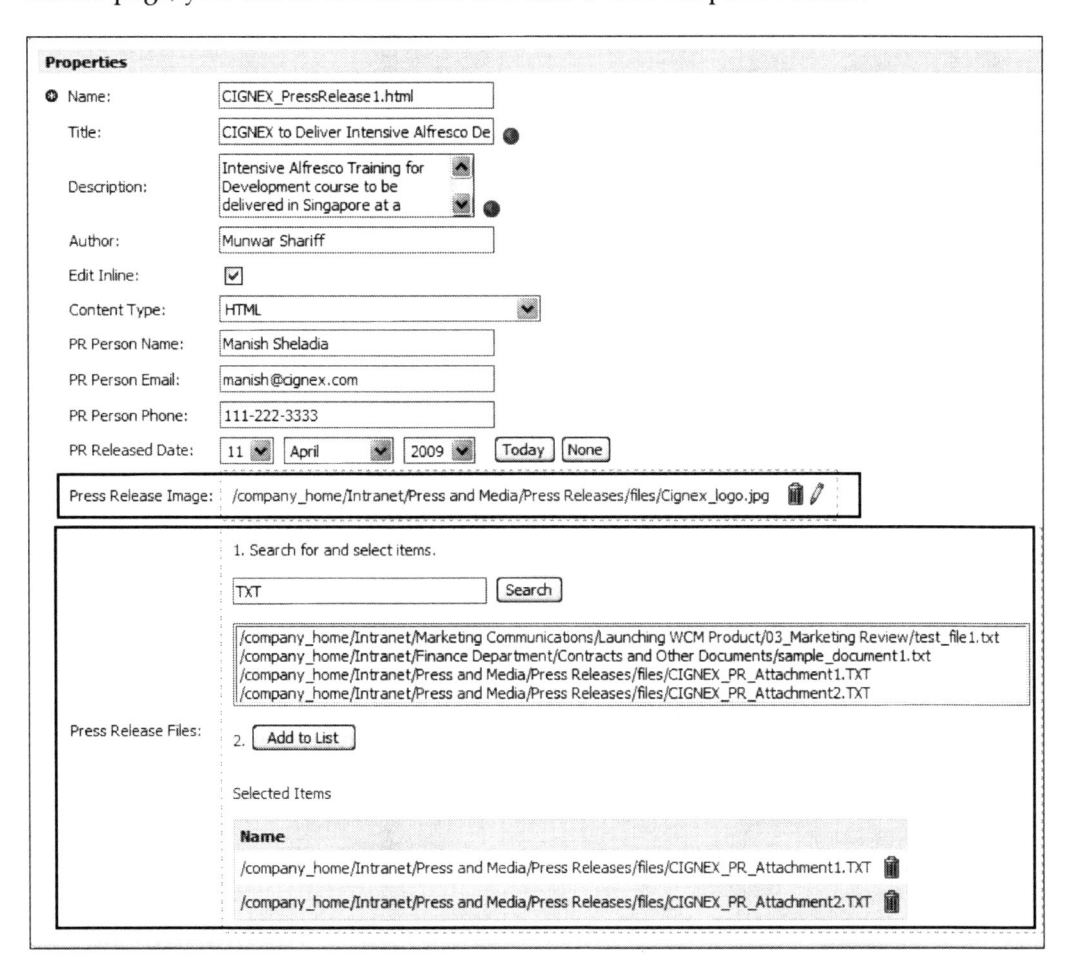

Presentation Template for custom content types

The space **Company Home > Data Dictionary > Presentation Templates** contains presentation templates, which are useful for consolidating and viewing content in various ways. The presentation templates are written in **Freemarker template language** and will have a `.ftl` extension.

Extending the Alfresco Content Model

You have created your own custom content type, called `Press Release`, which consists the following things:

- Press release content in HTML format
- Properties about PR person details, such as `PRName`, `PREmail`
- Press Release Image
- Related Files

You can create your own custom presentation template for previewing the press release in a specific format, according to your business requirements. The following are the steps required to create your custom presentation template:

1. Create a file called `chapter7_PressReleaseTemplate.ftl` on your personal computer that contains the following code. This is Freemarker template code to display press release information in two columns. The first column displays the image (associated with this press release) followed by the actual press release content in HTML format. The second column displays the properties (PR Contact details), followed by the list of associated files.

```
<#-- Shows Press Release content with Custom Properties,
Associated Image and Files -->

<H3> ${document.properties.name} </H3>
<HR>

<#if document?exists>
   <table>
      <tr>
        <td valign="top">
        <#if document.assocs["custom:PRImage"]?exists>
          <#list document.assocs["custom:PRImage"] as t>
               <img src="/alfresco${t.url}">
          </#list>
        </#if>

        <BR><BR>

        ${document.content}
        </td>
        <td valign="top">
            <B> PR CONTACT :</B>  <BR>
            Contact: ${document.properties["custom:PRName"]} <BR>
            Email: ${document.properties["custom:PREmail"]} <BR>
            Phone: ${document.properties["custom:PRPhone"]} <BR>
        <BR>
            <B> Associated Files: </B>
```

```
        <#if document.assocs["custom:PRFiles"]?exists>
            <#list document.assocs["custom:PRFiles"] as t>
                <a href="/alfresco${t.url}"> ${t.name} </a> <BR>
            </#list>
        </#if>
        </td>
    </tr>
    </table>
<#else>
    No document found!
</#if>
```

2. Go to the **Company Home > Data Dictionary > Presentation Templates** space and click on the **Add Content** link . Upload the `chapter7_PressReleaseTemplate.ftl` file, which you had created earlier, as a new presentation template.

3. Go to the **Company Home > Intranet > Press and Media > Press Releases** space and make sure that the content item you created earlier as `Press Release` has all of the properties filled up.

4. Use the **Preview in Template** button and select the `chapter7_PressReleaseTemplate.ftl` template from the drop-down list to display the press release, as shown below:

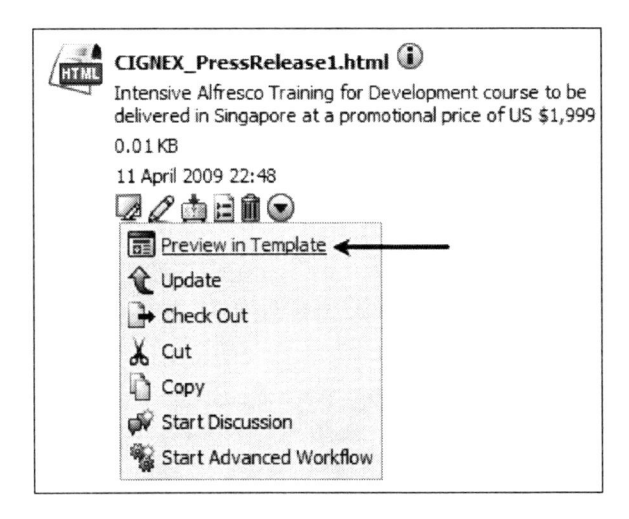

When you click on the **Preview in Template** option, you will get the following screenshot:

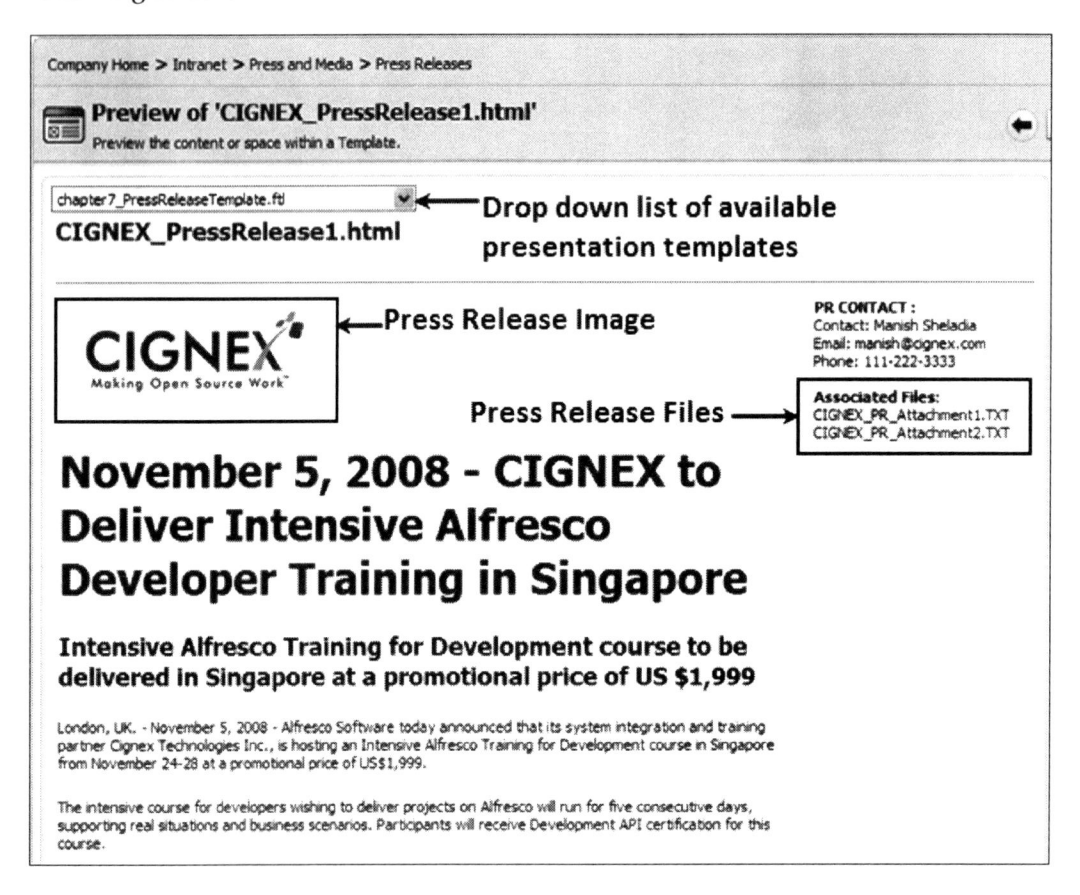

Association example

You can create various custom content types, aspects, and associations according to your business requirements.

Let us say that you belong to the training department and would like to maintain the training material in the Alfresco repository. As an example, create custom content types called the `Book` and `Chapters`. In the content model, define the `Book` content type to have `Chapters` as child associations.

`Chapters` are the actual text, HTML, or XML documents that are version-controlled. The `Book` content type logically groups all of the chapters by using the child association property, and creates a presentation template for the `Book` content that is used to display all of the associated chapters.

Dynamic models

You are able to customize Alfresco by using custom content types. These customizations are typically deployed via the `alfresco/extension` folder and require the Alfresco server to be re-started to take effect. Since version 2.9, Alfresco supports dynamic models to facilitate the dynamic customization of models without requiring a restart of the Alfresco server.

Dynamic models are nothing but XML based model files that are uploaded to Alfresco's repository in the `Company Home/Data Dictionary/Model` space.

The following are the advantages of Dynamic models:

- There is no need to restart Alfresco Server every time you make changes to the model files.
- Both the content as well as the model files are stored in the repository. It is easier to maintain and move content along with the model files.
- All of the model files in the `<extension>` folder will be considered active and will be loaded by Alfresco. However, you can activate and inactivate the dynamic models by keeping the model XML file in the repository.
- In a multi-tenant setup, the models defined in the `<extension>` folder are available to all tenants. If you would like to customize content types and custom aspects for a specific tenant only, then adynamic model is the best choice.

Dynamic custom model

Creating a dynamic custom model is the same as creating a regular custom model. For this example, create a custom content type that has two properties. Create a file named `dynamicModel1.xml` on your personal computer with the following content.

```
<?xml version="1.0" encoding="UTF-8"?>
<!-- Dynamic Model -->
<model name="dynamic:dynamicModel" xmlns="http://www.alfresco.org/model/dictionary/1.0">
    <!-- Optional meta-data about the model -->
    <description>Dynamic Model</description>
    <author></author>
    <version>1.0</version>
    <imports>
        <!-- Import Alfresco Dictionary Definitions -->
```

Extending the Alfresco Content Model

```xml
        <import uri="http://www.alfresco.org/model/dictionary/1.0"
prefix="d"/>
        <!-- Import Alfresco Content Domain Model Definitions -->
        <import uri="http://www.alfresco.org/model/content/1.0"
prefix="cm"/>
    </imports>

    <!-- Introduction of new namespaces defined by this model -->
    <!-- NOTE: The following namespace dynamic.model should be changed
to reflect your own namespace -->
    <namespaces>
        <namespace uri="dynamic.model" prefix="dynamic"/>
    </namespaces>

    <types>
        <!-- Definition of new Content Type: Model1 -->
        <type name="dynamic:Model1">
            <title>Dynamic Model ONE</title>
            <parent>cm:content</parent>
            <properties>
                <property name="dynamic:property11">
                    <title>Dynamic Property 11</title>
                    <type>d:text</type>
                </property>
                <property name="dynamic:property12">
                    <title>Dynamic Property 12</title>
                    <type>d:text</type>
                </property>
            </properties>
        </type>
    </types>
</model>
```

Deploying a custom model

Deploying a custom model is as simple as uploading the model file to a specific space in Alfresco. Log in to Alfresco Explorer and go to the **Company Home > Data Dictionary > Model** space. Upload the `dynamicModel1.xml` file.

Activating and deactivating a custom model

By default, the model will not be active unless the **Model Active** checkbox is selected during the upload. To activate a previously-inactive model, select **View Details** and then select the **Modify** properties icon. In the **Modify Content Properties** page, select the **Model Active** checkbox.

Similarly, to inactivate a custom model, deselect the **Model Active** checkbox.

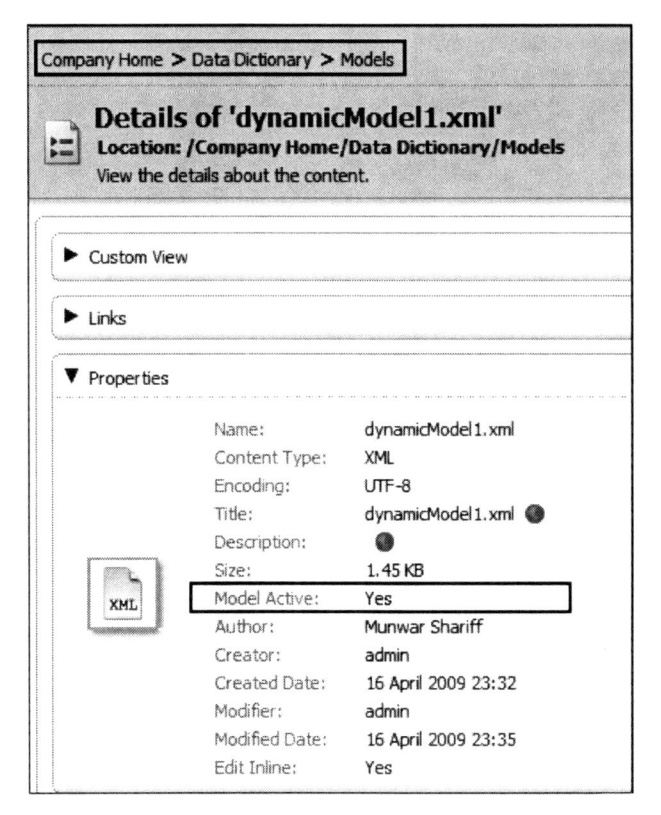

Updating a custom model

You can directly edit or update the XML model file. If the model is active, then it will be re-loaded. If the file is checked-out, then the working copy will be ignored until such a time as the file is checked-in.

Dynamic web client

A dynamic web client configuration file will have the same name as a custom web client configuration file. For example, create a `web-client-config-custom.xml` file, with the content as given below, to support the dynamic content type that you created earlier.

```
<alfresco-config>
   <config evaluator="string-compare" condition="Content Wizards">
      <content-types>
         <type name="dynamic:Model1" />
```

```
            </content-types>
        </config>
        <config evaluator="node-type" condition="dynamic:Model1">
            <property-sheet>
                <show-property name="mimetype" display-label-id="content_
type"
                        component-generator="MimeTypeSelectorGenerator"
/>
                <show-property name="dynamic:property11" />
                <show-property name="dynamic:property12" />
            </property-sheet>
        </config>
        <!-- Lists the custom content type in business rules Action wizard
-->
        <config evaluator="string-compare" condition="Action Wizards">
            <subtypes>
                <type name="dynamic:Model1"/>
            </subtypes>
        </config>
</alfresco-config>
```

Deploying web client customizations

Deploying a dynamic web client configuration is as simple as uploading it to a specific space in Alfresco. Log in to Alfresco Explorer and go to the **Company Home > Data Dictionary > Web Client Extension** space. Upload the `web-client-config-custom.xml` file.

The custom configuration will not be applied until it is explicitly re-loaded (refer to the following section) or when the server is restarted.

Reloading web client customizations

If the `web-client-config-custom.xml` file has been added, edited, or updated, it can be dynamically reloaded by using the web client configuration console via:

`http://<server>:<port>/alfresco/faces/jsp/admin/webclientconfig-console.jsp`

This has a single command, `reload`, which will cause the web client configuration to be re-loaded.

Dynamic models in a multi-tenancy environment

Alfresco supports a multi-tenancy architecture, where a single instance of the software serves multiple client organizations (tenants). In Chapter 14, the section named *Administering and maintaining the system* contains information about setting up Alfresco in a multi-tenant environment.

When configured for a multi-tenant environment, Alfresco virtually partitions its data and configuration so that each client organization works within a customized virtual application instance. By default, the models defined in the `<extension>` folder are available to all of the tenants.

If you would like custom content types and custom aspects for a specific tenant only, then dynamic models are the best choice.

To test this out, create few tenant accounts (say, `TenantA` and `TenantB`), according to the instructions given in Chapter 14, *Administering and Maintaining the System*. Log in as a specific tenant administrator (say `TenantA`) and create a dynamic content type and use it. Now, log in as a different tenant administrator (say `TenantB`), and you will notice that the dynamic content type created by `TenantA` is not available to `TenantB`.

Summary

The Alfresco content model is highly extensible. The custom aspects provide you with the flexibility to add additional sets of properties for the documents in specific spaces. You can customize the content model to suit your business needs. By using content associations, you can relate one document with one or more other documents. You have also seen the benefits of a newly-added feature called dynamic models for the dynamic customization of models, without requiring a restart of the Alfresco server.

8
Implementing Workflow

Workflow is the automation of a business process, during which documents are passed from one participant to another for action, according to a set of procedural rules. Every Content Management System implementation has its own workflow requirements. For some companies, workflow could be a simple approval process. For some companies, it could be a complex business process management system. Workflow provides ownership and control over the content and processes. In this chapter, you will learn about the basic, out-of-the-box workflow capabilities of Alfresco and the ways to extend it as per your business requirements.

By the end of this chapter, you will have learned how to:

- Enable simple workflow for documents
- Create email templates and set email notifications
- Extend workflow to include multiple approval steps
- Implement a complex workflow scenario for document lifecycle management
- Start an advanced workflow from the list of predefined workflows
- Assign documents and properties to the workflow
- Take ownership of a task
- Reassign a task
- Change the workflow state of a task
- List the tasks that are assigned to you and the tasks that have been completed by you
- Cancel or abort the workflows that you have started
- Create your own custom advanced workflow
- Start workflow through business rules
- Dynamically deploy workflows
- Customize dashlet to see the workflow status

Introduction to the Alfresco workflow process

Alfresco includes two types of out of the box workflow. The first is the **Simple Workflow,** which is content-oriented, and the other is the **Advanced Workflow,** which is task-oriented.

The Simple Workflow process in Alfresco involves the movement of documents through various spaces. It is simple, as each workflow definition is restricted to a single state. Multiple states are achieved by loosely tying together multiple workflow definitions. Loose coupling is achieved by attaching a workflow definition to a space and a workflow instance to a content item. A content item is moved or copied to a new space at which point a new workflow instance is attached, which is based on the workflow definition of the space.

[A workflow definition is unaware of other related workflow definitions.]

The Advanced Workflow process is task-oriented, where you create a task, attach documents that are to be reviewed, and assign it to appropriate reviewers. You can track the tasks assigned to you and the tasks that are initiated by you. You can change the status of the tasks, reassign the tasks to other users, and cancel a task. You can send various notifications to all of the parties involved, and track the tasks to closure. Alfresco provides this level of workflow ubiquitously, throughout its entire product. The same robust workflow capabilities are available in **Document Management (DM)**, **Records Management (RM)**, **Web Content Management (WCM)**, and throughout our applications, which includes Alfresco Share.

You can use the out of the box features provided by both types of workflow, or you can create your own custom advanced workflow, according to the business processes of your organization.

Simple Workflow

Consider a purchase order that moves through various departments for authorization and eventual purchase. To implement Simple Workflow for this in Alfresco, you will create spaces for each department and allow documents to move through various department spaces. Each department space is secured, only allowing the users of that department to edit the document and to move it to the next departmental space in the workflow process.

The workflow process is so flexible that you could introduce new steps for approval into the operation without changing any code.

Out of the box features

Simple Workflow is implemented as an aspect that can be attached to any document in a space through the use of business rules. Workflow can also be invoked on individual content items as actions.

Workflow has two steps. One is for approval while the other one is for rejection. You can refer to the upcoming image, where workflow is defined for the documents in a space called **Review Space**. The users belonging to the **Review Space** can act upon the document. If they choose to **Reject**, then the document moves to a space called **Rejected Space**. If they choose to **Approve**, then the document moves to a space called **Approved Space**. You can define the names of the spaces and the users on the spaces, according to your business requirements. The following figure gives a graphical view of the **Approved Space** and the **Rejected Space**:

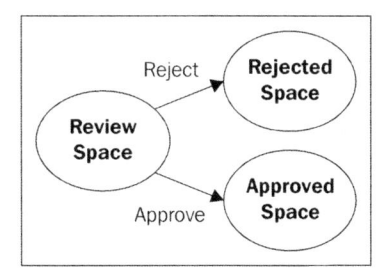

Define and use Simple Workflow

The process to define and use Simple Workflow in Alfresco is as follows:

- Identify spaces and set security on those spaces
- Define your workflow process
- Add workflow to content in those spaces, accordingly
- Select the email template and the people to send email notifications to
- Test the workflow process

As an example, let us define and use a Simple Workflow process to review and approve the engineering documents on your intranet. Go to the **Company Home > Intranet > Engineering Department** space and create a space named **ProjectA** by using an existing **Software Engineering Project** space template. For more information on creating a space using an existing space template, refer Chapter 5.

Identify spaces and security

If you go to the **Company Home > Intranet > Engineering Department > ProjectA > Documentation** space, then you will notice the following sub-spaces:

- **Samples**: This space is for storing sample project documents. Set the security on this space in such a way that only the managers can edit the documents, and others can only copy the documents from this space.

- **Drafts**: This space contains initial drafts and documents of **ProjectA** that are being edited. Set the security in such a way that only a few selected users (such as **Engineer1, Engineer2**—as shown in the upcoming image) can add or edit the documents in this space.

- **Pending Approval**: This space contains all of the documents that are under review. Set the security in such a way that only the Project Manager of **ProjectA** can edit these documents.

- **Published**: This space contains all of the documents that are **Approved** and visible to others. Nobody should edit the documents while they are in the **Published** space. If you need to edit a document, then you need to **Retract** it to the **Drafts** space and follow the workflow process, as shown in the following image:

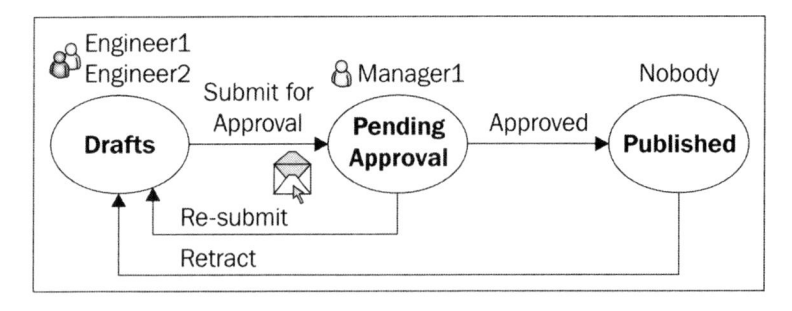

Set the security on these sub-spaces according to your requirements. For more information about securing spaces, refer to Chapter 4.

Defining the workflow process

Now that you have identified the spaces, the next step is to define your workflow process. The preceding image illustrates the spaces and the workflow.

We will add workflow to all of the documents in the **Drafts** space. When a user selects the **Approve** action called **Submit for Approval** on a document, then the document moves from the **Drafts** space to the **Pending Approval** space.

We will add workflow to all of the documents in the **Pending Approval** space. When a user selects the **Approve** action called **Approved** on a document, then the document moves from the **Pending Approval** space to the **Published** space. Similarly, when a user selects the **Reject** action called **Re-submit** on a document, then it moves from the **Pending Approval** space to the **Drafts** space.

We will add workflow to all of the documents in the **Published** space. When a user selects the **Reject** action called **Retract** on a document, then it moves from the **Published** space to the **Drafts** space.

You can have as many review steps (spaces) as needed and you can choose the workflow action names according to your business's requirements.

Adding simple workflow to items

Now that you have defined your workflow process, the next step is to add workflow to the documents in these spaces.

To add workflow to the **Drafts** space, carry out the following steps:

1. Ensure that you are in the **Company Home > Intranet > Engineering Department > ProjectA > Documentation > Drafts** space.
2. Click on the **More Actions > Manage Content Rules** link.
3. Click on the **Create Rule** link and you will see the **Create Rules Wizard**.
4. In **Step One**, from the **Select Condition** drop-down list, select the **All Items** option, and then click on the **Add to List** button. Click on the **Next** button.

Implementing Workflow

5. In **Step Two**, from the **Select Actions** drop-down list, select the **Add simple workflow to item** option, and then click on the **Set Values and Add** button. The **Set action values** dialog box appears, as shown in the following screenshot:

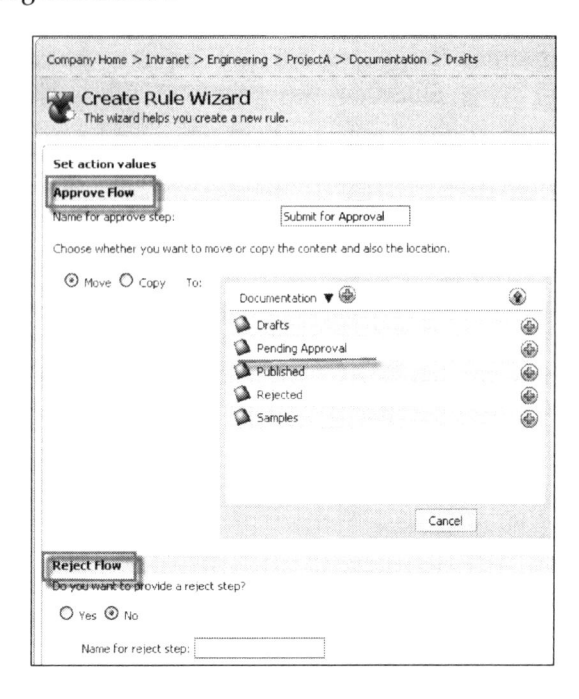

6. In the **Approve Flow** section, provide a workflow step name of **Submit for Approval**, and move the content to the **Pending Approval** space. This is as per your workflow design, as shown in the screenshot under the section *Identify spaces and security* for the **Drafts** space.
7. The workflow for the **Drafts** space does not require a 'reject' step. Hence, select the option **No** for **Reject Flow**.
8. Click on the **OK** button, and then click on the **Next** button.
9. In **Step Three**, select a **Type** of **Inbound**, and provide an appropriate name and description for this rule. Finish the rule.

Similarly, create workflow for the **Pending Approval** space, as per the design, as shown in the screenshot under the section *Identify Spaces and Security*. Remember that this space has both the **approve step** and **reject step,** options available, as shown in the following screenshot:

[264]

Next, create a workflow for the **Published** space, as per the design shown in the screenshot under the section *Identify Spaces and Security*. Remember that this space only has the **approve step** option, which moves the content to the **Drafts** space upon **retract**. Specify **retract** as the name for the **approve step** option.

Sending a notification for approval to the Manager

You can send a notification by email to the Project Manager whenever a document is waiting for approval. Follow the steps below to send an email notification to the Project Manager of **ProjectA** whenever a document gets into the **Pending Approval** space:

1. Ensure that you are in the **Company Home > Intranet > Engineering Department > ProjectA > Documentation > Pending Approval** space.
2. Click on the **More Actions > Manage Content Rules** link.
3. Click the **Create Rule** link and you will see the **Create Rule Wizard**.
4. In **Step One**, from the **Select Condition** drop-down list, select the **All Items** option, and then click on the **Add to List** button. Next, click on the **Next** button.
5. In **Step Two**, from the **Select Actions** drop-down list, select the **Send an email to specified user's,** and then click on the **Set Values and Add** button.

Implementing Workflow

6. You will notice a **Set action values** dialog box, as shown in the following screenshot:

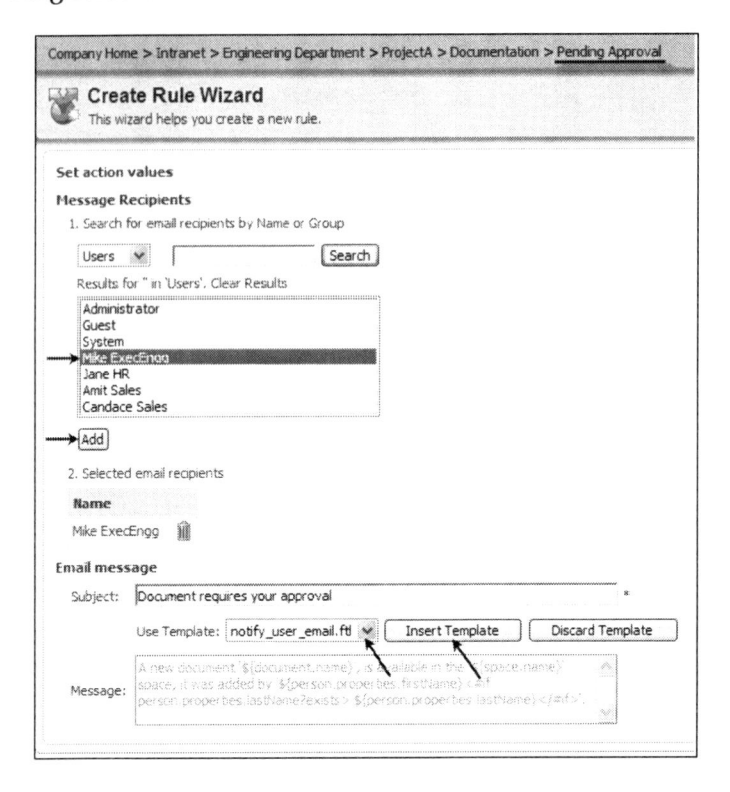

7. Search for and select the Project Manager's name as the email recipient, and then click on the **Add** button. Provide an appropriate subject for the email. As an email message, you can either provide your own text or use a built-in email template (`notify_user_email.ftl`), as shown in the preceding screenshot.

8. Click on the **OK** button and then click on the **Next** button. Select the **Type** as **Inbound**. Provide an appropriate name and description for this rule.

9. Finish the rule.

Test your simple workflow

To test the workflow process, go to the **Drafts** space and upload a sample document. You will notice that the available workflow actions in the **more actions** drop-down menu are as shown in the following screenshot. When you click on the **Submit for Approval** action, the document will be moved automatically to the **Pending Approval** space, as per the workflow rule.

When the document moves into the **Pending Approval** space, two business rules will be applied.

One business rule is to send an email notification to the Project Manager, indicating to him or her that the document is pending for approval. If your email server is correctly configured, then the Project Manager will receive email notifications with information about the document.

The second business rule is the workflow on all of the incoming documents that arrive in this space. When the Project Manager logs in he will notice the workflow actions in the **more actions** drop-down menu, as shown in the following screenshot:

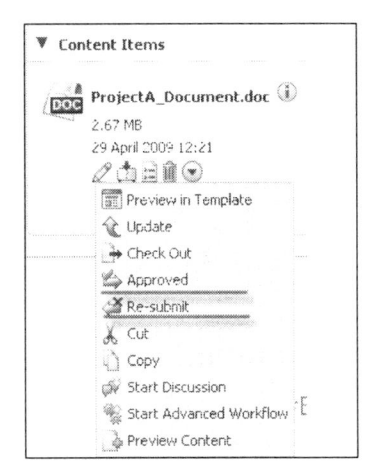

If the Project Manager is fine with the document, then he can click on the **Approved** action and the document will be moved to the **Published** space automatically. If the Project Manager requires more details, or if he's not satisfied with the document, then he can click on the **Re-submit** action to send the document to the original author to edit and **Re-submit** it. In this situation, the document will be moved to the **Drafts** space automatically. Once the document is in the **Drafts** space, the workflow process starts all over again.

If you select the **Approved** action, you will notice that the document is moved to the **Published** space. When the document is in the **Published** state, it is typically visible to all of the required employees, as it has already been reviewed and approved. You can **Retract** the document to the **Drafts** space (as shown in the following screenshot) for further edits and approvals.

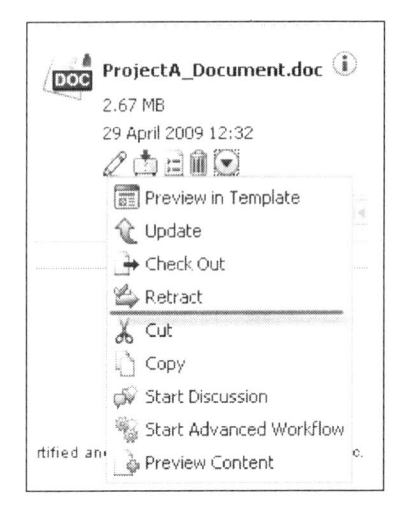

Email notification templates

For email notifications, you can either use your own email message or use a standard email notification template (as shown in the screenshot under the section *Send notification for approval to the Manager*). You can also create your own email templates to reuse whenever required. For more details about the **DataDictionary** and templates, please refer to Chapter 5.

The space at **Company Home > Data Dictionary > Email Templates** contains various email templates. The email templates are written in the FreeMarker template language and will have an extension of .ftl. Now we shall learn how to create your email template. For more details about Data dictionary and templates, please refer to Chapter 5.

Create a file named chapter8_notify_pending_approval_email.ftl on your personal computer, and populate it with the following code. This is FreeMarker template code, which includes the details of the document and the author in order to send them to the reviewer. Fill in Your Title, Company Name, and other details, as required.

```
<#-- Sends email to people when a document is pending approval -->
A document titled '${document.name}' is pending your approval in the
'${space.name}' space.
You can view it through this link:
http://<server-name>:<port>/alfresco${document.url}
Please review and approve it as soon as possible.
Best Regards
'${person.properties.firstName}<#if person.properties.lastName?exists>
${person.properties.lastName}</#if>'
Your Title
Your Company Name
Your Signature
```

Go to the **Company Home > Data Dictionary > Email Templates** space, and click on the **Add Content** link. Upload the `chapter8_notify_pending_approval_email.ftl` file, which you have created earlier, in this space.

The email template is now ready to be used. You can go back to the email notification business rule that was created for the **Pending Approval** space, and edit it to include the new email template that you have created.

Implementing complex workflows

You can implement complex workflows by chaining the spaces with business rules, as long as each step in the workflow results in either an approved or a rejected result. Once such a workflow is clearly defined—identifying various steps (spaces), people, and the business rules involved—it is easy to implement using Alfresco.

For example, let's consider a company named **Secure Loaning Ltd.** that provides loans such as **Home Loan**, **Auto Loan**, and **Two Wheeler Loan**. Therefore, the company has three departments run by three different groups of people. Each group has roles based on the department that they belong to. These groups of people review and then approve or reject the document, based on the category of the documents processed by the customers. On approval of the document, it is converted into PDF format and sent to the **Sanctioned** department. One copy of the PDF file is sent to the customer and another copy is kept within the department itself. On rejection of the document, it is send to the **Rejected** department. Notifications are sent to various parties when a document is received into a department, as well as when a document is sent to the **Approved** or **Sanctioned** departments.

Consider the sample workflow shown in the following image, where a document on the basis of its category, goes through different spaces, that is, departments for **Review**, **Reject**, **Approved**, and **Sanctioned**. In the image, each circle indicates the department, which can be considered as a folder. The document workflow process is identical for **Home Loan, Auto Loan,** and the **Two Wheeler Loan** documents. However, the actors (various groups of people) differ, based on the category of the document.

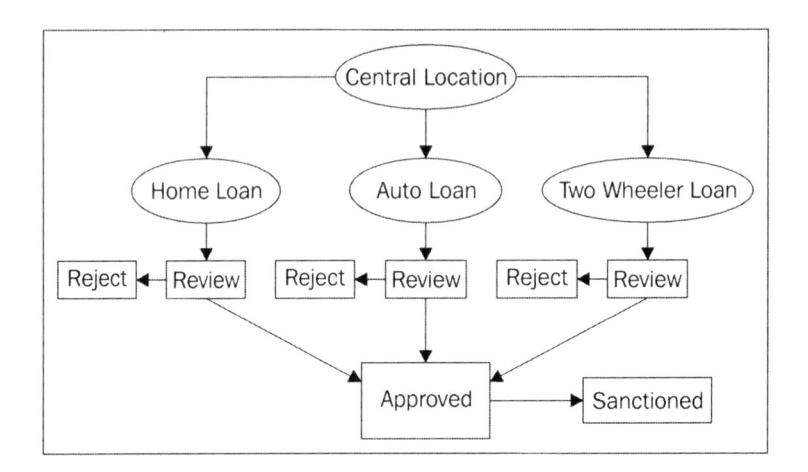

The workflow process

The workflow implemented here is the **Home Load Document Workflow**. The following steps should be followed for the Home Load Document Workflow. The same can be followed by the auto and two wheeler documents.

1. The user will drop all of the documents into a centralized location (**Central Location**) and will specify the desired type of loan. For this purpose, you can create a content type which has metadata such as `Customer Name, type of residence, locality, references, salary, and type of Loan`. Based on the type of loan, the document will be moved to the appropriate **Loan** folders (according to the business rules).

2. Next, a member of the relevant group will update the document and the related metadata. He or she then sends the document to the appropriate **Review** folder for review (through Simple Workflow).

- A member of the next group will review that document, add comments to it, and either **Approve** or **Reject** it (through Simple Workflow).
- If approved, the document will be moved to the **Approved** folder, and if rejected, the document will be moved to the **Rejected** folder.
- When any document enters the **Approved** folder, it is transformed into PDF format and copied into the **Sanctioned** folder (according to the business rule).

Advanced workflows

Simple Workflows are good for implementing content-oriented workflow processes. However, there are certain limitations of the Simple Workflow that are as follows:

- They are unable to create multi-state workflow definitions
- They are restricted to one or two exit transitions (approve, reject)
- They are unable to define parallel workflows
- They rely on folder structure for multi-stage workflow and action triggering
- They have no notion of a task or assignment

To resolve these limitations, Alfresco has embedded the **JBPM (JBoss Business Process Management)** engine into its core. JBPM is an open source, standalone workflow engine. It can run in any servlet container, as it doesn't require the JBoss Application server. The JBPM engine is responsible for managing deployed processes, instantiating and executing processes, persisting process states, providing metadata to a relational database (via Hibernate), and tracking task assignment and task lists. With JBPM, the Alfresco platform is extended to support complex task-oriented processes.

JBPM is built on the idea that any process can be described as a graph or a set of connected nodes. JBPM maintains a list of tasks assigned to each participant. How the users interact with the task list depends on the respective application. In Alfresco, the task to do a dashlet is configured for the currently logged in user. As users complete their tasks, the tasks are removed from the to-do list.

JBPM is a flexible, extensible workflow management system with an intuitive process language. Workflows are described in **process definitions,** using an XML based language called **Java Process Definition Language** (jPDL). jPDL is an example of a graph-based execution language.

jPDL is a process language that is built on top of a common framework. It is an intuitive process language that can be used to express business processes graphically, in terms of tasks, wait states for asynchronous communication, timers, and automated actions. To bind these operations together, jPDL has a powerful and extensible control flow mechanism. jPDL has minimal dependencies and can be used as easily as using a Java library.

jPDL includes a designer tool, which is a graphical tool for authoring business processes. It's an Eclipse plugin. Later in the section, we will see how to configure the Eclipse plugins.

For more information, please visit the following web site:

http://docs.jboss.com/jbpm/v3.2/userguide/html/

Workflow user interactions

As a user, you will be able to perform the following interactions using the Alfresco Explorer interface (such as a web browser):

- Start workflow
    - Select from a list of pre-defined workflows
    - Attach resources (additional related documents)
    - Assign users to the workflow
- List my tasks (what have I got to do?)
- List the tasks that I can assign to myself
- Perform a task
    - View associated task resources (if any)
    - Change a task's state
    - Mark a task done (or other outcome)
- Look back (display the trail of steps leading up to my task assignment)
- Look forward (why hasn't something happened yet?)

- Re-assign the task to someone else
- Take ownership of a task (if it is assigned to my group)
- Cancel or abort the workflow

Out of the box features

The Advanced Workflow process is task-oriented. You create a task, attach documents to be reviewed, and assign it to appropriate reviewers. It could also be implemented by using business rules.

There are two advanced workflows available out of the box.

- **Ad hoc task-based workflow**: Assign tasks to your colleague on an ad hoc basis
- **Review and Approve workflow**: Assign tasks to your colleague for review and approval.

The following example will give you a better understanding of the concept:

The **RajComp** Company got a project from the **United Nations Organization** (**UNO**). For this project, they have to send a **Request** for a **Proposal** to the client. The Project Manager asks the Team Leader to prepare an RFP document, and within a week to send the document across to the manager for approval. The Project Manager will review the document and will either approve it and send it to the UNO, or reject it in order to get some corrections made.

For this purpose, create a **RajComp** space in the **Company Home**. Create **Zoe Bull** and **Zarina Macaro** as the users. For more information about creating a space and users refer to *Chapter 4* and *Chapter 5*.

The following screenshot illustrates the process of creating a **Review** and **Approve** based workflow. **Zarina Macaro** prepares the RFP document and starts the workflow by providing the important information such as **Due Date** to complete the task, **Priority** of the task, and **notification** information. The workflow then assigns the document to **Zoe Bull** to **Review** or **Approve**. Please carry out the following steps to configure an ad hoc workflow.

Implementing Workflow

1. Click on the document's **More Actions** button, and then click on the **Start Advanced Workflow** link, as shown in the screenshot below.

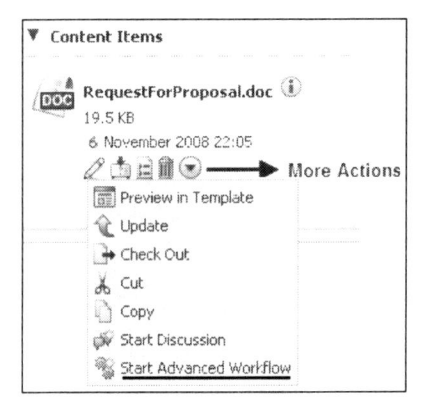

2. This wizard lists all of the available workflows, including custom workflow processes. From the list of available workflows, select the **Adhoc Task** option, and then click on the **Next** button.

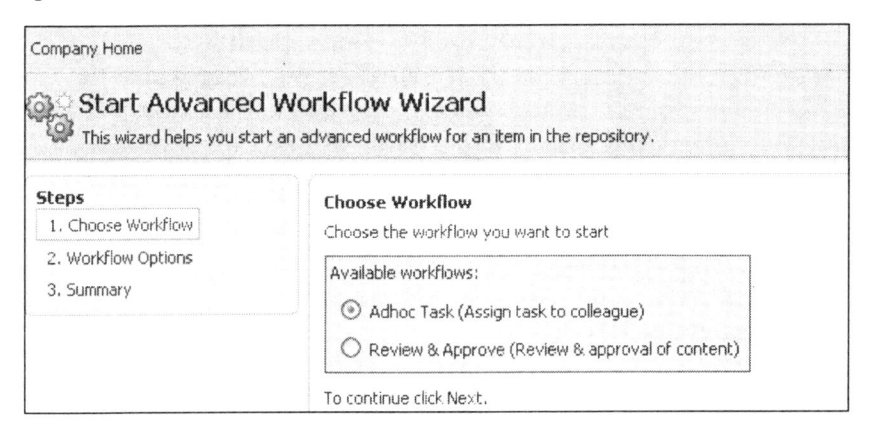

3. You will see the **Workflow options** pane of the **Start Adhoc Task Workflow Wizard,** as shown in the upcoming screenshot. Provide a meaningful **Description** for the task and choose the **Priority**, as well as the **Due Date**. Select the **Notify Me** checkbox to receive notification of the workflow status updates for the document.

4. From the list of users, search for **Zoe Bull** and assign her the task. You can also add additional resources (documents) to this workflow task by clicking on the **Add Resource** button, as shown in the following screenshot. This step will help if you want to send a set of documents, for approval as a group. Once you have entered all required information, click on the **OK** button to start the workflow process.

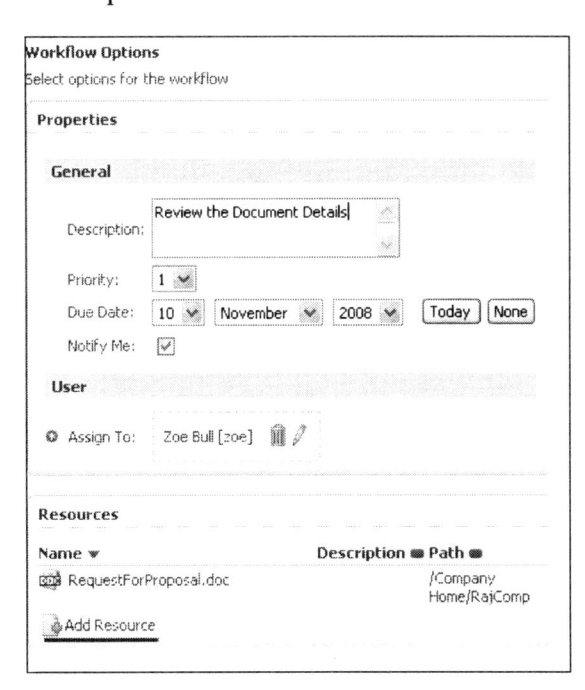

5. Log in as **Zoe Bull**. Click on the **My Alfresco** menu link in the toolbar to view your personal dashboard. The **My Tasks To Do** dashboard lists all of your pending tasks, as shown in the following screenshot:

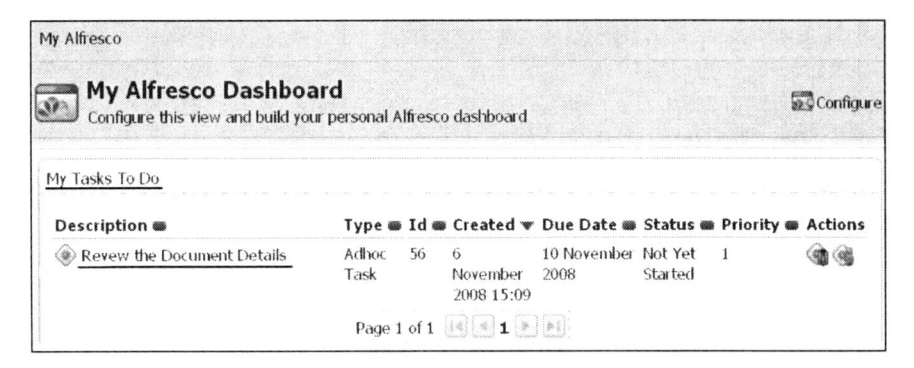

Implementing Workflow

6. Click on the **Review the document details** link shown in the preceding screenshot. To complete the task, choose a **Status** of **Completed** and then click on the **Task Done** button.

Creating custom advanced workflows

You can define and deploy your own task-oriented workflows in the Alfresco repository. However, you need to use a particular format in order to define your workflow, and follow a particular process to deploy it in Alfresco.

> A useful tutorial on creating and deploying your own custom workflow is provided at `http://wiki.alfresco.com/wiki/WorkflowAdministration`.

As an example, we will configure a workflow. The use case scenario is as follows.

Let us consider an example where a **Global Placement** company recruits nurses for various hospitals. The company has an internal process for the recruitment. Required documents for a nurse for a hospital are verified by the employees of this company. If the documents are found to be legal, the nurse is assigned to the hospital for seven weeks. After seven weeks, the process starts again for the same nurse for another assignment. This process goes on and on.

For this project, create a **GlobalPlacement** space in the **Company Home**. Inside the **GlobalPlacement** space, create the **Nurse, Recruiter | Annet_Recruiter**, and **CredentialSpecialist | Lee_Credential** spaces. Create the **Annet_Recruiter** and **Lee_Credential** users. For the home spaces, create the **Annet_Recruiter** and **Lee_Credential** spaces. Invite **Annet_Recruiter** and **Lee_Credential** as coordinators for the **GlobalPlacement** space. For more information about creating a space and users refer to Chapter 4 and Chapter 5.

Defining the workflow process

Now that you have identified the spaces and the users, the next step is to identify the workflow processes.

Annet_Recruiter will be logged in. She starts a process workflow (we will be creating this workflow in the next section) for the document by specifying the metadata values such as `nurse_id`, `nurse_name`, `assignemt_id`, `driver_licence`, `is_birthcert`, and `emp_expiration_date`. She then assigns the task to her colleague **Lee_Credential**. **Annet_Recruiter** can track the status of the task from her Alfresco Explorer interface. If the task is not completed within a specified time, or is rejected for some other reason, then **Annet_Recruiter** can cancel the workflow request or reassign it to somebody else. On the other hand, **Lee_Credential** receives a notification about the new task in her **My Tasks To Do** window. She examines the task and completes the task. She can approve or reject the workflow. If approved, the document will be moved to the **Company Home | GlobalPlacement | Nurse** folder. If it is rejected, it will remain in the **Annet_Recruiter** home space pending further action.

Annet_Recruiter and **Lee_Credential** can both track the status through the customized dashlet named **GlobalPlacement**. We shall discuss this shortly, after implementing a workflow.

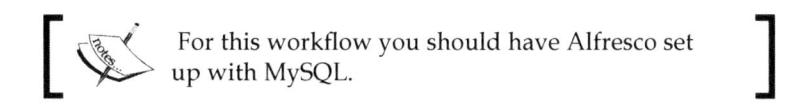

> For this workflow you should have Alfresco set up with MySQL.

For any workflow to be deployed, you should have the following files:

- Task model: The task model provides a description of each task in the workflow. Each task description consists of **Name**, **Title**, **Properties**, and **Association**.

- Resource bundle (optional): A workflow resource bundle provides all of the human-readable messages that are displayed in the user interface for managing the workflow. Messages include **task titles**, **task property names**, **task choices**, and so on.

- Process definition: The process definition describes the states (steps) and transitions (choices) of a workflow.

- `Web-client-config-custom.xml`: Web client configuration specifies the presentation of tasks to the user in the Alfresco Explorer.

The following steps need to be followed in order to create a custom advanced workflow:

Step 1: Create and deploy the task model

For each task in the process definition (as defined by `<task>` elements), it is possible to associate a task description. The description specifies the information that may be attached to a task, that is, it's properties (name and data type) and associations (name and type of associated object). A user may view and edit this information in the **task** dialog within the Alfresco Explorer.

The task model is expressed as a content model, as supported by the Data Dictionary. To create a task model, you need to:

- Create a new content model for the Process Definition.
- Create a custom content Type for each Task.
- Within each Type, describe the Properties and Associations (information) required for that Task

The task model can be dynamically deployed without restarting the server.

The dynamic deployment of task models

Dynamic custom models are stored in the **Models** space (**Company Home > Data Dictionary > Models**). This is a feature that enables the dynamic customization of models without requiring a restart of the Alfresco server. This feature is provided in Alfresco 3.0.

Upload a custom XML model file to the **Models** space. By default, the model will not be active unless the **Model Active** checkbox is selected during the upload. To activate a previously inactive model, select the **View Details** option and then select the **Modify** properties icon. On the **Modify Content Properties** page, select the **Model Active** checkbox.

To deactivate a model, select the **View Details** option and then select the **Modify** properties icon. On the **Modify Content Properties** page, deselect the **Model Active** checkbox.

Deployment of the model files can be achieved by the administrator by navigating to the following URL: `http://<server_name>:<port>/alfresco/faces/jsp/admin/repoadmin-console.jsp`

Use the command `activate model GlobalWorkflowModel.xml`. This command is used to activate the repository model and load it into the runtime data dictionary.

Use the command `deploy model alfresco/extension/GlobalWorkflowModel.xml`. This command uploads the model to the repository and loads it into the runtime Data Dictionary. This will also activate the repository model.

Carry out the following steps to deploy a model dynamically:

1. Go to **Company Home | Data Dictionary | Models**
2. In the header, click on **Create Content**

3. The **Create Content Wizard** is displayed, as shown in the following screenshot:

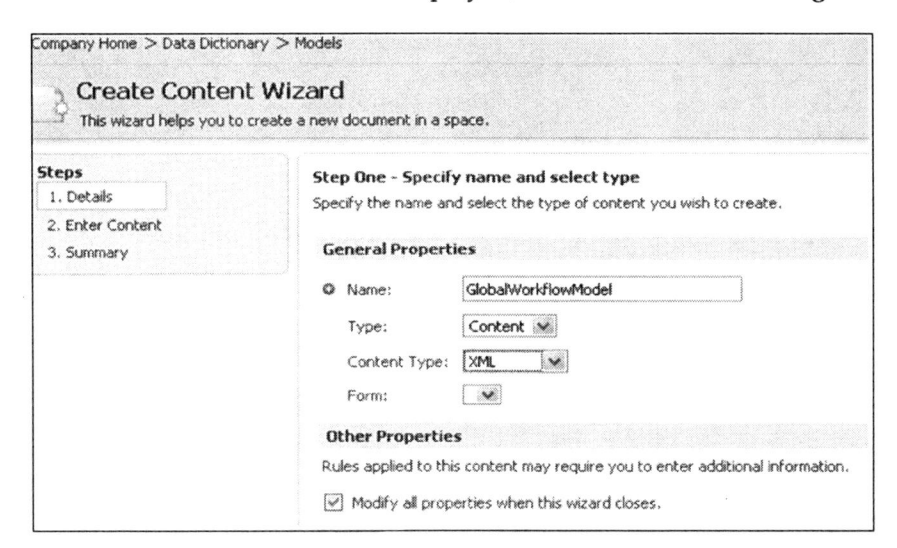

4. In the **Name** text box, enter **GlobalWorkflowModel**
5. Select **xml** as the **Content Type**
6. Click on the **Next** button to enter content into the specified file

7. Copy the following piece of code into the **Content Wizard**, as shown in following screenshot:

> You can download the complete code samples from the Packt web site.

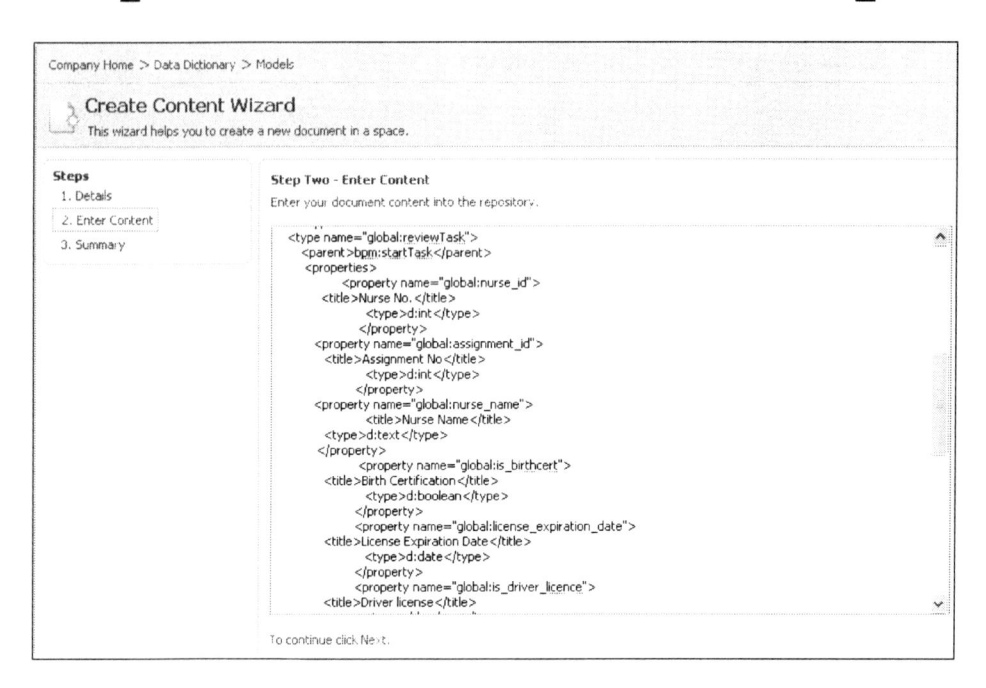

```
<type name="global:reviewTask">
<parent>bpm:startTask</parent>
<properties>
<property name="global:nurse_id">
<title>Nurse No.</title>
<type>d:int</type>
</property>
<property name="global:assignment_id">
<title>Assignment No</title>
<type>d:int</type>
</property>
<property name="global:nurse_name">
<title>Nurse Name</title>
<type>d:text</type>
```

```xml
        </property>
        <property name="global:is_birthcert">
        <title>Birth Certification</title>
        <type>d:boolean</type>
        </property>
        <property name="global:license_expiration_date">
        <title>License Expiration Date</title>
        <type>d:date</type>
        </property>
        <property name="global:is_driver_licence">
        <title>Driver license</title>
        <type>d:boolean</type>
        </property>
        <property name="global:wfDescription">
        <type>d:text</type>
        </property>
        </properties>
        <mandatory-aspects>
        <aspect>bpm:assignee</aspect>
        </mandatory-aspects>
        </type>
        <type name="global:submitReviewTask">
        <parent>global:reviewTask</parent>
        <overrides>
        <property name="global:nurse_id">
        </property>
        <property name="global:assignment_id">
        </property>
        <property name="global:nurse_name">
        </property>
        <property name="global:is_birthcert">
        </property>
        <property name="global:license_expiration_date">
        </property>
        <property name="global:is_driver_licence">
        </property>
        <property name="global:wfDescription">
        </property>
        </overrides>
        </type>
```

8. Click on the **Next** Button, and then click on the **Finish** button

9. Select the **Model Active** property, as shown in the following screenshot:

9. Click on the **OK** button
10. To verify the changes, first click on **logout**, and then click on **login** and log back in.

Step 2: Create and deploy the workflow resource bundles

For localized workflow interaction, it is necessary to provide resource bundles containing UI labels for each piece of text that is exposed to the user. With the appropriate resource bundles, a single workflow instance may spawn tasks where the user interface for each task is rendered in a different language, based on the locale of the user. The resource bundles can also be dynamically deployed without restarting the server.

The dynamic deployment of resource bundles

The associated message resource bundles are stored in the **Messages** space (**Company Home > Data Dictionary > Messages**). Upload the custom resource bundle by uploading each of the message property files (for all of the locales) to the **Messages** space. The messages will not be applied until either they are explicitly reloaded or the server is restarted.

The messages can be dynamically reloaded by using the repo admin console via the web site: `http://<server-name>:<port>/alfresco/faces/jsp/admin/repoadmin-console.jsp`.

The command line `reload messages <resource bundle base name>` will cause the message resource to be re-registered.

Carry out the following steps to create the content:

1. Go to **Company Home | Data Dictionary | Messages**
2. In the header, click on **Create Content**

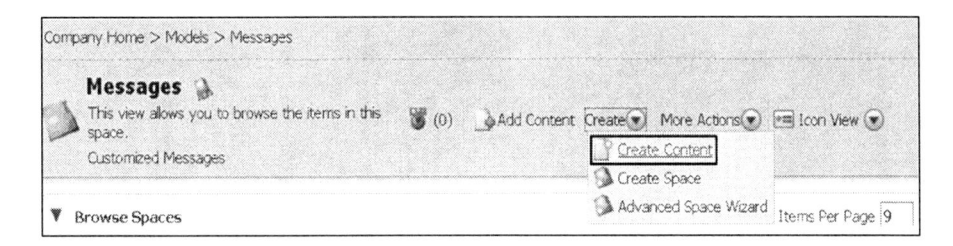

3. The **Create Content Wizard** is displayed, as shown in the following screenshot:

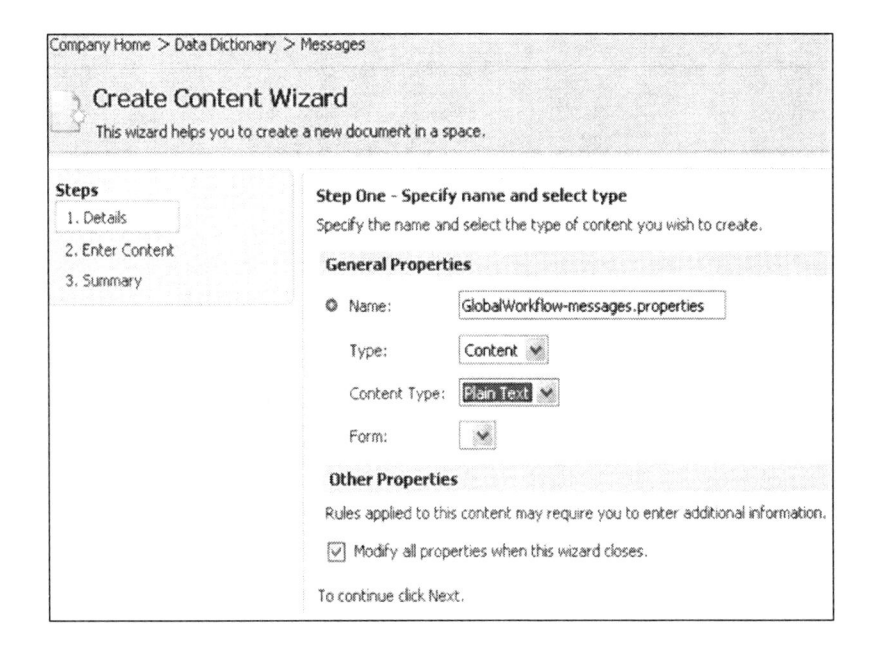

4. In the **Name** text box, enter **GlobalWorkflow-messages.properties**
5. Select **Plain Text** as the **Content Type**
6. Click on the **Next** button, to add the content into the specified file

Implementing Workflow

7. Copy the following piece of code into the **Content Wizard**, as shown in the following screenshot:

[You can download the code samples from book web site.]

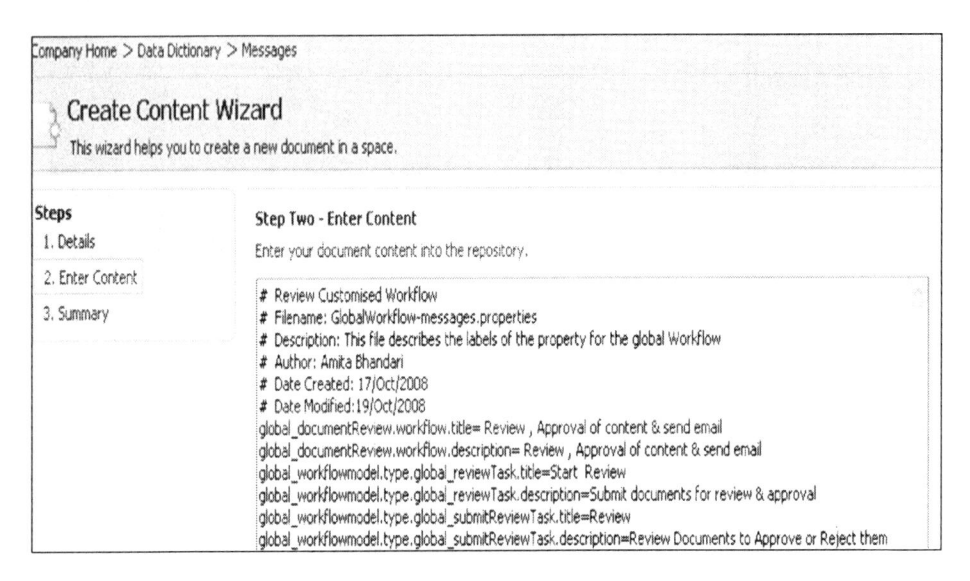

```
# Review Customised Workflow
# Filename: GlobalWorkflow-messages.properties
# Description: This file describes the labels of the property for the global Workflow. The first part of each key matches the name of the workflow content model (global). The process-related string keys matches the name of process(documentReview),
# Author: Amita Bhandari
# Date Created: 17/Oct/2008
# Date Modified:19/Oct/2008
global_documentReview.workflow.title= Review , Approval of content & send email
global_documentReview.workflow.description= Review , Approval of content & send email
global_workflowmodel.type.global_reviewTask.title=Start  Review
global_workflowmodel.type.global_reviewTask.description=Submit documents for review & approval
global_workflowmodel.type.global_submitReviewTask.title=Review
global_workflowmodel.type.global_submitReviewTask.description=Review Documents to Approve or Reject them
```

8. Click on the **Next** button, and then click on the **Finish** button.

9. Click on the **OK** button.
10. Deployment of the property files can be achieved by an administrator by navigating to the URL. `http://<server-name>:<port>/alfresco/faces/jsp/admin/repoadmin-console.jsp`
11. Use the following command to deploy the file:
    `reload messages GlobalWorkflow-messages`
12. To verify the changes, click on the **logout** button, and then click on the **login** button and log back in again.

Step 3: Create and deploy the process definition

Alfresco currently supports the ability to manage workflow process definitions dynamically via the Workflow Console, assuming that the definitions are using existing task models and messages. With the introduction of dynamic models, it is now possible to dynamically manage new workflow process definitions by using new task models and messages, and client configuration. In addition, it is also possible to deploy workflow definitions directly from a repository location.

The dynamic deployment of process definitions

Process definitions are stored in the **Workflow Definitions** space (**Company Home > Data Dictionary > Workflow Definitions**). Upload a custom XML process definition file to the **Workflow Definitions** space. By default, the process definition will not be deployed unless the **Workflow Deployed** checkbox is selected during the upload.

To make sure that a process definition is not deployed, select the **View Details** option and then click on the **Modify** properties icon. In the **Modify Content Properties** page, deselect the **Workflow Deployed** checkbox.

Using the workflow console

The workflow console can be used (as an alternative to the Alfresco Explorer) to deploy or withdraw process definitions. Its primary use is to test newly-developed workflow definitions. However, it also supports the debugging and diagnosis of current in-flight workflows. The workflow console can be deployed via the following web site:

`http://<server-name>:<port>/alfresco/faces/jsp/admin/workflow-console.jsp`

Manual Deployment of Workflow

Process definitions can be configured into Alfresco so that they are deployed whenever Alfresco starts.

Implementing Workflow

The Spring bean **workflowDeployer** deploys process definitions. It may be used with Alfresco's configuration extension mechanism to deploy custom workflows. A code snippet is provided for deploying workflows programmatically

```xml
<bean id="extension.workflowBootstrap" parent="workflowDeployer">
 <property name="workflowDefinitions">
    <list>
            <props>
              <prop key="engineId">jbpm</prop>
              <prop key="location">alfresco/extension/ Global-
                        review-process-definition.xml</prop>
              <prop key="mimetype">text/xml</prop>
              <prop key="redeploy">true</prop>
            </props>
      </list>
 </property>
</bean>
```

There are two ways of building the process definition .One is by hand, that is, by creating a jPDL XML document. The second option is by designer, that is, by using a tool to generate the jPDL XML document.

The first option: Creating a jPDL XML by hand

Let's create a jPDL XML document by hand. Carry out the following steps to create a jPDL XML document by hand:

1. Go to **Company Home > Data Dictionary > Workflow Definitions**.
2. In the header, click on the **Create Content** option.

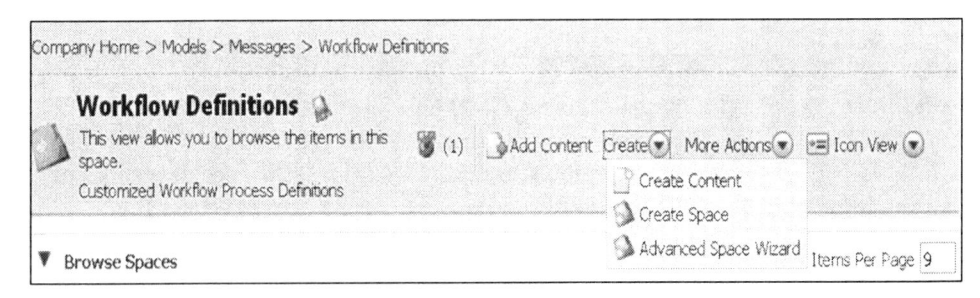

3. The **Create Content Wizard** is displayed, as shown in the following screenshot:

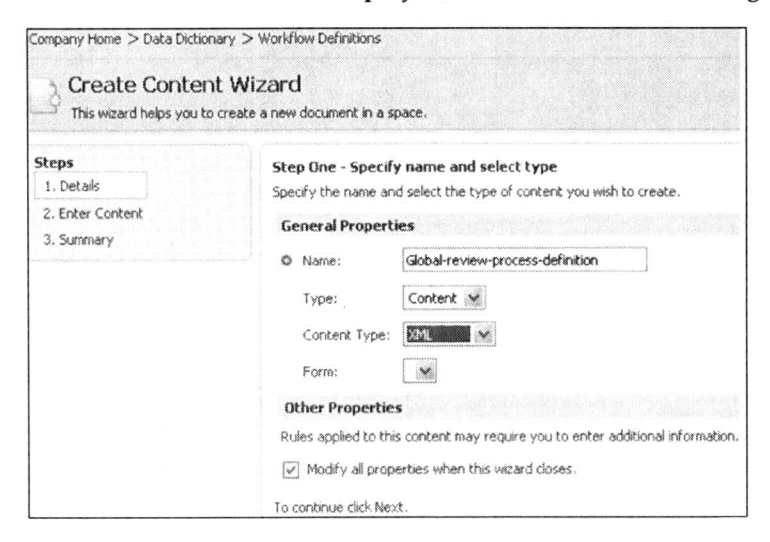

4. In the **Name** text box, enter **Global-review-process-definition**.
5. Select **XML** as the **Content Type**.
6. Click on the **Next** button to add content into the specified file.
7. Copy the following piece of code into the **Content Wizard**, as shown in the following screenshot:

> You can download the code samples from the Packt web site.

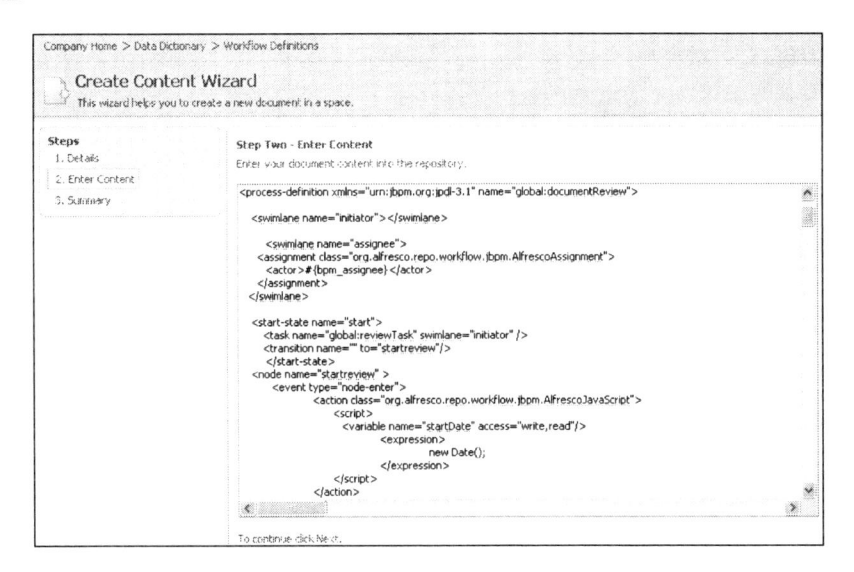

Implementing Workflow

```xml
<process-definition xmlns="urn:jbpm.org:jpdl-3.1" name="global:documentReview">  <swimlane name="initiator"></swimlane>
<swimlane name="assignee">
<assignment class="org.alfresco.repo.workflow.jbpm.AlfrescoAssignment">
<actor>#{bpm_assignee}</actor>
</assignment>
</swimlane>
<start-state name="start">
<task name="global:reviewTask" swimlane="initiator" />
<transition name="" to="startreview"/>
</start-state>
<node name="startreview" >
<transition name="review" to="review" >
<action class="org.alfresco.repo.workflow.jbpm.AlfrescoJavaScript">
<script>
</script>
</action>
</transition>
</node>
<task-node name="review">
<task name="global:submitReviewTask" swimlane="assignee">
</task>
<transition name="Reject" to="end" >
</transition>
</transition>
</task-node>
<end-state name="end"/> </process-definition>
```

8. Click on the **Next** button, and then click on the **Finish** button.

9. Select the **Workflow Deployed** checkbox. By default, the process definition will not be deployed unless the **'Workflow Deployed'** checkbox is selected during the upload.

10. In the **Workflow Engine Id** field, enter **jbpm**, as shown in the following screenshot:

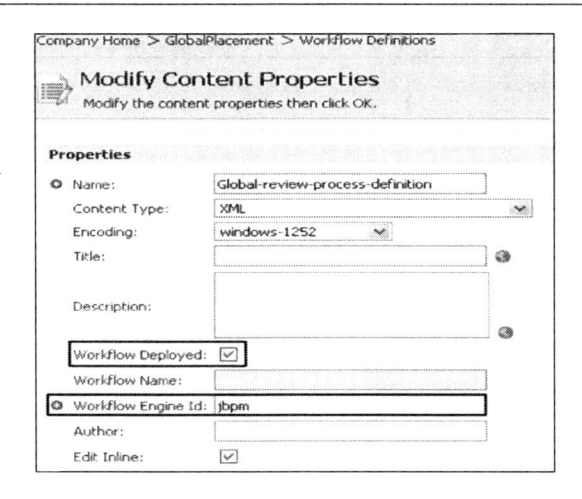

11. Click on the **OK** button.
12. To verify the changes, click on the **logout** button, and then click on the **login** button and log back in again.

The definition above describes the three steps of the **Review, Approve and sends email** task workflow. The following are the things to be considered when creating a process definition:

1. There's always a start and an end.
2. The process definition's name and task names are important. These tasks are defined in the workflow model files. The properties are displayed on the basis of these tasks.
3. **Swimlanes** are used to declare workflow **roles**.
4. Tasks are associated with a swimlane.
5. Certain actions are performed on the basis of these tasks, as defined in the process definition.

The second option: Using the JBoss jBPM process designer

JBoss jBPM also includes a graphical designer tool for authoring business processes. The most important feature of the graphical designer tool is that it includes support for both the tasks of the business analyst as well as those of the technical developer. This enables a smooth transition from business process modeling to practical implementation. Carry out the following steps to configure jBPM:

1. To implement the graphical designed tool, you have to download the jBPM plugins from http://labs.jboss.com/jbossjbpm/downloads.
2. Once the installation is over, restart Eclipse.

Implementing Workflow

3. Go to **File | New | Project**. Expand the **JBoss jBPM** process designer folder, and select **Process Project**, as shown in the following screenshot:

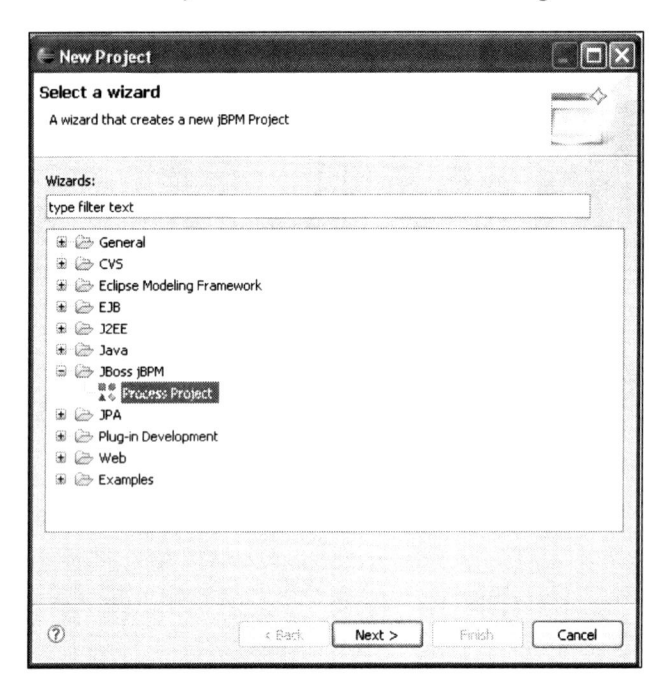

4. Enter the **Project Name,** and then click on **Next**.
5. Select the jBPM Location, as mentioned in the following screenshot. Click on the Finish button.

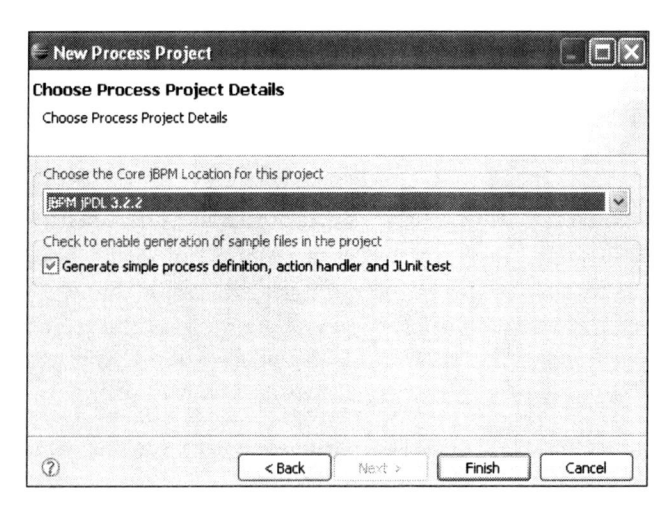

6. Copy the process definition code and paste it into the `src/main/jpd` package.
7. The process should look similar to the following screenshot:

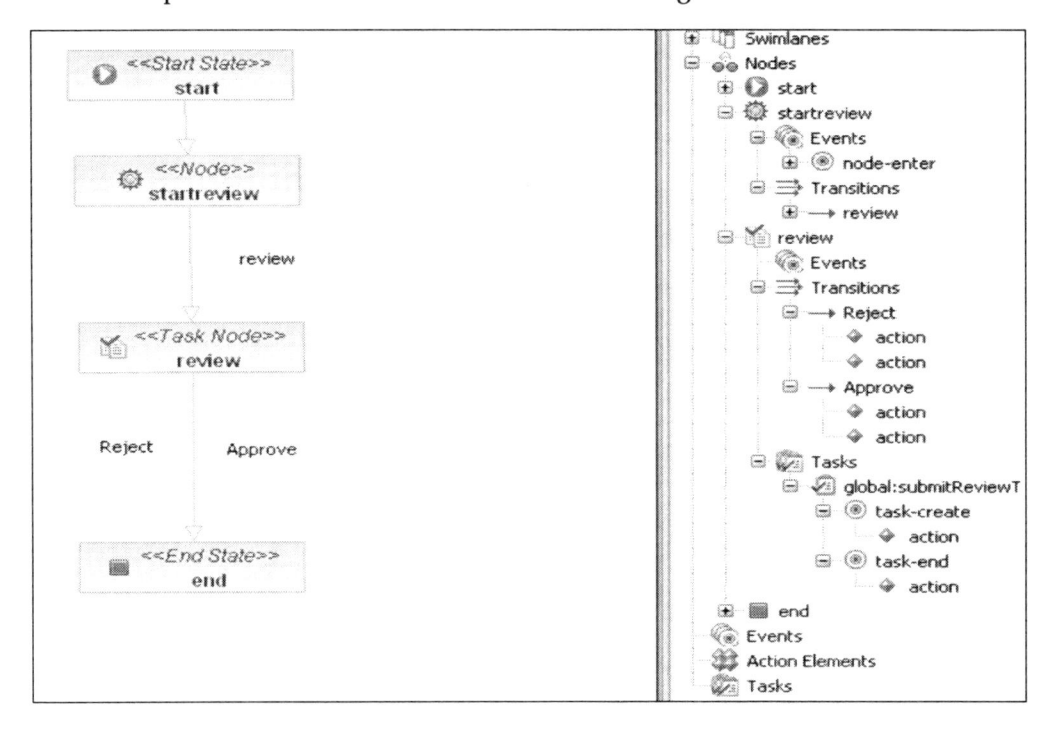

8. Deploy it.

The following steps need to be followed in order to deploy a workflow via JBoss jBPM Process Designer. These steps will deploy the workflow without the need to restart the server.

1. Ensure that the Alfresco Server is up and running.
2. Click on the **source** tab and copy the content of the file `Global-review-process-definition`.
3. Click on the **Deployment** tab and enter the following information:
    - **Server Name** = machine name where Alfresco is installed
    - **Server Port** = port number assigned to Alfresco (the default is **8080**)
    - **Server Deployer** = `/alfresco/jbpm/deployprocess`
    - Click on **Test Connection**.
    - When everything is OK, then click on the **Deploy Process Archive** button.

Implementing Workflow

The following screenshot shows the details mentioned earlier:

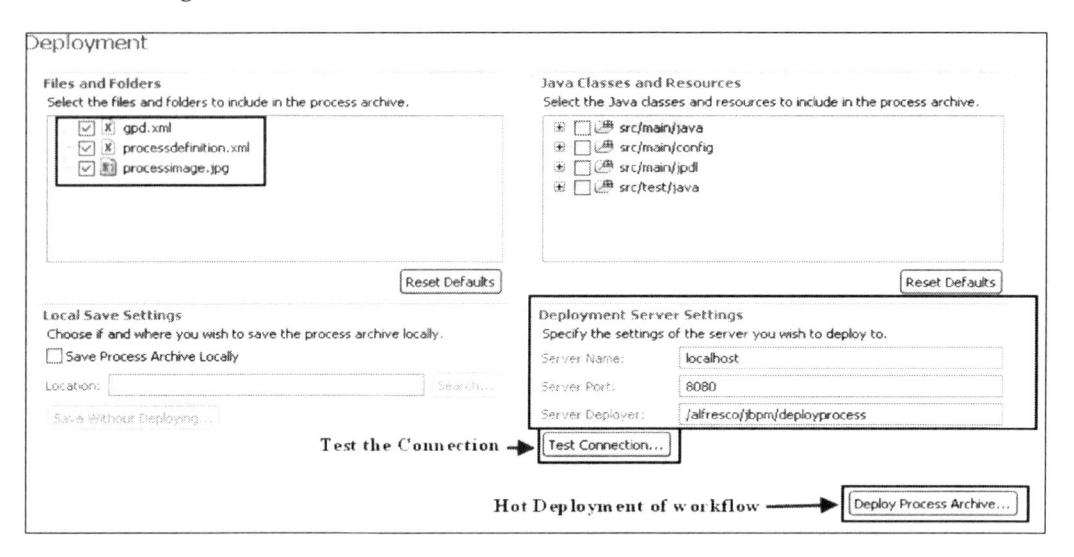

Step 4: Display the workflow images

If **Hot Deployment** is done, then we can see the workflow images, which show the current status of the workflow, in Alfresco Explorer under the *workflow outline* section. The screenshot is shown in the next section of this chapter, which is titled *Manage Adhoc Task of Out of Box Features Workflow Task Lists Dashboards*.

Modify the following files:

```
/jsp/workflow/start-workflow-wizard/workflow-options.jsp
/jsp/workflow/manage-task-dialog.jsp
```

Change the rendered and expanded value to true.

Modify this code:

```
<a:panel rendered="false" id="workflow-outline" label="#{msg.workflow_
outline}" progressive="true" expanded="false"
border="white" bgcolor="white" titleBorder="lbgrey" expandedTitleBorde
r="dotted" titleBgcolor="white" styleClass="mainSubTitle">
```

to:

```
<a:panel rendered="true" id="workflow-outline" label="#{msg.workflow_
outline}" progressive="true" expanded="true"
border="white" bgcolor="white" titleBorder="lbgrey" expandedTitleBorde
r="dotted" titleBgcolor="white" styleClass="mainSubTitle">
```

Step 5: Create and deploy the Alfresco Explorer task dialogs

The **Start Workflow Wizard** uses XML configuration to display the relevant controls to collect data from the user. The **Manage Task** dialog uses the same approach to display the data that it needs to collect. The Alfresco Explorer can also be dynamically deployed without restarting the server.

Dynamic Alfresco Explorer

Dynamic Alfresco Explorer customizations are stored in the **Web Client Extension** space (**Company Home > Data Dictionary > Web Client Extension**). Upload a custom `web-client-config-custom.xml` file to the **Web Client Extension** space. The custom configuration will not be applied until either it is explicitly reloaded, or the server is restarted. If the `web-client-config-custom.xml` file has been added, edited, or updated, then it can be dynamically reloaded by using the Alfresco Explorer config console, by navigating to the following location: `http://<server-name>:<port>/alfresco/faces/jsp/admin/webclientconfig-console.jsp`.

This has a single command, `reload`, which will cause the Alfresco Explorer configurations to be reloaded. Carry out the following steps in order to create and deploy the Dynamic Alfresco Explorer tasks:

1. Browse to the file `web-client-config-custom.xml`, which can be found in the location `tomcat/shared/classes/alfresco/extension`.

2. Copy the code below into this file

> You can download the code samples from the Packt web site.

```
<config evaluator="node-type"
condition="global:reviewTask" replace="true">
<property-sheet>
<show-property name="global:nurse_id" display-label="Nurse Id"/>
<show-property name="global:assignment_id"
display-label="Assignment No" />
<show-property name="global:nurse_name"
display-label="Nurse Name" />
<show-property name="global:is_birthcert" display-label="Is BirthCertificate"/>
<show-property name="global:license_expiration_date" display-label="Licensce   Expiration Date"/>
```

Implementing Workflow

```xml
<show-property name="global:is_driver_licence" display-label="Driver Licensce"/>
<show-property name="global:wfDescription" display-label="Description"/>
<separator name="sep2" display-label-id="users_and_roles" component-generator="HeaderSeparatorGenerator" />
<show-association name="bpm:assignee" display-label-id="wf_reviewers" />
</property-sheet>
</config>
<config evaluator="node-type" condition="global:submitReviewTask"
replace="true">
<property-sheet>
<show-property name="global:nurse_id" display-label="Nurse Id"/>
<show-property name="global:assignment_id" display-label="Assignment No" />
<show-property name="global:nurse_name" display-label="Nurse Name" />
<show-property name="global:is_birthcert" display-label="Is BirthCertificate"/>
<show-property name="global:license_expiration_date" display-label="Licensce Expiration Date"/>
<show-property name="global:is_driver_licence" display-label="Driver Licensce"/>
<show-property name="global:wfDescription" display-label="Description"/>
</property-sheet>
</config>
```

3. Deployment of the Alfresco Explorer can be achieved by the administrator by navigating to the URL `http://<server-name>:<port>/alfresco/faces/jsp/admin/webclientconfig-console.jsp`

4. Use the following command to deploy the file: `reload`

Step 6: Test the workflow

Let's test the workflow by carrying out the following steps:

1. Log in as **Annet_Recruiter**.

2. Upload a document to the **Company Home > Global Placement > Recruiter > Annet_Recruiter** space. Click on the document's **More Actions** button and then click on the **Start Advance Workflow** link.

3. Select the **Review, Approval of content & send email** option from the list of predefined workflows. Click on the **Next** button.

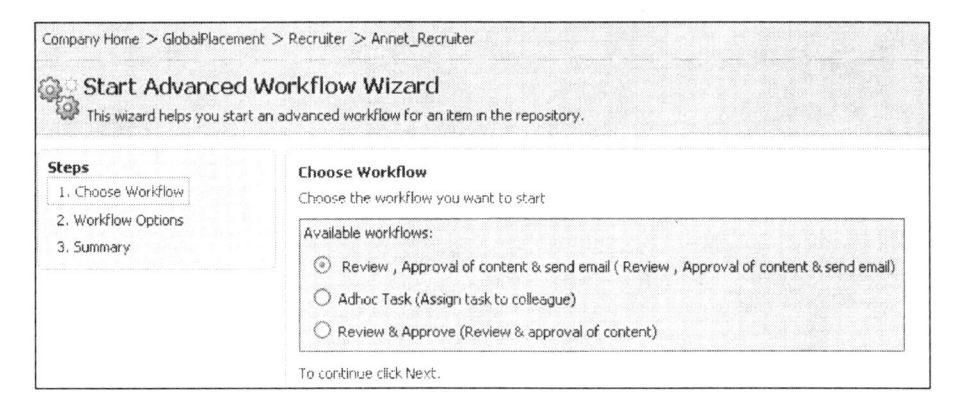

4. Provide meaningful values for the metadata, namely `nurse_id`, `nurse_name`, `assignemt_id`, `driver_licence`, `is_birthcert`, and `emp_expiration_date`.

5. From the list of users, search for **Lee_Credential** and assign her the task. You can also add additional resources (documents) to this workflow task by clicking on the **Add Resource** button, as shown in the following screenshot. This activity helps if you want to send a set of documents for approval as a group.

Implementing Workflow

6. Once you fill up the entire relevant information, click on the **OK** button to start the workflow process, as shown in the following screenshot:

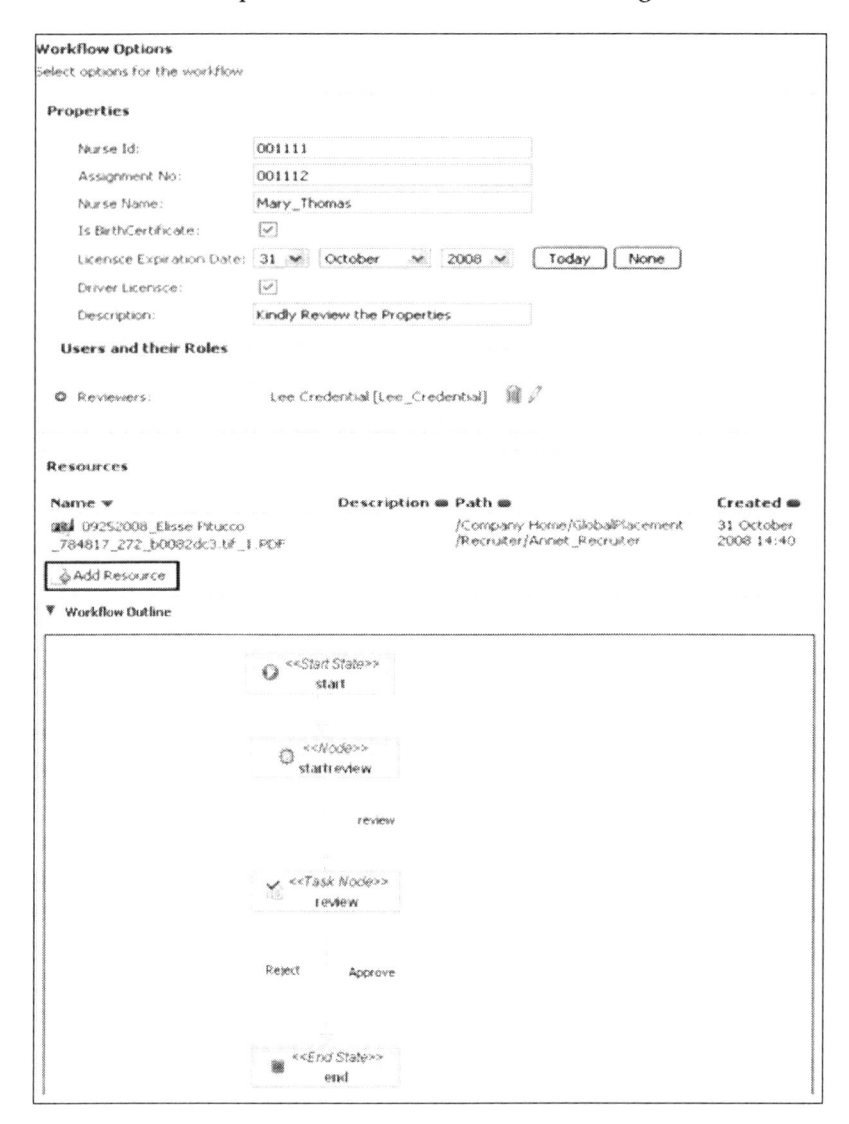

7. Click on **Next**, and then click on the **Finish** button.
8. Next, logged in as **Lee_Credential**, click on the **My Alfresco** menu in the toolbar to view your dashboard, that is, **My Tasks To Do**. You will notice that one task in the dashboard, which was assigned by **Annet_Recruiter.** You can also reassign the task to another, according to your business process. Shortly, we will discuss the various workflow related dashboards.

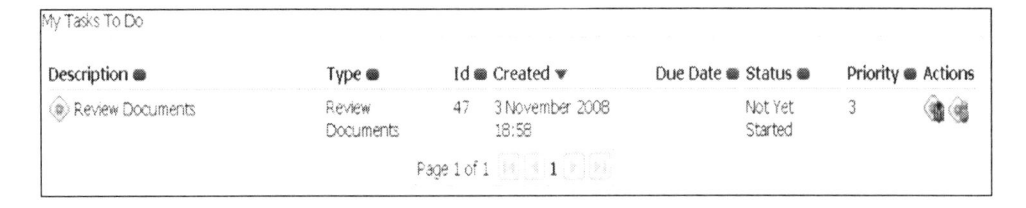

My Tasks To Do						
Description	Type	Id	Created ▼	Due Date	Status	Priority	Actions
Review Documents	Review Documents	47	3 November 2008 18:58		Not Yet Started	3	

Page 1 of 1   1

9. You can complete the process by verifying the metadata specified by **Annet_Recruiter**. If the relevant information is there, then you can **Approve** or **Reject** the task.

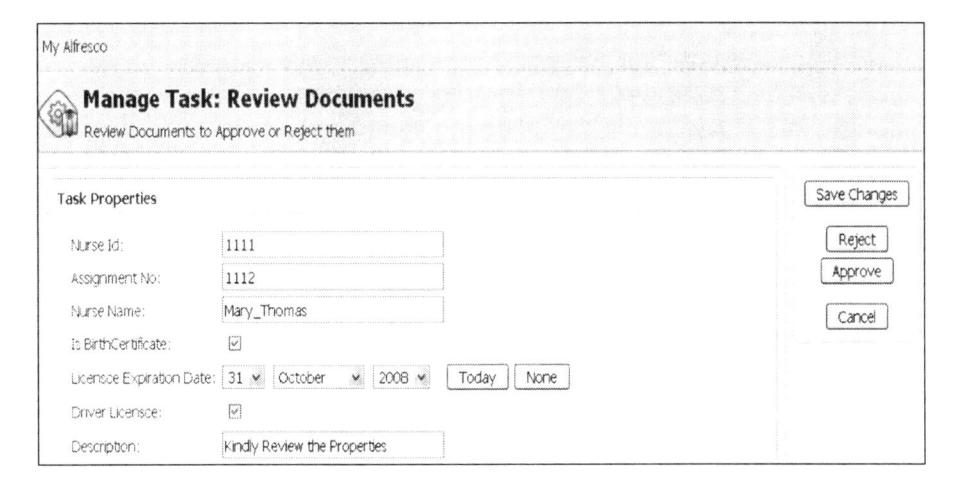

Manage Task: Review Documents
Review Documents to Approve or Reject them

Task Properties

- Nurse Id: 1111
- Assignment No: 1112
- Nurse Name: Mary_Thomas
- Is BirthCertificate: ☑
- Licensce Expiration Date: 31 October 2008 Today None
- Driver Licensce: ☑
- Description: Kindly Review the Properties

Save Changes / Reject / Approve / Cancel

10. Now, If you have approved the task, then you will find the document in the `nurse` folder.
11. If you have rejected the task, then the document will be available in the `recruiter` folder itself.

Track the status of this workflow through a customized dashlet

During the process of the **Review** and **Approval** workflows, two XMLs files are generated. These are `userlogger.xml` and `logger.xml`. These have the detailed information about the workflow in terms of initiator, assignee, start date, and end date of the workflows. These XML files will help us in generating the dashlet report.

Implementing Workflow

Carry out the following steps to configure the dashlet for the workflow mentioned above:

1. Create a custom dashlet script file of `/tomcat/shared/classes/alfresco/extension/templates/global_logs.ftl`. For this purpose, you have to create a `templates` folder within the following path: `/tomcat/shared/classes/alfresco/extension`.

   > You can download the code samples from the Packt web site.

2. Create a custom dashlet JSP. For this purpose, create a `global_logs.jsp` file, which consists of the following piece of code. Place the file in the dashlet folder, and create the following hierarchy `extension\dashboards\dashlets` of folders inside the `tomcat\webapps\alfresco\jsp` folder.

   ```
   <%@ taglib uri="/WEB-INF/repo.tld" prefix="r" %>
   <%-- Note that this template is loaded from the classpath --%>
   <r:template template="alfresco/extension/templates/global_logs.ftl" />
   ```

3. Open the file `web-client-config-custom.xml`, which is located in: `tomcat/shared/classes/alfresco/extension/`. Replace the existing code in the file with the code in the file `web-client-config-custom.xml`. Then, before the `</alfresco-config>` tag, add the following piece of code:

   ```
   <config evaluator="string-compare" condition="Dashboards">
   <dashboards><dashlets>
   <dashlet id="global_logs_horizontal" label="Global Placement" description="Log file for Global Placement" jsp="/jsp/extension/dashboards/dashlets/global_logs.jsp" />
   </dashlets></dashboards></config>
   ```

4. Restart the server.

5. Log in as **Lee_Credential**. Click on the **Configure** button to configure the dashboard.

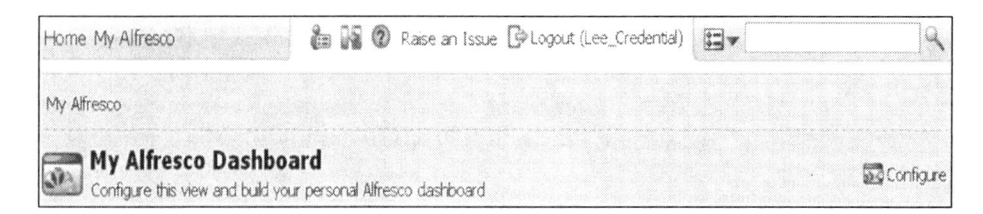

[298]

6. Select the **Global Placement** component, and then click on the **Add** button, as shown in the following screenshot:

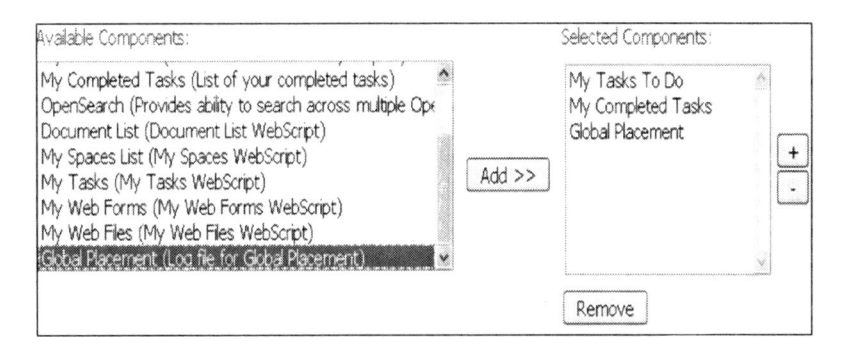

7. Click on the **Next** button, and then click on the **Finish** button.

You will find the following screen in **My Alfresco**. Through the **Global Placement** dashlet, you can easily track the performance of the user and also determine the timelines related to each stage of the workflow.

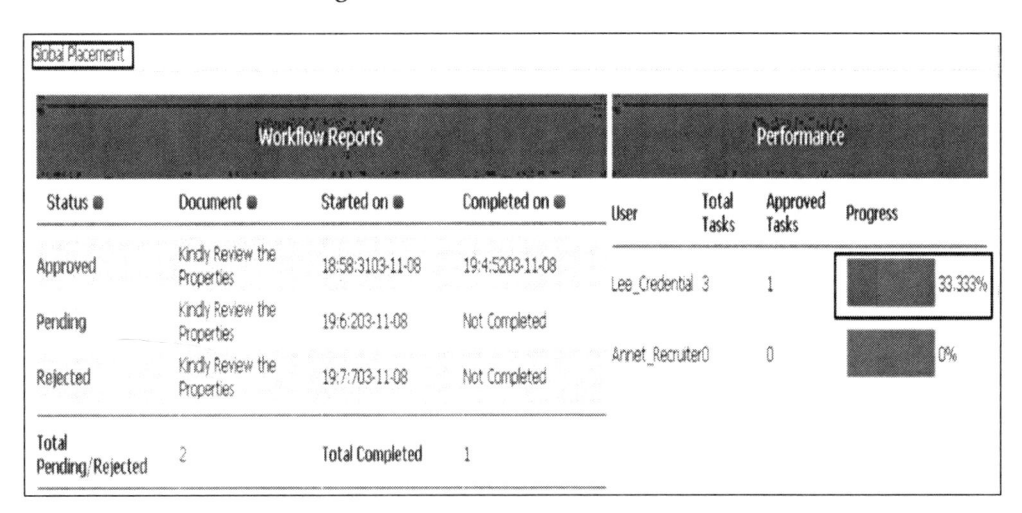

Out of the box features of the workflow task list's dashboards

Let's have a look at a few out of the box features.

List of My Tasks To Do

Click on the **My Alfresco** menu link in the toolbar to view your personal dashboard.

Implementing Workflow

This dashboard includes the tasks that you need to process, as shown in the following screenshot. You may notice that the new task listed in the **My Tasks To Do** window was assigned to you by **Annet_Recruiter**.

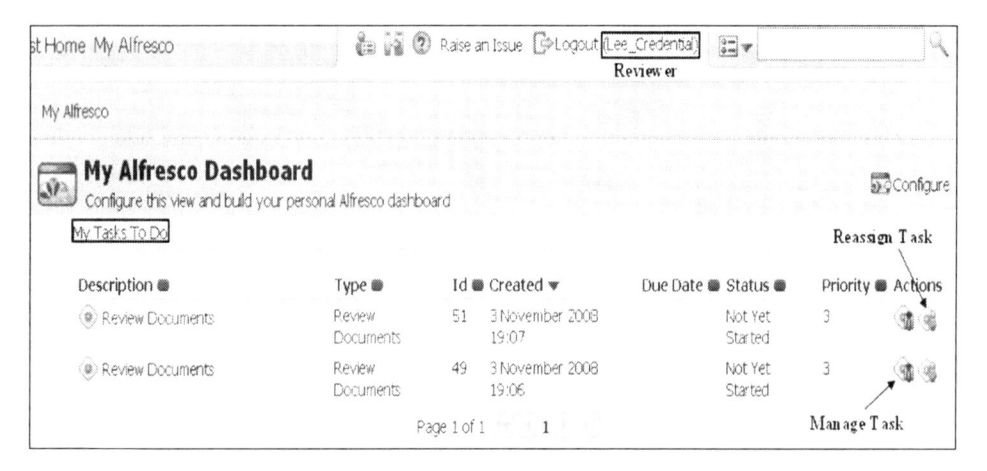

Reassign Adhoc Task

For various business reasons, you may need to reassign a task. You can do this by clicking on the **Reassign Task** button, as shown in the preceding screenshot. Once you click on the **Reassign Task** button, you will see the **Reassign Task** window, as shown in the following screenshot. You can search for the appropriate user to reassign the task to.

Manage Adhoc tasks

You can manage a task by clicking on the **Manage Task** button. Once you click on the **Manage Task** button, you will see the **Manage Task** window, as shown in the following screenshot. You can update the document and the properties based on the access permissions that you have on the document.

To complete the task, click on either the **Approve** button or the **Reject** button, as shown in the following screenshot:

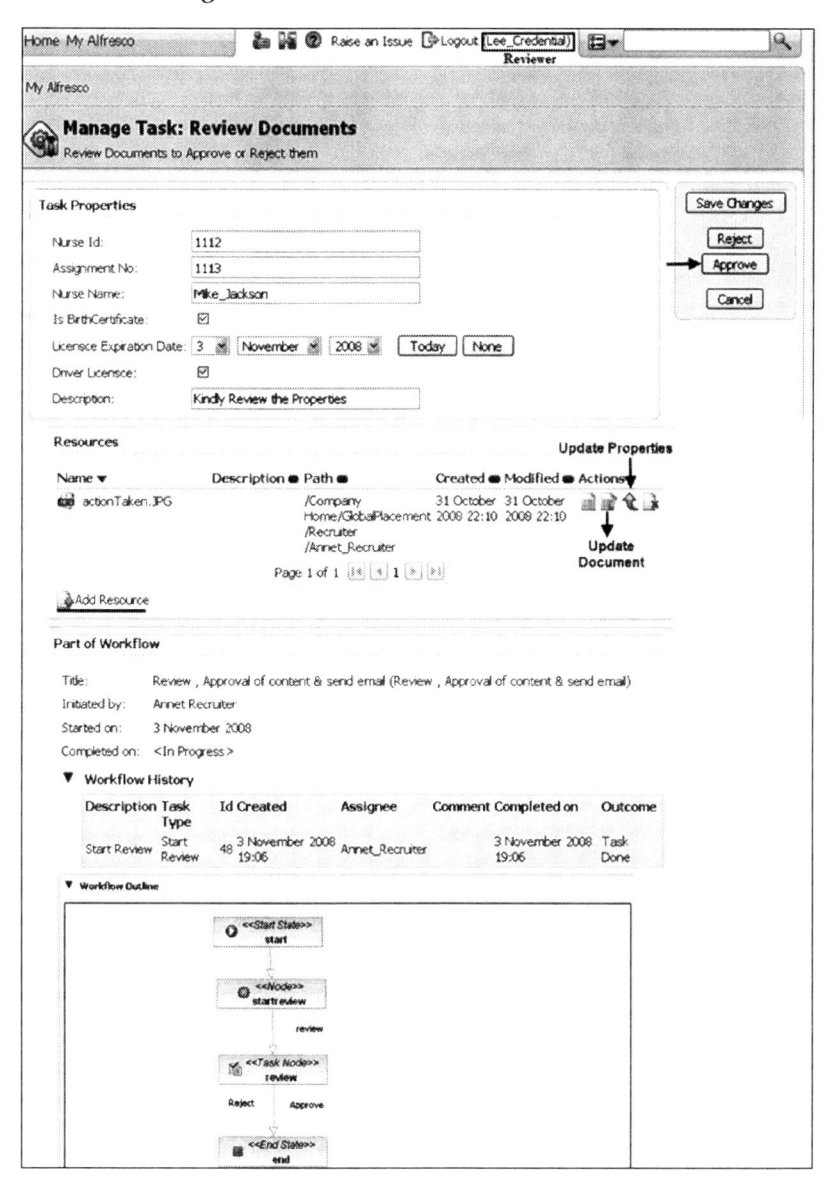

Implementing Workflow

List of My Completed Tasks

Once you have completed a task that was assigned to you, you will notice that the task is removed from the **My Tasks To Do** window, and is moved to the **My Completed Tasks** window, as shown in the following screenshot:

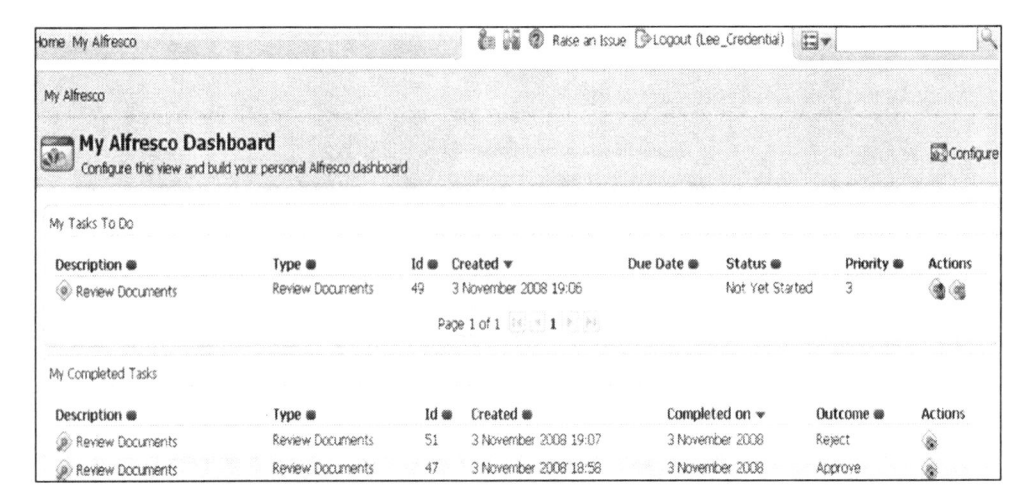

View the Status of or Cancel a Workflow

As an initiator, you can view the status of a workflow by clicking on the **View Status** button. You can cancel a task by clicking on the **Cancel Workflow** button.

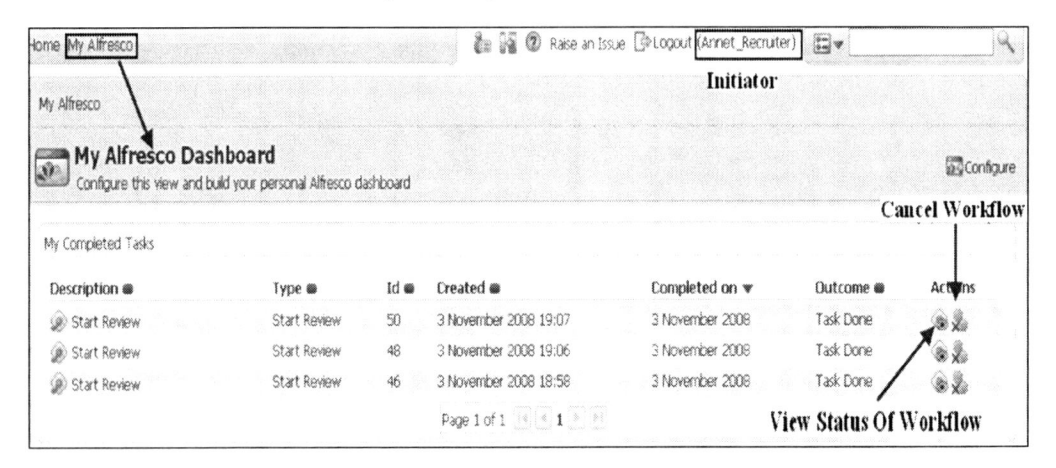

[302]

Workflow information in the Document Details page

For a specific document in your space, you can determine the workflow details by clicking on the document's **View Details** button.

The document's details page also lists the workflow details, as shown in the following screenshot. If you have sent this document to multiple people for approval, then all of these workflow tasks will be listed here for your reference.

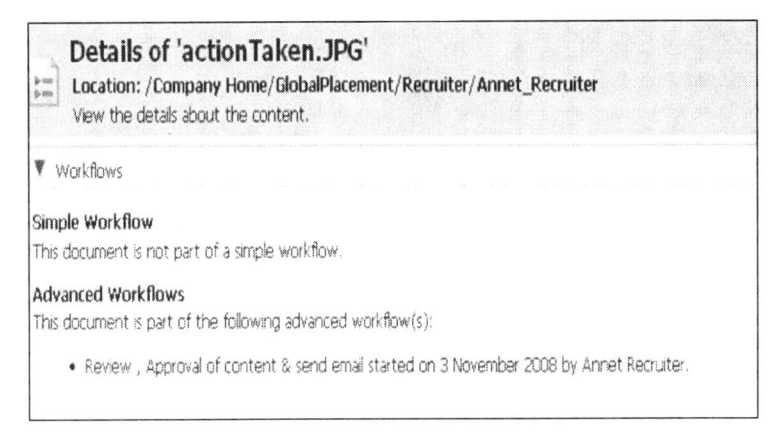

Details of 'actionTaken.JPG'
Location: /Company Home/GlobalPlacement/Recruiter/Annet_Recruiter
View the details about the content.

▼ Workflows

Simple Workflow
This document is not part of a simple workflow.

Advanced Workflows
This document is part of the following advanced workflow(s):

- Review , Approval of content & send email started on 3 November 2008 by Annet Recruiter.

Integration with rules

An Advanced Workflow may be initiated via a rule that is defined within the Alfresco Explorer. This allows for the automated initiation of a workflow, rather than relying on a user to manually start it.

The following script may be executed by a rule to initiate the **Review** and **Approve** workflow for the content that is acted upon by the rule. This script assigns the workflow to the person who kicked off the rule.

```
var workflow = actions.create("start-workflow");
workflow.parameters.workflowName = "jbpm$wf:review";
workflow.parameters["bpm:workflowDescription"] = document.name;
workflow.parameters["bpm:assignee"] = person;
workflow.execute(document);
```

Summary

Alfresco includes two types of workflows out-of-the-box. One is the Simple Workflow, which is content-oriented, and the other one is the Advanced Workflow, which is task-oriented.

The Simple Workflow feature of Alfresco enables you to define a simple **approve** or **reject** workflow for your document. The email templates and notification business rules are helpful for notifying all of the people involved in the workflow process. You can also implement complex workflows by chaining the spaces with multiple **approve** and **reject** steps.

Complex task-oriented workflow can be implemented by using the Advanced Workflow features. You can create a task, attach multiple documents, and send it to multiple people for review. Using the dashboard views, you can view all of the tasks assigned to you, and all of the tasks assigned to others by you. You can track the tasks to closure by using the Alfresco Explorer user interface.

Integrating External Applications with Alfresco

In the previous chapters, we experienced the content management features of Alfresco as a standalone application. We used the Alfresco Explorer, which is a built-in web application to access and manage the content within the Alfresco repository. However, in a real life scenario, many customers integrate their own business applications with Alfresco in variety of ways. In this chapter, we will focus on various ways of integrating external applications with Alfresco, in order to leverage the features of this highly-scalable and high-performance content management system.

By the end of this chapter, you will have learned about:

- Alfresco integration protocols
- The Alfresco Web Script framework, which provides RESTful web services for integration
- Various application integration examples, including Liferay Portal, Drupal CMS, iPhone, iGoogle, and Facebook
- Alfresco support for content management interoperability services

The Alfresco content platform

Alfresco is architected in such a way that the repository services are separated from the user interface, thereby giving infinite options to either embed or integrate with external applications. The Alfresco repository can be embedded into the customer application or it can be integrated with the customer application, as shown below:

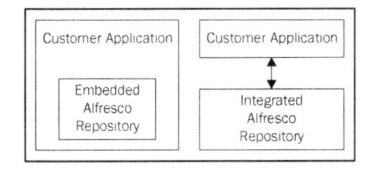

Embeddable enterprise content management system

Alfresco enterprise content management server is now available as a standalone embeddable option for OEMs. Alfresco was designed from the ground up, to be embedded in modern architectures for the new world of enterprise software. It offers:

- A 100% Java WAR file that can be simply run on an application sever
- A system that can share the same JVM as the embedding application or be accessed remotely
- The most scalable standards-based JSR-170 repository
- An environment for rapid development with API sets for REST, Web Services, and Java JSR-170

The Alfresco enterprise content management system enables **OEM (Original Equipment Manufacturer)** / **ISV (Independent Software Vendor)** / **VARs (Value-added reseller)** to focus core engineering resources on their product, rather than building and maintaining a proprietary ECM system. Many customers, including some of the largest software companies in the world, have already "white-labeled" Alfresco by embedding it in their core products.

Integrated enterprise content management system

At the time of writing this book, there expected to be around 75,000 production applications using Alfresco. These production applications include portals, media publishing sites, extranets, intranets, mobile applications, public static web sites, dynamic web sites, collaborative frameworks, social networking sites, financial applications, digital asset management systems, and knowledge management systems.

These applications:

- Are written using various languages such as Java, PHP, .NET, Python, and Ruby on Rails
- Run on various platforms such as Microsoft Windows, Linux, Unix, Solaris, and IBM
- Use various databases such as Oracle, MySQL, Microsoft SQL, Post GreSQL, and Sybase

The integration options available in Alfresco are independent of the programming language, operating system, application server, and underlying database used.

The following picture illustrates some of the current production integrations with Alfresco:

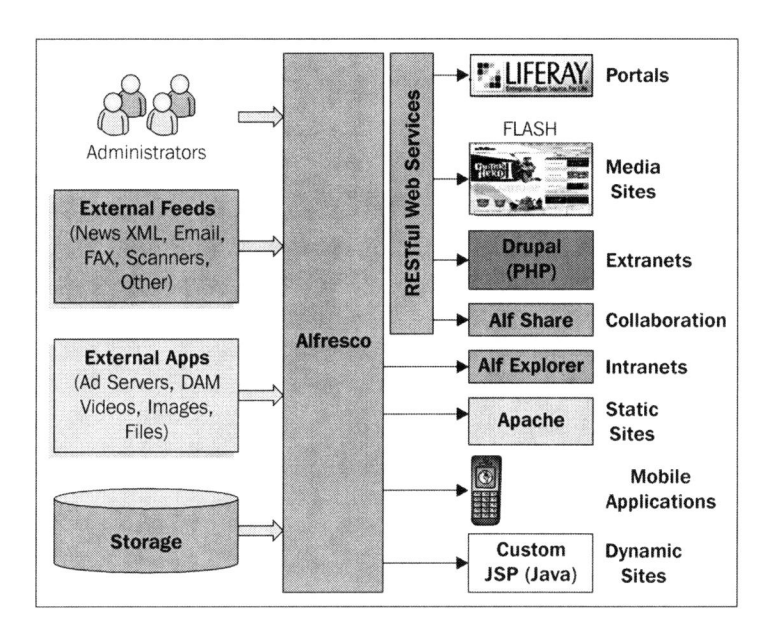

Various protocols for integration

Alfresco offers the following protocols for integrating with the repository:

- FTP: Transfers files in and out of Alfresco repository through the FTP protocol
- CIFS: Maps the Alfresco repository as a local drive
- WebDAV: Connects to Alfresco repository though the HTTP-based WebDAV protocol
- Web Services API: Provides web services support to connect to a repository using Java, PHP, and .Net based applications
- Java API: Connects to Alfresco using the Java API
- JCR API: Connects using the industry-standard JCR API
- RESTful Web Services: The Alfresco Web Scripts framework provides an interface with zero installation of client software
- Microsoft Share Point Protocol: Connects to Alfresco repository from Microsoft office applications
- Alfresco Surf: A collaborative web framework

- CMIS: Content Management Interoperability Service
- RSS: Syndication of content
- OpenSearch: An open standards-based search interface

Some of these options are explained next, to give you an idea of what to explore further.

Using web service as an integration solution

Web services are widely accepted and mostly used as an interoperability solution for any application. Alfresco also supports SOAP-based web services to access its repository. The web services provided by Alfresco are easy to understand and develop, accessible to almost all clients and languages, and mainly designed for accessing repository remotely by composite applications and business processes.

Using FTP, WebDAV, and CIFS protocols for integration

These protocols and integration options are covered in Chapter 5.

Alfresco can act as an FTP client as well a FTP Server. By default, Alfresco has support for this protocol.

WebDav is basically used for editing and managing files on remote web servers. If you have a WebDav client, you can access Alfresco with the following URL:

`http://localhost:8080/alfresco/webdev/`

The **Common Internet File System (CIFS)** is an excellent way of achieving desktop integration. Here, we use Alfresco as a CIFS server, and will expose the repository so that all the clients (users) would be able to map the repository as a normal Windows drive (as a shared network drive).

RESTful web services

Alfresco provides a Web Script framework, which is based on REST architecture. Nowadays, REST architecture has become popular and is widely used as an integration mechanism. RESTful Web Script is a very suitable and flexible solution to integrate Alfresco with any other application, and is most likely the best solution out of all of the available options. With the help of Web Scripts, you can easily access the Alfresco repository and perform operations such as searching a document, managing a document, and so on, even from outside Alfresco. For more details about Web Script, please refer the following section, which explains Web Script in detail, with some examples.

Web Scripts

Web Scripts are basically RESTful web services. Alfresco provides REST architecture-based framework for Web Scripts. In this section, we will talk about Web Script, implementing Web Script, some out of the box Web Script examples, along with some custom web script examples.

What is a Web Script

A REST Web Script is simply a service bound to a **URI** (**Universal Resource Identifier**) and based on HTTP. So, the technology that the external application is implemented in is irrelevant, that is, they are cross platform and cross language. You are not locked in to any programming language or development environment.

The Web Script framework lets you roll your own APIs, thereby allowing you to fine-tune the remote APIs that you expose to the external application. REST has proven itself to be simple, flexible, and extremely scalable. It provides a convenient bridge between any native application and the content management, along with easier content streaming than SOAP. Using Web Scripts, the Alfresco system now provides access to its repository services from anywhere, and has easier-to-access content and workflow information. Web Scripts support access and update using standard HTTP methods, and can be constructed using lightweight scripting languages, including JavaScript.

By definition, REST-style Web services are resource-oriented services. You can identify and locate resources by a URI, and the operations that might be performed against those resources are defined by the HTTP specification. The core operations include GET, POST, PUT, and DELETE.

Web Script allows you to:

- Build custom URI-identified and HTTP-accessible content management web services
- Turn your Alfresco repository into a content management powered HTTP Server
- Easily access, manage, and cross-link your content by using a tailored RESTful API

You do not need any special tools or sound Java knowledge. All you need is your favorite text editor to generate the Web Script coding. No compilation, generators, server restarts, or complex installs are required.

With Web Scripts, we can either build our own RESTful interface using lightweight scripting technologies such as JavaScript and FreeMarker, allowing you to arbitrarily map any content in the repository to resources on the web, or we can use pre-built out of the box Web Scripts that already encapsulate many of the required mappings. Typically, Web Scripts are used for querying, searching, and accessing content within the repository.

Primarily, there are two types of Web Scripts:

- Data Web Scripts

    Data Web Scripts encapsulate access to and modification of content/data held in the repository. Therefore, they are provided and exposed only by the Alfresco Repository server. They provide a repository interface for client applications to query, retrieve, update, and perform processes, typically using document formats such as XML and JSON. Out of the box, Alfresco provides a series of Data Web Scripts—for tagging, activities, site management, and so on.

- Presentation Web Scripts

    Presentation Web Scripts allow you to build user interfaces such as a dashlet for Alfresco Explorer or Alfresco Share, a portlet for a JSR-168 portal, a UI component within Alfresco SURF, a web site, or a custom application. They typically render HTML (and perhaps include browser-hosted JavaScript). Unlike Data Web Scripts, Presentation Web Scripts may be hosted on the Alfresco Repository server or on a separate presentation server. When hosted separately, the Presentation Web Scripts interact with Data Web Scripts. Out of the box, Alfresco provides a series of Presentation Web Scripts such as Portlets, Office Integration, SURF Components, and so on.

How to implement Web Scripts

Implementation of a Web Script consists of mainly four parts.

1. Create a Web Script:

    To create a web script, three files are required:

    - A description document, which describes the URL that initiates the Web Script, along with a short name, description, output format, authentication, and transactional needs.
    - A controller—optional Java script or a Java bean.
    - A rendering template (FreeMarker or XSLT to obtain the output in the desired format— XML/HTML/JSON and so on).

2. Store the Web Script:

    There are two ways to store a Web Script in Alfresco:

    - Store it in Alfresco Explorer.

        You can store the Web Script files in the **Company Home | Data Dictionary | Web Script Extensions folder**.

        Create the required folder structure under the path listed above and then place the Web Script files, description document, rendering template, and controller script (if you have) in that folder.

    - Store it on file system

        If you want to store it on the file system, you need to store it under the **<<alfresco_server>> > tomcat | shared | extension | templates | webscripts** folder. You can create the desired folder structure inside the above-mentioned folder and then put all of the Web Script files in there.

3. Register the web script:

    Once you are done with storing the required Web Script files, you need to register them in Alfresco.

    For registering the Web Scripts stored in Alfresco Explorer, go to `http://localhost:8080/alfresco/service/index`. Click on the **Refresh Web Scripts** button. You will see a message showing how many Web Scripts have recently been found and registered.

    For registering the Web Scripts stored on the file system, you need to restart the Alfresco server.

4. List the Web Scripts for external access:

    Next, you can use the Web Script that we developed using the correct URL mentioned in the description document file. For example, you can go to `http://localhost:8080/alfresco/service/index/package/org/alfresco/portlets` or to `http://localhost:8080/alfresco/service/index`. You can choose either **Browse by URL** or **Browse by Package**, and then select the Web Script that we created.

Hello World example

We will consider a "Hello World" example in this section, and walk through all four steps. In this example, we will just try to greet the user who is executing the Web Script.

1. Create a Web Script:
    - Create a file named `greeting.get.desc.xml`, which contains the details of the URL, authentication, and so on.

      ```xml
      <webscript>
        <shortname>Welcome</shortname>
        <description>Polite greeting</description>
        <url>/sample/greeting</url>
        <authentication>user</authentication>
      </webscript>
      ```

      Here, we don't require any controller as we are only displaying a greeting message.

    - Create a response template file named `greeting.get.html.ftl`, which contains the following output script:

      ```
      Welcome ${person.properties.userName}
      ```

2. Store the Web Script:

    We will store above two files in the **Company Home | Data Dictionary | Web Script Extensions** folder . We will create a folder structure such as **org | alfresco | sample** if it's not already there, and will then put the above two files in this sample folder.

3. Register the Web Script:
    - To register the Web Script, go to `http://localhost:8080/alfresco/service/index`
    - Click on the **Refresh Web Scripts** button.

4. List the Web Scripts for external access:
    - Now you can access this Web Script with the help of the specified URL:

      `http://localhost:8080/alfresco/service/sample/greeting`

    - When you access this URL from the browser, you will see the following greeting message:

      Welcome admin.

      This indicates that your Web Script is working perfectly.

      This Web Script is authenticated as user. So here, **admin** is the user name.

Sample out of the box portlet Web Scripts

Alfresco provides some out of the box Web Scripts for portlet integration with JSR 168 portlets. Some examples of portlet Web Scripts are as follows:

Myspaces portlet

This Web Script displays the documents and spaces in the repository as a portlet. You can upload new documents in any space by using a web client, or you can upload new documents in any space with the help of this Web Script.

URL: `http://localhost:8080/alfresco/service/ui/myspaces?f={filter?}&p={path}`

Example: `http://localhost:8080/alfresco/service/ui/myspaces?f=0&p=%2FCompany%20Home`

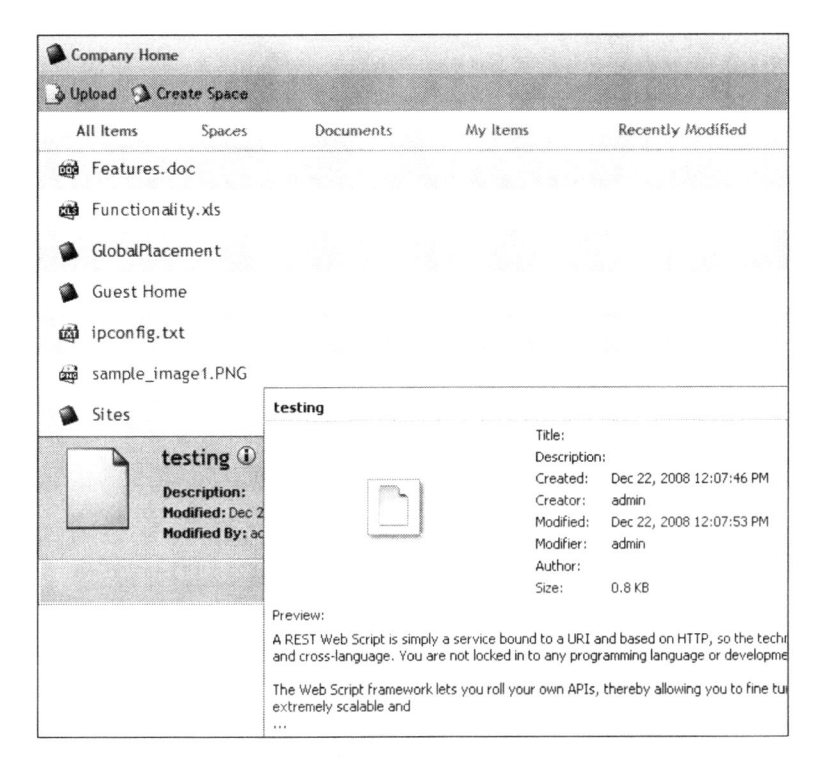

Document list portlet Web Script

This Web Script displays the documents available in the repository. You can filter by the particular type of document. You can also provide a path and query, along with the type of document, as input parameters.

URL:

```
http://localhost:8080/alfresco/service/ui/doclist?f={filter?}&p={path?}&q={query?}
```

Example:

```
http://<server_name>:<port>/alfresco/service/ui/doclist?f=3
```

In the above example, you need to pass a filter parameter of 3 if you are expecting a PDF document type. So, the following screen displays the PDF documents available in the repository:

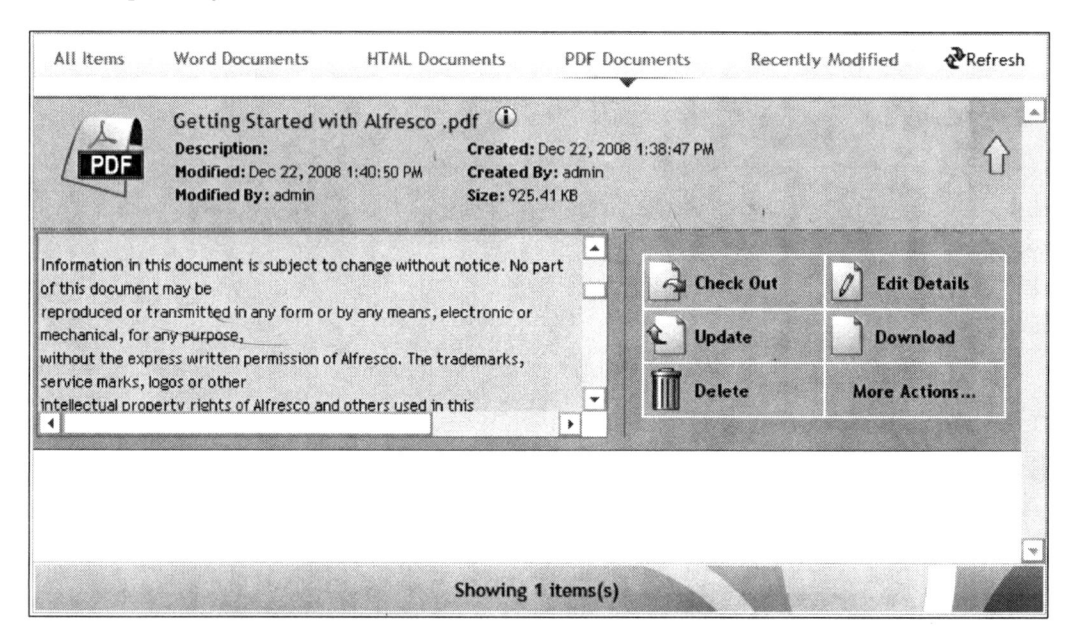

Web Script to list the latest documents

This example shows how to integrate an external Java-based web application with Alfresco. Here, we have one web application that displays the recently-modified documents on the daily dose documents page. If the daily dose date of any document is greater than or equal to today, this document should be listed on the daily dose page of the web application. All of the documents are managed by the Alfresco repository, and the daily dose date will be one of the metadata elements for this document. Next, we will generate a Web Script that will be responsible for displaying these documents in the web application. This Web Script will return HTML output, which we can easily incorporate into the existing web application.

Daily dose integration Web Script in detail

The following table shows detailed information about the "daily dose integration" Web Script:

Description:	This Web Script is responsible for displaying the latest documents, updated on daily basis on an external web application
Links:	Homepage of the external application
Package:	`recentdocuments.dailydose`
Web Script base URL:	`/recentdocuments/dailydose/listDailyDose`
Output:	<ul><li>HTML having following details of documents:</li><li>Document title (with link)</li><li>Type of document</li><li>Author</li><li>Expiration date</li></ul>
Conditions:	Documents whose "End Daily Dose Date" is greater than or equal to the current date
Controller:	Java script as a controller, which will fetch the documents that satisfy the Conditions from the Alfresco repository

Follow the steps listed below to create a Web Script:

1. Create the `listDailyDose.get.desc.xml` file, containing:

   ```
   <webscript>
           <shortname>Listing of Daily Dose Document Through
   Webscript</shortname>
           <description>Contains the list of daily dose documents
              </description>
           <url>/recentdocuments/dailydose/listDailyDose</url>
           <authentication>guest</authentication>
           <transaction>required</transaction>
   </webscript>
   ```

2. Create the `listDailyDose.get.js` file, containing:

   ```
   var l_customerDocs =
                   companyhome.childByNamePath("CustomerDocuments");
   model.m_documents_node=l_customerDocs;
   ```

3. Create the `listDailyDose.ftl.html` file. See the following code snippet:

   ```
   <#list m_documents_node.children as cust_documents>
   <#if (dateCompare(cust_documents.properties["CUST:EndDailyDoseDate
   "],date)) == 1>
   <tr>
   ```

```
<td>
<img src="${url.context}${cust_documents.icon32}"/>
</td>
<td align="center">
<a class="title" href="/alfresco/${cust_documents.url}">${cust_
documents.properties.name}</a>
</td>
<td> </td>
<td align="center"> ${cust_documents.properties["CUST:
DocumentType"]}
</td>
<td> </td>
<td> ${cust_documents.properties.creator}</td>
<td> </td>
<#if cust_documents.properties["CUST:ExpirationDate"]?exists>
<td align="center">
${cust_documents.properties["CUST:ExpirationDate"]?date}
</td>
<#else>
<td> </td>
</tr>
</#if>
</#list>
```

4. Store the Web Script:

   To store this Web Script, browse to **Company Home | Data Dictionary | Web Script Extensions** and create a folder hierarchy called **recentdocuments | dailydose**. Store all three of the files in this folder.

5. Browse to the **Company Home | Data Dictionary | Models** folder. Add the `custModel.xml`. Make the model active by selecting the **Active** property.

6. Browse to **Company Home | Data Dictionary | Web Scripts Extensions** folder. Add the `web-client-config custom.xml` file. Deployment of Alfresco Explorer can be achieved as an administrator by using the following URL: `http://localhost:8080/alfresco/faces/jsp/admin/webclientconfig-console.jsp`.

7. Use the following command to deploy the file:

   `reload`

> Download the `custModel.xml` and `web-client-config-custom.xml` file from Packt web site.

8. Create a space called as `CustomerDocuments` in **Company Home**. Upload a few documents to the folder. Apply the aspect "Customer Document Details" to all of the documents in the folder.
9. Register the Web Script. To do this, go to `http://localhost:8080/alfresco/service/index`
10. Click on the **Refresh Web Scripts** button. You will see a message showing how many Web Scripts were found and registered recently.
11. List the Web Scripts for external access:

    Now you can use the Web Script, that we developed, by using the correct URL mentioned in the description document file. For our example, the URL is:

    `http://<server_name>:<port>/alfresco/service/index/uri/recent-documents/dailydose/listDailyDose`

A screenshot of the daily dose page of web application, which is generated with the use of above mentioned Web Script, is shown below:

Title	Author	Expiration Date
AlfrescoBook	admin	Dec 31, 2008
BookAuthors	admin	Dec 31, 2008
Booksupporter	admin	Dec 31, 2008

Integrating Web Script with an external Java application

You can call this HTTP URL in the JSP of your web application, and can embed the HTML output returned by this Web Script in your JSP.

Below is the code snippet provided to call the Web Script from the jsp:

```
<html>
<title> The Daily Dose </title>
<body bgcolor="#edf6fc" text="blue">
<head bgcolor="#edf6fc"> Welcome to Daily Dose Page</head>
<H2 bgcolor="#edf6fc"> The Daily Dose</H2>
<iframe bgcolor="#edf6fc" width="60%" height="60%"frameborder=0
src="http://localhost:8080/alfresco/service/recentdocuments/dailydose/
listDailyDose"/>
</body>
</html>
```

Web Script to integrate document search

Because Alfresco is behaving as a content repository, it's a very suitable use case for where we have an external application with any kind of rich user interface. We also have a search interface incorporated into it, which will search inside the content repository and display the result based on some input parameters. You can also define some filtering criteria for searching for documents in the Alfresco repository.

In this example, we will search for documents in Alfresco using some parameters, such as client name, keyword, and so on, which are metadata of the documents. This will return XML/HTML output. You can process XML output in your application and orchestrate the UI layer. And if you want to display the output in HTML format, you can use the HTML output of the same Web Script, which you can directly incorporate into your application.

Document search Web Script in detail

The following table explains the "document search" Web Script in detail:

Description:	This Web Script is responsible for searching for documents in the repository, based on some input parameters
Links:	Homepage of the external application
Package:	`custdocuments.searchDocs`
Web Script base URL:	• `/custdocuments/searchDocs.xml?keyword={keyword?}&amp;clientname={clientname?}` • `/custdocuments/searchDocs?keyword={keyword?}&amp;clientname={clientname?}`
Input Parameters:	keyword `client_name`
Output:	XML/HTML (we will use the FreeMarker template language to generate the XML/HTML file) Document title (with link) Type of document Author Expiration date
Conditions:	None
Controller:	We will use JavaScript as a controller, which will search the documents from the Alfresco repository based on the criteria specified in the input parameters

The four steps below are used to create the "document search" Web Script:

1. Create a Web Script:

   Basically, three files are required. The first of these is the Description Document, `searchDocs.get.desc.xml` as. This should contain the following code:

   ```
   <webscript>
     <shortname>
           Searching of Documents in the repository Through Webscript
     </shortname>
      <description>
           Searches the documents in the repository
      </description>
      <url>
      /custdocuments/searchDocs?keyword={keyword?}&amp;clientname={clientname?}
      </url>
      <url>
      /custdocuments/searchDocs.xml?keyword={keyword?}&amp;clientname={clientname?}
      </url>
      <authentication>user</authentication>
      <transaction>required</transaction>
   </webscript>
   ```

   The second file that is needed is the Controller. This can be a Java-Script script or Java Bean. In this example, we will use JavaScript. Create a file named `searchDocs.get.js`, and enter the following code into it:

   ```
   var l_folder = "app:company_home/cm:CustomerDocuments";
   var l_search_docs = new Object();
   if (args.startpage == undefined)
   {
      l_search_docs.startPage = 1;
   }
   else
   {
      l_search_docs.startPage = parseInt(args.startpage);
   }
   if (args.count == undefined)
   {
      l_search_docs.itemsPerPage = 5;
   }
   else
   {
   ```

```
        l_search_docs.itemsPerPage = parseInt(args.count);
}
l_search_docs.startIndex = (l_search_docs.startPage-1) *
l_search_docs.itemsPerPage;
l_search_docs.searchTerms ="";
if (args.keyword == null || args.keyword.length == 0) {
        status.code = 400;
        status.message = "\"keyword\" argument is null or
        undefined";
        status.redirect = true;
}
else if (args.clientname == null || args.clientname.length
 == 0) {
        status.code = 400;
        status.message = "\"clientname\" argument is null or
        undefined";
        status.redirect = true;
}
else
{
        l_search_docs.searchTerms = args.keyword;
        l_search_docs.clientName = args.clientname;
        query = buildSearchQuery();
        var results = search.luceneSearch(query);
        l_search_docs.results = results;
        l_search_docs.totalResults = results.length;
        l_search_docs.totalPages = Math.ceil(results.length /
        l_search_docs.itemsPerPage);
        model.m_search_docs = l_search_docs;
}
function addQueryCriterion(param, value, isContained) {
        var valueStub;
        if (isContained) {
                valueStub = "*" + value + "*";
        }
        else {
                valueStub = value;
        }
        criterion = " AND @CUST\\:" + param + ":" +
        valueStub;
        return criterion;
}
function buildSearchQuery() {
        searchQuery = "PATH:\"//" + l_folder + "//*\"";
```

Chapter 9

```
        if (args.keyword != null) {
            searchQuery += addQueryCriterion("Keywords",
             args.keyword, true);
    }
        if (args.clientname != null) {
            searchQuery += addQueryCriterion("ClientName",
             args.clientname, true);
    }
        return searchQuery;
}
```

The third file we need is a rendering template. We can use FreeMarker, or xslt which will render the output in desired format XML/HTML/JSON etc. We will use FreeMarker with HTML output in this example. Create a FreeMarker template file named `searchDocs.ftl.xml`, and enter the following code into it:

```
<?xml version="1.0" encoding="UTF-8"?>
<items>
        <#if m_search_docs.results?exists>
        <#assign count=0>
        <#assign index=0>
        <#list m_search_docs.results as l_result_document>
        <#if (index>=m_search_docs.startPage) &&
        (index<m_search_docs.startPage+m_search_docs.
        itemsPerPage)>
        <#assign count=count+1>
        <#assign curl=url.serviceContext>
        <item>
                <name>${l_result_document.properties.name}
                 </name>
                <title>
                        <#if l_result_document.properties.
                         title?exists>
                                ${l_result_document.properties.
                                  title}
                        </#if>
                </title>
                <size> ${l_result_document.size} </size>
                <author>${l_result_document.properties.
                 creator}</author>
                <clientname>
                <#if l_result_document.properties["CUST:
                ClientName"]?exists>
                        ${l_result_document.properties["CUST:
                        ClientName"]}
```

[321]

Integrating External Applications with Alfresco

```
                </#if>
                </clientname>
                <expirationdate>
                <#if l_result_document.properties["CUST:
                ExpirationDate"]?exists>
                ${l_result_document.properties["CUST:
                    ExpirationDate"]?datetime}
                </#if>
                </expirationdate>
                <modificationdate>
                <#if l_result_document.properties
                ["cm:modified"]?exists>
                        ${l_result_document.properties
                            ["cm:modified"]?datetime}
                </#if>
                </modificationdate>
            </item>
            </#if>
            <#assign index=index+1>
            </#list>
            <#else>
                    No results to display.
            </#if>
    </items>
```

If you want to use a FreeMarker template file for HTML output, create a file named `searchDocs.ftl.html`, and enter the following code into it:

```
        <html>
        <head>
                <title>Alfresco Search</title>
        </head>
        <body>
        <b>Search Results: </b>
        <#if m_search_docs.results?exists>
                <#assign count=0>
                <#assign index=0>
                Showing page <b>${m_search_docs.startPage}</b>
of <b>${m_search_docs.totalPages}</b> from <b>${m_search_docs.
totalResults}</b> results for Keyword : <b>${m_search_docs.
searchTerms}</b> and Client:    <b>${m_search_docs.clientName}</b>
                <br> <br>
                <table>
                 <tr>
                 <th> </th>   <th> Name of Document </th>
                 <th> </th>   <th> Author </th>
                 <th> </th>   <th> Client Name </th>
```

[322]

```
                    <th> </th>   <th> Expiration Date</th>
                    </tr>
                    <#list m_search_docs.results as l_result_document>
                    <#if (index>=m_search_docs.startIndex) &&
                    (index<m_search_docs.startIndex+m_search_docs.
                      itemsPerPage         )>
                    <#assign count=count+1>
                    <#assign curl=url.serviceContext>
                    <tr>
                    <td>
                    <img src="${url.context}${l_result_document.
                      icon16}"/>
                    </td>
                    <td align="center">
                    <a class="title" href="/alfresco/${l_result_document.
                      url}">${l_result_document.properties.name}</a>
                    </td>
                    <td> </td>
                    <td> ${l_result_document.properties.creator} </td>
                    <td> </td>
                    <td align="center">${l_result_document.
                    properties["CUST:ClientName"]}    </td>
                    <td> </td>
                    <#if l_result_document.properties["CUST:
                      ExpirationDate"]?exists>
                    <td align="center"> ${l_result_document.
                      properties["CUST:ExpirationDate"]?d    ate} </td>
                    <#else>
                    <td> </td>
                    </#if>
                    </tr>
                    <tr>
                    <td> </td>
                    <td> <HR> </td> <td> <HR> </td>
                    <td> <HR> </td> <td> <HR> </td>
                    <td> <HR> </td> <td> <HR> </td>
                    <td> <HR> </td> <td> <HR> </td>
                    </tr>
                    </#if>
                    <#assign index=index+1>
                    </#list>
                    </table>
                    <br>
            <#if (m_search_docs.startPage > 1)>
```

Integrating External Applications with Alfresco

```
            <a href="${url.service}?keyword=${m_search_docs.searchTerms}
            &clientname=${m_search_docs.clientName}&startpage=0&count=$
            {m_search_docs.itemsPerPage}"></#if>First
            <#if (m_search_docs.startPage > 0)></a></#if> |
            <#if (m_search_docs.startPage > 1)><a
            href="${url.service}?keyword=${m_search_docs.searchTerms}
            &clientname=${m_search_docs.clientName}&startpage=$
            {m_search_docs.startPage - 1}&count=${m_search_docs.
            itemsPerPage}"></#if>Prev
            <#if (m_search_docs.startPage > 0)></a></#if> |
            <#if (m_search_docs.startPage < m_search_docs.totalPages)>
            <a href="${url.service}?keyword=${m_search_docs.searchTerms}
            &clientname=${m_search_docs.clientName}&startpage=$
            {m_search_docs.startPage +1}&count=$
            {m_search_docs.itemsPerPage}"></#if>Next<#if
            (m_search_docs.startPage+1 < m_search_docs.totalPages)></a></
            #if> |
            <#if (m_search_docs.startPage < m_search_docs.totalPages)>
            <a href="${url.service}?keyword=${m_search_docs.searchTerms}
            &clientname=${m_search_docs.clientName}&startpage=$
            {m_search_docs.totalPages -   1}&count=$
            {m_search_docs.itemsPerPage}"></#if>Last<#if
            (m_search_docs.startPage+1 < m_search_docs.totalPages)></a></
            #if>
    <#else>
        <i>No results to display.</i>
    </#if>
        </body>
    </html>
```

2. Store the Web Script:

To store this Web Script browse to **Company Home > Data Dictionary > Web Script Extensions** and create a folder named **custdocuments**. Store all the above three files here.

> Download the files from the Packt web site.

3. Register the Web Script:

Once you develop the Web Script, you need to register it for use. To do this, go to `http://localhost:8080/alfresco/service/index`.

Click on the **Refresh Web Scripts** button. You will see a message showing how many Web Scripts were found and registered recently.

4. List the Web Scripts for external access:

   Now you can use the Web Script that we developed, using the correct URL mentioned in the description document file. For our example, URLs are:

   `http://<server_name>:<port>/alfresco/service/custdocuments/searchDocs.xml?keyword={keyword?}&clientname={clientName?}`

   and

   `http://<server_name>:<port>/alfresco/service/custdocuments/searchDocs?keyword={keyword?}&clientname={clientName?}`

Calling the Web Script from external application

You can call this HTTP URL in the JSP of your web application, and can embed the HTML output returned by this Web Script in your JSP. You can also use the Web Script with XML output and process the returned XML in your application itself.

The following screenshot shows the XML output returned by this Web Script:

```xml
<?xml version="1.0" encoding="UTF-8" ?>
<items>
  <item>
    <name>AlfrescoBook</name>
    <title />
    <size>0</size>
    <author>admin</author>
    <clientname>cignex</clientname>
    <expirationdate>Dec 31, 2008 1:45:00 PM</expirationdate>
    <modificationdate>Jan 6, 2009 1:46:09 PM</modificationdate>
  </item>
  <item>
    <name>Booksupporter</name>
    <title />
    <size>0</size>
    <author>admin</author>
    <clientname>cignex</clientname>
    <expirationdate>Dec 31, 2008 1:47:00 PM</expirationdate>
    <modificationdate>Jan 6, 2009 1:48:15 PM</modificationdate>
  </item>
  <item>
    <name>BookAuthors</name>
    <title />
    <size>0</size>
    <author>admin</author>
    <clientname>cignex</clientname>
    <expirationdate>Dec 31, 2008 1:46:00 PM</expirationdate>
    <modificationdate>Jan 6, 2009 1:48:37 PM</modificationdate>
  </item>
</items>
```

The next screenshot shows the HTML output returned by this Web Script:

	Name of Document	Author	Client Name	Expiration Date
	AlfrescoBook	admin	cignex	Dec 31, 2008
	Booksupporter	admin	cignex	Dec 31, 2008
	BookAuthors	admin	cignex	Dec 31, 2008

Search Results: Showing page 1 of 1 from 3 results for Keyword : **test** and Client: **cignex**

First | Prev | Next | Last

Various application integration examples

This section contains various production examples that are currently available. Hence, before developing integration with Alfresco, you can check these examples to evaluate if you can reuse any of them for your application.

Integrating with Liferay

Liferay is the world's leading open source enterprise portal. Corporations use it to provide a unified web interface to data and tools scattered across many sources. Within Liferay portal, a portal interface is composed of a number of **portlets**—self-contained, interactive elements written to a particular standard. For more information, refer to the Liferay web site at http://www.liferay.com.

Liferay provides Alfresco Portlets, which can be connected to your existing Alfresco repository. The Liferay framework supports web services, and thus offers various integration options.

Various available options

Alfresco protocols have changed since version 3. To use Alfresco with Liferay, there are different options. Some of these are explained below.

Using the Web Script Container

Alfresco has de-coupled the Web Script Container from the core Alfresco application, so that it can be deployed independently as a portlet in Liferay or on other portals. The advantage of this approach is that any existing remote-enabled Web Script can easily be adapted to run as a portlet.

Using the CMIS proposed standard

Recently, Alfresco, IBM, Microsoft, Documentum, and others announced the submission of a new content management standard proposal called **CMIS (Content Management Interoperability Service)**. Alfresco has released an initial implementation of this proposed standard, which includes support for REST-like RPC and SOAP-based web services. This provides the Liferay community with a cross-platform mechanism for integrating not just with Alfresco, but with any other Content Management System that supports the specification.

Other REST APIs

In addition to the proposed CMIS standard, Alfresco has exposed a myriad of REST-like APIs for services such as workflow, tagging, thumbnailing, user management, and more. These services are documented on the Alfresco 3.0 REST API wiki page.

Create a portlet in Liferay and call the code given below from the controller of the portlet.

```
String _urlString=ResourceBundle.getBundle(REST_BUNDLE).
getString(URL);

System.out.println("This is the url correct: " + _urlString);
String _content = null;

Request _request = new Request(Method.GET, _urlString);
_request.setChallengeResponse(new ChallengeResponse(ChallengeScheme.
HTTP_BASIC, ResourceBundle.getBundle(REST_BUNDLE).getString(USER_
NAME), ResourceBundle.getBundle(REST_BUNDLE).getString(PASSWORD)));

Response _response = new Client(Protocol.HTTP).handle(_request);
        if(_request.getChallengeResponse() != null)
            System.out.println("request.getChallengeResponse().
getCredentials()   "+_request.getChallengeResponse().getCredentials());
        if (_response.getStatus().isSuccess())
        {
           if(_response!=null)
            _content=_response.getEntity().getText();
              else
            System.out.println("CONTENT :" + _content);
        }
```

> Download the `TestRest.java` file from the official web site.

[327]

Liferay built-in Portlet for Alfresco

Liferay is a portal server in which we can include our portlet, in order to call the Alfresco Web Script.

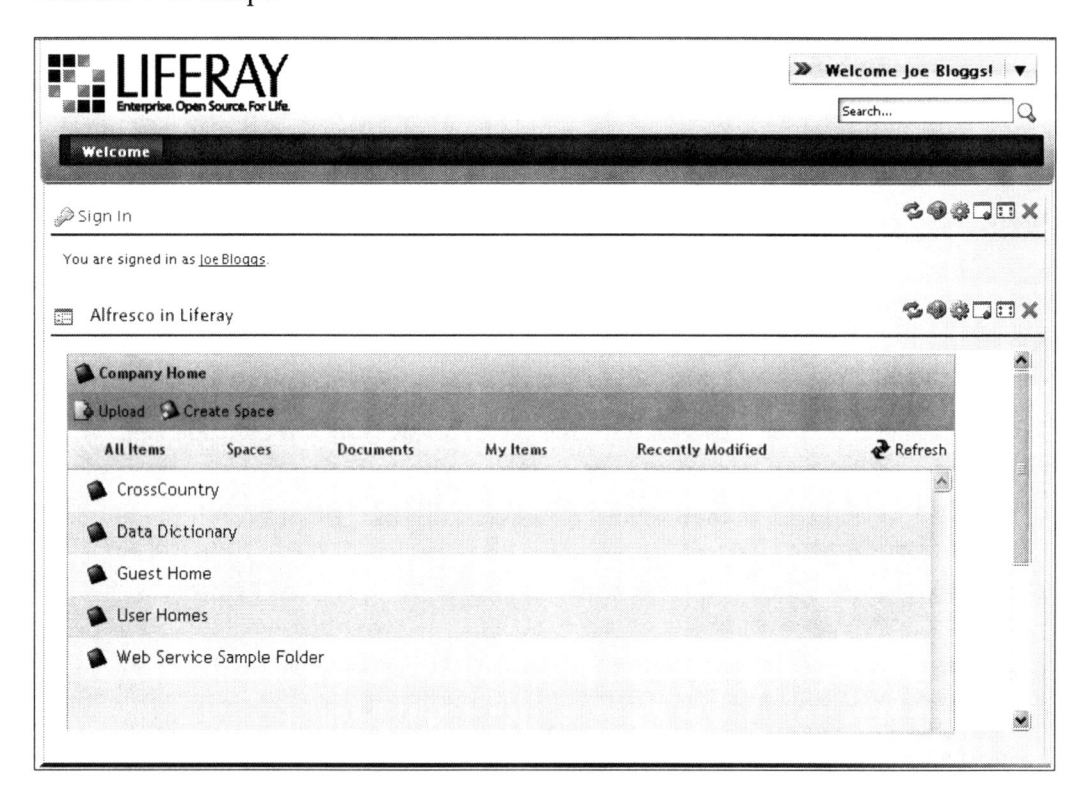

You will find your Web Script's screen on the portlet page, as shown in the immediately preceding screenshot.

Using your own API

You can write your own API for communicating with Alfresco using Liferay.

This method consists of creating an API that communicates with Alfresco. This API is independent from Liferay. You can use it in a portlet, a servlet, or a normal Java application. This API allows you to search, delete, and send documents to Alfresco, and so on, through Web Services.

For example, you can search in a space (filtering by one property) and you obtain a list of all of the documents found. You can then work with that list as you wish in your Liferay portlet. The advantage is that it allows you to have Liferay and Alfresco on different machines.

Integrating with Drupal

Drupal is a very powerful open source web content management framework. It is developed using the PHP language. More information about Drupal can be found at http://www.drupal.org.

A combination of Drupal and Alfresco is a good choice in scenarios where there is a significant amount of file-based content that requires services such as workflow, versioning, security, check-in/check-out, but needs to be shared in the context of a community. Alfresco acts as a back-end content repository, and Drupal acts as a front-end presentation layer. Here, Drupal really becomes equivalent, in terms of where it sits in the architecture and the role it plays, to traditional portals such as Liferay or JBoss Portal.

It is difficult for other systems to access content in Drupal when it is running on a separate machine, as compared to when it sits in Alfresco. There are Drupal modules that make it easier to syndicate, but Alfresco is designed to expose content in this way. Once it is in Alfresco, content can be routed through Alfresco workflows, and then be approved so that it is available to one or more front-end Drupal sites. Content could come from a Drupal site, be persisted to Alfresco, routed around for editorial review, and then made available.

Not all Drupal modules need to persist their data back to Alfresco. Things such as comments and ratings will probably never need to be treated as real content. Instead of trying to persist everything, you could either modify selected modules to integrate with Alfresco, or create new ones that work with Alfresco. For example, you might want to have Drupal put file uploads in Alfresco instead of the local file system. Or, it might make sense to have a "send to Alfresco" button that would send the current node to Alfresco that is visible to certain roles.

You may also want to get some Drupal data from within Alfresco, or may want to tag objects using the same set of tags that Drupal knows about, or may want to perform a mass import of Drupal objects into the Alfresco repository. All of this is possible by integrating Alfresco and Drupal.

The following code snippet can be used to access your Alfresco library through Drupal.

Helloworld is a simple Web Script created in Alfresco to test the Drupal alfresco integration. The code for this is as follows:

```
function data_from_webscript_block1() {
  $output = '';
  $url = 'http://<server_name>:<port>/alfresco/service/
   /facebook/helloworld';
```

```
      $http_result = drupal_http_request($url);
      if ($http_result->code == 200) {
        $doc = $http_result->data;
        $output .= $doc;
      }
      else {
        $msg = 'No content from %url.';
        $vars = array('%url' => $url);
        watchdog('data_from_webscript', $msg, $vars, WATCHDOG_WARNING);
        return t("The webscript is not accessible.");
      }
      return $output;
    }
```

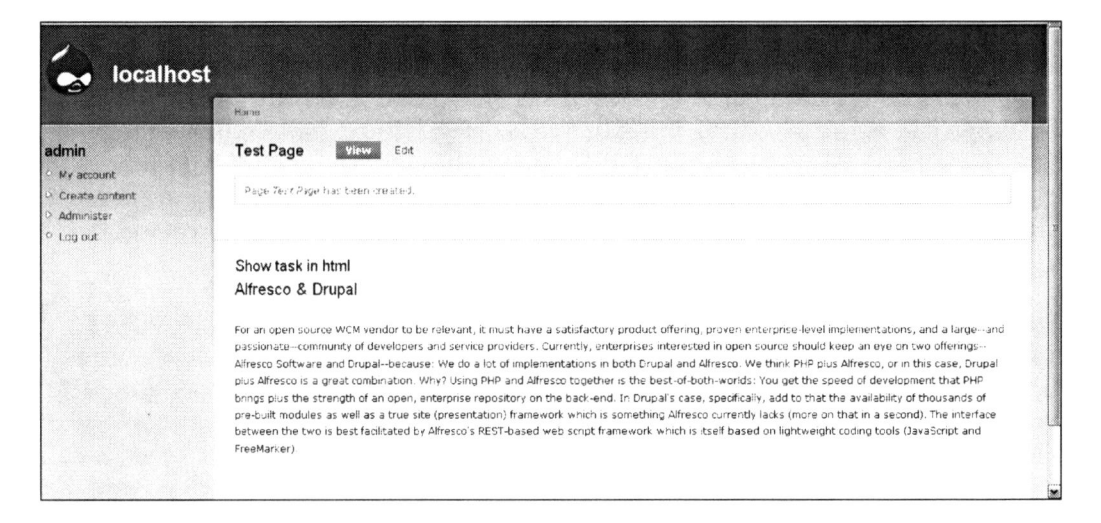

Integrating with Joomla!

Joomla! is a very popular open source-based dynamic portal and web Content Management System. For more information, visit the Joomla! web site at http://www.joomla.org.

Joomla! tools and Alfresco can be integrated based on the CMIS standard that allows Alfresco repositories to act as backend for Joomla! web sites. Because the integration was developed using CMIS and not a proprietary API, it can be used to access content stored in either an Alfresco repository or any other CMIS-compliant repository.

The Joomla! module for Alfresco was built using the draft CMIS REST API, to allow organizations running Joomla-based web sites to access Alfresco's robust open source content management repository. This integration is a perfect example of how cooperation between open source projects can yield innovative solutions more rapidly as compared to a proprietary model.

This integration, built using the CMIS REST API, will enable millions of Joomla! web sites to access the powerful backend content repository services of Alfresco, ensuring security, compliance, and auditability. Users will be able to effectively manage, preview, and track increasing volumes of content and digital assets on collaborative Joomla! web sites using Alfresco's content library. Similarly, Alfresco users will be able to search, publish, share, download, and edit content directly on Joomla! sites.

The Joomla! module for Alfresco perfectly illustrates the promise of CMIS with this integration. Joomla! users can now leverage Alfresco's scalable document repository to manage content on Joomla! sites in a secure, compliant, and audited environment. The Joomla! module for Alfresco can be downloaded from http://www.alfresco.com/products/platform/try/.

Integrating with Adobe Flex

Providing a Flex-based client to access an Alfresco content repository can improve user experience by delivering an easily customizable and highly-interactive interface, seamless integration in the user desktop, and cross-platform integration.

There can be two approaches to this. The first approach uses custom Java services and the second one uses Alfresco Web Scripts (REST).

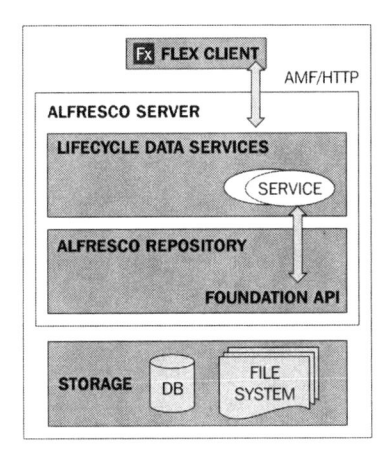

LiveCycle DATA SERVICES is Adobe server-side component that allows communication between the Flex client and a Java application. There are several options to create an Alfresco client:

- Protocols : FTP, WebDAV, CIFS
- APIs: Web Services, Web Scripts
- A custom solution that uses the Alfresco Foundation API directly

The next steps could be to create an AIR application to leverage the following:

- Integration with user's desktop
- Drag-and-drop documents (inbound/outbound)
- Access file system
- Embedded SQL DB to provide offline functions

For more details on Alfresco and Flex integration, refer Chapter 11.

Email integration: MS Outlook, Lotus Notes, Novell, and Thunderbird

Alfresco can be configured as a Mail Server or a Mail Client Application using a third party product. This makes for effective email management for users, who will benefit from the convenience and speed. Users can simply drag-and-drop emails directly into the Alfresco repository for automatic filing. Familiarity with the tools makes the interaction easy. Users can find and view documents and emails from the email client or file system view. The document search is regardless of the document format. A user can configure rules, based on which they can store and share outgoing emails.

Chapter 9

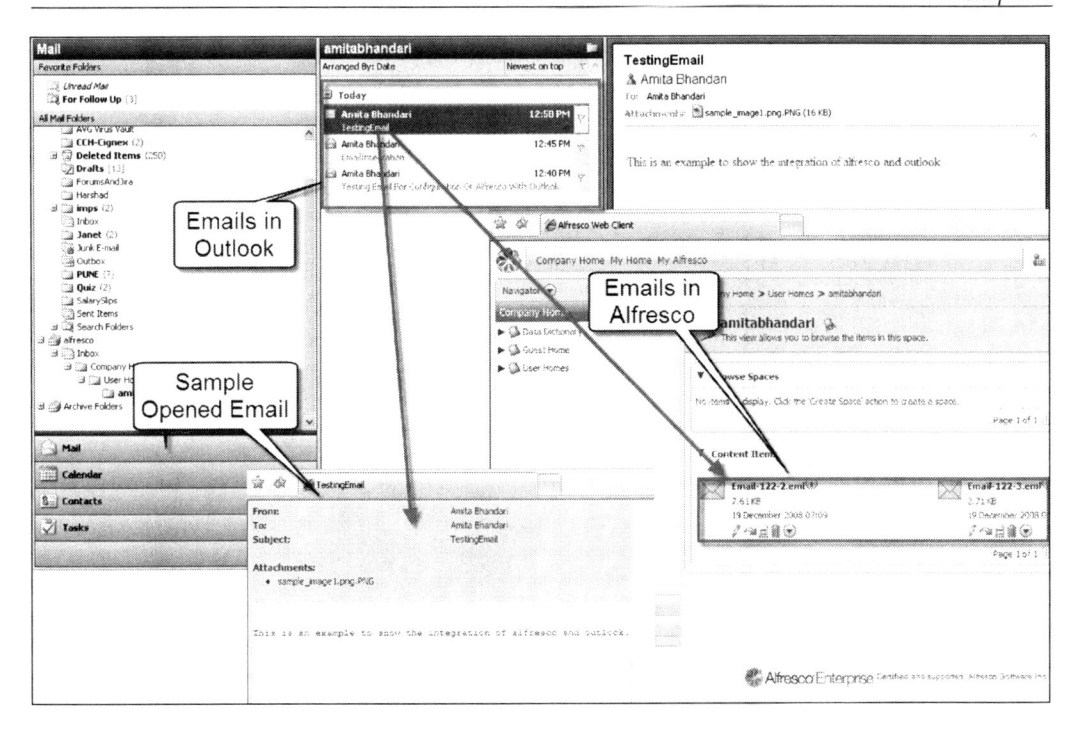

This can allow the organization to create a secure and auditable, central store of information and correspondence, which can easily demonstrate compliance with regulatory requirements and respond to requests for information. Information can be made available to everyone and duplication of data avoided. Enhanced productivity, along with facilitated and improved knowledge sharing and collaboration, are all byproducts. Even if a staff member leaves, key information is readily available within the organization. A cross-team or cross-project view of all communications, internally, along with customers or other external parties, is readily available.

Integrating with iPhone

We built a simple Alfresco navigator for iPhone. In fact, it is an iPhone-friendly web client. This navigator is backed by three Web Scripts—for DM space/doc navigation, for WCM navigation, and the third one for searching—and leverages the open source **iUI** package to provide the look and feel. The performance of the navigator is quite good on an iPhone. The script shows different branches of a single DOM tree based on where you are. When you navigate down to a new space or web project directory, it will add new nodes to the tree. The capabilities of the navigator include:

- Navigation of spaces, docs, and web projects
- Preview of images, PDF's web sites

- Search and display posts and topics attached to the docs

To install the package on your Alfresco, simply follow the steps described below:

1. Unzip `iui.zip` to `tomcat/webapps/alfresco/scripts`.
2. Import `iphone-navigator.zip` to **Company Home | Data Dictionary | Web Scripts | Web Scripts Extensions**.
3. Open the URL `http://<server_name>:<port>/alfresco/service/index` in your browser, and click on the **Refresh Web Script** button on the screen.
4. Browse to the **web script package | org | alfresco | demo | iphone** and click on it to open Navigation (iPhone) web script.

5. Next, click and open the URL `http://<server_name>:<port>/alfresco/service/iphone/navigation?p={path?}`

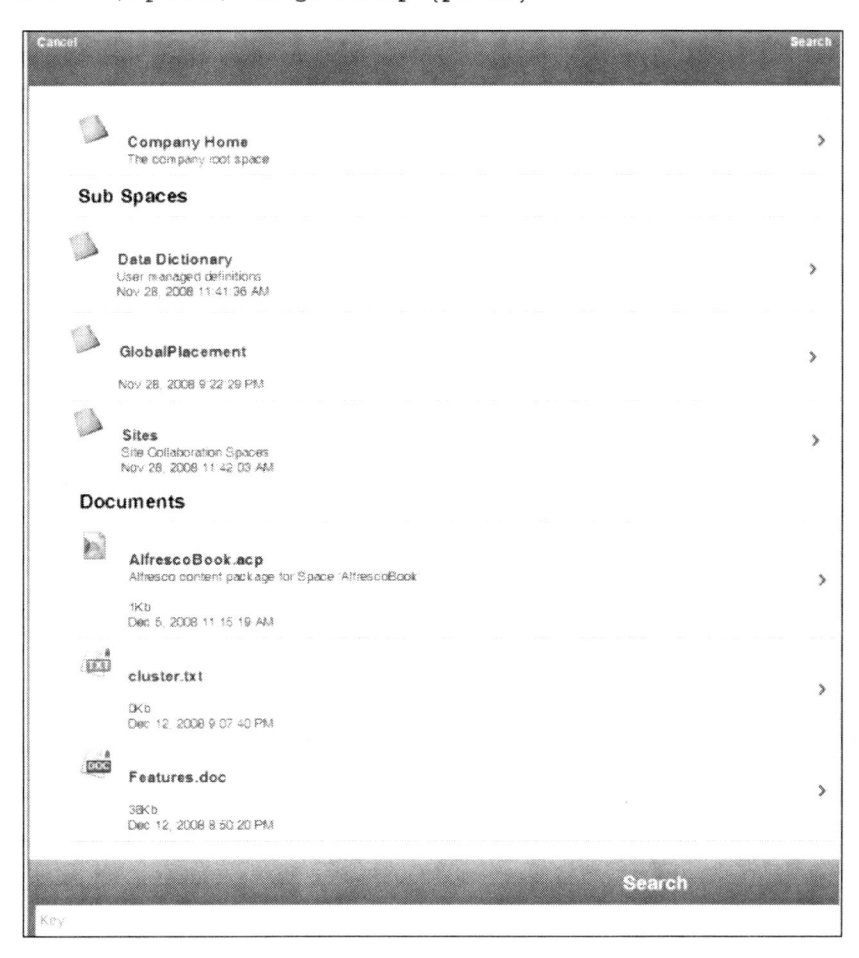

> You can download the `iui.zip` and `iphone-navigator.zip` file from Packt publisher's official web site.

Integrating with iGoogle

With this new release of Alfresco 3.0, you can now have access your content repository, and Alfresco as a Gadget, on the iGoogle webpage. This allows you to manage, create, and edit the content stored in the repository from your iGoogle homepage. Also, you can integrate internal and external content and services. The **Gadgets** are basically interactive mini-applications, which you can place on your iGoogle homepage, and use them to search and manage your personalized information.

Alfresco provides three easy-to-use Google Gadgets by default. These are:

- Alfresco space browser: Create and browse spaces. Create, update, and view documents.
- Alfresco my tasks: Workflow tasks management.
- Alfresco search: Searching of documents in the repository.

Besides of these out of the box, provided by Alfresco Gadgets, you can also create your own Web Scripts and can use them as Gadgets in the iGoogle.

Steps to integrate iGoogle Gadgets with Alfresco

Alfresco Google Gadgets are completely powered by Web Scripts.

1. If you have already installed ZIP file for Google Gadgets, move to the next step. Otherwise, download the `aggadget.zip` file from the Packt Publisher's official web site inside the `module` directory.
2. Log in to Alfresco with **admin** as username and password.
3. Browse to **Company Home | Data Dictionary | Web Scripts Extensions**.
4. Click on **More Actions | Import**. Upload the `aggadget.zip` file (which contains he required files for Web Scripts), to import those Web Scripts.
5. Now, the space named `aggadget` will be created containing all the related Web Script files provided by Alfresco.
6. The next step is to register these Web Scripts with the Alfresco server to activate it. To register, browse to `http://<server_name>:<port_number>/alfresco/service/index` and click on the **Refresh list of Web Scripts** button to register these new Web Scripts. You will be able to see a message telling with how many web scripts were found and registered recently.
7. Now, these Web Scripts are ready to be used in your iGoogle webpage.
8. Some of the sample URLs are given below to create folder , search any text, or to see the task list:
    - `http://localhost:8080/alfresco/wcservice/aggadget/search?dummy=1`
    - `http://localhost:8080/alfresco/wcservice/aggadget/folder/?dummy=1`
    - `http://localhost:8080/alfresco/wcservice/aggadget/tasks?dummy=1`

The following screenshot will give you a brief idea of what we have just seen:

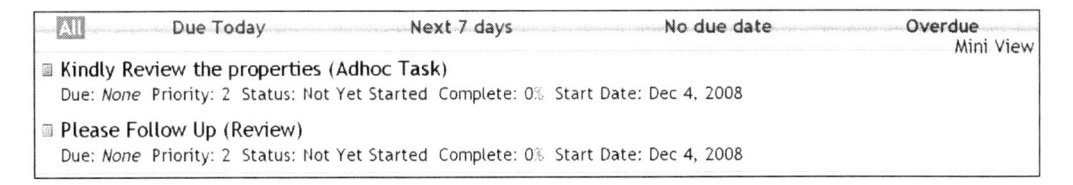

Using iGoogle Gadgets

The following steps will guide you when using iGoogle Gadgets.

1. You can use **Gadgets Editor** to add your own Gadget. Click on **File**, select **Upload** option. You will see the following screen:

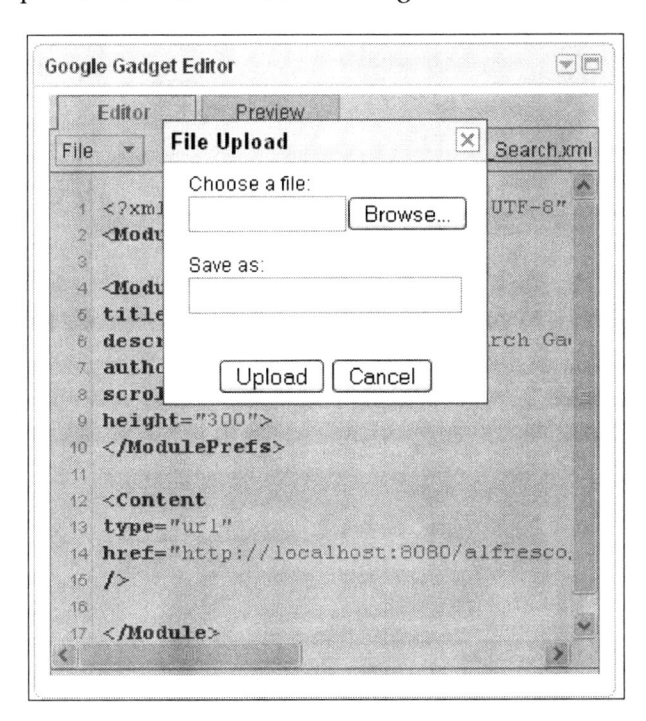

Integrating External Applications with Alfresco

2. Browse to the XML file for the module that you want to have as a Google Gadget, and upload it. You will be able to see the file in the **Google Gadget Editor,** as shown in the following screenshot. Here, we have used `Alfresco_Search.xml` for search the module.

3. You can edit the file if you want. Here, you just need to modify the `href`. Make it pointing to your alfresco server, which is already running.

4. To preview this gadget, click on the **Preview** tab. You can enter any keyword you want to search from Alfresco's repository, and you will be able to see the results with pagination support, as shown in the next figure:

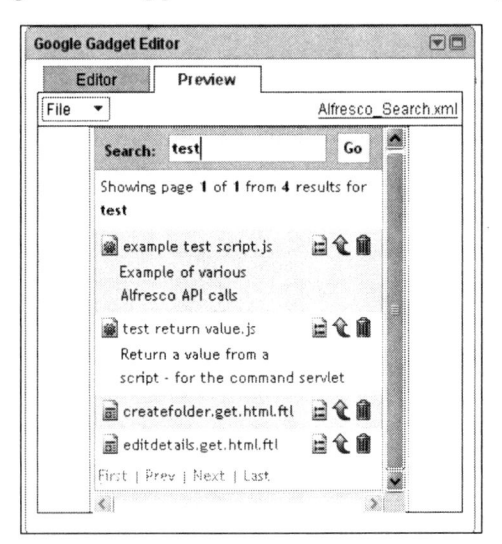

Integrating with FFMPEG video transcoder

FFMPEG is a popular video and audio transcoder having a high degree of performance. It is widely used in various commercial tools, to convert audio and video files from one format to another. It is basically a command line interface. We can easily integrate any such command-line application with Alfresco.

Let's take an example of one television company named STV. We assume they have **Asset Repository System (ARS)**, which is a centralized repository for all of the media content and serves the media packages to the customers of STV, who are spread all over the world. The company always uploads the video in Quick time (.mov) format. However, CMS system requires the video to be transformed to 3G (for cell phones), MPEG4 (for iPod), and Flash (the default format for the web site).

You need to download FFMPEG binary version for Windows and put into <alfresco_install>/bin directory. The command used for transformation is:

ffmpeg.exe -i [input_file.extension] [options] [output_file.extension]

Various options for video transcoding

Following are the various options for video transcoding:

- -b bitrate:

    Set the video bitrate in bit/s (default = 200 kb/s).

    => 512k

- -r fps:

    Set frame rate (Hz value, fraction or abbreviation), (default = 25).

    => 15.02

- -s size:

    Set frame size. The format is `wxh' (ffserver default = 160x128, ffmpeg default = same as source).

    => 320x240

- -aspect aspect:

    Set aspect ratio (4:3, 16:9 or 1.3333, 1.7777).

    => 4:3

Various options for audio transcoding

Following are the various options for audio transcoding:

- `-ar freq`:

    Set the audio sampling frequency (default = 44100 Hz).

    => 44100

- `-ab bitrate`:

    Set the audio bitrate in bit/s (default = 64k).

    => 64k

- `-ac channels`:

    Set the number of audio channels (default = 1 Mono; 2 = stereo).

    => 2

Integrating transformation as an action in Alfresco

In this section, we will see how we can use a FFMPEG transformations as a custom action in the Alfresco. We can then trigger some business rule on the spaces, which will execute this custom action to perform a transformation of all video files. Follow the steps mentioned next to execute this transformation:

1. The very first step is to configure the extra mime types, which we want to use. Here, we are using 3GP, MP2, MP4, avi, mov, and so on. All others, except 3GP, are already supported by Alfresco and defined in the `mimetype-map.xml` file in Alfresco. So, we need to add 3GP as a mime type, supported by Alfresco, in the `mimetype-map` file.

    ```
    <config evaluator="string-compare" condition="Mimetype Map">
          <mimetypes>
                  <mimetype mimetype="video/3gp" display="Mobile video">
                          <extension>3gp</extension>
                  </mimetype>
          </mimetypes>
     </config>
    ```

2. As FFMPEG is a command line interface, we can use Alfresco's `org.alfresco.util.exec.RuntimeExec` class to execute this command. To accomplish this, we need to configure it as a bean that will be referred to by our custom action executer. We can make these beans entries in the `custom-service-context.xml` file.

    ```
      <bean id="transformer.ffmpegVideo"
            class="org.stv.repo.content.transform.
    VideoContentTransformer "
    ```

```
            parent="baseContentTransformer"
            init-method=»init»>
      <property name=»executer»>
         <bean name=»transformer.ffmpegVideo.Command» class=»org.
alfresco.util.exec.RuntimeExec»>
            <property name=»commandMap»>
               <map>
                  <entry key=»Windows.*»>
                     <value>ffmpeg -i «${source}» ${options}
«${target}»
                                             </value>
                  </entry>
               </map>
            </property>
            <property name=»defaultProperties»>
               <props>
                  <prop key=»options»></prop>
               </props>
            </property>
         </bean>
      </property>
   </bean>
<bean id=»transform-video» class=»org.stv.repo.action.executer.
VideoTransformActionExecuter»
         parent=»transform»>
      <property name=»videoContentTransformer»>
         <ref bean=»transformer.ffmpegVideo» />
      </property>
</bean>
```

3. Once this is done, you have to create the custom action executer classes and perform the configurations for this. You can also refer to the wiki for more information on these. The wiki is available at: http://wiki.alfresco.com/wiki/Custom_Actions and http://wiki/alfresco.com/wiki/Wizard_Framework.

4. After finishing creation and configuration of Action Executer, you are ready with the example code. Start the Alfresco server and we will see how you can configure the rule for transformation.

5. We will create a folder structure of **Company Home | STV | Videos**. Inside the video space, create spaces for each of the different types of format (for video) that you want to support, that is, MPEG4, 3GP, and so on.

Integrating External Applications with Alfresco

6. Browse to **Company Home | STV | Videos** and click on **More Actions | Manage Content Rules**. In the next screen, click on **Create Rule** link. In the Create **Rule Wizard**, you can see the action created by us. Select the action as **Transform Video using FFMPEG and copy** as shown in the following figure:

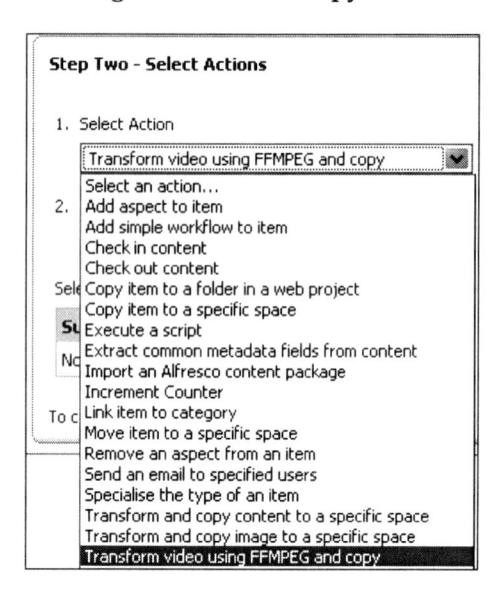

7. In the next step, you need to select the correct value for the **Required format**, which is the target format for transformation. Because we have configured 3GP, MP4, and AVI in the configuration file, we will have each of these three options that are available to us for transforming the video. After this, provide the correct, optional for a particular video transformation selection, based on the source and target type of the video file. You also need to provide the destination space, in order to copy the transformed video. Here, we have created the MP4 space inside the **Videos** folder. Therefore, provide the **Videos** folder as the destination folder.

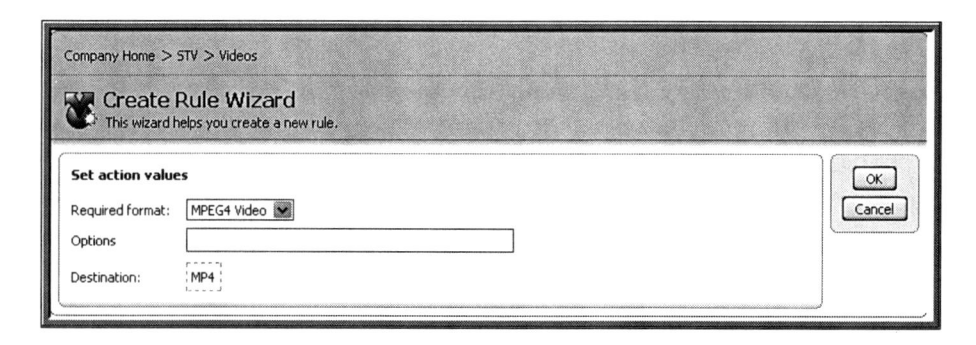

[342]

8. Now, whenever you upload any video in **Videos** space, it will be transformed in MP4 video format, and copied to **MP4** space inside **Videos** space as shown in the following screenshot:

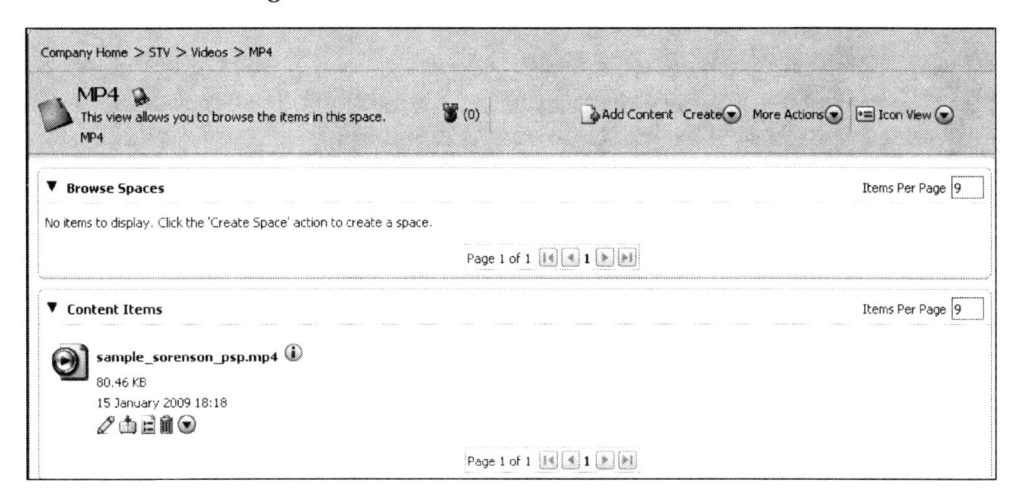

9. You can create as many rules as you create transformations that you want to perform for different video types.

> You can download the `ffmpeg.zip` from the Packt web site. Refer to `ReadMe.txt` for all of the file details.

Integrating with ViewOnePro image viewer

ViewOnePro is the world's first java applet image viewer to be extendable with additional modules without user installation, and that offers support for additional file formats (PDF Module, Universal Viewing Module), and for additional viewer functionality (Annotations Module, Permanent Redaction Server Module, Document Streaming Server Module, and the Print Accelerator Module). ViewOnePro is a powerful in-browser viewer with the ability to extend an applet's capabilities. This represents a major breakthrough for web-based document management users.

To protect the integrity of your records for compliance, ViewOnePro provides viewing (and crucially not editing) access to the wide range of documents stored in your repository. To integrate ViewOnePro with Alfresco, follow the steps given below:

1. Download ViewOnePro pro from http://www.daeja.com.
2. Extract the downloaded zip file and copy the v1files folder to `<<alfresco_server>>/tomcat/webapps/alfresco` folder. This folder contains required JAR files and applet classes.

Integrating External Applications with Alfresco

3. Next, create your own presentation template, specifying the applet tag for the applet ViewONE, provided by viewOnePro package.
4. You need to set some parameters in this template file, for look and feel of the applet, and also for the available options for the applet such as viewmode, pageButtons, fileMenus, and so on.
5. Template file will have extension as `.ftl`, similar to other FreeMarker template used by Alfresco. Following is the sample `v1preview.ftl` file:

```
<html>
<body onLoad="setTimeout('delayer()', 500)">
<APPLET CODEBASE="/alfresco/v1files"
ARCHIVE="ji.jar, daeja1.jar, daeja2.jar, daeja3.jar"
CODE="ji.applet.jiApplet.class"
NAME="ViewONE"
WIDTH="980"
HEIGHT="980"
HSPACE="0"
VSPACE="0"
MAYSCRIPT="true"
ALIGN="middle">

<PARAM NAME="cabbase" VALUE="viewone.cab">
<PARAM NAME="ACMPreloadFile" value="ji">
<PARAM NAME="fileMenus" value="false">
<PARAM NAME="pageButtons" value="true">
<PARAM NAME="draggingEnabled" value="true">
<param name="viewmode" value="thumbsleft">
<PARAM NAME="ACMRedirectTarget" value="_self">
<PARAM NAME="ACMDownloadPrompt" value="true">
<PARAM NAME="ACMUpdate" value="false">
<PARAM NAME="JavaScriptExtensions" VALUE="true">

<#assign counter = 1>

<#list space.children as child>
        <#if child.isDocument >
             <#if child.mimetype = "image/gif"
|| child.mimetype="image/jpeg" ||                   child.mimetype="application/pdf" || child.mimetype="image/tiff">
             <param name="page${counter?string}" value="/alfresco${child.url}">
                   <#assign counter = counter + 1 >
             </#if>
        </#if>
</#list>
</APPLET>
<script>
```

```
           function delayer()
           {
                   ViewONE.setFileButtons(false);
                   ViewONE.setAreaZoom (true);
           }
</script>
</body>
</html>
```

6. Upload this template file to the **Presentation Templates** folder, under **Company Home | Data Dictionary**.

7. To see the ViewOnePro functionality, you can apply this template as a custom view on any space.

    ◦ To accomplish this, click on the **More Actions** button for any space. You will have option to **Preview in Template,** as shown below:

    ◦ In the next screen, you will be asked to choose a template from the list of available presentation templates. Select your FTL presentation template file. In our case, this will be `v1preview.ftl`.

8. Now, you will be able to preview that space with ViewOnePro functionality. In our example, we are using ViewOnePro for previewing images. Therefore, we will preview `Images` folder as shown in the following screenshot:

Integrating with the Facebook social network application

Facebook is the most popular social network, where people share content, and connect with their friends, family, and businesses.

This integration will enable users of the Alfresco Enterprise Content Network to use Facebook to publish content. It is Alfresco's aim to make publishing and sharing enterprise content as simple and as familiar as possible.

A large enough segment of any workforce is active on one web-based social network or the other—if not Facebook, then MySpace, or LinkedIn, or one of the myriad boutique networks out there—to compel corporations to take them seriously as communication platforms.

Through the Facebook integration, Alfresco users can upload and share enterprise content with customers, fellow employees, and partners, in a secure and audited way. Platform functionality includes application registration, Facebook authorization and single sign-on, FBML support, and Facebook model support. The tools that are available to employees using the platform will be familiar if they are or have ever been users of Facebook. In a secure environment, the employees can upload documents. They can view My Documents, All Documents, or Recently Added Documents, along with documents owned or uploaded by colleagues and friends, through the Facebook newsfeed.

Now, social networks web sites such as Facebook can easily be built up with Alfresco's REST-based web services. This results into emerging the enterprise content management capabilities with the social graph of facebook integration. In this case study, we will see how we can develop Alfresco Facebook application with the help of Web Scripts. We will extend Web Scripts to support Facebook capabilities. As we are suing Web Script Framework, we don't use any core development with Java, but will just use the scripting language.

Creating a new Facebook application

The following are the steps for creating a new Facebook application:

1. Acquire the Alfresco Facebook package:

    Download the `doclib` folder that contains the required files from the Packt web site. Create the folders if they don't already exist, and copy the files from the following path: `tomcat\webapps\alfresco\WEB-INF\classes\alfresco\templates\webscripts\org\alfresco\facebook\doclib`

2. Set up the Facebook application

    Go to `http://developers.facebook.com/`, and then click on the **Start Now,** button as shown below:

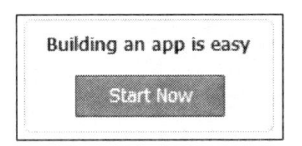

3. Next, you need to set up the application. You will see the **Go to the Facebook Developer App,** as shown in the figure below. Click on the link.

Integrating External Applications with Alfresco

4. Now, log in to your Facebook account, as prompted.
5. Click on the link, as shown in the next figure:

+ Set Up New Application

6. Next, you will see the various settings that you need to configure for your application.

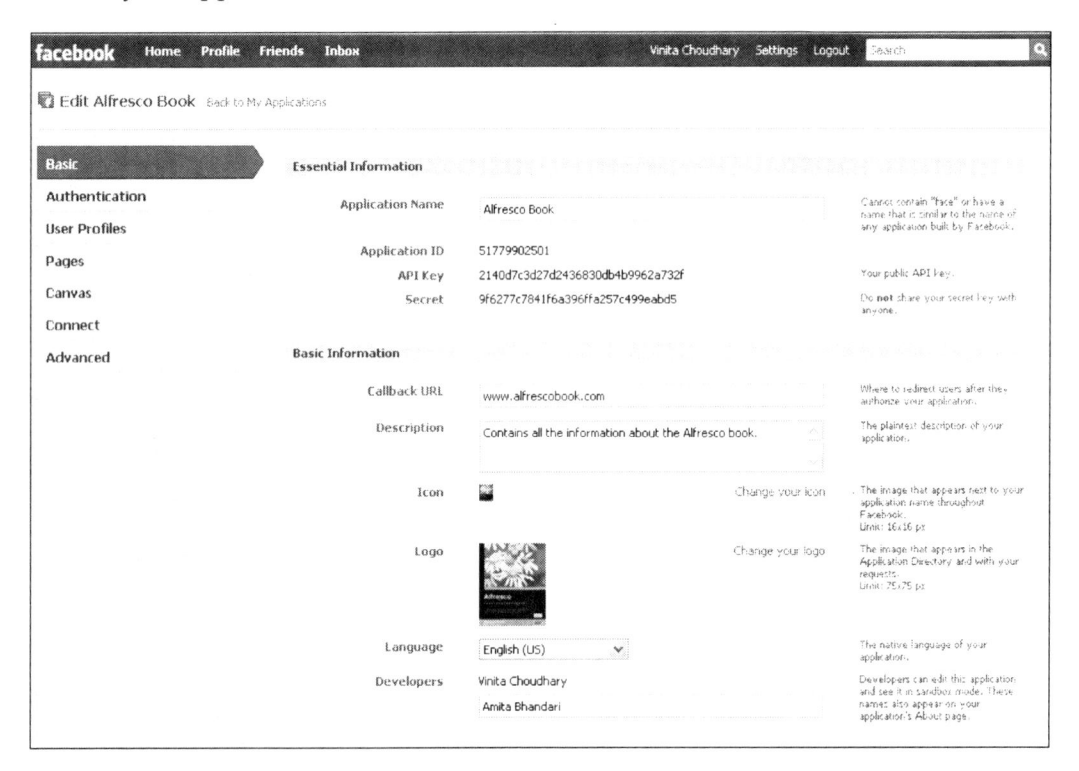

7. Enter the appropriate data and save. Provide proper application name that you can easily identify. Here, the **Developer Contact Email** and **User Support Email** is automatically filled up by Facebook (which is user who currently logged in Facebook). **Callback URL** is required for forwarding requests to Alfresco from Facebook. Provide unique **Canvas URL**. Provide **Post-Add URL**, which is mostly same as the **Canvas URL**. Once you complete all the necessary fields and submit, you will get screen like following:

Chapter 9

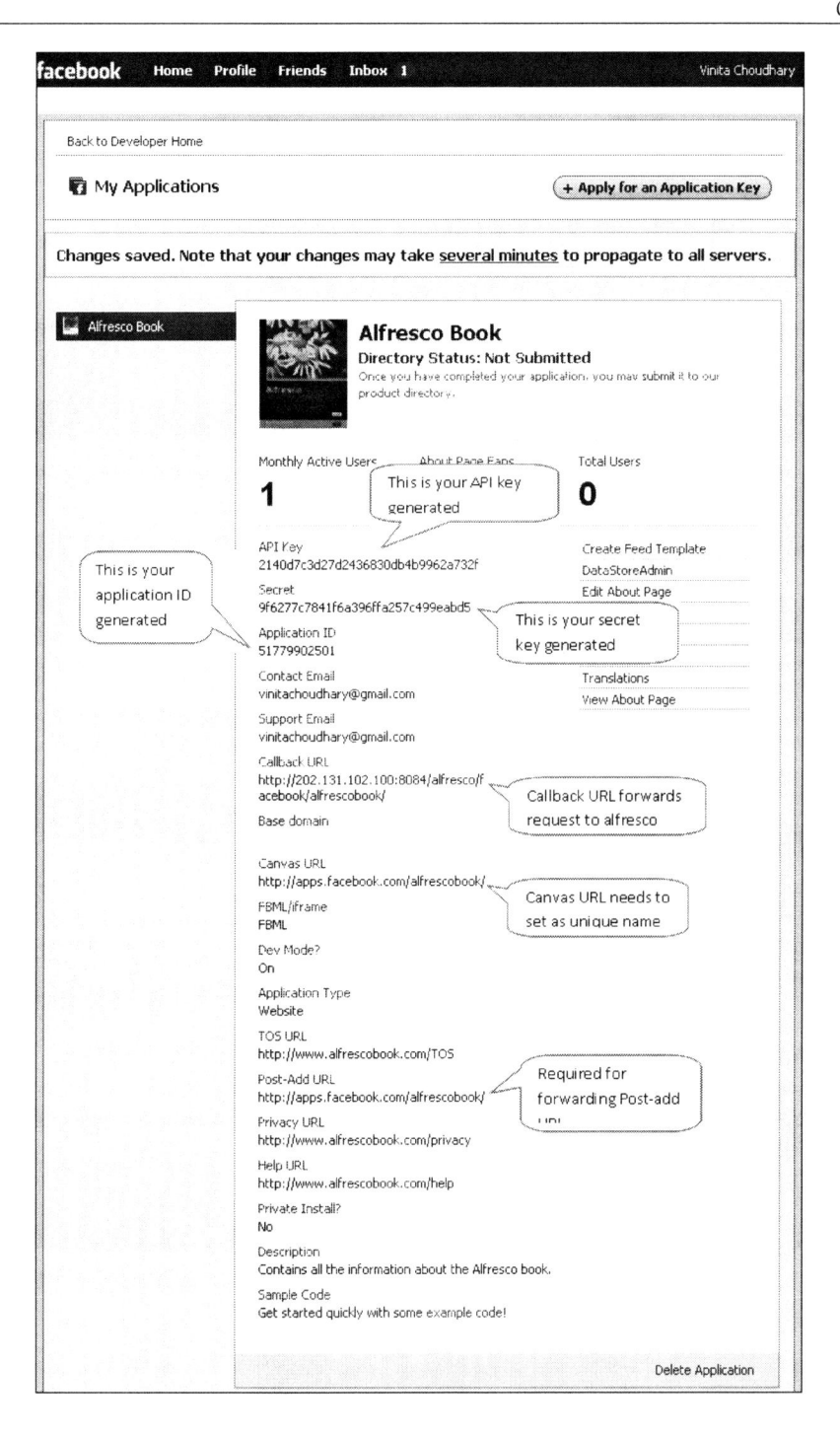

Alfresco Book
Directory Status: Not Submitted
Once you have completed your application, you may submit it to our product directory.

Monthly Active Users: 1
Total Users: 0

API Key
2140d7c3d27d2436830db4b9962a732f
This is your API key generated

Secret
9f6277c7841f6a396ffa257c499eabd5
This is your secret key generated

Application ID
51779902501
This is your application ID generated

Contact Email
vinitachoudhary@gmail.com

Support Email
vinitachoudhary@gmail.com

Callback URL
http://202.131.102.100:8084/alfresco/facebook/alfrescobook/
Callback URL forwards request to alfresco

Base domain

Canvas URL
http://apps.facebook.com/alfrescobook/
Canvas URL needs to set as unique name

FBML/iframe
FBML

Dev Mode?
On

Application Type
Website

TOS URL
http://www.alfrescobook.com/TOS

Post-Add URL
http://apps.facebook.com/alfrescobook/
Required for forwarding Post-add URL

Privacy URL
http://www.alfrescobook.com/privacy

Help URL
http://www.alfrescobook.com/help

Private Install?
No

Description
Contains all the information about the Alfresco book.

Sample Code
Get started quickly with some example code!

Other options: Create Feed Template, DataStoreAdmin, Edit About Page, Translations, View About Page, Delete Application

Changes saved. Note that your changes may take several minutes to propagate to all servers.

Integrating External Applications with Alfresco

> Here, the generated API key, Secret key, and Application ID are randomly generated each time, so these will not be the same as those shown in the above screenshot.
>
> In addition, /facebook/alfrescobook/ should match with the URL provided for Alfresco. Therefore, the syntax would be http://<HOST>:<PORT>/alfresco/<WEBSCRIPT URL>

Once you have set up your application and submitted it, you can see your own application, as shown in the screenshot below

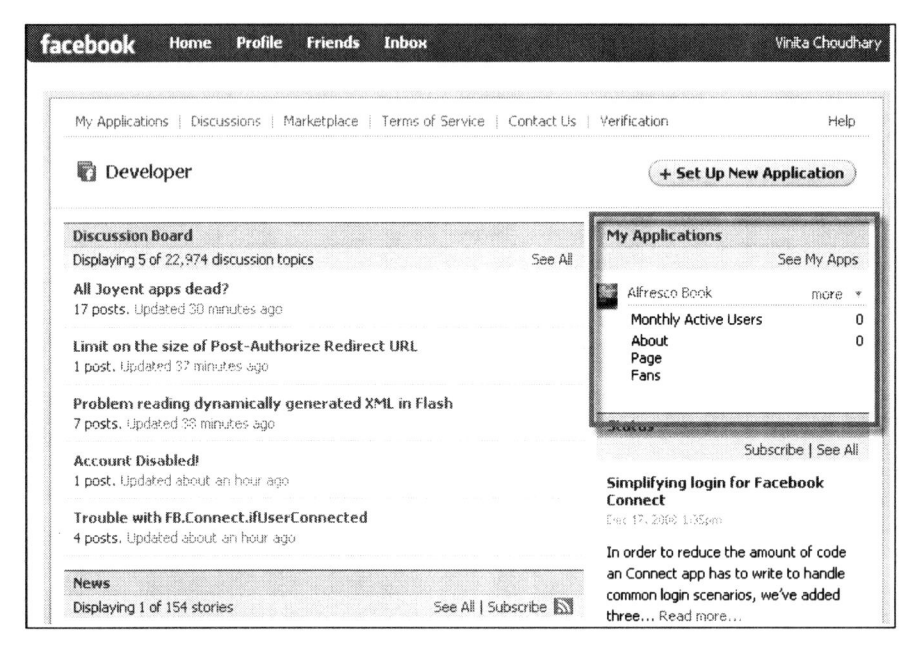

It is important to note that we need to pay more attention to the following property—**Application Name**, **Callback URL**, **Canvas URL**, and **Post Add URL**. Select the option Yes for the field **Add application to Facebook**, and select the Developer Mode checkbox.

Registering the Facebook application with Alfresco

Once you run a new instance of Alfresco 3.0, create the appropriate folder structure as described below:

1. Create a folder named Facebook<applicationID> inside **Company Home**.
2. Go to following path. If the folders don't exist, create them.
   Data Dictionary > Web Scripts > com > Facebook > _apps

3. Create the `app.<API_KEY>.js` file inside `_apps` folder. Please note that the API key is different in each case.

4. Now go to `Data Dictionary > Web Scripts > org > alfresco > Facebook > doclib`. You may need to create the spaces in case they do not exist

5. Now, through CIFS, copy the modified `doclib.rar` files to the `doclib` folder. Once you have copied all the files, the folders should appear as shown in the following screenshot:

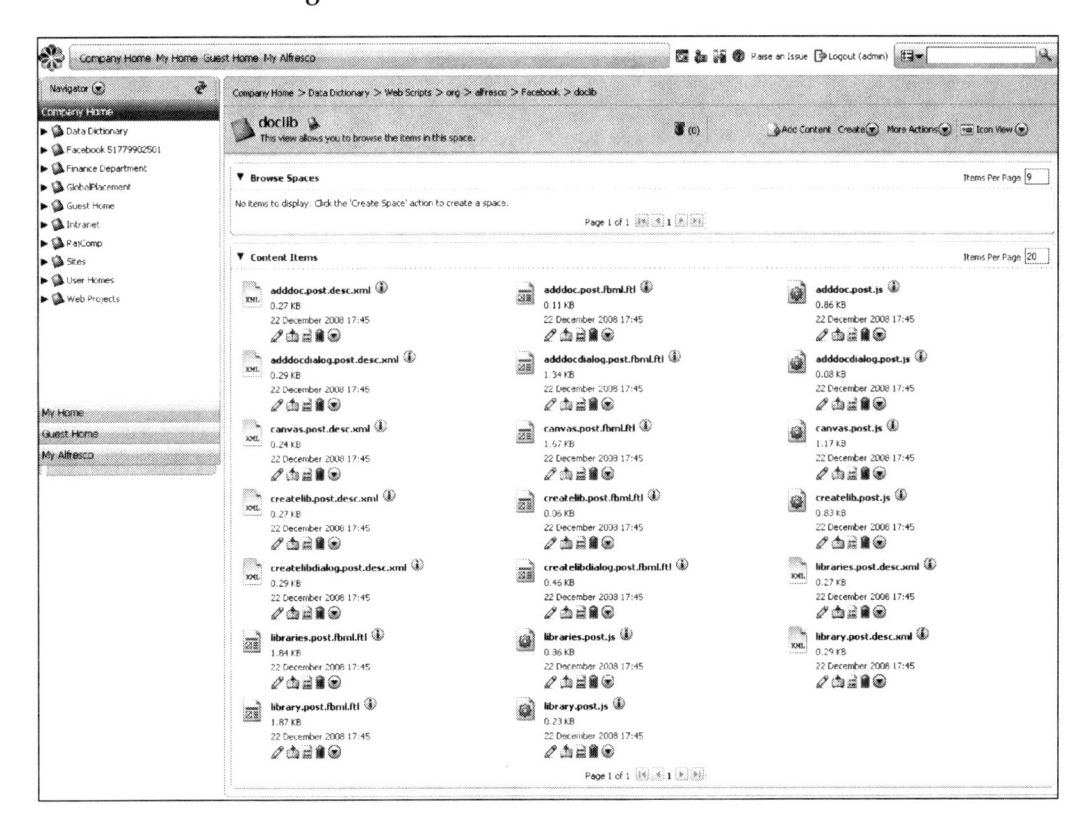

6. Once you all are set up, register your new Web Scripts to Alfresco. If you get the following error: **Error! Hyperlink reference not valid**, then click on **Refresh Web scripts**.

7. Now we are ready to run our application. Open new browser window and point URL to your given **Canvas URL**. In our case: `http://apps.facebook.com/alfrescobook/` (which is our Canvas URL).

CMIS

The CMIS (Content Management Interoperability Services) standard defines a domain model and set of bindings such as Web Service and REST/ Atom, which can be used by applications to work with one or more Content Management Systems/ repositories.

The CMIS interface is designed to be layered on top of the existing Content Management Systems and their existing programmatic interfaces. It is neither intended to prescribe how specific features should be implemented within those CM systems, nor to exhaustively expose all of the CM system's capabilities through the CMIS interfaces. Rather, it is intended to define a generic/universal set of capabilities provided by a CM system, and a set of services for working with those capabilities .

The following image shows not only a typical requirement in a larger enterprise, but also how the CMIS standard can enable content to be ubiquitous in an enterprise.

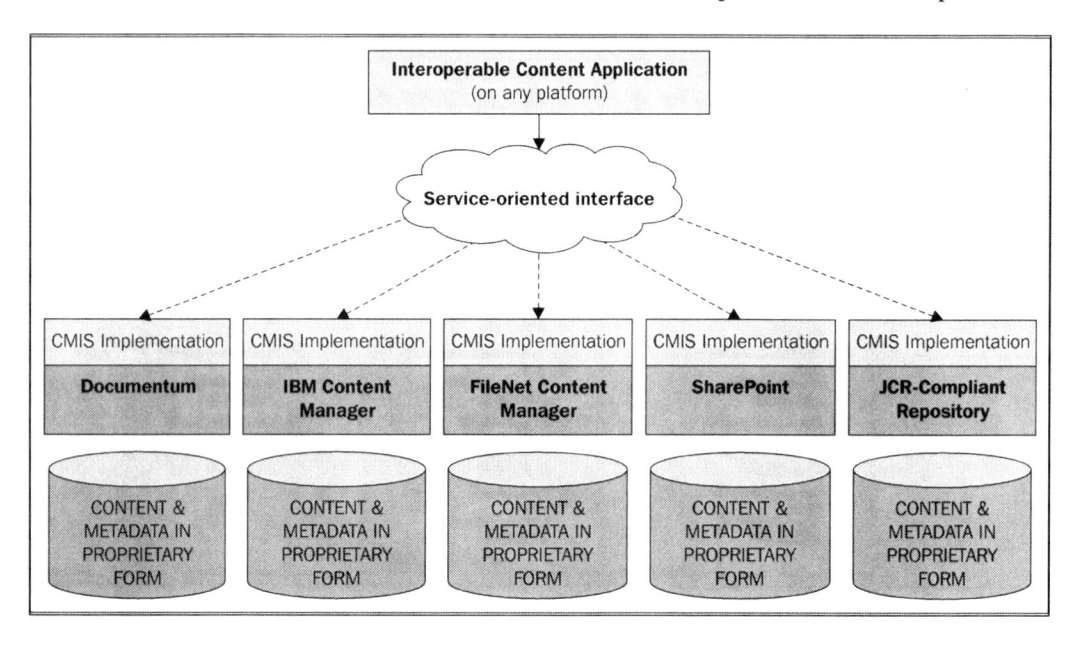

Just as the major database vendors standardized on SQL in the 1980's, today's leading ECM vendors have developed a draft specification with the goal of delivering and enabling interoperability across content repositories. The draft specification is backed by Alfresco, EMC, IBM, Microsoft, OpenText, Oracle, and SAP.

Alfresco leads the charge, being the first vendor to provide a draft implementation of CMIS at such an early stage of the standard. In September 2008, Alfresco released the industry's first draft implementation of the CMIS specification. The company has also made available the CMIS Developer Toolbox, which includes a working implementation of the CMIS standard, and contains resources to assist developers in the CMIS community to start the creation of portable content applications, based on the draft specification.

Scope of CMIS

To ensure that CMIS meets the previously-stated goal of allowing the creation of rich ECM applications using this standard, here is the list of representative use cases that are accounted for in the CMIS capabilities, along with some that were not targeted for CMIS Version 1. These are categorized into the following groups:

- Core ECM use cases that are directly supported by the CMIS interfaces: These are the fundamental ECM use cases that are common to most/all ECM applications today.
- ECM applications and use cases that can be built on top of the CMIS interfaces: These are examples of applications that can use the basic capabilities exposed via the CMIS interfaces to provide higher-level solutions to customer problems.
- Out-of-scope use cases for CMIS 1.0: These are use cases/applications that, although in many cases are important for ECM scenarios, have been deemed out-of-scope for the initial version of the CMIS standard.

Core ECM Use Cases	ECM applications and use cases that c an be built on top of the CMIS interfaces	Out-of-scope use cases for CMIS 1. 0
<ul><li>Collaborative Content Creation</li><li>Portals</li><li>Mashups</li></ul>	<ul><li>Workflow and business process management</li><li>Archival applications</li><li>Compound/ virtual documents</li><li>Electronic legal discovery</li></ul>	<ul><li>Records management and compliance</li><li>Digital asset management</li><li>Web content management</li><li>Subscription/ notification services</li></ul>

Alfresco CMIS implementation

CMIS exposes services for:

- Discovering object type definitions and other repository information (including which optional capabilities are supported by a particular repository)
- Creating, reading, updating, and deleting objects
- Filing documents into zero, one, or more folders, if the repository supports the optional multi-filing capability.
- Navigating and traversing the hierarchy of folders in the repository
- Creating versions of documents and accessing a document's version history
- Querying a repository to retrieve one or more objects that match user-specified search criteria, including full-text search queries

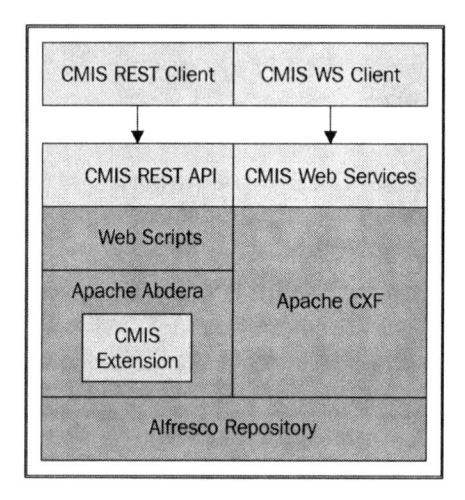

Sample Alfresco CMIS dashlet

As an example, we will use CMIS to query the Alfresco repository and display the documents in the Alfresco Book Project Site (refer Chapter10) on the site dashboard. The query will search the Alfresco Book Project site in the `Sites` folder of the **Company Home**.

A sample of our query is as follows:

```
var selectString = "SELECT * FROM Document WHERE IN_TREE( ,\'" +
sitespaceid + "\') AND " +
  "(CreatedBy=\'" + user.id + "\' OR LastModifiedBy=\'" + user.id +
"\') AND ObjectTypeId = \'document\'";
  var cmisQuery = "<?xml version=\"1.0\" encoding=\"UTF-8\"
standalone=\"yes\" ?><query xmlns:cmis=\"http://www.cmis.org/2008/05\
"><statement>" + selectString + "</statement><pageSize>" + 0 + "</
pageSize></query>";

  // get the documents for the currently active site
  var conn = remote.connect("alfresco");
  var queryResult = conn.post(stringUtils.urlEncodeComponent(id),
cmisQuery, "application/cmisquery+xml");
```

To accomplish this, follow the steps given below:

1. Browse to the folder **AlfrescoShare | tomcat | webapps | share | WEB-NF | classes | alfresco | webscripts** and create a folder here. We created a folder called `AlfrescoBook`.

   > You can download the code samples of `mydocuments.get.desc.xml`, `mydocuments.get.properties`, `mydocuments.get.js`, `mydocuments.get.html.ftl` from the Packt web site.

2. Copy the files into the new folder that you created. Restart Alfresco.

3. On the **Alfresco Book Project Site** toolbar, click on the **Customize Site Dashboard**.

Integrating External Applications with Alfresco

4. In the **Add Dashlets**, select the **Alfresco Book Site Documents** dashlet. (Refer to Chapter 10 to understand the process for adding dashlets.)

5. You can now see the dashlet that you added on your site, as shown in the next screenshot:

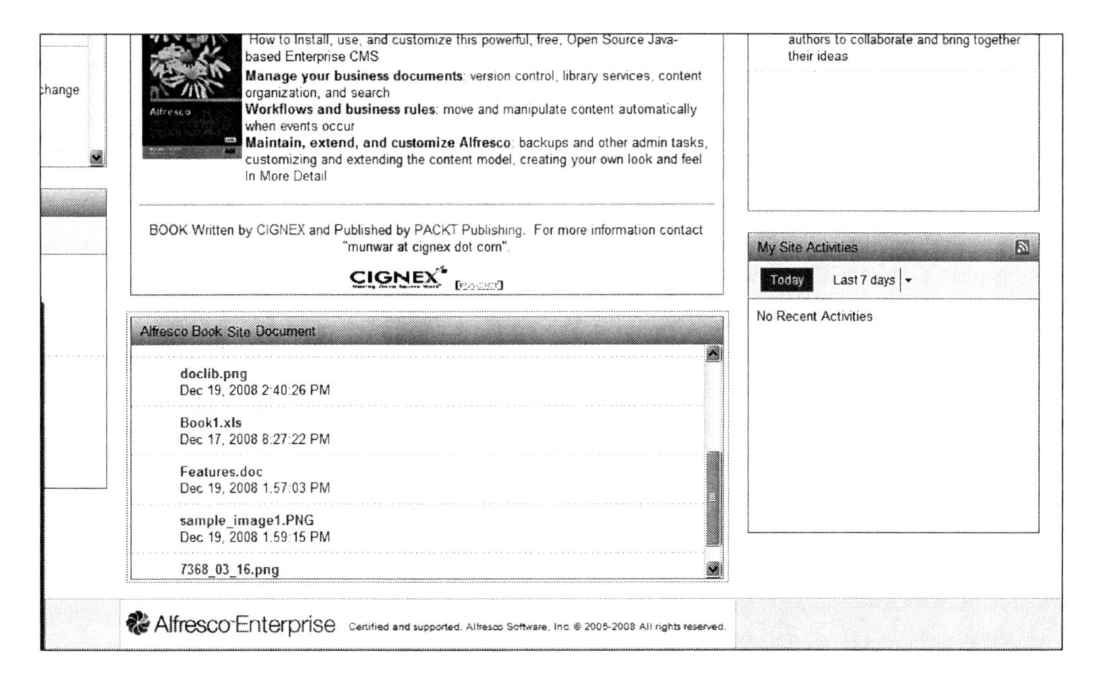

Summary

In this chapter, you have learned that Alfresco can be used as an embedded repository or an external content repository. Alfresco provides open standards based protocols to integrate with external applications. Some of the application integration examples are mentioned in this chapter. As it is an open source technology, you can reuse many of them for your business applications, saving time and money.

10
Advanced Collaboration Using Alfresco Share

Today, collaboration and team effort have become critical factors, both inside and outside of the workplace. More and more users want simplicity and familiarity with the tools they use day in and day out. They achieve this by searching in Google, reading in Wikipedia, writing on a blog, finding people on Facebook, being notified in a simple RSS reader, viewing friends, activities on Facebook, and bringing all of this together in iGoogle. Alfresco Share delivers all of this functionality to enterprise users, projects, and teams.

Imagine a business user, if given the permission, being able to set up their project web site quickly, being able to invite users to the site, and assign permissions to users within that web site. What previously required a customized solution is now offered out of the box by Alfresco Share.

By the end of this chapter you will have learned about:

- The Alfresco Share User Interface
- Creating and managing collaborative web sites
- Effective management of project content
- Customizing and managing your dashboard
- Configuring blogs
- Using Wikis
- Using the Alfresco repository with Microsoft Office tools

Alfresco Share

Alfresco Share (referred to simply as **Share** from now on) is built on the Alfresco enterprise-class document repository, and delivers out of the box collaborative content management. It simplifies the capture, sharing, and retrieval of information across virtual teams. Team members or project members can rapidly find relevant content or excerpts, look at past or similar projects, and stay on top of any relevant changes, in order to make them more efficient.

Share is focused on collaboration tasks and includes integration with popular blogging, Wiki, and forum or discussion products, out of the box. It provides a great interface into more traditional document management libraries (think folders) as well. Keep in mind that all of the web site's contents and documents are still stored in the Alfresco repository. Therefore they are secured, versioned, searchable, and auditable.

Share is an independent client application that accesses the repository through web scripts. It is built on the **Alfresco Surf** (referred to simply as **Surf** from now on) platform. Alfresco Share is a web application that runs on a machine that is separate from that of the repository.

Share provides a paradigm for creating collaborative applications by aggregating Surf components, and incorporating new Surf components as they are developed. With Share, users can modify their workspaces to fit their collaborative requirements inside or outside of the organization. Users can invite their peers to share and collaborate on the project and the content. With the addition of Share, Alfresco delivers a **Web 2.0** application that leverages Flash and AJAX with a polished interface, which any business person can enjoy.

Features like Document Libraries, Search, Activity Feeds, Virtual Teams, personalized dashboard, N-tier Architecture, and draft CMIS support make it a really competent tool for collaborative content management. Share allows you to:

- Bulk-upload content, select content from thumbnails, and view it in a Flash viewer. The content is automatically generated in Flash format. This allows users to view content regardless of the original format.
- Search for people and experts to contribute to their projects as easily as searching for content. Share provides updates on what is new in a project, especially details of content that has been added, edited, or commented upon. Share can track deliverables and import the information into your personal calendar by using iCal.

- Use an interactive interface to configure a customizable dashboard, and sites, based on what is critical to a specific role or project. Share allows you to create a virtual team for projects and communities.
- Develop applications in an environment that uses lightweight scripting and reusable components, as well as deliver scalability and allow more users to access existing resources.

The URL to access the Alfresco Share application is different from the URL used to access Alfresco Explorer. The Alfresco Share application can be launched in the web browser by visiting the URL, `http://<server name> /share/`

If you have already installed Alfresco in Windows, then you can invoke the Alfresco Share application by selecting the application, as shown in the following screenshot:

You need to provide your authentication credentials, which are similar to those used in the Alfresco Share application. For the administrator, the default username and password are both `admin`.

Once you have been authenticated, the **Administrator Dashboard** will be displayed, as shown in the following screenshot. At the top of the page you will find the application toolbar. This toolbar contains links to the various Share pages.

Advanced Collaboration Using Alfresco Share

Your **Administrator Dashboard** will look similar to the following screenshot:

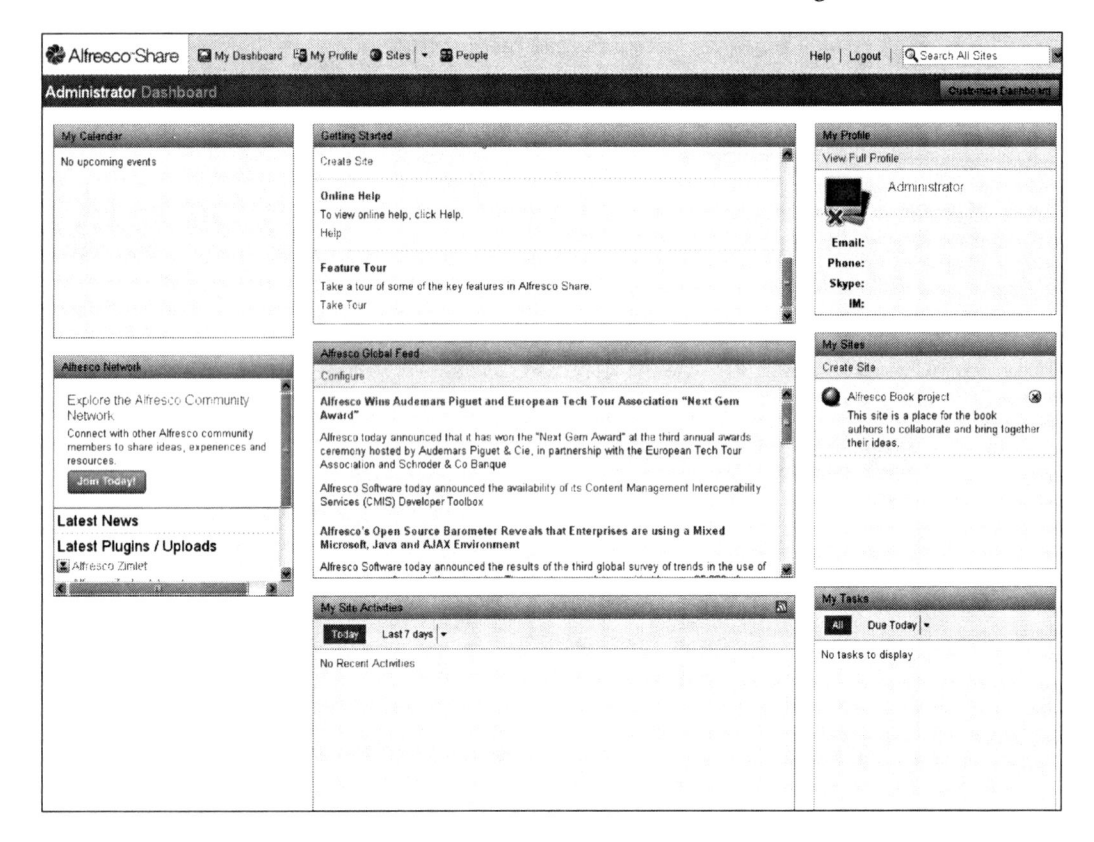

These components are as follows:

- **My Dashboard**: This component displays your personal, configurable dashboard
- **My Profile**: This component displays your **Profile** page, where you can view and edit your user details
- **Sites**: This component displays the **Site Finder** page, where you can search for specific sites and manage the membership of Share sites
- **People**: This component displays the **People Finder** page, where you search for specific Share users
- **Help**: This component displays the online help available for Alfresco Share
- **Logout**: This component logs you out of the Alfresco Share application.
- **Search**: This component enables you to perform a quick search for content in the current site, or across all of the sites

My Dashboard

This is your personal dashboard and consists of dashlets that allow you to track all of the information that is relevant to you. These dashlets appear on your personal dashboard and on site dashboards. Each dashlet provides a summarized view of a page. However, the presence of a corresponding page is not mandatory. Wherever a page exists, it generates the contents of the related dashlet.

When customizing your personal dashboard, each dashlet that you select is displayed as a pane on the dashboard. The following dashlets are available:

- **Getting Started**: This dashlet displays the instructions for getting started, and provides you with links to perform common tasks.
- **My Profile**: This dashlet contains a summary of the personal details provided in your user profile.
- **My Sites**: This dashlet displays all of the sites that you have either created or are a member of. You can access a site from this dashlet. Creating or deleting a site can be done by using this dashlet.
- **My Calendar**: This dashlet provides a list of events that you have created, as well as events for each site that you are a member of.
- **My Tasks**: This dashlet displays a list of all of your incomplete tasks.
- **My Activities**: This dashlet maintains the most recent activities that have been performed for any site that you are a member of.
- **Documents I'm Editing**: This dashlet displays all of the files that you currently have checked out from any Document Library.
- **Alfresco Network**: This is a portal that gives Alfresco Share customers access to the latest Alfresco news.
- **RSS Feed**: This dashlet is configured to display the Alfresco web site feed. This is the default setting.
- **CMIS Feed**: This dashlet displays links specific to the **Content Management Interoperability Services (CMIS)** specification and implementation.

Customize your dashboard

You can customize your personal dashboard to suit your purposes. You can modify the dashboard layout, select the dashlets that will appear in your dashboard, or configure the order in which the selected dashlets are displayed.

Advanced Collaboration Using Alfresco Share

To customize the dashboard layout and its contents, carry out the following steps:

1. Click on the **My Dashboard** option on the toolbar
2. Click on the **Customize Dashboard** button on the dashboard banner. As a result, the **Customize User Dashboard** page appears

The image in the **Current Layout** section represents the current layout. The **Dashlets** section displays the current selection of dashlets, as they will appear on your dashboard.

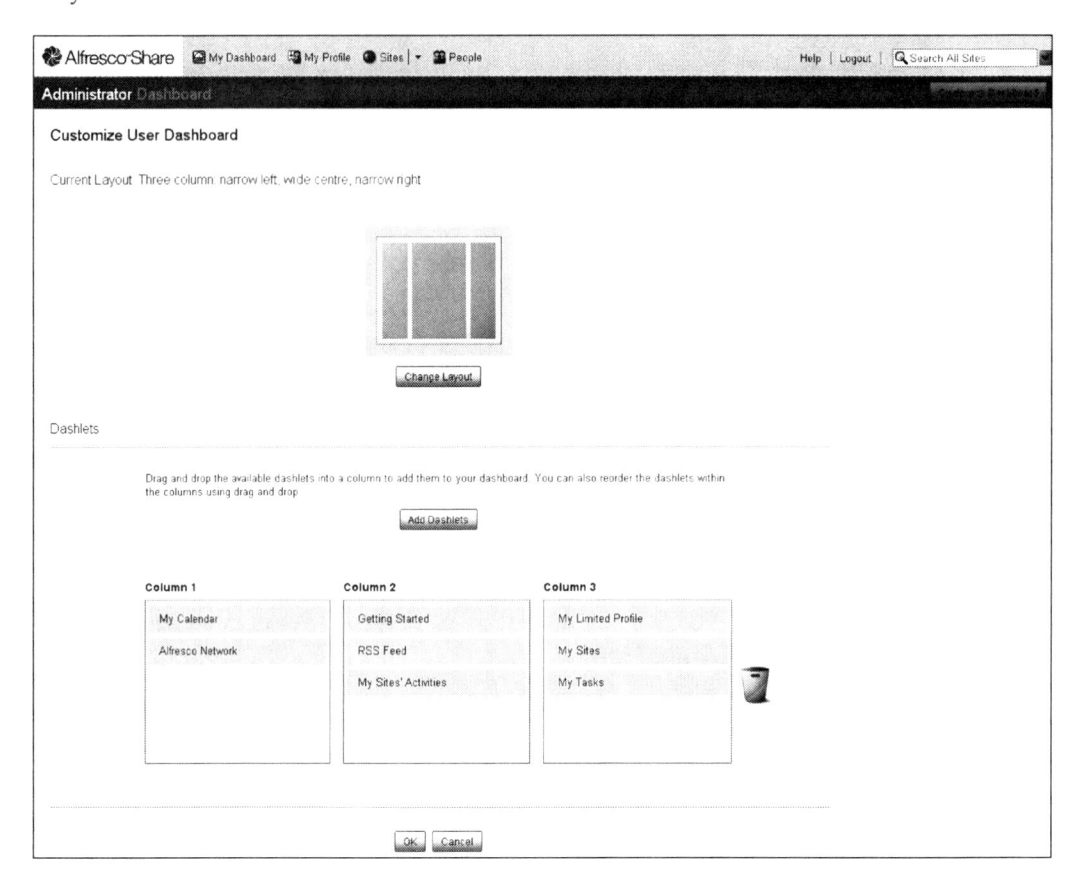

To change the dashboard layout, carry out the following steps:

1. Click on the **Change Layout**. This opens a page that lists the available dashboard layouts.
2. You can select a layout by clicking on it or on the **Select** button beside it.

[364]

To add, remove, or rearrange dashlets, carry out the following steps:

1. Click on the **Add Dashlets** option to display the available dashlets
2. Click on the desired dashlet in the **Add Dashlets** section and drag it to the desired column
3. To remove a dashlet, click on the dashlet and drag it to the bin
4. Click and drag the dashlets up and down, within and across columns, to set the display order
5. Click on the **OK** button to save your changes

Now your dashboard has been customized as per your selections, and will display the selected dashlets in the order specified and with the layout chosen.

My Profile

The profile page contains your detailed personal and business information. Share publishes these credentials for all of the site members to view.

Viewing your full profile

You can access your **User Profile** to review the information that is being published to the site members. You can access your **My Profile** page from anywhere in Share.

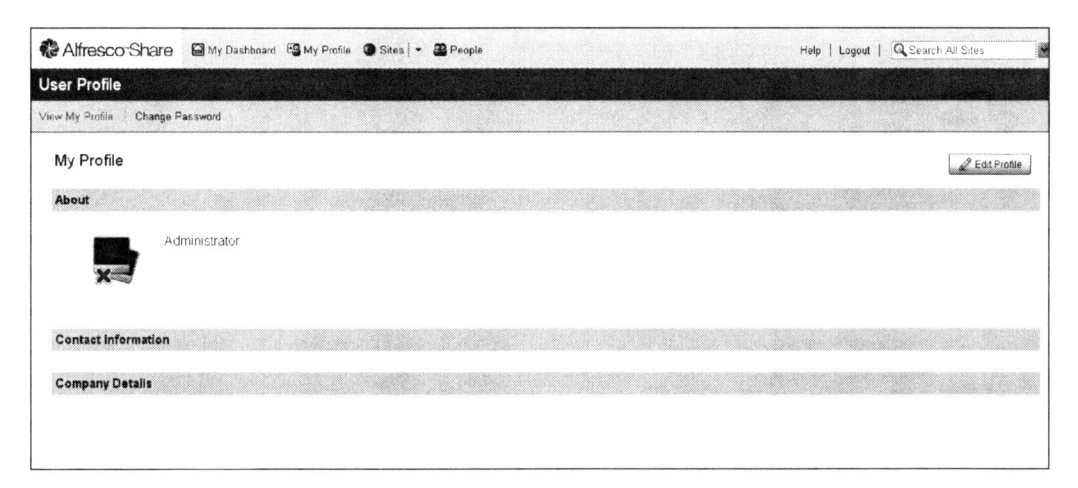

In order to view your complete profile, click on the **My Profile** option on the toolbar. Alternatively, on your dashboard, you can click on the **View full profile** option in the **My Profile** dashlet. As a result, the **User Profile** page will be displayed.

Editing your profile

You can edit your profile in order to manage the information about you that is available to the site members. In addition to personal and business information, you can also upload a photograph.

In order to edit your user profile, carry out the following steps:

1. Click on the **My Profile** option on the toolbar. The **User Profile** page appears.
2. Click on the **Edit Profile** button. Fields that currently specify your information are displayed. Mandatory fields are marked with an asterisk (*).

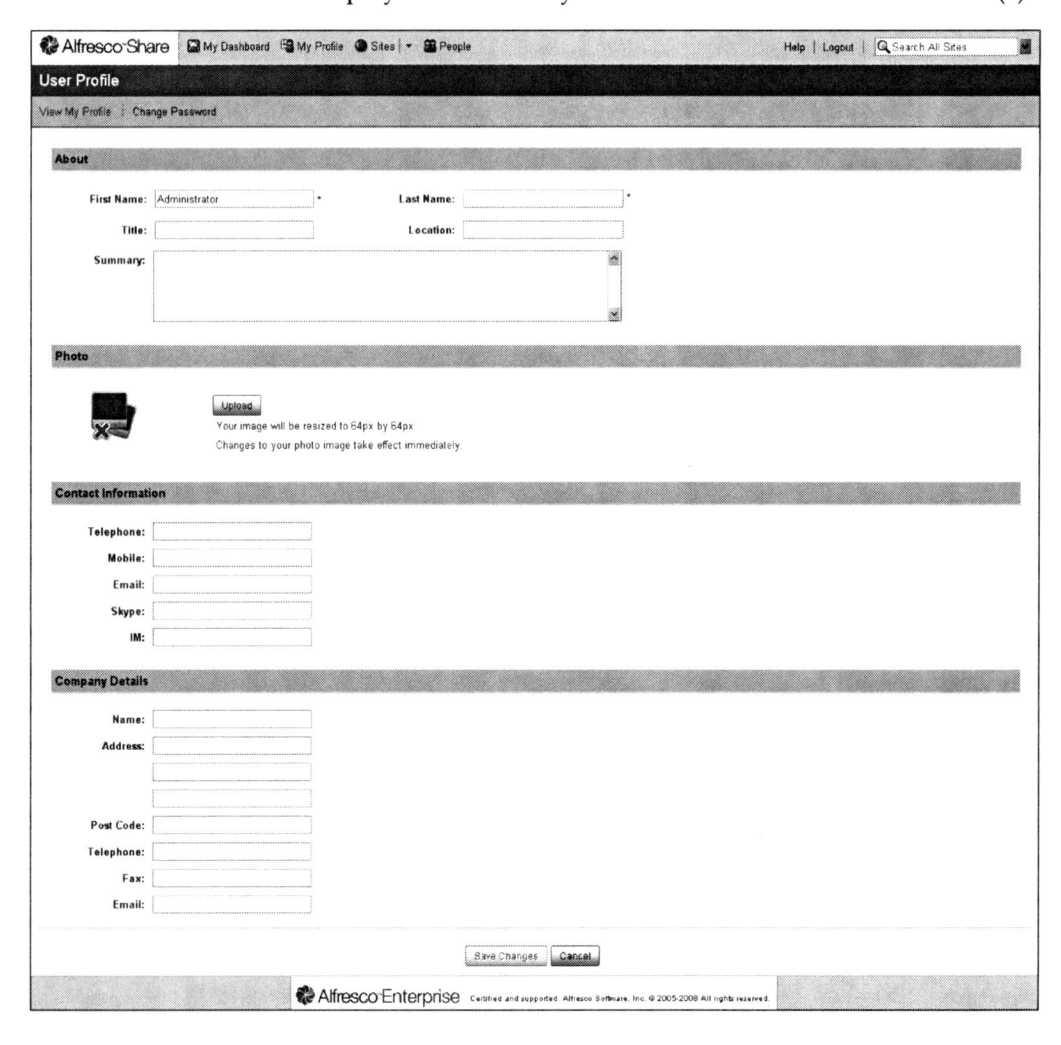

3. Edit the **User Profile** details, making changes and adding new information as desired.

In order to upload a photo to be displayed along with your profile, carry out the following steps:

1. Click on the **Upload** button in the **Photo** section. Click on the **Browse** button on the **Upload File** page.
2. **Browse** to and then **Upload** the image. The selected file appears in the **Upload File** page. Click **Remove** to delete the file listed.
3. Click **Upload File(s)** to upload the picture.
4. Click on the **Save Changes** to save the profile details. The **User Profile** page now displays your updated **User Profile**.

> If a profile picture already exists, uploading a new photo will replace the existing picture. The **User Profile** page now displays your updated profile.

Changing your password

You can also reset your password, for example for security reasons. To change your password, carry out the following steps:

1. Click on the **My Profile** option on the toolbar, which opens the **User Profile** page. Next, click on the **Change Password** option, which will display the **Change Password** page.
2. In the **Enter Old Password** box, type your current password. In the **Enter New Password** box, type your new password. In the **Confirm New Password** box, type the new password again.
3. Click on the **OK button** to complete the password reset process. You are then returned to your **User Profile** page.

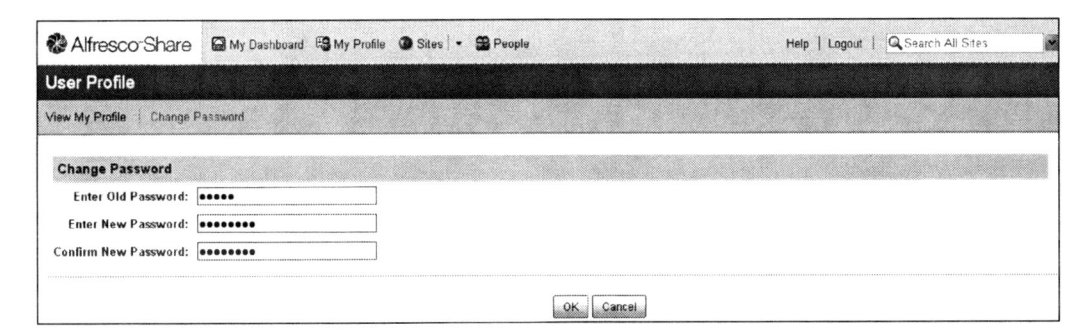

Advanced Collaboration Using Alfresco Share

Sites

A **site** is a collaborative area for a project or some task that is being undertaken. Sites can be either public or private sites.

Private sites are visible only to site members. A **Site Manager** must extend an invitation to you in order for you to be able to and become a member of the private site.

Public sites can be viewed by everyone, but can be worked on only by the site members. The tasks that can be performed by a member user, depends on the role assigned to him/her.

From the **Sites** option on the toolbar, you can create a new site or display the **Site Finder** component. This component allows you to search for a particular site or display a list of all of the web sites that you can access, the sites created by you, sites (public and private) of which you are a member, and Share public sites. From the site list, you can enter a site, delete a site, and manage your site membership.

Creating a site

You can create a site from anywhere in the application by using the **Sites** option on the toolbar. You can make the site a public or a private site. If you create a site, you become the Site Manager. A site can also have multiple Site Managers.

We shall create a sample site named **Alfresco Book project** and use that as a basis for explaining how to use a site with Alfresco Share.

To create a site, carry out the following steps:

1. On the toolbar, expand the **Sites** option, and then click on the **Create Site** option. Alternatively, on your personal dashboard, you can click on the **Create Site** option on the **My Sites** dashlet. As a result, the **Create Site** page appears as shown in the following screenshot:

	Create Site	
Name:	Alfresco Book project	*
URL name:	alfrescobookproject	*
	The 'URL name' is a part of the url to the site, ie: http://domain.com/share/page/site/<url-name>/dashboard Please do not use any spaces or special characters.	
Description:	This site is a place for the book authors to collaborate and bring together their ideas	
Type:	Collaboration Site	
Access:	☑ Make Site Public	
	OK Cancel	

[368]

2. Complete the site information by filling in the fields, namely the **Name**, **URL name**, and **Description**. Fields marked with an asterisk (*) are, mandatorily. The site name is a descriptive name that will be displayed as the title of your site. This is a mandatory field. Enter **Alfresco Book project** as the site name.

3. The **URL name** is a short version of the name to be used as the URL. It cannot have any special characters or spaces. In the **URL name** option, **alfrescobookproject** has been entered as the URL.

4. Specify the type of site access. By default, each new site has public access. To create a private site, clear the **Make Site Public** checkbox.

5. Finally, click on the **OK** button.

6. The application now displays the site dashboard of the newly-created site.

Searching for a site

You can search for a site from the **Sites** tab on the toolbar.

To search for a site, carry out the following steps:

1. Click on the **Sites** tab on the toolbar. The **Site Finder** component appears.

2. In the search box, type the full or partial name of the site that you are searching for, and then click the **Search** button. Leave the search box empty and click on the **Search** button to return a list of all of the public sites, sites that you created, and sites of which you are a member (both public and private).

3. The results list appears below the search box, and displays all of the existing sites that match the criteria entered. This list includes only public sites, sites created by you, and private sites of which you are a member of.

To the righthand side of a site, the action **Join** indicates that you are not a member of that site. Similarly, the action **Leave** indicates that you are currently a member of that site. In order to enter a site from this page, you must click on the site name.

Managing your site membership

You can choose to join or leave a site. Managing membership is easy in Alfresco share. To manage your site membership, carry out the following steps:

1. Click on the **Sites** tab on the toolbar. The **Site Finder** page appears.
2. Perform a search. The results list appears below the **Search** box.
3. In the results list, you can manage your membership on sites by clicking on the **Join** option to become a member of a site. Click on the **Leave** option to remove yourself from the site, that you no longer wish to be a member of.

Deleting a site

Deleting a site means to permanently remove it from the repository. Deleting a site also removes all of the site content, including the Document Library content, Wiki pages, Blog posts, and discussion topics. Only a Site Manager or the application administrator can delete a site.

To delete a site, carry out the following steps:

1. Click on the **Sites** tab on the toolbar. The **Site Finder** page appears. Perform a search. The results list appears below the search box. If a site can be deleted, then the **Delete** button is displayed for that site.
2. Click on the **Delete** button for the site that you want to delete. A message prompts you to confirm the deletion.
3. Click on the **OK** button to delete the selected site. A message informs you that the selected action deletes all of the site content. Click on the **Yes** button. As a result, the selected site is deleted in its entirety.

People

The **People** tab on the toolbar displays the **People Finder** page. You can use this search feature to find a particular user. Once the user has been found, you can view the user's full profile.

Searching for a user

The **People Finder** page enables you to search for a particular user and allows you to view the user's profile from the list displayed.

To search for a user, carry out the following steps:

1. Click on the **People** tab on the toolbar, and as a result the **People Finder** page appears. In the search box, type the full or partial name of the desired user. You must enter a minimum of three characters. The search is not case-sensitive.
2. Click on the **Search** option. The results list appears beneath the search box and displays all of the users that match the search criteria provided. Click on a user's name to view the user's profile.

Using your personal dashboard

You can view the details of and perform operations on the dashlets that make up your personal dashboard.

Entering a site

You can enter a site from the **My Sites** dashlet on your personal dashboard. This dashlet lists all of the sites that you created or of which you are a member. We shall use the **Alfresco Book project Site**, which was created in the earlier example, as the sample site to help us to understand all of the operations that can be performed on or for a site.

If the site that you want to access is not listed in the **My Sites** dashlet, you can search for it using the **Site Finder** page. If the desired site does not exist, then click on the **Create Site** option to create it.

To access a site, carry out the following steps:

1. Click on the **My Dashboard** component on the toolbar, if your personal dashboard is not already displayed.
2. On the **My Sites** dashlet, click on the site that you wish to enter. The application displays the site.

Configure the personal dashboard RSS feed

The Alfresco Global Feed can be configured to display any **RSS feed** on your dashboard.

This appears as the **RSS Feed** dashlet on the **Customize User Dashboard** page.

Advanced Collaboration Using Alfresco Share

To configure the **RSS feed**, carry out the following steps:

1. Click on the **My Dashboard** component on the toolbar, if your personal dashboard is not already displayed.
2. In the Alfresco Global Feed dashlet, click on **Configure**. The **Enter URL** dialog box is displayed. Enter the link of the feed that you want to subscribe to in the URL field.
3. In the **Number of items to display** field, select the number of items to be displayed in the dashlet for the specified feed. Select **All** in order to display all of the items available for the feed.
4. You can select the **Open links in new window** option to have the target story displayed in a new window. Click on the **OK** button, and the Alfresco Global Feed dashlet displays the feeds for the URL specified, as shown in the following screenshot:

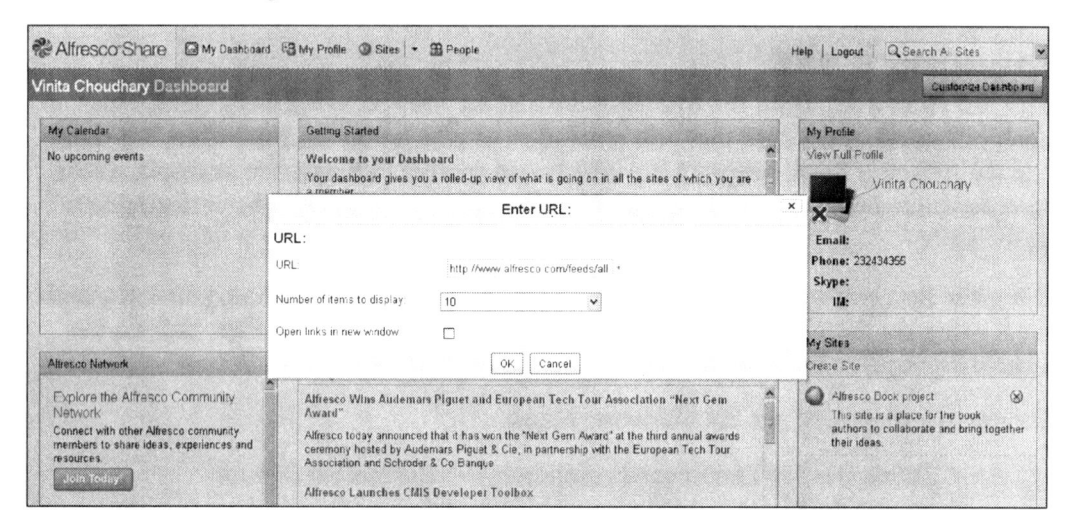

View scheduled events

The **My Calendar** personal dashlet summarizes the scheduled items from all of the sites that you are associated with. It contains a rolled-up view of events that you have created, as well as events for each site that you are associated with, either as a member or as the Site Manager.

To view the events, you must first configure your personal dashboard to display the **My Calendar** personal dashlet.

To view scheduled events, carry out the following steps:

1. Click on the **My Dashboard** tab on the toolbar, if your personal dashboard is not already displayed. The **My Calendar** personal dashlet displays the name, date, and time of each event, as well as the site in which it was created.
2. With the help of the **My Calendar** dashlet, you can view additional information about an event:
    - Click on the event name to display the **Calendar** page where the event was created. This is a convenient method of accessing and editing the events that you have created.
    - Click on the site name to display the corresponding site dashboard.

Using the Alfresco Network

The Alfresco Network personal dashlet displays the most recent Alfresco news and information, conveniently on your personal dashboard.

To view this information, you must first configure your personal dashboard to display the Alfresco Network personal dashlet.

To use the Alfresco Network dashlet, carry out the following steps:

1. Click on the **My Dashboard** tab on the toolbar, if your personal dashboard is not already displayed. The Alfresco Network personal dashlet displays links to information including the news items, knowledge base, and downloads.
2. Click on a link present on the Alfresco Network dashlet, in order to open the associated content in a separate window.

Using a site

We shall use the **Alfresco Book project** site as an example to explain the various aspects of using the site. By default, sites include Wiki, Blog, Document Library, Calendar, and Discussion Forum pages. However, you can customize the site to contain any combination of these components.

When you enter the **Alfresco Book project** site, the site dashboard is displayed. The site dashboard consists of site dashlets, which organize and display information that is relevant to the site.

When you customize the **Alfresco Book project** site dashboard, you can specify the desired dashlets. Each dashlet that is selected is displayed as a tab on the dashboard. The tabs available on the site are:

Getting Started

The **Getting Started** tab displays helpful information for getting started in the **Alfresco Book project** site, and provides links to common tasks.

Site Profile

The **Site Profile** tab contains a summary of the personal details provided in your full user profile.

Site Colleagues

The **Site Colleagues** tab lists all of the **Alfresco Book project** site members and the roles assigned to them.

Site Calendar

The **Site Calendar** tab contains a rolled-up view of events for the **Alfresco Book project** site.

Site Activities

The **Site Activities** tab tracks the most recent activities that have been performed on the site.

Recently Modified Documents

The **Recently Modified Documents** tab displays the documents present in this site's Document Library that have been added or edited in the past seven days.

Wiki

The **Wiki** tab displays the specified Wiki page. The **Configure** link present on the dashlet enables you to select the desired page.

RSS Feed

By default, the **RSS Feed** tab is configured to display the Alfresco web site feed.

Customize a site

Customizing a site enables you to choose the pages that you want to include in the site. By default, all components (**Wiki**, **Blog**, **Document Library**, **Calendar**, and **Discussions**) are included when you create a site. Only the Site Manager can customize the site. Once you customize the site, you can customize the site dashboard, which provides a summary of the available pages.

To customize a site, carry out the following steps:

1. Access the **Alfresco Book project** site.
2. Click on the **Customize Site** option on the dashboard banner. The **Customize Site** page displays the current pages for that site.
3. To remove a page from the site, click on the **Remove** icon below the page.

To add a page to the site, carry out the following steps:

1. Click on the **Add Pages** option to display the available pages. In the **Select New Page** section, click on the **Select** button to the right of the component that you want to include in the site.
2. Click on the **OK** button to save your changes.

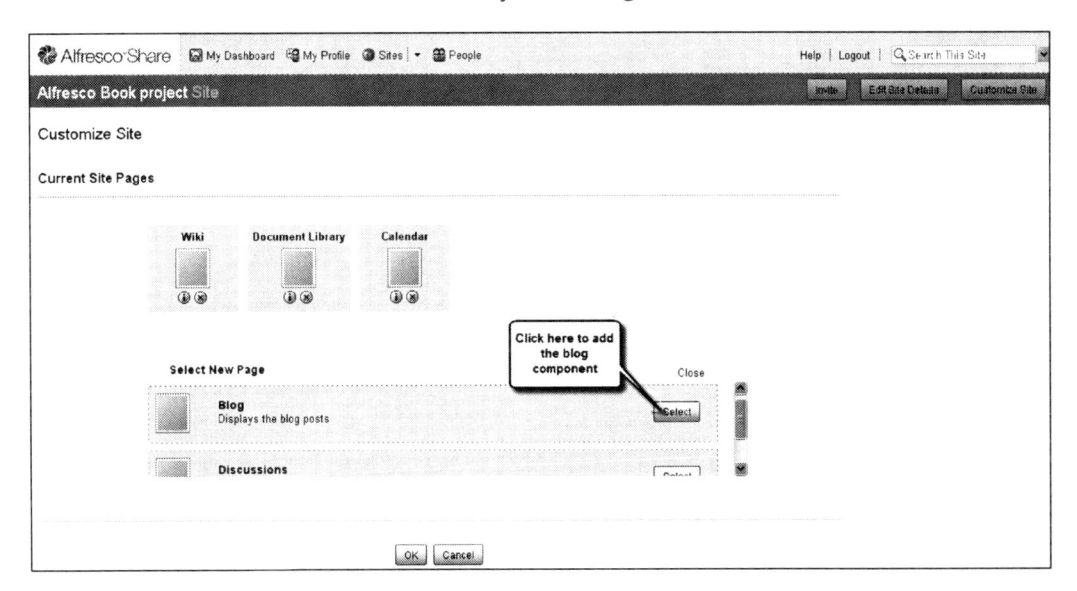

You are returned to the site dashboard. The banner displays the selected pages in the order of their configuration.

With the site customized, you can now customize the site dashboard to display information that is relevant to the site.

Customizing a site's dashboard

The **Alfresco Book project** dashboard is an interactive user interface that contains information specific to the site. Similar to your personal dashboard, site information is organized and displayed in dashlets, which represent the configured pages.

> The site should be customized before the site dashboard is configured.

For each site, you can modify the dashboard appearance, select the site dashlets to appear on the dashboard, or configure the display order of the selected dashlets.

In order to customize the appearance and content of the site dashboard, carry out the following steps:

1. Enter the **Alfresco Book project** site.
2. On the dashboard banner, click **Customize Dashboard** to display the **Customize Site Dashboard** page. The image in the **Current Layout** section represents the currently-selected layout. The **Dashlets** section displays the currently-selected dashlets as they will appear on the site dashboard.

In order to change the site dashboard layout, click on the **Change Layout** option to display the available dashboard layouts. Either click on the graphic of the desired layout, or click on the **Select** button to the right of it.

To select site dashlets, carry out the following steps:

1. Click on the **Add Dashlets** option to display the available dashlets.
2. To add a dashlet, click the desired dashlet in the **Add Dashlets** section and drag it to the desired column.
3. To remove a dashlet, click on the unwanted dashlet and drag it to the garbage bin.
4. Click and drag the dashlets within and across columns to configure the display order. Click on the **OK** button to save your changes. You will be returned to the site dashboard, which displays the selected pages in the order configured.

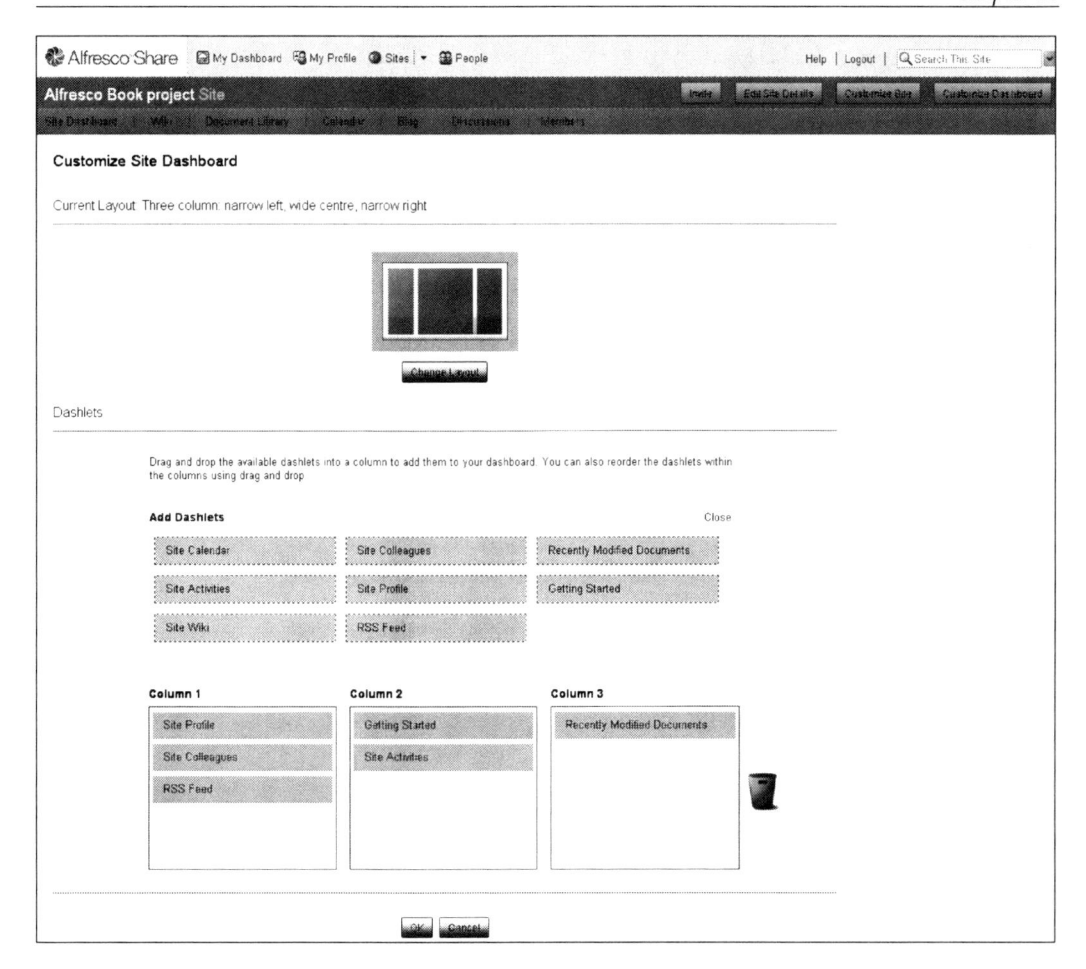

Editing the site details

You can edit the name and description of the site from anywhere within the site. You can also change the site's access to public or private.

To edit the site, details, carry out the following steps:

1. Enter the **Alfresco Book project** site.
2. On the dashboard banner, click on the **Edit Site Details** option. The **Edit Site Details** page displays the current details for this site.
3. Make the desired changes to the site's **Name** and **Description**.
4. Change the site's access, if desired. To make this a private site, clear the **Public** check box, and click on the **OK** button.

As a result, the site dashboard displays the updated details on the banner and the **Site Profile** dashlet.

Configuring the site dashboard RSS feed

You can configure the **RSS Feed** site dashlet to display any RSS feed on a site dashboard. To perform this task, you must first customize your site dashboard to display the Alfresco Global Feed dashlet. This appears as the **RSS Feed** dashlet on the **Customize Site Dashboard** page.

The steps to configure the **RSS Feed** dashlet on a site dashboard are the same as for your personal dashboard (see above).

Configuring the Wiki site dashlet

To perform this task, the **Wiki** page must contain at least one page and the **Wiki** site dashlet must be configured to be displayed on the site dashboard.

To configure the **Wiki** site dashlet, carry out the following steps:

1. Enter the desired site. On the **Wiki** site dashlet, click on the **Configure** option. The **Select Wiki Page** page appears. This page lists all of the pages in this site's Wiki.
2. Select the page whose content you want to display on the **Wiki** dashlet. If no Wiki pages have been created, the message **There are no pages available to select** is displayed.
3. Click on the **OK** button. The **Wiki** dashlet is displayed the selected page.

Subscribing to an RSS feed

Share allows you to subscribe to RSS feeds. These feeds enable you to automatically receive regular updates on various Share activities.

The RSS Feed feature is available in the following Share locations:

- Wiki page
- Blog page
- Document Library page
- Discussions page
- My Site Activities dashlet on your personal dashboard
- Site Activities dashlet on the site dashboard

To subscribe to an RSS feed, carry out the following steps:

1. Click on the **RSS Feed** link or icon. This initiates the subscription process. The user interface presented depends on your browser.
2. Choose to subscribe to the feed. Select a location in which to store the feed, and then subscribe to it.

Tagging site content

When you use Share, you can use tags to categorize similar or related content across pages within a site. This enables you to easily locate the content again.

You can associate a tag with the following types of content:

- Wiki pages
- Blog posts
- Discussion topics
- Calendar events
- Document Library items
- Document Library folders

You can create your own tags for each component. The Wiki, Blog, and Discussions components also allow you to select from a list of tags that are already used within the current site.

The Wiki, Blog, Document Library, Calendar, and Discussion page, all contain a browsing pane. The **Tags** list in this pane displays the tags that are referenced by items in the current component. Clicking on a tag displays the items associated with that tag. The number in parentheses indicates the number of component items that are tagged with this tag.

Selecting a page

Once you enter a site, you can navigate between the pages to view information and perform functions on the site content. The pages included in the site are listed in the site banner.

Advanced Collaboration Using Alfresco Share

To select a page, carry out the following steps:

1. Enter the **Alfresco Book project** site. The site banner beneath the application toolbar displays the name of the selected site. Below the **Alfresco Book project** site name, the **Site Dashboard** link is highlighted. This indicates that this is the current page. To the right of this link are links to the pages included in this site. The banner also includes the **Members** link, for the purpose of managing the site's membership.

2. On the Alfresco Book Project dashboard banner, click on the page that you want to access. The application displays the selected page, and the current component is highlighted on the banner. Each component has its own functionality. See the appropriate section of the documentation for instructions on using each page.

3. On the site dashboard banner, click on any page link to navigate to that page, or click on the **Site Dashboard** component to return to the dashboard of the current site.

The Wiki page

The **Wiki Page List** displays a summary of all of the pages created for the current site's Wiki. A browsing pane on the lefthand side of the page enables you to populate the Wiki list with a subset of the Wiki content. Selecting a page in the Wiki list displays the entire Wiki page in the page view.

When you enter the Wiki page, the page view displays the **Wiki** main page. Click on **Wiki Page List** to display the Wiki list.

In both of the views you are allowed to create, delete, view the details for, and edit a Wiki page. You must be in the page view to rename a Wiki page. To perform operations on a Wiki page, you must be on the **Wiki** page.

Accessing the Wiki page

Accessing the Wiki page gives you access to all of the Wiki content. Within the Wiki, you can create, delete, rename, and edit the Wiki pages. You can perform most actions from both the Wiki list and the page view.

To access the Wiki page, carry out the following steps:

1. Enter the **Alfresco Book project** site.

2. Click on **Wiki** in the banner. The Wiki page appears, displaying the main Wiki page for this site in the page view. In this view, the actions that you can perform on the current Wiki page appear as buttons below the banner (**New Page**, **Delete**, and **Rename**) and as links in the upper-right corner of the content area (**View Page**, **Edit Page**, and **Details**).

3. Click on the **Wiki Page List** to display the Wiki list. The Wiki list displays a summary of all of the pages in the Wiki for the current site. In this view, the actions that you can perform on a Wiki page appear as buttons below the banner (only new page is available in this view) and as links to the right of each page summary.

Browse the Wiki pages

Assuming that you are on the **Wiki** page of the **Alfresco Book project** site, the browsing pane to the left-hand side of the **Wiki Page List** enables you to filter the Wiki content in order to make it easier to locate specific Wiki pages.

The Wiki page lists all of the Wiki pages in the current site, organized chronologically. Therefore, the most recent page appears at the top of the list.

The browsing pane to the left of the page enables you to display a subset of the Wiki's content by selecting a specific view or tag. Whether you are browsing by view or by tag, the Wiki list displays a summary of all of the pages matching the selected option. The summary includes the Wiki page name, the author, the creation and modification dates, a sample of the content, and the tags associated with the page.

The browsing pane provides us with the following views:

- **Recently Modified**: Displays a list of pages modified in the past seven days
- **All**: Displays a list of pages created in the Wiki for the current site
- **Recently Added**: Displays a list of pages created in the past seven days
- **My Pages**: Displays a list of pages created by the currently logged in user

The **Tags** list displays all of the tags currently associated with one or more Wiki pages.

To browse through the Wiki pages, carry out the following steps:

1. Click on the **Wiki Page List** option on the page view, to navigate to the Wiki list, if it is not already displayed.
2. Select the desired option in the browsing pane.
3. In the **Pages** list, click the view representing the Wiki pages that you want to display. The Wiki list displays all of the pages in the current site that correspond to the selection.

4. Click on the tag of interest in the **Tags** list. The Wiki list displays all of the pages in the current site, which are associated with the selected tag.
5. Click on a Wiki page title to display that full page. The selected Wiki page appears in the page view.

Creating the Wiki main page

When you create a new site, the site's Wiki contains a main page that is empty. You will likely opt to make this the introductory page for the site's Wiki.

To add content to the Wiki main page, carry out the following steps:

1. Click on the **Main Page** option below the banner, if the main page is not already displayed. Then click on the **Edit Page** option.
2. Type the content for the main page into the **Text** box. Use the formatting features provided to mark up the content, insert bulleted and numbered lists, and include hyperlinks, as required.

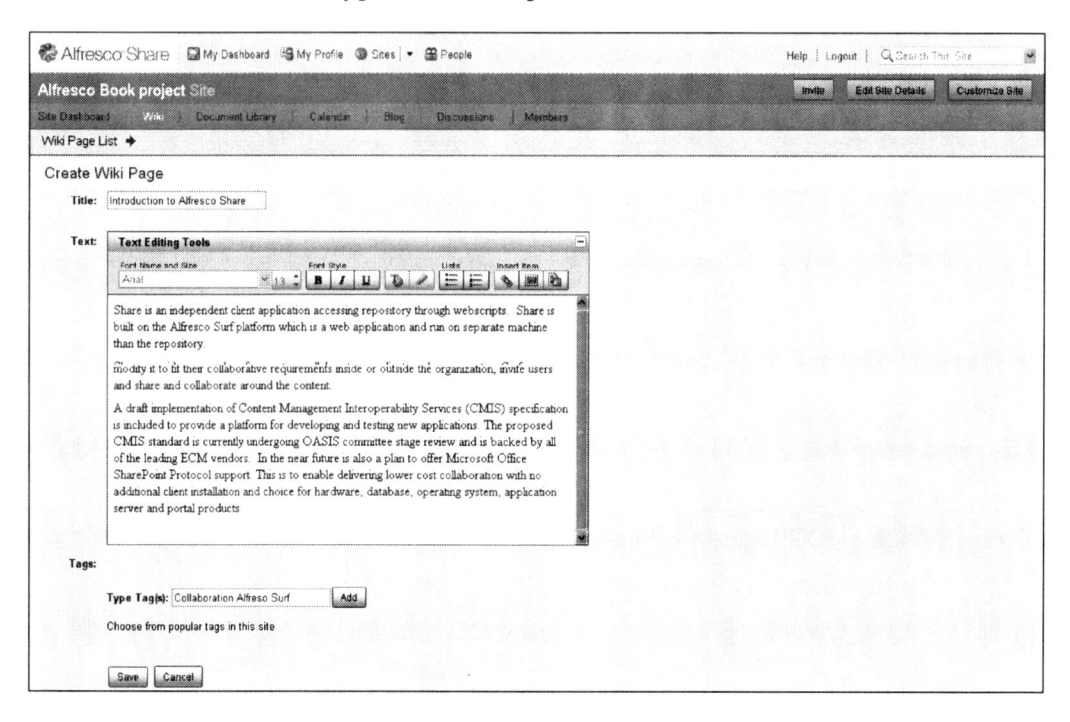

Optionally, add tags to and remove tags from the main page, as follows

- Type a tag into the box provided. Click on the **Add** button to add multiple tags, separating each tag with a space.
- Click on the **Choose from popular tags in this site** option in order to display the existing tags that are used in this site. Click on a tag to associate it with the main page.
- The newly-associated tags appear below the **Text** box. Click on a tag to remove it. When you are done, click on the **Save** button. The page view displays the main page.

Creating a new Wiki page

You can create a new Wiki page from both the Wiki list and the page view.

To create a new Wiki page, carry out the following steps:

1. Click on the **New Page** option. The **Create Wiki Page** appears.
2. Enter a **Title** for the page. If your title contains a disallowed character, such as quotation marks, periods, colons, asterisks (*) and other special characters, then the **Save** button is disabled.
3. Type the Wiki page content in the **Text** box. Use the formatting features provided to mark up the content, insert bulleted and numbered lists, and include hyperlinks, as required. To create a link to another Wiki page, type the **Page Name**. If the page indicated does not exist, then Share creates it. However, this is an empty Wiki page and it will not appear in the Wiki list until you select **Edit Page** and provide some content for it.

Optionally, you can add tags to the Wiki page by carrying out the following steps:

1. Type a tag, or multiple tags separated by a spaces, in the box provided, and then click on the **Add** button. Click on the **Choose from popular tags in this site** option to display the existing tags used in this site. Click on a tag to associate it with the new Wiki page.
2. The newly-associated tags appear beneath the **Text** box. Click on a tag to remove it.

Advanced Collaboration Using Alfresco Share

3. Click on the **Save** button. The new Wiki page is displayed, and the users will be able to see it. Click on the **Wiki Page List** option to return to the Wiki list.

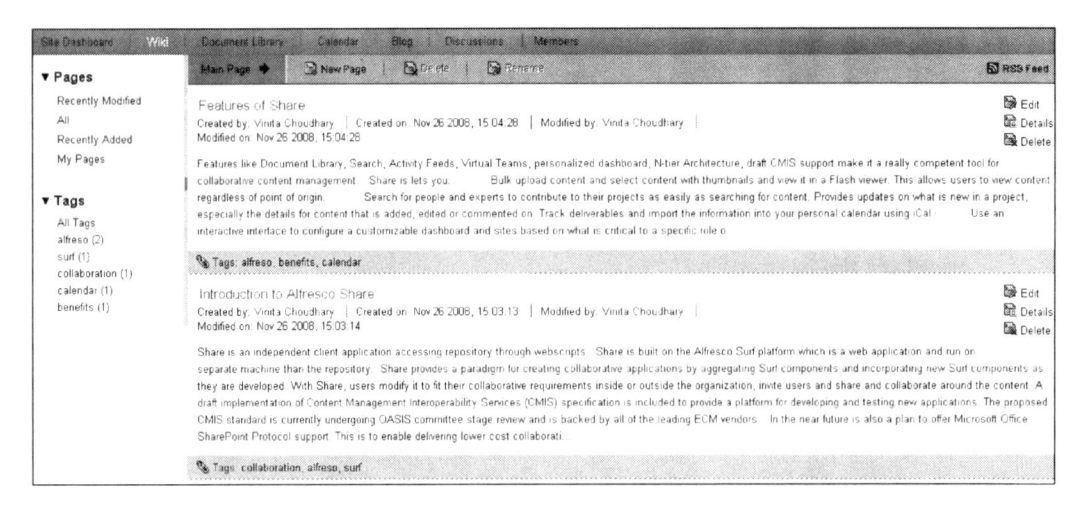

Editing a Wiki page

Adding and editing Wiki content is done in a simple browser. You can perform this task from both, the Wiki list and the page view.

To edit a Wiki page, carry out the following steps:

1. Click on the **Edit** option for the page that you want to modify. If the Wiki page that you want to edit is already open in the page view, then simply click on the **Edit Page** option. The content of the selected Wiki page is displayed in an editing box.

2. Make the required changes to the content. To create a link to another Wiki page, type the **Page Name**. If the page indicated does not exist, then Share creates it. However, this is an empty Wiki page and it will not appear in the Wiki list until you select **Edit Page** and provide content for it.

You can edit the tags for this Wiki page by carrying out the following steps:

1. To add a new tag, type a tag into the provided box and then click on the **Add** button. To add multiple tags, separate each tag with a space.

2. To add an existing tag, click on the **Choose from popular tags in this site** option, in order to display the tags used in this site. Click a tag to associate it with the Wiki page.

3. To remove an existing tag from the set below the **Text** box, click on the tag that you want to remove. Then click on the **Save** button. The page view displays the updated Wiki page.

Renaming a Wiki page

You can rename a Wiki page from the **Page view** option. To rename a Wiki page, carry out the following steps:

1. Click on the title of the page that you want to rename and then click on the **Rename** button. The **Rename** page is displayed.
2. Type the new name of the Wiki page and click on the **Save** button.

The page view reflects the name change and this Wiki page retains the page history of the original page. Share creates a new page with the original page name, which links to the updated page.

Deleting a Wiki page

You can delete a Wiki page that you no longer want to appear in the Wiki of the current site. You can perform this task from both the Wiki list and the **Page View**.

To delete a Wiki page, carry out the following steps:

1. In the Wiki list, locate the Wiki page that you want to delete.
2. Click on the **Delete** button for that page. If the Wiki page you want to delete is already open in the page view, then simply click on the **Delete** button on that page. A message prompts you to confirm the deletion.
3. Click on the **Yes** button to delete the current Wiki page.

Viewing a Wiki page's details

You can display the details of a Wiki page in order to see the version history, view the tags associated with the page, and list the Wiki pages that link to the selected page. You can view the page details from both the Wiki list and the page view.

To view the details of a Wiki page, carry out the following steps:

1. Click on the **Details** option for the page whose details you want to view. If the Wiki page you want to view is already open in the page view, then simply click on the **Details** option on that page. The page view displays the Wiki page content in an expanded form that includes the **Version History**, **Tags**, and **Linked Pages**. From here, you can click on the **Edit Page** option to make any necessary changes.

2. Click on the **View Page** option to hide the details again. The Wiki page is displayed in the page view.

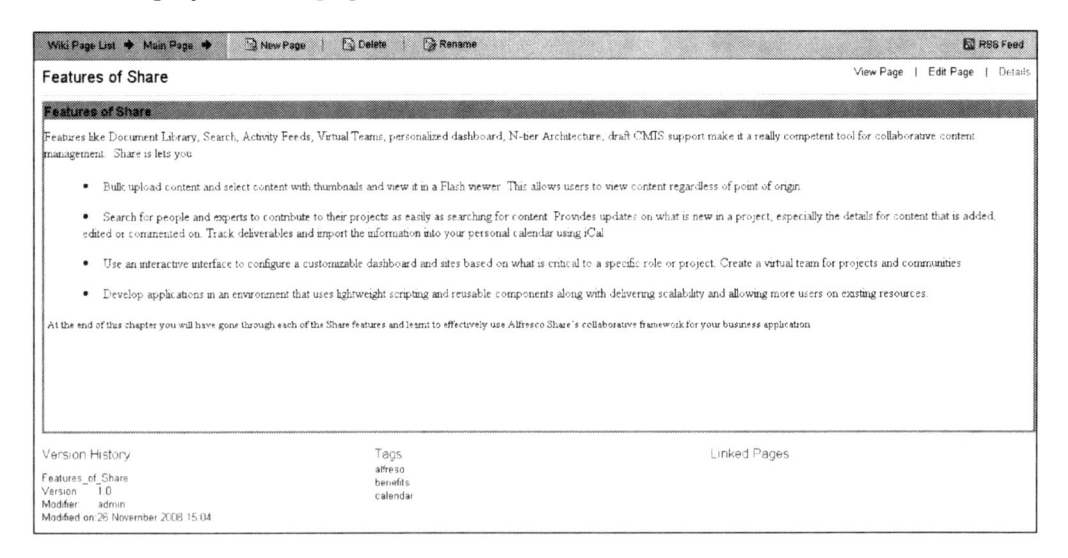

The Document Library page

The Document Library enables you to gather and store information, and collaboratively manage any content related to a site, such as documents, media files, and graphics. In this section, we assume that you are in the **Document Library** page of the desired site.

Accessing the Document Library page

You need to access the **Document Library** page in order to view all of the content items for the current site. In the library, you can view, upload, edit, and delete items. You can also add comments to an item and edit its metadata.

To access the **Document Library** page, carry out the following steps:

1. Enter the **Alfresco Book project** site.
2. On the banner, click on the **Document Library** link in order to display the **Document Library** page. The content item list displays a summary of the items in the top level folder, which is the default selection of the browsing pane. The item summary includes the thumbnail of the content, the item title, the date and time that the item was uploaded to or last modified within the site, the user who uploaded or modified the item, the version number (set to 1.0 when a new item is uploaded), file size, a description, and the tags associated with the item.

3. Click on the **Show Folders** option to display both folders and content items in this list. Click on the **Hide Folders** option to hide the folders.
4. Click on the **Simple View** option to display only the basic item details (title, modification date and time and user responsible for the modifications) for the content items. Click on the **Detailed View** option to display the summary view.

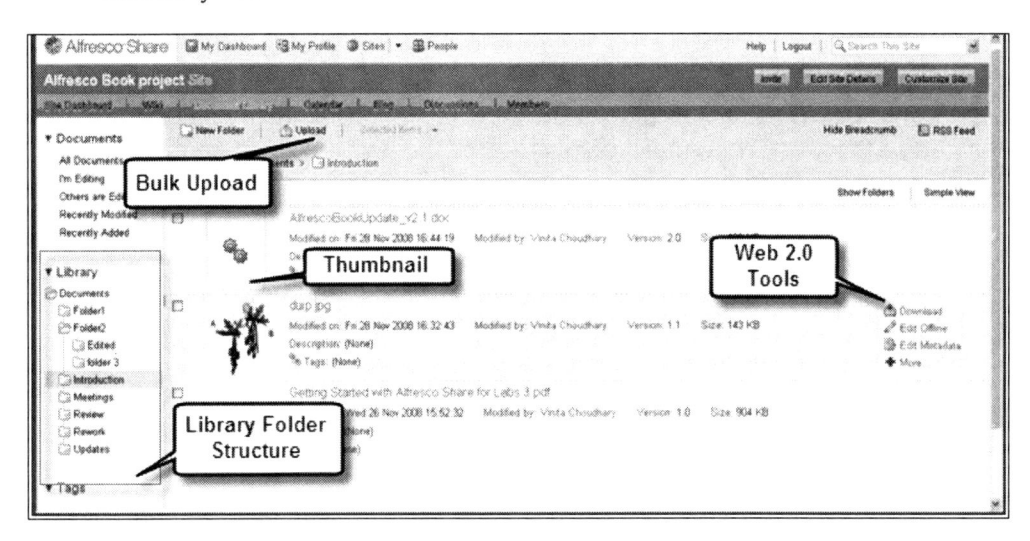

Browsing the library

The browsing feature in the **Document Library** page allows you to easily navigate through the library and to filter the items displayed in the item list. This task assumes that you are in the **Document Library** page of the desired site.

You can display a subset of the library items by selecting a specific view, a folder, or a tag, in the browsing pane on the left.

The **Documents** list in the browsing pane provides the following views for browsing library content:

- **All Documents**: Displays all of the items in the Document Library.
- **I'm Editing**: Displays the items checked out by the current user.
- **Others are Editing**: Displays the items checked out by other site members.
- **Recently Modified**: Displays items modified in the past seven days.

- **Recently Added**: Displays items added to the library in the past seven days.
- **Library**: Displays the folder structure in a tree view.
- **Tags**: Displays all of the tags currently associated with one or more items. The number in parentheses following a tag indicates the number of items in the library that are tagged with the tag.

To browse the **Document Library** items, carry out the following steps:

1. Select the desired option in the browsing pane.
2. In the **Documents** list, click on the view representing the items that you want to view. The item list displays all of the items in the current site that correspond to the selection.
3. In the **Library** section, navigate to the tree and click on a folder to display the items that it contains. The Breadcrumb Path, which is located above the content item list, displays your current position within the folder structure. Each breadcrumb item is a link, allowing you easy access to any part of the current navigation path. The breadcrumbs allow you to return to any folder in the current path without having to repeat all of the steps. Click on a link to return to the corresponding folder. Click on the **Hide Breadcrumb** option to collapse the breadcrumb path. You can click on the **Show Breadcrumb** option in order to display it again.
4. Click on the tag of interest in the **Tags** list. The item list displays all of the items in this site's library, which are associated with the selected tag.
5. Position the cursor over an item in this list to display its available actions.

Creating a folder structure

The **Library** section of the browsing pane displays the folder structure for the current site. A new site contains only the root folder, named Documents. You can add new folders beneath the root in order to create the site's folder structure.

To create a new folder, carry out the following steps:

1. In the **Library** section of the browsing pane, navigate through the tree and click to select the location of the new folder. The **New Folder** will be created as a subfolder of the folder highlighted in the tree.
2. Click on the **New Folder** link. The **New Folder** page is displayed. Type a **Name** for the folder. This is the name that will appear in the tree.
3. Type a **Title** and **Description** to the folder. Click on the **OK** button. The page closes and the new folder appears in its appropriate position in the tree.

Adding items to the library

Adding content items from your computer to a site's Document Library is a simple process. Share allows you to upload individual files or several files at a time.

The first step in adding an item to your site's library is to determine where you want it to reside. The **Library** section of the browsing pane in the **Document Library** page displays the available folders. Create a new folder if necessary.

To upload content to the library, carry out the following steps:

1. Navigate through the library's folder structure and click on the folder where the item or items to be uploaded will reside.
2. Click on the **Upload** button. The **Upload File(s)** page appears. Click on the **Browse** option.
3. Locate the file or files on your computer that you want to upload, and then click **Open**. Use the *Shift* button to select multiple, consecutive items, or use the *Ctrl* button to select multiple, non-consecutive items. The selected items appear in the list. Click on the **Remove** option to delete an item from this list, if necessary.
4. Click on the **Upload File(s)** button when this list contains all of the items that you want to upload. An indicator informs you of the upload progress. When it displays **100%** for all files, then you can proceed. The following screenshot shows what the uploading process looks like:

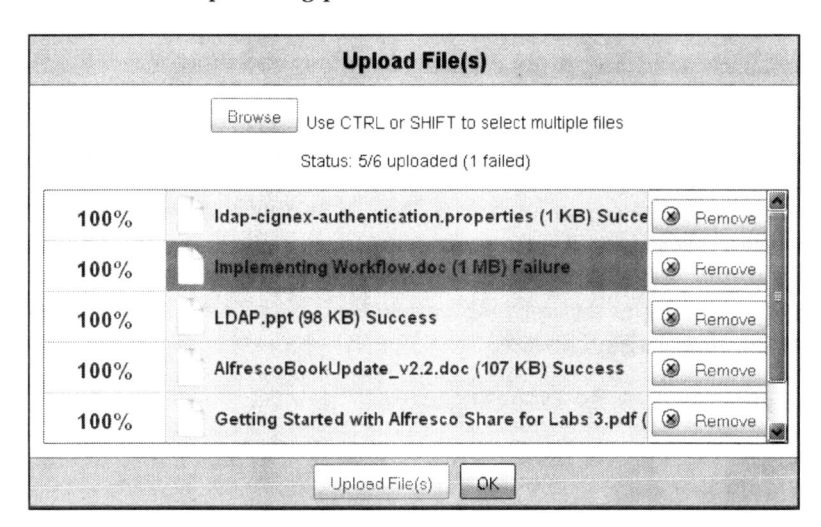

Advanced Collaboration Using Alfresco Share

5. Click on the **OK** button. As shown in the preceding figure, the page closes and the item list for the specified folder displays the uploaded content item(s). The thumbnails of each of the documents uploaded are displayed next to the document name.

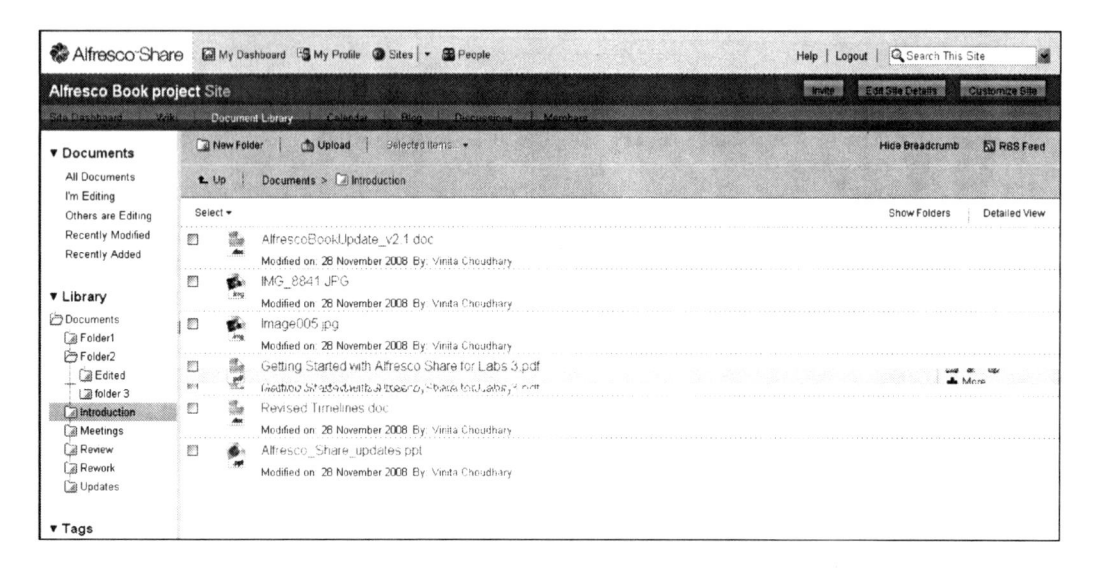

Working with individual library items

Once the Document Library structure has been set up and content has been added, site members will be able to access and work with the content items within the library. In addition to adding more content, members can view, download, edit, and delete content items.

Viewing an item

The preview feature allows you to view a content item directly in the application, without having to download it onto your computer or check it out. For documents containing multiple pages, navigation features enable you to view all of the pages. The preview page includes a comment feature that allows site members to add comments to the item being viewed.

To view an item, carry out the following steps:

1. Navigate through the library's folder structure to locate the content item that you want to view.
2. In the item list, click on the title or thumbnail of the desired item, and the preview page will open. On the left-hand side of the page, you will be able to see the name and a preview of the selected item. If the content item cannot be previewed, then a message is displayed asking you to download the file.

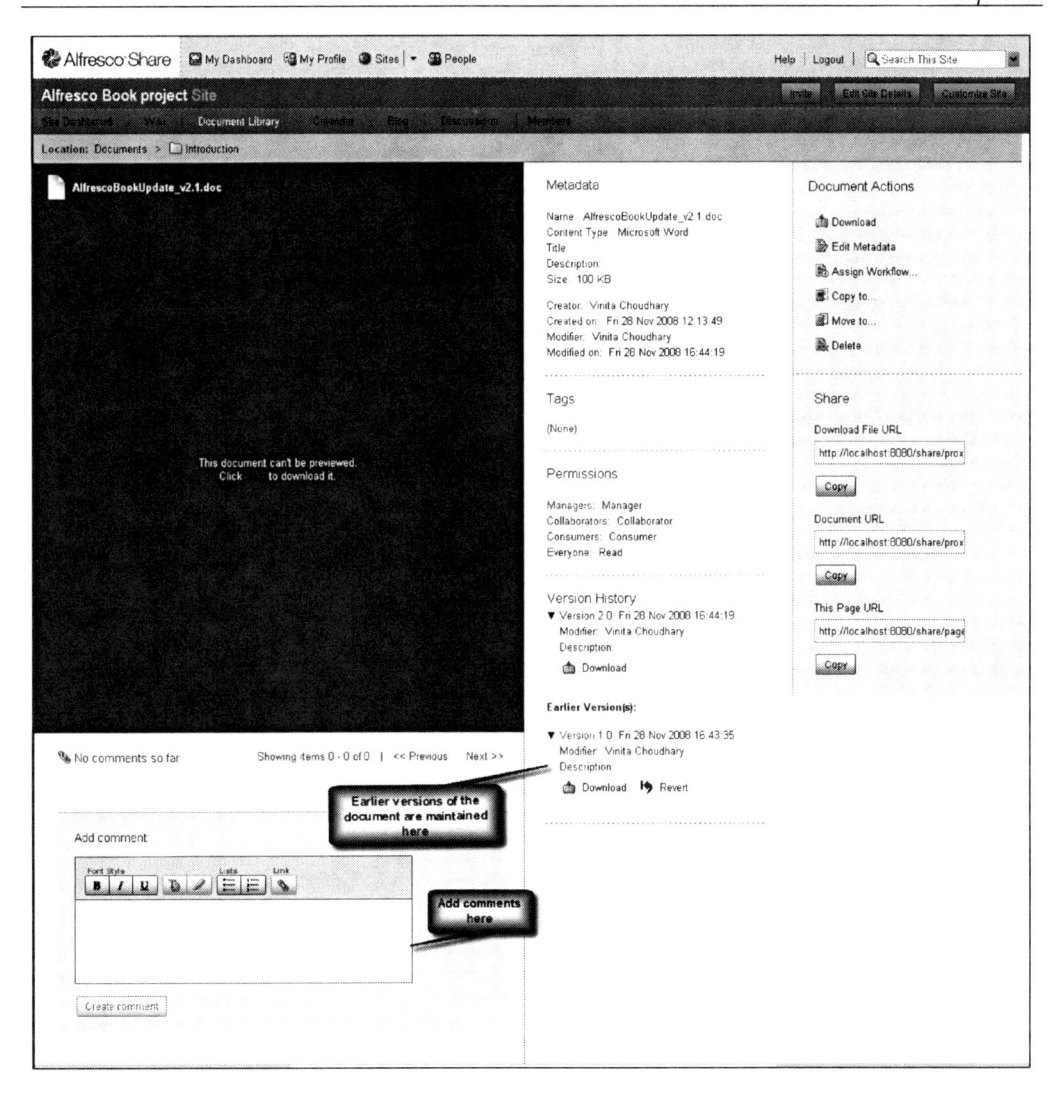

3. The right-hand side of the page contains the item details, which includes metadata, tags, permissions, version history, document actions, and related URLs. Comments made on the selected item appear at the bottom of the page, along with the **Add Comment** box. In the header, the **Location** indicates the folder in which the selected item resides.

Advanced Collaboration Using Alfresco Share

If the content item contains multiple pages, then use the features provided to navigate through the pages, as follows:

- Click on the **Prev** and **Next** buttons to move backward and forward through the pages. In the **Jump to page** box, you can type the number of the page that you want to view, and then press the *Enter* key.
- Click on the **Full Screen** option to view only the item without the item details. To return from the full screen view to the default view, click on the **Close** button.
- Use and share the URLs provided. You can bookmark the URLs or share them with other users via email or instant messaging. When invoked, these links prompt the user to save the content item locally (**Download File URL**), open the content item directly in the browser (**Document URL**), or display the current page (**This Page URL**).
- Scroll to the bottom of the page to view comments related to the selected item. In order to return to the item list, click on the **Location** folder in the header.

Add a comment to a library item

In the **Document Library** page, you can add a comment to a content item. To add a comment to an item in the library, carry out the following steps:

1. Locate and preview the item that you wish to comment on. At the bottom of the page, enter your comments in the **Add comment** box.
2. Then, click on the **Create comment** button. The **Edit** and **Delete** actions are available for each comment and are ready to be used as required. Only the Site Manager and the user who originally created the comment can perform these actions.

Editing a library item comment

You can edit a comment on a library item to modify or add to its content. To edit a comment made on a library item, carry out the following steps:

1. In the library, locate and preview the content item containing the comment that you want to edit. Scroll to the bottom of the page to view the comments.
2. Click on the **Edit** button, located to the right of the comment that you want to change. This action is available only when the currently logged in user has permission to edit the comment. The **Edit Comment** box appears, displaying the selected comment.
3. Make the desired changes to the comment. Click on the **Update** button and the updated comment will be displayed.

Deleting a library item comment

You can delete a comment to permanently remove it from a content item. Only a Site Manager and the user who originally created the comment can delete it.

To delete a comment made on a library item, carry out the following steps:

1. In the library, locate and preview the content item containing the comment that you want to delete.
2. Scroll to the bottom of the page to view the comments.
3. Click on the **Delete** option, located to the right of the comment that you want to remove. This action is available only when the currently logged in user has the permission to delete the comment. A message prompts you to confirm the deletion of the selected comment.
4. Click on the **Delete** button. As a result, you will get a message indicating that the selected comment has been deleted.

Editing an item

Editing an item, while offline, creates a working copy of the file that is placed in the **I'm Editing** view. Although the original item remains in the folder, site members are only able to view and download it. An icon indicates to users that the item is locked. Once checked out to your computer, you can edit the item and then upload the new version.

To edit an item, carry out the following steps:

1. Navigate through the library's folder structure to locate the item that you want to edit.
2. In the item list, position the cursor over the item of interest, in order to display the available actions.
3. Click on the **Edit Offline** option. You are prompted to open or save the file.
4. Choose to save the file on your computer. Depending on your browser, you are prompted to specify a destination. If you do not specify a destination, then the item is downloaded to a default location. Once the download is complete, close the dialog box.
5. Share places a working copy of the item in the **I'm Editing** view, which contains your other working copies. An icon indicates that the file is being edited by you.

Downloading an item

You can download an item from the Library tree or from one of the browsing views (**All Documents, I'm Editing, Others are Editing, Recently Modified, Recently Added**) onto your computer.

The label for the download action (**Download Original** or simply **Download**) varies, depending on whether the item is locked or not. In both the cases, the procedure to download the item is the same. When you select a locked item, you are downloading the last version checked into the Document Library. It is important to realize that this version may be out of date. Because the item is being edited by another site member, a more recent version may exist outside of the library.

To download a content item, carry out the following steps:

1. Navigate through the library's folder structure to locate the item that you want to download. In the item list, position the cursor over the item of interest, in order to display the available actions.

2. Click on either the **Download** or **Download Original** option. You are prompted to **Open** or **Save the file**.

3. Choose to **Save the file** to your computer. Depending on your browser, you are either prompted to specify a destination or the item is downloaded to a default location.

Upload updated content

Once your offline edits are complete, you must upload your changes to the document library. This will check in the working copy of the item, removing it from the **I'm Editing** view.

This task assumes you are in the **Document Library** page of the desired site.

To update a content item, carry out the following steps:

1. Click on the **I'm Editing** option in the **Documents** section of the browsing pane. The item list displays all of the items that you currently have checked out.

2. In the item list, position the cursor over the working copy of the file that you want to update, in order to display the available actions. Click on the **Upload New Version** option. The **Update File** page appears. Click on the **Browse** button.

3. Locate the file that you want to upload on your computer. Then click on the **Open** button. The selected item appears in the list. Click on the **Remove** button to delete the item, if necessary.

4. Indicate whether the revision is a **Minor Version** or a **Major Version**.
5. In the **Comments** box, type any information relevant to the updates.
6. Click on the **Upload File(s)** button. An indicator informs you of the upload progress. When **100%** appears beside the file, you can proceed.
7. Click on the **OK** button. The page closes and the item is removed from the item list in the **I'm Editing** view.

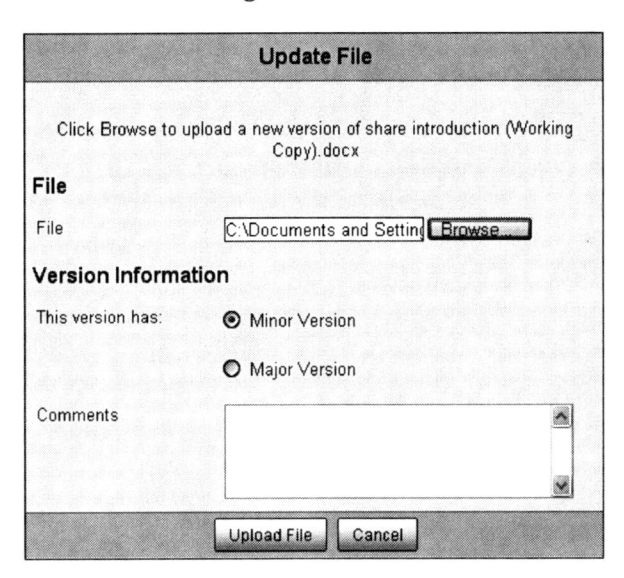

Deleting an item

Deleting a content item, or multiple content items, in order to permanently remove it from a site's library, is possible.

To delete a single content item, carry out the following steps:

1. Navigate through the library's folder structure in order to locate the content item that you want to delete.
2. In the item list, position the cursor over the item of interest to display the available actions.
3. Click on the **More** button and then click on the **Delete Document** button. As a result, a message prompts you to confirm the deletion. Click on the **Delete** button.

Editing item details

Editing a library item's metadata means to renaming the item, editing its associated tags, and changing its description.

To edit the details of a library item, carry out the following steps:

1. Navigate through the library's folder structure in order to locate the item that you want to work with.
2. In the item list, position the cursor over the item of interest, in order to display the available actions.
3. Click on the **Edit Metadata** option. The **Details for [name]** page appears.
4. Edit the item details on this page as desired. Click on the **OK** button. The metadata details are updated for the selected item.

Copying an item

You can copy an item to another site within Share, or to any space in the Alfresco Explorer repository. The copied item remains in its original location and the copy is placed in the selected destination folder (Share) or space (Explorer).

This feature is also available for multiple selections that are being copied to a common destination.

To copy a library item, carry out the following steps:

1. Navigate through the library's folder structure in order to locate the item that you want to copy.
2. In the item list, position the cursor over the item of interest, in order to display the available actions.

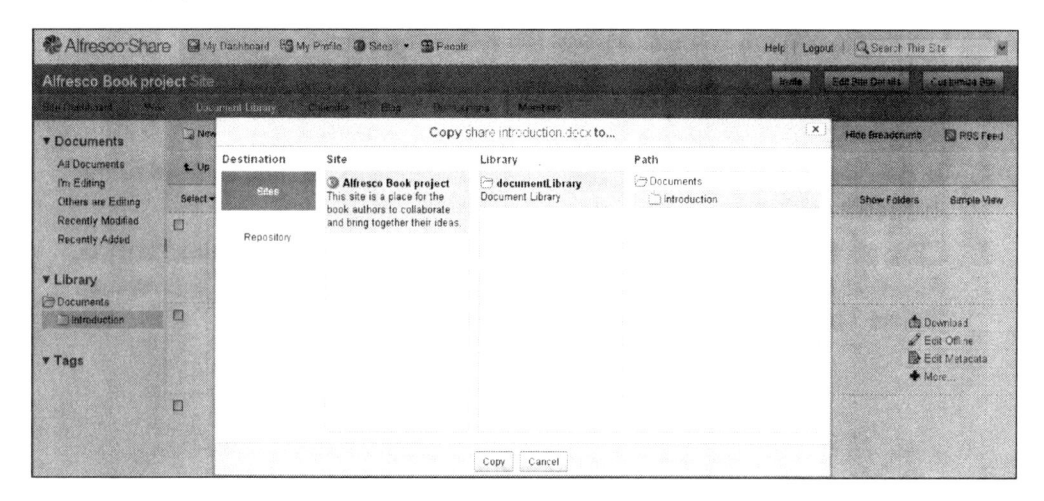

3. Click on the **More** button and then select the **Copy to** option. The **Copy [name] to** page appears, as shown in the preceding screenshot.
4. Select the **Destination**.
5. Click on the **Sites** tab in order to copy the selected item to another site in Share.
6. Click on the **Repository** tab in order to copy the selected item to a space in the Explorer.
7. Specify the path, as follows, depending on whether you are copying to a Share site or an Explorer repository:
    - When copying to a site, click on the desired site in the **Site** list. For the **Path**, navigate through the folder structure and click on the destination folder.
    - When copying to a repository, navigate through to the repository structure and click on the destination space.
8. Click on the **Copy** button. As a result, a copy of the item is placed in the specified location.

Moving an item

You can move an item to relocate it to another folder within the current site, but you cannot relocate an item to a different site or a location outside Share. This is also applicable to multiple selections that are to be moved to a common destination.

To move a library item, carry out the following steps:

1. Navigate through the library's folder structure in order to locate the item that you want to move.
2. In the item list, position the cursor over the item of interest, in order to display the available actions.
3. Click on the **More** button and then select the **Move to** option. The **Move [name] to** page appears.
4. Navigate through the folder structure and select the destination for the selected item. Click on the **Move** button. As a result, the item is moved from its original location to the specified folder.

Assigning workflow to an item

Share includes two preconfigured workflows—**Adhoc Task** (for assigning a task to a colleague) and **Review & Approve** (for setting up the review and approval of content). You manage the tasks that result from workflow on the **My Tasks** dashlet on your personal dashboard. Setting up a workflow enables you to attach the workflow directly to a content item and then assign the item to another user for review.

Advanced Collaboration Using Alfresco Share

To assign a workflow to an item in the content library, carry out the following steps:

1. Navigate through the library's folder structure, in order to locate the item that you want to work with. In the item list, position the cursor over the item of interest, in order to display the available actions.

2. Click on the **More** option and then select **Assign Workflow**. The **Assign Workflow to [name]** page is displayed, as shown in the example below:

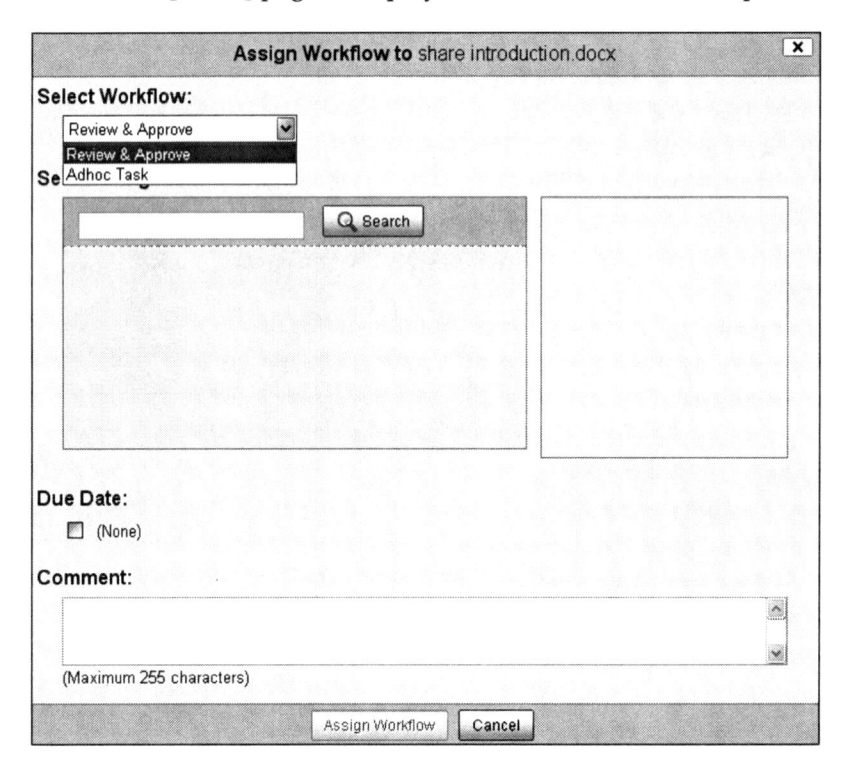

3. In the **Select Workflow** list, select the type of workflow that you want to define, that is, whether you want either the **Review & Approve** workflow or the **Adhoc Task** workflow.

4. In the search box, type the full or partial name of the site member that you want to be responsible for the task generated by the workflow. Leave the search box empty to return a list of all of the site members. Click on the **Search** button.

5. In order to select the desired user, click on the **Add >>** option. You can assign the workflow to only one user.

6. To specify a due date for the task, you can select the **Due Date** checkbox. This will display the calendar. You then select the desired due date. Deselect the checkbox to remove the due date.

7. In the **Comment** box, describe what you want the recipient of this task to do, such as 'Please review the attached file'. Then click on the **Assign Workflow** option.

Managing permissions for an item

There are four roles or groups that are available for categorizing Share users. The four roles or groups are as follows:

- Manager
- Collaborator
- Contributor
- Consumer

Share allows you to manage permissions at the library item level by changing a group's default permissions for a particular library item, or a group of library items.

To manage the group permissions for an item, carry out the following steps:

1. Navigate through the library's folder structure, in order to locate the item whose permissions you want to define. In the item list, position the cursor over the item of interest, in order to display the available actions.

2. Click on **More** and then select **Manage Permissions**. As a result, the **Manage Permissions for [name]** page appears. A button on the right-hand side of each group displays the current permissions.

3. In order to change the permissions of a group, click on the button that is located to the right of the group, and select the desired permission from the list that is displayed. Selecting the **No privileges** option blocks the users with that defined role from having any access to the currently-selected content item. The content item will not even appear in the Document Library to these users. Note that Site Managers always have full privileges within a site. Click on the **Use Defaults** option in order to return the settings to their default values.

4. Click on the **Save** button, and the group permissions will be set as defined for the specified library item.

Working with multiple library items

Selecting multiple items allows you to perform a single task on multiple items in the **Document Library** page. There are several methods available to do this.

Selecting multiple items

Select multiple items in the current view by using the item checkboxes to the left of each item's thumbnail, or use the **Select** feature at the top of the item list. You can select items, folders, or a combination of the two.

You can select multiple items as follows:

- In the browsing pane, select a view, folder, or tag to display the desired library items. In the item list displayed, select the desired content item.
- Click on a checkbox to select the associated item.
- Click on the **Select** option at the top of the item list and click on the list element that you want to select, that is, **Documents**, **Folders**, or **All**.
- Click on the **None** option to clear your selection. Click on the **Invert Selection** option to toggle the checkboxes to their opposite state. The checkboxes of the specified items appear selected in the item list.

Performing actions on multiple items and folders

Once you select the library items and (or) folders that you want to work with, you can select an action to perform.

The **Selected Items** list in the header displays the actions that can be performed on multiple items. They are:

- **Copy to...**: This action copies the selected items or folders to a single location that you specify. This can be in the same site, a different site, or a space in the repository.
- **Move to...**: This action moves the selected items or folders to a single location within the current site.
- **Delete**: This action deletes the selected items or folders.
- **Assign Workflow...**: This action assigns an identical workflow to the selected items, as specified.
- **Manage Permissions...**: This action assigns identical permissions to the selected items or folders, as specified.
- **Deselect All**: This action clears the checkboxes of the currently-selected items or folders.

In order to perform an action on the selected library items and (or) folders, carry out the following steps:

1. Click on the **Selected Items** option, which is situated in the header. A list appears, showing the available actions.

2. Select the desired action. Click on the **Deselect All** option to clear the selected items. When you select this option, you cannot perform another action until you reselect the desired library items.

3. Refer to the appropriate topic in the section named **Working with library items**, for details of how to complete the selected action.

The Calendar page

The Calendar page allows you to schedule and track events related to the current site. Site members can create events that display on the calendar for all of the site users to view. You can view the calendar by day, week, or month. The **Agenda** view displays upcoming events. The tasks in this section assume that you are on the Calendar page of the desired site.

Accessing the Calendar page

Accessing the Calendar page allows you to view the upcoming events for the current site. The calendar defaults to the monthly view.

To access the Calendar page, carry out the following steps:

1. Enter the **Alfresco Book project** site.

2. In the banner, click on the **Calendar** tab. The Calendar page appears, displaying the current month. Events scheduled in this month appear on the calendar.

Browsing the calendar

The main view of the Calendar page defaults to a calendar displaying the current month. To the left of the calendar, we have a browsing pane, which provides another calendar for navigating the months, without affecting the main view.

Advanced Collaboration Using Alfresco Share

To browse the calendar, carry out the following steps:

1. Use the navigation buttons in the header to change the main calendar view. Use the **Day**, **Week**, and **Month** buttons to change the main display to a daily, weekly, or monthly view, respectively.

2. Use the **Previous** and **Next** buttons to move backward and forward through the calendar, one day, week, or month at a time, depending on the current view, as shown in the following screenshot:

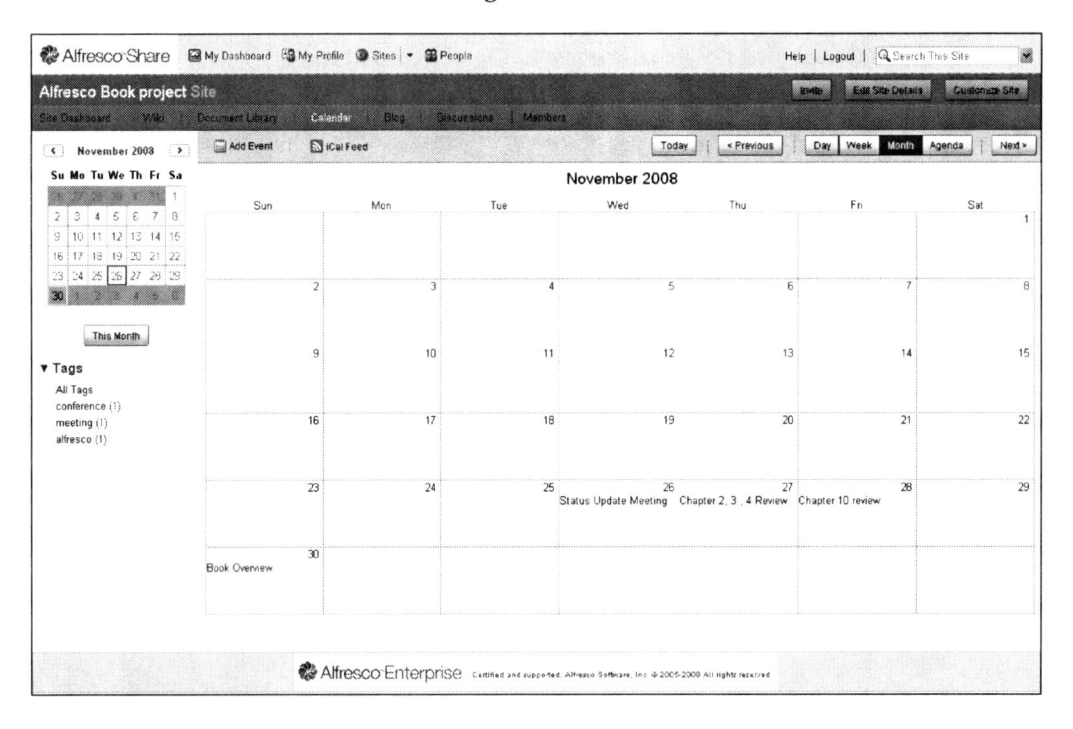

3. Click on the **Agenda** button to display a list of the upcoming events that are scheduled for this site.

4. Click on the **Today** button to display the current date.

5. Use the calendar in the browsing pane to navigate through the months without affecting the main view.

6. Click on the < button in the browsing pane, to the left of the calendar, to display the previous month.

7. Click on the > button in the browsing pane, to the left of the calendar, to display the next month.

8. Click on the **This Month** button, below the browsing pane calendar, to reset this calendar to the current month. As a result, the current day is highlighted.

9. Click in a date in the browsing pane calendar to load the selected date onto the calendar in the main view. If the Agenda is currently displayed, then no update occurs in the main view.
10. In the **Tags** list, click on the tag of interest to highlight associated events in the main view. The events in the current calendar view that are associated with the selected tag are displayed in black text. All other events are displayed in gray text.
11. Click on the **iCal Feed** option in the header to take advantage of the calendar's data exchange features.

Viewing an event

The calendar displays only the name of the event, so to view the complete details of the event, you must open the event. Once the event has been opened, you can edit or delete it.

To view a scheduled event, carry out the following steps:

1. Locate the event of interest in one of the following ways:

    To locate the event of interest, navigate through the calendar on the main view.

    Navigate through the calendar in the browsing view and select a date, in order to update the main view calendar.

    Click on the **Agenda** tab, to display all of the future events that are currently scheduled.

2. In the main view, click on the event of interest. The **Event Information** page displays the full details of the selected event. You can then click on **Close**.

Adding an event

Once created, events appear on the site calendar. Any site member can schedule an event that is relevant to the site.

To add a new event, carry out the following steps:

1. Using the browsing pane calendar, navigate to and click on the date that you want to schedule the event on. Select the event date on the browsing pane calendar to populate the event start and end dates with the selected date. You can choose to skip this step, in which case the start and end dates default to the current date.
2. Click on the **Add Event** tab to open the **Add Event** page. Fields marked with an asterisk (*) are mandatory.
3. Type a name for the event in the **What** box. Type the location of the event in the **Where** box.

Advanced Collaboration Using Alfresco Share

4. Provide a description to the event that you are scheduling in the **Description** box.
5. Select the **All Day** option to schedule a full day event.
6. Provide a date and time for both, the event's **Start Date** as well as the **End Date**. Click on the calendar icon to select a date from a calendar.
7. In the **Tags** box, type the tags that you want to associate with the event. If you need to add multiple tags, then separate each tag with a space.
8. Click on **OK**.

The page closes and the calendar displays the scheduled event on the specified day or days.

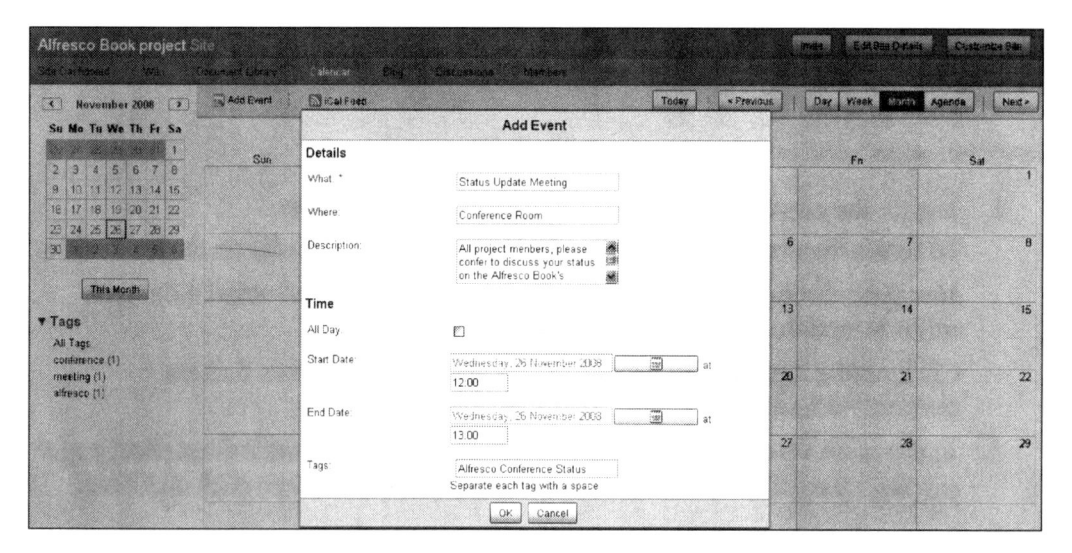

Editing an event

To edit a scheduled event, select and open the event. You can change any of the event's details, including the location, date, and time. You can also add and remove the tags associated with the event.

To edit a scheduled event, carry out the following steps:

1. Select and view the event that you want to edit. The **Event Information** page displays the full details of the selected event.
2. Click on **Edit**. The **Add Event** page is displayed. Make the desired changes to the event.
3. Click on the **OK** button to save the changes. The calendar displays the updated event. Changes will not be evident on the calendar unless you changed the event name.

Deleting an event

To delete a scheduled event, you must select and then open the event. Carry out the following steps to delete a scheduled event:

1. Locate and view the event that you want to delete. The **Event Information** page displays the full details of the selected event.
2. Click on the **Delete** button. The calendar no longer displays the deleted event.

Browsing the site's events

The **Agenda** view displays all of the upcoming events scheduled for the current site.

The events that are scheduled for the current day and later appear in the **Agenda** list in chronological order. The information displayed includes the scheduled date and start time, along with the event name.

To browse through the events, carry out the following steps:

1. Click on the **Agenda** tab in the header. The **Agenda** view displays the upcoming events.
2. In the **Tags** list, you can click on the tag of interest to highlight the associated events in the agenda. The scheduled events that are associated with the selected tag are displayed in black text. All other events are displayed in gray text.
3. Click on the **Day**, **Week**, or **Month** buttons in the header to return to the desired calendar view.

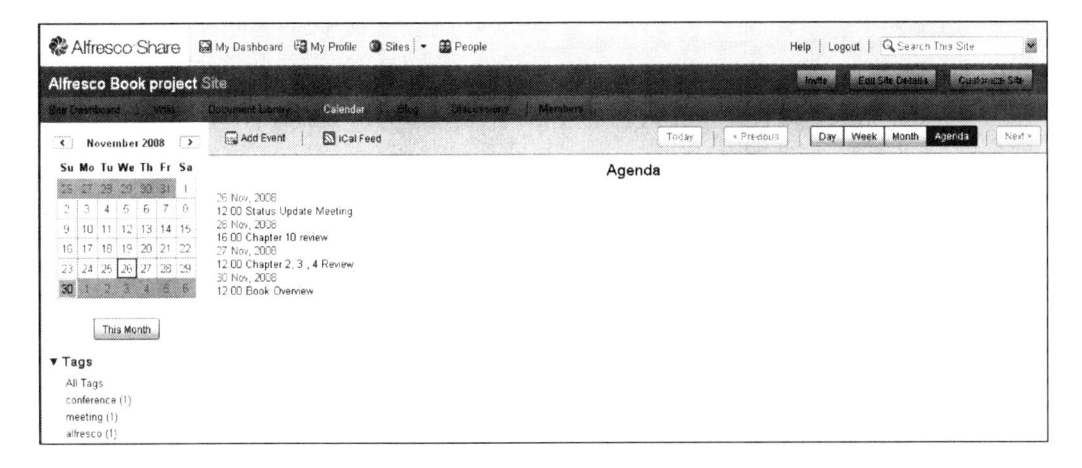

The Blog page

Site members can create, edit, and add comments to the blog postings. The **Blog** page enables you to add commentary, descriptions of events, and other materials that are related to your site.

The postings can be saved as drafts, and when ready, they can be published to the internal blog. Members can also choose to publish posts to an external blogging site, including WordPress and TypePad. To work with or perform operations on the Blog, you must be on the desired **Blog** page.

Accessing the Blog page

Accessing the **Blog** page allows you to view all of the published blog posts for the **Alfresco Book project Site**. Within the blog, you can create new posts, as well as edit, publish, and delete the posts, which you have previously created. You can also add comments to the existing blog posts.

To access the **Blog** page, carry out the following steps:

1. Enter the **Alfresco Book project Site**. On the banner, click on the **Blog** tab. The **Blog** page appears. The default view, **Latest**, is selected. The post list displays a summary of the posts created or edited in the past seven days. The summary includes the post title, the date and time at which the post was published (if applicable), the author who created the post, a sample of the content, the number of replies to the post, and the tags associated with the post.
2. The **Previous** and **Next** navigation buttons will help you to browse through multi-page posts (where necessary).
3. Click on the **Simple List** option to display only the titles of the posts. Click on the **Detailed List** option to display the summary view.

Browsing the blog

The browsing feature in the **Blog** page allows you to filter the blog posts. This allows you to navigate through the blog content more easily.

You can display subset of the blog posts by selecting a specific view, a period of time (month), or a tag in the lefthand browsing pane.

The **Posts** list in the browsing pane provides the following views:

- **All**: Displays all of the posts in the blog
- **Latest**: Displays the posts created or edited in the past seven days

- **My Drafts**: Displays the posts created by the current user that are currently saved as drafts (that is, not yet published)
- **My Published**: Displays the posts created and published, either externally or internally, by the current user
- **Published Externally**: Displays all of the posts that have been published to an external blog

The **Archives** list organizes posts by month and year.

The **Tags** list displays all of the tags currently associated with one or more blog posts.

To browse through the blog posts, carry out the following steps:

1. Select the desired option in the browsing pane. In the **Posts** list, click on the view that represents the posts that you want to view. The post list displays all of the blog posts in the current site that correspond to the selection.
2. In the **Archives** list, you can click on the month of interest. The post list displays all of the blog posts in the current site that were published during that month.
3. In the **Tags** list, you can click on the tag of interest. The post list displays all of the posts in the current site that have been tagged with the selected tag.
4. Click on the **Simple List** option to display only the titles of the posts. Click on the **Detailed List** option to display the summary view.

Creating a Blog post

You can create a new blog post to add information or a comment related to the current site.

When you create a new post, you can save it as a draft without publishing it, or you can immediately publish it to the **Alfresco Book project Site** blog. You also have the option of publishing the post to both the internal blog and a configured external blog.

To create a new post, carry out the following steps:

1. Click on the **Create Post** button. The **Create Blog Post** page appears. Type a **Title** for the post.
2. Type the post content in the **Text** box. Use the formatting features provided to mark up the content, insert bulleted and numbered lists, and include hyperlinks, as required.

Optionally, you can add tags to the blog post, as follows:

1. Type a name for the tag in the box provided, and then click on **Add**. To add multiple tags, separate each tag by a space.
2. Click on the **Choose from popular tags in this site** option to display the existing tags that are used in this site. Click on a tag to associate it with the new post.

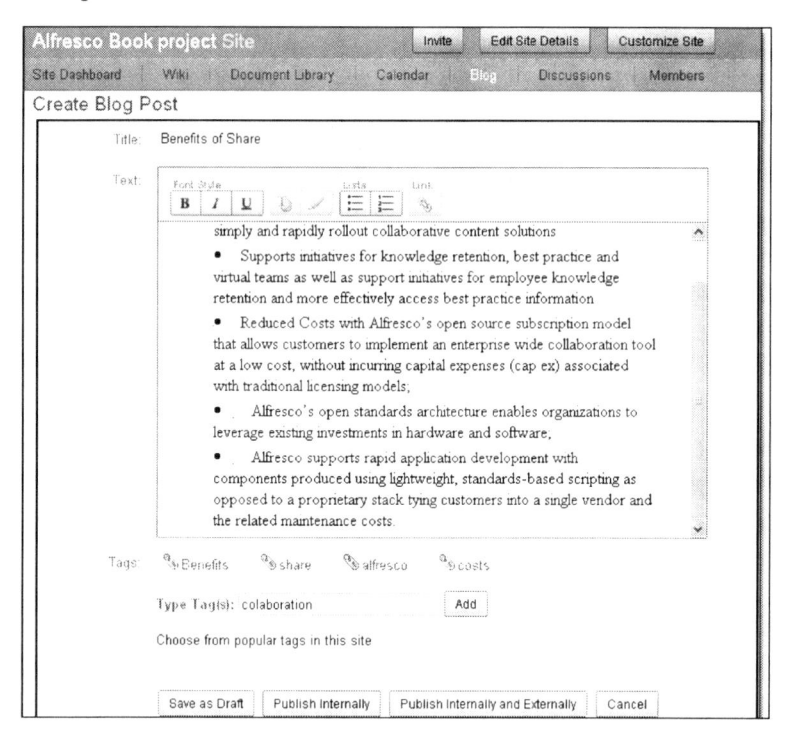

The newly-associated tags appear beneath the **Text** box. Click on a tag to remove it.

To save or publish the new blog post:

1. Click on the **Save as Draft** button to save the post without publishing it. The post will not appear in the post list.
2. Click on the **Publish Internally** button to publish the post to the internal blog, making it available for other users of this site.
3. Click on the **Publish Internally and Externally** button to publish the post to both the internal and external blogs.

The new post appears as users will see it. The text "Draft" appears after the title if the post remains unpublished. Click on the **Go to Post List** option to return to the main view.

Editing a Blog post

Only an Alfresco Book Project Site Manager or the user who created the blog post can modify it, or add to its content.

To edit an existing post, carry out the following steps:

1. In the post list, locate the blog post that you want to edit and click on the **Edit** button. The **Edit Blog Post** page appears, displaying the selected post.
2. Make the desired changes to the post title and/or content.

To edit the tags for the post, do the following:

1. To add a new tag, or multiple tags separated by spaces, type the tag(s) into the box provided, and then click on the **Add** button.
2. To add an existing tag, click on the **Choose from popular tags in this site** button to display the tags used in this site. Click a tag to associate it with the new blog post.
3. To remove an existing tag from the set below the **Text** box, click on the tag that you want to remove.

To save or publish the updated blog post, carry out the following steps:

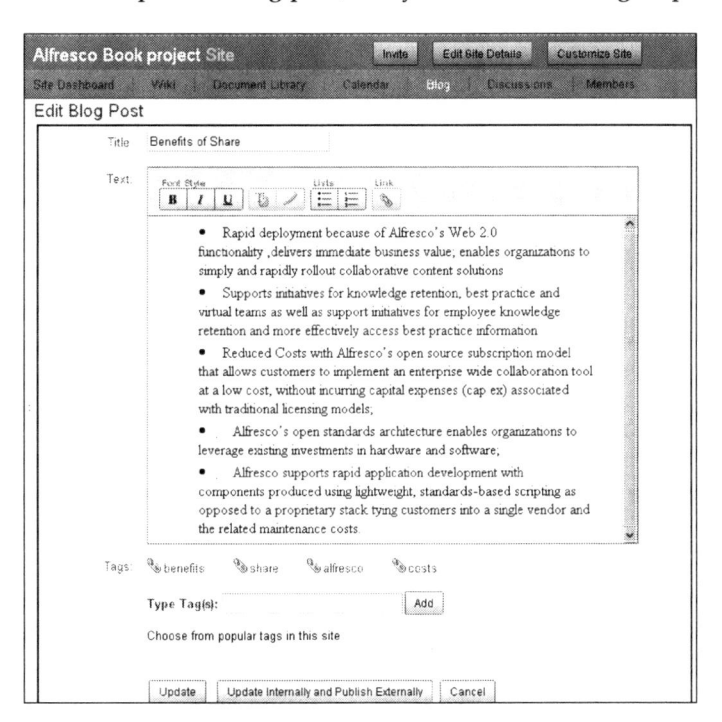

1. Click on the **Update** button to save the changes.
2. Click on the **Publish Internally** option to save the changes and publish the post to the internal blog, thus making it available for the other site members. This option appears only for draft posts.

   Click on the **Update Internally and Publish Externally** option to publish the post to both the internal and external blogs.
3. The updated post appears as the users will see it. The text (updated) appears after the title. Click on the **Go to Post List** option to return to the main view.

Viewing a blog post

Browsing the blog displays either a summary view or a simple list of the existing posts, in the main window of the **Blog** page. Viewing a post allows you to see the full contents of the post.

You can perform actions on a post from the main page, but viewing a post allows you to confirm that you have selected the correct post before performing any irreversible actions, such as deleting or publishing the post.

Although the same actions are available in both views (**Edit**, **Publish Externally**, and **Delete**), you must view a post to add a comment to it.

To view a blog post, carry out the following steps:

1. Browse the blog posts to locate the post that you want to view.
2. Click the title of the post or click **Read** below the post. If the main page displays the posts in a simple list, then you must click the title of the post. The post view displays the selected blog post in its entirety, along with any related comments.
3. Click on the **Go to Post List** option to return to the main view.

Deleting a blog post

To delete a blog post means to permanently remove it from the **Alfresco Book Project site** blog. Deleting a post also deletes all of its comments. Only a Site Manager or the user who created the blog post can delete it.

To delete a post, carry out the following steps:

1. In the post list, locate the blog post that you want to delete.
2. Click on the **Delete** button. A message prompts you to confirm the deletion of the selected post. Click on the **Delete** button. A message indicates that the selected blog post has been deleted.

Configuring the external blog

In addition to creating blog posts and publishing them internally within the site, you can publish the blog posts to an existing WordPress or TypePad blog. To publish the site blogs externally, you must configure the external blog details. To publish a draft post externally, you must also publish it internally.

To configure an external blog, carry out the following steps:

1. Click on the **Configure External Blog** option. The **Configure External Blog** page appears.
2. In the **Type** list, select the appropriate option:
    - Select **WordPress** in order to configure the external blog to run on the WordPress blog publishing system.
    - Select **TypePad** in order to configure the external blog to run on a TypePad blogging service.
3. Complete the remaining fields with the details of the external blog.
4. The **User Name** and **Password** provided must be the user details of the author or administrator responsible for posting the external blog. Click on the **OK** button.

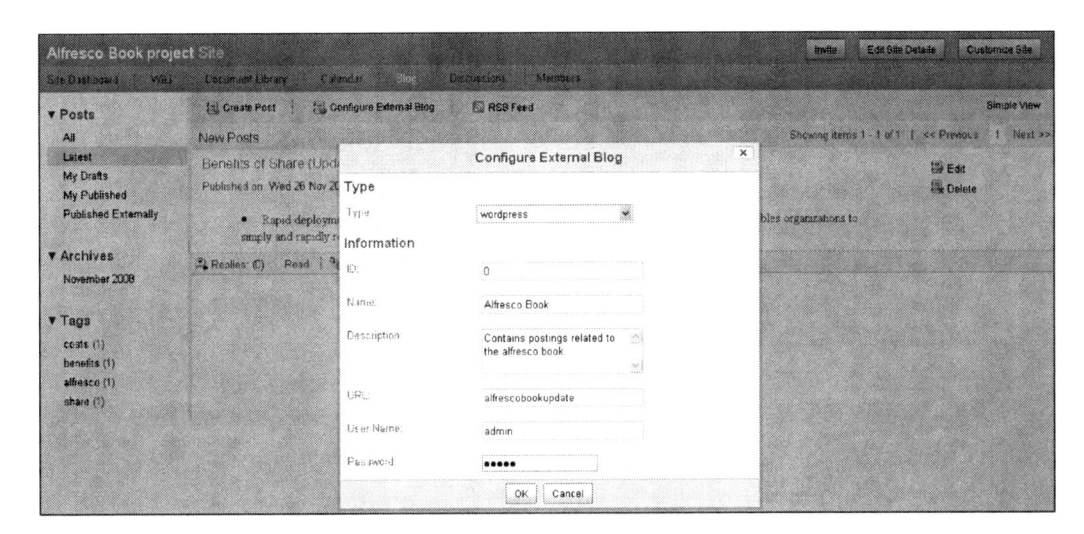

Publishing a post to an external Blog

In addition to publishing a blog post to the Alfresco Book Project site's internal blog, you can publish a post to a configured external blog. In order to publish a draft post externally, you must also publish it internally. To publish a post externally, carry out the following steps:

1. In the post list, locate the blog post that you want to publish externally.
2. Click on the **Publish Externally** button. Optionally, open the post to perform this action.

A message indicates that the selected blog post has been published.

Working with comments

Adding comments to a blog post can help make a site blog more interactive. Although all of the users with access to the **Alfresco Book project** site can view the blog conversations, only the site members can add comments.

The number of replies added to a post is displayed in the post list beneath the post summary. You must view a post to add, view, and manage the related comments.

Adding a comment to a post

In the **Blog** page, you can add a comment to reply to any published blog post.

To add a comment, carry out the following steps:

1. In the post list, locate the blog post to which you want to add a comment.
2. Click on the post title to view the post. The post view displays the selected blog post in its entirety, along with any related comments.
3. Type the post comment in the **Add comment** box. Use the formatting features that are provided to mark up the content, insert bulleted and numbered lists, and include hyperlinks, as required.
4. Click on the **Create comment** button. The comment is displayed below the post. Click on the **Go to Post List** option to return to the main view.

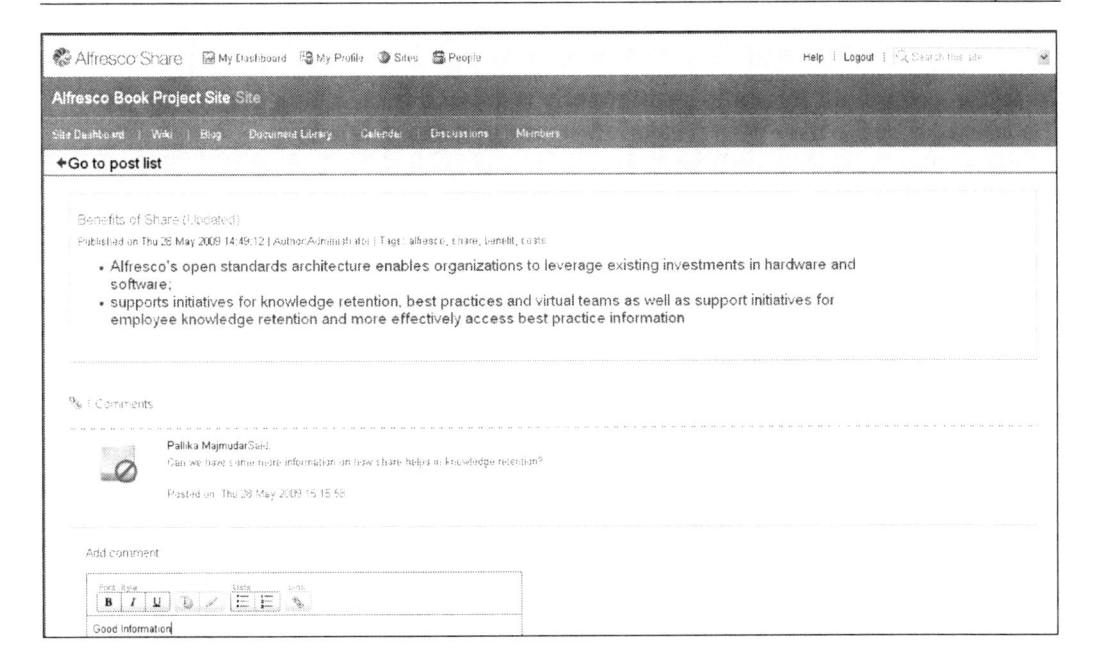

Editing a comment

To edit a blog comment means modifying or adding to its content. Only a Site Manager or the user who created the comment can edit it.

To edit a comment, carry out the following steps:

1. In the post list, locate the blog post that contains the comment that you want to edit. Click on the post title to view the post. The post view displays the selected blog post and the related comments.
2. Click on the **Edit** button to the right of the comment that you want to change. The **Edit Comment** box appears, displaying the selected comment.
3. Make the desired changes to the comment. Click on the **Update** button. The updated comment then displays below the post.
4. Click on the **Go to Post List** option to return to the main view.

Deleting a comment

To delete a comment means to permanently remove it from a blog post. Only the Site Manager or the user who created the comment can delete it.

To delete a comment, carry out the following steps:

1. In the post list, locate the blog post that contains the comment that you want to delete. Click on the post title to view the post. The post view displays the selected blog post and the related comments.

2. Click on the **Delete** button. A message prompts you to confirm the deletion of the selected comment.

3. Click on the **Delete** button. A message indicates that the selected comment has been deleted. Click on the **Go to Post List** button to return to the main view.

The Discussions page

The topics on the Discussions page can take the form of questions or comments with threaded discussions. Site members can use the **Discussions** page to post user-generated content related to the site.

Members of a site can create new topics and can also reply to a posting, in order to take part in a discussion on a specific topic.

Accessing the Discussions page

To view the discussion topics for the current site, you must use the Discussions page. Within a discussion, you can create new topics, as well as edit and delete topics that you have created. You can also reply to existing topics to take part in the discussion.

To access the Discussions page, carry out the following steps:

1. Enter the **Alfresco Book project** site, and click on the **Discussions** tab in the banner. The Discussions page appears, displaying the most recent topics in the topic list. This list displays a summary of all of the topics matching the selected browse option. The summary includes the topic title, the date and time at which the topic was created, the author who created the topic, the number of replies to the topic, sample content for the topic, and the tags associated with the topic.

2. Use the **Previous** and **Next** navigation buttons to move backward and forward through multi-page of topics.

3. Click on the **Simple List** button to display only the titles of the topics. Click on the **Detailed List** button to display the summary view.

Browsing the topics

Browsing through the **Discussions** page allows you to filter the discussion topics, as well as to easily navigate through the content. The browsing pane on the left-hand side of the page allows you to display a subset of the discussion topics, by selecting a specific view or tag.

The **Topics** list in the browsing pane provides the following options for browsing through the discussion topics:

- **New:** Displays all of the topics created or updated in the past seven days
- **Most Active**: Displays the topics that have been opened most often in the past seven days
- **All**: Displays all of the topics
- **My Topics**: Displays the topics that were created by the current user

In the **Tags** list, the browsing pane displays all of the tags that are currently associated with one or more discussion topics.

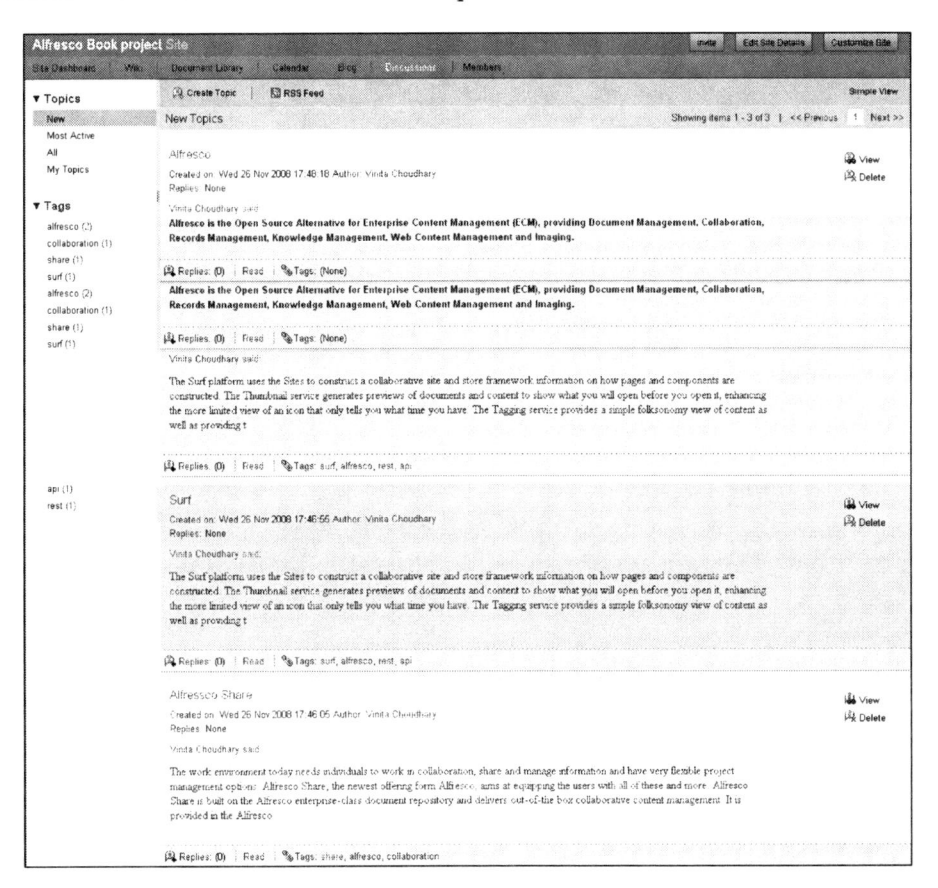

To browse the discussion topics, carry out the following steps:

Use the browsing pane to browse through the discussion topics:

1. In the **Topics** list, click on the view representing the topics that you want to view. The topics list displays all of the discussion topics in the current site that correspond to the selection.
2. In the **Tags** list, click on the tag of interest. The topic list displays all of the topics in the current site that have been tagged with the selected tag.
3. Click on the **Simple List** button to display only the title of the topics. Click on the **Detailed List** button to display the summary view.

Viewing a topic

Browsing the discussion forum displays the existing topics in the main window of the Discussions page. These topics display in either, a summary view or a simple list view. Viewing a topic allows you to see the full contents of the discussion.

Although you can perform actions on a topic from the main page, viewing the topic enables you to confirm that you have selected the correct topic before you edit, delete, or reply to it.

To view a discussion topic, carry out the following steps:

1. Browse through the discussion topics to locate the topic that you want to view.
2. Click on the **View** button to the right of the topic. Alternatively, you can click on the title of the topic or click on the **Read** button below the topic. If the main page displays topics in a simple list, then you need to click on the **View** button or the topic title. The topic view displays the selected topic in its entirety, along with any replies.
3. Click on the **Go to Topic List** button to return to the main view.

Creating a new topic

To create a new topic means to start a discussion relevant to the current site with the site members. This task assumes that you are on the **Discussions** page of the desired site.

To create a new discussion topic, carry out the following steps:

1. Click on the **Create Topic** button. The **Create New Topic** page appears. Type a **Title** for the topic.
2. Type the topic content in the **Text** box. Use the formatting features provided to mark up the content, insert bulleted and numbered lists, and include hyperlinks, as required.

Optionally, you can tags to the discussion topic, as follows:

- Type a tag in the box that is provided, and click on **Add**. To add multiple tags, separate each tag with a space.

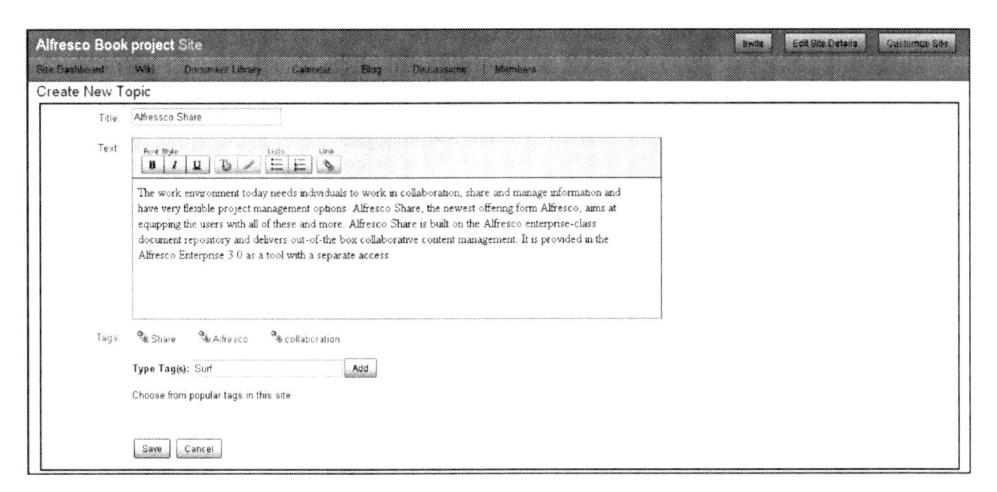

- Click on the **Choose from popular tags in this site** option to display the existing tags used in this site. Click on a tag to associate it with the new topic.
- The newly-associated tags appear below the **Text** box. Click on a tag to remove it.
- Click on the **Save** button. The new topic appears as it appears to the users. Click on the **Go to Topic List** option to return to the main view.

Editing a topic

To edit an existing discussion topic means modifying it or adding to its content. Only a Site Manager or the user who created the topic can edit it.

To edit a discussion topic or reply, carry out the following steps:

1. In the topic list, locate the discussion topic that you want to edit.
2. Click on the **View** button to the right of the topic. Alternatively, you can click on the title of the topic or click on the **Read** button below the topic. If the main page displays topics in a simple list, then you must click on the **View** button or the topic title. The topic view displays the selected topic in its entirety, along with any replies.
3. Click on the **Edit** button to the right of the topic that you want to edit. The selected topic appears in its entirety in an edit box. Make the desired changes to the topic title and/or content.

You can the tags for a topic, as follows:

- To add a new tag, type the tag in the box provided and click on the **Add** button. To add multiple tags, separate each tag with a space.
- To add an existing tag, click on the **Choose from popular tags in this site** option to display the tags that are used in this site. Click on a tag to associate it with the topic.
- To remove an existing tag from the set below the **Text** box, click on the tag that you want to remove.
- Click on the **Save** button. The updated topic is displayed as it appears to the users. The text **(Updated)** appears after the title. Click on the **Go to Topic List** option to return to the main view.

Deleting a topic

To delete a topic means to permanently remove it from the Discussions page. Deleting a topic also deletes all of its replies. Only the Site Manager or the user who created the topic can delete it.

To delete a discussion topic:

1. In the topic list, locate the topic that you want to delete. Click on the **View** option on the right-hand side of the topic. Viewing the topic before deleting it allows you to ensure that you have selected the correct topic. The topic view displays the selected topic in its entirety, along with any replies.
2. Click on the **Delete** button to the right of the topic. A message prompts you to confirm the deletion of the selected topic. Click on the **Delete** button. A message indicates that the selected topic has been deleted.

Creating a reply

Creating a reply allows you to begin or take part in a discussion related to the site. You can reply to the original discussion topic or any replies that have already been created for that topic. Each reply is nested to visually indicate the discussion flow.

To create a reply in a discussion, carry out the following steps:

1. In the topic list, locate and view the topic that you want to reply to. The topic view displays the selected topic in its entirety, along with any existing replies.
2. Click on the **Reply** button. Type your content in the **Add Reply** box. Use the formatting features provided to mark up the content, insert bulleted and numbered lists, and include hyperlinks, as required.
3. Click on the **Create** button.

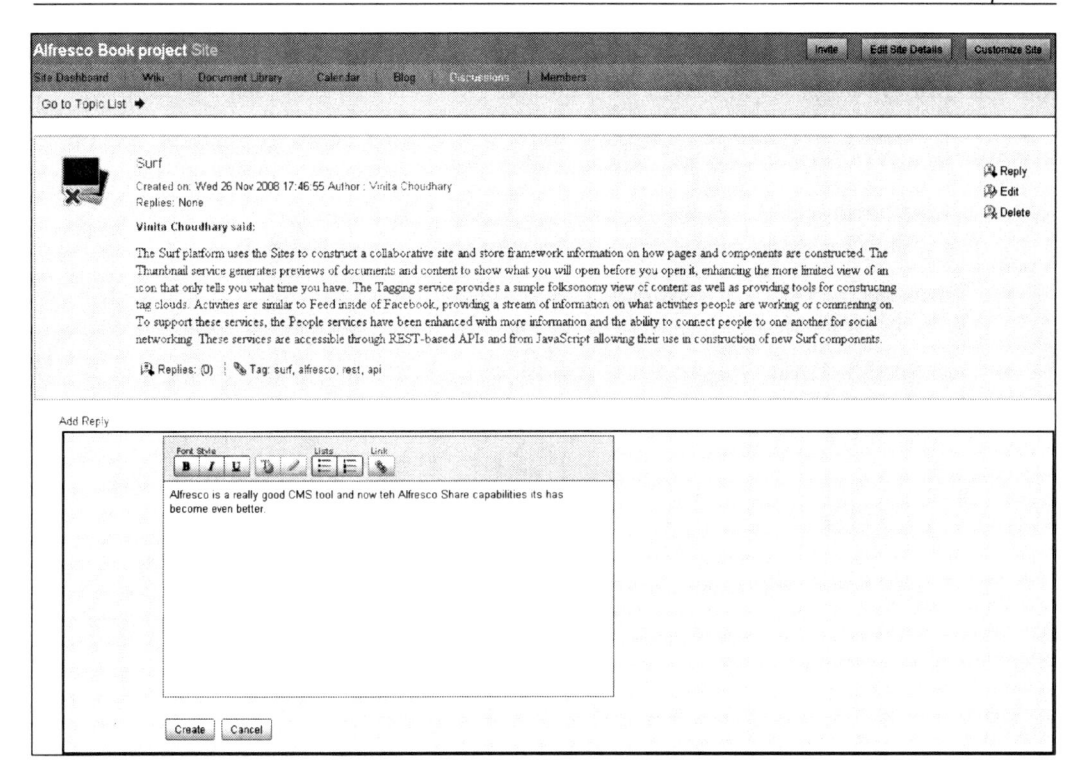

The reply appears below and indented from its parent topic or reply.

Editing a reply

You can edit a reply just as you edit a discussion topic. To edit a topic reply, carry out the following steps:

1. In the topic list, locate and view the desired topic. The topic view displays the selected topic in its entirety, along with its replies.
2. Click on the **Edit** button to the right of the reply that you want to change. The selected reply appears in its entirety in an edit box.
3. Make the desired changes to the topic title and/or content. Then, click on the **Update** button.

The updated reply appears as users will see it. The text **(Updated)** appears after the name of the member who originally created the reply.

Managing site users

In the **Members** page, the member management tasks are divided across three pages. The tasks and the sections mentioned below assume that you are on the **Members** page of the desired site. These pages are:

- **Site Members:** This is the default page. The **Site Members** page allows you to search for a site member and view the site's current members.
- **Pending Invites:** The **Pending Invites** page allows you to view the users that have been invited to join the current site but have not yet accepted the invite.
- **Invite**: The **Invite** page allows you to invite internal and external users to become members of the current site. The **Invite** link on the banner also displays this page.

The links to these pages appear below the site banner. The link of the currently-displayed page appears in green.

Accessing the Members page

Accessing the **Members** page allows you to manage the members of any site of which you are a Site Manager.

To access the **Members** page, carry out the following steps:

1. Enter the **Alfresco Book project Site**.
2. On the banner, click on the **Members** page.
3. The **Members** page displays the default page, **Site Members**.

Invite users to a site

The **Invite** page enables you to invite both, internal and external users to join the current site. This is multi-part process where you select the users to invite, assign a role to each user, and then issue the invitations. However, the invitation requires the configuration of the SMTP server. The following is what you need to do to invite users. The available user roles are **Manager**, **Collaborator**, **Contributor**, and **Consumer**.

To invite users to join the site, carry out the following steps:

1. Click on the **Invite** button below the banner. Search for, and add internal users.
2. In the **Search** box, type the full or partial name of the user that you want to invite. Leave this box empty to return a list of all of the internal users. Selecting the option to display all of the users may take some time if there are many users in the system.

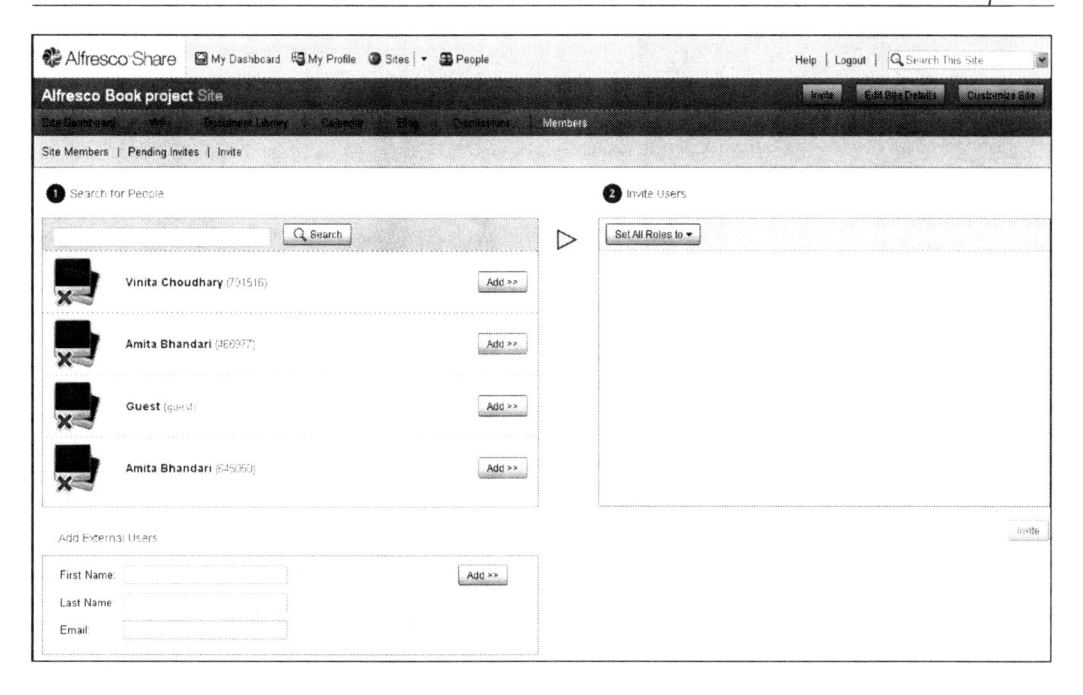

3. Click on the **Search** button. The application displays a list of all of the users matching the specified search criteria.
4. Click on the **Add** button located to the right of a user in this list. The user appears in the **Invite Users** list.

To add an external user, carry out the following steps.

1. Type the **First Name** and **Last Name** of the external user that you are inviting to the site.
2. In the **Email** box, type the email address of the external user. This is the email address to which the invitation will be sent.

3. Click on the **Add** button. The user appears in the **Invite Users** list.

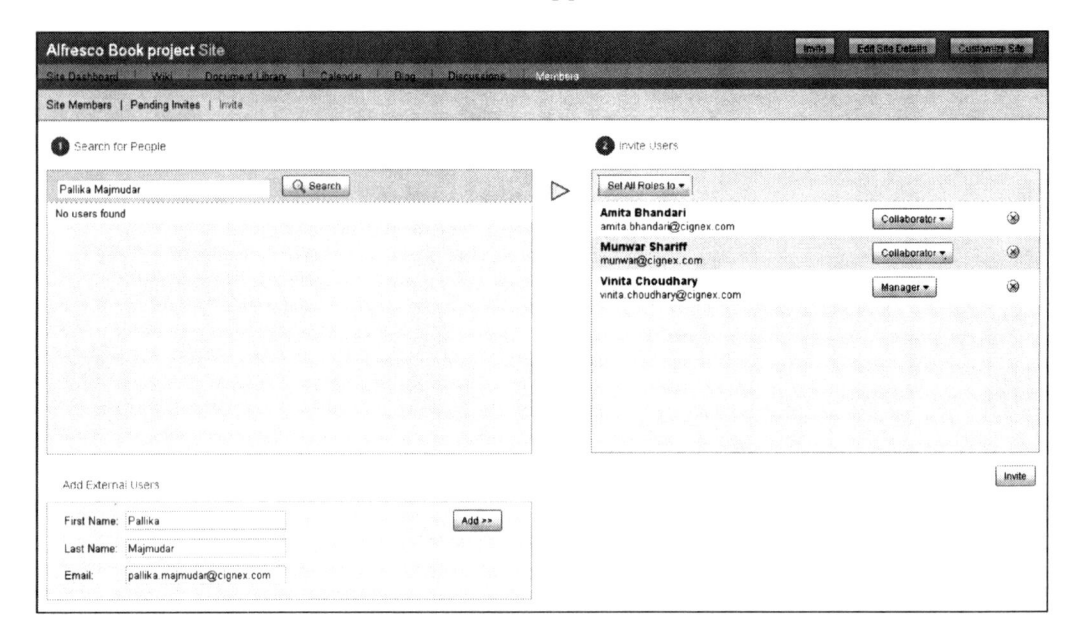

In the **Invite Users** list, specify a role for each user.

To set the role for an individual user, click on the **Select Role** option, which is located to the right of the user, and then on the desired role.

- To set the same role for all of the users in the list, click on the **Set All Roles to** option at the top of the list and then click on the desired role.
- Click on the **Add** button, which is located beneath the **Invite Users** list, to extend invitations to all of the users that are displayed in the list.

Each user in the **Invite Users** list receives an email invitation from `invites@alfresco.com`. The users have the option to accept or reject the invitation to become a member of the site.

Viewing the site members

The **Site Members** page allows you to search for a particular site member, or to display all of the members of the current site.

To search for or view the site's members, carry out the following steps:

1. Click on the **Site Members** tab, which is beneath the banner, if this page is not already selected.
2. In the **Search** box, type the full or partial name of the site member that you want to locate. Leave the search box empty to return a list of all of the site members. Displaying all of the users may take some time if there are many members in the current site. Next, click on the **Search** button.

The page displays a list of the site's current members. From this list, you can change a member's role or remove a member from the site.

Changing a site member's role

At any time, a Site Manager can change the role assigned to a site member. This task assumes that you are on the **Members** page of the desired site.

To change the role assigned to a site member, carry out the following steps:

1. On the **Site Members** page, locate the site member whose role you want to change for the current site. The page displays a list of the current site members. A button to the right of the member's name indicates the currently-assigned assigned role for this member.
2. Click on the button displaying the currently-assigned role. A list displays the available roles, such as, **Manager**, **Collaborator**, **Contributor**, and **Consumer**.
3. Click on the appropriate role for the site member. Share assigns the selected role.

You can even assign a role different from the ones assigned to a site member for a specific content item in the Document Library. The Site Manager will have full privileges. To manage the permissions assigned to the site members, carry out the following steps:

1. Click on the **More** option from the list of actions that can be performed on the document. From the list of options, select the **Manage Permissions option**.

Advanced Collaboration Using Alfresco Share

2. You can now manage permissions for the selected document in the library. You have the option of selecting the default options or changing the roles according to your requirements. For example, you can assign the role of a consumer to the coordinator. You can also completely remove privileges for a particular role by selecting the **No privileges** option from the available role list for the particular role.

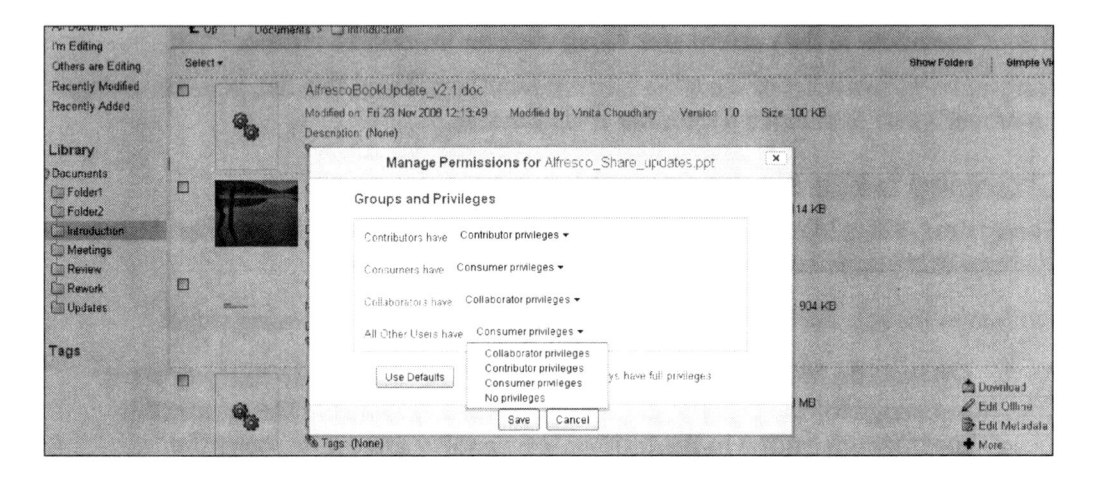

Removing a site member

At any time, a Site Manager of a site can remove a member from that site. A removed member no longer has access to the site. However, if the site is public, then a user can choose to rejoin the site.

This task assumes that you are on the **Members** page of the desired site.

To remove a member from a site, carry out the following steps:

1. On the **Site Members** page, locate the site member that you want to remove from the current site. The page displays a list of the current site members.
2. Click on the **Remove** button, which is located to the right of the user that you want to remove from the site.

Share removes the specified member. If the Site Manager or the person who created the site leaves, then another site member can be assigned the role of the Manager. To do this, carry out the following steps:

1. The Site Administrator should go to the **Members** tab on the dashboard of the site. Search for the members by clicking on the **Search** tab.
2. In the list, click on the current Site Manager's role and change it to something other than **Manager**.

3. From the list, click on the member who will be the new Site Manager, and change their role to Manager by clicking on the **Manager** role from the drop-down list.

4. Now you can delete the old Site Manager, by changing the role and clicking on the **Remove** tab.

Viewing and managing the invited users

On the **Pending Invites** page, you can view the full list of invited users or search for a particular user. This page allows you to view the users that have been invited to join the current site. Once you have invited a user to join your site, you can revoke the invitation up until it has been accepted.

This task assumes that you are on the **Members** page of the desired site.

To search for or view invited users, carry out the following steps:

1. Click on the **Pending Invites** option, below the banner.

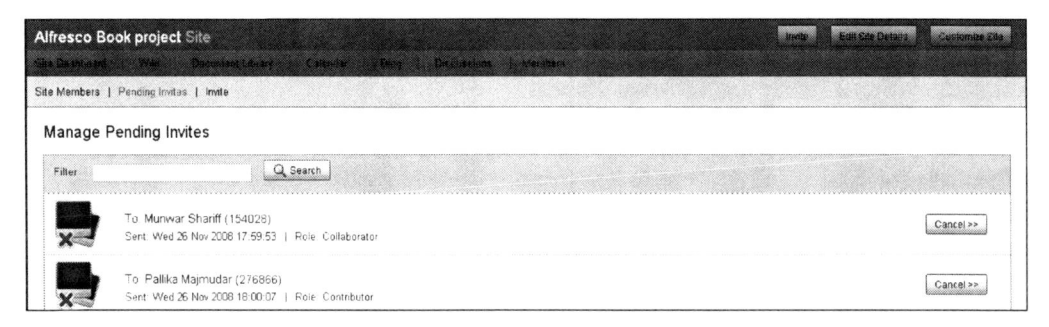

2. In the **Filter** box, type the full or partial name of the invited user that you want to locate. Leave this box empty to return a list of all of the users invited to this site. Displaying all of the users may take some time if many users have been invited to join the current site.

3. Click on the **Search** button. The page displays a list of the users that have been invited to be members of the site.

4. Click on the **Cancel** option, which is located to the right of the user whose invitation you wish to revoke. Share cancels the invitation and removes the user from the list.

Benefits of using Alfresco Share

Some very evident benefits of Alfresco Share are as follows:

- Rapid deployment, because of Alfresco's Web 2.0 functionality, delivers immediate business value. It enables organizations to simply and rapidly roll out collaborative content solutions
- Supports initiatives for knowledge retention, best practices and virtual
- Reduced costs with Alfresco's open source subscription model allows customers to implement an enterprise-wide collaboration tool at a low cost, without incurring the **capital expenses** (**cap ex**) associated with traditional licensing models
- Alfresco's open standards architecture enables organizations to leverage existing investments in hardware and software
- Alfresco supports rapid application development with components produced using lightweight, standards-based scripting, as opposed to a proprietary stack tying customers into a single vendor and the related maintenance costs.

SharePoint protocol support with Alfresco Enterprise 3.0

Let's now take a look at how you can manage your Microsoft Office documents in Alfresco, without being an **Alfresco Expert**.

This is facilitated by the SharePoint protocol support that is offered by Alfresco. Alfresco is the first ECM system to implement the Microsoft Office and Windows SharePoint Services protocols as a compatible server. With this implementation, users can now look forward to an open alternative that delivers equivalent benefits but with true platform choice.

The Alfresco repository now offers:

- Microsoft Office SharePoint protocol support, without the need for an additional client installation
- Alfresco Surf platform for building dynamic, REST-oriented web applications and collaborative web sites
- A RESTful API delivering content and collaboration services for customizing and developing Alfresco applications
- Preview of Alfresco Share, a new social computing application
- A Document Library that can scale to over 100 million documents

Alfresco's new Surf platform is built on Alfresco Web Scripts technology, which utilizes light-weight scripting and templating. The Surf platform is designed to work in a number of different web environments, as well as a Web Part in a Microsoft SharePoint Portal.

Handling documents within Microsoft Office

The SharePoint Protocol support built into Alfresco Enterprise Edition 3.0 SP1 lets users work with documents in the Alfresco Share repository without using the Share interface. We will now go through how to manage documents within Microsoft Office. For the case scenarios, we shall use Microsoft Word 2003. You can also carry out the same tasks using Word 2007.

Creating a Document Workspace

A Document Workspace is an Alfresco Share site that contains a document. For our example, we shall use The **Alfresco Book project Site** that we have created.

To create a Document Workspace, carry out the following steps in MS Word 2003:

1. Open MS Word, create a new document, enter the required content, and then save this document as `Alfresco Update.doc` on your machine.

2. On the MS Word toolbar, click on the **View** menu and select the task pane or press *Ctrl+F1*. The task pane opens in MS Word to the right of the document. If you are using MS Word 2007, you have to click on the Windows icon in the upper-left corner of the screen and then select the **Publish | Create Document Workspace** option.

Advanced Collaboration Using Alfresco Share

3. Select the **Shared Workspace** option from the drop-down menu at the top of the task pane. A pane similar to the following screenshot will be displayed:

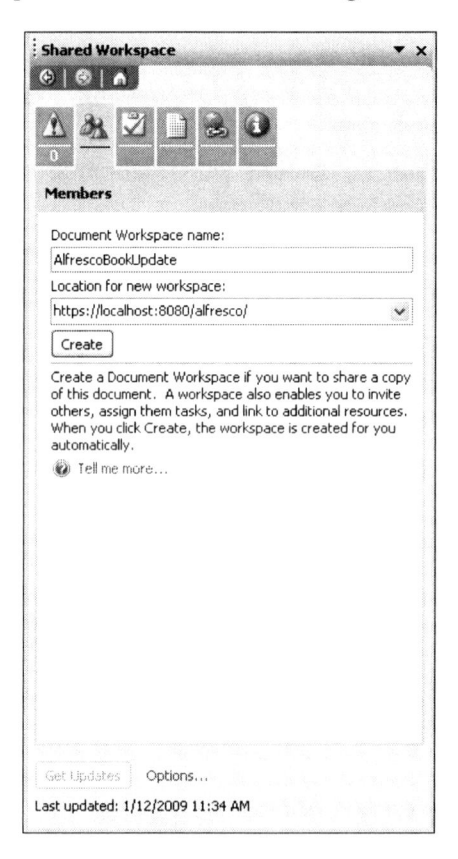

4. Change the default entry in the **Document Workspace name** field to **AlfrescoBookUpdate**.

> When creating a site, all non-alphanumeric characters in the **Document Workspace name** field, including spaces, are converted into underscores, for both the site name and the URL name.

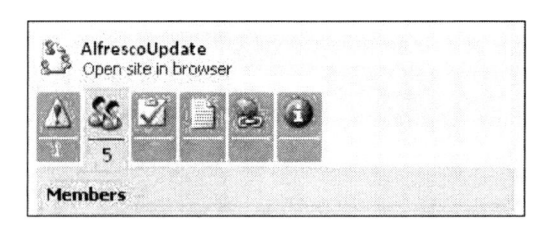

There are six tabbed panels available on this pane. They are: **Status**, **Members**, **Tasks**, **Documents**, **Links**, and **Document Information** (as shown in the preceding screenshot). Position your cursor over a tab to display the tab name.

1. In the **Location for new workspace** field, type the URL `http://<Alfresco serverinstance>/alfresco`, for example, `http://alfrescoserver:8080/alfresco`.

2. You also need to add the Alfresco server as a trusted site before you can create the workspace. Otherwise, you will be prompted to do the same. Click on the **Create** button.

3. Now, you can log in with your credentials. You can also save them to avoid re-entering them every time. Word creates the Document Workspace in Share, adds the document `Alfresco Update.doc` to the new site, and displays the familiar Shared Workspace task pane. Office may prompt you to log in again. If so, use the same username and password.

4. Verify whether the new site has been created. Open `http://< Alfresco server instance >/share/` on the browser. Sign in with your credentials. The **Alfresco Update Site** then displays in your **My Sites** dashlet on your personal dashboard, as shown in the following screenshot:

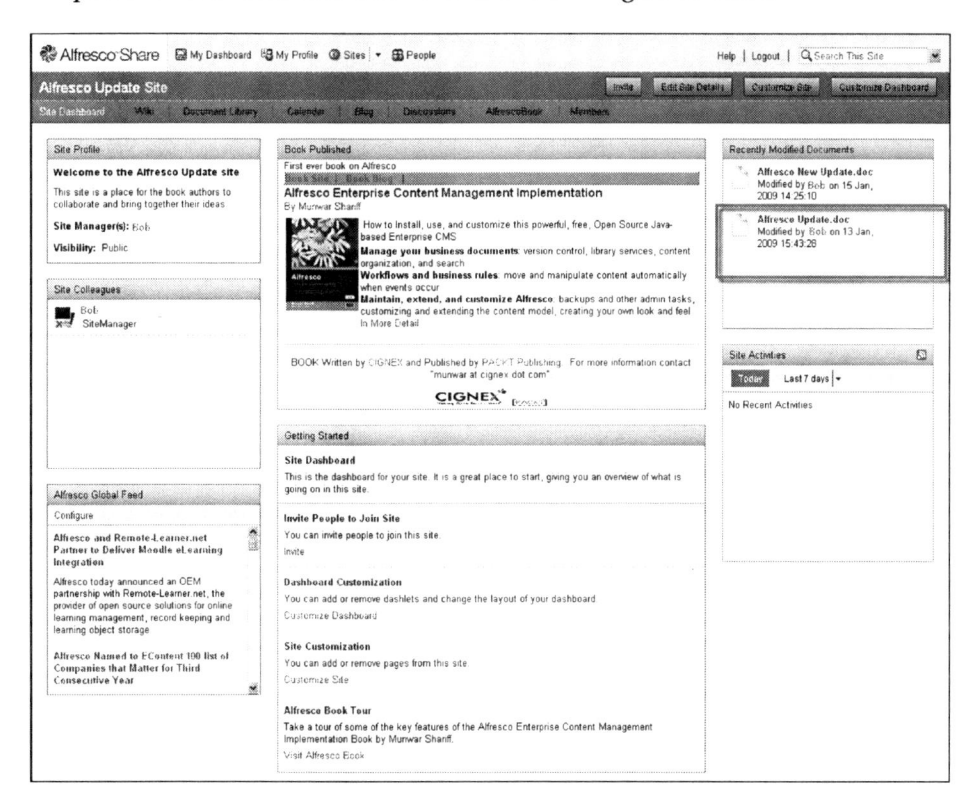

Advanced Collaboration Using Alfresco Share

On clicking the site link, the site is opened and you can see the **Alfresco Update.doc** file in the site's Document Library in the **Recently Modified Documents** dashlet, as highlighted in the following screenshot:

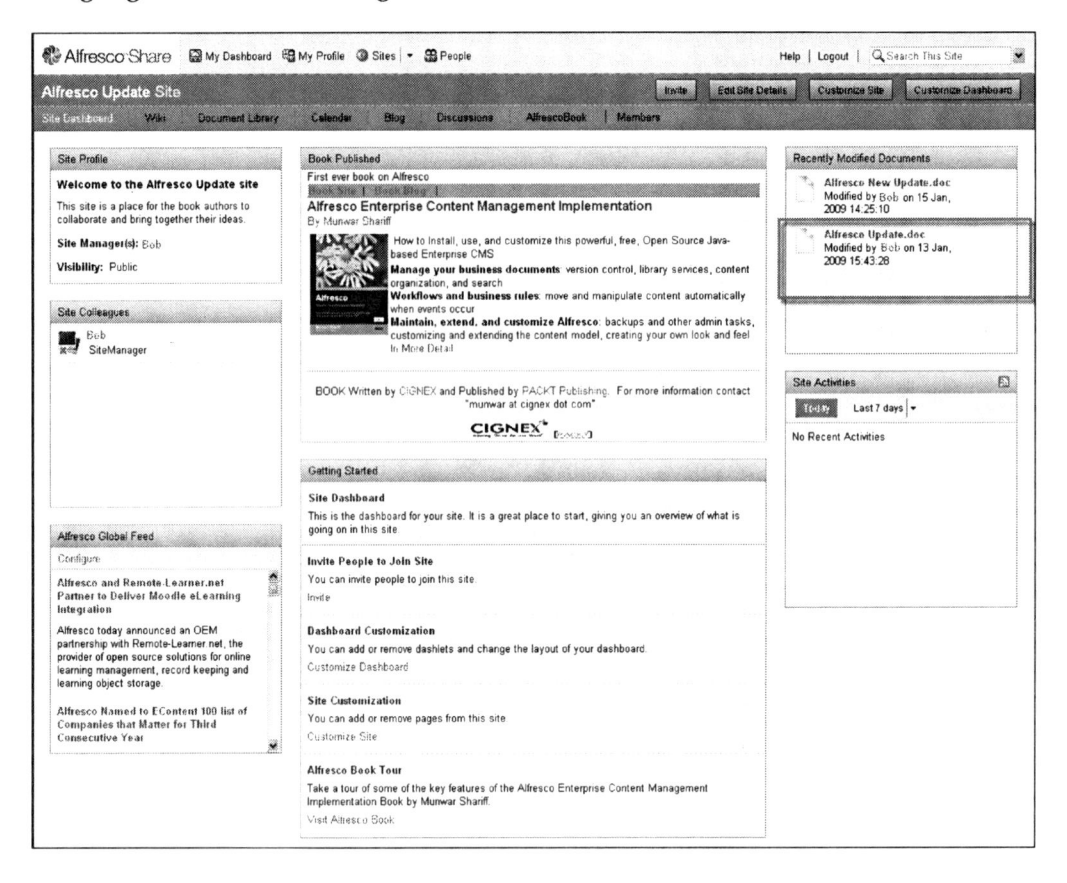

Editing a document

To edit a document, carry out the following steps:

1. Open a document stored in the Document Workspace from MS Word. MS Word automatically displays the Shared Workspace task pane, which contains many of the document management features that are available.

2. To edit a document, open the Document Workspace document that was created and added to Share in the previous section. To do this, click on **File | Open**.

3. Enter http://<Alfresco server instance>/alfresco as the file name and click on **Open**. As a result, a list of all of the existing Share sites is displayed.

[430]

4. Select the **Alfresco Update** option and click on the **Open** button to navigate to that site. The MS Word window in this case will switch to a Web view.

5. Select **Alfresco Update.doc** from the Document Library and open it. MS Word displays the selected Share document.

Checking out the document

When you check a document during or before editing, the document is locked for all other users. Site members can still view or download the original version of the document while you edit it and have it checked out.

- To check out the file **Alfresco Update.doc** from the site, select the **Document Information** tab from the task pane, and then click on **File | Check Out**
- A new **Check in** link in the task pane indicates that the document is now checked out. Moreover, the **Alfresco Update** site in Share displays a lock icon to the left of the file named **Alfresco Update.doc**.

Checking in the document

After editing the checked out document, check it in to update the document in the Document Workspace Library. This removes the lock from the document. As a result, the updated version is available to the other users.

- To check in the document, after saving the document, click on **File | Check In**. Enter check in comments, if any, and then click on **Ok**.
- The **Check In** link in the task pane changes to **Check out**, indicating that the document is now checked back in. Once the page refreshes, the **Alfresco Update** site in Share will no longer display the lock icon.

Document Versions

When a document is added to the document workspace, it has a version. Each time it is updated, a version history is maintained. The versions can be managed through MS Word. Alfresco does not support the deletion of individual document versions.

Ensure that **Alfresco Update.doc** is open. We will use this document to view the version history and then explore the other document version features available.

To check the version history, carry out the following steps:

1. On the Shared Workspace task pane of the document **Alfresco Update.doc**, select the **Document Information** tab.

Advanced Collaboration Using Alfresco Share

2. In the **Document Library**, select on **File | Version History**. The **Versions saved for Alfresco Update.doc** window appears, displaying all of the previous versions of the document. The window displays the version number, the user who made the modification, the date and time of the modification, and a truncated comment (if any was entered when the document was checked in).

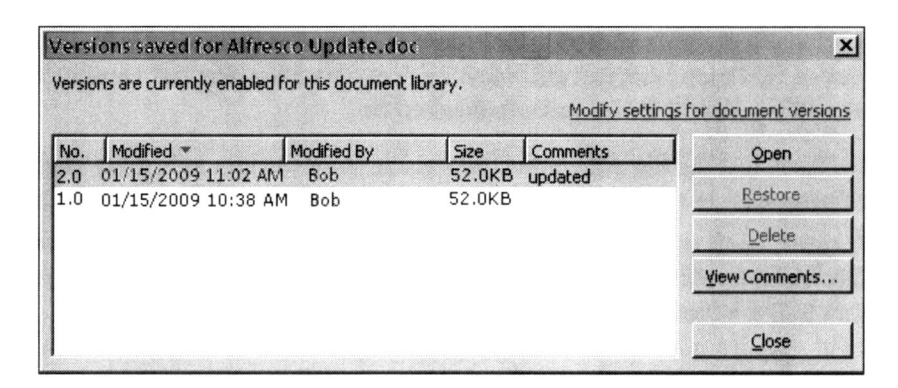

```
Versions saved for Alfresco Update.doc                                    X
Versions are currently enabled for this document library.
                                            Modify settings for document versions
  No.  Modified ▼          Modified By   Size     Comments        Open
  2.0  01/15/2009 11:02 AM  Bob          52.0KB   updated
  1.0  01/15/2009 10:38 AM  Bob          52.0KB                   Restore

                                                                  Delete

                                                                  View Comments...

                                                                  Close
```

> The **Modify settings for document versions** link on this window (shown in the preceding screenshot) navigates to the document details page in Share for the current document, whereas the same link in SharePoint takes you to the site settings page.

3. You can click on the **View Comments** button to view the full comment for a version. Click on the **Modify settings for document versions** link to view the details for `Alfresco Update.doc`.

4. Log in to Share. On the left-hand side, you will see the name and a preview of the document. The right-hand side of the page contains the item details, including metadata, tags, permissions, version history, document actions, and related URLs. Comments made on the item selected are displayed at the bottom of the page.

Viewing a previous document version and then restoring the document to that version

Any version that was saved for `Alfresco Update.doc` file can be viewed. To view the original version of the document, select version 1.0 in the version list, and then click on the **Open** button.

The document opens in a new window as a read-only version. Close the window, when you have finished reviewing the content.

Managing the document versions

Selecting a previous version of the document in the **Versions saved for Alfresco Update.doc** window enables both, the **Restore** and **Delete** buttons. We can restore the original version of the document as our current version. In order to replace the current document with a previous version, carry out the following steps:

1. In the **Document Library**, click on **File | Version History**.
2. In the **Versions saved for Alfresco Update.doc** window, select the original document (**version 1.0**) in the version list, and then click on the **Restore** button.
3. Click on the **Yes** button to confirm that you want to replace the current version of the document with the selected version. You might be prompted to log in again.
4. MS Word replaces the content of the current version with the content of version 1.0. Select the **Document Information** tab and click on **Version history**. Notice that restoring the original content has created a new version, 3.0. A read-only copy of version 2.0 of the document remains open.
5. Close the version 2.0 copy of `Alfresco Update.doc`. Click on the **Close** button on the **Versions saved for Alfresco Update.doc** window. The `Alfresco Update.doc` that has been reverted to its original content remains open.

Adding content to a document library

You can create a separate folder in the document library to contain content, and then add a document to the folder. To do this, carry out the following steps:

1. On the **Shared Workspace** task pane of the document `Alfresco Update.doc`, select the **Documents** tab. The files and folders that currently reside in the site's document library are displayed here. You can manage the contents of the **Document Workspace** document library from here.

2. Next, click on the **Add new folder** option. Enter **New Updates** as the **Folder Name** and then click on the **OK** button. The newly-created folder now appears in the **Documents** list. You can now upload a document to it.

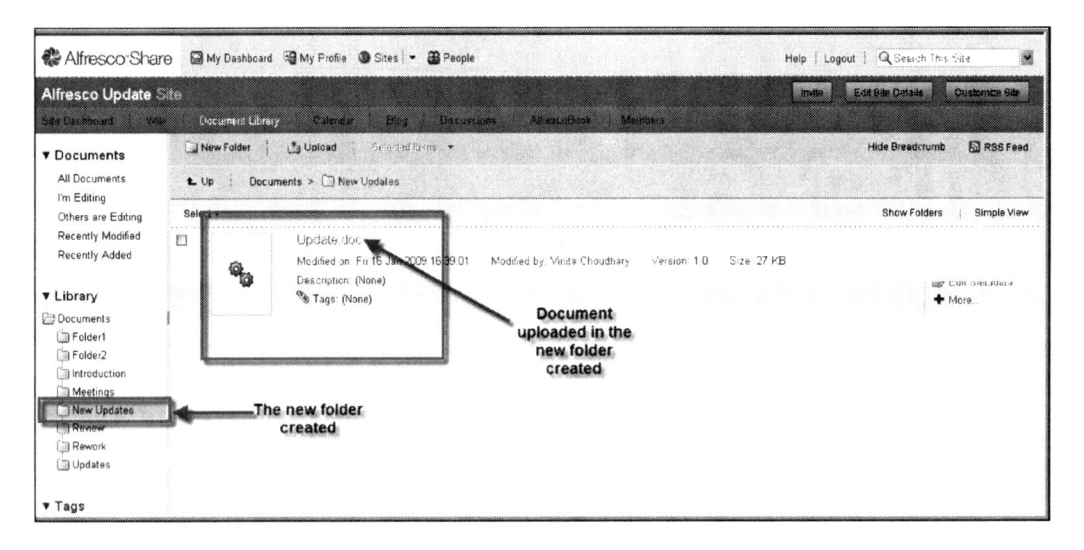

3. Click on the **New Updates** folder and then click on the **Upload** button. Browse and locate an MS Word file on your computer to upload, and then click on the **Open** button.

4. Click on **OK**. The document appears in the Documents list within the **New Updates** folder. The label **New** indicates that the document has been recently uploaded.

> To remove a document from the **Document Workspace**, position your cursor over the document name, open the context menu, click on the **Delete** button, and confirm the deletion when prompted.

Collaborating on a document

A **Document Workspace** allows you to collaborate on documents with one or more colleagues. We shall use the **Alfresco Update** site that we created previously, as an example in this section. The site, after the exercises performed earlier, now contains two documents, namely the `Alfresco Update.doc` and the document uploaded in the `New Updates` folder.

Saving a document to the Document Workspace

We have created the **Document Workspace** and can now save MS Word documents directly to the site. To save an MS Word document to the **Document Workspace**, carry out the following steps:

1. Create a new Word document, enter content, and click on **File | Save As**.
2. Enter `http://<Alfresco server: 8080>/alfresco/AlfrescoUpdate/DocumentLibrary/Update.doc` as the **File name**. The URL takes the following form: `http://<Alfresco server: 8080>/alfresco/<site URL name>/DocumentLibrary/<folder structure>/<filename>`.

> `<Alfresco server:8080>` is the server and port where Alfresco is installed and running on your machine. Alfresco's SharePoint Protocol Support name must be used with all URLs.
>
> `<site URL name>` is the URL name of the **Document Workspace** (Share site) where the document is being saved. In our case it is the **Alfresco Update** site.
>
> `DocumentLibrary` is the Site's **Document Library** page component.
>
> `<folder structure>` is the path and destination of the folder, where a folder structure has been established within the site's library. In our example, the folder is the `New Updates` folder.
>
> `<filename>` is the filename of the current document. In our case, it is `Update.doc`

3. When you click on the **Save** button, MS Word saves the new document (titled `Update.doc`) to the Document Library of the specified Share site.
4. Next, open the task pane and click on the **Open site** button in the browser to verify that the new document has been saved to the **Alfresco Update** site.

5. Log in with your credentials and the **Alfresco Update** site dashboard is displayed. The **Update.doc** document is listed in the **Recently Modified Documents** dashlet.

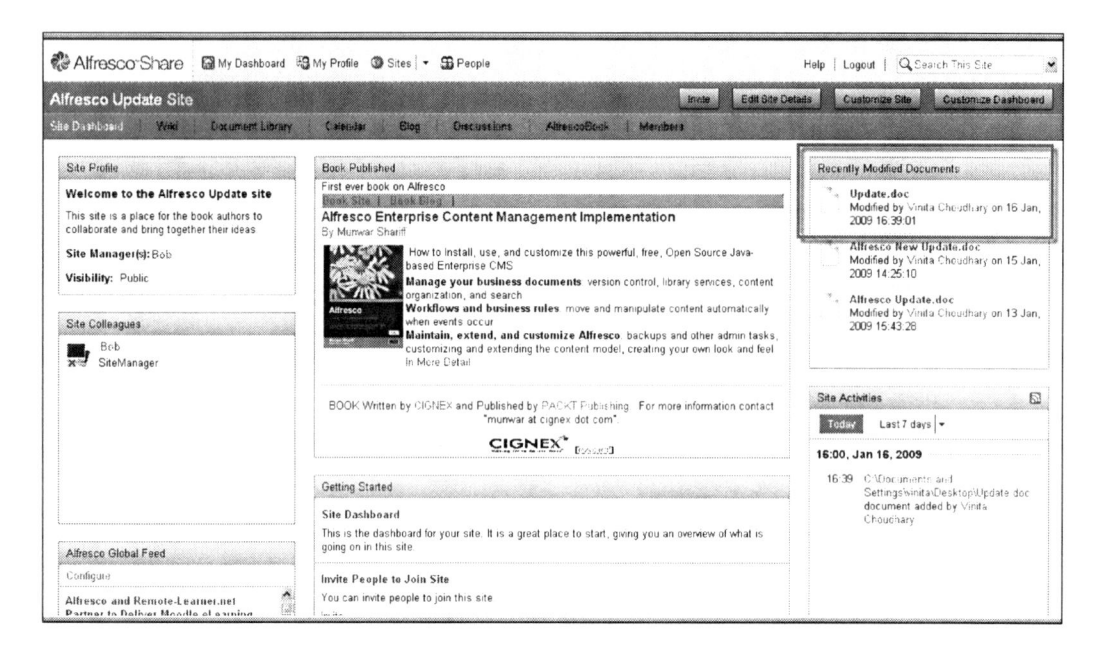

Customize the Document Workspace

The document workspace URL name is automatically generated from the name of the site provided. This name is not editable. In this tutorial, both the site name and the URL name are **AlfrescoUpdate**. Once the Document Workspace has been created, you can manage the site directly from Microsoft Word.

Editing the site name

Ensure that the document Update.doc is opened on your computer, and that the **Shared Workspace** task pane is open in the document window, with the site name **AlfrescoUpdate** displayed at the top. This is the name that you will edit by carrying out the following steps:

1. To edit the site's display name, position your cursor on the site name **AlfrescoUpdate** in the **Shared Workspace** task pane of the document Update.doc.

2. Open the now active menu and select the **Change Site Title** option. Change the site title to **Alfresco SPP Support** and click on the **OK** button. You can open the site to confirm that the site name has been changed in Share.

3. Open the site in the browser by clicking on the **Open site in browser** option below the **Document Workspace** name, and log in. Your browser displays the dashboard of the **Alfresco SPP Support** site in Share `http://localhost:8080/share/page/site/alfrescoupdate/dashboard`. The **Document Library** page component link appears beneath the site name.

Changing the site settings

There are five page components available for a site namely, the **Document Library**, **Calendar**, **Blog**, **Discussions**, and **Wiki** in Alfresco Share. When you create a Document Workspace from MS Word, the site includes only the Document Library component by default. From MS Word, you can easily access the Share page to customize the site. Again, you will work from the document `Update.doc`.

1. To customize the site, on the Shared Workspace task pane of the document `Update.doc`, position your cursor over the site name, that is, **Alfresco SPP Support**. Open the context menu and select the option **Change Site Settings**.

2. Log in to Share. The browser opens, displaying the **Customize Site** page for the **Alfresco SPP Support** site. Only the **Document Library** page component is included in the site.

3. Add and remove pages from the site as desired. Refer to the earlier sections on collaboration with Share for details.

Manage the Document Workspace membership

Only the members of the **Document Workspace** can work with the documents stored there. The tasks relating to site members are displayed on the **Members** tab of the **Shared Workspace** task pane.

Adding members to the site

Currently, only Bob, whose login credentials you used to create the Document Workspace, is a member of the **Alfresco SPP Support** site. The user who creates the site is automatically given the role of Site Manager. We will now add users to the site, by carrying out the following steps:

1. On the **Shared Workspace** task pane of the document `Update.doc`, select the **Members** tab. The **Admin** appears at the top of the tab.

2. Click on the **Add new members** option. Type **Tom** and **Ann** to add **User Tom** (tom/tom) and **User Ann** (ann/ann) as members of the site. Select **SiteCollaborator** as the site role for these users, and then click on the **Next** button.

3. When adding multiple users, all of the users will be assigned the same role. Once added, you can change the role of an individual site member.

4. Confirm the member details that are displayed, and then click on the **Finish** button. The **Members** tab displays the newly-added site members, **Tom** and **Ann**.

Viewing and editing user profiles

A user can only edit his or her profile details. However, he or she can view the profiles of all of the site members. To edit a user profile, carry out the following steps:

1. To edit your profile go to the **Shared Workspace** task pane of the document `Update.doc`, position your cursor over **Admin**, open the context menu, and then select the **Edit User Information** option.

2. As a result, Alfresco Share opens. The **User Profile** page component displays your user details. From here, you can change your password and can also edit your profile.

Changing a member's role

There are four roles available in Share sites, namely, **Manager**, **Collaborator**, **Contributor**, and **Consumer**. Only a Site Manager can manage site membership by changing a member's role. To do this, position your cursor over (for example) **Ann** on the **Shared Workspace** task pane of the document `Update.doc`. Open the context menu and select the **Edit Site Group Membership** option.

Log in as **Bob**. Share opens and displays the **Search for Site Members** page. Type in the username in the field provided, and then click on the **Search** button. Share returns a list of the site's members matching the search criteria entered. The assigned role is displayed for each member. As the Site Manager, you can change the member roles and remove members from the site.

Removing a site member

Only the Site Manager can remove a member from the site. To remove a Document Workspace site member, position your cursor over (for example) **Ann** in the **Members** tab. Open the context menu, and select **Remove Member** from Workspace. Click on **Yes** to confirm the removal.

Working with a Document Workspace document locally

When you add or save a document to the **Document Workspace**, the original version of the document remains on your computer. This document copy is linked to the copy in the site's Document Library. Once linked, you can work on one version, and then update the other, to keep them synchronized.

Downloading document updates from the site

Use the file `Alfresco Update.doc`, which you used to create the **Alfresco SPP Support** site. It should still reside on your desktop. A copy also exists in the site's library. Double-click on the `Alfresco Update.doc` document that is saved on your desktop. The following pop-up window will appear:

Because a copy of the `Alfresco Update.doc` document exists in the collaboration site, it is possible that your local copy is no longer current. You need to synchronize your local copy with the site copy to ensure that you have the current version.

- Click on the **Get Updates** button. MS Word checks for and applies changes made by other members to the local copy of the document.

Updating the site copy

When a local copy of a document is linked to a **Document Workspace**, MS Word detects the changes made to the document and prompts you to resolve the discrepancy. In the previous task, you updated the local copy with the version from the workspace. In this task, you will update the workspace copy with the local version. To update the site copy, carry out the following steps:

1. Make some changes to your open document (`Alfresco Update.doc`) and then save the document. The **Status** tab displays a warning, indicating that there is a discrepancy between the local copy and the workspace copy of the document.

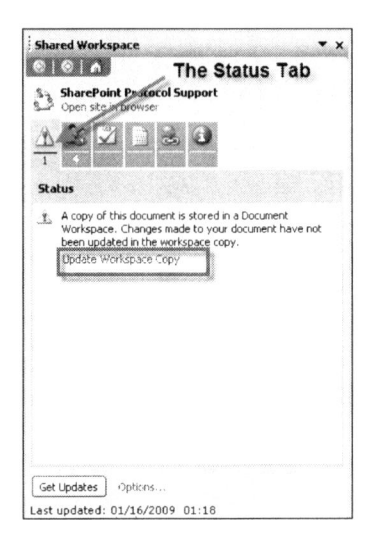

2. Click on the **Update Workspace Copy** link on the **Status** tabbed page.
3. MS Word checks for and applies changes made in the local copy to the version in the site's document library. Click on the **Open site in browser** option and verify that the new document has been saved to the site.

Saving an updatable copy locally

Currently, user Bob has the original copy of the document `Alfresco Update.doc` on his desktop. The **Save Updatable Copy** feature in MS Word enables other site members to obtain a copy of this document for their own machines. This copy, similar to the original document on your own machine, is linked to the `Alfresco Update.doc` document in the **Document Workspace**. This can only be done if there is access to a second machine that uses Internet Explorer as the default browser, and that has your Alfresco Server as a **Trusted Site**. To save an updatable copy to the local machine itself, you have to carry out the following steps:

1. On another machine, open MS Word and select **Open** in the **File** menu. Enter `http://<Alfresco server URL:8080>/alfresco`.
2. At the login page, log in as **Tom** (tom/tom). Browse to `/AlfrescoUpdate/documentLibrary` and open the `Alfresco Update.doc` file.
3. User **Tom** now has the server copy of the document `Alfresco Update.doc` open. On the **Shared Workspace** task pane, select the **Documents** tab. The document **Alfresco Update.doc** is highlighted in the **Documents** list. Position your cursor over the document name, open the menu that becomes active, and select the **Save Updatable Copy** option. Save the document locally when the **Save As** window appears.
4. Log in as **Tom** again, if prompted to.

Tom now has a local copy of the `Alfresco Update.doc` file, just as **Bob** does. Make some changes to the `Alfresco Update.doc` file, save the document, and upload it to the **Document Workspace**.

Managing document updates

When multiple users hold local copies of a **Document Workspace** document, the **Document Updates** pane provides you with options for managing the edits. When changes to your local copy conflict with the version stored in the site, this feature enables you to compare the two versions, and either overwrite one copy, or merge the two copies. All of this can be done by carrying out the following steps:

> You can perform this task only if you were able to complete the previous task (Saving an updatable copy locally).

1. Return to your original machine, where the document `Alfresco Update.doc` is open. On the **Shared Workspace** task pane, select the **Documents** tab.
2. The document `Alfresco Update.doc` is highlighted in the **Documents** list. Position your cursor over the document name, open the context menu, and then select **Document Updates**.
3. The **Document Updates** task pane is displayed. Click on the **Open Updated Copy** option to obtain the updates.

Deleting the Document Workspace

Once you complete the collaboration on the document, you would typically delete the **Document Workspace**, as it is no longer required. This action permanently deletes the site and all of its contents. With the tutorial now complete, you can perform this task to remove the sample site, **Alfresco SPP Support**, and its contents, from Share. Ensure that the document `Alfresco Update.doc` is open, and then carry out the following steps:

1. On the **Shared Workspace** task pane, position your cursor over the site name, namely, **Alfresco SPP Support**. Open the context menu and select the **Delete Workspace** option.

2. Click on the **Yes** button in order to confirm the deletion. The site is removed.

Document Workspace dashlet in Share

You can click on a **Document Workspace** name to enter the related site, and click on the **Delete** button to the right of a **Document Workspace** name to delete the site in the **My Workspaces** dashlet in Share.

Summary

With the addition of Share, Alfresco delivers a Web 2.0 application that leverages Flash and AJAX with a richer user interface than more traditional document management libraries. Share is heavily focused on collaboration tasks, and includes integration with popular blogs that you can publish to internally and externally, Wiki, and Forum/Discussion products are provided out of the box. Share's ability to perform rapid user site creation, site user invitation, permissions and management is noteworthy.

In SharePoint, you can open a document from the web interface, have it automatically load in the appropriate Office application, make your edits, and then check the file in to automatically **upload** the new version. In Alfresco Share, you have to navigate down to the document manager area of your desired site, and then open the file. Then, check out the file, edit it, and check it back in. The difference in the two methods seems to be that the SharePoint way uses the web interface as the starting point, whereas Alfresco Share uses Microsoft Office as the starting point.

11
Customizing the User Interface

The Alfresco Explorer user interface is designed to handle most of the common user interaction scenarios. However, each business application will have some specific user interface requirements. You can configure certain user-interface elements in Alfresco Explorer, such as space icons, menu options, and the custom look and feel of a space. Of course, you can also change the entire look and feel of the application through Java programming.

For each user of the system, you can provide a personalized dashboard view. In this chapter, you will examine various options for customizing the user interface, including custom dashlets (dashboard components). You will experience the power of **FreeMarker Template Language** in consolidating the content information and presenting it to the end users.

The Alfresco Share delivers out of the box collaborative content management. You can configure certain user interface elements, such as dashlets, page components, and the custom look and feel of the space. For each user of the system you can provide a personalized dashboard view, a customized site dashboard, and customized components. You will find that this is mostly built using CSS, Java Script, FTL, and XML files.

By the end of this chapter, you will have learned how to:

- Configure space portal views
- Add custom icons to spaces
- Extend the action menu items
- Write custom dashlets
- Using webscript as dashlets
- Write custom templates to preview content

- Write webscripts for Share
- Configure Share portlets through webscript
- Integrate share with flex
- Write custom JSPs
- Integration with external system

Configuring Alfresco Explorer

You can configure the look and feel of the Alfresco Explorer without programming by simply editing the XML configuration file. You can change the way Alfresco Explorer looks and operates, you can change the navigation elements, and you can modify the space views, as per your organizational or departmental requirements.

Configuring views

This section gives you an insight into configuring various views in Alfresco.

Configuring space views

Every space can be viewed in four different ways. These are as follows:

1. **Details View:** This displays detailed information about documents, displayed as rows.
2. **Icon View:** This displays the icon, description, and modification time properties of the documents.
3. **Browse View:** This displays information about sub-spaces.
4. **Custom View:** This displays a custom view selected by the user for that space.

For Windows users, this is similar to having various view options for folders in Windows Explorer. The **Details view**, **Icon view**, and **Browse view** are provided out of the box. The **Custom View** is a customized view of that space, which is selected by the user.

The default view for a space is the **Icon View**. You can choose a specific view (say, **Details View**) by selecting it from the drop-down list, as highlighted in the screenshot below. However, the selection is going to be saved only for that session, and the next time you log in to the Alfresco web client, you will see the default view of the space. You can configure the default view for spaces. You can also specify the number of items to be displayed on a page.

Chapter 11

You can find the details about the default configuration in the file named, `web-client-config.xml`, which is located in your configuration folder. To customize the default view, you need to update the `web-client-config.xml` file in the `extensions` folder. Go to `extensions` folder (for Tomcat installation it is in the following folder: `<alfresco_install_folder>\tomcat\shared\classes\alfresco\extension`). Here, you will have to edit the `web-client-config-custom.xml` file, and add the following block of XML code. If you want to display the details of all of the documents in your space (as shown in the screenshot on the previous page), then you can set **View Details** to default. If you want to see more documents on a page, then you can increase the number of documents displayed per page from 10 to 25.

```
<config evaluator="string-compare" condition="Views">
      <!-- the views available in the client -->
  <views>
      <!-- default values for the views available in the client -->
    <view-defaults>
      <browse>
      <!-- allowable values: list|details|icons -->
        <view>details</view>
        <page-size>
        <list>10</list>
        <details>25</details>
        <icons>9</icons>
        </page-size>
      </browse>
    </view-defaults>
  </views>
</config>
```

[445]

> Deployment of Alfresco Explorer can be achieved as the administrator by using the URL: `http://localhost:8080/alfresco/faces/jsp/admin/webclientconfig-console.jsp`
>
> Use the following command to deploy the file:
>
> `reload`

Applying a Custom View to a space

A **Custom View** is a portal window that shows up on the top of each space when a **Custom View** option is selected. This is useful for representing the content in a space in a specific manner, such as showing recent documents and a summary of the documents. For example, you can apply a custom view on the **Finance Department | Checks** space to display a list of checks received in the past week.

This enables you to have an alternate view of spaces through templates. Other such examples include:

- Show a space and its sub-spaces (collapse the tree).
- Traverse the entire repository, displaying content whose date is effective.
- Show the file names of all of the images, along with their thumbnails, and create HTML links to the actual images.
- Display summaries of the information within a space, such as the total number of documents, the number of documents under review, the number of documents belonging to a category, and the number of documents published or approved.

Let us say you would like to see all of the documents in your home space that have been either created or modified in the past one week. Carry out the following steps to apply a custom view to do this your home space.

1. Go to the space to which you would like to apply the **Custom View**. For example, go to your home space by clicking on the **My Home** menu link in the tool bar.
2. Using the **More Actions | View details** menu option, go to the details page.

3. Click on the **Add Custom View** icon, as shown in the following screenshot, to select a custom view. The **Remove Custom View** icon (also shown in the following screenshot) is useful for removing an existing custom view from a space.

4. Clicking on the **Add Custom View** icon will open an **Apply Template** window, as shown in the screenshot below. You can select a template to be applied to the space as a **Custom View**. There are already some built-in templates provided for most generic use cases. You can also apply your own custom templates to this space. The process of adding a custom template is explained later in this chapter.

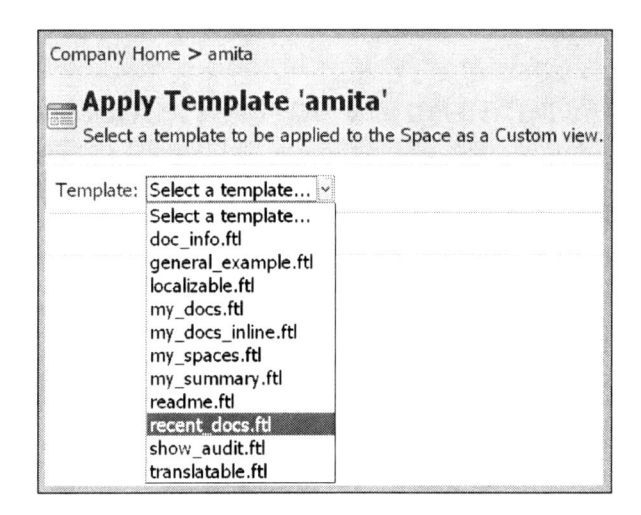

5. From the list of presentation templates, select the `recent_docs.ftl` template, which displays the list of documents in the current space that were either created or updated in the past week.

[447]

6. Once you select the presentation template, click on the **OK** button and close the **View Details** page. You will notice that the presentation template you have chosen is applied to the space as a **Custom View** (refer to the following screenshot).

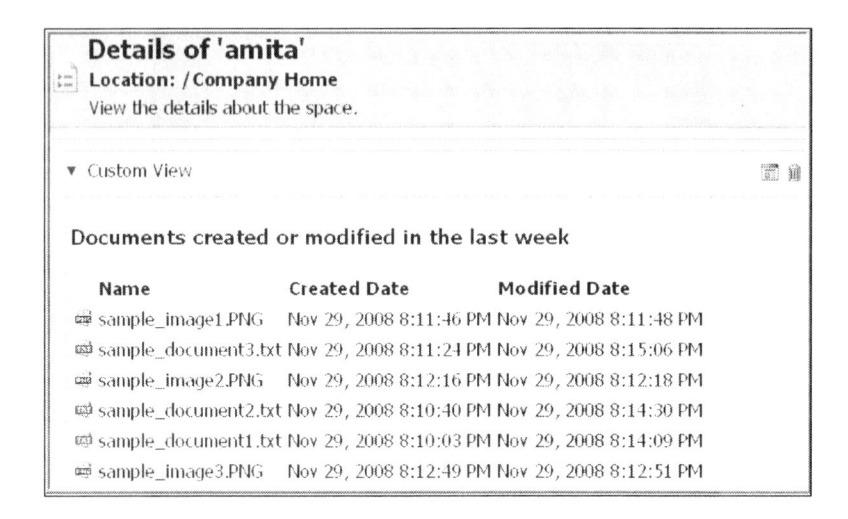

Configuring forum topics sort direction

By default, the topic view in the forums functionality lists the posts in descending order, that is, the most recent post is at the top of the list. If you wish to change this, then add the following XML text to the `web-client-config-custom.xml` file. You can also define the number of posts listed per page.

```
<topic>
        <!-- allowable values: details|bubble -->
   <view>bubble</view>
   <sort-column>created</sort-column>
        <!-- allowable values: ascending|descending -->
   <sort-direction>ascending</sort-direction>
   <page-size>
     <bubble>5</bubble>
     <details>20</details>
   </page-size>
</topic>
```

Adding a custom icon to a space

In order to add another space icon to the list from which we choose from when creating a space, add the following code to the `web-client-config-custom.xml` file.

```
<!-- Example of adding a custom icon to the Create Space dialog -->
<config evaluator="string-compare" condition="cm:folder icons">
   <icons>
     <icon name="space-icon-custom" path="/images/icons/
                                          space-icon-custom1.gif" />
   </icons>
</config>
```

A similar approach can be used to add icons to the forums space types (`fm:forums`, `fm:forum` and `fm:topic`).

Once you add the custom icon names to the `web-client-config-custom.xml` file, you need to make sure that the icons with the same filename are copied to the file system icons folder. For an installation of Tomcat, the `icons` folder is at `<install_folder>\tomcat\webapps\alfresco\images\icons`. Also, for uniformity, ensure that all of the icons are sized to 32 x 32 pixels.

As per the example, create a `.gif` file icon named `space-icon-custom1.gif` (32 x 32 pixels in size) and copy it to `icons` folder. Once you reload the `web-client-config-custom.xml` file, you will notice the new icon when creating a space, as shown in the following screenshot:

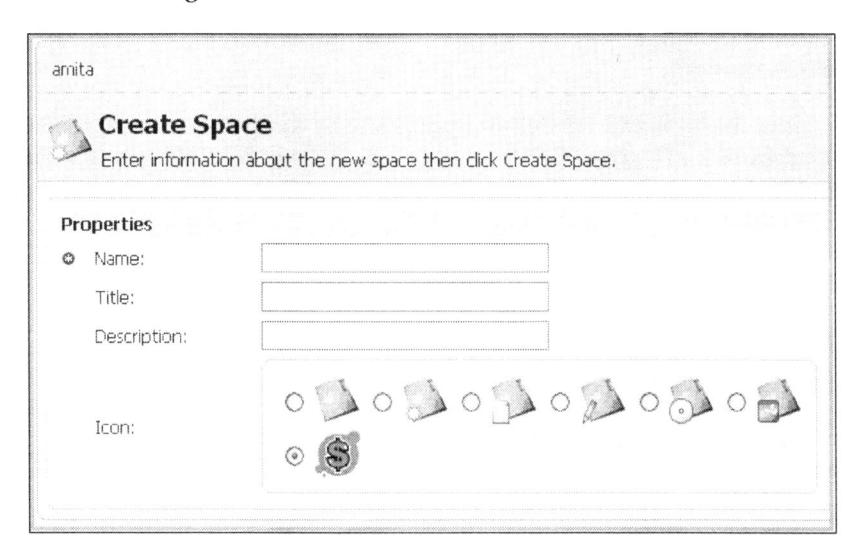

Configuring HTML links to appear in Alfresco Explorer

You can control certain HTML links that appear in the web client. For example, there is a small help icon in the menu at the top. By clicking on this icon, you can navigate to Alfresco's web site. You can update the lines that follow in the web client configuration file to point the help index to your internal online help guide (if you have any). The URL to the client **Help** file is `<help-url>http://www.alfresco.org/help/webclient</help-url>`.

User configurable dashboards

In the Alfresco Explorer user interface, the **My Alfresco** area is known as the **dashboard**. The end users can construct their own dashboard page from a list of pre-configured components known as **dashlets**. As a developer, you can configure these components, or create new components, and make them available for selection to users when they are configuring their pages. For more details about configuring your personal dashboard, refer to Chapter 3.

Writing custom dashlets

There are certain dashlets provided to you out of the box. Because the dashboard is a place where you can see dynamic information, you might consider having custom dashlets to provide you with important information. For example, you might want to see the list of contracts approved in the last seven days. You might also want to see the latest press releases.

Usually, custom dashlets are written in a scripting language such as **FreeMarker,** and are called from a **JSP (Java Server Page)**. The JSP can be configured in the web client so that the custom dashlet is visible for you to select in the dashboard.

The following steps need to be followed in order to write and configure a custom dashlet:

1. Create a custom dashlet script.
2. Create a custom dashlet JSP (which internally uses dashlet script).
3. Configure the custom dashlet JSP in the web client.
4. Restart Alfresco.
5. Use the custom dashlet in the **My Alfresco** dashboard.

Create a custom dashlet script

As an example, write a custom dashlet script, using the FreeMarker template language, to display the latest press releases from the **Company Home > Intranet > Press and Media > Press Releases** space.

The dashlet script could be plain HTML text, a FreeMarker template, JavaScript, or a JSP page. For this example, let us use a FreeMarker template.

Using the following code, create a file named `chapter11_press_releases.ftl` in your Alfresco configuration's `templates` folder. For the installation of Tomcat, the folder is `<install_folder>\tomcat\webapps\alfresco\WEB-INF\classes\alfresco\ templates`.

```
<#------------------------------------------------------------------>
<#-- Name: chapter11_press_releases.ftl                           -->
<#--Displays a table of all the documents from a "Press Releases"-->
<#-- folder under Company Home/Intranet/Press and Media space     -->
<#-- NOTE: Obviously this folder needs to exist and               -->
<#--       the docs in it should have the title and content      -->
<#------------------------------------------------------------------>
<table>
   <#assign l_space = companyhome.childByNamePath["Intranet/Press and
                                      Media/Press Releases"]>
     <#list l_space.children as doc>
       <#if doc.isDocument>
       <tr>
         <td>
           <a class="title"href="/alfresco/${doc.url}">$
                                   {doc.properties.title}</a></td>
         </tr>
         <tr>
           <td style="padding-left:8px">
             <#if (doc.content?length > 500)>
               <small>${doc.content[0..500]}...</small>
             <#else>
               <small>${doc.content}</small>
             </#if>
           </td>
         </tr>
         <tr><td> <HR> </td></tr>
       </#if>
     </#list>
</table>
```

Create a custom dashlet JSP

Once the custom dashlet script has been created in the `templates` folder, the next step is to create a custom dashlet JSP, which uses the custom dashlet script.

Create the `chapter11_press_releases.jsp` file, containing the following code, and place the file in the dashlets folder. For a Tomcat installation, the folder is `<install_folder>\tomcat\webapps\alfresco\jsp\dashboards\dashlets`.

```
<%--
Name    : chapter11_press_releases.jsp
Purpose: Dashlet to display the latest press releases
--%>
<%@ taglib uri="/WEB-INF/repo.tld" prefix="r" %>
<%-- Note that this template is loaded from the classpath --%>
<r:template template="/alfresco/templates/chapter11_press_releases.ftl" />
```

Configure custom dashlet JSP in Alfresco Explorer

Now you need to configure the web client to use the custom dashlet and to make it visible in the dashboard wizard.

Add the following code to the `web-client-config-custom.xml` file, before the last xml tag, which is `</alfresco-config>`.

```
<config evaluator="string-compare" condition="Dashboards">
<!-- Dashboard layouts and available dashlets for the My Alfresco
                                                           Pages -->
  <dashboards>
    <dashlets>
<!-- Add additional dashlet for press releases -->
      <dashlet id="press-releases" label="Press Releases"
                      description="Lists Press Releases with URL"
          jsp="/jsp/dashboards/dashlets/chapter11_press_releases.jsp"
                                       allow-narrow="true" />
    </dashlets>
  </dashboards>
</config>
```

The following table describes each dashlet element used in the XML configuration.

Dashlet element	Description
`id`	An identifier string that uniquely identifies the dashlet.
`jsp`	The JSP page to be used for the implementation of the dashlet.
`label` or `label-id`	The label text or label I18N message ID for the dashlet. This label is shown in the list of available components that is presented to the user in the Dashboard Configuration Wizard.
`description` or `description-id`	The description text or description I18N message ID for the layout. This description text is shown in the list of available components that is presented to the user in the Dashboard Configuration Wizard.

Restart Alfresco

To make the configuration changes effective, you need to restart Alfresco. The newly-created custom dashlet example requires one or two press releases to be available in the **Company Home > Intranet > Press and Media > Press Releases** space. In Chapter 7, you created few press releases in the **Company Home > Intranet > Press and Media > Press Releases** space. Refer to the *Create Press Release as HTML Content* section in Chapter 7 for further details.

Use the Custom Dashlet in the My Alfresco Dashboard

Click on the **My Alfresco** link provided in the tool bar menu to view the Dashboard. Click on the **Configure** icon shown in the **My Alfresco Dashboard,** and the **Configure Dashboard Wizard** will display the custom dashlet in **Step Two**. Then, select the **Components** screen, as shown in the following screenshot:

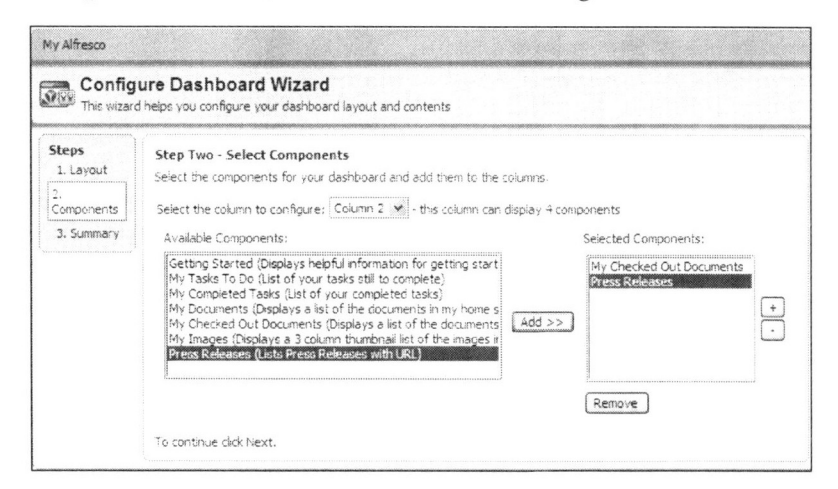

Customizing the User Interface

Select the **Press Releases** dashlet for **Column 2**, as shown in the preceding screenshot. Once you finish the configuration, the custom dashlet in your dashboard will look similar to the one shown in following screenshot:

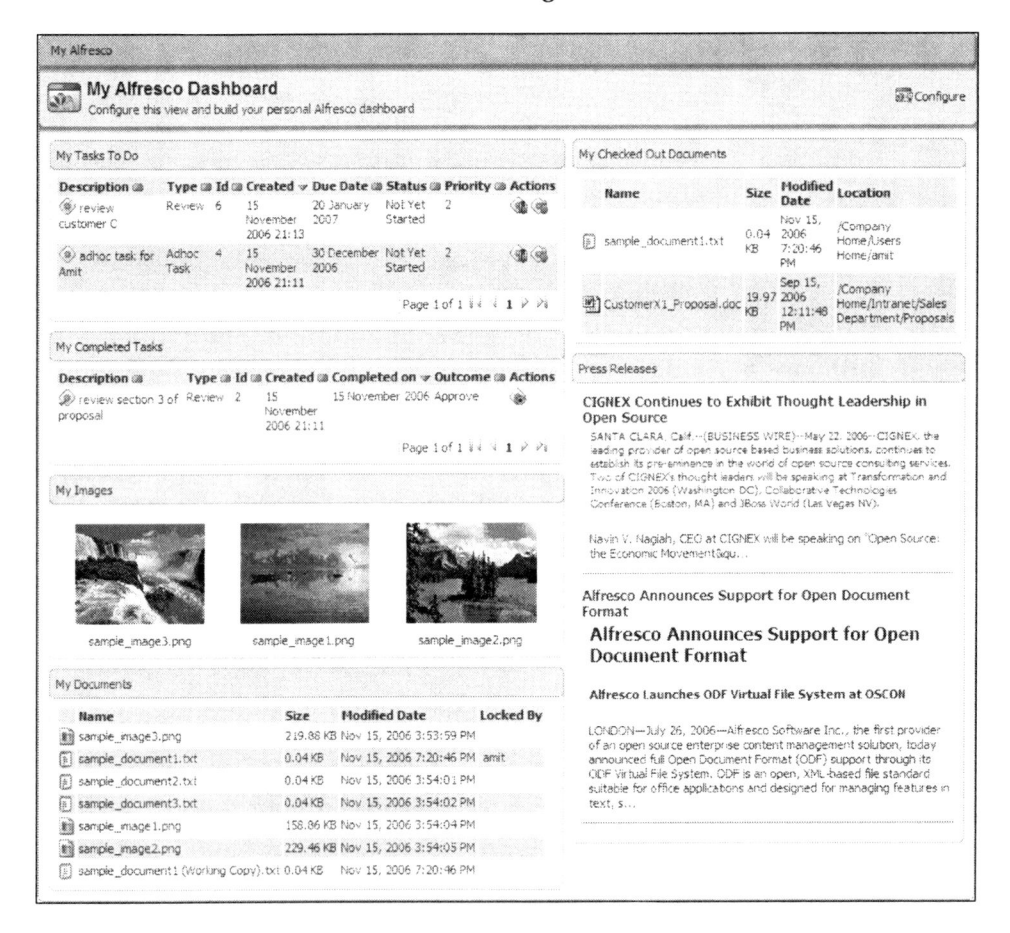

Using webscripts as dashlets

Alfresco provides a webscript feature as an easy way to interface other applications with the repository. In the previous section we saw how to customise a dashlet by using FreeMarker templates. Using the example that is given below, we will use webscript as a dashlet.

The following steps are required to configure a dashlet as webscripts:

1. Create a custom dashlet JSP.
2. Configure a custom dashlet JSP.
3. Configure custom **My Spaces** dashlet in Alfresco Explorer.

Create a custom dashlet JSP

Create a new JSP page named `Chapter11-myspaces-webscript.jsp`, containing the following code. Place the file in the `dashlets` folder. For a Tomcat installation, the folder is: `<install_folder>\tomcat\webapps\alfresco\jsp\dashboards\dashlets`.

```
<%--
Purpose    : Dashlet to display the summary information of Home
Space
Created by: Amita Bhandari
Created on: November 27, 2008
--%>
<%@ taglib uri="/WEB-INF/repo.tld" prefix="r" %>
http://localhost:8080/alfresco/service/ui/myspaces?f=0
<r:webScript scriptUrl="/wcs/ui/myspaces?f=0" />
```

Here `<r:webscript>` is a built-in tag. In order to call webscript, put the webscript URL in the `scriptUrl` attribute of this tag. We have used an out of the box webscript, which is provided by the **My Spaces** webscript URL in the code above.

Configure the custom dashlet JSP

Add the following code to the `web-client-config-custom.xml` file, before the last xml tag, which is `</alfresco-config>`:

```
<config evaluator="string-compare" condition="Dashboards">
    <!-- Dashboard layouts and available dashlets for the My Alfresco
Pages -->
      <dashboards>
          <dashlets>
            <!-- Add additional dashlet for press releases -->
              <dashlet id="MySpaces" label="MySpaces"
                                           description="Webscript
Dashlet for My Spaces"
                  jsp="/jsp/dashboards/dashlets/Chpater11-myspaces-
webscript.jsp"
     allow-narrow="true" />
          </dashlets>
      </dashboards>
</config>
```

Configure the My Spaces dashlet

Configure the newly-created **My Spaces** custom webscript dashlet in the dashboard the same way, as we configured the JSP custom dashlet in the **My Alfresco** dashboard, as shown in the following screenshot:

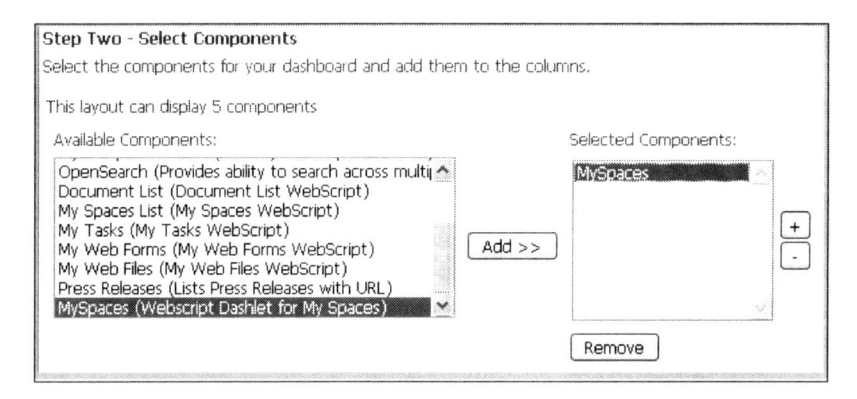

Custom dashlet

Once you configure the dashlet, you can see your webscript dashlet, as shown in the following screenshot:

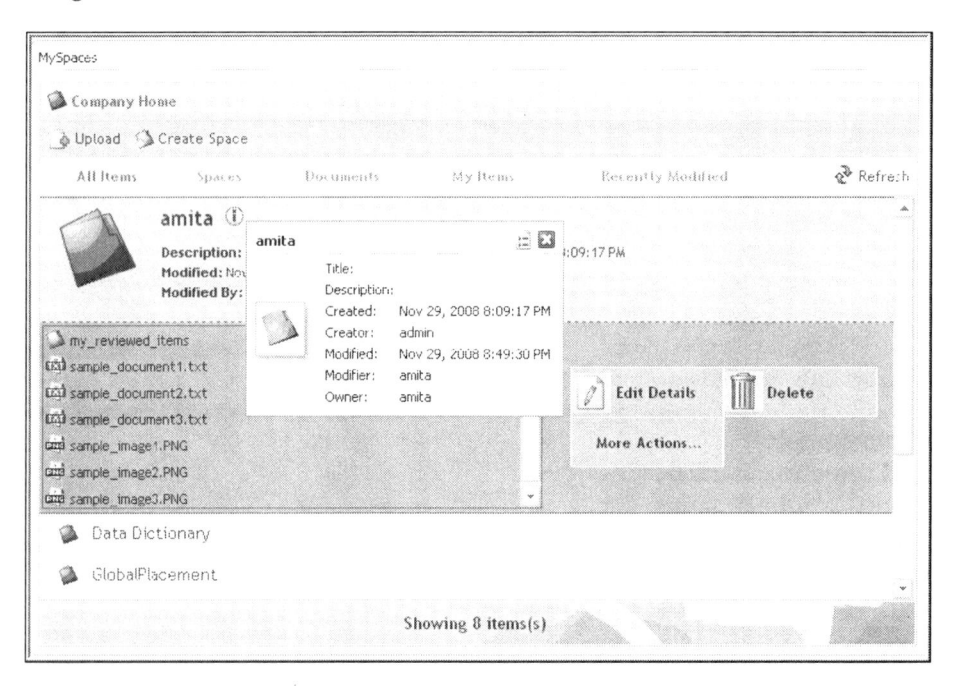

Using a FreeMarker dashlet from the repository

Dashlet components can contain any selection of JSF components, including the template component. This means that it is possible to use the results of a FreeMarker template as the dashlet contents. In the example above, you have used the FreeMarker template from the file system.

However, you can also use the FreeMarker template from your Alfresco Explorer's **Company Home > Data Dictionary > Presentation Templates** space.

To display a template that is stored in the repository, copy the `NodeRef` of the template file and create the page as follows, pasting your `NodeRef` value into the template attribute in the following example:

```
<%@ taglib uri="/WEB-INF/repo.tld" prefix="r" %>
<r:template template="workspace://SpacesStore/
                    e4d1c727-e98b-11da-821a-936824f635fe" />
```

Presentation templates

The space **Company Home > Data Dictionary > Presentation Templates** contains both, built-in and custom presentation templates. A presentation template can be used to preview the content and to provide the look and feel of the content. An example of a presentation template is provided in Chapter 7, where a custom template is used to preview the **Press Release** content. Presentation templates are written in the FreeMarker template language and will have an .ftl extension.

FreeMarker is an open-source template engine. It is a generic tool for generating text output (which can be anything from HTML to auto-generated source code) based on templates. FreeMarker is designed to be practical for the generation of HTML web pages, by following the **MVC (Model View Controller)** pattern. The idea behind using the MVC pattern for dynamic web pages is that you separate the content authors from the programmers. This separation is useful, even for projects where the programmer and the HMTL page author are the same person, as it helps to keep the application clear and easier to maintain.

Customizing the User Interface

In the diagram below, the content authors create document content in Alfresco. The programmers create the presentation template file with stylesheets, HTML code, and take care of the look and feel. The final content will be generated by the FreeMarker engine (which is embedded in Alfresco), by applying the presentation template to the document content, as shown in the diagram.

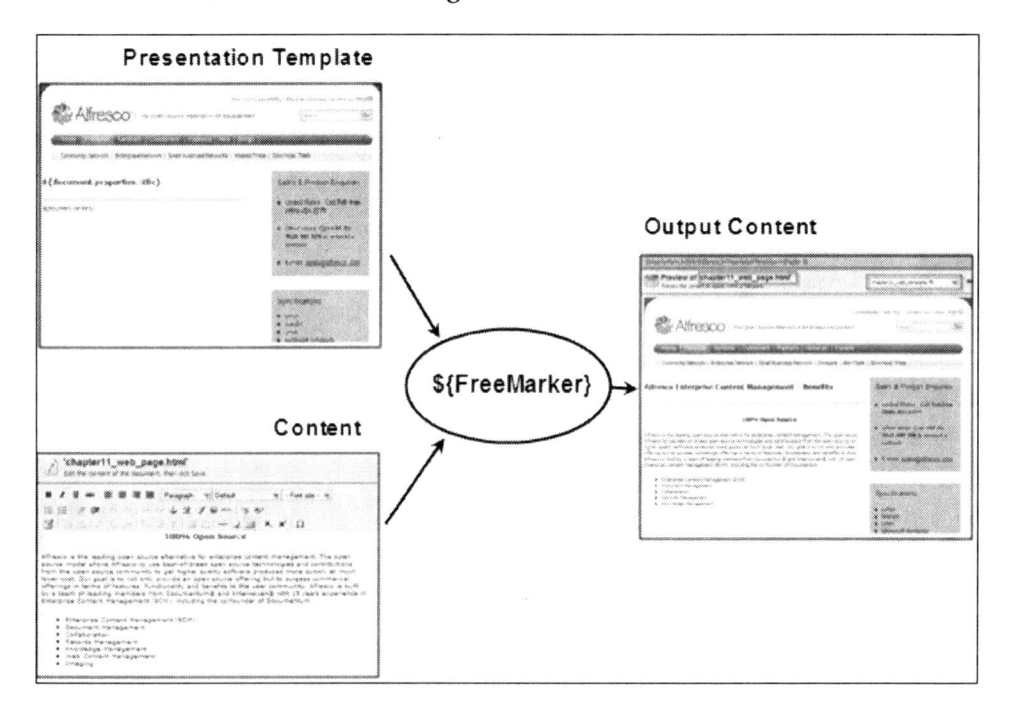

The FreeMarker template engine within Alfresco

The FreeMarker template engine is embedded within Alfresco. FreeMarker takes the Alfresco data model as input and generates text (HTML or XML) as output. FreeMarker also supports XSLT to translate XML content.

The Alfresco objects available to FreeMarker

The default model provides a set of named objects that wrap Alfresco node objects, to provide a rich, object-oriented layer that is suitable for scripting usage. If you are accessing the templates through the web-client UI, then the following named objects are provided by default.

Named object	Description
`companyhome`	The Company Home template node
`userhome`	The current user's Home Space template node
`person`	A node representing the current user's Person object
`space`	The current space template node (if you are accessing the templates through the Space Preview action)
`document`	The current document's template node (if you are accessing the templates through the Document Preview action)
`template`	The node representing the template itself
`args`	A map of any URL parameters passed via the Template Content Servlet (only available if the template was executed via the servlet)
`session`	Session-related information (`session.ticket` for the authentication ticket)
`classification`	Read access to classifications and `root` categories

For example, consider the following FreeMarker template.

```
<html>
  <head>
    <title>Welcome!</title>
  </head>
  <body>
    <h1>Welcome ${person.properties.userName}!</h1>
  </body>
</html>
```

At run-time, the value of the variable `person.properties.userName` will be the name of the current user who is accessing the system. Therefore, the template generates a dynamic greeting message.

> The Alfresco Wiki we bsite (http://wiki.alfresco.com) contains a complete reference to the FreeMarker template.

FreeMarker template node model API

These objects, and any child node objects of them, are called **template node objects**. These template node objects provide the following API:

Node method	Description
`properties`	A map of the properties of the node. For example userhome, properties, name. Properties may return several different types of objects. This depends entirely on the underlying property type in the repository. If the property is multi-valued, then the result will be a sequence, which can be indexed as for any other sequence or array.
`children`	A sequence (list) of the child nodes. For example, a list of the documents in a space.
`url`	The URL of the content stream of this node.
`content`	Returns the content of the node as a string.
`size`	The size, in bytes, of content attached to this node.
`isLocked`	True if the node is locked, false otherwise.
`name`	Shortcut access to the name property.
`parent`	The parent node, it can be null if this is the root node.
`childrenByXPath`	Returns a map capable of executing an XPath query in order to find child nodes, for example, `companyhome.childrenByXPath["*[@cm:name='Data Dictionary']/*"]`
`childByNamePath`	Returns a map capable of returning a single child node found by the name path, for example, `companyhome.childByNamePath["Data Dictionary/Content Templates"]`

FreeMarker directives

As with any other programming language, FreeMarker template language also supports fundamental directives, such as the following ones:

```
#if, #else, #elseif
#switch, #case
#list
#assign
#function
#include
<#-- comment -->
```

Chapter 11

> For your reference, a complete guide to Freemarker directives is available at: http://FreeMarker.sourceforge.net/docs/

Custom template to preview web pages

Let us develop a custom template to preview HTML documents.

Log in as the *admin*, go to the **Company Home | Data Dictionary | Presentation Templates** space, and create a new template and name it appropriately (say, chapter11_web_template.ftl). The template should display the web-page layout, as shown in the screenshot below. The template can be applied to any text or HTML document in the Alfresco repository, in order to generate a web page with layout, as shown in the following screenshot:

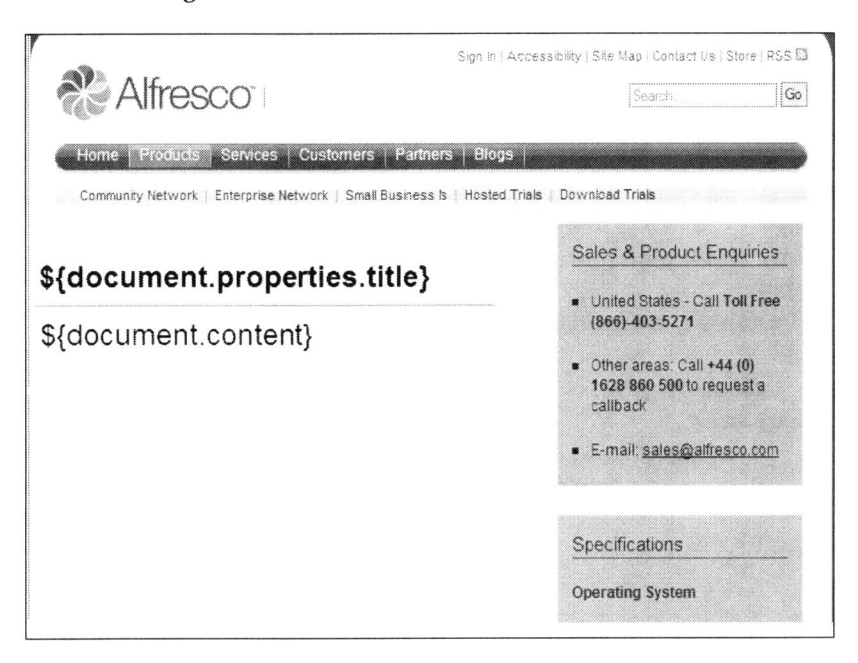

You can consider using the following code to create a custom template. The code uses the images in the Alfresco repository to display the horizontal bar at the top and the vertical bar on the righthand side. Note that the image URLs may change in the code, based on the location of the actual images in your repository. You can use your own images or you can even create the HTML header and table structure in your application.

[461]

Customizing the User Interface

The template extracts the document titles and displays them as page headings. Refer to the FreeMarker template code `${document.properties.title}`. Similarly, the template extracts the document content and displays it in center portion of the page, as shown in the screenshot below the code. Refer to the FreeMarker template code `${document.content}`.

```
<#--------------------------------------------------------------->
<#-- Extracts Title and Description from Content and           -->
<#--                 shows in web template                     -->
<#--------------------------------------------------------------->
<table width="100%" border="0" cellspacing="0" cellpadding="0">
  <tr>
    <td colspan="2" valign="top">
      <img src=
"http://localhost:8080/alfresco/download/direct/workspace/SpacesStore
                          /bfcc8130-4537-11db-972a953696db55bc/
                          chapter11_template_top_image.png" />
    </td>
  </tr>
  <tr>
    <td valign="top">
      <BR>
      <H4> ${document.properties.title} </H4>
      <HR>
      ${document.content}
    </td>
    <td valign="top">
      <img src=
          "http://localhost:8080/alfresco/download/direct/workspace/
                SpacesStore/c87378c9-4537-11db-972a-953696db55bc/
                          chapter11_template_right_image.png" />
    </td>
  </tr>
</table>
```

Create a new HTML document in one of the spaces in your Alfresco Explorer. Use the **Preview in Template** action button to preview the document. Choose the custom template (in this example it is `chapter11_web_template.ftl`) to display the document content. The sample preview screen is shown in the following screenshot:

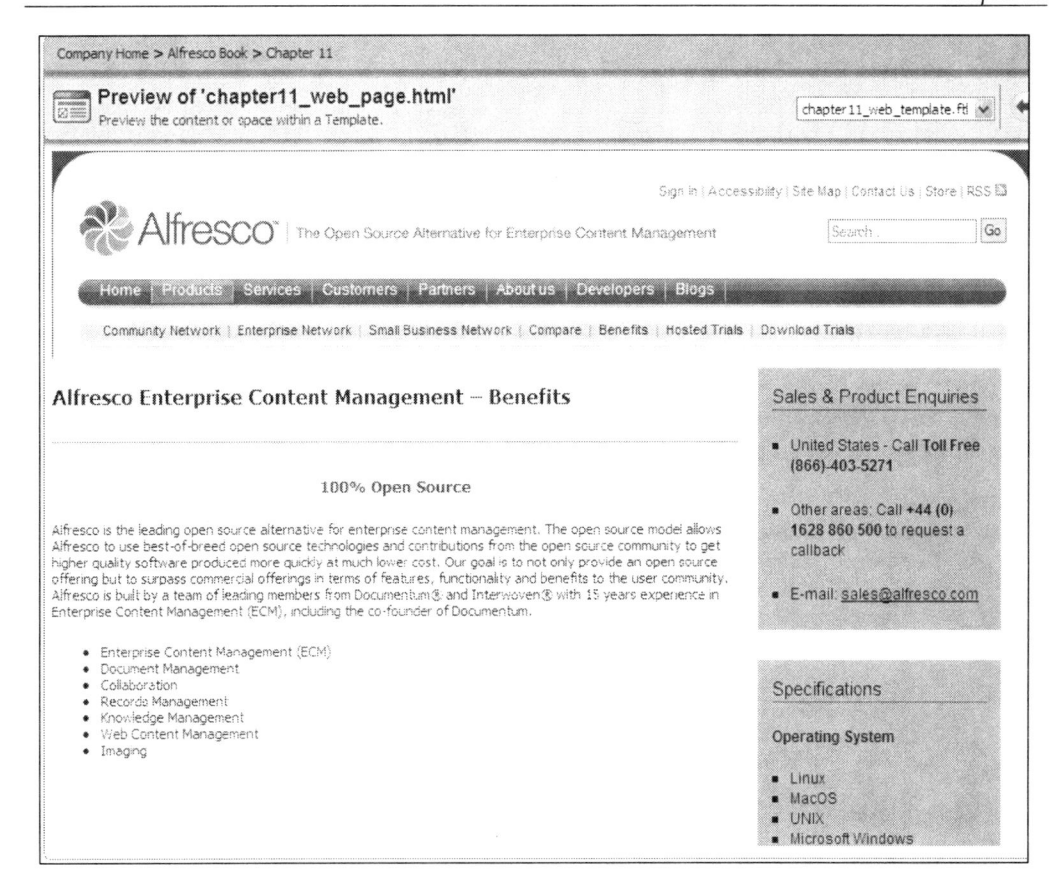

Custom template for XML content

The FreeMarker template engine can be used for XSLT (XML transformations) to transform XML content to HTML, with an appropriate look and feel.

This is a classic solution for storing the data in the Alfresco's repository in native XML format and using FreeMarker custom templates to display the XML data in HTML format.

To test the XML transformation features, you will first need to create an XML document in Alfresco. You can either create this as an XML file (say, `book.xml`) on your desktop and upload it to the Alfresco web client, or you can directly create this XML document in Alfresco. Create a document called `mybook.xml` in one of your **Company Home | Intranet** spaces, with the following content:

```
<?xml version="1.0" standalone="yes"?>
<book title="Book Title">
  <chapter>
```

```
        <title>Chapter 1</title>
        <para>p1.1</para>
        <para>p1.2</para>
        <para>p1.3</para>
    </chapter>
    <chapter>
        <title>Chapter 2</title>
        <para>p2.1</para>
        <para>p2.2</para>
    </chapter>
</book>
```

Create a template in the **Company Home | Data Dictionary | Presentation Templates** space called `xmlbook.ftl`, containing the following code:

```
<#if document.mimetype = "text/xml">
    <#assign dom=document.xmlNodeModel>
        <h1>${dom.book.@title}</h1>
    <#list dom.book.chapter as c>
        <h2>${c.title}</2>
        <#list c.para as p>
            <p> ${p} </p>
        </#list>
    </#list>      </#assign>
</#if>
```

The template displays the title of the book and chapters using HTML tags. When you apply the `xmlbook.ftl` template to the `book.xml` document, you will see output is similar to that shown in the screenshot below:

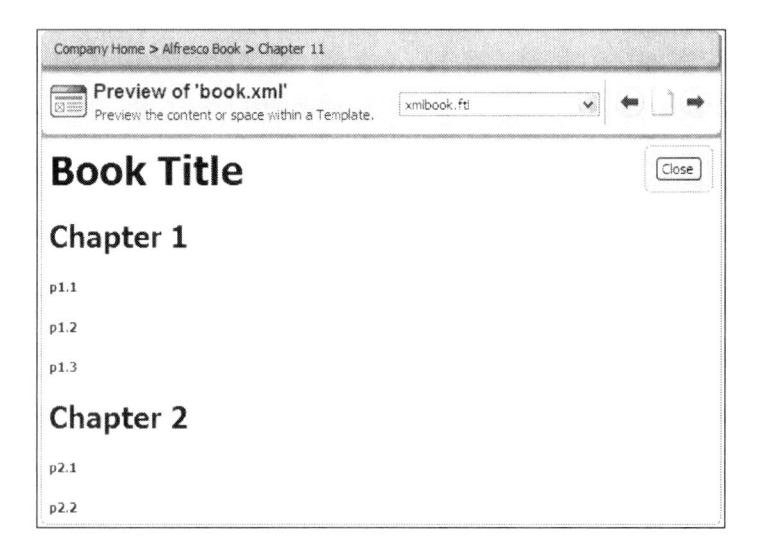

Custom templates for custom space view

Custom space view is a portal window, which shows up on the top of each space when a **Custom View** is selected. If you are implementing Alfresco for various departments and groups, then you might consider having custom home pages for each department or group space.

As an example, let us build a **Custom View** for all of the department spaces. Let us say each department space contains two files: `home_image.png` and `home_page.html`. Let us apply a presentation template, as a **Custom View** for the department space, which displays these two local files in that department as the department home page.

Create a template in the **Company Home > Data Dictionary > Presentation Templates** space called `chapter11_dept_home_template.ftl`, and containing the following code:

```
<#------------------------------------------------------------------>
<#--      Displays Home Page for each department using      -->
<#-- (1) Home Page Image file home_image.png and            -->
<#-- (2) Home Page HTML file home_page.html                 -->
<#-- By Munwar Shariff, Nov 16, 2006                        -->
<#------------------------------------------------------------------>
<H4> Welcome to ${space.properties.title} </H4>
<#list space.children as child>
  <#if child.properties.name = 'home_image.png'>
    <img src="/alfresco${child.url}">
  </#if>
</#list>
  <#list space.children as child>
    <#if child.properties.name = 'home_page.html'>
      ${child.content}
    </#if>
</#list>
```

Next, create a sample space (say **Department A**). Within that space, create two content files, with names `home_image.png` (the department image) and `home_page.html` (the department description). Next select **chapter11_dept_home_template.ftl** template as a **Custom View** for your space (the **Department A** space).

The steps to apply a presentation template as a **Custom View** are explained in the *Applying Custom View on a space* section of this chapter. You will notice that the **Custom View** of your space is as shown in the screenshot on the next page.

This can be applied to each and every department and group within your organization. Consider having the department space as the space template, so that you can reuse the department space template to create spaces for many departments. More information about space templates is provided in Chapter 5.

Department members can update the image file and the HTML file, as required, to alter the home page information dynamically. Similarly, you can use the various presentation templates to display the information in a specific space.

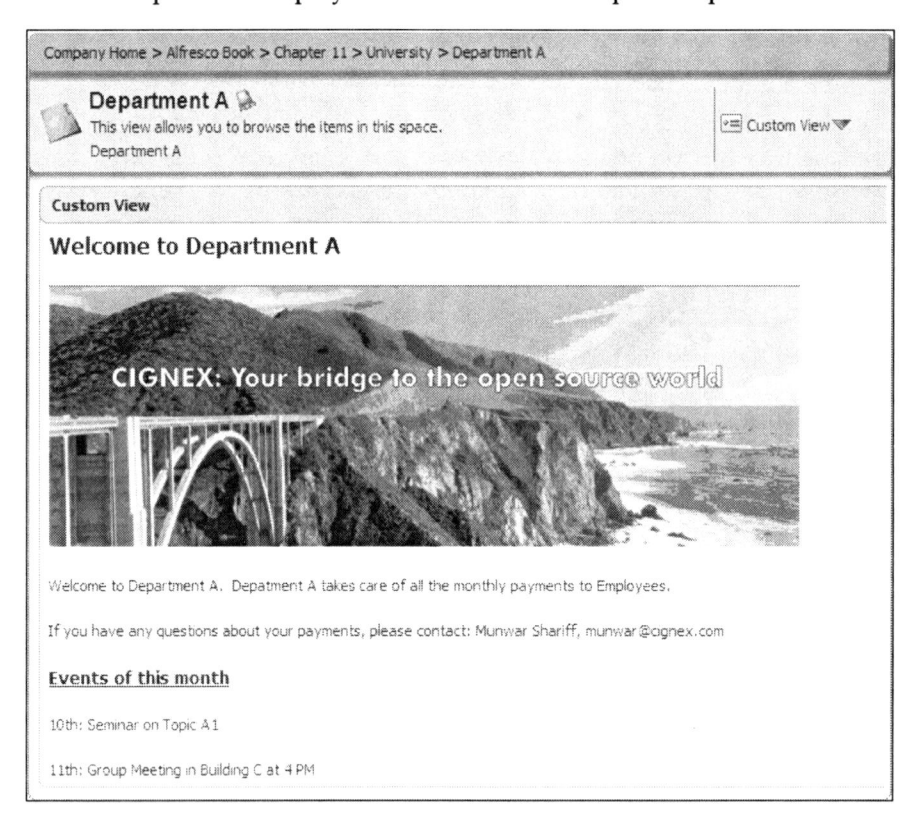

Customizing Alfresco Share

You can configure the look and feel of the Alfresco Share simply by editing the XML configuration files, FTL files, CSS files, and JavaScript files. You can change the way that Alfresco Share dashboards look and operate. You can customize the set of page components for the site. You can add new dashlets to the application. For this we will customize the Alfresco Book site, which we configured in chapter 10.

Presentation templates

An introduction to Presentation templates was provided in the previous section. For Alfresco Share, templates are stored in the following location:

```
<install_folder>\tomcat\shared\classes\alfresco\web-extension\
templates
```

The `alfresco-template.ftl` file can be considered as the base template. This is placed within the following location:

```
<install_folder>\tomcat\shared\classes\alfresco\web-extension\
templates
\org\alfresco\import\alfresco-template.ftl
```

As an example, consider the following FreeMarker template:

```
<#import "import/alfresco-template.ftl" as template />

<@template.header>
  <script type="text/javascript"
    src="${url.context}/templates/welcome/welcome-view.css"></script>
  <script type="text/javascript"
    src="${url.context}/templates/blog/welcome-view.js"></script>
</@>
<@template.body>
   <div id="hd">
      <@region id="header" scope="global" protected=true />
      <@region id="title" scope="template" protected=true />
      <@region id="navigation" scope="template" protected=true />
      <h1 class="sub-title">${page.title}</h1>
   </div>
   <div id="bd">
      WelCome ${user.properties["firstName"]}
   </div>
</@>
<@template.footer>
   <div id="ft">
      <@region id="footer" scope="global" protected=true />
   </div>
</@>
```

At run-time, the value of the variable `user.properties["firstName"]` will be the name of the current user who is accessing the system. Therefore, the template generates a dynamic greeting message.

Custom template

Let us customize a **Getting Started Dashlet**. As an example, you want to display the information about the Alfresco book in the **Getting Started Dashlet** for the site that you have configured. For this, you have to customize the **Getting Started Dashlet.**

Carry the following steps in order to customize the dashlet:

1. Browse to the folder `<install_folder>\tomcat\shared\classes\alfresco\web-extension\site-webscripts\org\alfresco\components\dashlets`.

2. Open the file `site-welcome.get.properties` and add the following code to the end of the file:

   ```
   header.featureBook=Alfresco Book Tour
   text.featureBook=Take a tour of some of the key features of
   the  Alfresco Enterprise Content Management Implementation
   Book by Munwar Shariff.
   link.featureBook=Visit Alfresco Book
   ```

3. Open the file `site-welcome.get.html` and add the following code before the `<#else>` directive:

   ```
   <div class="detail-list-item last-item">
       <h4>${msg("header.featureBook")}</h4>
       <div>${msg("text.featureBook")}</div>
       <div><a href="http://www.alfrescobook.com/"
   target="_new">${msg("link.featureBook")}</a></div>
   ```

4. Restart Alfresco.
5. Log in to Alfresco Share.
6. Click on the Alfresco site that you have configured.

7. Once you click on the **Alfresco Book Project** link, the application displays the **Site Dashboard** of the site. You will find the customized **Getting Started Dashlet**.

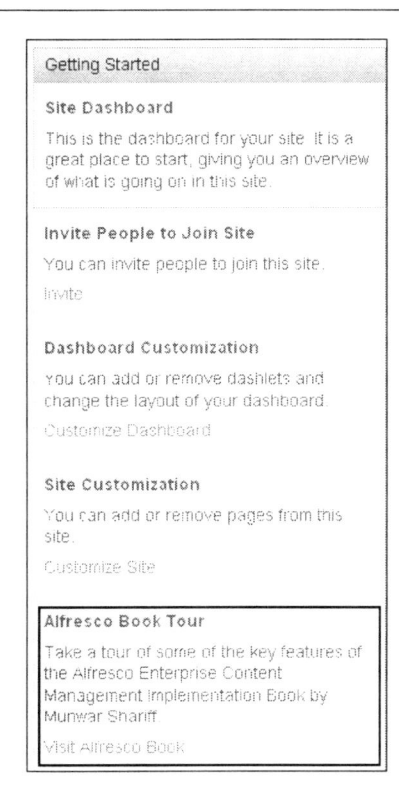

8. Click on the **Visit Alfresco Book** link. It will take you to www.alfrescobook.com. For the **Alfresco Book** dashlet, the configuration of the dashlet is explained in the next section.

> You can download the complete code samples from the Packt web site.

Configure custom webscripts

Web Scripts provide RESTful access to content held in your Alfresco Enterprise Content Repository. This allows you to place controls on your enterprise content to manage it, and at the same time provide uniform access for a wide variety of client applications and services. With Web Scripts, you can build your own RESTful interface by using light-weight scripting technologies such as JavaScript and FreeMarker.

Customizing the User Interface

Alfresco Share accesses the repository through web scripts. As an example, we will configure a webscript that will add a new dashlet to the Book web site, with a title of **Book Published**. Carry the following steps:

1. Navigate to the following folder:

   ```
   <install_folder>\tomcat\shared\classes\alfresco\web-extension\site-webscripts\org\alfresco\components\dashlets.
   ```

2. Create a new file named `alfrescobook.get.desc.xml` and add the following code:

   ```
   <webscript>
      <shortname>Alfresco Book</shortname>
      <description>Alfresco Book Dashlet</description>
      <family>site-dashlet</family>
      <url>/components/dashlets/Alfresco-Book</url>
   </webscript>
   ```

3. Create another file, named `alfrescobook.get.html.ftl`. The code snippet is provided below:

   ```
   <div class="dashlet">
      <div class="title">
      Book Published
      </div>
      <div class="body">
      <div>
            First ever book on Alfresco<br>
         <div style="color: rgb(153, 51, 0);" class="header">
               <table style="width: 100%; text-align: left;" border="1"
            cellpadding="5" cellspacing="0">
               <tbody>
               <tr>
               <td style="background-color: rgb(255, 153, 102);"><span
               style="font-weight: bold;"><a
               href="http://www.packtpub.com/alfresco/book">Book
               Site</a> |    <a
               href="http://alfrescobook.blogspot.com/">Book
               Blog</a>  
                | </span><span style="font-weight: bold;"> 
               </span><span style="font-weight: bold;"></span><span
               style="font-weight: bold;"></span></td>
               </tr>
               </tbody>
               </table>
               <h2>Alfresco Enterprise Content Management
            Implementation</h2>
         </div>
            </div>
      </div>
   ```

Chapter 11

4. Restart Alfresco.
5. Log in to Alfresco Share.
6. Open the URL `http://localhost:8080/share/service/`. Click on the **Browse 'site-dashlet' Web Scripts** option.

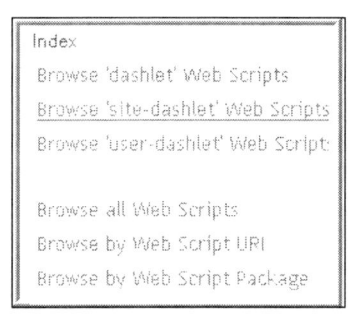

```
Index
Browse 'dashlet' Web Scripts
Browse 'site-dashlet' Web Scripts
Browse 'user-dashlet' Web Script

Browse all Web Scripts
Browse by Web Script URI
Browse by Web Script Package
```

7. You will see the **Alfresco Book** web script. To display the details, click on the hyperlink, as shown in the following screenshot:

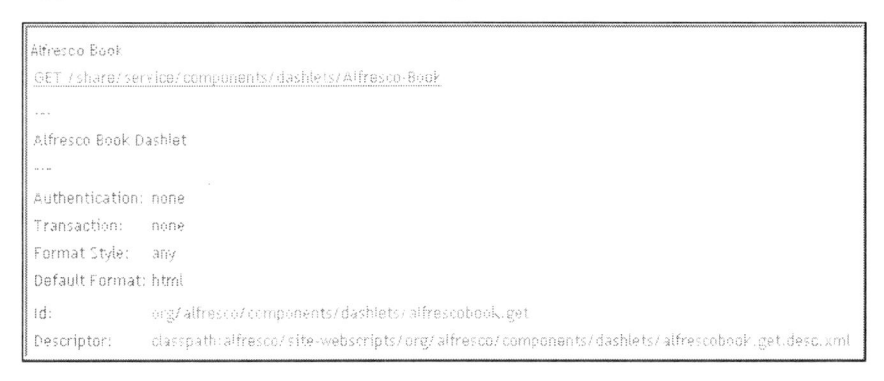

```
Alfresco Book
GET /share/service/components/dashlets/Alfresco-Book
...
Alfresco Book Dashlet
...
Authentication: none
Transaction:    none
Format Style:   any
Default Format: html
Id:             org/alfresco/components/dashlets/alfrescobook.get
Descriptor:     classpath:alfresco/site-webscripts/org/alfresco/components/dashlets/alfrescobook.get.desc.xml
```

> You can download the complete code samples from the Packt web site.

Configure custom dashlets

All of the dashlets provided by Alfresco Share are configured by using webscripts. We just need to provide the family when configuring the webscripts.

Three families are available out of the box:

1. Site-dashlet
2. User-dashlet
3. Dashlet

Customizing the User Interface

In the previous section, we created the webscript that belongs to the site-dashlet family. This dashlet will be displayed in your site under the name **Alfresco Book Project**.

```
<webscript>
    <shortname>Alfresco Book</shortname>
    <description>Alfresco Book Dashlet</description>
    <family>site-dashlet</family>
    <url>/components/dashlets/Alfresco-Book</url>
</webscript>
```

To add the new dashlet that you have created, perform the following steps:

1. Go to the **Customize Dashboard** option in your site dashboard toolbar. Select and add the dashlet.

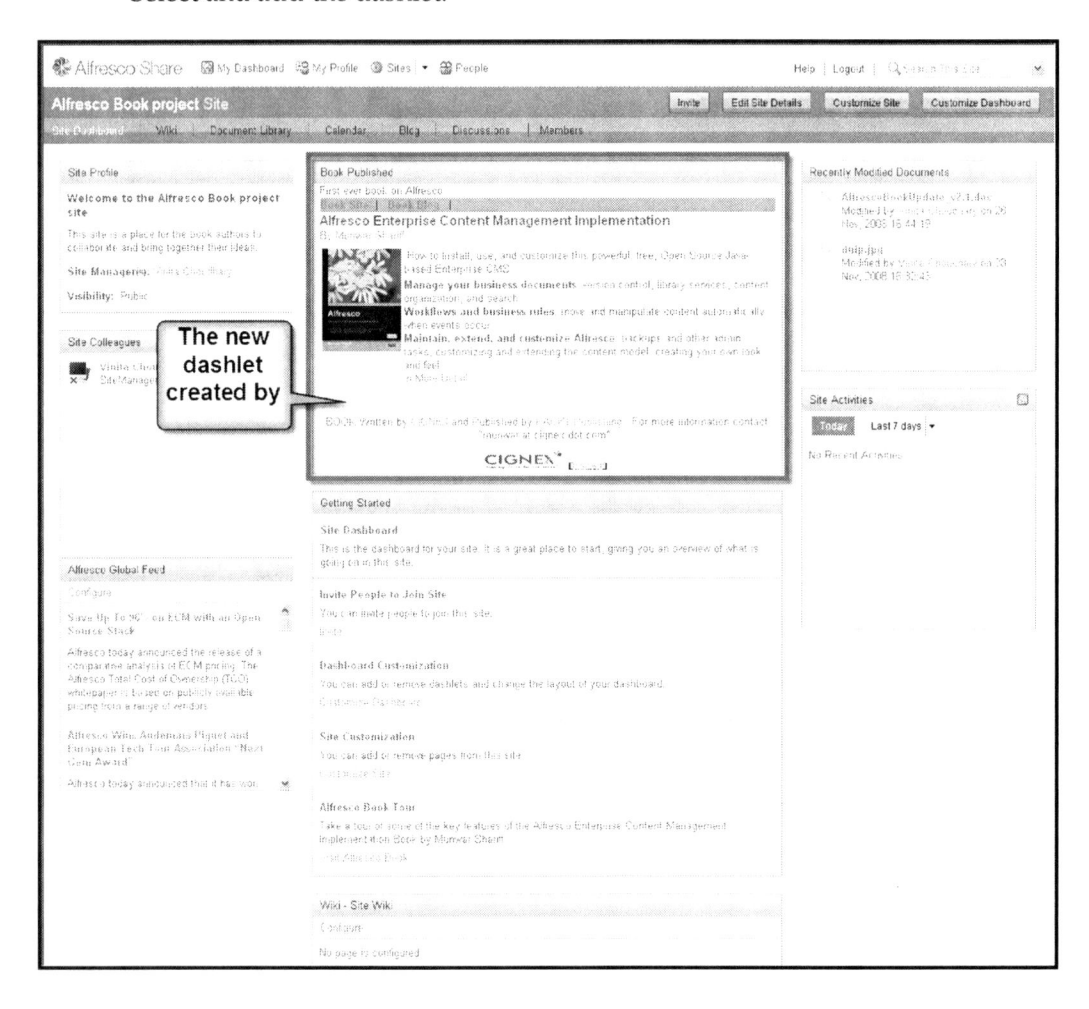

2. If you change the family to **user-dashlet**, it will be displayed as:

   ```
   <webscript>
       <shortname>Alfresco Book</shortname>
       <description>Alfresco Book Dashlet</description>
       <family>user-dashlet</family>
       <url>/components/dashlets/Alfresco-Book</url>
   </webscript>
   ```

3. Restart Alfresco.
4. Log in to Alfresco Share.

To add the new dashlet that you have created, go to the **Customize Dashboard** on your dashboard toolbar and then select and add the dashlet.

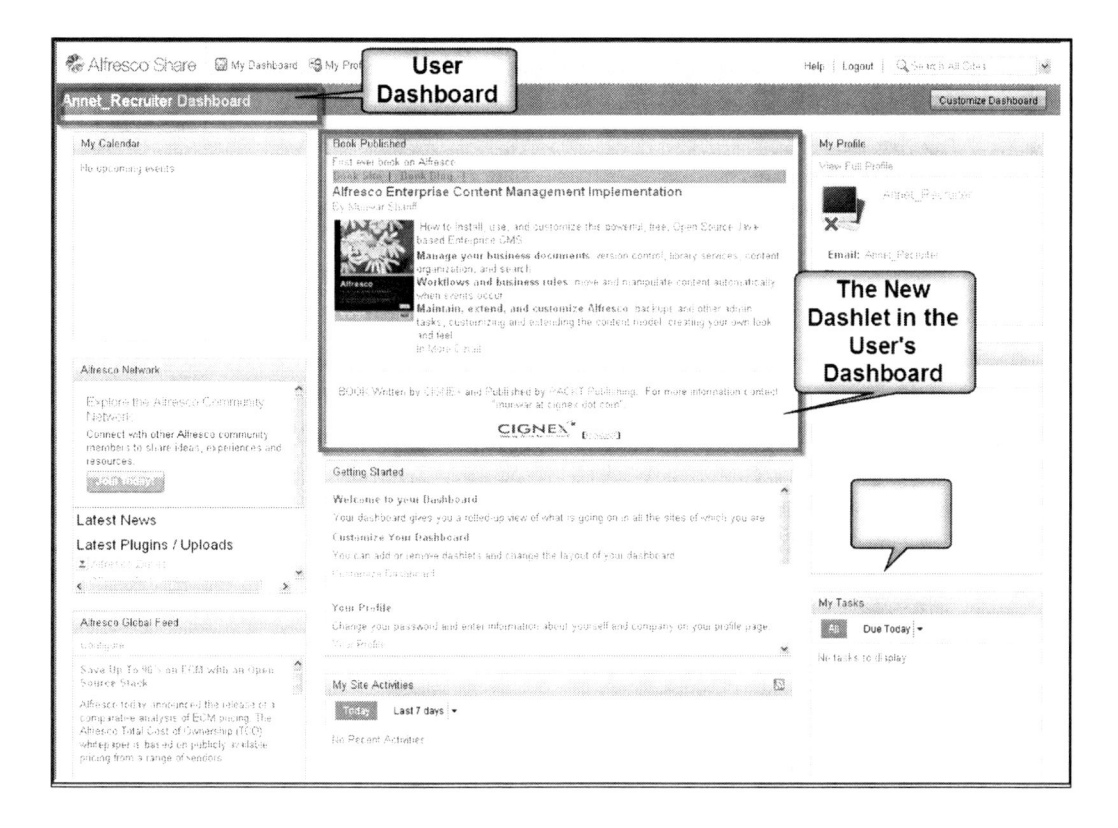

Configure custom components in Alfresco Share

You can add a page component. As an example, we will create one component, the **Alfresco Book** for the **Alfresco Book Project** site. The following screenshot displays a configured page component:

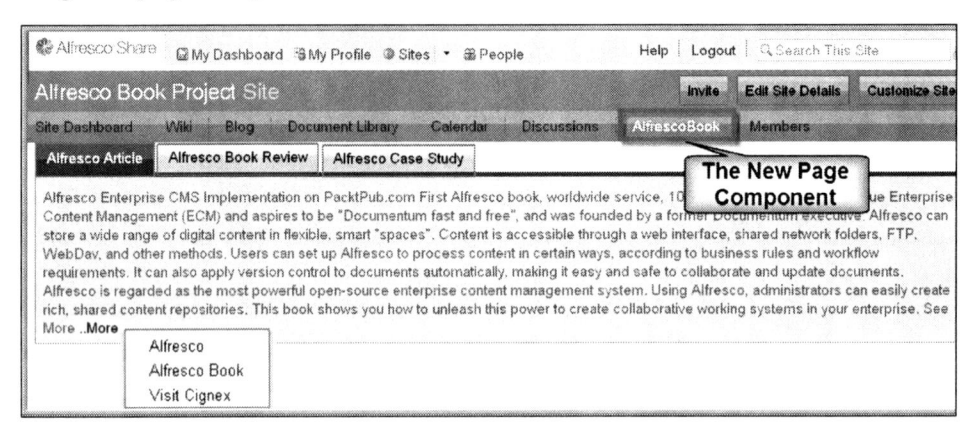

Carry out the following steps to create a new page component, as shown in the preceding screenshot:

1. Navigate to the following folder: `<install_folder>\tomcat\shared\classes\alfresco\web-extension\site-data\components`.

2. Create a new file, named `template.title.alfrescobook`, and add the following code:

   ```
   <?xml version='1.0' encoding='UTF-8'?>
   <component>
       <scope>template</scope>
       <region-id>title</region-id>
       <source-id>alfresco</source-id>
       <url>/components/title/collaboration-title</url>
   </component>
   ```

3. Create a new file, named `template.navigation.alfrescobook`, and add the following code:

   ```
   <?xml version='1.0' encoding='UTF-8'?>
   <component>
       <scope>template</scope>
       <region-id>navigation</region-id>
       <source-id>alfresco</source-id>
       <url>/components/navigation/collaboration-navigation</url>
   </component>
   ```

4. Create a new file, named `template.alfresco.book`, and add the following code:

   ```
   <?xml version='1.0' encoding='UTF-8'?>
   <component>
       <scope>template</scope>
       <region-id>alfresco</region-id>
       <source-id>alfresco</source-id>
       <url>/components/alfresco/book</url>
   </component>
   ```

5. Navigate to the following folder: `<install_folder>\tomcat\shared\classes\alfresco\web-extension\site-data\template-instances`.

6. Create a new file, named `alfrescobook.xml`, and add the following code

   ```
   <?xml version='1.0' encoding='UTF-8'?>
   <template-instance>
       <template-type>org/alfresco/alfrescobook</template-type>
   </template-instance>
   ```

7. Go to the following folder: `<install_folder>\tomcat\shared\classes\alfresco\web-extension\site-data\pages`.

6. Create a new file, named `alfrescobook.xml`, and add the following code:

   ```
   <?xml version='1.0' encoding='UTF-8'?>
   <page>
       <title>AlfrescoBook</title>
       <description>AlfrescoBook</description>
       <template-instance>alfrescobook</template-instance>
       <authentication>user</authentication>
   </page>
   ```

7. Go to the following folder: `<install_folder>\tomcat\webapps\share\WEB-INF\classes\alfresco\templates\org\alfresco\import`.

8. Modify the file named `alfresco-template.ftl`. The code snippet is provided below. Add the following line under the section `<!-- Common YUI components: RELEASE -->`

   ```
   <script type="text/javascript" src="${url.context}/yui/tabview/tabview-min.js"></script>
   ```

9. Go to the following folder: `<install_folder>\tomcat\shared\classes\alfresco\web-extension\templates\org\alfresco\`.

[475]

Customizing the User Interface

10. Create a new file, named `alfrescobook.ftl`. The code snippet is provided below:

    ```
    <#import "import/alfresco-template.ftl" as template />
    <@template.header>
    </@>
    <@template.body>
       <div id="hd">
          <@region id="header" scope="global" protected=true />
          <@region id="title" scope="template" protected=true />
          <@region id="navigation" scope="template" protected=true />
       </div>
    </@>
    <@template.footer>
       <div id="ft">
          <@region id="footer" scope="global" protected=true />
       </div>
    </@>
    ```

11. Navigate to the following folder: `<install_folder>\tomcat\shared\classes\alfresco\web-extension\site-data\presets`.

12. Modify the file `presets.xml` and add the code in the pages tag of the site dashboard section. The pages section should look like the following:

    ```
    <pages>
        <page id="site/${siteid}/dashboard">
          <title>Collaboration Site Dashboard</title>
          <description>Collaboration site's dashboard page</description>
           <template-instance>dashboard-3-columns</template-instance>
           <authentication>user</authentication>
           <properties>
    <sitePages>[{"pageId":"wiki-page"}, {"pageId":"blog-postlist"},
    {"pageId":"documentlibrary"}, {"pageId":"calendar"},
    {"pageId":"discussions-topiclist"},{"pageId":"alfrescobook"}
    ]</sitePages>
                </properties>
             </page>
        </pages>
    ```

13. This entry is optional. If you want to see the component in the new site, that you will be configuring after adding this code, then the component will be displayed without configuring the **Customize Site**.

14. Navigate to the following folder: `<install_folder>\tomcat\shared\classes\alfresco\web-extension`.

15. Create the file `web-framework-config-custom.xml`. Modify the file to include the following code:

```
<alfresco-config>
    <config evaluator="string-compare" condition="SitePages"
    replace="true">
       <pages>
          <page id="calendar">calendar</page>
          <page id="wiki-page">wiki-page?title=Main_Page</page>
          <page id="documentlibrary">documentlibrary</page>
          <page id="discussions-topiclist">discussions-
                    topiclist</page>
          <page id="blog-postlist">blog-postlist</page>
             <page id="alfrescobook">AlfrescoBook</page>
       </pages>
    </config>
</alfresco-config>
```

16. Restart the Alfresco Server.
17. Log in to Alfresco Share.
18. Open the Alfresco project site. You will find a new component has been added, as shown in the screenshot above. If you are not able to see this, then go to the Customize Site and select add pages. The component will be there.

> You can download the complete code samples from the Packt web site.

Rich user interface using Flex

You can customize the user interface by using *Adobe Flex 3, RIA clients*. Flex is a highly-productive, free, open-source framework for building and maintaining expressive web applications that deploy consistently on all of the major browsers, desktops, and operating systems. **FlexSpaces** is a RIA client for Alfresco that runs in browsers (Firefox, IE, Safari, Chrome, etc.) with a Flash player. FlexSpaces was developed with Adobe Flex 3 and ActionScript 3 on the client side. This makes it easy for the designers and developers to work together. To learn more about FlexSpaces, visit the following web site: `http://forge.alfresco.com/projects/flexspaces/`.

Alfresco Share 3.0 Integration support

The following are the two features of Alfresco Share 3.0:

- Five site page components that run FlexSpaces views inside Share, running in a browser
- An additional tab running Share in FlexSpaces

Customizing the User Interface

The **Alfresco Book Project Site** will look similar to the following screenshot:

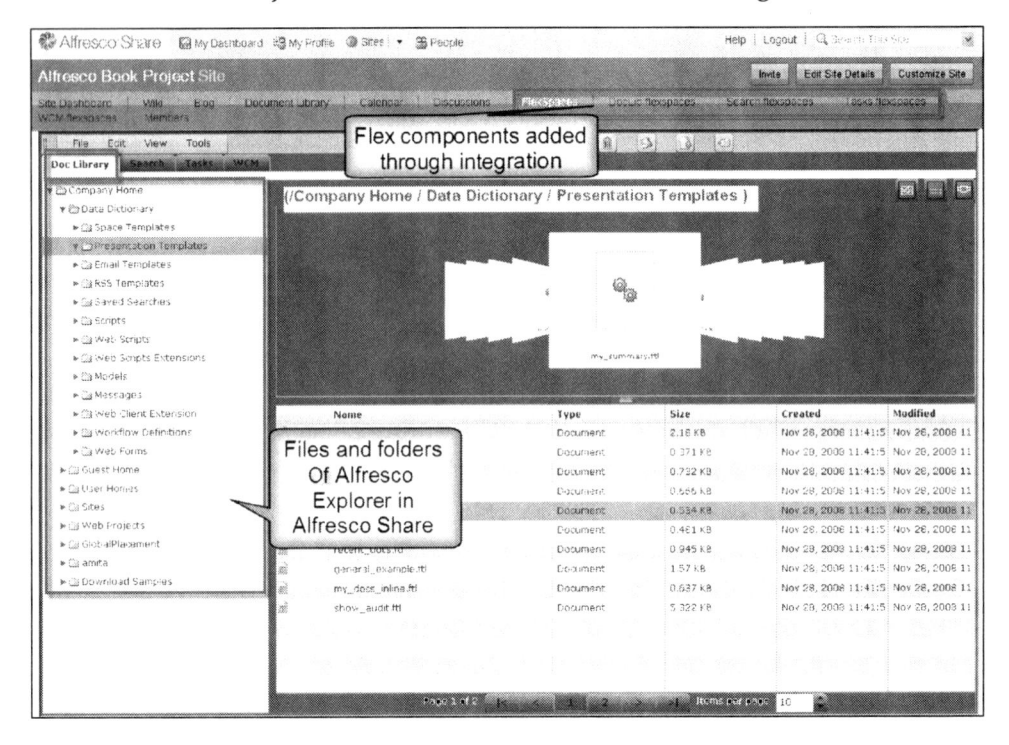

The **Alfresco Book Project Site** has a **Search** option, which helps us to search for the file that we are looking for. We just need to enter the name of file that we are looking for, in the **Search Query** box, and then click on the **Advanced** button, as shown in the following screenshot:

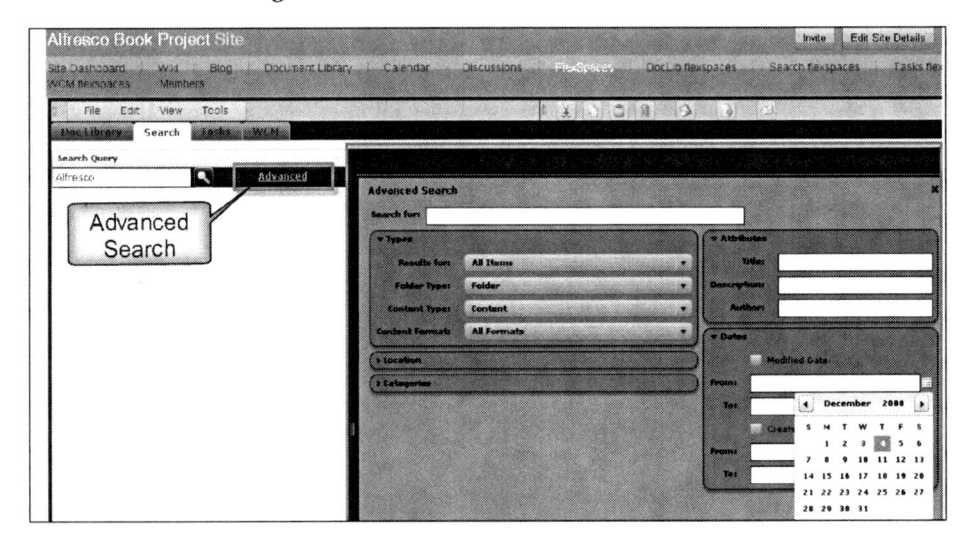

Customizing JSP Client

You can develop a custom user interface by using JSPs and Alfresco Foundation APIs. Let's go ahead and learn more about this.

Alfresco foundation APIs:

The following are the Alfresco foundation APIs:

- NodeService
- SearchService
- DictionaryService
- ContentService
- FileFolderService

Suppose there is an existing portal for a travel agency named **Fun Travels Ltd**. This portal is developed on another platform. The agency has various **Galleries**, **Articles**, **Guidelines**, **Forms**, etc. They want to store, this content on, and fetch this content from, the Alfresco repository.

In order to implement this, you have to customize the user interface of this portal in such a way that when you click on any of their existing links, such as **Galleries**, **Articles**, **Guidelines**, and so on, the screen should appear so that we can enter some useful data. On the basis of this information, you have to fetch content from, or add content into, the Alfresco repository.

The JSP's will have their own UI to deal with Alfresco, and these JSPs will be called on each link, asking for the data to be entered. On submission, Alfresco beans will be called, which will fetch the content and send it to the portal.

The following are the code snippets provided:

1. Define a managed bean that contains the properties of the UI elements and properties for the Alfresco services.

    Custom UI Properties:

    ```
    Public class ArticleBean
    {
     private String contentTitle = null;
     public String getContentTitle()
     {
            return contentTitle;
     }
        public void setContentTitle(String contentTitle)
        {
    ```

Customizing the User Interface

```
            this.contentTitle = contentTitle;
        }
```

//Alfresco Service properties:

```
Private SearchService searchService = null;
    /**
    *    @return the searchService
    */
    public SearchService getSearchService()
    {
        return searchService;
    }
    /**
    * @param searchService the searchService to set
    */
    public void setSearchService(SearchService searchService)
    {
        this.searchService = searchService;
    }
Public void addContent()
{

}
```

2. Add the following code to the `faces-config-custom.xml` file. For a Tomcat installation, this file is in the following folder: `<alfresco_install_folder>\tomcat\webapps\alfresco\WEB-INF`.

```xml
        <managed-bean>
    <managed-bean-name> ArticleBean</managed-bean-name>
<managed-bean-class>
 com.alfresco.bean.ArticleBean
</managed- bean-class>
            <managed-bean-scope>session</managed-bean-scope>
            <managed-property>
              <property-name>searchService</property-name>
              <value>#{SearchService}</value>
            </managed-property>
        </managed-bean>
```

3. Add the following code to a new file named `faces-config-navigation-custom.xml` file. For a Tomcat installation, create the file in the following folder: `<alfresco_install_folder>\tomcat\webapps\alfresco\WEB-INF`

```
<navigation-rule>
<from-view-id>/jsp/extension/displayAllTravels.jsp</from-view-id>
    <navigation-case>
        <from-outcome>addContent</from-outcome>
<to-view-id>/jsp/extension/addContent.jsp</to-view-id>
    </navigation-case>
</navigation-rule>
```

4. Write various JSP pages. These JSPs will access the bean properties for setting elements and for displaying content.

```
<h:inputText ="#{articleBean.contentTitle}" />
<h:outputText ="#{articleBean.contentTitle}" />
<h:commandButton action="#{articleBean.getContent" value
   ="ADD"/>
```

5. Attach the JSP to the links provided on the portal. Click on each link, and a custom JSP Page will be called, as shown in the following screenshot:

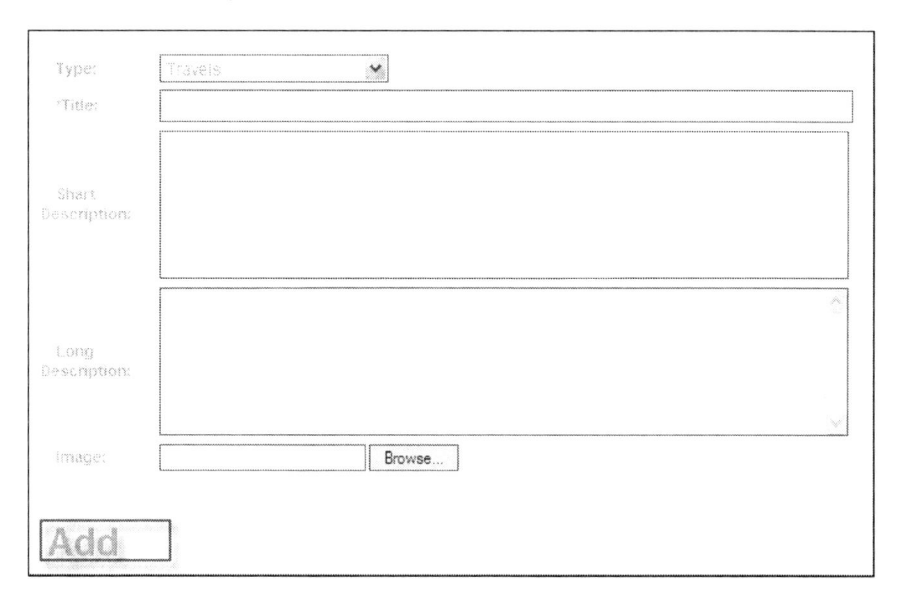

Customizing the User Interface

6. The following screenshot shows the Alfresco custom JSP integrated with the external application:

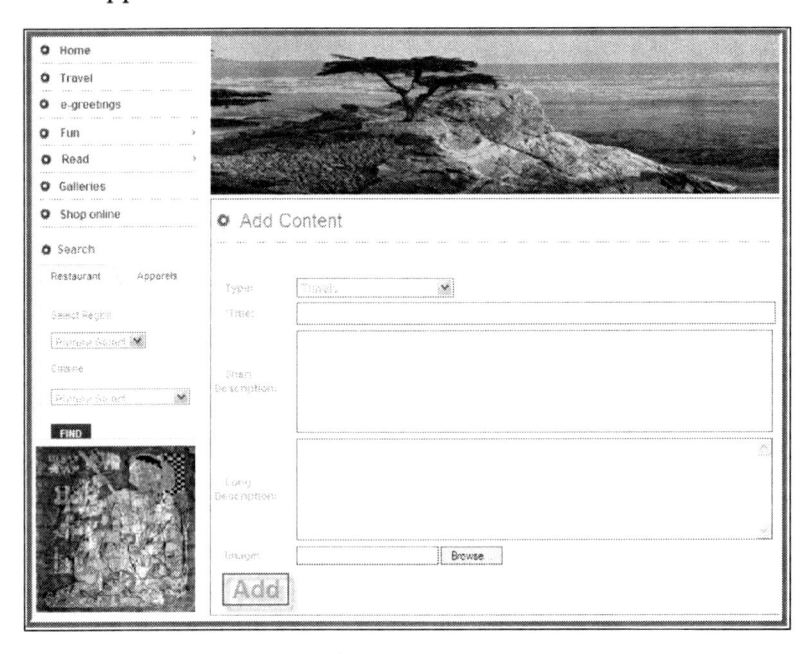

7. When the **Add** button is clicked, the content is fetched from the Alfresco repository and is displayed in the portal, as shown in the following screenshot:

Various user interface options

Alfresco can be integrated with various other external systems. It can be integrated with Flash, Liferay, Drupal, iPhone, Facebook, iGoogle, Outlook, Adobe, Quark, FFMPEG, and ViewOnePro. For more details about configuring external systems, refer to Chapter 9.

Summary

The Alfresco Explorer user interface can be customized to display your personal dashboard information, such as the pending tasks, checked out documents, and a list of press releases. Presentation templates can be applied to spaces, as well as to content. By using a **Custom View** on a space, you can gather all of the important information into one place.

You can store content in the Alfresco repository in native XML format and use FreeMarker custom templates to display the XML data in various formats, such as PDF and HTML. You have the option of separating the actual content and the display information so that you can leverage the ability to have multiple views of the same content.

The Alfresco Share user interface can be customized to display your dashlets. The page components can be added to the site and the presentation templates can be applied. Integration with Flex, and the ability to include and modify components on the site, allows a rich user interface experience.

12
Search

The success of Content Management Systems depends on their ability to locate the required content with the least amount of clicks. The way you choose the content name, the way you categorize the content, the location where you place the content, and the meta-data property values that you provide will all help you to locate the content more easily. You will realize the benefits of having a powerful search engine when you have a large number of files in your Content Management System. In this chapter, you will examine the advanced search features of Alfresco, and extend the capabilities of search.

By the end of this chapter, you will have learned how to:

- Use the advanced search form
- Extend search capabilities
- Define and save search criteria as reusable reports
- Use Alfresco's OpenSearch features
- Configure Alfresco as a federated search client across multiple external repositories and search engines
- Configure Alfresco's search engine

Overview

Unlike many commercial Content Management Systems, Alfresco includes a free and very powerful search engine called **Lucene** as part of its installation. Therefore, you don't have to buy and install a third-party search engine. Moreover, you don't have to deal with integration issues and upgrades.

Search

By using Alfresco, you will be able to search both content and properties. You can perform a full-text search on any word in the content, regardless of the format. You can search for content in a particular space. You can also search for content belonging to certain categories or of a specific type. You can search for content created or modified between certain dates, created by a specific person, and so on. You can extend the search capabilities to search for custom content types and custom property values.

By default, all content in Alfresco is full-text searchable. Any content that has been uploaded to Alfresco, such as the following types, will be internally converted to text, indexed and made searchable:

- Microsoft Office documents, MS Word, Excel, PowerPoint
- Open Office documents
- XML/HTML
- PDF
- Emails
- Content in foreign languages

Search using Alfresco Explorer

Alfresco Explorer provides a web-based user interface for searching and locating content. When you log in (to http://<servername>:<port>/alfresco), you will notice a search box in the upper-right corner.

Simple search

Performing a search in Alfresco is easy. Simply type one or more search terms (the words that best describe the information that you want to find) into the search box, and press the *Enter* key or click on the search icon as shown in the following screenshot:

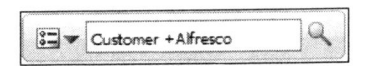

You can use Google-style query syntax to search the content stored in the Alfresco repository. The following table provides several examples of search syntax with description, along with an explanation of them:

Search String	Description
Customer	Returns all of the documents that contain the text 'Customer' (as file name or file content)
- Customer	Returns all of the documents that do not contain the text 'Customer'
Customer Alfresco	Returns all of the documents that contain the text 'Customer' or 'Alfresco'. This is equivalent to Customer +Alfresco
Customer + Alfresco	Returns all of the documents that contain the text 'Customer' or 'Alfresco'
Customer - Alfresco	Returns all of the documents that contain the text 'Customer' and do not contain the text 'Alfresco'
inter	Returns all of the documents that contain content that includes the text string 'inter', such as International, Interest, and so on. This is also known as a **wild card search**.

Search file names only

It is faster to search the content by filenames if you know the filename or some portion of the filename. When you click on the search options icon, you will see the list of options that are available to you, as shown in the following screenshot:

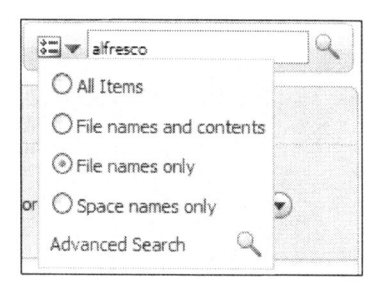

You can select an option by clicking on the option button, as shown in the preceding screenshot. You have the following options:

- **All Items**: Performs a search of the entire content and all of the properties.
- **File names and contents**: Performs a search of the entire content and the filename property.
- **File names only**: Performs a search on only the name property of files.
- **Space names only**: Performs a search on only the name property of spaces.

Advanced search

You can view the advanced search form by clicking on the **Advanced Search** link provided in the search drop-down list, as shown in the preceding screenshot. By using the advanced search form (as shown in the next screenshot), you can search content:

- Within a space, and optionally its sub-spaces
- Matching a given category, optionally sub-categories
- Of a specific content type or a mime type
- Matching the built-in properties such as title, description, and author
- Created or modified within certain date ranges
- Matching custom properties

The menu bar of the advanced search form contains a **Reset All** button, which is useful for clearing all of the options selected in the form. You can save the search options and execute the saved searches as reports. More information about saved searches is provided in subsequent sections of this chapter.

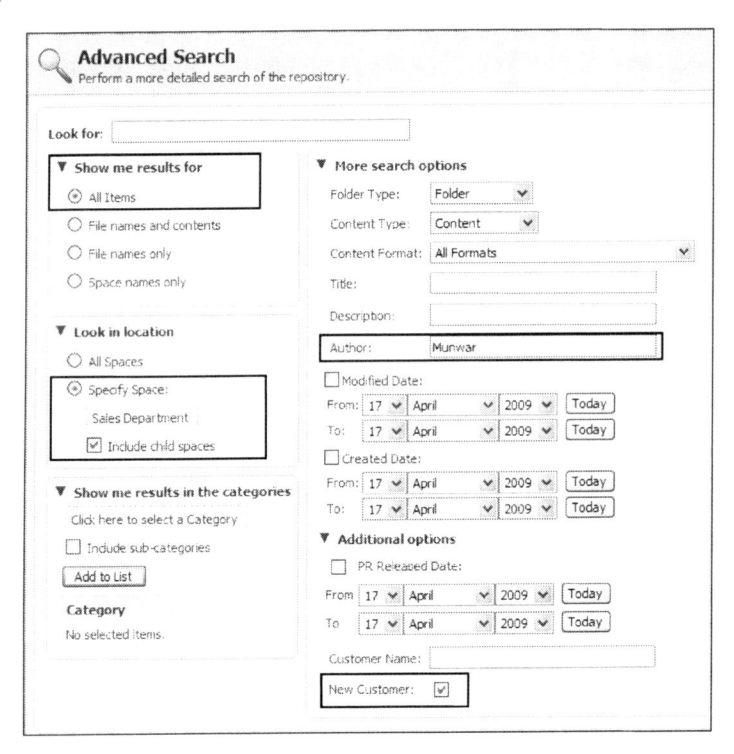

Search by content location

The options provided in the **Look in location** block of the advanced search form allow you to search for content based on its location. Clicking on the **Specify Space** radio button will list the spaces available for you to choose, as shown in the upcoming screenshot. From the list of spaces, click on a space name to browse to sub-spaces. You can click on the **+** icon in order to select a space and optionally choose to search in all of the sub-spaces by selecting the **Include child spaces** checkbox. You can choose only one space and its sub-spaces to search at a time.

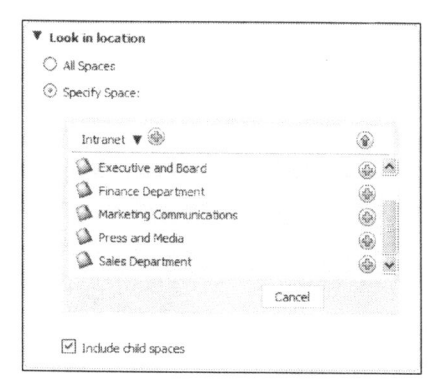

Search by content category

The options that are provided in the **Show me results in the categories** block of the advanced search form allow you to search content belonging to one or more categories. Clicking on the **Select Category** link will list the categories, as shown in the upcoming screenshot. From the list of categories, click on a category name to browse through the sub-categories. You can click on the **+** image to select a category. Optionally, you can choose to search all of the sub-categories by selecting the **Include sub-categories** checkbox. Click on the **Add to List** button to add the category to the list of selections. You can choose as many categories as you want.

Search by content properties

The options provided in the **More search options** block of the advanced search form allow you to search for content based on the property values of the content objects. You can search for content that belongs to a specific content type by selecting the **Content Type** drop-down option. You can search for content created by a specific author by providing the full or partial name of the author in the **Author** text box, as shown in the upcoming screenshot. You can search for the content created within a certain date range by selecting the **Created Date** checkbox and providing the **From** and **To** dates.

If you choose more than one option, then the content that satisfies all of the conditions will be listed in the search result. For example, if you have provided the author's name and a **Created Date** range, then only content created within that date range and authored by that specific person will be listed. This is equivalent to using logical AND criteria to select the content. The current limitation with the advanced search form is that you cannot use OR criteria. For example, you cannot search for content within a specific date range or which was created by a specific person.

Extending the search form

In Chapter 7, you created a custom content type called **Press Release** and a custom aspect called **Customer Details**. You can search the content of the press release type. You can also search the content having a specific custom property value.

For the advanced search form to recognize and list the custom content types and custom aspects, you need to customize the web client.

Configure the web client user interface

Edit the `web-client-config-custom.xml` file in the extension (`<alfresco_install_folder>\tomcat\shared\classes\alfresco\extension`) folder. Add the following XML code to extend the advanced search form:

```
<config evaluator="string-compare" condition="Advanced Search">
  <advanced-search>
    <content-types>
      <type name="custom:pressrelease" />
    </content-types>
    <custom-properties>
      <meta-data type="custom:pressrelease"
                                   property="custom:PRDate" />
      <meta-data aspect="custom:CustomerDetails"
                                   property="custom:CustomerName" />
       <meta-data aspect="custom:CustomerDetails"
                                   property="custom:NewCustomer" />
    </custom-properties>
  </advanced-search>
</config>
```

This code in the `<content-types>` block will result in this content type being listed in the advanced search form. The code in the `<custom-properties>` block will result in the given custom properties being listed in the advanced search form.

After making the changes to the configuration file, restart Alfresco.

Search custom content and properties

After you login to Alfresco Explorer, open the advanced search form and click on the **Additional options** block. You will notice the custom properties, as highlighted in the next screenshot. Similarly, when you click on the **Content Type** drop-down list, you will notice the custom content type listed, as shown in the upcoming screenshot.

You can search content by providing various values in the **Additional options** block. For example, you can list the documents belonging to new customers by selecting the **New Customer** checkbox, and then pressing the *Enter* button on your keyboard or clicking on the **Search** button in the advanced search form.

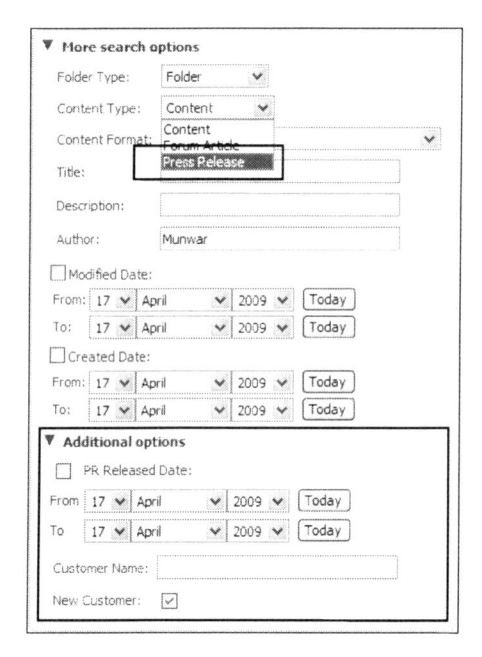

Save a search as a report

Sometimes, you will have to repeatedly search for content that satisfies a specific search criteria. Instead of typing or selecting the same options in the advanced search form repeatedly, you can save the search criteria to reuse when needed. This is like a personalized report for you. You can choose to share this report with others by setting the saved search to **Public**. You can keep certain reports to yourself by not sharing them with others. These reports will be listed as private reports.

Define complex search criteria

For example, let us generate a report to list all of the sales documents authored by Munwar for new customers.

In order to define these search criteria, open the **Advanced Search** form. Under the **Look in location** block, select the **Company Home | Intranet | Sales Department** space and select sub-spaces. Under the **More search options** block, type **Munwar** for **Author**. Under the **Additional options** block, select the **New Customer** checkbox.

You can further complicate the search criteria by selecting a date range for **Created Date**.

Once you are done with your search criteria, click the **Search** button to display the search results.

Save search criteria as public or private report

The search results page is shown in the following screenshot. You can save the search criteria by clicking on the **More Actions | Save New Search** option, as shown in the following screenshot:

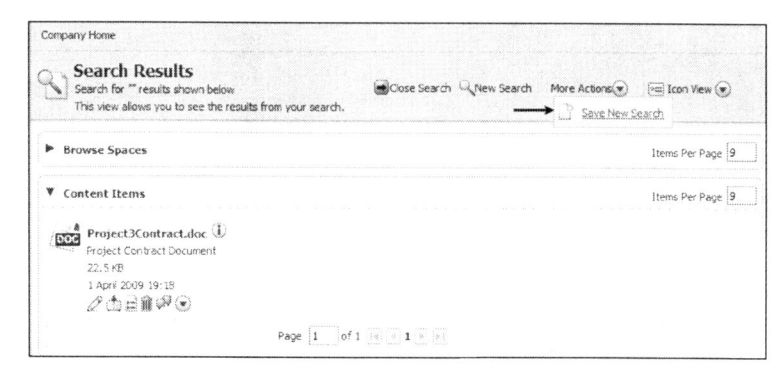

Clicking on the **Save New Search** link will open up the **Save New Search** dialog, as shown in the screenshot below:

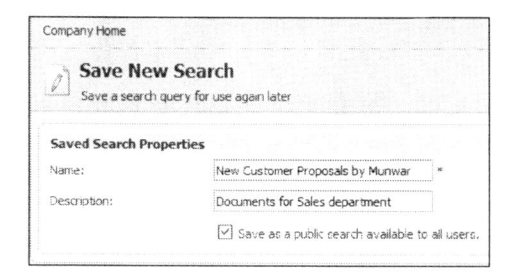

In the **Save New Search** dialog, enter a meaningful **Name** and, optionally, a **Description** for your custom report (saved search).

If you select the **Save as a public search available to all users** option, then this report becomes a public report and is visible to all other users, via the advanced search form. If you have not selected this option, then this report is visible only to you, as a private report.

All saved searches can be found in the **Company Home | Data Dictionary | Saved Searches** space.

Reuse a saved search

You can reuse the search criteria that are saved earlier by selecting them in the **Advanced Search** form. In the **Advanced Search** form, click on the **My Saved Search Options link,** and then click on **Public Searches**. The rightmost drop-down box will list all of the available public reports (saved searches).

Selecting a saved search will automatically create the search criteria by selecting the options in the advanced search form. Similarly, you can reuse **Your Searches**, which are types of private reports for you.

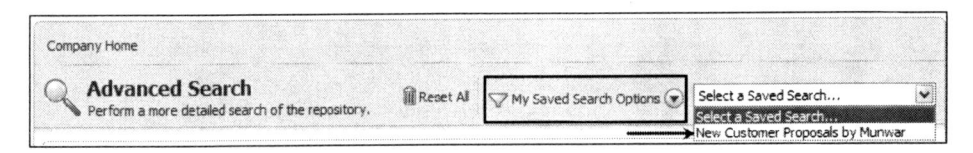

OpenSearch

OpenSearch is a standard format for sharing search results across different systems. It helps various search engines and search clients to communicate, by introducing a common set of formats for performing search requests and syndicating search results.

> Refer to the OpenSearch web site at http://www.opensearch.org for specifications and documentation.

Alfresco has adopted open standards throughout its framework, and OpenSearch is one such standard. This enables a standards-based interface for searching the content in the repository. For example, you can search the content in Alfresco from any application, which may be written in any other programming language and/or running on any other platform.

Alfresco exposes its search engines via OpenSearch and also provides a new aggregate open search feature in the Alfresco Explorer.

Alfresco's open search engines

You can see the available open search engines by navigating to the following URL, `http://<servername>:<port>/alfresco/service/api/search/engines`.

There are two open search engines available out of the box. One is a keyword (Google-like) search and the other is a person (registered member) search. Click on a specific Engine to view its description and usage.

Keyword search description

This search is similar to the keyword search of the Alfresco Explorer. Documents containing the specified keywords in their name or content are returned.

The search URL format is as follows:

`http://<servername>:<port>/alfresco/service/api/search/keyword?q={searchTerms}&p={startPage?}&c={count?}&l={language?}`

The following parameters needs to be provided. The optional parameters are usually listed with a question mark.

- `searchTerms`: keyword or keywords to search on
- `startPage` (optional): the page number of the search results required by the client
- `count` (optional): the number of search results per page (default: 10)
- `language` (optional): the locale to search with (XML 1.0 Language Id, for example, en-GB)

The output response can either be in HTML, ATOM or RSS. The default output format is HTML.

Sample keyword search in HTML

Consider the following sample keyword search:

```
http://localhost:8080/alfresco/service/search/keyword.
html?q=alfresco&c=5
```

In the URL, `keyword.html` indicates that the desired output is HTML. The search term is `alfresco` and the number of search results to be listed per page should be 5. The following screenshot displays the search results. If the search returns more results than the count specified (which is 5 in our example), then you will see links to subsequent results pages at the bottom of the screen.

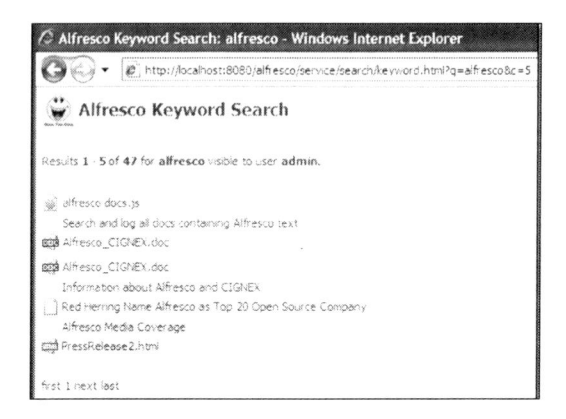

Sample keyword search in RSS

You can also consider using the RSS output if you have the RSS reader, or if you would like to display the search results in a custom application, such as a Portal. The URL format remains the same, except that the file extension is `rss`.

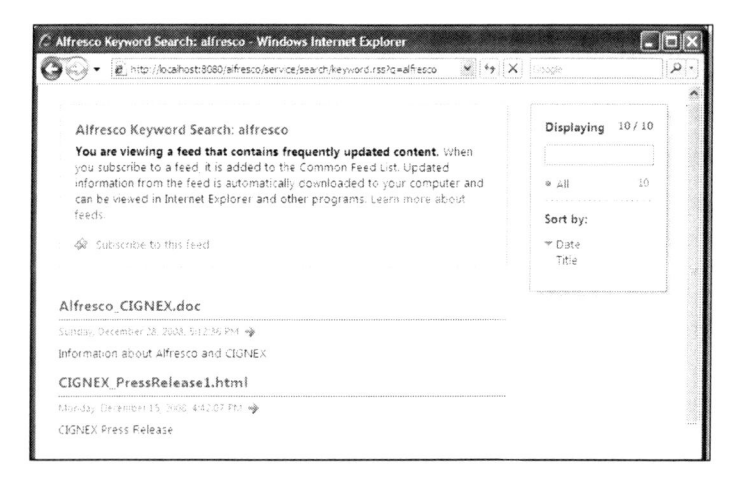

The search interface is provided through Alfresco web scripts. You can customize the search result format by customizing these web scripts. More information about web scripts is provided in Chapter 9.

Alfresco Explorer as an OpenSearch aggregator

The Alfresco Explorer can be used as an OpenSearch aggregator in order to search across multiple repositories. When you log in to the Alfresco Explorer, you will notice the `OpenSearch` box on the left-hand side, along with a navigation window.

Registering new search engines

New search engines can be registered with Alfresco by placing them in the `<extension>/web-scripts-config-custom.xml` file.

Let us register the following search engines with Alfresco.

- Another external Alfresco server: If you have more than one Alfresco server installed in your organization, then this will be useful for searching content across multiple Alfresco repositories.
- Yahoo search engine: Performs a search on the entire web for the given keyword, by using the Yahoo search engine.
- Wikipedia: Performs a search of the Wikipedia database for the given keyword.

Search

There is a sample file that you can use in the `<extension>` folder. Rename the sample file `web-scripts-config-custom.xml.sample` to `web-scripts-config-custom.xml` and edit it as follows.

```xml
<!--   File: extension/web-scripts-config-custom.xml     -->
<!--   Example configuration of multiple OpenSearch engines -->
<!--                                                     -->
<alfresco-config>
    <config evaluator="string-compare" condition="OpenSearch">
        <opensearch>
            <engines>
                <!--                                         -->
                <!--   Example: Remote Alfresco Server       -->
                <!--                                         -->
                <engine label="Remote Alfresco Repository" proxy="remote">
                    <url type="application/atom+xml"> http://partners.alfresco.com/alfresco/api/service/search/keyword.atom?q={searchTerms}&amp;p={startPage?}&amp;c={count?}&amp;l={language?}&amp;guest=true
                    </url>
                    <url type="application/rss+xml">         http://partners.alfresco.com/alfresco/api/service/search/keyword.rss?q={searchTerms}&amp;p={startPage?}&amp;c={count?}&amp;l={language?}&amp;guest=true
                    </url>
                </engine>
                <!--                                         -->
                <!--   Example: Yahoo Search Engine          -->
                <!--                                         -->
                <engine label="Yahoo Search" proxy="yahoo">
                    <url type="application/rss+xml">
http://api.search.yahoo.com/WebSearchService/rss/webSearch.xml?appid=yahoosearchwebrss&amp;query={searchTerms}&amp;start={startIndex?}&amp;results={count?}
                    </url>
                </engine>
                <!--                                         -->
                <!--   Example: Registration of Wikipedia    -->
                <!--                                         -->
                <engine label="Wikipedia Search" proxy="wikipedia">
                    <url type="application/rss+xml">
http://api.search.yahoo.com/WebSearchService/rss/webSearch.xml?appid=yahoosearchwebrss&amp;query={searchTerms}&amp;site=wikipedia.org&amp;start={startIndex?}&amp;results={count?}
                    </url>
                </engine>
```

```
            </engines>
          </opensearch>
       </config>
</alfresco-config>
```

You can configure Alfresco's OpenSearch to directly submit the search request to the external search engine. It may be necessary to configure a search engine proxy. This means that the OpenSearch client indirectly submits a search request via the Alfresco Web Server (i.e. the proxy), rather than directly to the search engine. This is particularly useful in scenarios where the client is an AJAX-based browser, which is limited by cross-domain scripting locks.

Creating a search engine proxy is as simple as adding the proxy attribute to the engine configuration. The value of this attribute is a unique name that identifies the engine.

After creating and editing the `web-scripts-config-custom.xml` file, restart Alfresco.

Federated search

Log in to the Alfresco Explorer to view the OpenSearch features that you have added. You will notice the new entries for **Remote Alfresco Repository**, **Yahoo Search**, and **Wikipedia Search**. When you search for keywords, the search is federated across multiple content sources and unified results are provided, as shown in the following screenshot:

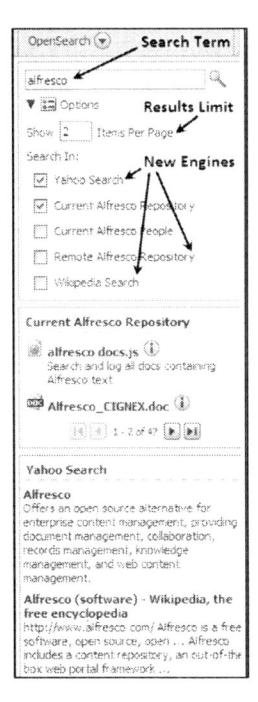

Configuring the Alfresco search engine

The Alfresco search engine is configurable and highly scalable. This section provides information about the underlying search engine and the process for configuring it.

The theory behind the search engine

Alfresco supports full-text search capabilities, using Apache's powerful Lucene search engine (`http://lucene.apache.org`). Lucene is an open source, highly scalable, and fast search engine. Lucene powers search in the discussion groups at Fortune 100 companies, in commercial issue trackers, email search from Microsoft, and the Nutch web search engine (which scales to billions of pages).

Lucene's logical architecture performs a search on a document based on its text content. This helps Lucene to be independent of the file format. So any kind of file (PDF, HTML, Microsoft Word documents, and so on) can be indexed—as long as its textual information can be extracted.

Lucene stores the search indexes and related data in a back-end file system, similar to Alfresco's binary files. You can find the search index files in your `<alfresco_installation>\alf_data\lucene-indexes` folder. Lucene also supports federated searches by combining various data sources.

At the time of writing, Alfresco supports two languages (Lucene and XPath). These are used to search the content in the Alfresco repository.

Limit search results

By default, a search returns all of the results that match the search criteria. Let us say you have millions of documents in your repository. If a particular search results into thousands of documents, the web client uses pagination to display search results in multiple pages. Quite often we never see the search results in the later pages of the search. Can you recollect having ever clicked on page number 10 (or later) in the search results page to locate content? It is very inefficient to get all of the search results and display them in pages.

You can limit the search results by customizing your web-client configuration file `web-client-config-custom.xml` in the extension (`<alfresco_install_folder>\tomcat\shared\classes\alfresco\extension`) folder.

Edit the `web-client-config-custom.xml` file and add the following XML text after the first line (which is `<alfresco-config>`). If you have already created this XML block in your `web-client-config-custom.xml` file, then you only need to insert the lines that are highlighted.

```xml
<config>
  <client>
    <!-- Override the from email address -->
    <from-email-address>munwar@cignex.com</from-email-address>
    <!-- the minimum number of characters required for a valid
                                                    earch string -->
    <search-minimum>3</search-minimum>
    <!-- set this value to true to enable AND text terms for
                                  simple/advanced search by default -->
    <search-and-terms>false</search-and-terms>
    <!-- Limit search results. -1 for unlimited. -->
    <search-max-results>100</search-max-results>
  </client>
</config>
```

This code ensures that the search engine will return a maximum of 100 results. It also sets the minimum search string length to 3 characters, and disables Boolean AND search option in order to improve the search performance.

Restart Alfresco to make sure the changes above have taken effect.

Indexing properties

In the Alfresco content model, the data dictionary settings for properties determine how individual properties are indexed in the search engine.

Refer to the custom aspect called `Customer Details` in Chapter 7. In the earlier sections of this chapter, we configured the advanced search form to search for the `Customer Name` property of this custom aspect. It is advisable to index the values of the `Customer Name` property in order to improve the search performance.

Edit the `customModel.xml` file in your `<extension>` folder where you declared the `Customer Details` aspect. Add the highlighted code to the aspect declaration, in order to index the property.

```xml
<property name="custom:CustomerName">
    <title>Customer Name</title>
    <type>d:text</type>
    <protected>false</protected>
    <mandatory>false</mandatory>
    <multiple>false</multiple>
    <index enabled="true">
        <atomic>false</atomic>
        <stored>false</stored>
        <tokenised>true</tokenised>
    </index>
```

```
            <constraints>
                <constraint ref="custom:name_length"/>
            </constraints>
        </property>
```

If the `enabled` option for the index is set to `true`, then this property will be indexed in the search engine. If this is `false`, there will be no entry for this property in the index.

If the `Atomic` option is set to `true`, then the property is indexed in the transaction. If this is set to `false`, the property is indexed in the background.

If the `Stored` option is set to `true`, then the property value is stored in the index and may be obtained through the Lucene low-level query API.

If the `Tokenized` option is set to `true`, then the string value of the property is tokenized before indexing. If it is set to `false`, then it is indexed as it is, that is, as a single string. The token is determined by the property type in the data dictionary. This is locale-sensitive as supported by the data dictionary. Therefore, you could choose to tokenize all of your content in German, if you wish to do so.

If you have not specified any indexing values for your custom properties, then Alfresco gives default values to your properties. By default, the properties are indexed atomically. The property value is not stored in the index, and the property is tokenized when it is indexed.

Configuring Lucene in Alfresco

The `repository.properties` file in your `config` folder defines a number of properties that influence how all indexes behave. You can improve the search performance by setting appropriate values in the `properties` file.

> We advise that you to NOT change the values in the `repository.properties` file. Instead, we recommend that you override the settings in the `custom-repository.properties` file in the `/extension` folder in the Alfresco classpath.

The following are the default search-index properties:

- `lucene.query.maxClauses=10000`
- `lucene.indexer.batchSize=10000`
- `lucene.indexer.minMergeDocs=1000`
- `lucene.indexer.mergeFactor=10`
- `lucene.indexer.maxMergeDocs=100000`

Max Clauses (Lucene standard parameter): Lucene queries limit the number of clauses in a Boolean query to this value. Some queries are expanded under the covers into a whole set of Boolean queries with many clauses. For example, searching for `luc.*` will expand to a Boolean query containing an OR for every token that the index knows about that matches `luc.*`.

Batch size (Alfresco indexing parameter): The indexer stores a list of what it has to do as the changes are made using the node service API. Typically, there are many events that would cause a node to be re-indexed. By keeping an event list, we can optimize these actions. The algorithm limits re-indexes to one per batch size, and it will not index if a delete is pending. When the list of events reaches this size, the whole event list is processed and the documents are added to the delta index.

Min Merger Docs (Lucene standard parameter): This determines the size of the in-memory Lucene index that is used for each delta index. A higher value of Min Merger Docs would mean that we have more memory but less IO for writing to the index delta. The in-memory information will be flushed and written to disk at the start of the next batch of index events. As the process progresses, the event list requires reading against the delta index. This does not affect the way information is stored on disk—just how it is buffered before it gets there.

Merge Factor (Lucene standard parameter): This determines the number of index segments that are created on disk. When there are more segments than this value, then some segments will be combined.

Max Merge Docs (Lucene standard parameter): This value determines the maximum number of documents that can be stored in an index segment. When this value is reached, the segment will not grow any larger. As a result, there may be more segments than expected by looking at the merge factor.

Summary

Alfresco supports full-text search capabilities by using an open source based, highly scalable, fast search engine called Lucene. The content, as well as the content's properties will automatically be indexed in a search engine. You can use the advanced search form to create complex search criteria to search your content. You can save the searches as reusable reports. You can extend the advanced search form to include your custom content types and custom properties. Alfresco's OpenSearch enables you to have a federated search across local Alfresco repositories, external Alfresco repositories, and external search engines.

13
Implementing Imaging and Forms Processing

Alfresco includes integrated scanning and **OCR** (**Optical Character Recognition**) technologies. This chapter helps you to implement an end-to-end solution by collecting paper documents and forms, transforming them into accurate, retrievable information, and delivering them into an organization's business applications. The information is full-text searchable, and goes through various approval workflows, based on the organization's defined business process management.

By the end of this chapter, you will have learned how to:

- Connect a scanner to a network drive and map it to a space within Alfresco
- Specify a business rule to automatically extract metadata from the scanned document
- Define and execute a workflow process for scanned documents
- Bulk upload scanned documents into the Alfresco repository
- Integrate OCR utilities into Alfresco
- Integrate and use Kofax Ascent Capture
- Integrate Alfresco with eCopy-enabled scanners

You can extend the value of your Enterprise Content Management (ECM) investment by implementing imaging and automated forms processing solutions, as per your organization's requirements. Electronic document images are starting to have the same legal status as a paper document.

Alfresco integrates with various image capturing systems to provide flexible and intelligent form processing. This results in greater control and management of crucial information and documents, both within and outside of the firewall. These joint solutions enable you to include forms and the data captured from them as content types that can be version controlled, repurposed, integrated into workflows, and managed by the ECM environment. This simplifies compliance with enhanced archiving and audit capabilities. You can also reduce the cost of printing, storing, and distributing paper forms.

You can implement various solutions by leveraging Alfresco's content management and business process management features. Some are listed below, for your reference:

- Order fulfillment
- Claim processing
- Underwriting
- Loan origination
- Contract management
- Accounts payable, managing checks and invoices

Electronic imaging and the paperless office

Managing paper documents is not easy. Distribution of paper documents is manual, and a slow process. The high cost of filing and retrieving them makes paper documents expensive to manage. The electronic imaging technology offers an effective solution to these problems. The concept of the **paperless office**, for scanning and digitizing the business documents and processing the images instead of the paper itself is picking up.

Electronic imaging gives us the following benefits:

- It reduces storage space.
- The documents are stored as magnetic or optical images. This eliminates the possibility of their deterioration due to age, adverse temperatures, or weather conditions.
- It facilitates instant retrieval of the documents.
- It provides security of the documents by providing separate view, edit, and delete access to the relevant people.
- It provides simultaneous access to documents for multiple users.
- It provides usage and tracking of documents.

- It provides a centralized database for documents belonging to various departments.
- It helps in speeding up business decisions that require an approval process.
- It provides file integrity—as the use of read-only files prevents document images from being altered.

In the early years of imaging, the absence of workflow was the main barrier to customer acceptance. The development of robust workflow systems has created a widespread adoption of electronic imaging by allowing web-based approval processes.

Forms processing

Automated forms processing is used to capture data on forms that are filled in manually using handwriting, machine print, and checkboxes. These forms are then returned to a centralized location for batch processing. Imaged handwriting or machine print is of little value until it is converted into computer-usable (ASCII) data.

Forms automation is **ICR (Intelligent Character Recognition)** intensive, and involves a process for converting a bitmapped image into ASCII data. Because, over 80% of all of the business documents are forms, the conversion of a manual data entry form involves enormous expense, which can be significantly diminished through the use of recognition-based automated forms processing.

The following is a typical process to convert and manage forms in a Content Management System:

1. **Scanning**: Pages of forms are scanned and converted into bitmapped (usually `TIFF`) images of forms. These images are either compressed and stored for later batch processing, or are passed immediately, in an uncompressed format, to an ICR engine for recognition.
2. **Image enhancement**: The document image is cleaned up and character images are enhanced, using image enhancement techniques.
3. **Information extraction**: An information extraction template identifies which individual fields on the form image require recognition, as well as the nature of those fields. They can be barcodes, signatures, hand prints, machine prints, numeric, alphabetic, or alphanumeric.
4. **Electronic content**: An image with the converted ASCII data is then moved to a content management system as a content item. The information extracted from the form is stored as the properties of the content item.
5. **Workflow**: The content goes through various workflow approval processes and is finally stored for future access.

Alfresco for imaging and forms processing

Alfresco already has imaging solutions with Kofax and eCopy. You can also use the network drive features of Alfresco to automatically upload all of the scanned documents to the repository, even without having a tight integration between your scanner and the Alfresco repository.

The following figure shows a sample architecture diagram that uses Alfresco for imaging and forms processing. A remote office can be connected to your central Alfresco repository to bulk upload the scanned documents. The documents could be forms, checks, invoices, engineering diagrams, legal contracts, or any other kind of paper document.

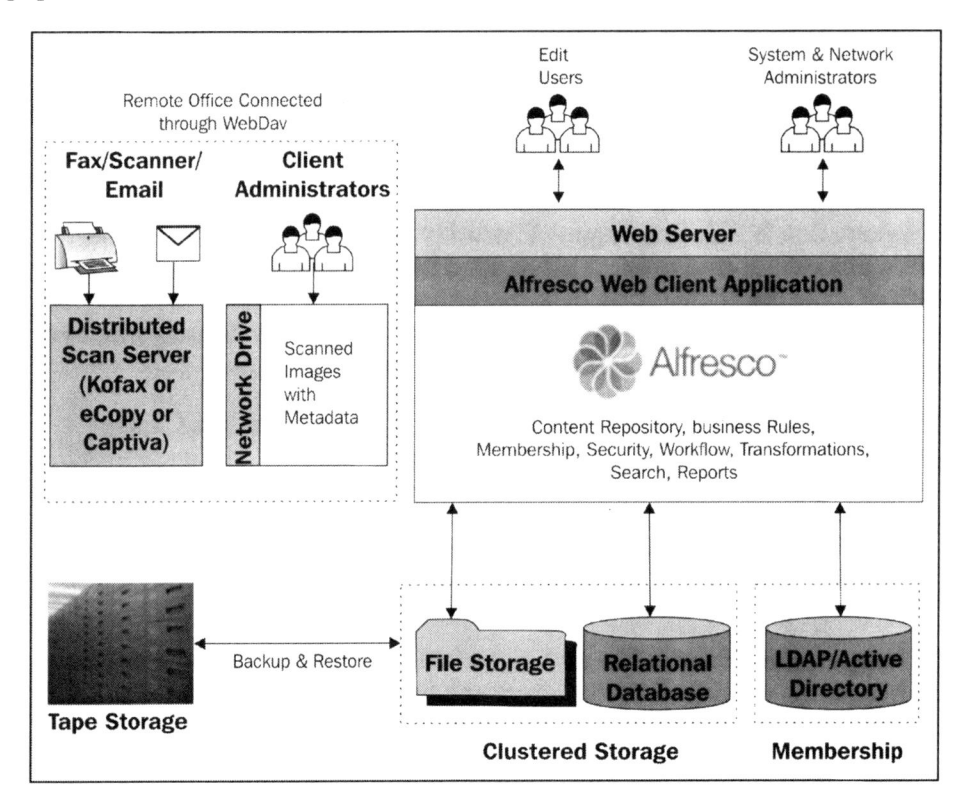

Once a document has been uploaded to a space, business rules can be triggered by moving the document through a workflow process. The documents and the search indexes can be stored in a high-end file storage such as EMC Centera. The metadata can be stored in a relational database such as Oracle or MySQL. The storage can be clustered for high performance and heavy loads. You can even consider having a single sign-on with an existing **Active Directory** or **LDAP** membership system.

Alfresco is highly scalable in terms of storage and performance. Alfresco is being used by a large French bank for loading all faxes of client trades into the repository. On a low-powered machine they were getting around 350 TIFF images loaded per minute (21,000 documents per hour) and the scalability tests showed that this could be scaled up pretty easily, with more horsepower.

Sample imaging solution with workflow

Let us consider sample imaging by using a case scenario. Let us say that you have remote client offices, which scan all of the checks, OCR them, extract metadata, and send them over to you for approval, payment, and storage.

The sample solution that is provided in this section uses all of the features you have learnt so far, including business rules, transformations, security, and workflow. The solution is useful for scanning a paper document (such as a check or a claim form), OCR it, extracting important data, transforming the document into a required format (such as in gif format) and delivering it to your business application and database.

Refer to the architecture diagram that is shown in the previous figure. A remote office can be connected to your central Alfresco repository to bulk upload scanned documents. Once a document is uploaded to a space, business rules are triggered. This transforms the document into the required format and moves it through a workflow process.

You are going to perform the following steps in a demo application:

1. Set up a space and security for your remote office. You can create a separate space for each remote office to scan the documents.
2. A remote office connects their scanner to a network folder, and maps it to an Alfresco space via WebDAV (HTTP protocol).
3. The scanned documents (checks, claims, and forms) will enter the Alfresco repository in TIFF format.
4. The Alfresco business rule extracts the metadata, and attaches this to the scanned image.

5. These documents will be automatically transformed from TIFF format to GIF format, and sent to the Review space. When a document is moved into the Review space, the workflow starts.

6. The reviewer can visit this space, and review the document. He or she can approve or reject the document.

7. The approved document will then be moved to the Approved space and then (in the case of a check) to the Cut Check space.

8. The rejected checks will be stored in the Rejected space and an email notification will be sent to the concerned people.

Setting up space and security

Log in to the Alfresco web client, go to the **Company Home > Intranet > Finance Department** space, and create a new space called **Office Accounts** for the imaging solution demo application.

Under the **Office Accounts** space, create the following sub-spaces:

- 01_Inbox
- 02_Under Review
- 03_Approved
- 04_Rejected
- 05_Cut Checks
- Offices

Under **Offices**, create two office sub-spaces called **OFFICE1** and **OFFICE2**:

- Offices
  - OFFICE1
  - OFFICE2

Set the security for each office so that only the personnel for that office have write access to that office's space. Go to the **Company Home | Intranet | Finance Department | Office Accounts | Offices | OFFICE1** space, and set the security. For example, you can add a user (say user1 from your remote office1) and give the user the **Contributor** role so that he or she can add documents to the **OFFICE1** space. To ensure security, make sure nobody else has write access to this space, except for some of the employees of Office1. For more information about securing spaces, refer to Chapter 4. You can set the security for the **OFFICE2** space in the same way.

Business rule to extract important metadata

Let us define a single business rule that performs the following three actions on all of the incoming documents in the **Offices** space and all of the sub-spaces:

1. Adds the Customer Details aspect.
2. Executes a script to extract important metadata, and populates the document properties.
3. Moves the document to the **01_Inbox** space.

Refer to Chapter 7, where you added a custom aspect called **Customer Details** in order to add customer-specific properties to the documents. The properties include CustomerName, CustomerContactName, CustomerContactPhone, CustomerProjectID, and NewCustomer.

You can create your own script in the JavaScript language to automatically populate the document properties for all of the incoming scanned documents. For example, create a file called chapter13_fill_metadata.js in your personal computer with the following code. The following JavaScript populates the three properties. The CustomerName property is filled with the name of the office space, and the other two properties, CustomerContactName and CustomeContactPhone, are filled with some fixed values, as shown below:

```
if (document.hasPermission("Write"))
{
    if (document.mimetype == "image/tiff")
    {
      var l_currentSpace = document.parent;
      document.properties["custom:CustomerName"]
                                            = l_currentSpace.name;
      document.properties["custom:CustomerContactName"]
                                            = "Office Admin";
      document.properties["custom:CustomerContactPhone"]
                                            = "111-222-3333";
      document.save();
    }
}
```

Go to the **Company Home > Data Dictionary > Scripts** space, click on the **Add Content** button, and upload the chapter13_fill_metadata.js file. Now, you have your own custom script that can be used in the business rules.

Go to the **Company Home > Intranet > Finance Department > Office Accounts > Offices** space and create a new business rule.

Implementing Imaging and Forms Processing

In the **Step One-Select Condition** drop-down list, select Items with the specified mime type, and click on the **Set Values and Add** button. In the **Set condition values** pop-up window, select the **TIFF Image** value as the **Type** and click on the **OK** button, and then click on the **Next** button.

In the **Step Two - Select Actions** pane create three actions, as shown in the following screenshot:

In the **Step Three - Enter Details** pane of the **Edit Rule Wizard** provide an appropriate **Title** and **Description**. Select the checkbox that says **Apply rule to sub spaces**, as shown in the following screenshot:

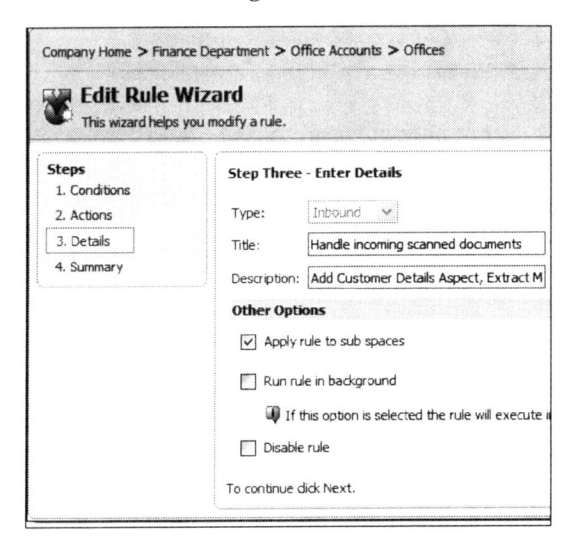

Now, when a document gets into the **OFFICE1** space, additional properties will be added to the document (due to the `CustomerDetails` aspect). Some properties of the document will be pre-populated with data (due to the `chapter13_fill_metadata.js` script). Finally, the document will be moved to the **01_Inbox** space, for further workflow and approval.

Transform documents into the required format

Create a new business rule in the **01_Inbox** space to transform the incoming `TIFF` file to a `GIF` image file. Copy it to the **02_Under Review** space for the further workflow approval process.

Follow the steps below to add the business rule:

1. Ensure that you are in the **Company Home > Intranet > Finance Department > Office Accounts > 01_Inbox** space.

2. Select the **More Actions | Manage Content Rules** option. Click on the **Create Rule** link, and you will see the **Create Rules Wizard**.

3. In the **Step One - Select Condition** drop-down list, select **Items with the specified mime type**, and click on the **Set Values and Add** button. In the **Set condition values** pop-up window, select **TIFF Image** as the **Type** and click on the **OK** button, and then click on the **Next** button.

4. In the **Step Two - Select Actions** pane, select **Transform and Copy Image to a specific space** from the drop-down list, and then click on the **Set Values and Add** button. In the **Set Action values** dialog box, select **GIF Image** as **Required Format** and the 02_Under Review space as the **Destination**. Leave the **Options** field empty in order to retain the size of the transformed image as it is. Click on the **OK** button, and then click on the **Next** button.

5. In the **Step Three - Enter Details** pane, select **Inbound** as the **Type**. Provide an appropriate **Title** and **Description** for this rule.

6. Finish the rule by clicking on the **Finish** button.

Define the workflow process

The next step is to define a workflow process for all of the incoming documents, as well as setting the option that sends notifications to all concerned parties. This is shown in the following screenshot. For more information on defining the workflow and the email notifications, refer to Chapter 8.

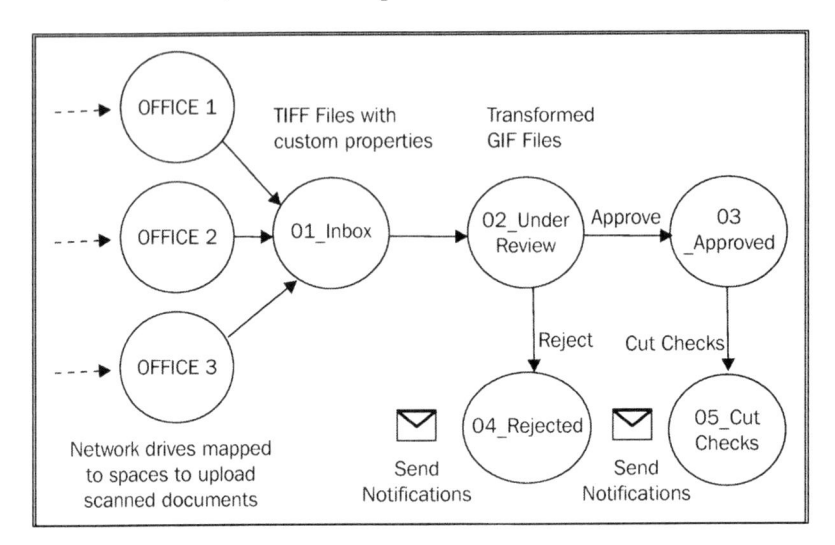

Add a simple workflow to all of the inbound items in the **02_Under Review** space. For the **Approve** step, move the document to the **03_Approved** space. For the **Reject** step, move the document to the **04_Rejected** space, as shown in the figure above.

Add a simple workflow to all of the inbound items in the **03_Approved** space. For the **Approve** step, move the document to the **05_Cut Checks** space. There is no **Reject** step here.

Add a business rule to all of the inbound items in the **04_Rejected** space to send an email notification to the appropriate people when a scanned document (check) is rejected.

Similarly, add a business rule to all of the inbound items in the **05_Cut Checks** space to send the email notifications to the appropriate people when a check is cut and released.

Connecting the scanner to network folder

The scanner in your remote office can be connected to a local network folder (refer to the first figure in this chapter). The network folder can be mapped to the Alfresco repository as a space via WebDAV or CIFS. More information about mapping a drive to Alfresco using CIFS or WebDAV is provided in Chapter 5.

You can map the network folder in your remote **OFFICE1** space to a secure space in Alfresco (**Intranet | Finance Department | Office Accounts | Offices | OFFICE1**)

To map the **OFFICE1** space in Alfresco in the local Windows Explorer as a network drive, follow the steps given below:

1. In Windows Explorer, click on the **Tools | Map Network Drive** option. The **Map Network Drive** dialog box appears.
2. Select an unused drive letter (say, O for **OFFICE1** space).
3. In the folder text box, enter `\\<AlfrescoServer>_a\Alfresco\Intranet\Finance Department\Office Accounts\Offices\OFFICE1`. Replace `<AlfrescoServer>` with the actual server name.
4. Select the **Reconnect at logon** checkbox.
5. Click on the **Finish** button. Because the space is secured, the system will prompt you for your authentication. Only users defined on the **OFFICE1** space will be able to connect to the **OFFICE1** space.
6. Enter your Alfresco username and password when prompted.

Bulk upload scanned documents into the repository

To test the network folder setup, drag-and-drop a few `TIFF` files from your personal computer to the O drive, which is mapped to the **OFFICE1** space. In a production environment, the scanner will be connected to the O drive in order to upload the scanned images directly to this drive.

You will notice that as soon as the scanned documents (`TIFF` files) get into the `OFFICE1` space, additional properties are added to the documents and the documents are moved to the **01_Inbox** space.

You will also notice that the original documents (`TIFF` format) are in the **01_Inbox** space. The transformed copies of the documents (in `GIF` format) are in the **02_Under Review** space for further steps in the workflow approval process.

Implementing Imaging and Forms Processing

If you examine the transformed documents in the **02_Under Review** space, then you will notice that a set of properties have been added and were pre-populated due to the business rules that have already been applied to the document. The screenshot on the next page is the **Details View** of one of the documents in the **02_Under Review** space.

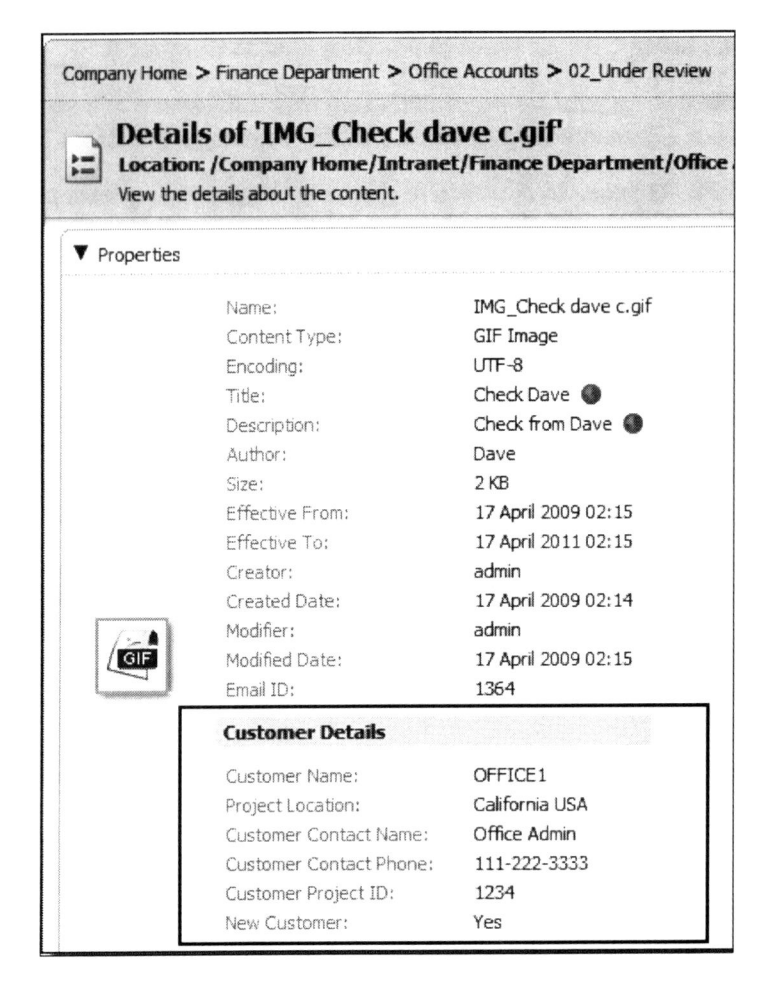

> Company Home > Finance Department > Office Accounts > 02_Under Review
>
> **Details of 'IMG_Check dave c.gif'**
> Location: /Company Home/Intranet/Finance Department/Office
> View the details about the content.
>
> ▼ Properties
>
> | | |
> |---|---|
> | Name: | IMG_Check dave c.gif |
> | Content Type: | GIF Image |
> | Encoding: | UTF-8 |
> | Title: | Check Dave |
> | Description: | Check from Dave |
> | Author: | Dave |
> | Size: | 2 KB |
> | Effective From: | 17 April 2009 02:15 |
> | Effective To: | 17 April 2011 02:15 |
> | Creator: | admin |
> | Created Date: | 17 April 2009 02:14 |
> | Modifier: | admin |
> | Modified Date: | 17 April 2009 02:15 |
> | Email ID: | 1364 |
>
> **Customer Details**
>
> | | |
> |---|---|
> | Customer Name: | OFFICE1 |
> | Project Location: | California USA |
> | Customer Contact Name: | Office Admin |
> | Customer Contact Phone: | 111-222-3333 |
> | Customer Project ID: | 1234 |
> | New Customer: | Yes |

You can examine the documents in the **02_Under Review** space and either **Approve** them or **Reject** them. You can write a presentation template to have a custom view of all of the documents in the **02_Under Review** space, as shown in the screenshot on the next page. More information about custom views is presented in Chapter 11.

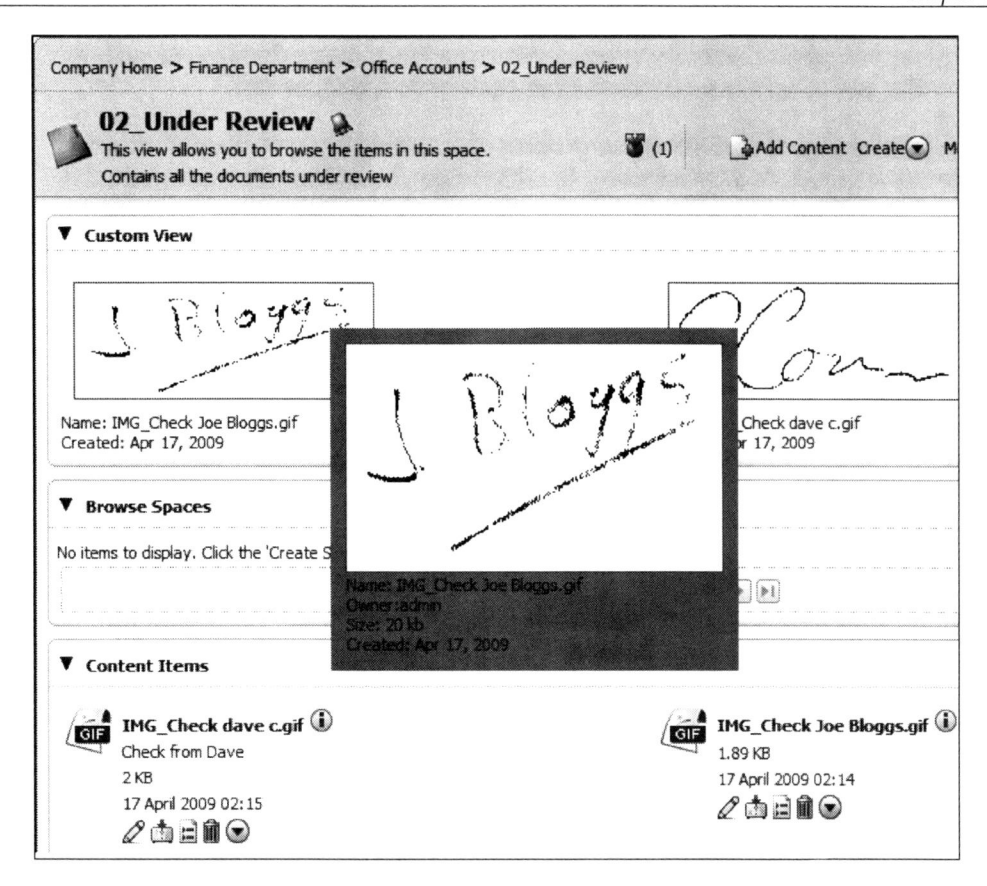

When you **Approve** a document in the **02_Under Review** space, the document moves to the **03_Approved** space, and an email notification is sent to the concerned people. When you **Reject** a document in the **02_Under Review** space, then the document moves to the **04_Rejected** space, and an email notification is sent to the concerned people. Test the workflow by moving documents through various workflow spaces, as shown in the earlier figure defining the workflow.

Now that you have an idea about how to implement a solution, create a custom solution to solve your business problem, and test it.

OCR integration

Most of the **OCR (Optical Character Recognition)** utilities available in the market will convert scanned archives into a PDF format, including both image and text in the same standard container. Alfresco supports a content transformation framework—where you can plug in a third-party content transformation engine to convert a document from one format to another.

This gives you great flexibility when converting your image document, such as a `TIFF` file, to a machine readable format such as `PDF`, `RTF`, or `TXT`.

The following figure illustrates the process of scanning a paper document using a network scanner, and transferring the document, in an image format, into the Alfresco repository. Once the image document gets into the Alfresco repository, you can trigger a business rule, which converts it to a PDF document. You can still keep the image document in the repository for future reference. The quality and the accuracy of the output PDF document will be depending upon the OCR utility that you use for the transformation.

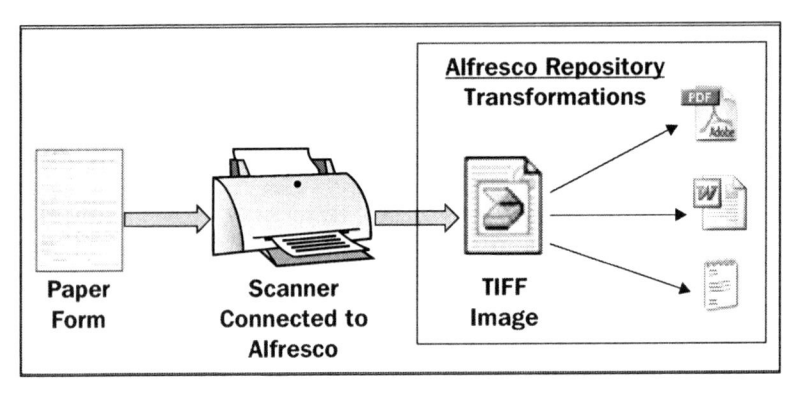

Intelliant OCR-Alfresco bundle

Intelliant sells an OCR-Alfresco bundle, which can be downloaded from their web site. You can find more information about their offerings from their web site, at http://www.intelliant.fr/en/alfresco-ocr-bundle.php.

Their OCR utility is integrated with the Alfresco repository as a content transformation. Intelliant's OCR utility converts `TIFF` images into `PDF`, `RTF`, and `TXT` documents. Follow the tutorial provided on their web site to download and install the bundle.

Carry out the following steps to enable OCR in Alfresco:

1. Download and install the Intelliant OCR utility.
2. Download and copy the Alfresco content transformations context file into Alfresco's `<extension>` folder.
3. Restart Alfresco.
4. Create a business rule for the space to automatically transform the incoming TIFF images to PDF documents.

You can follow this same process to integrate any OCR utility into Alfresco.

Integration with Kofax Ascent Capture

Kofax is the world's leading provider of information capture solutions. Their product—Kofax Ascent Capture—is integrated with Alfresco, offering customers access to a comprehensive production capture solution. The product includes automatic document classification, data extraction, and validation for both Internet-based distributed capture as well as capture in centralized environments.

The integration was developed by Alfresco, Kofax, and Kofax Certified Solution Provider Aarden Ringcroft. The Kofax Ascent Capture integration module is available through Alfresco Forge.

By leveraging the distributed features of Ascent Capture, together with the power of the Alfresco web services API, integrators can easily deliver a scenario where the documents are scanned in New York, validated in Bangalore, and then released to an Alfresco repository in London—all using standards based protocols.

Kofax release script configuration

Alfresco Ascent Capture integration is built as a release script. Release scripts connect to the Alfresco repository through web services, define content types and aspects, map indexing fields to content metadata, and transfer content as Image (`TIFF`), OCR Text, and PDF.

The following information will be captured via an Administration Dialog, allowing configuration of the release script:

- The Alfresco server connection details (username, password, and repository instance)
- The destination of the Alfresco folder, where the information captured by Kofax should be placed
- Mapping of the Kofax captured information (Metadata, TIFF, OCR, and PDF renditions) to the Alfresco Content Model
- Mapping of the Kofax Document Class to the Alfresco Content Type
- Mapping of the Kofax Index Value (as extracted from the document by Kofax) to the Alfresco property (of the appropriate data type)
- Transferring a Kofax TIFF, OCR, or PDF document to the Alfresco property (of binary data type)

Implementing Imaging and Forms Processing

The following screenshot shows the release script administration window's **Repository** tab. Notice that the connection to Alfresco is via a URL over HTTP. There is no need to open special ports or to use special protocols to communicate. All of the files will be copied to the Alfresco's space that is specified by the **Destination** field, as shown in the following screenshot:

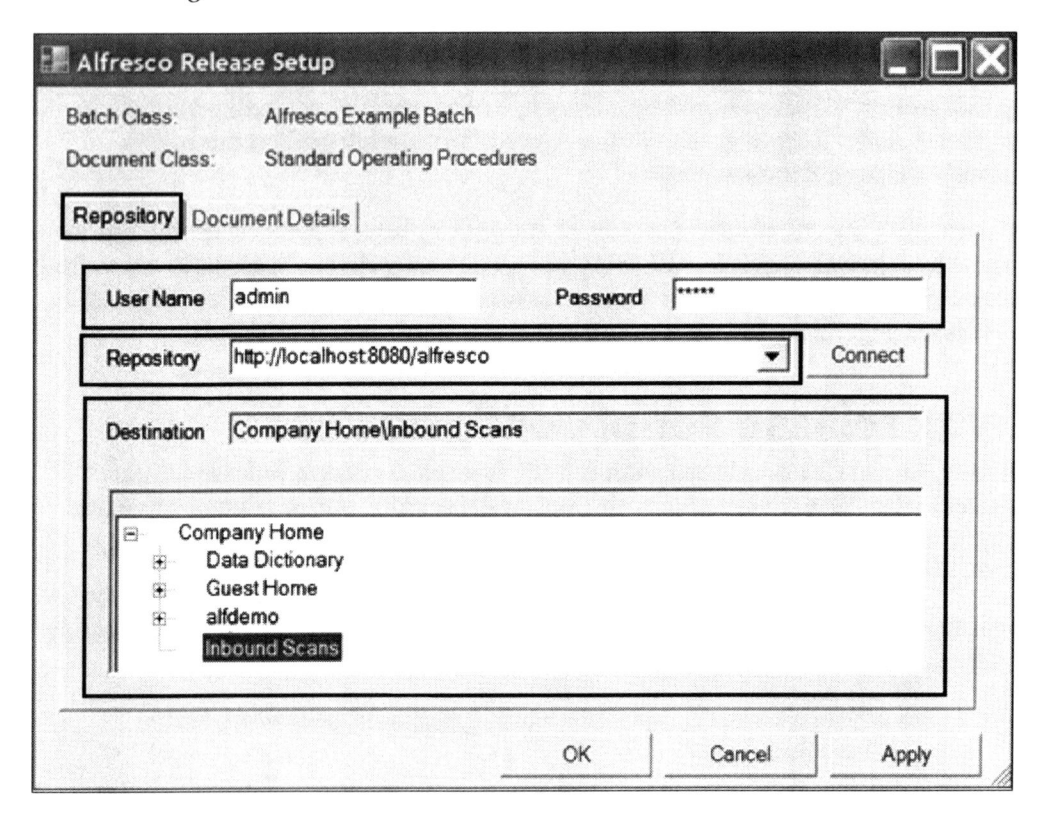

![Alfresco Release Setup screenshot showing Repository tab with Batch Class: Alfresco Example Batch, Document Class: Standard Operating Procedures, User Name: admin, Repository: http://localhost:8080/alfresco, Destination: Company Home\Inbound Scans]

The screenshot on the next page shows the release script administration window's **Document Details** tab. Notice that the **Content Type** can be selected from the list of available types in the current Alfresco repository. Similarly, **Aspects** can be applied from the list of available aspects in the current repository.

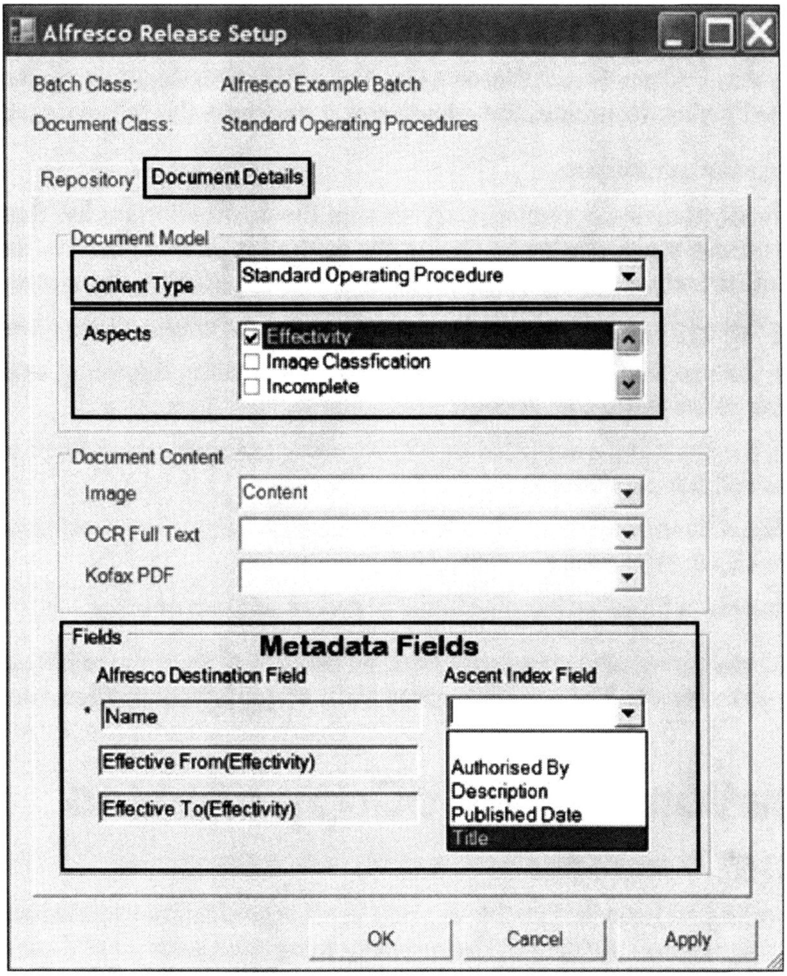

The **Document Content** section allows you to configure the formats that are released to the repository, which are Image (`TIFF`), OCR, Full Text, and PDF (Image/Image & Text). Multiple formats can be mapped to different content types. Text-based formats are full-text searchable within Alfresco.

Refer to the screenshot above, where the metadata is listed dynamically, based on the content type selected. You can map the Kofax indexing fields to metadata. Therefore, when the document is scanned, the metadata is populated automatically with values.

Release script functionality

The release script connects to Alfresco using the connection details supplied. For each supplied Kofax document, the release script performs the following actions:

1. Starts the transaction.
2. If the document does not already exist in the destination folder, then the release script creates one using the content type as defined in the **Administration** dialog; otherwise it updates the existing document.
3. Applies appropriate aspects (as defined in the **Administration** dialog).
4. Sets the property values (as supplied by Kofax, using mapping, as defined in the **Administration** dialog).
5. Sets the content (as supplied by Kofax, using mapping, as defined in the **Administration** dialog).
6. Returns the new content Id to Kofax, thus providing a cross-reference between the systems.
7. Commits or rolls-back transactions based on success or error.

If—for some reason—a document could not be processed, then the release script reports the error back to Kofax so that some form of quality control can take place.

Integration with an eCopy-enabled scanner

eCopy provides products that enable anyone in an organization to transform paper documents into information that is easily integrated with all of their existing business workflows and applications. SIRA Systems Corporation (http://www.sirasystems.com) created a connector to integrate Alfresco into the eCopy suite. This connector allows users to scan in an image via eCopy and place it directly into Alfresco.

Using the Alfresco connector, any documents can be scanned directly to a selected Alfresco repository by using your eCopy-enabled digital copier or scanner. The Alfresco connector acts as an interface between your copier or scanner, and your Alfresco Content Management System. Once **eCopy ShareScan OP** is installed on your device, you can add the Alfresco connector, thus making your eCopy-enabled copier or scanner capable of adding the information directly into the selected Alfresco repository, with user authentication.

Summary

Alfresco integrates with various image capturing systems. This feature adds to the flexibility of Alfresco, and provides intelligent form processing. This results in greater control and management of crucial information and documents, inside and outside the firewall.

You can implement an OCR solution within Alfresco by using the transformations framework. The Kofax Ascent integration also allows documents to be captured and stored in Alfresco, enabling customers to review and approve documents for long term archival or records management purposes. Using the eCopy Alfresco connector, any documents can be scanned directly into a selected Alfresco repository through your eCopy-enabled digital copier or scanner.

14
Administering and Maintaining the System

Maintaining and upgrading a system is equally as important as implementing it. A well-maintained system will give the highest return on investments. This chapter provides a high level overview of administering and maintaining your Alfresco implementation. It includes information about backing up your valuable content, upgrading your system to newer versions, enabling a full audit trail, and setting up a multi-tenant system configuration. You will also find general maintenance tips, such as maintaining log files and periodically updating your admin password.

By the end of this chapter, you will have learned how to:

- Export and import your personal or departmental information
- Back up your data on a regular basis for storage and retrieval
- Perform general maintenance tasks, such as examining log files
- Set up replication for high availability
- Upgrade your Alfresco application to newer versions
- Control system usage, by using a user quota system
- Manage a multi-tenant system
- Enable full auditing of user and system activities

Exporting and importing content

Export and import functions are useful in order to bulk extract and load the personal, departmental, or team information from one location to another location within the repository, or to some other repository. In some situations, you can use this to integrate with third-party systems. For example, you can send the exported content from the Alfresco repository to another Content Management System, or an internal system. Similarly, you can package external content, and import it into the Alfresco repository.

Alfresco Content Package (ACP)

The Alfresco Explorer has web-based utilities for exporting and importing content using an **Alfresco Content Package (ACP)**. An ACP is a single file (with an extension of .acp) that bundles together the metadata, content files, business rules, and the security settings for content.

The process for export and import is simple. Export produces one or more ACP files, which hold the exported information. As with all of the files, you can place them somewhere secure, or transfer them using mechanisms such as email, FTP, and so on. Security settings only allow the export of those items that are readable by the user, performing the export.

The import of an ACP file is the reverse of an export. The information held in the ACP file is placed into the repository location chosen at the time of. By default, the import process creates a copy of the ACP-held information.

An ACP file is simply a ZIP archive whose structure is as follows:

```
/<packagename>.xml
/<packagename>/
    contentNNN.pdf
    contentNNN.txt
    ...
```

The packagename is assigned on export. The XML file conforms to the export and import view schema, which describes the transported nodes in terms of their types, aspects, properties, associations, and permissions. Content properties are handled specifically where the binary content of the property is held in a separate file, under the packagename folder of the ZIP archive, and the XML contains a reference to the file.

While the repository provides several different ways to create an ACP file (export), it is also possible to create one manually. This is very useful for system-to-system integration.

Exporting and importing space content

Any Alfresco user may perform an export and import of folders and files that they have access to. You can choose any space (personal or departmental) to export.

The scope of information to export is configurable, but typically involves specifying the location within the repository to export. For example, if you choose to export content in one specific space (say **Company Home > Intranet > Finance Department**), then the exported data includes:

- The current space and all of the sub spaces
- All of the documents (files, images, HTML/XML content, custom content, all versions) within the space and its sub spaces
- Complete metadata (aspects, audit, and versions) associated with the documents
- Business rules set on the spaces
- Invited users to a space or content

Export of a department space using Alfresco Explorer

The process to export a space within Alfresco Explorer is as follows:

1. Select a specific space to export (say, **Sales Department**, in your sample **Intranet** application).
2. Select the **More Actions | View Details** link to view the **Details** page of the space.
3. Select the **Export** action to launch the **Export** dialog, as shown in the following screenshot:

4. Fill in the export options, as follows:
    - **Package name**: The name of the resulting export ACP file.
    - **Destination**: The location within the repository to place the ACP file.
    - **Include children**: If selected, then it will also export sub folders.
    - **Include this space**: If selected, then it exports the selected folder, otherwise it only exports the children.
    - **Run export in background**: If selected, then the export will take place in the background, eventually creating the export ACP file.

5. Click on the **OK** button.

On success, the destination location will contain the ACP file. At this point, the ACP file can be saved to a local filesystem for a safe backup or for transfer via email.

Importing a department space using Alfresco Explorer

The process for importing an ACP file within Alfresco Explorer is as follows:

1. Select a space to import the information into.
2. Select the **More Actions | View Details** link to view the **Details** page of the space.
3. Select the **Import** action to launch the **Import** dialog, as shown in the following screenshot:

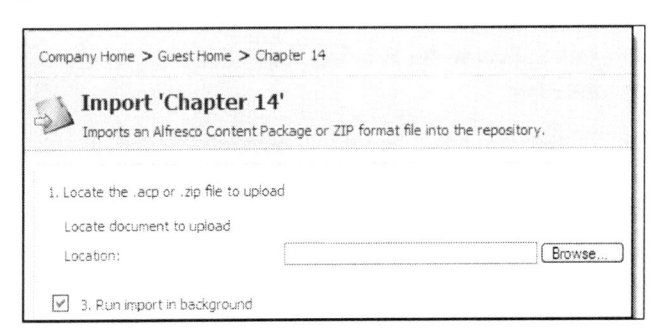

4. Fill in the import options, as follows:
    - **Location**: Select an ACP file to import from the filesystem, by clicking on the **Browse** button.

- **Run in background**: If selected, then the import will take place in the background, eventually creating all of the folders and files held in the ACP file.

5. Click on the **OK** button.

On success, the information previously exported to the ACP file will now reside in the destination space.

Using business rules to import data

By using Alfresco's rules and actions, it is possible to set up an automated import, whereby an ACP file is automatically imported into the repository when it is placed into a designated space.

For example, the following rule (shown in the upcoming screenshot) is defined against an **Import Drop Zone** space, wherein, if the incoming file name property matches *.acp, then the ACP file's contents are imported into the **Import Content** space.

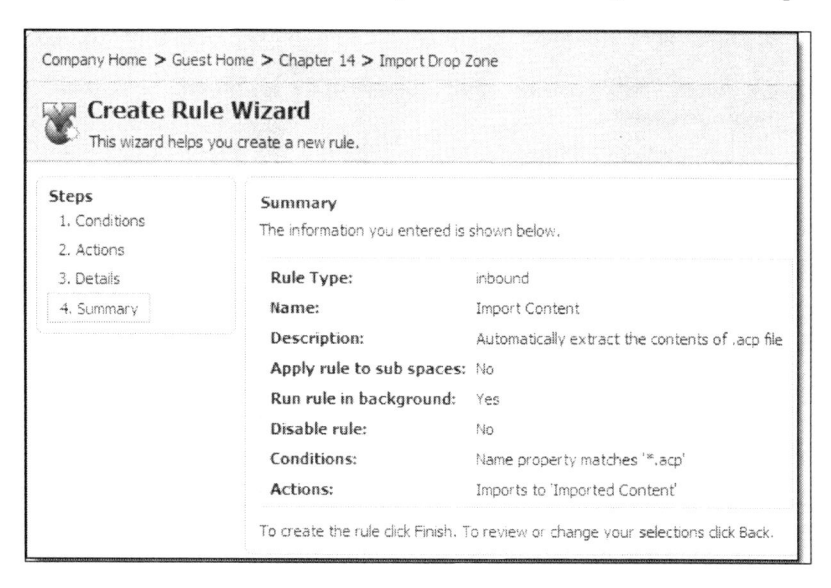

When an ACP file is placed into the **Import Drop Zone** space, the import process is automatically kicked off, and the items held in the ACP file are imported into the **Imported Content** space.

An important point to remember is that the import will be initiated regardless of how the ACP file was placed into the folder. For example, the import will initiate if the ACP file was placed there via CIFS, FTP, WebDAV, Alfresco Explorer, or API. This is particularly powerful for system-to-system data integration.

Using command line tools

The Alfresco export and import tools are developed directly against the Alfresco repository foundation APIs. This means that they can be executed stand-alone with an embedded repository. To perform an export and import operation via these tools requires the configuration of the, to ensure that the appropriate storage locations (for example, database and file system folder) are used.

The export tool

The export tool is useful when you want to extract certain data from the Alfresco repository, without using the Alfresco Explorer application. The Java class file for the export tool is located at `org.alfresco.tools.Export`.

Because the Alfresco repository imposes strict security policies, you need to provide your authentication credentials (username and password), no matter how you access the repository.

The usage of the tool is as follows:

```
Usage: export -user <username> -pwd <password> -s[tore] <store>
[options] <packagename>
```

Where,

- `<username>` is your login user ID
- `<password>` is your password
- `<store>` is the store to extract from, which is in the `scheme://store_name` format
- `<packagename>` is the filename to export to (with or without extension)

Other important `[options]` include:

- `-path`: the path within the store to extract from (the default is "/", which is the root folder)
- `-nochildren`: does not extract children
- `-overwrite`: forces the overwrite of an existing export package if it already exists
- `-quiet`: does not display any messages during export
- `-verbose`: reports the export progress

For example, to export the Intranet space from the repository, you would use the following command:

```
export -user admin -pwd admin -s workspace://SpacesStore -path
/companyhome -verbose Intranet.acp
```

The import tool

The import tool is useful when you want to upload certain data into the Alfresco repository, without using the Alfresco Explorer application. The Java class file for the import tool is located at org.alfresco.tools.import.

The usage of the tool is as follows:

```
Usage: import -user <username> -pwd <password> -s[tore] <store>
[options] <packagename>
```

The [options] are as follows:

- -path: the path to import into, within the store (this default is "/", which is the root folder)
- -verbose: reports the import progress
- -uuidBinding: CREATE_NEW, REMOVE_EXISTING, REPLACE_EXISTING, UPDATE_EXISTING, THROW_ON_COLLISION (the default is CREATE_NEW)

For example, to import the intranet space into the repository, you would use the following command:

```
import -user admin -pwd admin -s workspace://SpacesStore -path
/companyhome -verbose -uuidBinding REPLACE_EXISTING Intranet.acp
```

It is possible to import from an ACP file or just an XML file. Importing just an XML file is useful if you want to import nodes without the associated binary content.

Data backup

This is one of the most important, yet one of the most neglected, areas of computing. Backing up your data should be at the top of your computer's maintenance list, right next to virus protection. Without data backups, you are running the risk of losing your data.

Data loss can happen in many ways. One of the most common causes is the physical failure of the media, on which the data has been stored on. In some situations, users of the system might have deleted the content due to some error. No matter what, your data is your intellectual property, and you have to protect it by taking proper backups regularly.

List of items to backup

Alfresco stores content information in both the database and the filesystem. You need to back up both the filesystem and relational database. As a part of implementation, you might have customized Alfresco. In this case, you also need to back up the customization files. If you have used an external membership system, such as Active Directory or OpenLDAP, then you might have to back up the user and group data as well.

You can set up automated processes to back up your data periodically. On Linux operating systems, you can write a **cron job** to run a backup script on a regular basis. Similarly, all other Operating Systems support backup utilities.

Most often, people tend to store the backup data on the same server. This might create issues if the server crashes. Therefore, it is recommended that you move the backup data on to some other external server to store.

Now, let us examine the various types of data which need to be backed up.

The content stored in the filesystem

Typically the content in the filesystem is stored in your `<install_folder>\alf_data` folder, as shown in the upcoming screenshot. The folder `contentstore` contains the binary content with all of the versions. The folders named `lucene-indexes` and `backup-lucene-indexes` contain search information. The folder named `audit.contentstore` contains audit trail details.

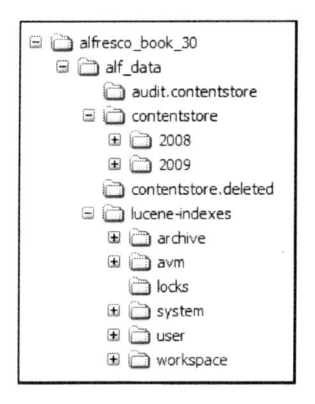

```
alfresco_book_30
  alf_data
    audit.contentstore
    contentstore
      2008
      2009
      contentstore.deleted
    lucene-indexes
      archive
      avm
      locks
      system
      user
      workspace
```

You need to back up the entire folder named `alf_data`, as well as all of its contents.

If you are a Windows user, then you can use the backup utility that comes with Windows XP (it is installed by default in Windows XP Home Edition). You will find it in the **Start** menu, under **All Programs | Accessories | System Tools | Backup**. When you start it, you are presented with the backup wizard, and can follow the instructions on the screen.

The metadata stored in the relational database

The relational database contains a set of tables defined according to the Alfresco schema. These tables hold information about users, security, audit, spaces, metadata, rules, scripts, and various business processes (jBPM).

Most database vendors (both commercial and open source) provide utilities to take a database dump. Based on the database that you have selected during installation (MySQL or Oracle or MySQL Server), you can use an appropriate utility to take a database dump.

MySQL database provides a utility called `mysqldump` to back up both the database table definitions and the contents. It can be used to dump a database or a collection of databases for backup, or for transferring the data to another SQL server (not necessarily a MySQL server). The dump contains SQL statements to create the tables, populate them, or even both.

The following is the command to add the database backup in MySQL:

`Syntax: mysqldump [options] db_name [tables] [> output_file_name]`

An example of the use of this command is:

`> mysqldump alfresco > alfresco_outfile.sql`

Customization files

You might be customizing your Alfresco application over a period of time. Typically, you might have added or updated the following files:

- Logos, images, and style sheets
- JSP Files (dashboard)
- Presentation templates
- Configuration files and property files
- Files in the extension folder
- Custom application code (WAR File, source Java files, and so on.)

The process that you follow to maintain and back up your customization files depends upon the development process you follow within your organization. It is useful to maintain your customization files in a configuration management system, such as CVS or SVN, which helps you to easily maintain the files, as well as back them up.

Membership data

If you have used the Alfresco out of the box membership system, then the data is stored in a relational database. You don't have to do any special tasks to back up the data, as you are already backing up the relational database tables.

If you have used an external membership system, such as Active Directory or OpenLDAP, to provide a single sign-on or centralized identity management system, then you must consider backing up your membership data.

You will have access to the backup tools, based on the membership system that you have used. Ensure that the data in the external membership system is backed up.

Log files

The location of the log files depends upon the application server. For a Tomcat installation, the log files are located in the `<install_folder>` itself. The Tomcat application server creates a log file every day. The current log file is named `alfresco.log` and at the end of the day, the log file is backed up as `alfresco.log.YYYY-MM-DD` (for example, `alfresco.log.2006-09-18`).

Based on the usage of the system and the logging level, the size of these log files might be pretty big. Therefore, it is a good practice to back up the older log files and remove them from the current location, to save disk space.

Backup frequency

The frequency with which you take back-ups, depends upon the nature of the application, your high availability requirements, and the Alfresco deployment option that you have chosen.

For example, you can consider only a single back up of the customization files. You can back up the files whenever you enhance the application, or upgrade the application to newer versions.

Since the content, metadata, and tasks change very frequently, a regular back up of the Alfresco filesystem and relational database is required. You have to consider the business risk, and the system resources available, when deciding on the back up frequency.

Backing up based on the Alfresco deployment

If your application is accessed by thousands of users, then it is important for you to deploy Alfresco in a clustered environment. If it is a critical application, such as a finance or insurance application, then you should consider deploying Alfresco in hot backup mode, with a master-slave configuration. The data back up policy and process might be different, based on the way that you have deployed Alfresco.

The typical process to backup the Alfresco repository is as follows:

1. Stop Alfresco to ensure that nobody can make changes during the back up
2. Export the MySQL (or other) database
3. Backup the Alfresco `alf_data` folder
4. Start Alfresco

To restore the Alfresco repository, carry out the following steps:

1. Stop Alfresco
2. Delete the `alf_data` folder, and restore the `alf_data` folder that you backed up earlier
3. Drop the database, and then import the database that you have exported
4. Start Alfresco

The various Alfresco deployment options are described below:

Alfresco deployed as a repository application server

In this method of deployment (as shown in the following figure), the web application becomes the host for an embedded repository, and remote access is via the application, that is, through HTTP. This is the default deployment option that is chosen by the Alfresco installer. This means that the repository automatically benefits from any enhanced features that are provided by higher-end web application servers.

Administering and Maintaining the System

For example, the repository is not only be embedded inside Apache Tomcat for the lightest weight deployment, but also embedded inside J2EE compliant application servers from JBoss, Oracle, and IBM, to take advantage of distributed transactions and so on.

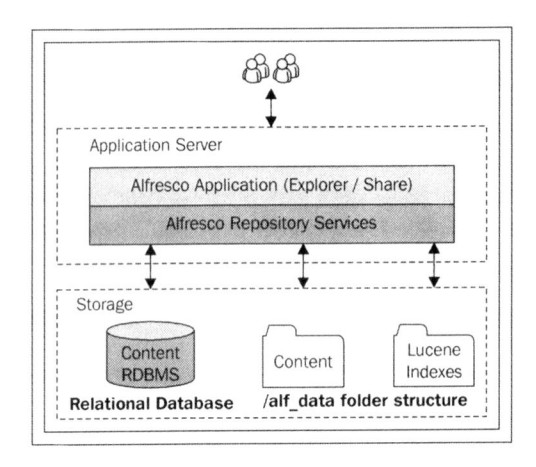

In this deployment option, you need to take a back up of the `alf_data` folder and the database. There will be one copy of the customization files.

Alfresco deployed as a Clustered Repository Server

A **Clustered Repository Server**, as shown in the following figure, supports a large numbers of requests, by employing multiple processes against a single repository store. Each embedded repository is hosted on its own Web Server, and the collection as a whole, that is the Cluster, acts as a single repository.

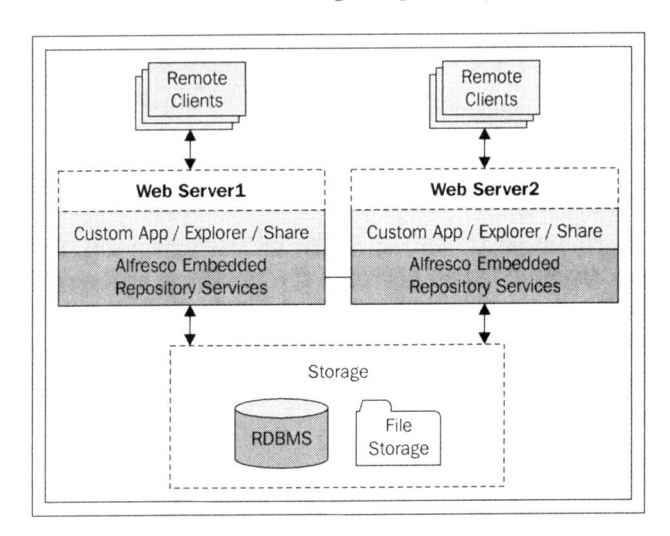

In this deployment option, you need to take a back up of the `alf_data` folder and the database. The customization files need to be provided per web server box.

Alfresco deployed as hot backup

In this method of deployment, as shown in the upcoming figure, one repository server is designated as the master, and another, completely separate, repository server is designated as the slave. The live application is hosted on the master, and as it is used, synchronous and asynchronous replication updates are made to the slave, that is, the backup. The backup remains in read-only mode. If, for some reason, the master breaks down, then it is a relatively simple task to swap over to the slave, and continue operations.

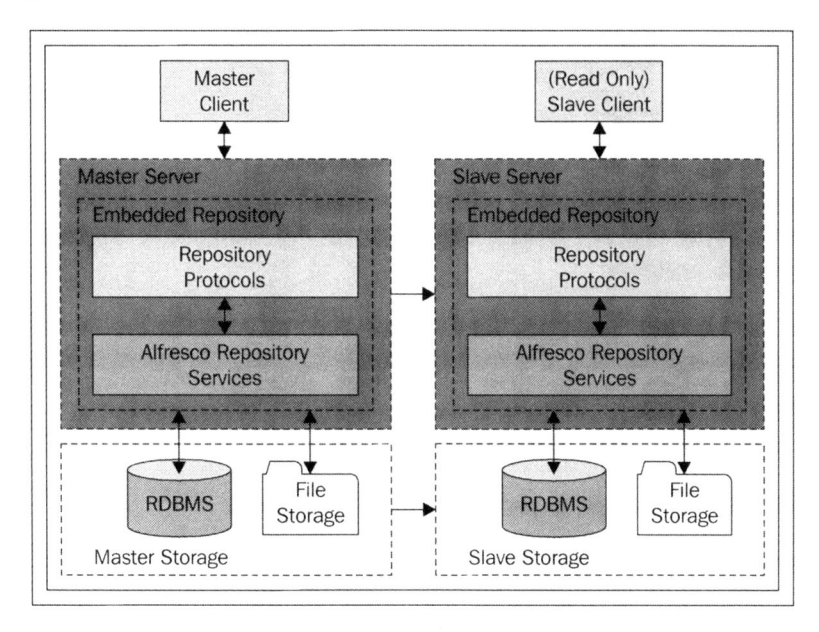

In this deployment option, you don't have to take a regular backup, as the data is being backed up automatically.

Upgrading to newer versions of Alfresco

You can consider upgrading to a newer version of Alfresco if you are expecting one of the following benefits:

- Security patches
- Bug fixes

- New features
- Compatibility with other systems

Even if you are not getting the benefits that are listed above, sometimes you might consider upgrading to a newer version, so that you do not have a big gap between the Alfresco version on which your application is currently running, and the latest Alfresco version. If this gap is too big, then it might be very expensive for you to upgrade later on. This is the scenario with most enterprise software.

Alfresco has an upgrade script feature that helps you to upgrade to newer versions automatically. However, it is essential to follow the best practices when upgrading your system. Always try upgrading your test or staging server first, before trying to upgrade the production server. It is essential that you back up your existing data before attempting an upgrade. Follow the information and the instructions given in the **Data Backup** section.

Upgrading to a minor release

Tpically, an Alfresco minor (or *dot*) release contains bug fixes and minor enhancements. There will not be any new features. An example is upgrading from Alfresco 3.0 to 3.0.1 release.

Because there are no new features, the database schema remains the same. In this situation, you can replace only the web application (.war) file in order to upgrade.

The WAR file (`alfresco.war`) for a Tomcat installation is located in the `<install_folder>\tomcat\webapps` folder.

Carry out the following steps to perform a minor upgrade:

1. Download the latest `alfresco.war` file from the Alfresco web site.
2. Stop Alfresco.
3. Back up all of the data, including the customization files (as explained in the earlier sections of this chapter).
4. Delete the web application folder, `<install_folder>\tomcat\webapps\alfresco`.
5. Replace the `alfresco.war` file, in the `<install_folder>\tomcat\webapps` folder, with the latest one.
6. Restore the customization files.
7. Start Alfresco.

Test your application after upgrading it, in order to ensure that the upgrade was successful.

Upgrading to a major release

Alfresco's major releases typically contain new features, performance enhancements, and bug fixes. An example is upgrading from Alfresco 2.x to the 3.0 version.

The upgrade scripts will be executed automatically by the server, when starting up against an existing database. Scripts that support the various hibernate dialects can be found in the `<configRoot>/alfresco/dbscripts/upgrade/*` folders. This means that you don't have to perform manual upgrades anymore.

For example, let us assume that you are using a Tomcat bundle of Alfresco 2.1 (installed in the `C:\alfresco2.1` folder) on your Windows operating system, and you want to upgrade to the Alfresco 3.0 release. In this case, you would carry out the following steps:

1. Stop Alfresco in your current installation folder, `C:\alfresco2.1`.
2. Back up all of the data, including customization files (as explained in the earlier sections of this chapter).
3. Download the complete Alfresco package and the Tomcat bundle for the Windows operating system.
4. Perform a new installation in a different folder (say, `C:\alfresco3.0`).
5. Copy the older Alfresco file content folder to the newer installation (copy `C:\alfresco2.1\alf_data` folder to `C:\alfresco3.0\alf_data`).
6. Create a new database table, and restore the relational database content from the older database. Update the Alfresco configuration file in the new installation, to point to this new database.
7. Restore the customization files in the new installation.
8. Start Alfresco in the new installation.

Although most of the upgrade happens automatically, you might have to perform some manual steps in order to restore your customization files in the new installation.

There are some configuration files and a properties file in Alfresco's `config` folder (`\tomcat\webapps\alfresco\WEB-INF\classes\alfresco\`), which you might want to update, that requires manual updates.

While I was writing this book, I upgraded the sample application from the Alfresco 2.1 version to the Alfresco 3.0 version. I used the following script to restore some of the customization files. I then manually updated some of the configuration files. Refer to the following batch file, which I used to restore the customization files on the Windows platform:

```
rem ---------------------------------------------------------------
rem Replaces/Adds Alfresco Custom Files to new Alfresco installation
rem ---------------------------------------------------------------
set L_LOCALDIR=%CD%
set L_SRCDIR=C:\alfresco_book_21
set L_DESTDIR=C:\alfresco_book_30
rem ------------ Replace Logos ----------------
CD %L_DESTDIR%\tomcat\webapps\alfresco\images\logo
move AlfrescoLogo32.png AlfrescoLogo32.png-ORIGINAL
move AlfrescoLogo200.png AlfrescoLogo200.png-ORIGINAL
move AlfrescoFadedBG.png AlfrescoFadedBG.png-ORIGINAL
copy %L_SRCDIR%\tomcat\webapps\alfresco\images\logo\AlfrescoLogo32.png .
copy %L_SRCDIR%\tomcat\webapps\alfresco\images\logo\AlfrescoLogo200.png .
copy %L_SRCDIR%\tomcat\webapps\alfresco\images\logo\AlfrescoFadedBG.png .
rem ------------ Copy files in extension folder ----------------
CD %L_DESTDIR%\tomcat\shared\classes\alfresco\extension
copy %L_SRCDIR%\tomcat\shared\classes\alfresco\extension\custom-model-context.xml .
copy %L_SRCDIR%\tomcat\shared\classes\alfresco\extension\customModel.xml .
copy %L_SRCDIR%\tomcat\shared\classes\alfresco\extension\web-client-config-custom.xml .
CD %L_LOCALDIR%
echo I am done...
pause
```

You can create your own batch scripts to automatically restore your customization files. Typically, most of the developers use tools such as Eclipse for building and deploying the customization files to newer installations.

Test your application after upgrading it, in order to confirm that the upgrade was successful.

General maintenance tips

If you maintain the system regularly, by cleaning up the database and by fixing the system errors, then your system will run faster. Some tips for how to perform such activities are given in this section.

Regular maintenance of deleted items

When you delete an item (content or space) in Alfresco, the item will not be deleted from the server, but will be moved to a temporary store called `archive space store`. This gives you the opportunity to recover the content that you have deleted, if necessary. More information about recovering deleted content is provided in Chapter 5.

Deleted items will be kept in the temporary store forever, and will eventually consume a significant amount of storage space. It is best to purge these items periodically. Purged items are deleted forever, and cannot be recovered. It is recommended that take backups of your data before purging.

Examining log files

Your log files present you with information on very important issues and problems about your system. The level of details logged will be based on the defined level of logging (`INFO`, `ERROR`, and `DEBUG`). Refer to Chapter 3, where you have set the level of logging to DEBUG.

The log files are named `alfresco.log` (current files) or `alfresco.log.YYYY-MM-DD` (older files). Examine one of the log files, and you will notice that the log entries fall into the following categories.

- `ERROR`: Error occurred (requires `FIX`)
- `WARN`: Warning messages (requires your attention)
- `INFO`: General information about the system

Some sample messages are as follows:

```
14:20:42,088 WARN    [org.hibernate.cache.EhCacheProvider] Could not
find configuration [org.jbpm.graph.def.Node]; using defaults.
14:21:45,056 ERROR [org.alfresco.repo.action.ActionServiceImpl] An
error was encountered whilst executing the action 'import'.
org.alfresco.service.cmr.view.ImporterException: Failed to import
package at line 8; column 19 due to error: A complete repository
package cannot be imported here…
15:03:19,308 INFO   [org.alfresco.repo.admin.patch.PatchExecuter] No
patches were required. .
```

You have to fix the errors listed in the log file, and make sure there are no ERROR messages in the log files. There are many utilities (based on the operating system), that examine the log file for ERROR messages, and send you notifications whenever necessary. Consider using such a tool, or developing such a tool, to be notified as soon as an ERROR occurs.

Resetting the administrator password

The administrator has the highest powers in the Alfresco application. It is a good practice to periodically change the administrator's password as a security process. You can change the password by using the Alfresco Explorer's **User Profile** option.

If you forget the administrator's password, then you can reset the password by carrying out the following steps:

1. Configure the authentication component to accept all logins, using `org.alfresco.repo.security.authentication.SimpleAcceptOrRejectAllAuthenticationComponentImpl`.
2. Log in as anyone who has admin rights
3. Reset the password
4. Revert the configuration

Resetting the complete repository data

If you are setting up an environment to test your Alfresco application, then you might want to remove or reset the data once the testing has been done. There might be other circumstances, where you want to remove the existing users, spaces, and rules from the repository and start from a fresh installation. Before deleting or resetting the complete repository, you might want to back it up.

The following is the process to reset the complete repository data:

1. Stop Alfresco.
2. Remove the `alf_data` folder.
3. Drop the Alfresco database, and create a new empty Alfresco database.
4. Start Alfresco.

When you start Alfresco, the `alf_data` folder will be created and the default database tables will be created automatically.

Migrating servers

The process of migrating an instance of Alfresco, running on one server to another server, follows a similar pattern to the Backup process, with additional steps for ensuring that any configuration is also copied over.

User quota system

Using Alfresco Explorer's Administrative console, you can track the users' usage within the DM repository, as shown in the following screenshot:

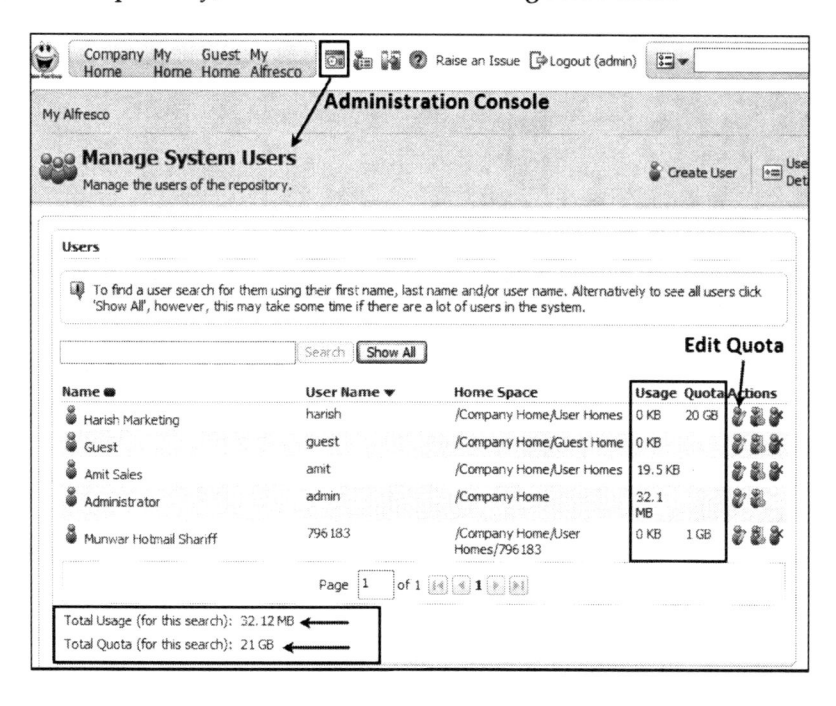

You can also set quotas for a given user. The usage is based on the content size (in bytes) and is typically displayed in **KB** (kilobytes), **MB**(megabytes), or **GB**(gigabytes).

When a user adds or edits content beyond his or her quota, an error message will be displayed, stating that the user has exceeded his or her quota.

Individual users can check their quota and usage, by using Alfresco Explorer's **User Profile** settings page.

Multi-Tenancy

Multi-Tenancy (MT) is a software architecture, where a single instance of the software runs on a **software-as-a-service (SaaS)** vendor's server, while serving multiple client organizations (tenants). MT is contrasted with a multi-instance architecture, where separate software instances (or hardware systems) are set up for different client organizations. With a multi-tenant architecture, a software application is designed to virtually partition its data and configuration, so that each client organization works with a customized virtual application instance.

Alfresco ECM can be configured as a true single-instance multi-tenant environment. This enables multiple independent tenants to be hosted on a single instance, which can be installed, either on a single server or across a cluster of servers. The Alfresco instance is logically partitioned in such a way that it will appear to each tenant as if they are accessing a completely separate instance of Alfresco.

Enabling Multi-Tenancy

By default, Alfresco supports a single-instance, **Single-Tenant (ST)** environment, where each tenant (for example customer) runs a single instance that is installed on one server or across a cluster of servers.

To enable a multi-tenant environment, you need to rename the following three sample MT extension files:

- Rename `alfresco/extension/mt/mt-context.xml.sample` to `alfresco/extension/mt/mt-context.xml`
- Rename `alfresco/extension/mt/mt-admin-context.xml.sample` to `alfresco/extension/mt/mt-admin-context.xml`
- Rename `alfresco/extension/mt/mt-contentstore-context.xml.sample` to `alfresco/extension/mt/mt-contentstore-context.xml`

Then, restart Alfresco to enable multi-tenancy.

Creating tenants

The default Alfresco admin user can be considered as the **super tenant**. All tenants can be administered by this super tenant admin user from the **Tenant Administration Console**.

Log in to the Alfresco Explorer (`http://<servername>:<port>/alfresco`) using an admin username and password. The URL to the tenant administration console is `http://<Alfresco Explorer URL>/faces/jsp/admin/tenantadmin-console.jsp`, which in our case is, `http://localhost:8080/alfresco/faces/jsp/admin/tenantadmin-console.jsp`, as shown in the following screenshot:

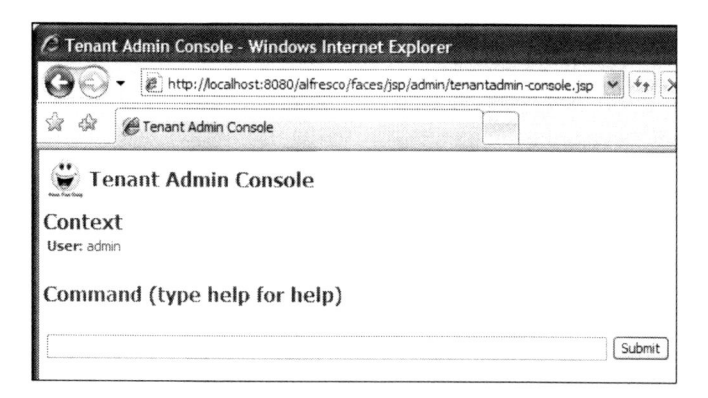

To test the multi-tenancy features, create a tenant account using the Tenant Admin Console.

`create cignex.com pwcignex /usr/tenantstores/cignex`

In this example, `cignex.com` is the domain, `pwcignex` is the tenant administrator's password, and `cignex` is the name of tenant store.

Now, `admin@cignex.com` will be the administrator for the tenant account `cignex.com`.

Tenant use case

Now, the Alfresco instance has multi-tenancy enabled, with two tenants. One is the default tenant, and the other is the `cignex.com` tenant.

Log in to Alfresco Explorer (`http://<servername>:<port>/alfresco`) with a user ID of `admin@cignex.com` and a password of `pwcignex`, as set by the super tenant administrator.

Administering and Maintaining the System

You will notice a new instance has been created, as shown in the following screenshot. The user administration, spaces, security, scripts, business rules, and search, are specific to the tenant, `cignex.com`.

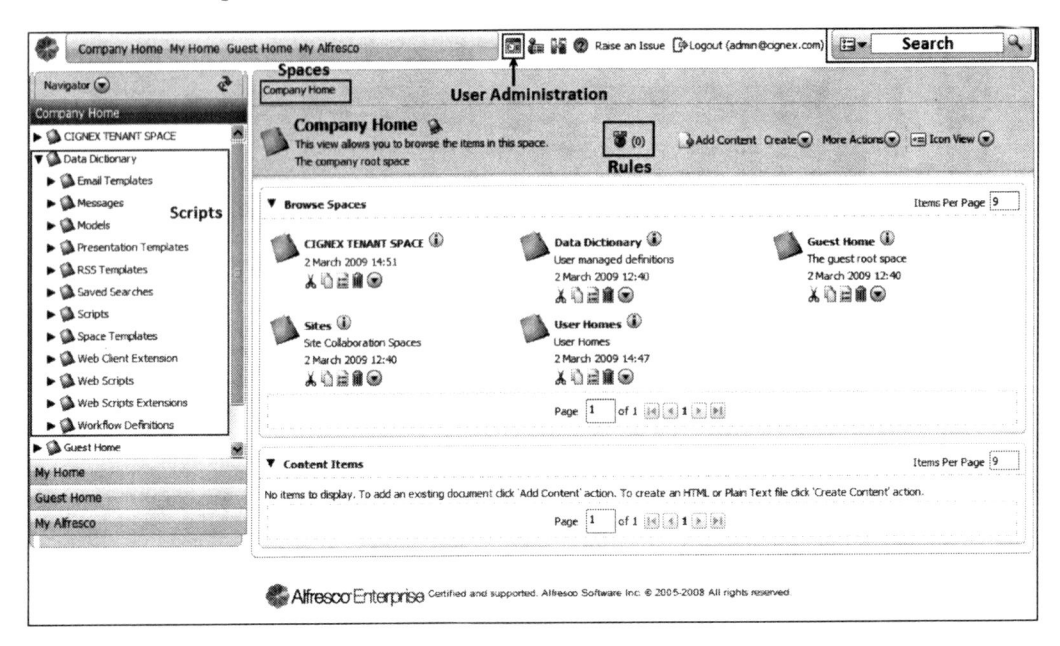

The tenant administrator (`admin@cignex.com`) can create other users, who will have local access to this tenant site, as needed. The users created for this tenant should log in to the `cignex.com` domain. For example, if the user id is `user1`, then that user must login with `user1@cignex.com` as the user ID.

Similarly, the spaces and the content created can only be accessed and searched by the tenant users. Even the interfaces, such as CIFS, FTP, and WebDAV, are specific to a tenant. For example, if you map CIFS with `admin@cignex.com` as the user ID, then you will access only the `cignex.com` tenant-specific space structure, as shown in the following screenshot:

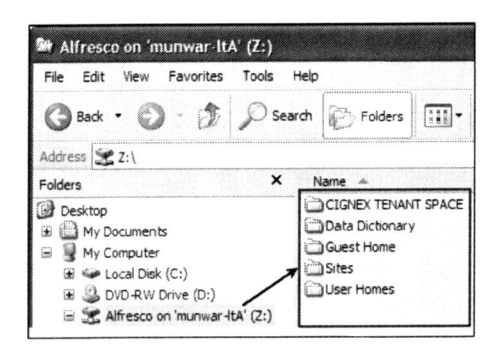

Managing tenants

As a **super tenant administrator**, you can enable or disable tenants, you can export or import tenant data, and you can perform other administrative tasks, such as, changing tenant admin passwords.

The following table lists some of the important commands that you can use in the **Tenant Admin Console**.

Command	Description
`help`	Lists all of the commands.
`show tenants`	Lists all of the tenants and shows their details.
`create <tenant domain> <tenant admin password> [<root contentstore dir>]`	Creates a tenant, with an admin user called `admin@<tenant domain>` with a supplied admin password. The root of the `contentstore` folder can be optionally specified.
	For example: `create cignex.com pwcignex /usr/tenantstores/cignex`.
`changeAdminPassword <tenant domain> <new pass word>`	Useful if the tenant's admin (`admin@<tenant domain>`) has forgotten their password.
`enable <tenant domain>`	Enables the tenant so that it is active and available for new logins.
`disable <tenant domain>`	Disables the tenant so that it is inactive. Existing logins will fail on the next usage.
`delete <tenant domain>`	Deletes the tenant. This currently requires a server restart to clear the index threads. Also, the tenant search index folders should be deleted manually.
`export <tenant domain> <destination directory>`	Exports the tenant to the given destination folder. Export filenames will be suffixed with `<tenant domain>_`.
	For example: `export cignex.com /usr/exportdir`
`import <tenant domain> <source directory>`	Creates a tenant by importing the tenant files from the given source folder. The import filenames must be suffixed with `<tenant domain>_`.

Exporting and importing tenant data

As part of the tenant maintenance activity, you could periodically export tenant specific data. For example, the following is the command (from the **Tenant Admin Console**) to export the entire `cignex.com` tenant data to the destination folder `c:/temp`:

`export cignex.com c:/temp`

You will notice that the following tenant files are created in the destination folder, with filenames suffixed with `<tenant domain>_`.

- `cignex.com_models.acp`
- `cignex.com_spaces.acp`
- `cignex.com_spaces_archive.acp`
- `cignex.com_system.acp`
- `cignex.com_users.acp`
- `cignex.com_versions2.acp`

Similarly, you can recreate the tenant by importing the tenant files from a given source folder. The syntax of the `import` command is specified in the table shown earlier.

Full auditing

Your content could be one of your most valuable assets. Based on regulatory and compliance requirements, you might want to have a full audit trail and accountability of user activities in your Content Management System.

Although content may be removed from the site, a full audit trail is always recoverable. That audit includes the content, all of the edited versions of the content, and a full record of exactly who did what and when.

In Alfresco, auditing is carried out in the service layer of the repository. This captures both user and application interaction with the repository. All of the user and system activities are logged and made available through the server auditing system. The data, time, user, comments, and the actual content changes, are stored and are accessible to users.

Controlling audit information

By default, auditing is disabled. To enable the default audit configuration, change the `enabled` attribute, which is highlighted in bold in the upcoming piece of code, to `true`.

For auditing to be enabled for a method, it must be enabled or unset on the method, enabled or unset on the service, and enabled on the top-level audit element. If it is marked as `enabled="false"` anywhere in the stack, then auditing will be disabled.

The audit configuration file is located at `<configRoot>\auditConfig.xml`. The following code extract shows some of the important parameters in the audit configuration file. Note that this is the not the complete file.

```xml
<!-- Default Audit Configuration -->
<Audit xmlns="http://www.alfresco.org/model/audit/1.0" xmlns:xsi="http://www.w3.org/2001/XMLSchema-instance" enabled="false" auditInternal="false" mode="all">

    <!-- The File/Folder Service -->
    <Service name="FileFolderService" mode="none">
        <Method name="rename" mode="all"/>
        <Method name="move" mode="all"/>
        <Method name="copy" mode="all" auditInternal="true"/>
        <Method name="create" mode="all"/>
        <Method name="delete" mode="all"/>
        <Method name="makeFolders" mode="all"/>
        <Method name="getWriter" mode="all"/>
    </Service>
    <Service name="VersionService" mode="none">
        <Method name="createVersion" mode="all"/>
        <Method name="revert" mode="all"/>
        <Method name="restore" mode="all"/>
        <Method name="deleteVersionHistory" mode="all"/>
    </Service>
```

Simple audit template for displaying auditing information

To enable auditing, open the `<configRoot>\auditConfig.xml` file, and change the `enabled` attribute value to `true`. Then restart the Alfresco server, in order to apply the changes.

Go to the **Company Home > Intranet > Press and Media > Press Releases** space, and edit one of the press release documents. For the same press release document, use the **Preview in Template** button and select the **show_audit.ftl** template from the drop-down list. Notice the column titled **Method** in the audit report, which captures all of the actions that happened for the document.

You will see the audit information, as shown in the following screenshot:

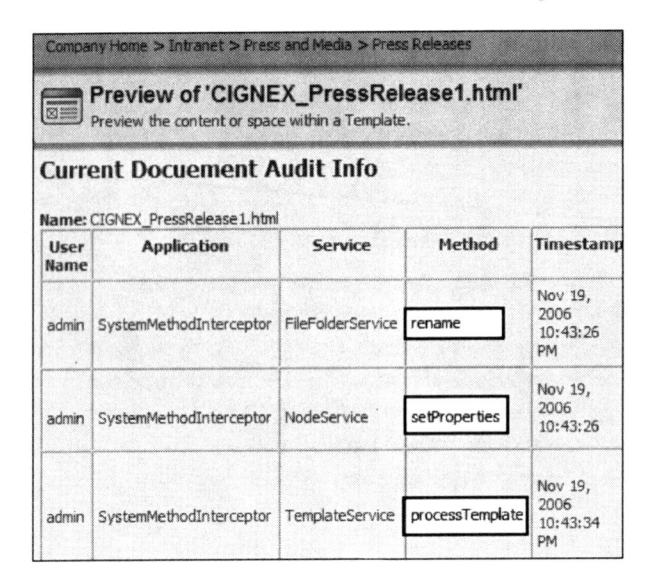

Go to the **Company Home > Data Dictionary > Presentation Templates** space, and examine the code in the `show_audit.ftl` file. This is a simple audit template that is provided in order to display the audit information. You can either edit this template, or create another one, depending on your audit reporting requirements.

Summary

Alfresco Explorer has administrative utilities to export data from the Alfresco repository, and to import data to the same repository or to another repository.

You must back up data at regular intervals, in order to protect your data from hardware failure. Consider the hot backup deployment option of Alfresco for high availability. If you need a high performance repository, then you should consider deploying Alfresco in a clustered environment.

The upgrade scripts in Alfresco help you to upgrade to newer versions automatically. It is recommended that you try an upgrade on a test or staging server, before upgrading the production server.

Alfresco ECM can be configured as a true single-instance multi-tenant environment. This enables multiple independent tenants to be hosted on a single instance.

Index

A

ACEGI Aspect-Oriented Security Framework 13
ACP
  about 526
  exporting 526
  importing 526
  importing, business rules used 529
ACP Generator's bulk upload utility 178
Active Directory
  and eDirectory, differences 109
  integrating with Alfresco 15
administration console, Alfresco Explorer
  about 62
  category management 63
  data management 63
  export functionality 63
  group management 62
  import functionality 63
  manage user groups functionality 62
  node browser functionality 63
  system information 63
  user management 62
Adobe Flex 331
Adobe Flex 3, RIA clients 477
Adobe Flex Alfresco intergration 331, 332
advanced search
  about 488
  search by content category 489
  search by content properties 490
advanced workflow
  about 260, 271
  adhoc workflow 273, 275
  custom advanced workflows, creating 276
  integrating, with rules 303
  out of the box features 273
  RajComp company example 273
  status, tracking through customized dashlet 297, 299
  workflow task list's dashboards 299
  workflow user interactions 272
AIFS 13
Alfresco
  about 10
  Active Directory, integrating with 15
  advantages 10
  auditing 548
  basic configuration 70
  benefits 19
  blue print, creating 82
  built-in business rules 193
  business rules, implementing 179
  configuring, as Windows service 53
  content, categorizing 149
  content, creating 64
  content, exporting 526
  content, importing 526
  content, managing 134
  content, migrating to 177
  content, securing 106
  dashboards 66
  data backup 531
  data dictionary space 165
  deleted content, recovering 163, 164
  discussion forums 170
  Drupal, integrating with 15
  eCopy-enabled scanner, integrating with 522
  example solution, implementing 28
  existing users, migrating to 119
  export tool 530

Facebook, integrating with 14
features 31, 509
forms processing 508
future 26
general maintenance tips 541
iGoogle, integrating with 14
imaging solutions 508
import tool 531
information web sites 28
installing 3, 31
installing on Microsoft Windows 3
integrating with, Liferay 118
inter-department collaboration,
    via space 174
iPhone, integrating with 14
Joomla!, integrating with 14
Kofax Ascent Capture, integrating
    with 14, 519
LDAP, integrating with 15
library services 144
Liferay, integrating with 15
link to content, creating 65
Lucene, configuring 502
maintaining 525
membership and security model 86
MS Office 2003 add-ins 160
multilingual content, managing 152
open search engines 495
overview 10, 12
Quark Publishing System 8, integrating
    with 14
resources, information 28
RSS syndication 175
scheduled actions 211, 215
search criteria, saving as report 493
search feature 485
security, imposing 88
security model, selecting 107
security permissions and roles,
    extending 99
space, creating 63, 64
space, managing 128
spaces, securing 101
space templates, for reusable space
    structure 167
system users, managing 89
upgrading, to major release 539, 540
upgrading, to minor release 538
upgrading, to new versions 537, 538
user access, individual 94
user groups, managing 97
user interface options 483
ViewOne Pro, integrating with 14

Alfresco, benefits
collaboration management 23, 24
customer case studies web site 26
document management 19, 20
enterprise content search 25
records management 21
web content management 22, 23

Alfresco, future
enterprise version versus community
    labs 26
free upgrades 28
support options 27

Alfresco, installing
extensions, installing with AMP install 55
installation options 35
on Linux 54
on Microsoft Windows 39, 41
out of the box installation architecture 32

Alfresco, installing on Linux 54, 55

Alfresco, installing on Microsoft Windows
Alfresco, configuring as Windows
    service 53
Alfresco, starting as console
    application 52, 53
Alfresco, stopping as console
    application 52
Alfresco components, installing 43
Alfresco Tomcat bundle, installing 42
folder structure, installing 51
installation 39, 42
requisites 39

Alfresco, on Microsoft Windows
requirements 3

Alfresco, overview
acess control 13
business process automation 14
content repository 11
content repository, diagrammatic
    representation 11
enterprise integrations 14
globalization support 13

[552]

library services 14
open source, benefits 10
open standards 12
scalable architecture 12
security 13
Alfresco applications
　blue print, creating 82
　compliance and records management 25
　corporate websites 25
　enterprise document repository 25
　enterprise knowledge management
　　　portal 25
　financial applications 25
　intranet 25
　marketing communications 25
　on demand publishing 25
　research portals 26
　scalable content repository 25
Alfresco Book project site
　blog page 406
　calendar page 401
　creating 368, 369
　customizing 375
　dashboard, customizing 376
　discussions page 414
　document library page 386
　multiple library items, working with 400
　page, selecting 379, 380
　RSS feed, subscribing 378, 379
　site content, tagging 379
　site dashboard RSS feed, configuring 378
　site details, editing 377
　site users, managing 420
　using 373
　wiki page 380
　wiki site dashlet, configuring 378
Alfresco bundled with Tomcat
　downloading 42
　installing 42
Alfresco CMIS implementation
　about 354
　sample Alfresco CMIS dashlet 354
Alfresco Community Labs Network 35
Alfresco Components installation
　about 43
　CIFS, installing 49
　Image Magick, installing 49

Microsoft Office Add-ins, installing 50
MySQL database, configuring 46-48
MySQL database, installing 44, 45
MySQL database, setting up 47
OpenOffice, installing 48
Share Point Protocol Support, installing 43
SWFTools, installing 51
WCM, installing 50
Alfresco configuration, extending
　ConfigRoot folder 71
　configuration approach 71, 73
　db.* 71
　default configuration files 71
　dir.root 71
　extension folder 71
　Java extensions, deploying 73, 74
　Java extensions, packaging 73, 74
　JBoss 71
　Tomcat 71
Alfresco Content Package. *See* **ACP**
Alfresco content platform
　about 305
　embeddable enterprise content
　　　management system 306
　integrated enterprise content management
　　　system 306
Alfresco deployment option
　Alfresco, deploying as clustered repository
　　　server 536, 537
　Alfresco, deploying as hot backup 537
　Alfresco, deploying as repository
　　　application server 535, 536
Alfresco Draft CMIS Implementation
　about 19
　Apache Abdera CMIS Extension 19
　CMIS query language 19
　CMIS REST API binding 19
　CMIS REST API Binding Test Harness 19
　CMIS Web Services API binding 19
Alfresco Enterprise 3.0
　about 15
　Alfresco Draft CMIS Implementation 19
　Alfresco Network 16
　Alfresco Repository Public API 18
　Alfresco Share 17
　Alfresco Surf 18
　Alfresco Web Studio 16

Microsoft Office SharePoint Protocol
      support 19
  overview 15
  SharePoint protocol support 426
Alfresco Enterprise Edition 9
Alfresco Enterprise Network 35
Alfresco Explorer
  about 57
  administration console 62
  Alfresco, logging into as admin 58
  Alfresco Share, customizing 466
  configuring 444
  custom components, configuring in
      Alfresco Share 474
  custom dashlets, configuring 471
  custom webscripts, configuring 469
  dashboards, user configurable 450
  FreeMarker dashlet 457
  JSP client, customizing 479
  presentation templates 466
  screen layout 58
  search 486
  user interface, customizing with Flex 477
  views, configuring 444
Alfresco Explorer as OpenSearch aggregator
  about 497
  Alfresco server, registering 497, 498
  federated search 499
  new search engines, registering 497
  Wikipedia, registering 498
  Yahoo search engine, registering 497, 498
Alfresco foundation APIs
  about 479
  code snippets 479
  ContentService 479
  DictionaryService 479
  FileFolderService 479
  implementing 479
  NodeService 479
  SearchService 479
Alfresco Labs Edition 9
Alfresco license file
  downloading 44
  installing 43, 44
Alfresco Network
  about 16
  features 16

Alfresco objects, available to FreeMarker
  args 459
  classifications 459
  companyhome 459
  document 459
  person 459
  session 459
  space 459
  template 459
  userhome 459
Alfresco repository
  about 426
  features 426
Alfresco Repository Public API
  about 18
  features 18
  JavaScript API 18
  RESTful API 18
Alfresco search engine
  configuring 500
  properties, indexing 501, 502
  search results, limiting 500
  theory 500
Alfresco Share
  about 17, 57, 360
  benefits 426
  components 362
  customizing 466
  features 17, 18, 360, 361
  my dashboard 363
  my profile 365
  people 370
  personal dashboard, using 371
  site, customizing 375
  site, using 373
  sites 368
Alfresco Share 3.0
  about 477
  features 477
Alfresco Surf
  about 18, 360
Alfresco Tomcat bundle installation
  about 42
  Alfresco bundled with Tomcat,
      installing 42
  Java SE Developer Kit, installing 42

[554]

Alfresco Web Studio
  about 16, 17
  features 17
Alfresco workflow process
  about 260
  advanced workflow 260
  simple workflow 260
application integration examples
  about 326
  Adobe Flex integration 331
  Drupal integration 329
  email integration 332
  Facebook integration 346
  FFMPEG video transcoder integration 339
  iGoogle integration 335
  iPhone integration 333
  Joomal! integration 330
  Liferay integration 326
  ViewOnePro image viewer integration 343
Aspect-Oriented Programming 194
auditing
  about 548
  audit information, controlling 548
  enabling 549
  simple audit template 549
authentication 88

B

backbox 35
basic configuration, Alfresco
  content store, configuring 74, 75
  default administrator password,
    changing 74
  default logos, configuring 79
  email server, configuring 76
  enterprise license file, installing 74
  extending 70
  file systems, configuring 78
  inbound email server, configuring 77
  log files, configuring 77
  look and feel, customizing CSS used 80
  multilanguage support, configuring 80, 81
  MySQL database, configuring 75
  outbound email service, configuring 76
  relational database, configuring 75
  virtual file system, configuring 78

batch size 503
bean 222
blog page, Alfresco Book project site
  about 406
  accessing 406
  blog comment, deleting 414
  blog comment, editing 413
  blog post, creating 407
  blog post, deleting 410
  blog post, editing 409
  blog post, publishing 408
  blog post, publishing to external blog 411
  blog post, saving 408
  blog post, viewing 410
  browsing 406
  comment, adding to post 412
  comments, working with 412
  external blog, configuring 411
  updated blog post, publishing 409, 410
blue print, creating
  about 82
  features, to be implemented 82, 83
  Have Fun Corporation enterprise 82
business rules
  actions, applying to individual content 198
  aspect, removing from content 198, 199
  extending, with custom JavaScript 206
business rules, built-in
  about 193
  actions 195, 196
  conditions, checking 194, 195
  triggering 197
  working 194
**business rules, extending with custom
    JavaScript**
  about 206, 207
  corporate forms space, setting up 207
  custom JavaScript, creating 208, 209
  custom JavaScript, executing as action 209
business rules, space
  chaining 192, 193
  documents, automatic versioning 190
  documents, organizing
    automatically 180-187
  email notifications, sending to specified
    people 191, 192

[555]

properties, adding to document 188
running, in background 188

C

calendar page, Alfresco Book project site
  about 401
  accessing 401
  browsing 401, 402
  event, adding 403, 404
  event, deleting 405
  event, editing 404
  event, viewing 403
  site events, browsing 405

CAS server
  integrating with, Liferay 119

categories, content
  about 149
  adding, to content 150, 151
  managing 149, 150

CIFS
  about 154, 308
  documents, checking in 157, 158
  documents, checking out 157, 158
  documents, drag-and-drop 157
  drive, mapping 155, 156
  installing 49
  SMB 154

classification object 210
cm-effectivity property 72
CMIS
  about 19, 352
  Alfresco CMIS implementation 354
  features 352
  scope 353
  use cases 353

CMIS, use cases
  core ECM use cases 353
  ECM applications and use cases 353
  Out-of-scope use cases 353

CMIS technical draft specification 19
collaboration management, Alfresco
  about 23
  CIFS 24
  knowledge management 24
  WebDAV 24

Common Internet File System. *See* **CIFS**
companyhome object 210
complex workflows
  Secure Loaning Ltd example 269

constraints
  applying 234-237
  constraint type 232

constraint types
  LENGTH 234
  LIST 233
  MINMAX 233
  REGEX 233

content
  Alfresco, migrating to 177
  binary files, uploading 137
  categories 149
  categories, adding 150
  categorizing 149
  content actions 141
  content properties, managing 142, 144
  copying, clipboard used 142
  creating 134
  deleting 142
  editing 138
  exporting 526, 527
  HTML file, editing online 138
  importing 526
  managing 134
  managing, network drivers used 154
  moving, clipboard used 142
  searching, by category 152
  shortcut, creating 142
  text documents, creating 134, 135, 136
  text file, editing online 138
  text files, editing offline 139, 140
  updated cotent, uploading 141
  XML file, editing online 138

content, migrating to Alfresco
  about 177
  ACP Generator's bulk upload utility 178
  content, drag-and-drop to network drive 177
  web services, used 177

content, securing
  about 106
  user roles 106
  users, inviting 107

Content Management Interoperability
    Services. See CMIS
content metadata 142
content model
    about 221
    constraints 232
    custom aspect 225
    custom associations 246
    custom configuration 220
    custom content type 239
    dynamic models 253
    property sheet configuration 237
content properties
    additional properties, adding 144
    content metadata 142
    managing 142
    metadata editing 143
    metadata extractors 143
content repository
    about 11
    features 11
content store
    configuring 74
content transformation
    about 199
    built-in transformations 206
    handling 199
    images, resizing 202, 203
    images, transforming 202, 203
    Micorsoft Office documents, converting to ODF 203
    OpenDocument Format 203
    word document, transforming to PDF 199-201
cron expression 216
cron job 532
custom-hibernate-dialect.properties
    modifying 48
custom-repository.properties
    modifying 48
custom advanced workflows, creating
    Alfresco Explorer task dialogs, creating 293
    Alfresco Explorer task dialogs, deploying 293
    process definition, creating 285
    process definition, deploying 285
    task model, creating 278

task model, deploying 278, 279, 282
testing 295, 296
workflow images, displaying 292
workflow process, defining 277
workflow resource bundles, creating 282
workflow resource bundles, deploying 282-285
custom aspect
    about 225
    adding, to Alfresco 226
    advantages 225
    content model, extending 227
    defining 226
    disadvantage 226
    need for 225
    properties 226, 227
    property elements 228
    using, as businness rule 230-232
    web client, configuring 229
custom associations
    about 246
    child association 246
    defining 246, 248
    example 252
    need for 246
    presentation template, for custom content type 249-251
    reference association 246
    types 246
    using 248
custom components, Alfresco Share
    configuring 474-477
custom configuration
    about 220
    configuration files, for custom content model 222
    configuration files, for default content model 220
    configuration files, hierarchy 224
custom content
    adding 242
custom content model, configuration files
    custom model context file 223
    custom model file 224
    custom web client configuration file 224
custom content type
    about 239

[557]

adding 242, 243
adding, to Alfresco 239
business rules, creating 245
content model, extending 240
defining 240
need for 239
press release, creating as HTML content 244, 245
web client, configuring 241, 242
custom dashlets
Alfresco, restarting 453
configuring 450, 471, 473
custom dashlet JSP, configuring 452, 453
custom dashlet JSP, creating 452
custom dashlet script, creating 451, 452
My Alfresco Dashboard, using 453, 454
writing 450, 452

D

daily dose integration Web Script
about 315
creating 315, 316
storing 316
daisy chaning 113
dashboards
about 66, 450
configuring, wizard used 67
My Alfresco dashboard, selecting at start location 66
user configurable 450
webscripts, using as dashlets 454
dashboards, configuring
components, selecting 68
layout, selecting 68
wizard used 67
dashlets 363, 450
dashlets, personal dashboard
Alfresco Network 363
CMIS feed 363
documents editing 363
getting started 363
my activities 363
my calendar 363
my profile 363
my sites 363

my tasks 363
RSS feed 363
data backup
about 531
Alfresco, deploying as clustered repository server 536
Alfresco, deploying as hot backup 537
Alfresco, deploying as repository application server 535
backup frequency 534
content stored in file 532, 533
customization files 533
log files 534
membership data 534
metadata, stored in relational database 533
process, in Alfresco repository 535
datadictionary 268
data dictionary space
about 165
sub spaces 165
data dictionary space, sub spaces
email templates 165
messages 166
models 166
presentation templates 166
RSS templates 166
saved searches 166
scripts 166
space templates 166
web client extension 166
web forms 166
web scripts 166
web scripts extensions 166
workflow definitions 166
default administrator password
changing 74
default logos, Alfresco
AlfrescoFadedBG.png file 79
AlfrescoLogo200.png file 79
AlfrescoLogo32.png file 79
configuring 79
customizing 79
login page background logo 79
login page logo 79
site logo 79
directory servers, LDAP
Active Directory 109

[558]

eDirectory 109
iPlanet 109
OpenLDAP 109
discussion forums
  about 170
  creating, in forum space 171
  forums, defining for groups 173
  forum space 170
  roles and permissions 172, 173
  security 172
  topics, creating 171
discussions page, Alfresco Book project site
  about 414
  accessing 414
  new topic, creating 416, 417
  reply, creating 418
  reply, editing 419
  topics, browsing 415, 416
  topics, deleting 418
  topics, editing 417, 418
  topics, viewing 416
document library page, Alfresco Book project site
  about 386
  accessing 386
  browsing 387, 388
  comment, adding to library item 392
  content, uploading 389, 390
  folder structure, creating 388
  individual library items, working with 390
  item, copying 396, 397
  item, deleting 395
  item, downloading 394
  item, editing 393
  item, moving 397
  item, viewing 390, 392
  item details, editing 396
  items, adding 389
  library item comment, deleting 393
  library item comment, editing 392
  permissions, managing 399
  updated content, uploading 394
  workflow, assigning to item 397, 398
document management, Alfresco
  about 20
  dashboard views 20
  document lifecycle management 20

  document lifecycle management features 20
  Presentation templates 20
document object 210
documents, handling, Share Point Protocol Support
  content, adding to document library 434
document search Web Script
  about 318
  calling, form external application 325
  creating 319-324
  storing 324, 325
documents handling, Share Point Protocol Support
  about 427
  content, adding to document library 433
  document, checking in 431
  document, checking out 431
  document, editing 430, 431
  document versions 431, 432
  document versions, managing 433
  document workspace, creating 427, 429
  previous document version, viewing 432
document workspace, Share Point Protocol Support
  about 434
  customizing 436
  document, saving 435
  document updates, downloading from site 439
  document updates, managing 441
  membership, managing 437
  site copy, updating 440
  site name, editing 436
  site settings, changing 437
  updatable copy, saving locally 440
  working with 439
document workspace dashlet 442
document workspace membership, Share Point Protocol Support
  members, adding to site 437
  members role 438
  site member, removing 438
  user profiles, editing 438
  user profiles, viewing 438

Draft CMIS Implementation. *See* **Alfresco Draft CMIS Implementation**
Drupal
  about 329
  integrating with Alfresco 15
Drupal Alfresco intergration 329
dynamic custom model
  about 253
  activating 254
  deploying 254
  inactivating 255
  updating 255
dynamic models
  about 253
  dynamic custom model 253, 254
  dynamic web client 255
  in, multi-tenancy environment 257
  tenant accounts, creating 257
dynamic web client
  about 255
  web client customizations, deploying 256
  web client customizations, reloading 256

E

ECM 9
ECM investment value
  extending 505
eCopy 508
eCopy-enabled scanner
  about 522
  integrating with Alfresco 522
eCopy ShareScan OP 522
eDirectory
  and Active Directory, differences 109
electronic imaging
  about 506
  benefits 506
email integration, Alfresco
  about 332
  Lotus Notes 332
  MS Outlook 332
  Novell 332
  Thunderbird 332
email service
  configuring 76

embeddable enterprise content management system 306
Enterprise Content Management. *See* ECM
enterprise content search
  about 25
  features 25
enterprise integrations 14
enterprise license file
  installing 74
export tool 530, 531
extensions, installing with AMP install 55

F

Facebook
  about 346
  integrating with Alfresco 14
Facebook Alfresco integration
  about 346
  Facebook application, registering 350, 351
  new Facebook application, creating 347-349
FFMPEG video transcoder 339
FFMPEG video transcoder Alfresco integration
  about 339
  audio, transcoding 340
  transformation, executing 340-342
  transformation, integrating as action 340
  video, transcoding 339
File Transfer Protocol. *See* FTP
flash player
  installing 51
Flex 477
FlexSpaces 477
folder structure installation
  about 51
  alf_data 51
  Alfresco 51
  Amps 51
  bin 52
  extras 52
  java 52
  licenses 52
  OpenOffice 52
  README files 52
  tomcat 52
  virtual-tomcat 52

forms processing
  about 507
  electronic content 507
  image enhancement 507
  information extraction 507
  scanning 507
  workflow 507
forum 170
forum space 170
FreeMarker
  about 457
  features 457
  FreeMarker template engine 460
FreeMarker dashlet
  about 457
  Alfresco objects available 458, 459
  custom template, for space custom
      view 465
  custom template, for XML content 463, 464
  custom templates, for previewing web
      pages 461, 462
  FreeMarker directives 460
  FreeMarker template engiine 458
  FreeMarker template node model API 460
  presentation templates 457
FreeMarker directives 460
FreeMarker template 451
FreeMarker template engine 458
FreeMarker Template Language 443
FreeMarker template node model API 460
FTP 34, 158, 308

G

general maintenance tips
  administrator password, resetting 542
  complete repository data, resetting 542
  deleted items, maintenance 541
  log files, examining 541
  servers, migrating 543
groups
  about 86
  EVERYONE 86

H

Hello World example, Web Scripts 312

Hibernate 3.2 ORM Persistence 13
Home Load Document Workflow 270

I

ICR 507
iGoogle
  about 335
  integrating with Alfresco 14
iGoogle Alfresco integration
  about 335
  iGoogle gadgets, integrating 336, 337
  iGoogle gadgets, using 338
Image Magick
  installing 49
import tool 531
Independent Software Vendor. *See* **VARs**
installation options, Alfresco
  about 35
  application servers 37
  databases 36
  Enterprise Network 35
  JBoss application server 37
  JBoss Portal 38
  Liferay 38
  Linux 36
  Linux, advantages 36
  MS SQL Server database 36
  MySQL database 37
  operating systems 36
  Oracle database 37
  PostgreSQL database 37
  software, selecting 38
  Tomcat application server 37
  Windows operating system 36
installing
  Alfresco 31
  Alfresco, on Linux 54
  Alfresco, on Microsoft windows 39
  Alfresco license file 43
  Alfresco Tomcat bundle 42
  CIFS 49
  extensions, with AMP install 55
  flash player 51
  Image Magick 49
  Java SE Developer Kit 42
  MySQL 44

OpenOffice 48
Share Point Protocol Support 43
SWFTools 51
WCM 50
integrated enterprise content management system
  about 306
  FTP, used for integration 308
  protocols, integrating 307
  RESTful web services 308
  web services, used as solution 308
Intelliant OCR-Alfresco bundle 518
inter-department collaboration
  about 174
  content collaboration 175
  discussion, on specific space, starting 174
  individuals, inviting 175
  space collaboration, through emails 174
  space users, managing 174
iPhone
  about 333
  integrating with Alfresco 14
iPhone Alfresco integration 333, 334
ISV 306

J

Jakarta POI 13
Java1.6 13
Java Content Repository 63
Java Content Repository API 13
Java Portlet Integration 13
JavaScript
  executing, as business rules 206
JavaScript, as business rules
  built-in, using as actions 206
  business rules, extending with custom JavaScript 206
  JavaScript API 210
JavaScript API
  about 210
  objects 210
JavaScript API objects
  classifications 210
  companyhome 210
  document 210
  people 210

person 210
script 210
search 210
session 210
space 210
userhome 210
Java SE Developer Kit
  installing 42
JBoss 220
JBoss Business Process Manager. *See* **JBPM**
JBoss Portal 38
JBPM 14, 271
JBPM 3.2 13
JCR 35
Joint Photographic Experts Group. *See* **JPEG**
Joomla!
  about 330
  integrating with Alfresco 14
Joomla! Alfresco intergration 330, 331
jPDL 271
JPEG 202
JSP client
  customizing 479
JSR-170 standard interface 12
JSR-223 Java Language Integration 13

K

knowledge management 24
Kofax 508
Kofax Ascent Capture
  about 519
  integrating, with Alfresco 519
  integrating with Alfresco 14
  Kofax release script, configuring 519-521
  release script functionality 522

L

LDAP
  about 107, 109
  configuring 109
  configuring, with Active Directory 110-112
  daisy chaning 113
  daisy chaning, implementing 114
  integrating with, Liferay 118
  integrating with Alfresco 15

synchronising 112
users, exporting from Active Directory 113
using with directory server 109
LENGTH 234
library services
  about 14, 144
  auto versioning 145
  check out, undoing 148
  document, unlocking 148
  documents, checking out 146
  versioning 144
  versioning, enabling ways 144
  working copy, checking in 147, 148
Liferay
  about 38, 326
  integrating with, Alfresco 118
  integrating with, LDAP 118
  integrating with Alfresco 15
  server, restarting 119
  SSO, configuring 119
Liferay Alfresco intergration
  about 326
  API, used 328
  built-in portlet 328
  CMIS proposed standard, used 327
  REST APIs 327
  Web Script Container, used 326
Lightweight Directory Access Protocol. *See* LDAP;
LIST 233
log files
  configuring 77
Lucene
  about 33, 500
  batch size 503
  configuring, in Alfresco 502
  features 500
  MAX Clauses 503
  Max Merge Docs 503
  Merge Factor 503
  Min Merger Docs 503
Lucene 2.1 Text Search Engine 13

M

Max Clauses 503
Max Merge Docs 503

membership and security model
  about 86
  authentication 88
  groups 86
  permission group 87
  permissions 87
  roles 88
  security, imposing 88
  users 86
Merge Factor 503
Microsoft Office Add-ins
  downloading 50
  installing 50
Microsoft Office SharePoint Protocol support 19
MINMAX 233
Min Merger Docs 503
MS Office 2003 add-ins
  about 160
  configuring 161
  downloading 160
  installing 160
  MS Word add-in, features 162
  support, for MS Office 2007 160
  Word file, editing 163
Multi-Tenancy
  about 544
  enabling 544
  features, testing 545
  tenant data, exporting 547
  tenant data, importing 547
  tenants, creating 544
  tenants, managing 547
  tenant use case 545, 546
multilanguage support
  configuring 80
multilingual content
  deleting 154
  managing 152
  versions 153, 154
multiple library item, Alfresco Book project site
  actions, performing 400
  selecting 400
  working with 400
my profile, Alfresco Share
  full profile, viewing 365

password, changing 367
profile, editing 366, 367
MySQL database
  configuring 46-48
  downloading 44
  installing 44, 45
  setting up 47

N

network drivers
  CIFS 154
  FTP 158
  used, for managing content 154
  WebDAV 159
Node 63
node methods
  childByNamePath 460
  children 460
  childrenByXPath 460
  content 460
  isLocked 460
  name 460
  parent 460
  properties 460
  size 460
  url 460
NTLM
  about 107, 115
  authentication, using 115
  configuring 115
  scenarios 116
  SSO, integrrating with Active Directory 116-118
  SSO with CAS 118

O

OCR
  about 505, 517
  integrating 517
  Intelliant OCR-Alfresco bundle 518
ODF
  about 203
  Microsoft Office documents, converting to 203-205
OEM 306
OpenDocument Format. *See* **ODF**

OpenOffice
  downloading 48
  headless service, configuring 49
  installing 48
Open Office 2.x 13
OpenSearch
  about 494
  Alfresco Explorer, as OpenSearch aggregator 497
  open search engines 495
open search engines
  about 495
  keyword search 495
  sample keyword search, in HTML 496
  sample keyword search, in RSS 496, 497
open source
  advantages 10
open standards, Alfresco
  ACEGI Aspect-Oriented Security Framework 13
  AIFS 13
  Hibernate 3.2 ORM Persistence 13
  Jakarta POI 13
  Java Content Repository API 13
  Java Portlet Integration 13
  JBPM 3.2 13
  JSR-223 Java Language Integration 13
  Lucene 2.1 Text Search Engine 13
  Open Office 2.x 13
  PDFBox iText 13
  Spring 2.0 Aspect-Oriented Framework 13
  WebDAV 13
Optical Character Recognition. *See* **OCR**
Original Equipment Manufacturer. *See* **OEM**
out of the box installation architecture
  Alfresco applications, components 34
  application, accessing 34
  CIFS 35
  client applications layer 32
  Data Storage layer 33
  FTP 34
  protocols 34
  Repository Services layer 33
  WebDAV 34
  web services 35
out of the box installation architecture,

Alfresco 32

P

PDFBox iText 13
people, Alfresco Share
  about 370
  user, searching for 370
people object 210
permission group
  about 87
  add 87
  delete 87
  edit 87
  read 87
permissions 87
permissions, for content items
  _DeleteNode 100
  _ExecuteContent 100
  _ReadContent 100
  _ReadProperties 100
  _SetOwner 100
  _WriteContent 100
  _WriteProperties 100
permissions, for spaces
  _CreateChildren 100
  _DeleteChildren 100
  _DeleteNode 100
  _ReadChildren 100
  _ReadProperties 100
  _WriteProperties 100
personal dashboard, Alfresco Share
  about 363
  Alfresco Network, using 373
  customizing 363, 365
  dashlets 363
  RSS feed, configuring 371
  scheduled events, viewing 372
  site, entering into 371
  using 371
person object 210
portlet Web Scripts
  about 313
  document list portlet Web Script 313, 314
  mysapces portlet 313
presentation templates
  about 466

  custom template 468
presentation templates, FreeMarker dashlet 457
process definitions 271
process definitions, custom advanced workflows
  creating 285
  deploying 285
  deploying, via JBoss jBPM process designer 289-291
  deploying, workflow console used 285
  deploying ways 286
  jPDL XML, creating by hand 286-289
  workflow, deploying manually 285
property sheet configuration
  about 237
  component generators 238, 239
  converters 238
  properties, conditional diplay 238
  property labels 237
protocols
  CIFS 154
  FTP 154
  WebDAV 154
prototcols, integrating with repository
  Alfresco Surf 307
  CIFS 307
  CMIS 308
  FTP 307
  Java API 307
  JCR API 307
  OpenSearch 308
  RSS 308
  WebDAV 307
  Web Services API 307

Q

Quark Publishing System 8
  integrating with Alfresco 14

R

records management, Alfresco
  about 21
  features 21, 22
REGEX 233
relational database

configuring 75
Repository Data Dictionary 220
Repository Public API. *See* **Alfresco Repository Public API**
RESTful Web Scripts 308
RESTful web services 308
Rich user interface
　Alfresco Share 3.0 Integration support 477
　Flex used 477
roles
　about 88, 100
　collaborator 88
　consumer 88
　contributor 88
　coordinator 88
　editor 88
RSS syndication
　about 175
　enabling 175, 176
　RSS feeds, using 176
　RSS templates 176, 177
RSS templates 177
rule wizard 194

S

SaaS 544
sample Alfresco CMIS dashlet 354, 357
sample imaging solution, with workflow
　about 509
　business rule, for extracting metadata 511-513
　documents, transforming into required format 513
　scanned documents, uploading into repository 515-517
　scanner, connecting to network folder 515
　security, setting up 510
　space, setting up 510
　workflow process, defining 514
scalable architecture, Alfresco 12
scheduled actions
　about 211
　action template 211
　cron expression 211, 216
　example, archiving expired content 211-215
　query template 211

screen layout, Alfresco Explorer
　about 58
　breadcrumbs 61
　categories logical view, navigator 61
　detail screen 61
　header screen 61
　navigator 59
　navigator tree view 60
　opensearch, navigator 60
　shelf, navigator 60
　toolbar 59
script object 210
search
　overview 485
　text, searching 486
search, using Alfresco Explorer
　advanced search 488
　search criteria, saving 492
　search form, extending 490
search criteria
　complex search criteria, defining 492
　reusing 494
　saving 492
　saving, as private report 493
　saving, as public report 493
search form, extending
　about 490
　custom content, searching 491
　custom properties, searching 491
　web client user interface, configuring 491
search object 210
Secure Loaning Ltd 269
security model, selecting
　about 107
　LDAP, configuring for centralized identity management 109
　NTLM, configuring, for single sign-on 115
　out-of-the-box security 108
　sample scenarios 107
security permissions and roles, extending
　about 99
　custom roles, creating 101
　default permissions 100
　default roles 100
Service Level Agreements 9
session object 210
Share Point Protocol Support

document, collaborating on 434
documents handling within MS Office 427
document workspace, deleting 442
document workspace dashlet 442
downloading 43
installing 43
Sharepoint protocol support 426
simple audit template 549
simple search
  file names, searching 487
  search syntax 487
simple workflow
  about 260
  adding, to items 263, 264
  complex workflows, implementing 269
  defining 261
  email notifications templates 268, 269
  notification, sending to manager for approvals 265, 266
  out of the box features 261
  spaces and security, identifying 262, 263
  testing 266, 267
  using 261
  workflow process 270, 271
  workflow process, defining 263
site, Alfresco Share
  about 368
  creating 368, 369
  customizing 375
  deleting 370
  getting started tab 374
  recently modified documents tab 374
  RSS feed tab 375
  searching for 369
  site activities tab 374
  site calendar tab 374
  site colleagues tab 374
  site manager 368
  site membership, managing 370
  site profile tab 374
  using 373
  wiki tab 374
site manager 368
site users, Alfresco Book project site
  invited users, managing 425, 426
  invited users, viewing 425, 426
  managing 420

members page, accessing 420-422
site member, removing 424
site members, viewing 422, 423
site members role, changing 423
space
  browser view 444
  business rules, using 179
  copying, clipboard used 132
  custom icon, adding 449
  custom view 444
  custom view, applying 446
  default view, creating 132
  deleting 132
  details view 444
  editing 130
  features 128
  hierarchy, importance 129, 130
  icon view 444
  managing 128
  moving, clipboard used 132
  properties, editing 130, 132
  sample space structure, for marketing project 133, 134
  shortcut, creating 132
  smart folder 128
  viewing ways 444
  views, configuring 444
space, as smart folder
  about 128
  features 128
  space aspects 129
  space content 129
  space dashboard view 129
  space events 129
  space network folder 129
  space search 129
  space security 128
  space syndication 129
  space workflow 128
space content
  department space, exporting 527, 528
  department space, importing 528, 529
  exporting 527
  importing 527
space object 210
spaces, securing
  about 101

space, defining 105
user roles 102
users, inviting 103, 104
space templates, for reusable space structure
about 167
new space templates, creating 168
space template, reusing 168, 169
Spring 37, 222
Spring 2.0 Aspect-Oriented Framework 13
super tenant 544
system users, managing
about 89
existing user, searching for 92
new users, creating 90-92
user, deleting 93
user details, modifying 93

T

template node objects
about 460
methods 460
tenant administration console
about 544
commands 547
tokenize 502
Tomcat 220

U

user access
about 94
existing users, searching in Alfresco Share 96
homepage 94
new user, logging in 94
passwod, updating 95
personal details, updating 95
user details, modifying 96
user group management
EVERYONE group 97
groups, creating 97
subgroups, creating 97
users, adding 98, 99
users, removing 99
userhome object 210

user interface
Alfresco Share 3.0 Integration support 477
customizing 443
customizing, Flex used 477
user quota system 543
users 86
users, migrating
Alfresco repository, bootstrapping 123
users, bulk uploading 120-123
web services API, using for creating users 124

V

VARs 306
versioning
about 144
enalbing ways 144
ViewOne Pro
about 343
integrating with Alfresco 14
ViewOnePro Alfresco integration
about 343, 344, 346
views, Alfresco Explorer
configuring 444
custom icon, adding to space 449
custom view, applying on space 446-448
forum topics, configuring 448
HTML links, configuring 450
space views, configuring 444, 445
virtual file system
CIFS 78
configuring 78
customizing 78
FTP 78
WebDAV 78

W

WCM
downloading 50
installing 50
web content management, Alfresco
about 22
features 23
supported protocols 22

WebDAV
  about 13, 34, 159, 308
Web Scripts
  about 309
  daily dose integration Web Script 315
  documents, listing 314
  document search Web Script 318
  external Java application, integrating
      with 317
  features 309
  Hello World example 312
  implementing 310
  portlet Web Scripts 313
webscripts, using as dashlets
  custom dashlet JSP, configuring 455
  custom dashlet JSP, creating 455
  My Spaces dashlet, configuring 456
Web services 35, 308
wiki page, Alfresco Book project site
  about 380
  accessing 380, 381
  browsing 381
  deleting 385
  details, viewing 385, 386
  editing 384
  main page, creating 382, 383
  new page, creating 383
  renaming 385
Windows NT LAN Manager. *See* **NTLM;**
workflow 259
workflow task list's dashboards
  adhoc task, managing 301
  adhoc task, reassigning 300
  document details page list 303
  my completed tasks list 302
  my task to do 299
  status, viewing 302
  workflow, canceling 302
workflow types, Alfresco
  advanced workflow 260
WWW Distributed Authoring and
      Versioning. *See* **WebDAV**

[PACKT PUBLISHING]
Thank you for buying
Alfresco 3
Enterprise Content Management Implementation

Packt Open Source Project Royalties

When we sell a book written on an Open Source project, we pay a royalty directly to that project. Therefore by purchasing Alfresco 3 Enterprise Content Management Implementation, Packt will have given some of the money received to the Alfresco project

In the long term, we see ourselves and you—customers and readers of our books—as part of the Open Source ecosystem, providing sustainable revenue for the projects we publish on. Our aim at Packt is to establish publishing royalties as an essential part of the service and support a business model that sustains Open Source.

If you're working with an Open Source project that you would like us to publish on, and subsequently pay royalties to, please get in touch with us.

Writing for Packt

We welcome all inquiries from people who are interested in authoring. Book proposals should be sent to author@packtpub.com. If your book idea is still at an early stage and you would like to discuss it first before writing a formal book proposal, contact us; one of our commissioning editors will get in touch with you.

We're not just looking for published authors; if you have strong technical skills but no writing experience, our experienced editors can help you develop a writing career, or simply get some additional reward for your expertise.

About Packt Publishing

Packt, pronounced 'packed', published its first book "Mastering phpMyAdmin for Effective MySQL Management" in April 2004 and subsequently continued to specialize in publishing highly focused books on specific technologies and solutions.

Our books and publications share the experiences of your fellow IT professionals in adapting and customizing today's systems, applications, and frameworks. Our solution-based books give you the knowledge and power to customize the software and technologies you're using to get the job done. Packt books are more specific and less general than the IT books you have seen in the past. Our unique business model allows us to bring you more focused information, giving you more of what you need to know, and less of what you don't.

Packt is a modern, yet unique publishing company, which focuses on producing quality, cutting-edge books for communities of developers, administrators, and newbies alike. For more information, please visit our website: www.PacktPub.com.

Alfresco Developer Guide

ISBN: 978-1-847193-11-7   Paperback: 556 pages

Customizing Alfresco with actions, web scripts, web forms, workflows, and more

1. Learn to customize the entire Alfresco platform, including both Document Management and Web Content Management
2. Jam-packed with real-world, step-by-step examples to jump start your development
3. Content modeling, custom actions, Java API, RESTful web scripts, advanced workflow

Java EE 5 Development with NetBeans 6

ISBN: 978-1-847195-46-3   Paperback: 400 pages

Develop professional enterprise Java EE applications quickly and easily with this popular IDE

1. Use features of the popular NetBeans IDE to improve Java EE development
2. Careful instructions and screenshots lead you through the options available
3. Covers the major Java EE APIs such as JSF, EJB 3 and JPA, and how to work with them in NetBeans
4. Covers the NetBeans Visual Web designer in detail

Please check www.PacktPub.com for information on our titles

OpenCms 7 Development

ISBN: 978-1-847191-05-2   Paperback: 292 pages

Extending and customizing OpenCms through its Java API

1. Targets version 7 of OpenCms
2. Create new modules to extend OpenCms functionality
3. Learn to use the OpenCms templating system

Java EE 5 Development using GlassFish Application Server

ISBN: 978-1-847192-60-8   Paperback: 424 pages

The complete guide to installing and configuring the GlassFish Application Server and developing Java EE 5 applications to be deployed to this server

1. Concise guide covering all major aspects of Java EE 5 development
2. Uses the enterprise open-source GlassFish application server
3. Explains GlassFish installation and configuration
4. Covers all major Java EE 5 APIs

Please check www.PacktPub.com for information on our titles

Lightning Source UK Ltd.
Milton Keynes UK
24 January 2011

166256UK00001B/12/P